EDP AUDITING
CONCEPTUAL FOUNDATIONS
AND PRACTICE

McGraw-Hill Series in Management Information Systems

Gordon B. Davis, *Consulting Editor*

Davis: Management Information Systems: Conceptual Foundations, Structure, and Development
Davis and Everest: Readings in Management Information Systems
Lucas: The Analysis, Design, and Implementation of Information Systems
Lucas: Information Systems Concepts for Management
Lucas and Gibson: A Casebook for Management Information Systems
Weber: EDP Auditing: Conceptual Foundations and Practice

EDP AUDITING

CONCEPTUAL FOUNDATIONS AND PRACTICE

Ron Weber
University of Queensland, Australia

McGRAW-HILL BOOK COMPANY
New York St. Louis San Francisco Auckland Bogotá
Hamburg Johannesburg London Madrid Mexico Montreal New Delhi
Panama Paris São Paulo Singapore Sydney Tokyo Toronto

FOR MY PARENTS

This book was set in Times Roman by Ruttle, Shaw & Wetherill, Inc.
The editors were Donald G. Mason and Edwin Hanson;
the production supervisor was Phil Galea.
New drawings were done by Danmark & Michaels, Inc.
R. R. Donnelley & Sons Company was printer and binder.

EDP AUDITING
Conceptual Foundations and Practice

Copyright © 1982 by McGraw-Hill, Inc. All rights reserved. Printed in the United States of America. No part of this publication may be reproduced, stored in a retrieval system, or transmitted, in any form or by any means, electronic, mechanical, photocopying, recording, or otherwise, without the prior written permission of the publisher.

    5 6 7 8 9 0 DODO 8 9 8 7 6 5

Library of Congress Cataloging in Publication Data

Weber, Ron.
    EDP auditing.

    Includes index.
    1. Electronic data processing departments—
Auditing. 2. Electronic data processing departments
—Auditing—Problems, exercises, etc. I. Title.
HF5548.2.W38   657'.453   80-28872
ISBN 0-07-068830-3

CONTENTS

PREFACE xi

PART 1 **INTRODUCTION**

    1   OVERVIEW OF EDP AUDITING   3

        Need for Control and Audit of Computers   4
        EDP Auditing Defined   7
        Effects of EDP on Internal Control   10
        Foundations of EDP Auditing   12

    2   A GENERAL APPROACH TO EDP AUDITING   21

        The System of Internal Controls and the Audit Approach   22
        Controls and the Potential for Loss   22
        The Nature of Computer Controls   24
        Overview of Steps in an EDP Audit   28
        Some Major Audit Decisions   32

    3   ORGANIZATION AND MANAGEMENT OF THE EDP AUDIT FUNCTION   45

        Need for a Separate EDP Audit Section   46
        Centralization versus Decentralization of the EDP
            Audit Function   50
        Staffing the EDP Audit Function   51
        Training   53
        Relationships with Management and Other
            Organization Groups   57

		Promotional Opportunities for the EDP Auditor	59
		Life Cycle of the EDP Audit Group	60

PART 2   THE MANAGEMENT CONTROL FRAMEWORK

4	TOP MANAGEMENT AND EDP MANAGEMENT		69
	Evaluating the Planning Function		70
	Evaluating the Organizing Function		78
	Evaluating the Staffing Function		84
	Evaluating the Directing Function		86
	Evaluating the Controlling Function		88
5	SYSTEMS DEVELOPMENT		98
	Auditing the System Development Process		99
	Normative Models of the System Development Process		99
	Evaluating the Major Phases in the System Development Process		103
6	PROGRAMMING MANAGEMENT		128
	The Program Life Cycle		129
	Organizing the Programming Team		144
	Managing the System Programming Group		148
	Software Development Aids		150
7	DATABASE ADMINISTRATION		164
	Motivations toward a Database Administration Role		165
	Some Audit Considerations		166
	Functions of the Database Administrator		167
	Organizational Considerations		171
	Data Dictionary		172
	Control over the Database Administrator		175
8	OPERATIONS MANAGEMENT		183
	Overview of Operations Management		184
	Computer Operations		185
	Data Preparation		189
	Control Section		190
	File Library		191
	Documentation Library		194
	Security Section		195

PART 3   THE APPLICATION CONTROL FRAMEWORK

9   DATA CAPTURE, PREPARATION, AND ENTRY CONTROLS   209

Overview of Data Capture, Preparation, and Entry   211
Evaluation of Data Capture Methods   212
Evaluation of Data Preparation/Entry Methods   216
Source Document Design   224
Interactive Language Design   227
Data Code Controls   231
Check Digits   234
Batch Controls   237
Other Data Capture and Preparation Controls   239

10   ACCESS AND COMMUNICATIONS CONTROLS   249

Access Controls   250
Communications Controls   260
Cryptography   270

11   INPUT CONTROLS   283

Input Validation Checks   285
Design of the Input Program   288
Control over Input   294
A Generalized Input System   295

12   PROCESSING CONTROLS   304

Validation Checks   305
Some Matters of Programming Style   306
Concurrency Control   311
System Software Integrity   316
Control over Hardware Malfunctions   321
Checkpoint/Restart Controls   323

13   OUTPUT CONTROLS   330

Controls over Reports   331
Interrogation Languages and Output Response Errors   340
Controls over Files   343
Some Output Effectiveness/Efficiency Considerations   343

14   AUDIT TRAIL CONTROLS   355

The Accounting Audit Trail   356
The Operations Audit Trail   366

15 BACKUP AND RECOVERY CONTROLS 376

Need for Backup and Recovery 377
Backup and Recovery Strategies 378
Some Administrative Aspects 393

PART 4 EVIDENCE COLLECTION

16 GENERALIZED AUDIT SOFTWARE 401

Motivations for Generalized Audit Software Development 402
Functional Capabilities 403
Audit Tasks That Can Be Accomplished 406
Functional Limitations 409
Installation/Audit Group Maturity Issues 410
Managing a Generalized Audit Software Application 412
Accessing Complex Data Structures 414
Purchasing Audit Software 419

17 SYSTEM SOFTWARE AND SPECIALIZED AUDIT SOFTWARE 431

System Software as an Audit Tool 432
Specialized Audit Software as an Audit Tool 440

18 CODE REVIEW, TEST DATA, AND CODE COMPARISON 448

Factors That Lower Program Quality: Some Empirical
  Evidence 450
Program Source Code Review 451
Test Data 458
Program Code Comparison 465

19 CONCURRENT AUDITING TECHNIQUES 473

Basic Nature of Concurrent Auditing Techniques 474
Need for Concurrent Auditing Techniques 474
Types of Concurrent Auditing Techniques 477
Implementing Concurrent Auditing Techniques 485
Advantages/Disadvantages of Concurrent Auditing
  Techniques 487

20 INTERVIEWS, QUESTIONNAIRES, AND CONTROL FLOWCHARTS 493

Interviews 494
Questionnaires 498
Control Flowcharts 506

21	PERFORMANCE MONITORING TOOLS	515
	The Objects of Measurement	516
	General Characteristics of Performance Monitors	517
	Types of Performance Monitors	518
	Performance Monitoring and Data Integrity	526

PART 5 EVIDENCE EVALUATION

22	EVALUATING ASSET SAFEGUARDING AND DATA INTEGRITY	535
	Measures of Asset Safeguarding and Data Integrity	536
	Evaluating Asset Safeguarding and Data Integrity: Formal Techniques	538
	Cost-Effectiveness Considerations	545
	Some Informal Guidelines for Evaluation	553

23	EVALUATING SYSTEM EFFECTIVENESS	560
	Goals of an Information System	561
	The Evaluation Process	562
	The Global Evaluation Judgment	576

24	EVALUATING SYSTEM EFFICIENCY	583
	The Evaluation Process	584
	Performance Indices	587
	Workload Models	588
	System Models	593

PART 6 FUTURES

25	THE CHANGING EDP AUDIT FUNCTION	609
	Toward Professionalism	610
	Legal Influences	612
	Social Influences	616
	Impact of the Changing Technology	619
	Research and Pedagogy	624

	INDEXES	629
	Name Index	
	Subject Index	

PREFACE

A friend and colleague once said to me: "To be a good auditor you have to be better at business than your client." I've often pondered that remark, for on the one hand it is a compelling notion, yet on the other it sets an impossible ideal for auditors to achieve. Perhaps in the more traditional areas of auditing we, as auditors, are gaining confidence in the soundness of our methodologies. Admittedly, the lawsuits still prevail, but the problems seem to be in the application of the methodologies rather than in the methodologies themselves.

In the domain of modern auditing, however, we have an Achilles heel: our methodologies for the control and audit of computer systems are still in their infancy. Further, the rate at which new computer technology is developed and introduced seems to outstrip the rate at which we can develop viable audit methodologies. It is the area of EDP auditing that currently represents the great challenge to auditors.

EDP auditing is the process of collecting and evaluating evidence to determine whether a computer system safeguards assets, maintains data integrity, achieves organizational goals effectively, and consumes resources efficiently. Safeguarding assets involves ensuring that they are protected from damage or destruction, unauthorized use, and being stolen. Data integrity is a state: it means data is accurate, complete, and consistent. Asset safeguarding and data integrity always have been the concern of auditors. However, the definition of EDP auditing proposed also encompasses a concern for the effectiveness with which EDP systems meet their objectives and the efficiency with which data is processed. Since EDP expenditure often is a major item in an organization's balance sheet and income statement, currently management is more frequently asking auditors to evaluate these aspects of EDP systems.

Some Pedagogical Issues

Before writing this book, I thought long and hard about the approach I should use to present the subject matter of EDP auditing. It seems to me there are two approaches. With the first approach, which I will call the "exposures approach," the writer focuses primarily on the types of losses that can occur in computer systems. The secondary focus is on the controls used to reduce these losses. With the second approach, which I will call the "controls approach," the primary focus is on the controls and the secondary focus is on the losses that the controls reduce.

Why can't *both* exposures and controls be the primary focus? Both certainly have major importance from an audit perspective. The problem is that there is not a one-to-one relationship between exposures and controls. A single control can reduce the loss from multiple exposures. Thus, if the writer focuses on *exposures,* some subject matter on controls will be repeated; alternatively, if the writer focuses on *controls,* some subject matter on exposures will be repeated. As my students have not hesitated to point out, the writer who does not carefully control the duplication of material that results, will bore the reader quickly. The only solution, I believe, is for the writer to adopt either exposures or controls as the primary focus; the secondary focus then becomes the material that must be duplicated as efficiently as possible so presentation of the subject matter of EDP auditing is complete.

In this book, I chose to focus on *controls* for three major reasons. First, I trust that students who have had a first course in auditing will be familiar with the major types of exposures facing an organization (these do not change with computers); I assume they are reading this book because their knowledge of computer control technology is not so well developed. Second, my experience is that students feel more comfortable with the controls approach; they seem to find it less "messy" than the exposures approach. I am unsure why this is the case, but I think it has to do with controls requiring a smaller "chunk" of understanding than exposures. Third, a major purpose of this book is to integrate the burgeoning literature on computer controls that appears in *both* the auditing and computer science areas. It dismays me that each area still tends to ignore the other; each has much to contribute to the other.

The controls approach has its problems. The subject matter on computer controls is somewhat more volatile than the subject matter on exposures. Some control technology is still evolving; for example, several problems remain to be solved relating to the use of cryptography in communications networks. But I believe there to be more than enough stability in the control technology to make the approach that I have adopted worthwhile.

Structure of the Book

The parts (and chapters) of the book follow a natural sequence. The first part motivates the EDP audit function within an organization. The second and third parts describe the computer control frameworks that should exist in an organization at the management level and application system level, respectively. By first evaluating the management control framework, the EDP auditor determines the extent and scope of testing needed at the application system level. Techniques of evidence collection are discussed in the fourth part of the book; and the fifth part discusses how the evidence collected can be evaluated. The final part discusses the futures of EDP auditing.

One point must be made on the subject matter of the chapters. As a potential reader, you may look for chapters on the specialized areas of EDP audit: online realtime systems, database management systems, service bureaus, etc. You may be disappointed to find these chapters missing. However, through experience I am convinced that this is not the best way to initially present the subject matter of EDP auditing. Many of the controls and audit methodologies needed for online systems are the same for database management systems, and so forth. This is not to deny there are specialized controls and specialized audit techniques for these specialized areas. However, organizing the basic subject matter of EDP auditing by these specialized areas results in substantial duplication of material and frustrations for both the instructor and student. The secret of being a good EDP auditor is to be capable of assembling the fundamental controls and EDP audit methodologies in a manner appropriate for a specific computer installation, be it a simple batch system or a complex database management system.

Using the Book

I intend this book to be of use primarily to both students and practitioners of EDP auditing. However, I hope it will also prove useful to EDP managers, systems analysts, and programmers who have responsibility for designing and implementing controls in systems.

The book presumes the reader has at least a basic knowledge of auditing, computer data processing, and a programming language (preferably COBOL). Thus, it is not intended for beginners in the field. The beginner should first study one of the many excellent introductory texts in the areas of auditing and computers.

At the college level, the book provides sufficient material for a solid semester's work at the upper undergraduate or graduate level. The instructor may wish to leave out some chapters—for example, Chapter 3 on organization and management of the EDP audit function—and give more emphasis to others. The chapter bibliographies are a source of additional reading for students if the instructor wants to spend more time on particular chapters.

Besides the usual lecture method, the instructor might like to try using the book employing a case study approach. The students are made responsible for studying the chapter materials; the class periods are used to discuss the exercises and cases at the end of each chapter.

Besides the exercises and cases, each chapter in the book also contains a set of review questions. In general, answers to the review questions can be found in the chapter. At times, however, a little thought may be required. The exercises and cases are more demanding. Often I have tried to make the student think from an exposures perspective, thereby compensating for my primary focus on controls in the chapter. The exercises and cases also may require the student to integrate material covered in earlier chapters. To assist the instructor, there is also an instructor's manual available containing suggested solutions to the assignment material.

I strongly recommend that the instructor supplement the assignment material with further case studies and some computer problems. The case studies should be more comprehensive than the short cases contained in the book so the student is forced to integrate the text material. They might be on specific types of systems; for example, an online banking system or a service bureau. A variety of computer problems can be set; for example, using a generalized audit software package to examine the quality of data on a file or using a test data generator to assist validating the logic of a program.

I hope that as a user of the book, you conclude that the benefits exceed the costs. I would appreciate your feedback, whether it be positive or negative, so that a second edition (if it occurs) might better meet your needs.

ACKNOWLEDGMENTS

This book grew from a set of notes prepared for a course on EDP Auditing that I taught with Professor Gordon B. Davis during my graduate student days at the University of Minnesota from 1973–1976. The opportunity to teach the course is simply one of many opportunities for professional and intellectual development that Professor Davis has given me during my association with him. I cannot express properly my deep appreciation to him for his ongoing support and encouragement.

I owe, also, a large intellectual debt to Professor Gordon C. Everest at the University of Minnesota. His research on database management systems and his clear thinking on data integrity have significantly influenced my own thinking.

I was privileged to have five reviewers of the manuscript who, in spite of my limitations as a writer, were always tremendously supportive of my efforts. Professors Gordon B. Davis, University of Minnesota; Russell C. Kick, Jr., University of North Florida; John O. Mason, Jr., University of Alabama; Frederick L. Neumann, University of Illinois; and Carl S. Warren, University of Georgia, all reviewed portions or the whole of the manuscript. Their suggestions improved considerably its overall quality.

The typing of the manuscript was handled expertly, efficiently, and cheerfully by five women. Chris Stone and Liz Kinloch prepared some of the initial chapters while I was at the Australian National University in Canberra. Lynn Gallegos and Sage Toninato typed chapter revisions while I was on leave at the University of Minnesota. The bulk of the work, however, has been done by Jo Waldron at the University of Queensland.

Finally, to the two women in my life—my wife, Kay, and my daughter, Amy—go my deepest thanks. The debt I owe them for their love, support, and patience is awesome.

Ron Weber

PART ONE
INTRODUCTION

EDP auditing is a function that has been developed to assess whether computer systems safeguard assets, maintain data integrity, and achieve the goals of an organization effectively and efficiently. Parties both internal and external to an organization are concerned with whether computer systems fulfill these objectives. The management of an organization attempts to use resources in an optimal manner within the constraints established by the society; for example, management may pursue a profit-maximizing objective subject to the

Chapter	Overview of contents
1 Overview of EDP Auditing	Discusses the need for control and audit of computers; defines EDP auditing; examines the underlying support disciplines; evaluates the effects of EDP on internal control
2 A General Approach to EDP Auditing	Examines the effects of the system of internal controls on the audit approach; discusses the relationship between expected losses and errors and irregularities; discusses the nature of computer controls; provides an overview of the steps in an EDP audit; describes some of the major EDP audit decisions
3 Organization and Management of the EDP Audit Function	Discusses setting up and organizing an EDP audit group; considers staffing and training issues; examines the relationship of the EDP audit group with other organizational groups

legal constraint that it maintains the privacy of data provided to it by individual members of the society. External parties, whether they be shareholders, unions, or pressure groups, also have vested interests in how organizations use computers. Their concerns vary from wealth maximization to possible work displacement to a loss of personal privacy.

The first three chapters of this book introduce the EDP audit function. They discuss the motivations for an EDP audit function, the objectives of EDP auditing, present an overview of the EDP audit process, and show how the EDP audit function might be set up within an organization.

CHAPTER 1

OVERVIEW OF EDP AUDITING

CHAPTER OUTLINE

NEED FOR CONTROL AND AUDIT OF COMPUTERS
    Organizational Costs of Data Loss
    Incorrect Decision Making
    Computer Abuse
    Privacy
    Controlled Evolution of Computer Use
EDP AUDITING DEFINED
    Asset Safeguarding Objectives
    Data Integrity Objectives
    System Effectiveness Objectives
    System Efficiency Objectives
EFFECTS OF EDP ON INTERNAL CONTROL
    Separation of Duties
    Access to Assets
    Types of Internal Controls
    The Audit/Management Trail
    Comparing Recorded Accountability with Assets
    Consequences of Error
FOUNDATIONS OF EDP AUDITING
    Traditional Auditing
    Information Systems Management
    Behavioral Science
    Computer Science

SUMMARY
REVIEW QUESTIONS
EXERCISES AND CASES
REFERENCES

Whereas 25 years ago we fulfilled most of our data processing needs manually, today computers perform much of the data processing required in both the private and public sectors of our economy. The need to maintain the integrity of data processed by computers pervades our lives. We have increasing fears that our substantially increased data processing capabilities are not well controlled. The media makes much of computer abuse. We have concerns about the privacy of data we exchange with organizations such as the tax department, medical authorities, and credit granting institutions. Probably all of us have suffered the frustrations of trying to get an organization to update its computer-maintained name and address file.

Uncontrolled use of computers has a widespread impact on a society. Inaccurate information causes misallocation of resources within the economy. Frauds are perpetrated because of inadequate system controls. Unfortunately, the person who suffers most is often the person who can least afford to suffer; for example, the small shareholder and the low-income earner. Perhaps more subtle is the growing distrust of institutions that gather and process large volumes of data. A sense of lost individuality now exists: the "big brother" of 1984 is upon us.

NEED FOR CONTROL AND AUDIT OF COMPUTERS

Computers continue to be used more extensively to process data. Between 1974 and 1979, International Data Corporation [1979] estimated worldwide use of U.S. manufactured computers increased from 264,690 units to 764,400 units. As part of this increase, worldwide use of U.S. manufactured minicomputers grew from an estimated 135,300 units in 1974 to an estimated 504,700 units in 1979. Steady growth in computer use, especially minicomputer use, is inevitable.

Since computers play such a large part in assisting us process data, it is important that their use be controlled. The following sections briefly discuss five major reasons for setting up a function to examine controls over computer data processing (Figure 1.1).

Organizational Costs of Data Loss

Data is a critical resource necessary for an organization's continuing operations. Everest [1982] proposes that data provides the organization with an

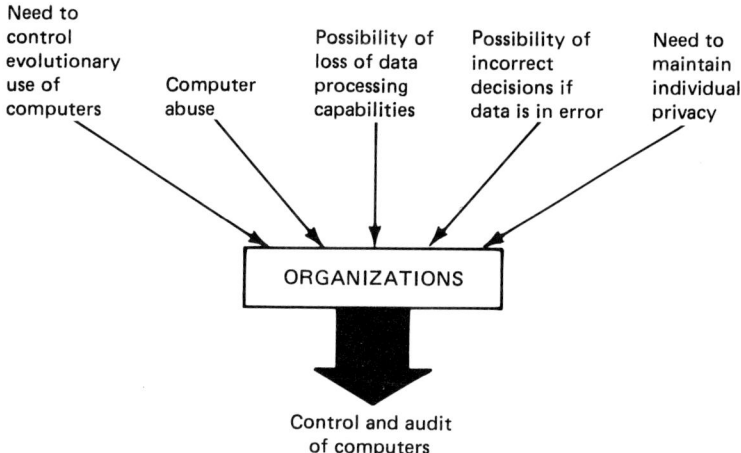

Figure 1.1
Factors influencing an organization toward control and audit of computers.

image of itself, its environment, its history, and its future. If this image is accurate, the organization increases its abilities to adapt and survive in a changing environment.

Consider the case of a large department store that has its accounts receivable file destroyed. Unless its customers are honest, and also remember what they have purchased from the store, the firm can suffer a major loss in cash receipts and its long-run survival may be affected. Consider, also, the department store losing its accounts payable file. It is unable to pay its accounts on time and can suffer a loss of credit rating as well as any discounts available for early payment. If it contacts creditors requesting assistance, the department store relies on the honesty of the creditors in notifying it of the amounts owed. Further, creditors must now question the competence of the department store's management and may be unwilling to extend credit in the future.

Such losses can arise through lax controls existing over computers. Management may not provide adequate backup for computer files; thus, the loss of a file through computer program error, sabotage, or natural disaster means the file cannot be recovered and the organization's continuing operations are impaired.

Incorrect Decision Making

The importance of accurate data depends on the types of decisions made by individuals having some interest in an organization. For example, if management makes strategic planning decisions, most likely they will tolerate some errors in the data, given the nature of strategic planning decisions—their long-run perspective and surrounding uncertainty. However, management control and operational control decisions usually require accurate data. These latter decisions involve detection, investigation, and correction of out-of-control processes. Inaccurate data may cause costly, unnecessary investigations to be undertaken, or result in out-of-control processes remaining undetected.

Other people besides management have interests in an organization. Shareholders need accurate financial statements to enable them to make their investment decisions. Governments, labor, and pressure groups such as environmentalists also need accurate data to make decisions about an organization. However, accurate data is a necessary but not sufficient condition to prevent misallocation of resources within an economy.

Computer Abuse

The major stimulus for development of the EDP audit function within organizations often seems to be computer abuse. Parker [1976, p. 12] defines computer abuse to be "any incident associated with computer technology in which a victim suffered or could have suffered loss and a perpetrator by intention made or could have made gain." Recently, some spectacular cases of computer abuse have caused management and more academics and researchers to be concerned with the problem. However, after extensive studies of computer abuse, Parker [1976] regards it to be only the third most serious problem confronting an organization using computers. The most serious problem is errors and omissions causing losses to organizations. Next is disruption to computer data processing caused by natural disasters such as fire, water, and power failures. Control techniques for handling these two types of problems are better developed than those for computer abuse.

The losses which result from computer abuse seem to be higher than those which result when abuses of manual data processing systems occur. Parker [1976] reports two studies made of general bank fraud and embezzlement (not involving the computer) and computer bank fraud and embezzlement. The average loss per case for general bank fraud and embezzlement was $104,000 and the average loss per case for computer bank fraud and embezzlement was $617,000. Even with the problems of collecting data on fraud and embezzlement, figures that show computer-related fraud and embezzlement to be approximately six times higher than general fraud and embezzlement are cause for concern.

Because computer abuse has had such an important influence on the development of EDP auditing, the reader should be familiar with some of the major cases of computer abuse. The exercises and case studies at the end of this chapter describe three of the more famous cases. The bibliography that follows includes several references that contain extensive discussions and analyses of computer abuse.

Privacy

Much data is now collected about us as individuals: taxation, credit, medical, educational, employment, residence, etc. This data also was collected before computers. However, the data processing capabilities of the computer, particularly the rapid throughput, integration, and retrieval capabilities, cause many people to now wonder whether the privacy of individuals (and organizations) is being eroded. Some people conceive ultimately there will be a large database on all individuals containing substantial information about them keyed on some universal identifier.

Aside from any constitutional aspect, many nations deem privacy to be a human right. They consider it to be the responsibility of those people concerned with computer data processing to ensure computer use does not evolve to the stage where different data about people can be collected, integrated, and retrieved quickly. A further responsibility exists to ensure data is used only for the purposes intended.

Controlled Evolution of Computer Use

Technology is neutral, neither good nor bad. It is the *use* of technology that produces social problems. Major decisions still have to be made on how computers should be used within the society; for example, to what extent should the implementation of computer technology be allowed to displace the work force?

It is a function of governments, professional societies, and pressure groups to be concerned with evaluating the use of technology; but, it is also well-accepted that individual organizations should have a social conscience that includes the use of computer technology.

EDP AUDITING DEFINED

EDP auditing is the process of collecting and evaluating evidence to determine whether a computer system safeguards assets, maintains data integrity, achieves organizational goals effectively, and consumes resources efficiently. Thus, EDP auditing supports the attainment of traditional audit objectives: attest objectives (those of the external auditor) that have asset safeguarding and data integrity as their focus, and management objectives (those of the internal auditor) that encompass not only attest objectives but also effectiveness and efficiency objectives. The EDP audit process can be conceived as a force that helps organizations to better attain these objectives (Figure 1.2).

Asset Safeguarding Objectives

The assets of a computer installation include hardware, software, people, data files, system documentation, and supplies. Like all assets they must be pro-

Figure 1.2
Impact of the EDP audit function on organizations.

tected by a system of internal control. Hardware can be damaged maliciously. Proprietary software and the contents of data files can be stolen. Supplies of negotiable forms can be used for unauthorized purposes. Because of the concentration of assets within the physical locality of the computer installation, asset safeguarding is an especially important objective.

Data Integrity Objectives

Data integrity is a fundamental concept in EDP auditing. It is a state implying data has certain attributes: completeness, soundness, purity, veracity. Without data integrity being maintained, an organization no longer has a true representation of itself or of real world events. However, maintaining data integrity can only be achieved at a cost. The benefits obtained should exceed the costs of the control procedures needed.

Two major factors affect the value of a data item to an organization: (*a*) the value of the informational content of the data item for individual decision makers, and (*b*) the extent to which the data item is shared among decision makers. The value of the data item determines how important it is to maintain the integrity of the data item.

The informational content of a data item depends on its ability to reduce the uncertainty surrounding a decision. The value of this uncertainty reduction in turn depends on the payoffs associated with the decision to be made. These notions have been well-developed within statistical decision theory (see, for example, Marschak and Radner [1972]).

If data is shared, corruption of data integrity affects not just one user but multiple users. The value of a data item is some aggregate function of the value of the data item to the individual users of the data item. Thus, in a shared data environment, maintenance of data integrity becomes more critical.

System Effectiveness Objectives

An effective data processing system accomplishes its objectives. Evaluating effectiveness implies knowledge of user needs. To evaluate whether a system reports information in a way that facilitates decision making by its users, the auditor must know the characteristics of the user and the decision-making setting.

Effectiveness auditing typically occurs after a system has been running for some time. Management requests a postaudit to determine whether the system is achieving its stated objectives. This evaluation provides input to the decision on whether to scrap the system, continue its running, or modify it in some way.

Effectiveness auditing also can be carried out during the design stages of a system. Systems designers have a difficult task ensuring users communicate their needs and understand and accept the proposed design. If a system is complex and costly to implement, management may want an independent evaluation of whether the design is likely to fulfill user needs. The auditor may be responsible for performing this independent evaluation for management.

System Efficiency Objectives

An efficient data processing system uses minimum resources to achieve its required output. Data processing systems consume various resources: machine time, peripherals, channels, system software, labor. These resources are scarce and different application systems compete for their use.

The question of whether a data processing system is efficient often has no clear-cut answer. The efficiency of any particular application system cannot be considered in isolation from other application systems. Problems of suboptimization occur if one system is "optimized" at the expense of other systems. For example, minimizing an application system's run time may require dedication of a channel to that system. However, the system may not utilize the channel fully and the slack resource normally available for use by other application systems is no longer available.

Data processing system efficiency becomes especially important when a computer no longer has excess capacity. The performance of individual application systems typically degrades (for example, slower response times occur) and management must decide whether efficiency can be improved or extra resources must be purchased. Since extra hardware and software are expensive, management needs to know whether available capacity has been exhausted because individual application systems are inefficient or existing allocations of computer resources are causing bottlenecks. Again, because auditors are independent, management may ask them to perform or assist the evaluation.

EFFECTS OF EDP ON INTERNAL CONTROL

Asset safeguarding, data integrity, system effectiveness, and system efficiency can be achieved only if an organization's management sets up a system of internal control. Traditionally, the major components of an internal control system have included separation of duties, clear delegation of authority and responsibility, hiring and training of high-quality personnel, management supervision, a system of authorizations, limited access to assets, and comparison of recorded accountability with assets. In an EDP system, these components must still exist; however, use of EDP affects the *implementation* of these components in several ways. The following sections highlight some of the major areas of impact (see also, American Institute of Certified Public Accountants [1974]).

Separation of Duties

In a manual system, separate individuals should be responsible for initiating transactions, recording transactions, and custody of assets. As a basic control, this helps prevent or detect fraud and inaccurate or incomplete transactions.

In a computer system, the traditional notion of separation of duties does not always exist. For example, a program may reconcile a vendor invoice against a receiving document and print a check for the amount owed to a creditor. Clearly, it may be inefficient and, from a control viewpoint, useless to place these functions in separate programs. Instead, separation of duties must exist in a different form. Once it has been determined that the program executes correctly, the capability to run the program in production mode and the capability to change the program must be separated.

In a minicomputer environment, separation of incompatible functions may be even more difficult to achieve (see, also, Price Waterhouse [1979]). Some minicomputers allow users to change easily programs and data; further, they provide no record of these changes. If the minicomputer does not have an inbuilt capability to provide a secure record of changes, it may be difficult, if not impossible, to provide this record using other means. Thus, auditors should ensure organizations purchase only those makes of minicomputers that provide basic control capabilities if the minicomputers are to be used on financial applications.

Access to Assets

As organizational units, computer installations are somewhat unique in the way they concentrate the assets of the organization. A fraud can be perpetrated by an unauthorized change to any program or data file that ultimately affects the disbursement of funds. Further, the programs and data files may constitute valuable assets themselves. For example, a competitor may be willing to pay substantial money for a copy of a customer file or a proprietary program. Thus, compared with other organizational units, the proper functioning of internal controls that prevent unauthorized access to assets often is more important in a computer installation.

Types of Internal Controls

Though the basic objectives of internal control do not change in a computer installation, the technology (the specific controls) used to accomplish these objectives does change. For example, accurate and complete operation of a disk drive requires a set of hardware controls not used in a manual system; similarly, system development controls include procedures for testing programs that would not be found in the development of manual systems.

The Audit/Management Trail

The audit or management trail provides a record of all events that occur within an application system. In the early days of computer use, a fear existed that the audit trail would disappear. However, this fear was ill-founded. Preservation of the audit trail simply requires good design of the applications and system software used in computer systems.

Unfortunately, the trend toward increased use of minicomputers does threaten the adequacy of the audit trail. Some minicomputers provide insufficient access controls and logging facilities to ensure preservation of an accurate and complete audit trail. When this is coupled with a decreased ability to separate incompatible functions, serious control problems result.

Comparing Recorded Accountability with Assets

Periodically data and the assets that the data purports to represent should be compared to determine whether or not incompleteness or inaccuracies exist. In a computer system, programs are used to prepare the basic counts used for comparison purposes. For example, programs may sort an inventory file by warehouse location and prepare counts by inventory item at the different warehouses. If unauthorized modifications occur to the programs or the data files that the programs use, a fraud may be perpetrated. Thus, internal controls must be implemented and their operation ensured if irregularities are to be prevented or detected.

Consequences of Error

Boritz [1979] points out that the consequences of errors in a computer system can be more serious than the consequences of error in a manual system. Errors in manual systems tend to occur stochastically; for example, periodically a clerk prices an inventory item incorrectly. Errors in computer systems tend to be deterministic; an erroneous program always will execute incorrectly. Furthermore, errors are generated at high speed and the cost to correct and rerun the program may be high. Whereas fast feedback can be provided to clerks if they make errors, errors in computer programs can involve extensive redesign and reprogramming. Thus, internal controls that ensure high-quality computer systems are designed and implemented are critical.

FOUNDATIONS OF EDP AUDITING

EDP auditing is not just a simple extension of traditional auditing. Recognition of the need for an EDP audit function came from two directions. First, auditors realized that computers had impacted their ability to perform the attest function. Second, both corporate and information processing management recognized computers were valuable resources that needed controlling like any other valuable resource within the organization.

Figure 1.3 shows EDP auditing to be an intersection of four other areas or disciplines. EDP auditing borrows much of its theory and practical methodologies from traditional auditing, information systems management, behavioral science, and computer science.

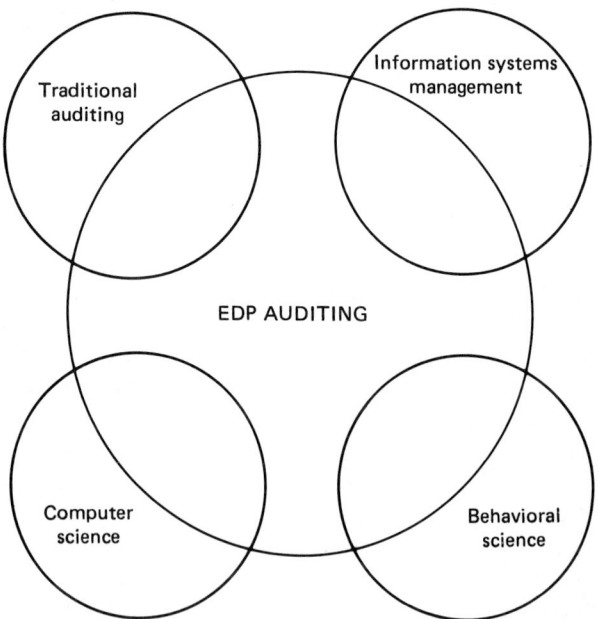

Figure 1.3
EDP auditing as an intersection of other disciplines.

Traditional Auditing

Traditional auditing brought to EDP auditing a wealth of knowledge and experience concerning internal control techniques. A computer system has both manual and machine components. There are clerical activities such as data preparation activities supporting a computer system. These activities should be subject to internal control principles such as separation of duties, having competent and trustworthy personnel, and establishing clear definitions of duties, just as a manual system should be subject to these principles. Applying these principles attempts to ensure the integrity of data before it reaches the computer facility, and in the subsequent distribution of the computer output.

Traditional auditing also impacts the computer component of a data processing system. Concepts such as control totals are relevant to the update and maintenance of files by computer programs. Computer programs must ensure all transaction data is processed and that it is processed correctly in the same way a manual system must ensure these things. Many of the controls used in traditional auditing can be carried over directly into computer data processing activities.

The general methodologies for evidence collection and evidence evaluation used by EDP auditors are rooted in traditional auditing (see, further, Chapter 2). The long evolution and extensive experience of traditional auditing highlight the critical importance of objective, verifiable evidence and independent evaluation of systems.

Perhaps most important, traditional auditing brings to EDP auditing a control philosophy. It is difficult to articulate the nature of this philosophy. However, one can glean elements by reading auditing literature or examining the work of auditors. The philosophy involves examining data processing with a critical mind, questioning a system's ability to safeguard assets, maintain data integrity, and achieve its objectives effectively and efficiently.

Information Systems Management

The early history of computer data processing shows some spectacular disasters when implementing computer systems. There were massive cost overruns and failures to achieve stated objectives. Recently, many researchers have been concerned with better ways of developing and implementing information systems. As a result, several advances have occurred. Techniques of project management have been carried across into the information systems area. Documentation, standards, budgets, and variance investigation are now emphasized. Better ways of developing and implementing systems have been developed. For example, the structured programming and chief programmer team approaches to software development seem to result in software being developed faster, with fewer errors, and with easier maintenance in the future. These advances impact EDP auditing because they ultimately affect asset safeguarding, data integrity, system effectiveness, and system efficiency.

Behavioral Science

Lucas [1975] concluded after a study of 2000 users in 16 different organizations that the major reason computer systems fail is through ignoring organizational behavior problems in the design and implementation of information systems. The failure of an information system can impact asset safeguarding, data integrity, system effectiveness, and system efficiency. Thus, the EDP auditor must know those conditions that lead to behavioral problems and possible system failure. Behavioral scientists, especially organization theorists, have contributed much to understanding people problems within organizations. Some researchers are now applying the findings of organization theory to information systems development and implementation. They emphasize the need for systems designers to consider *concurrently* the impact of a computer system on task accomplishment, the technical system, and the quality of work life of individuals within the organization, the social system.

Computer Science

Computer scientists also have been concerned with asset safeguarding, data integrity, system effectiveness, and system efficiency (see, further, Hoffman [1977] and Denning and Denning [1979]). For example, research has been carried out on how to develop error-free software and ways to maintain overall hardware/software system integrity. The theoretical basis for structured programming developed in computer science. Reliability theory and control theory have been the basis for designing secure operating systems, secure system software, and error-free hardware.

The high level technical knowledge of computer science provides both benefits and problems for EDP auditing. On the one hand, it allows the auditor to be less concerned about the reliability of certain components in a data processing system. On the other hand, if the knowledge is abused, it may be very difficult for the auditor to detect the abuse. Fraud perpetrated by a skilled systems programmer may be almost impossible to detect by an auditor who does not have a corresponding level of technical knowledge.

SUMMARY

EDP auditing is an organizational function that evaluates asset safeguarding, data integrity, and effectiveness and efficiency in computer systems. There are five major motivations for having an EDP audit function within an organization: (*a*) the consequences of losing the data resource, (*b*) the possibility of misallocating resources because of decisions based on incorrect data, (*c*) the possibility of fraud and embezzlement if computer systems are not controlled, (*d*) the need to maintain the privacy of individuals, and (*e*) the need to control the evolutionary use of the computer.

Asset safeguarding, data integrity, system effectiveness, and system efficiency can be achieved only if a sound system of internal control exists. Use of a computer for data processing does not affect the basic objectives of internal control; however, it affects how these objectives must be achieved.

EDP auditing borrows much of its theory and methodologies from other areas. Traditional auditing contributes knowledge of internal control practices and overall control philosophy. Information systems management provides methodologies necessary to achieve successful design and implementation of systems. Behavioral science indicates when and why information systems are likely to fail because of people problems. Computer science contributes technical knowledge about control theory, and hardware and software that maintain data integrity.

REVIEW QUESTIONS

1.1. Why is there a need for control and audit of computers?
1.2. For each of the following groups, give a specific example of how incorrect data processing by a company's computer system may lead to incorrect decisions being made:
   a. management
   b. shareholders
   c. labor unions
   d. environmentalists
   e. tax department
   f. affirmative action groups
1.3. What are the implications of a company losing its:
   a. personnel master file
   b. inventory master file
1.4. Should we be any more concerned about computer fraud and embezzlement versus other forms of business fraud and embezzlement?
1.5. Why does the computer cause us to have increased concern about the privacy of individuals?
1.6. Give an example of the computer being used for data processing where you consider it to be:
   a. socially desirable
   b. socially undesirable
1.7. What are the four major objectives of EDP auditing? Explain the meaning of each one of them.
1.8. Define data integrity. What factors affect the importance of data integrity to an organization?
1.9. What is the distinction between system effectiveness and system efficiency? Why is the EDP auditor concerned with system effectiveness and system efficiency?
1.10. Briefly explain the nature of the impact of using computers on the overall objectives of internal control.
1.11. What problems arise for ensuring incompatible functions are separate in a computer installation?
1.12. Briefly explain how assets may be lost by a person having unauthorized access to a payroll program.

1.13. How does a changed control technology impact auditors when they evaluate internal control systems?
1.14. What problems does the use of minicomputers sometimes produce for maintenance of an adequate audit/management trail?
1.15. In manual systems, records and assets are compared sometimes by taking a statistical sample of records and checking their correspondence with assets. Briefly explain how this activity might be undertaken in a computer system.
1.16. Give two reasons (and give examples) why the consequences of error in a computer system may be more serious than the consequences of error in a manual system.
1.17. Briefly explain the contributions of the following areas to EDP auditing:
   a. traditional auditing
   b. information systems management
   c. computer science
   d. behavioral science

EXERCISES AND CASES

1.1. Further research on computer abuse is useful because it helps provide answers to the following questions:
   a. *Who* perpetrates abuses?
   b. *How* are abuses perpetrated?
   c. *Why* are abuses perpetrated?
   d. What *controls* would have prevented or detected abuses?
   e. What *audit procedures* would have detected the abuse?
   Required: Undertake some reading on computer abuse and on the basis of your reading write a brief report providing some answers to the above questions.
1.2. **Equity Funding Corporation**
   In 1973, the largest single company fraud known was discovered in California. The collapse of the Equity Funding Corporation of America involved an estimated $2 billion fraud. The case is extremely complex and it took several years before the investigation was complete. However, some of the pertinent findings derived from the Trustee's Bankruptcy report follow.
   Equity Funding was a financial institution primarily engaged in life insurance. In 1964, its top management commenced to perpetrate a fraud that would take almost 10 years to discover. The intent of the fraud was to inflate earnings so that management could benefit through trading their securities at high prices.
   The fraud progressed through three major stages: the "inflated earnings phase," the "foreign phase," and the "insurance phase." The inflated earnings phase involved inflating income with bogus commissions supposedly earned through loans made to customers. Equity Funding had a funded life insurance program whereby customers who bought mutual funds shares could obtain a loan from the company to pay the premium on a life insurance policy. After some years the customer would sell off the mutual fund holdings to repay the loan, and hopefully the mutual fund shares would have appreciated sufficiently so only a partial sale of shares would be required. Thus, the customer had the cash value of the insurance policy and the remaining mutual fund shares as assets from the investment.
   The inflated earnings obtained via bogus commissions were supported by manual entries made on the company's books. Even though supporting documen-

tation did not exist for the entries, the fraud managed to miss the scrutiny of the company's auditors. However, the inflated assets did not bring about cash inflows, and the company started to suffer severe cash shortages because of real operating losses.

To remedy the cash shortage situation, the fraud moved into the second stage called the foreign phase. The company acquired foreign subsidiaries and used these subsidiaries in complex transfers of assets. Funds were brought into the parent company to reduce the funded loans asset account and falsely represent customer repayments of their loans. However, even this scheme proved inadequate.

The third stage of the fraud, called the insurance phase, involved the resale of insurance policies to other insurance companies. This is normal practice in the insurance business when one company needs cash immediately and another company has a cash surplus. Equity Funding created bogus policies and in the short run attempted to solve its cash problems by selling these policies to another insurance company. In the long run, however, the purchasing company expected cash receipts from premiums on the policies. Since the policies were bogus, Equity Funding had to find the cash to pay the premiums. Thus, it was a matter of time before the fraud could no longer be concealed. Interestingly, the fraud was revealed by a disgruntled employee involved in the fraud who had been fired by Equity Funding management.

The computer was not used in the fraud until the insurance phase. The task of creating the bogus policies was too big to be handled manually. Instead, a program was written to generate policies and these policies were coded as the now infamous "Class 99."

The trustee's report reveals two clear-cut conclusions. First, the fraud was unsophisticated and doomed to failure. Second, Equity Funding's auditors were grossly negligent. The fundamental principles of good auditing were not applied. The fraud was the financial ruin of many families.

Required: Write a brief report outlining some traditional audit procedures which, if they had been used, should have detected the fraud. Be sure to explain why you believe the procedures you recommend would have been successful.

1.3. Jerry Schneider

One of the more famous cases of computer abuse involves a young man called Jerry Schneider. Schneider always had a flair for electronics and by the time he left high school he had already formed his own firm to market his inventions. His firm also sold refurbished Western Electric telephone equipment. In 1970, he devised a scheme whereby Pacific Telephone in Los Angeles would supply him with good equipment—free!

Pacific Telephone used a computerized equipment ordering system. Equipment sites placed orders using a Touch-Tone card dialer. The orders were then keypunched onto cards and the computer updated the inventory master file and printed the orders. The orders were then supplied to a transportation office that shipped the supplies.

Schneider intended to gain access to the ordering system and have Pacific Telephone deliver supplies to him thinking they were supplying one of their legitimate sites. He used a variety of techniques to find out the working of the system and breach security. He sifted through trash cans and found discarded documents that provided him with information on the ordering system. He posed as a magazine writer and gathered information directly from Pacific Telephone. To support his activities he bought a Pacific Telephone delivery van at an auction, "acquired" the master key for supply delivery locations in the Los Angeles area, and bought a Touch-Tone telephone card dialer with a set of cards similar to those used by the equipment sites to submit orders.

Schneider took advantage of the budgeting system used for ordering sites. Typically, these sites had a budget allocated larger than they needed. Providing this budget was not exceeded, no investigation of equipment ordering took place. Schneider managed to gain access to the online computer system containing information on budgets and determined the size of orders that would be tolerated.

For seven months Pacific Telephone delivered him equipment that he resold to his customers and to Pacific Telephone. He kept track of the reorder levels for various Pacific Telephone inventories, depleted these inventories with his ordering, and then resold the equipment back to Pacific Telephone.

Schneider's downfall occurred when he revealed his activities to an employee. He was unable to keep up with the pace of his activities and so he confided in an employee to obtain assistance. When the employee asked for a pay raise, Schneider fired him and the employee then went to Pacific Telephone and told them of the fraud.

There are varying reports on how much Schneider took from Pacific Telephone. Parker [1976] estimates it was possible equipment worth a few million dollars was taken. For the fraud Schneider received a two-month jail sentence followed by three years probation. Interestingly, upon completing the jail term he set up a consulting firm specializing in computer security.

Required: Write a brief report outlining some basic internal control procedures which, if they had been applied, should have prevented or detected Schneider's activities. Be sure to explain why the application of the internal control procedures you recommend would have been successful.

1.4. Union Dime Savings Bank

Banks seem especially prone to computer abuse. Roswell Steffen used a computer to embezzle $1.5 million of funds at the Union Dime Savings Bank in New York City. In an interview with Miller [1974] after he was discovered, he claimed: "Anyone with a head on his shoulders could successfully embezzle funds from a bank. And many do." Steffen was a compulsive gambler. He initially "borrowed" $5000 from a cash box at the bank to support his gambling with a view to returning the money from his earnings. Unfortunately, he lost the $5000 and he spent the next three and one-half years trying to replace the money, again by "borrowing" from the bank to gamble at the racetrack.

As the head teller at Union Dime, Steffen had a supervisory terminal in the bank's online computer system that he used for various administrative purposes. He took money from the cash box and used the terminal to manipulate customer account balances so the discrepancies would not be evidenced in the bank's daily proof sheets.

He used several techniques to obtain money. He first concentrated on accounts over $100,000 that had little activity and had interest credited quarterly. He used the supervisory terminal to reduce the balances in these accounts. Occasionally an irate customer complained about the balances so Steffen then faked a telephone call to the data processing department, informed the customer it was a simple error, and corrected the situation by moving funds from another account.

Other sources of funds included two-year certificate accounts and new accounts. With two-year certificate accounts, he prepared the necessary documents but did not record the deposit in the bank's files. Initially he had two years to correct the situation but matters became more complicated when the bank started to pay interest on these accounts quarterly. With new accounts, he used two new passbooks from the bank's supply of prenumbered books. Upon opening an account, he entered the transaction using the account number of the first passpook but recorded the entry in the second passbook. He then destroyed the first passbook. Perpetrating the fraud became very complex and he made many mistakes. However, the bank's internal control system and audit techniques were sufficiently weak that he could explain away discrepancies and continue. He was caught because police raided Steffen's bookie and noticed a lowly paid bank teller making very large bets.

Required: Write a brief report outlining some basic internal control procedures which, if they had been applied, should have prevented or detected Steffen's activities. Be sure to explain why the application of the control procedures you recommend would have been successful.

REFERENCES

Allen, Brandt. "The Biggest Computer Frauds: Lessons for CPAS," *Journal of Accountancy* (May 1977), pp. 52–62.

American Institute of Certified Public Accountants. *Statement on Auditing Standards No. 3: The Effects of EDP on the Auditor's Study and Evaluation of Internal Control* (New York: American Institute of Certified Public Accountants, 1974).

―――. *The Auditor's Study and Evaluation of Internal Control in EDP Systems* (New York: American Institute of Certified Public Accountants, 1977).

―――. *Report of the Special Advisory Committee on Internal Accounting Control* (New York: American Institute of Certified Public Accountants, 1979).

Blish, Eugene A. "Computer Abuse: A Practical Use of the AICPA Guide," *EDPACS* (September 1978), pp. 6–12.

Boritz, J. Effrim. *Computer Guide '79* (Canada: Morka Publications, Inc., 1979).

Denning, Dorothy E., and Peter J. Denning. "Data Security," *Computing Surveys* (September 1979), pp. 227–249.

Everest, Gordon C. *Database Management: Objectives, System Functions, and Administration* (New York: McGraw-Hill Book Company, 1982).

Hoffman, Lance J. *Modern Methods for Computer Security and Privacy* (Englewood Cliffs, N. J.: Prentice-Hall, Inc., 1977).

International Data Corporation. *EDP Industry Report,* June 29, 1979, pp. 1–20.

Krauss, Leonard I., and Aileen MacGahan. *Computer Fraud and Countermeasures* (Englewood Cliffs, N. J.: Prentice-Hall, Inc., 1979).

Leibholz, Stephen W., and Lois D. Wilson. *Users' Guide to Computer Crime: Its Commission, Detection and Prevention* (Radnor, Pa.: Chilton Book Company, 1974).

Lucas, Henry C. *Towards Creative System Design* (New York: Columbia University Press, 1975).

McKnight, Gerald. *Computer Crime* (New York: Walker Publishing Company, Inc., 1973).

McNeil, John. *The Consultant* (New York: Coward, McCann and Geoghegan, Inc., 1978).

Marschak, Jacob, and Roy Radner. *Economic Theory of Teams* (New Haven and London: Yale University Press, 1972).

Miller, Curt. "Union Dime Picks Up the Pieces in $1.5 Million Embezzlement Case," *Bank Systems and Equipment* (June 1973), pp. 34–35, 92.

———. "How I Embezzled $1.5 Million—And Nearly Got Away with It," *Bank Systems and Equipment* (June 1974), pp. 26–28. An interview with Roswell Steffen.

Parker, Donn B. *Crime by Computer* (New York: Charles Scribner's Sons, 1976).

———, Susan Nycum, and S. Stephen Oura. *Computer Abuse* (Stanford, Calif.: Stanford Research Institute, 1973). Available from National Technical Information Service, U.S. Department of Commerce, Springfield, Va. 22151, Order No. PB-231-320.

Price Waterhouse. *Accounting Controls in a Minicomputer Installation* (New York: Price Waterhouse, 1979).

Weiss, Harold. "The Latest from Equity Funding" *EDPACS* (December 1974), pp. 1–9.

CHAPTER 2

A GENERAL APPROACH TO EDP AUDITING

CHAPTER OUTLINE

THE SYSTEM OF INTERNAL CONTROLS AND THE AUDIT APPROACH
CONTROLS AND THE POTENTIAL FOR LOSS
THE NATURE OF COMPUTER CONTROLS
    Management and Application Controls
    Preventive, Detective, and Corrective Controls
OVERVIEW OF STEPS IN AN EDP AUDIT
    The Preliminary Review Phase
    The Detailed Review Phase
    The Compliance Testing Phase
    Review and Testing of User (Compensating) Controls
    The Substantive Testing Phase
SOME MAJOR AUDIT DECISIONS
    The Evaluation Judgment
    Timing of Audit Procedures
    Audit Use of the Computer
    Selecting Application Systems for Audit
SUMMARY
REVIEW QUESTIONS
EXERCISES AND CASES
REFERENCES

It is a sobering experience to be in charge of the EDP audit of a computer installation that has several hundred programmers and analysts, a large computer, and thousands of files. Obviously all computer installations are not this size. However, in all but the smallest installation it is normally impossible for the auditor to perform a detailed check of all the data processing carried out. How, then, can the EDP audit be performed so that the auditor obtains reasonable assurance a computer installation safeguards its EDP assets, maintains data integrity, and achieves system effectiveness and efficiency?

This chapter describes a general approach to carrying out an EDP audit. It describes some techniques for simplifying and providing order to the complexity faced by the auditor when making evaluation judgments on computer systems. Further, it discusses some of the major decisions the auditor must make when planning and implementing an EDP audit.

THE SYSTEM OF INTERNAL CONTROLS AND THE AUDIT APPROACH

One way for the auditor to evaluate how well application systems in a computer installation safeguard assets and meet data integrity, system effectiveness, and system efficiency objectives would be to examine directly the end products of the systems: the data produced, its use by decision makers, and the resources consumed by the systems. Clearly, in all but the smallest installations this approach would be time consuming. Usually it is less costly for the auditor to examine the system of internal controls set up by management to ensure application systems achieve the asset safeguarding, data integrity, system effectiveness, and system efficiency objectives. If the internal control system is intact, the auditor can have more confidence in the quality of the application systems being evaluated. Direct testing of the end products of application systems still usually has to be carried out; however, the extent of this testing can be reduced and it can be better directed.

CONTROLS AND THE POTENTIAL FOR LOSS

Management sets up a system of internal controls to reduce the potential for loss. The value of a control can be assessed in terms of its cost and the extent to which it reduces *expected* losses. It can reduce expected losses in two ways: (*a*) by reducing the probability of the loss occurring, and (*b*) by reducing the amount of the loss if the loss occurs.

Controls reduce expected losses by acting on the *causes* of losses. The auditor's task is to evaluate *how well* controls act on the causes of losses to reduce expected losses. Unfortunately, this is a complex task. Both the causes of losses and the controls acting on these causes confound and interact in complex ways so that overall evaluation of an internal control system is difficult.

To illustrate the problem, consider some of the major reasons why an organization may suffer losses. Mair et al. [1976] list the following:

1 Erroneous record keeping
2 Unacceptable accounting
3 Business interruption
4 Erroneous management decisions
5 Fraud and embezzlement
6 Statutory sanctions
7 Excessive costs or lost revenues
8 Loss or destruction of assets
9 Competitive disadvantage

Each of these "high"-level causes of loss, however, can be broken up into "lower"-level causes of losses. For example, Figure 2.1 shows that erroneous management decisions are caused in part by inaccurate and incomplete data. These two causes in turn are a function of lower-level causes. For example, incomplete data may be caused by a clerk's failure to record data or an erroneous program processing the data (see also, Loebbecke and Zuber [1980]).

The notion of a hierarchy of causes of losses is a useful way for the auditor to conceptualize the internal control system evaluation process. It emphasizes the interdependencies between causes of loss and the ways in which they eventually impact an organization. For example, at a low level in the hierarchy, good forms design reduces the number of data recording errors made. This impacts the expected losses resulting from higher-level causes in the hierarchy; because the likelihood of incomplete data arising during the data capture

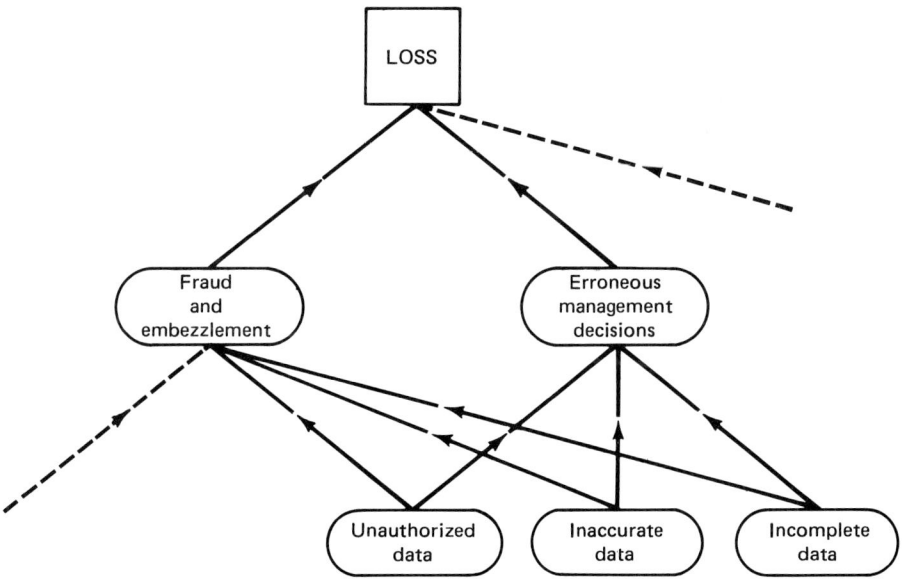

Figure 2.1
Loss and its causes as a hierarchy.

process is reduced, there is less likelihood of erroneous management decisions being made.

The problem with this approach is that there is no simple one-to-one relationship between controls and causes of loss and higher-level causes and lower-level causes. For example, good forms design impacts at least *two* causes of loss: incomplete data and inaccurate data. Further, the effects of *several* higher-level causes of losses are a function of the effects of incomplete and inaccurate data. Incomplete and inaccurate data can cause erroneous management decisions, statutory sanctions, loss of assets, etc. Thus, tracing the functional relationships between controls and causes of loss and lower-level causes and higher-level causes is often a difficult if not impossible task. Unfortunately, the reduction in the expected loss from a cause that occurs because a control is exercised must be assessed in terms of the ultimate effect on profitability; and this requires the auditor to understand the functional relationships that exist. In spite of the practical shortcomings of the approach, however, it still provides a useful way for the auditor to think about the evaluation of the internal control decision-making process.

THE NATURE OF COMPUTER CONTROLS

The evaluation of the system of internal controls also is facilitated if the auditor conceptualizes controls over computer data processing in different ways. The following sections present two major bases for classifying computer controls; they discuss also why these classifications are useful during the audit.

Management and Application Controls

Classifying computer controls into management controls and application controls is useful for three reasons. First, it is often more efficient for the auditor to evaluate management controls before application controls. Second, within the major categories of management controls and application controls, computer controls can be organized further to provide an orderly basis for conducting the audit. Third, it will become apparent from the discussion which follows that a useful conceptualization of controls within a computer installation is as an "onion" where the layers of skin constitute the various levels of management and application controls (Figure 2.2). Forces that erode data integrity, system effectiveness, and system efficiency must penetrate these control layers. To the extent that the outer layers of control are intact, it is likely the inner layers of control will be intact.

The Management Control Framework Management controls attempt to ensure the development, implementation, and operation of information systems proceeds in a planned and controlled manner. There are several levels of management controls corresponding to the organizational hierarchy and major functions performed within a computer installation:

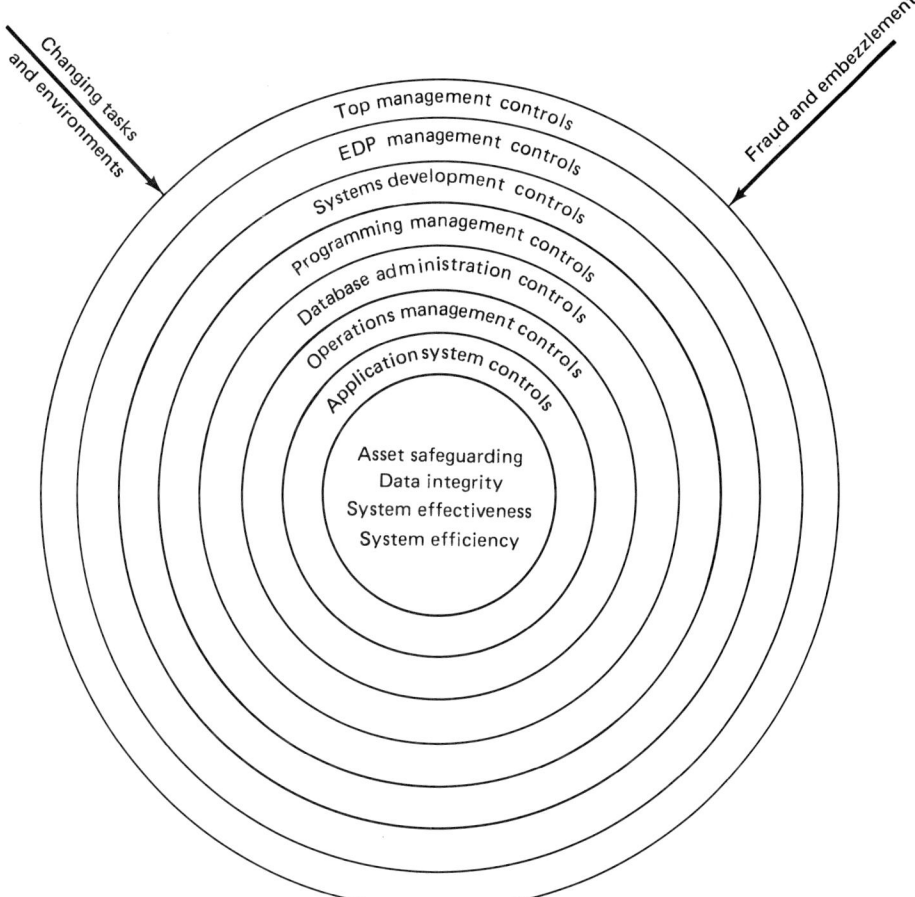

Figure 2.2
The computer control framework.

Management control level	Description of controls
Top Management	Top management of the organization must ensure the computer installation is well-managed. It is responsible primarily for long-run policy decisions on how computers will be used in the organization.
EDP Management	EDP management has overall responsibility for the planning and control of all computer activities. It also provides inputs to top management's long-run policy decision making and translates long-run policies into short-run goals and objectives.
Systems Development Management	Systems development management is responsible for the design, implementation, and maintenance of individual application systems.

Programming Management	Programming management is responsible for programming new systems, maintaining old systems, and providing general systems support software.
Database Administration	Database administration is responsible for the control and use of an organization's database or library of application system files.
Operations Management	Operations management controls the day-to-day operations of computer systems. It is responsible for data preparation, the data flow through the installation, production running of systems, maintenance of hardware, and sometimes maintenance of program and file library facilities and installation security.

Management controls are fundamental controls that apply across all application systems; thus, the absence of a management control is a serious concern for the auditor. It may not be worthwhile to review and evaluate application controls if a fundamental weakness exists in the management control framework.

From the viewpoint of audit efficiency, it is also useful to evaluate management controls first. If the auditor evaluates a management control once, it usually does not have to be evaluated again since it should function across all applications. For example, if the auditor finds that an installation enforces high-quality documentation standards, it is unlikely the auditor will have to review the quality of documentation for each application system.

The Application Control Framework Application system controls attempt to ensure that individual application systems safeguard EDP assets, maintain data integrity, and process data efficiently. Application controls are exercised at various stages in the flow of data through a computer system:

Application control stage	Description of controls
Data Capture	Data capture controls ensure all transactions are recorded and that the transactions are authorized, complete, and accurate. They also ensure source data is transmitted to the point of data preparation for input to the computer, and that source data is returned and properly filed.
Data Preparation	Data preparation controls ensure all data is converted to machine-readable form, and is authorized, complete, and accurate. They also ensure input data is transmitted to a computer room or input device for input to the computer, and that input data is returned and properly filed.
Access	Access controls ensure only authorized personnel gain access to computing resources such as application system files and programs.

Input	Input controls ensure all data entered into the computer is authorized, accurate, and complete. They also ensure errors identified are corrected and reentered for computer processing.
Transmission	Transmission controls ensure data sent between two points in a computer system is authorized, accurate, and complete.
Processing	Processing controls ensure programs process all data entered into the computer and that processing is authorized, accurate, and complete.
Output	Output controls ensure output produced by the computer is authorized, accurate, and complete, distributed to the responsible personnel, and properly filed.
Audit Trail	Audit trail controls ensure data can be traced through a system from its source to its final destination, and vice versa, and that the integrity of a corrupted audit trail can be restored.
Backup and Recovery	Backup and recovery controls ensure the physical existence of data can be restored if the data is lost or its integrity is corrupted.

The specific controls used in an application system depend upon the likely causes of loss in the application system and the activities performed by the system. For example, if data capture and entry is performed by a machine (e.g., a point-of-sale device) that rarely generates an error, few input controls may be used. Similarly, an application system that did not use data communications obviously would not require transmission controls for communication lines.

Application controls also are examples of *horizontal* controls. They follow the data flow through the organization and cut across organizational lines of authority and responsibility. Management controls, on the other hand, tend to be examples of *vertical* controls; controls that follow the hierarchical lines of authority on the organization chart.

Preventive, Detective, and Corrective Controls

The classification of controls as preventive, detective, or corrective is useful for the auditor because it highlights *when* the controls are exercised during the flow of data through a computer system.

Preventive controls exist to stop errors occurring. For example, good forms design means clerks are less likely to make errors in coding source data for a system; separation of duties reduces the likelihood of collusion occurring. Preventive controls usually are general types of controls exercised at early stages in the flow of data through a computer system. Their generality often allows them to be robust to changes in the computer systems where they are used. For example, separation of duties may remain constant even though specific clerical duties may change. However, because preventive controls are general controls, they allow many types of errors still to occur.

Detective controls identify errors after they have occurred. For example, an input validation program will identify data that falls outside an allowable range of values. Detective controls tend to be specific types of controls exercised at later stages in the flow of data through a computer system.

Corrective controls attempt to ensure that errors identified are corrected. For example, writing update mismatches to a suspense file and issuing reminders if they are not removed from the file should ensure errors are corrected and reentered into the system. Once an error has been detected, some type of corrective control is always necessary. However, corrective controls also must be subject to detective controls since errors may occur once again in the error correction process.

If the auditor is considering what types of controls might be exercised to reduce the expected loss from some type of error, it is often useful to group the controls that can be exercised into the three categories: preventive, detective, and corrective. The auditor then can trace the flow of the error through the computer system to see how the various controls act upon the error, especially in terms of their ability to reduce the expected loss from the error.

OVERVIEW OF STEPS IN AN EDP AUDIT

Bearing in mind, then, the lessons of the previous sections on how an EDP audit might be approached, Figure 2.3 flowcharts the major steps in an EDP audit. The general approach shown in the flowchart is representative of the approaches advocated by many of the professional audit organizations (see, for example, American Institute of Certified Public Accountants [1974, 1977a]). It has been formulated in light of substantial experience in performing EDP audits.

The following sections describe briefly each step in an EDP audit. Though Figure 2.3 and the ensuing discussion imply a sequential progression of audit steps, some of the steps may be carried out concurrently. For example, for efficiency purposes data required for the preliminary review evaluation and detailed review evaluation may be collected at the same time.

The Preliminary Review Phase

The first step in an EDP audit is the preliminary review of the computer installation. The objective of the preliminary review is to obtain the information necessary for the auditor to make a decision on how to proceed with the audit.

At the conclusion of the preliminary review, the auditor can proceed in one of three ways:

1 Withdraw from the audit; there may be problems of independence because the auditor may lack the technical competence to perform the audit.

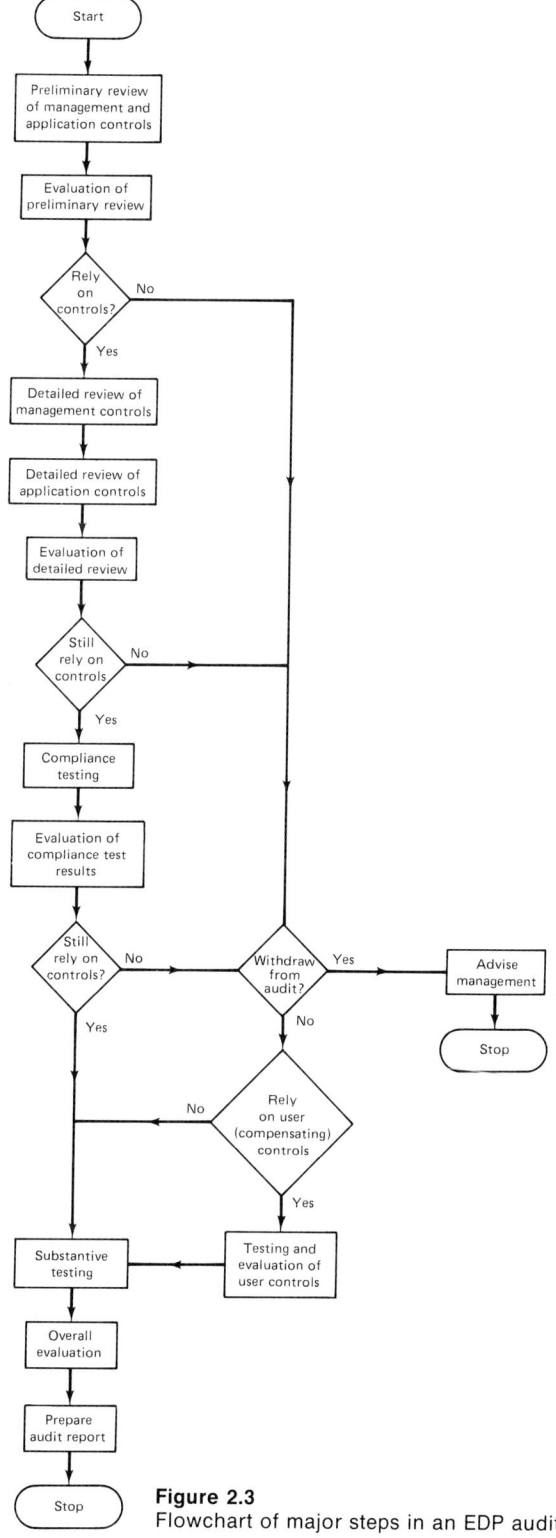

Figure 2.3
Flowchart of major steps in an EDP audit.

2 Perform a detailed review of the internal control system with the expectation that reliance can be placed upon the internal control system and the scope and extent of substantive testing can be reduced as a consequence.

3 Decide not to rely on the internal control system. There are two possible reasons for this decision. First, it may be more cost-effective to perform substantive tests directly. Second, EDP controls may duplicate controls existing in the user area. The auditor may decide it is more cost-effective to rely on these *compensating* controls and proceed to review and test these controls instead.

The preliminary review phase incorporates a review of management controls and application controls. During the review of management controls the auditor attempts to understand the organization and management practices used at each level within the management hierarchy of the computer installation. During the review of application controls the auditor attempts to understand the controls exercised over the major types of transactions that flow through the significant application systems within the installation.

The primary means of evidence collection during the preliminary review phase are interviews with installation personnel, observations of installation activities, and reviews of installation documentation. The evidence may be documented by completing questionnaires, constructing flowcharts and decision tables, and preparing narratives.

The preliminary review carried out by internal auditors differs from the preliminary review carried out by external auditors in three ways. First, internal auditors typically need to undertake less preliminary review work than external auditors, especially in terms of management controls, since they should be familiar with the installation already. Second, whereas external auditors focus primarily on causes of loss and controls relevant to the attest decision, internal auditors have a broader perspective that incorporates system effectiveness and efficiency considerations. Third, if internal auditors suspect serious weaknesses exist in the internal control system when they complete the preliminary review phase, rather than proceed directly to substantive testing, they still may carry out detailed testing of the internal control system with a view to making specific recommendations for improvement.

The Detailed Review Phase

The objective of the detailed review phase is to obtain the information necessary for the auditor to have an *in-depth* understanding of the controls used in a computer installation. Once again a decision must be made on whether to withdraw from the audit, proceed to the compliance testing phase with the expectation that reliance can be placed upon the internal control system, or proceed directly to a review of user (compensating) controls or substantive test procedures. For some applications the auditor may decide to rely on the internal control system; for others, alternate audit procedures may be more appropriate.

Again, both management controls and application controls are reviewed. As discussed earlier in the chapter, if possible, management controls should be reviewed first as pervasive weaknesses in these controls may cause the auditor to deem further review of application controls to be unnecessary. The methods of obtaining and documenting evidence in the detailed review stage are primarily those used during the preliminary review phase.

In the detailed review phase, it is important for the auditor to identify the causes of loss existing within the installation and the controls established to reduce the effects of these causes of loss. At the conclusion of the detailed review the auditor must evaluate whether the controls established reduce the expected losses from these causes to an acceptable level. Since during this phase the auditor still does not know how well the controls work in practice, the evaluation assumes the controls function reliably, unless there is already evidence to the contrary.

As with the preliminary review phase there are differences in the approaches adopted by the internal auditor and the external auditor. The internal auditor is more likely to consider causes of loss that affect system effectiveness and efficiency. Besides evaluating whether or not the set of controls chosen is sufficient to reduce expected losses to an acceptable level, the internal auditor also often considers whether or not the set of controls chosen is "optimal"; that is, the system may be overcontrolled or it may be possible to achieve a satisfactory level of control using fewer or less costly controls. If the internal auditor considers the system of internal controls to be unsatisfactory, again, rather than proceed directly to review and testing of compensating controls or substantive test procedures, compliance testing still may be undertaken as a basis for making specific recommendations for improvement.

The Compliance Testing Phase

The objective of the compliance testing phase is to determine whether or not the system of internal controls operates as it is purported to operate. The auditor seeks to determine whether or not alleged controls in fact exist and whether or not they work reliably.

Besides the manual evidence collection techniques described previously, often the auditor must use computer-assisted evidence collection techniques to determine the existence and reliability of controls. For example, to evaluate the validation controls in an input program, the most cost-effective way may be to use a test data generator to produce test data for input to the program.

At the conclusion of the compliance testing phase, the auditor again must evaluate the internal control system in light of the evidence collected on the reliability of individual controls. The general process of evaluation and the choices of further audit procedures available are the same as those for the previous phases.

Review and Testing of User (Compensating) Controls

In some cases the auditor might decide not to rely on internal controls within the computer installation because users exercise controls that compensate for any weaknesses in the EDP internal control system. For example, even though weak controls may exist over the transit of source data to the computer installation, users may carefully reconcile their own control totals with those produced as output from application system programs.

From an external audit viewpoint, evaluating compensating controls may be a more cost-effective way of completing the audit. The internal auditor may be concerned, however, that compensating controls do not represent a needless duplication of controls; in other words, it may be worthwhile to eliminate either some user controls or some computer controls.

The Substantive Testing Phase

The objective of the substantive testing phase is to obtain sufficient evidence so the auditor can make a final judgment on whether or not material losses have occurred or could occur during computer data processing. The external auditor expresses this judgment in the form of an opinion as to whether a material misstatement of the accounts exists. Usually the internal auditor is concerned with a broader perspective: given the state of the internal control system, have losses occurred or could they occur in the future because of weaknesses in the controls used to safeguard assets and to achieve data integrity, system effectiveness, and system efficiency?

Davis et al. [1981] identify five types of substantive tests that can be used within a computer installation:

1. Tests to identify erroneous processing
2. Tests to assess the quality of data
3. Tests to identify inconsistent data
4. Tests to compare data with physical counts
5. Confirmation of data with outside sources

Many of these tests require computer support; for example, generalized audit software can be used to select and print confirmations. However, the fundamental processes involved in carrying out substantive testing and issuing the audit report for computer systems are the same as those for manual systems.

SOME MAJOR AUDIT DECISIONS

By presenting only an overview of the major steps in an EDP audit, the previous section glossed over the difficulties involved in making some of the major decisions required when carrying out an EDP audit. Since these decisions can impact substantially the audit approach adopted for a specific system, the following sections highlight the nature of these decisions and some of the considerations involved in making the decisions.

The Evaluation Judgment

Perhaps the most difficult decision for auditors to make during an EDP audit is the evaluation judgment. The evaluation judgment must be made at the end of the preliminary review phase, at the end of the detailed review phase, at the end of the compliance testing phase, and at the end of the substantive testing phase. It impacts whether the auditor will continue with the audit, whether the internal control system can be relied upon, what controls are critical to the audit and how they should be tested for compliance, the extent of substantive testing needed, and, finally, whether or not the system has satisfactorily safeguarded assets, maintained data integrity, and achieved system effectiveness and efficiency.

Since the evaluation decision is a *judgment* decision, there is no single accepted method of making the decision. However, Table 2.1 shows a conceptual representation of the judgment decision to be made. The columns of the matrix are causes of loss; in this case, circumstances that would cause a loss if they occurred during the data capture stage of an application system. The rows are controls exercised over the causes to reduce the expected loss. The elements of the matrix might be some rating of the effectiveness of each control at reducing the expected loss from each cause, the reliability of the

TABLE 2.1
MATRIX CONCEPTUALIZATION OF CONTROLS THAT REDUCE EXPECTED LOSSES DURING DATA CAPTURE (RECOGNITION AND MEASUREMENT OF AN ECONOMIC EVENT)

Control \ Cause of loss	Recognition/ measurement inaccurate	Recognition/ measurement incomplete	Event not recognized/ measured	Measurement/ recognition unauthorized
Hire high-quality staff	✓	✓	✓	✓
Ensure staff are trained	✓	✓	✓	
Ensure division of duties exists	✓	✓	✓	✓
Procedures well-designed	✓	✓	✓	
Procedures well-documented	✓	✓	✓	
Supervise staff properly	✓	✓	✓	✓
Well-designed tasks	✓	✓	✓	
Pleasant work environment	✓	✓	✓	
Restrict physical access				✓

✓ Denotes functional relationship.

control with respect to each cause in light of compliance testing results, or the marginal benefits and costs of exercising the control. In Table 2.1 the elements simply show the existence of a relationship between the different controls and causes of loss.

In terms of the matrix, conceptually the auditor performs three types of evaluations: a columnar evaluation, a row evaluation, and a global evaluation. The *columnar* evaluation involves asking the question: For a given cause of loss, do the controls exercised over the cause reduce the expected loss from the cause to an acceptable level? As discussed previously, the auditor asks this question prior to and after testing the reliability of controls.

The *row* evaluation involves asking the question: Do the benefits of having a control exceed the costs? To facilitate this evaluation, the elements of the matrix might contain the net marginal benefits (marginal benefits less marginal costs) of each control with respect to each cause of loss.

The *global* evaluation involves asking the question: What is the optimal set of controls for the organization? The answer to this question requires somehow a joint evaluation of columns and rows to be made. Whereas from a columnar perspective it may not be worthwhile to have a control, from a row perspective the benefits of the control when it is exercised over *all* causes of loss may exceed its cost.

With respect to the global evaluation question, there are still two more complicating factors. First, the marginal benefits and costs of a control often depend on what controls are being exercised already; that is, the benefits and costs of a control are conditional. Second, there is an overriding constraint on how many controls should be introduced into a system. This constraint applies when for all controls that still might be exercised, the marginal benefits of any one control exceed the marginal costs of that control.

The matrix conceptualization of the evaluation judgment also can be used to illustrate the different functions of the external and internal auditor. The external auditor is concerned primarily with columnar evaluation: Has the expected loss from a cause of loss been reduced to a satisfactory level? Further, the external auditor focuses on those causes of loss relating to lack of safeguards over assets or violation of data integrity. Whether or not the choice of controls is optimal in a global sense is a secondary consideration.

The internal auditor performs all three types of evaluation. Columnar evaluations include also causes of losses relating to ineffective and inefficient systems. The internal auditor is concerned, furthermore, with whether the marginal benefits of a control exceed the marginal cost (row evaluation) and whether the choice of controls is optimal from a global viewpoint (joint row and columnar evaluation).

Unfortunately, *how* a columnar, row, or global evaluation should be performed is still a research area. With respect to the columnar evaluation, some professional bodies have designated minimum control standards; that is, control standards that must be met for the auditor to consider controls over a cause of loss as being satisfactory (see, further, Canadian Institute of Chartered Accountants [1970] and EDP Auditors Foundation for Education and Research [1977]).

Timing of Audit Procedures

One of the important decisions the auditor must make when planning an EDP audit is the timing of audit procedures to be performed. The timing of EDP audit activities has been a controversial area. Some auditors argue little change is needed to the traditional schedule of interim work, end-of-period work, and postperiod-end work. Nevertheless, they recognize that audit use of the computer for evidence collection purposes often requires substantial advance preparation; for example, scheduling computer time for audit purposes, preparation of audit programs and test decks, and obtaining files for testing (see also, Davis et al. [1981]). Other auditors argue fundamental changes are needed to the timing of audit procedures when computer systems must be evaluated. These auditors emphasize audit participation in the design phases of an EDP system. If this latter view is accepted, audits will be performed at three stages in the life of a system: (a) during the design phase, (b) during the operations phase, and (c) during postaudits (Figure 2.4).

There are two major reasons given for design phase participation by EDP auditors. First, changing a system to include necessary controls after it has been implemented can be expensive. Second, it is often difficult, if not impossible, for the auditor on the basis of a periodic review to understand a system that has taken several thousand work-hours to design and implement. To avoid these problems, some EDP auditors argue both external and internal auditors

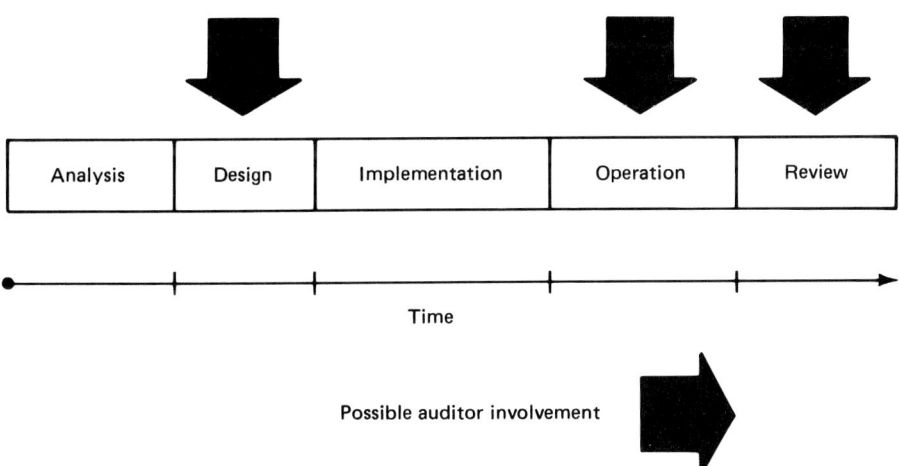

Figure 2.4
Auditor involvement in the systems life cycle.

should, at a minimum, review and evaluate the design of computer controls at various major checkpoints in the system development process.

The major concern about design phase participation by EDP auditors has been the potential effects on the auditor's independence. Controversy surrounds whether or not design phase participation impairs an auditor's ability to evaluate a system from a detached, objective viewpoint, particularly if the initial design reflects closely the auditor's recommendations.

Rittenberg [1977] surveyed internal and external auditors, EDP management, and top management to investigate the perceived effects of design phase participation on auditor independence. In general he found these groups believed design phase participation decreased auditor independence, but there were several ways in which auditor independence could be strengthened to compensate, at least partially, for the effects of design phase involvement:

1 Increase the auditor's technical knowledge of EDP
2 Assign different auditors to design phase audit work and postinstallation audit work
3 Recruit auditors with more extensive EDP experience
4 Set up an EDP audit section within the internal audit department specializing in EDP auditing
5 Obtain greater top management support

The groups surveyed believed the first two methods of increasing auditor independence were especially important; namely, increasing the technical knowledge of EDP auditors and assigning different auditors to the postaudit of a system.

Audit Use of the Computer

Another important decision the auditor must make when planning the audit is whether to use the computer to assist the audit or whether to audit without using the computer. The two approaches are commonly called auditing around the computer and auditing through the computer.

The terms are unfortunate since they derive from the period when auditors were auditing around the computer because of technical incompetence rather than arriving at a decision through a cost-benefit analysis of the two approaches. Thus the term "auditing around the computer" has negative connotations. However, because the terms are still commonly used, they will be retained throughout the following discussion.

Auditing around the Computer Auditing around the computer involves arriving at an audit opinion through examining the internal control system for a computer installation and the input and output *only* for application systems. On the basis of the quality of the input and output of the application system, the auditor infers the quality of the processing carried out. Application system processing is not examined directly. The auditor views the computer as a black box.

The auditor can usually audit around the computer when either of the following situations applies to application systems existing in the installation:

1 The system is simple and batch oriented.
2 The system uses generalized software that is well-tested and used widely by many installations.

Sometimes batch computer systems are just an extension of manual systems. These systems have the following attributes:

1 The system logic is straightforward and there are no special routines resulting from the use of the computer to process data.
2 Input transactions are batched and control can be maintained through the normal methods; for example, separation of duties and management supervision.
3 Processing primarily consists of sorting the input data and updating the master file sequentially.
4 There is a clear audit trail and detailed reports are prepared at key processing points within the system.
5 The task environment is relatively constant and few stresses are placed on the system.

For these well-defined systems, generalized software packages often are available. For example, software vendors have developed payroll, accounts receivable, and accounts payable packages. If these packages are provided by a reputable vendor, have received widespread use, and appear error free, the auditor may decide not to test directly the processing aspects of the system. The auditor must ensure, however, that the installation has not modified the package in any way and that adequate controls exist over the source code, object code, and documentation to prevent unauthorized modification of the package.

Not all generalized software packages make application systems amenable to auditing around the computer. Some packages provide a set of generalized functions that still must be selected and combined to accomplish application system purposes. For example, database management system software may provide generalized update functions, but a high-level program still must be written to combine these functions in the required way. In this situation the auditor is less able to infer the quality of processing from simply examining the system's input and output.

The primary advantage of auditing around the computer is simplicity. Auditors having little technical knowledge of computers can be trained easily to perform the audit, though they should be managed by a computer audit specialist.

There are two major disadvantages to the approach. First, the type of computer system where it is applicable is very restricted. It should not be used for systems having any complexity in terms of size or type of processing. Second, the auditor cannot assess very well the likelihood of the system degrading if the environment changes. The auditor should be concerned with the ability of the system to cope with a changed environment. Systems can be designed and programs can be written in certain ways so that a change in the environment will not cause the system to process data incorrectly or for it to degrade quickly. These aspects will be discussed in later chapters.

Auditing through the Computer For the most part the auditor now is involved in auditing through the computer. The auditor can use the computer to test: (a) the logic and controls existing within the system, and (b) the records produced by the system. Depending upon the complexity of the application system being audited, the approach may be fairly simple or require extensive technical competence on the part of the auditor.

There are several circumstances where auditing through the computer must be used:

1 The application system processes large volumes of input and produces large volumes of output that make extensive direct examination of the validity of input and output difficult.

2 Significant parts of the internal control system are embodied in the computer system. For example, in an online banking system a computer program may batch transactions for individual tellers to provide control totals for reconciliation at the end of the day's processing.

3 The logic of the system is complex and there are large portions that facilitate use of the system or efficient processing.

4 Because of cost-benefit considerations, there are substantial gaps in the visible audit trail.

The primary advantage of this approach is that the auditor has increased power to effectively test a computer system. The range and capability of tests that can be performed increases and the auditor acquires greater confidence that data processing is correct. By examining the system's processing, the auditor also can assess the system's ability to cope with environmental change.

The primary disadvantages of the approach are the high costs sometimes involved and the need for extensive technical expertise when systems are complex. However, these disadvantages are really spurious if auditing through the computer is the only viable method of carrying out the audit.

Selecting Application Systems for Audit

As a general rule the auditor should select for audit those application systems most critical to the continued existence of the organization. Since budget constraints usually apply, the auditor wants to select those application systems where the highest payoff will be obtained. The following sections provide some guidelines for selecting application systems for audit.

User Audits as a Selection Basis A useful way of finding out which application systems have problems is to perform a user audit. When application systems do not function correctly, users are affected because reports are late or incorrect, source data coding is difficult, error resubmission is onerous, etc. The control clerks in the user area responsible for gathering and batching source data, error correction, and error resubmission often know the fundamental weaknesses in an application system. User management can provide information on any problems experienced with the quality and timeliness of reports produced by the system.

The auditor also needs to investigate carefully a further aspect of the user environment. Sometimes an application system has detrimental effects on the quality of work life of its users. This can produce a variety of problems that impact asset safeguarding, data integrity, and system effectiveness and efficiency. At one extreme users attempt to directly sabotage the system. At the other extreme they simply show disinterest in the system. Eventually the application system degrades through lack of active user support. Sometimes these problems are covert and are difficult to identify.

The auditor can carry out the user audit in a formal or informal manner. If the user audit is part of the evaluation of an application system's effectiveness, user opinions may be solicited through questionnaires or structured interviews. If the auditor is simply carrying out a user audit to identify potential application systems for further investigation, the approach may be more informal. However, even if the approach is informal, it still needs to be planned and the results documented in working papers. The auditor's problem always is to ask those questions that elicit a response enabling problems to be identified. Asking the "right" questions requires forethought and planning.

Application System Characteristics as a Basis for Selection Perry [1974] provides other guidelines that the auditor can use to choose a specific application system for audit. The following are based upon his initial list:

Selection guideline	Explanation
Financial System	The auditor should give major attention to those systems providing financial control over the assets of the corporation, e.g., cash receipts and disbursements, payroll, accounts receivable and payable.
High-Risk System	Some application systems are riskier than others because: 1 They are susceptible to various kinds of losses, e.g., fraud and embezzlement. 2 Their failure may cripple the organization, e.g., failure to process payroll causes employees to strike. 3 They interface with other systems, and errors generated permeate these other systems.
High Potential for Competitive Damage	Some systems give an organization a competitive edge in the marketplace, e.g., an effective strategic planning system. Others through patents, copyrights, etc., are major sources of revenue for the organization. Others through their loss would destroy the image of the organization.

Technologically Advanced System	If a system utilizes advanced technology, e.g., a database management system, distributed hardware and software, or technology with which the installation has little experience, it is more likely the system will be a source of control problems.
High-Cost System	Systems that are costly to develop are often complex systems presenting many control problems.

Besides the audit of application systems where problems are apparent, internal auditors should perform a cyclical review of systems that seem to function well. This review examines ways of improving these systems.

SUMMARY

The steps involved in carrying out an EDP audit are similar to those involved in carrying out the audit of a manual system. First, the auditor performs a preliminary review of the computer installation to obtain an understanding of how the installation is managed and the major application systems being processed. Second, if the auditor expects to rely on the internal control system, a detailed review is carried out. Third, the auditor tests the reliability of those controls critical to the audit judgment. Fourth, substantive test procedures are performed. Finally, an audit opinion must be given. After all steps, the auditor evaluates the internal control system and decides whether to proceed with the audit or take alternate steps.

Throughout the EDP audit several difficult decisions must be made. Each evaluation of the reliability of the internal control system requires a complex joint evaluation of piecemeal evidence. The auditor must make a decision on whether to become involved at the design phase. Whether or not to audit through or around the computer must be evaluated carefully. The critical systems on which the audit will focus also must be chosen.

REVIEW QUESTIONS

2.1. Why does the auditor usually evaluate the internal control system when undertaking an EDP audit?
2.2. Briefly explain the relationship between controls, causes of loss, and expected loss. Be sure to define precisely what you mean by expected loss. Give an example to illustrate the relationship.
2.3. What is meant by a hierarchy of causes of loss? Why is it useful for the auditor to conceptualize the causes of loss as a hierarchy? What problems exist with conceptualizing the causes of loss in this way?
2.4. Briefly explain the difference between management controls and application system controls. Give an example of each type of control and explain why it is either a management or application system control.

2.5. For each of the following activities, identify the level of management that has primary responsibility for performing the activity:
   a. control and use of the organization's database
   b. maintenance of old application systems
   c. provision of general systems support software
   d. implementation of long-run policy decisions
2.6. Why might a serious weakness in the management control framework result in the auditor not examining application controls?
2.7. Classify each of the following application controls by type (e.g., data capture, input, processing, etc.):
   a. a control to prevent unauthorized access to computing resources
   b. a control to ensure erroneous data that is corrected is reentered into the computer
   c. a control to ensure data recorded on a form is authorized
   d. a control to ensure data printed on a report can be traced back to its origin
2.8. Why are management controls an example of vertical controls and application controls an example of horizontal controls?
2.9. Briefly explain the difference between preventive, detective, and corrective controls. Give an example of each. Why is it sometimes useful for the auditor to classify controls in this way?
2.10. Briefly explain the nature and purpose of the preliminary review phase. Are there any differences in the way internal and external auditors might perform the preliminary review?
2.11. Explain the nature of compensating controls. Give an example of a compensating control and show how its existence might affect the audit approach.
2.12. Briefly explain the relationship between the detailed review phase and the compliance testing phase of an EDP audit.
2.13. What courses of action might the auditor take after completing the compliance testing phase of an audit?
2.14. List three types of substantive tests that the auditor may perform and give an example of how the test might be performed.
2.15. List the major differences between the way an internal auditor might perform the various phases in an audit and the way an external auditor might perform the phases.
2.16. Briefly explain how the means of evidence collection change between the detailed review and compliance testing phases. Why do they change?
2.17. If the relationship between controls and causes of loss is conceptualized as a matrix, briefly explain how the row evaluation, columnar evaluation, and global evaluation relate to audit objectives.
2.18. Briefly explain why the evaluation judgment usually is very difficult for the auditor to make.
2.19. Why do some auditors argue they must become involved in design phase auditing? What problems can arise when the auditor gets involved at the design stage of a system? How might these problems be overcome?
2.20. Why does an EDP audit often involve more advance preparation than the audit of a manual system? Be sure to point out the specific areas where more advanced preparation often is necessary.
2.21. Give an example of a system where auditing around the computer would be appropriate and an example where auditing through the computer would be necessary. Explain why the approaches are appropriate for the examples you give.

2.22. Briefly explain why user audits can help the auditor to identify application systems where the payoff from an audit could be high.

2.23. Consider a manufacturing organization. Give two examples of application systems that would be important from the viewpoint of the external auditor and two that would be relatively unimportant.

EXERCISES AND CASES

2.1. Many audit organizations now follow the "cycle" approach when evaluating an internal control system (see, for example, American Institute of Certified Public Accountants [1979] and Arthur Andersen & Co. [1978]). This approach involves classifying transactions by cycles, converting the broad objectives of internal control into specific objectives for these classifications of transactions, and evaluating the controls in place in light of these objectives. Five major cycles of a business can be identified: revenue, expenditure, production or conversion, financing, and external financial reporting. For the revenue cycle the American Institute of Certified Public Accountants [1979] lists the following eight objectives:
1. The types of goods and services to be provided, the manner in which they will be provided, and the customer to whom they will be provided should be properly authorized.
2. Credit terms and limits should be properly authorized.
3. The prices and other terms of sale of goods and services should be properly authorized.
4. Sales-related deductions and adjustments should be properly authorized.
5. Deliveries of goods and services should result in preparation of accurate and timely billing forms.
6. Sales and related transactions should be recorded at the appropriate amounts and in the appropriate period and should be properly classified in the accounts.
7. Cash receipts should be accounted for properly on a timely basis.
8. Access to cash receipts and cash receipts records, accounts receivable records, and billing and shipping records should be suitably controlled to prevent or detect within a timely period the interception of unrecorded cash receipts or the abstraction of recorded cash receipts.

The Canadian Institute of Chartered Accountants [1970] gives four control objectives for the processing phase in a computer system:
1. Ensure the completeness of data processed by the computer.
2. Ensure the accuracy of data processed by the computer.
3. Ensure that all data processed by the computer is authorized.
4. Ensure the adequacy of management (audit) trails.

Required: Write a short report showing how the two sets of objectives can be reconciled.

2.2. You are on the staff of an external audit firm that audits a small-medium size financial institution. One day you receive a copy of a letter from the president of the financial institution to the partner-in-charge of the audit. The letter indicates that the client is considering replacing its existing computer with 20 desk-top minicomputers and converting its application systems to the minicomputers. You are alarmed at this "radical" move and its audit implications so you go to the partner-in-charge to request time to investigate the proposed changes and, if need be, suggest some design alternatives. The partner-in-charge hesitates when you make your request. She explains that she believes you should not become involved at this stage because it will affect the firm's independence. However, she concedes there may be problems with the changes proposed and she asks you to prepare a brief for her.

Required: Write a report to the partner outlining some of the control and audit problems that may arise with the proposed changeover to the minicomputers and suggest why you should become involved with the client at this stage.

2.3. The accounting department of a small company is responsible for payment of creditors. It receives a copy of each purchase order issued, a receiving document when the goods arrive, and the vendor's invoice. All documents are date-stamped upon receipt and filed securely. When the receiving document and vendor's invoice arrive, a clerk matches details and checks the accuracy of items and computations on the documents. A second clerk then prepares a disbursement voucher and a check for payment and gives the check, the voucher, and the supporting documents to a manager who examines them before signing the check.

Required: List the control objectives for the above operations. Prepare a controls matrix where the columns show causes of loss and the rows show the controls in existence to reduce expected losses. The elements of the matrix should show which controls act on the causes of loss. How well does the system of internal control allow the control objectives to be accomplished?

2.4. You are a staff EDP auditor in a public accounting firm. The firm has just acquired a new client—a small manufacturing organization. The client uses a minicomputer for its data processing.

All of the application systems are straightforward batch systems with well-defined input and output. However, the client uses a database management system that was purchased initially for its bill-of-materials application system. Furthermore, all application systems now use the DBMS.

Required: You are on the first audit of the new client. The partner-in-charge asks you to advise him on whether to plan the audit through the computer or around the computer. Write a short report giving your recommendations and the reasons for your recommendations.

REFERENCES

American Institute of Certified Public Accountants. *Statement on Auditing Standards No. 3: The Effects of EDP on the Auditor's Study and Evaluation of Internal Control* (New York: American Institute of Certified Public Accountants, 1974).

———. *The Auditor's Study and Evaluation of Internal Control in EDP Systems* (New York: American Institute of Certified Public Accountants, 1977a).

———. *Management, Control and Audit of Advanced EDP Systems* (New York: American Institue of Certified Public Accountants, 1977b).

———. *Report of the Special Advisory Committee on Internal Accounting Control* (New York: American Institute of Certified Public Accountants, 1979).

Anthony, Robert N. *Planning and Control Systems: A Framework for Analysis* (Cambridge, Mass.: Harvard University Press, 1965).

Arthur Andersen & Co. *A Guide for Studying and Evaluating Internal Accounting Controls* (Chicago: Arthur Andersen & Co., 1978).

Canadian Institute of Chartered Accountants. *Computer Control Guidelines* (Toronto, Canada: The Canadian Institute of Chartered Accountants, 1970).

Davis, Gordon B., Donald Adams, and Carol A. Schaller. *Auditing and EDP*, 2d ed. (New York: American Institute of Certified Public Accountants, 1981).

EDP Auditors Foundation for Education and Research. *Control Objectives*, 2d ed. (Hanover Park, Ill.: EDP Auditors Association, 1977).

Jancura, Elise G. *Audit and Control of Computer Systems* (New York: Petrocelli/Charter, 1974).

———— and Fred L. Lilly. "SAS No. 3 and the Evaluation of Internal Control," *Journal of Accountancy* (March 1977), pp. 69–74.

Loebbecke, James K., and George R. Zuber. "Evaluating Internal Control," *Journal of Accountancy* (February 1980), pp. 49–56.

Mair, William C., Donald R. Wood, and Keagle W. Davis. *Computer Control and Audit*, 2d ed. (Altamonte Springs, Fla.: The Institute of Internal Auditors, Inc., 1976).

Perry, William E. "Selecting an EDP System for Audit," *EDPACS* (April 1974), pp. 1–8.

Porter, W. Thomas, and William E. Perry. *EDP Controls and Auditing*, 2d ed. (Belmont, Calif.: Wadsworth Publishing Company, Inc., 1977).

Price Waterhouse. *Accounting Controls in a Minicomputer Installation* (New York: Price Waterhouse, 1979).

Rittenberg, Larry E. *Auditor Independence and Systems Design* (Altamonte Springs, Fla.: The Institute of Internal Auditors, 1977).

CHAPTER 3

ORGANIZATION AND MANAGEMENT OF THE EDP AUDIT FUNCTION

CHAPTER OUTLINE

NEED FOR A SEPARATE EDP AUDIT SECTION
  Need for Computer Audit Specialists
  Placement of Computer Audit Specialists
CENTRALIZATION VERSUS DECENTRALIZATION OF THE EDP AUDIT FUNCTION
STAFFING THE EDP AUDIT FUNCTION
  Number of EDP Auditors Required
  Source of EDP Audit Staff
TRAINING
  Amount of Training Needed
  Types of Training Needed
RELATIONSHIPS WITH MANAGEMENT AND OTHER ORGANIZATION GROUPS
  Types of Problems Experienced
  Methods of Improving Relations
PROMOTIONAL OPPORTUNITIES FOR THE EDP AUDITOR
  Internal Career Advancement
  External Career Advancement
LIFE CYCLE OF THE EDP AUDIT GROUP
SUMMARY
REVIEW QUESTIONS

EXERCISES AND CASES
REFERENCES

The emphasis given to EDP auditing in the accounting literature over recent years sometimes gives the impression that EDP auditing is a function separate and distinct from the traditional audit function. This is a mistaken impression. EDP auditing is an integral part of the total audit function: that part of the function supporting the auditor's judgment on the quality of computer systems. Ultimately the completion of an EDP audit contributes to the overall objectives of an external audit or an internal audit.

The emergence of an EDP audit function, however, has given rise to some controversial organization and management issues. There has been debate on how the function should be integrated with the total audit effort and how the function should be organized and managed. In some cases the issues debated have been resolved; however, there still are many contentious areas.

This chapter examines some of the major organization and management problems and controversies brought about by the existence of the EDP audit function. It assumes familiarity with good organization and management practices for both external and internal auditing (see Arens and Loebbecke [1976] and Sawyer [1973]); thus the chapter only highlights the difficulties that arise when these practices are applied to the EDP audit function.

NEED FOR A SEPARATE EDP AUDIT SECTION

A major question that has arisen when organizing and managing the EDP audit function is whether or not a separate group of computer audit specialists should exist to perform the function. Two issues must be resolved. First, is there a need for computer audit specialists? Second, if computer audit specialists are needed, where should they be placed within the organization hierarchy of the audit group?

Need for Computer Audit Specialists

Three motivations exist for having separate computer audit specialist positions created within the hierarchy of audit organizations. First, someone must be technically proficient to perform EDP audits. Second, audit independence may be increased if auditors are technically proficient with computers. Third, better relations may exist between the audit staff and data processing staff if the auditor is technically proficient with computers.

Technical Proficiency Considerations A fundamental requirement of any audit is that the auditor be technically proficient to carry out the audit. In general, how much knowledge of computers must an auditor have to be able to carry out an EDP audit competently? Further, can the general staff auditor be expected to remain technically proficient in both auditing and EDP?

A debate exists over what level of technical knowledge the auditor must have to be able to perform an EDP audit competently. The debate stems from a deeper issue: what are the responsibilities of an auditor? Some external auditors argue the auditor has neither the time nor the resources available to perform in-depth testing of technologically complex computer systems. It is not the role of the auditor to carry out detailed testing of computer systems. Instead, the external auditor evaluates management controls, examines the work of internal auditors, etc. If expert advice is needed, the services of a data processing professional can be employed. The external auditor simply needs sufficient knowledge of computers to be able to liaise with experts and maintain an independent attitude. It is reasonable to expect general staff auditors to have this level of knowledge.

Various professional organizations of external auditors have taken a different viewpoint. They argue a distinction should be made between the EDP knowledge requirements of a *general* staff auditor and the EDP knowledge requirements of a *computer audit specialist.* For example, both the American Institute of Certified Public Accountants and the Canadian Institute of Chartered Accountants argue all auditors must be able to carry out an audit of a simple batch computer system (see Jancura [1975a, 1975b]). However, beyond that level the services of a computer audit specialist usually are needed.

There is less room for debate over the level of computer knowledge required by *internal* auditors. The substantial growth in the number of organizations that employ computer audit specialists clearly shows management believes high technical expertise is necessary to achieve certain objectives of the internal audit group.

External auditors usually require greater breadth of knowledge about computers than internal auditors since they encounter more different types of systems. At least for some time period the internal auditor examines and evaluates only one or a small number of hardware/software configurations. On the one hand this suggests the external auditor cannot be expected to have an in-depth knowledge of computer systems. On the other hand it suggests the need for a separate group of computer audit specialists who can evaluate the variety of configurations confronted. It seems more reasonable to expect internal auditors to have in-depth knowledge of the computer systems they audit; hence, it might be argued there is less justification for a separate group of computer audit specialists in an internal audit department.

Audit Independence Considerations One of the major arguments advanced for having separate computer audit specialists is that it will increase the independence of the audit group. Rittenberg [1977] asked EDP audit managers, heads of internal audit, staff EDP auditors, company management, heads of EDP departments, and external auditors about methods of increasing audit independence. Several of their responses involved arguments for greater technical proficiency on the part of the auditor (see, also, Chapter 2):

1 Increase technical EDP knowledge   75% of respondents agreed
2 Recruit employees with more
  extensive EDP experience   44% of respondents agreed
3 Set up audit section specializing
  in EDP auditing   32% of respondents agreed

Underlying these responses is the belief that decreased audit independence results from relying on data processing professionals for technical assistance. Some auditors argue this is not the case; it is an independence in *attitude* that is important because to some extent the auditor must always rely on others for assistance.

Relationships with EDP Staff Sometimes the respect of EDP staff for the auditor depends on the auditor's technical proficiency with computers. If the data processing professional sees the auditor has clearly formulated objectives, and further has the technical knowledge to accomplish those objectives, then relationships between the EDP group and the audit group may be enhanced.

Placement of Computer Audit Specialists

Though there now seems to be some agreement that computer audit specialists are needed, a debate still continues over *where* computer audit specialists should be placed within the hierarchy of external or internal audit groups. One side sees the computer audit specialists primarily performing a staff function; that is, providing advice and assistance to the general staff auditor on technologically complex matters (Figure 3.1*a*). The other side sees the computer audit specialist primarily performing a line function; that is, being an integral part of an audit team and assuming responsibility for those parts of the audit that involve the computer (Figure 3.1*b*).

EDP Auditing as a Staff Function There are several arguments given for having EDP audit as a staff function:

1 *Better Utilization of EDP Audit Resources* Maintaining an effective and efficient EDP audit group requires a heavy commitment to ongoing training. Further, skilled EDP auditors are difficult to hire. In a staff capacity the EDP auditor advises and assists on matters that involve data processing only. This specialization of function improves utilization of a scarce resource.

2 *Greater Work Satisfaction for EDP Auditor* Since EDP auditors working in a staff capacity will be involved purely with EDP audit work, they should have higher job satisfaction. They will not be forced to keep up with the changing technology of auditing as well as data processing.

3 *Organization Commitment to EDP Auditing More Likely* In a staff capacity the EDP audit group has a separate existence. Thus, it is more difficult for top management to overlook the EDP audit function. A greater ongoing organization commitment to EDP auditing should result.

4 *Facilitates Coordination and Control* If EDP auditors exist as a separate group having their own manager, they can be better coordinated and controlled.

5 *Allows Increased Specialization to Cope with Complex Technology* Within the EDP audit group different EDP auditors can specialize in different aspects of computer technology. Especially for external audit groups, this helps ensure someone is always able to cope with the diverse types of complex technology encountered.

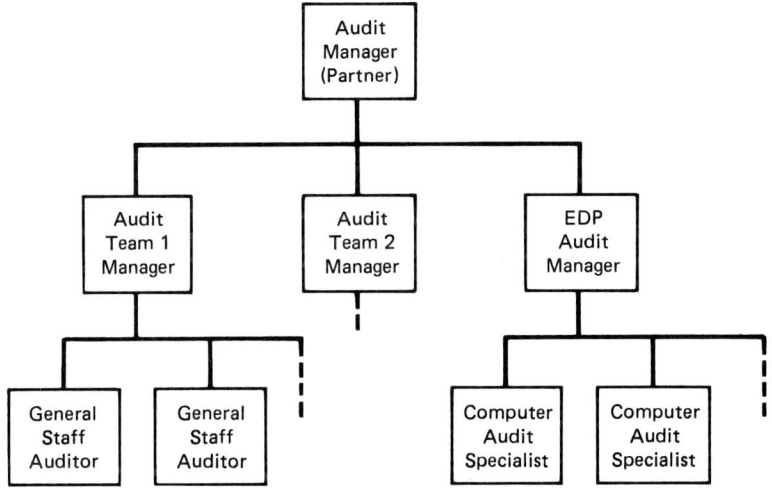

Figure 3.1a
EDP auditing as a staff function.

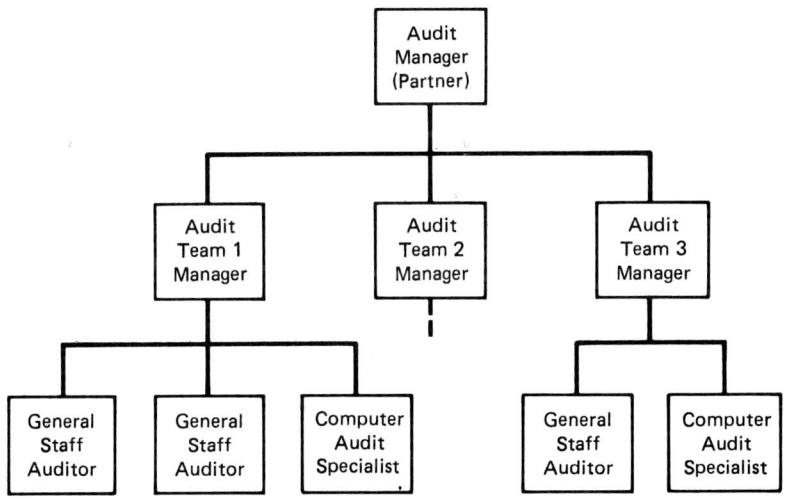

Figure 3.1b
EDP auditing as a line function.

EDP Auditing as a Line Function If EDP auditing is a line function, computer audit specialists will be assigned to any audit involving a computer system simply as a member of the audit team performing the audit. Thus, the responsibilities of the computer audit specialist will encompass both EDP audit as well as more traditional audit functions. Three major arguments are given for having EDP auditing as a line function:

1 *Greater Goal Congruence* As an integral member of the audit team having full responsibility for completion of an audit, the computer audit specialist should have a better understanding of the overall audit objectives and assume greater responsibility for achieving the objectives.

2 *Facilitates Communications* The existence of a separate EDP audit group sometimes causes friction to arise between computer audit specialists and general staff auditors. The computer audit specialist sees the general staff auditor as being technically deficient and resistant to change; the general staff auditor sees the computer audit specialist as being more interested in technology than accomplishing the objectives of the audit. Consequently, communications between the two groups are inhibited or break down. Having computer audit specialists as a member of the audit team facilitates communications and improves relations between the two groups.

3 *Improves EDP Expertise of Staff Auditors* If computer audit specialists perform a staff function, general staff auditors tend to abrogate responsibility for decisions made about the quality of computer systems. However, if computer audit specialists perform a line function, each member of the audit team tends to assume more responsibility for each other's decisions. Thus, general staff auditors have an incentive to improve their EDP expertise. Similarly, computer audit specialists have an incentive to improve their audit skills.

CENTRALIZATION VERSUS DECENTRALIZATION OF THE EDP AUDIT FUNCTION

Both internal and external audit groups face a decision on whether or not to centralize or decentralize their EDP audit expertise. If the group decentralizes, still a further decision must be made: how much decentralization should occur?

There is no clear-cut answer to whether or not an EDP audit group should be centralized or decentralized. The following factors influence the decision:

1 If EDP audits must be performed in locations that are dispersed physically, there is a tendency toward decentralization to overcome communications and control problems.

2 If the audit group has a shortage of EDP audit expertise, there is a tendency toward centralization to make more effective use of the limited expertise that is available.

3 If general staff auditors have basic computer training, there is a tendency to have a centralized group of computer audit specialists performing a staff function.

4 If it is difficult to implement computer-assisted evidence collection techniques at physically dispersed locations, there is a tendency to set up a centralized EDP audit group that performs service bureau type functions.

5 Newly formed EDP audit groups tend to be centralized; decentralization occurs as the group matures.

Stanford Research Institute [1977] reports that one form of centralized EDP audit function used by some organizations is a *competency center*. Essentially, a competency center performs EDP audit service bureau functions. General staff auditors can send data files to the competency center to be processed. Computer audit specialists in the center also provide consulting advice. The center has other responsibilities; for example, it develops EDP audit standards to be used generally, refines EDP audit methodologies, and develops, implements, and tests computer-assisted audit techniques. A competency center may be implemented by both internal and external audit groups.

STAFFING THE EDP AUDIT FUNCTION

In most countries staffing the EDP audit function has been a major problem. Historically there has been a shortage of accounting professionals (see, for example, Journal of Accountancy [1977] and J. O. Miller [1978]). A similar situation has existed in the data processing field (see, for example, Smith and de Ferranti [1976a, 1976b]). Finding personnel who have both sets of skills has been very difficult; EDP auditor salaries have reflected the problem (see Yasaki [1977]).

As a result of the shortage, management has focused on two questions related to staffing. First, how many EDP auditors does an organization need? Second, given that few EDP auditors exist having equal facility with auditing and data processing, should personnel with an auditing background or a data processing background be hired into EDP auditing?

Number of EDP Auditors Required

There is no fixed formula that an external or internal audit group can use to determine how many EDP auditors it should have on its staff. For internal audit groups, Weiss [1977] argues a ratio of about one EDP auditor to every $16^{1}/_{2}$ systems analysts and programmers on average is a reasonable ratio. However, other major factors affect this decision; for example:

Factor	Explanation
Size of the Organization	Larger organizations usually have more EDP systems and therefore a greater need for EDP auditors.
Nature of the Organization	Some types of business activities require more controls to be exercised than others. For example, banking and

	public accounting organizations are more likely to require a greater number of EDP auditors than engineering organizations (see, also, the survey by Weiss [1977]).
Extent of EDP Use	Organizations making greater use of EDP for their data processing are more likely to require a larger number of EDP auditors.
Types of Computer Systems Implemented	Organizations that have installed complex systems such as online realtime systems and database management systems are more likely to need a greater number of EDP auditors than organizations that have only batch computer systems.
Stability of the EDP Environment	Mature data processing installations primarily carrying out maintenance work rather than new system development will require fewer EDP auditors.

The number of EDP auditors required by an organization may follow a cyclical pattern. The data processing activities of the organization often stabilize after some period of development, remain stable for a time, and then undergo another major change. For example, the organization may decide to purchase different hardware and software or commence integration of a number of application systems. As development and implementation activity increases, the number of EDP auditors needed also will increase (see, also, Chapter 4).

The number of EDP auditors needed by an *external* audit group depends on the number of clients using computers for their data processing and the complexity of the data processing performed. It also will depend on the level of computer training provided to general staff auditors and whether or not computer audit specialists are centralized or decentralized.

Source of EDP Audit Staff

Since a shortage of EDP auditors exists and few tertiary institutions graduate individuals with both audit and computer expertise, many organizations have been forced to train their own EDP auditors. They have faced a decision on whether to train data processing professionals in auditing or auditors in data processing. There are two issues involved: (*a*) whether it is easier to train an auditor or a data processing professional in EDP auditing; and (*b*) who will be the most effective and efficient EDP auditor?

Those who favor training computer professionals as EDP auditors give several reasons. First, they argue that computer professionals already have a solid grounding in computer controls. Systems analysts and programmers are already responsible for designing and implementing controls in systems; thus, they understand what controls are needed in systems. Second, they argue that the technical knowledge required to evaluate computer controls in a system of even moderate complexity can be obtained only through practical experience in the design and implementation of systems. Third, they argue that EDP auditors need more knowledge of computers than accounting; the accounting knowledge required to interact with auditors is less than the computer knowledge required to interact with data processing professionals.

Those who favor training accountants as EDP auditors give two reasons. First, they argue that the overall control philosophy needed to be an effective and efficient EDP auditor is best acquired through training in accounting and auditing. Second, they argue that in most cases the ultimate objective of any type of audit is to make some judgment about the state of the accounting records. Substantial training in accounting and auditing is essential if a quality judgment is to be made.

It is difficult to establish empirically whether personnel who were first trained in auditing or computers make better EDP auditors. Interestingly, Rittenberg [1975] asked both types of EDP auditor whether they perceived auditing knowledge or data processing knowledge to be more difficult to acquire. Those who were trained first in computers thought auditing knowledge was more difficult to acquire; those who were trained first in auditing thought data processing knowledge was more difficult to acquire. In practice it seems organizations generally prefer to train computer professionals in auditing (see Weiss [1977]).

TRAINING

With the advent of the EDP audit function some auditors argue the commitment to continuing education will have to be increased. However, training is a costly activity. Management's problem is to balance the benefits and costs of ongoing education for the EDP auditor. Two questions must be addressed: (*a*) how much ongoing training does an auditor need; and (*b*) what types of training are needed?

Amount of Training Needed

Weiss [1977] found that although some organizations provided 60 or more days of training per year for each of their EDP auditors, about three weeks per year was the average. He argues this amount is insufficient for EDP auditors to keep up with the pace of change in computer technology.

There is very little research evidence to guide management in their decision on the amount of ongoing training needed. Some of the major factors influencing this decision are:

Factor	Explanation
Level of Technology Used by Data Processing Installation	If the data processing installation to be evaluated by the auditor uses complex technology, the auditor will have to invest more in training.
Changes in the Data Processing Environment	Higher investments in training may be required if the data processing installation to be audited changes the technology it uses.

Maturity of the EDP Audit Group	As individual EDP auditors gain more experience, they require less training to keep up with computer technology. As an EDP audit group matures, the objectives, standards, methodologies, etc., of the group become stabilized and less training is needed to refine and communicate this knowledge.
Changes in EDP Audit Objectives	If the objectives of the EDP audit function change, further training may be required to enable these objectives to be met. For example, if an EDP audit group previously has performed only financial audits and it commences to perform operational (efficiency) audits, further training may be needed.

Types of Training Needed

Compared to the question of how much training is needed, somewhat more formal analysis has been undertaken on the types of training an EDP auditor needs. Stanford Research Institute [1977] studied the skill levels needed by EDP auditors to be able to implement and use various EDP audit techniques. SRI identified seven basic areas where the EDP auditor must be competent to be technically proficient:

Knowledge area	Explanation
Data Processing Principles and Concepts	Overview of computer terminology, hardware, software, file processing, system development
Computer Application Systems Structure	Basic understanding of how an application system is developed, implemented, and operated
Computer Application Systems Controls and Procedures	Understanding of the controls that can be exercised over all aspects of application system processing
Data Management	Understanding of the methods used to define, create, update, and retrieve data; techniques for control and use of data
Computer Service Center Controls	Understanding of controls needed for data processing operations: job scheduling, librarian function, report distribution, data transit controls, etc.
Application System Development Controls	Understanding of controls needed to ensure development of quality application systems
Computer Application Programming	Familiarity with a programming language used for commercial purposes; for example, COBOL

Perry [1977] provides an extensive analysis and summary of the SRI findings. His analysis proceeds in two steps. First, he identifies three types of EDP auditor: (*a*) those having basic skills, (*b*) those having intermediate skills, and (*c*) those having advanced skills. Table 3.1 shows the level of proficiency each type of auditor requires in each of the seven knowledge areas identified by SRI. For example, those auditors having basic skills in EDP auditing need

TABLE 3.1
EXTENT OF DATA PROCESSING KNOWLEDGE REQUIRED TO ACHIEVE VARIOUS LEVELS OF EDP AUDIT PROFICIENCY

Knowledge area	Auditor's overall skill level		
	Basic	Intermediate	Advanced
Data processing principles and concepts	Elementary	Substantive	Substantive
Computer application systems structure	Elementary	Substantive	Substantive
Computer application systems controls and procedures	Elementary	Elementary	Substantive
Data management	Elementary	Elementary	Substantive
Computer service center controls	Elementary	Elementary	Substantive
Application system development controls	Nil	Elementary	Substantive
Computer application programming	Nil	Elementary	Substantive

(Adapted from Perry [1977]. Copyright 1977 by the Institute of Internal Auditors, Inc., 249 Maitland Avenue, Altamonte Springs, Florida 32701, U.S.A. Reprinted with permission. Adapted with permission, also, Automation Training Center, Inc.)

not be able to program in any language; those having intermediate skills should be able to write elementary programs; and those having advanced skills should have substantive programming knowledge.

Second, he examines each type of auditor's facility with the different EDP audit techniques. Following SRI he distinguishes between an auditor's ability to *develop and implement* the technique and an auditor's ability to *use* the technique. Table 3.2 provides an overview of the second part of his analysis. Part 4 of this book discusses many of the techniques listed in the table. However, the primary purpose of the table is to illustrate two of Perry's major findings:

1 A substantial number of EDP audit techniques do not require programming skills for their development and implementation or use.

2 For some techniques there is a difference between the skill level needed to develop and implement the technique and the skill level needed to use the technique.

These findings run contrary to a viewpoint often expressed; namely, that auditors need substantial computer knowledge and substantial programming skills to be able to carry out EDP auditing competently. If the SRI results are valid, selective training at an elementary level in certain skill areas enables the EDP auditor to use many EDP audit techniques. In-depth training across skill areas may be reserved only for a select few EDP auditors.

TABLE 3.2
SKILL LEVELS NEEDED FOR DEVELOPMENT, IMPLEMENTATION, AND USE OF EDP AUDIT TECHNIQUES

EDP audit technique	Data processing skills needed					
	Basic		Intermediate		Advanced	
	I*	U*	I	U	I	U
Scoring	✓	✓	✓	✓	✓	✓
Test data method	✓	✓	✓	✓	✓	✓
Computer-aided mapping	✓	✓	✓	✓	✓	✓
Audit guide	✓	✓	✓	✓	✓	✓
Extended records	✓	✓	✓	✓	✓	✓
Manual tracing and mapping	✓	✓	✓	✓	✓	✓
Competency center	✓	✓	✓	✓	✓	✓
Integrated test facility	✓	✓	✓	✓	✓	✓
Disaster test	✓	✓	✓	✓	✓	✓
Transaction selection		✓	✓	✓	✓	✓
Audit area selection		✓	✓	✓	✓	✓
Embedded audit data collection		✓	✓	✓	✓	✓
Snapshot		✓	✓	✓	✓	✓
Multisite audit software		✓		✓	✓	✓
Base case system evaluation			✓	✓	✓	✓
Generalized audit software			✓	✓	✓	✓
Terminal audit software			✓	✓	✓	✓
Postinstallation audit procedures			✓	✓	✓	✓
Job accounting data analysis			✓	✓	✓	✓
Code comparison			✓	✓	✓	✓
Computer-aided flowcharting			✓	✓	✓	✓
Simulation/modeling					✓	✓
Parallel operation					✓	✓
Parallel simulation					✓	✓
Special-purpose audit programs					✓	✓
Computer-aided tracing					✓	✓
Systems development life cycle					✓	✓
Systems development control guidelines					✓	✓
Systems acceptance control group					✓	✓

*I = Development and Implementation, U = Use.

(Adapted from Perry [1977]. Copyright 1977 by the Institute of Internal Auditors, Inc., 249 Maitland Avenue, Altamonte Springs, Florida 32701, U.S.A. Reprinted with permission. Adapted with permission, also, Automation Training Center, Inc.)

The findings also raise another issue. It now becomes important to establish *which* EDP audit techniques provide the highest payoffs when they are used. If only those EDP audit techniques requiring advanced data processing skills provide high payoffs, then the most cost-effective way of accomplishing an EDP audit may be to use only these techniques and give EDP auditors in-depth training in the knowledge areas required. Alternatively, some EDP audit techniques that require only basic skills for their use may provide high payoffs in terms of audit objectives. Selective training then can take place.

RELATIONSHIPS WITH MANAGEMENT AND OTHER ORGANIZATION GROUPS

One of the major objectives of an *internal* audit group that performs the EDP audit function is to achieve good relationships with the various levels of management in the organization. Good relationships are important for two reasons. First, they facilitate work being accomplished. Second, strong support from top management is a primary factor affecting the auditor's independence. Rittenberg [1977] found EDP audit managers, heads of internal audit, staff EDP auditors, public accountants, and top management unanimous in their rating of top-management support as the primary factor affecting audit independence.

Unfortunately EDP auditors have had their share of problems in establishing good relationships with management and other organizational groups (see, for example, Gustafson [1976] and Perry [1976]). The following sections examine some of the types of problems experienced and some strategies for overcoming these problems.

Types of Problems Experienced

Some of the problems experienced by internal EDP auditors in establishing good relationships with management and other organizational groups can be expected because they confront any internal audit group (see Sawyer [1973]). However, there are some characteristics of EDP auditing that cause additional problems:

1 *Pressures on Function to Develop Quickly* Some primary stimuli for the EDP audit function to develop have been the major cases of computer fraud. Often the establishment of an EDP audit group has been a panic reaction by management. On other occasions it may be a response to problems being experienced with the organization's data processing: the discovery of errors or suspicions of gross inefficiency in the use of computing resources. The problem here is that the situations giving rise to the EDP audit function are stress situations. Consequently, management has high expectations of fast results from the EDP audit group. The EDP audit manager may have to follow a strategy of getting operational quickly and worrying about standards, documentation, etc., at a later stage. The EDP audit group may feel pressured to attack problem areas where they have insufficient expertise. As a result the actual achievements of the EDP audit group may fall below the expected achievements.

2 *Communications Problems* The establishment of an EDP audit group produces a new set of communications problems within the organization. Management may be unclear on what objectives the group should have. Because of the technology involved, doubts may exist about how to evaluate the function. Data processing management may not understand clearly why the EDP audit group is interfering with their function. Traditional auditors may be uncertain about how they should interact with the EDP audit function.

3 *Frictions Produced with Other Groups* These communications problems and the changes brought about to work patterns and relationships because of the existence of the EDP audit function often produce frictions between the EDP audit group and other groups within the organization. Data processing personnel may resent their activities being subjected to scrutiny. They may feel the overheads added to their function by the presence of EDP auditors exceed the benefits obtained. Traditional auditors may resent the uncertainty produced about their own function because of the presence of an EDP audit function. They also may perceive characteristics of the EDP auditor and the EDP audit function that violate what they consider to be behavior norms for audit professionals: higher allegiance by EDP auditors to the data processing profession rather than the accounting profession, unacceptable involvement by EDP auditors in the design phase of new systems (thereby violating audit independence), unorthodox audit reporting on design flaws in systems prior to their implementation rather than after their implementation (again violating audit independence), unduly long time commitments to complete assignments, etc.

Methods of Improving Relations

Many of the problems experienced by EDP auditors with management and other groups within the organization result from the newness of the EDP audit function. To some extent these problems will be resolved as the function becomes more established. In the meantime some remedial steps can be undertaken to alleviate some of the problems that arise:

1 *Promote Open Communications* In general, organization theorists believe that conflict in organizations is resolved best through open communications between the parties involved (see, for example, Lawrence and Lorsch [1969]). The EDP audit group must interact heavily with three other groups in the organization: top management, other audit personnel, and data processing personnel. It is important the EDP audit group clearly communicates its objectives and the methodologies to be used to accomplish these objectives to personnel affected by EDP audit activities. These individuals then have an opportunity to debate an issue or seek clarification on an issue that they feel is contentious.

2 *Audit within Technical Capabilities* Especially during the formative stages of the EDP audit function, it is important to undertake only those audit tasks that are well within the technical capabilities of the EDP audit group. The success of the group during its early activities is a major factor affecting the attitudes of top management, audit personnel, and data processing personnel toward the group. If the group performs its function well, it is likely that personnel affected by the group will have a more positive attitude toward the EDP audit function.

3 *Prioritize Tasks to Be Accomplished* Given the technical capabilities of the group, those EDP audit tasks that can be accomplished should be prioritized. This process helps identify activities where the payoffs are highest. The opinions of top management, data processing management, and audit management should be solicited and priorities formulated in a cooperative manner.

4 *Manage the EDP Audit Function Well* Relationships with other organizational groups will improve if these groups perceive the EDP audit function to be well-managed. Different organization groups compete for the scarce resources of the organization. Poor relationships develop if other groups in the organization believe the resources assigned to the EDP audit function are not used effectively and efficiently.

PROMOTIONAL OPPORTUNITIES FOR THE EDP AUDITOR

A major problem facing management with respect to any group of technical experts is providing promotional opportunities for the members of the group. Finding suitable job positions for technicians often is difficult. Promotion usually requires greater facility with generalist skills rather than specialist skills. However, unless management provides a suitable career path for specialists, morale deteriorates and staff turnover occurs. Thus, the organization suffers losses on its investment in human capital.

Because the EDP audit function is relatively new within organizations, providing career advancement for the EDP auditor is a problem that has received little attention. There is uncertainty about the kinds of promotional opportunities suitable for EDP auditors given their training and experience. Few organizations have experimented with different types of career paths so their relative strengths and weaknesses can be evaluated.

Internal Career Advancement

One set of promotional opportunities for the EDP auditor exists within the EDP audit group. The Institute of Internal Auditors [1974] surveyed 15 organizations and identified eight positions currently used within the hierarchy of the EDP audit group (see, also, Figure 3.2):

Position	Function/Duties
Audit Trainee—EDP	Under close supervision assists in collecting and evaluating evidence on small computer systems or segments of large computer systems
Internal Audit Specialist—EDP	Under close supervision assists in collecting and evaluating evidence on all types of data processing activities; performs detailed examinations of records where selection and test criteria have been defined
Internal Audit Analyst—EDP	Under limited supervision conducts audits of all types of data processing activities by following established audit procedures

Assistant Internal Auditor—EDP	Under limited supervision conducts audits of all types of data processing activities; participates in new projects and special investigations; responsible for analyzing audit evidence, making recommendations, and preparing documentation to support audit findings
Internal Auditor—EDP	Under limited supervision performs audits of large complex computer systems
Associate Internal Audit Manager—EDP	Develops standards for conduct of EDP audits; supervises EDP internal audit assignments
Internal Audit Manager—EDP	Establishes long-run goals for EDP audit group; plans and assigns work and sets performance objectives; responsible for motivating, counseling, and developing staff
Consultant for Internal Auditing—EDP	Acts in a staff capacity; provides any detailed technical assistance needed to perform audits

Currently few organizations could support an EDP audit group having eight levels in its hierarchy. Often external auditors have only a consultant position for EDP auditors. Many internal audit groups have only a few levels in the hierarchy.

External Career Advancement

Promotional opportunities for the EDP auditor exist outside the EDP audit group. Perry [1974a] gives the following ranking of career paths outside the EDP audit group for an internal auditor; however, an external auditor who leaves public accounting also might take one of these career paths:

1 Database administration
2 Data processing consulting
3 Data processing management
4 Financial management

He lists financial management last since he argues non-EDP management often looks with suspicion on personnel having computer expertise. This outlook is slowly changing. Database administration makes best use of the auditor's training and experience in preserving data integrity (see Chapter 7).

LIFE CYCLE OF THE EDP AUDIT GROUP

There is at least some evidence to suggest that organizations follow a certain life cycle in their control and use of EDP facilities. Nolan [1973] argues that for computer installations this life cycle can be depicted graphically by an S curve if the size of the computer installation budget is plotted over time (see, further, Chapter 4). However, an S-curve representation of the life cycle seems to hold generally for all types of organizations. J. G. Miller [1978] points out that for all living systems (which includes organizations) the growth curve appears to take a sigmoid or logistic shape.

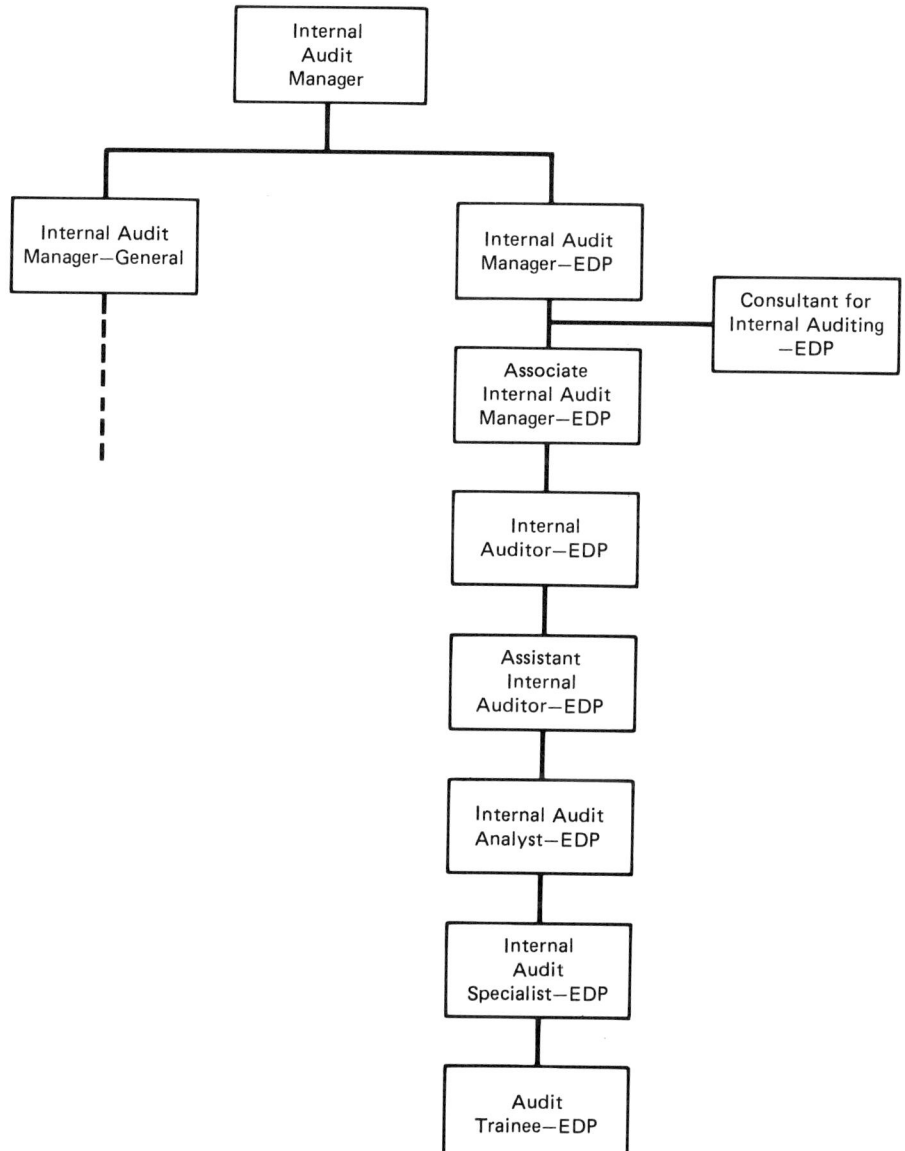

Figure 3.2
EDP audit hierarchy within the internal audit department. *(Adapted from the Institute of Internal Auditors [1974]. Copyright 1974 by the Institute of Internal Auditors, Inc., 249 Maitland Avenue, Altamonte Springs, Florida 32701. Reprinted with permission.)*

It is useful for management to identify the stage reached by an organization in its life cycle. At each stage the organization exhibits certain characteristics; consequently, management can anticipate the likely capabilities and limitations of the organization at each stage. With respect to an EDP audit group the stage reached in the life cycle affects decisions on what EDP audit tasks the group can handle competently, what EDP audit techniques it will have sufficient expertise to use, and what controls should be exercised over the group. To illustrate this point, consider the following life cycle stages and their associated characteristics for an *internal* audit group:

Stage	Characteristics of stage
Initiation	Establishment of the EDP audit group; financial audits carried out only on major accounting application systems; controls are lacking; EDP audit objectives have not been clearly formulated; standards do not exist; no formal basis established for assigning priorities to tasks; substantial pressures applied to get work accomplished quickly; lines of authority and responsibility unclear; behavioral problems exist because of uncertainty surrounding interactions with other organization groups
Expansion	More widespread coverage of application systems by EDP audit; expansion sometimes rapid; attempted use of more complex EDP audit techniques; some formalization of objectives, standards, lines of authority and responsibility, etc.; controls still loose
Maturity	Involvement in complex application systems; EDP audit participation in the system development life cycle; concurrent auditing being carried out as well as ex post auditing; operational audits for system effectiveness and efficiency undertaken; objectives and standards have been formalized; well-established interactions with other organization groups; tight project control exists; advance planning undertaken

If the organization experiences some major change in its use of computing facilities, the EDP audit group may pass through these stages again. For example, the organization may attempt a changeover from batch-oriented systems to online systems or change from using centralized systems to distributed systems. The structure, objectives, standards, control procedures, etc., of the EDP audit group also may have to change. New EDP audit techniques may have to be developed and implemented. Existing EDP auditors may have to undertake substantial training in the new technology. The three stages in subsequent iterations of the life cycle may not be as pronounced as those in the first iteration; however, in general the EDP audit group still will exhibit the characteristics of each stage as it adapts to the changes made.

SUMMARY

The emergence of an EDP audit function within organizations has given rise to some controversial organization and management issues. There has been debate over the need for computer audit specialists and a separate EDP audit group, whether the group should be centralized or decentralized, the number of EDP auditors required, whether or not their background should be audit or EDP, and how much and what types of training are needed.

The existence of the function also has caused several other problems. Often data processing personnel and other audit personnel react unfavorably toward the EDP audit function. They resent their work being examined by EDP auditors and the uncertainty surrounding the nature of their interactions with the EDP audit group. The newness of the function, its requirements for expertise, and the smallness of the function cause problems in providing career paths for EDP auditors that will maintain their morale and prevent staff turnover.

To some extent management can deal with these problems by recognizing the EDP audit function passes through a life cycle. By identifying the stage in the life cycle reached by the EDP audit group, management can undertake actions to alleviate some of the problems caused by the group being in a particular stage.

REVIEW QUESTIONS

3.1. Briefly explain why some auditors argue it is not necessary for them to have detailed technical knowledge of computer systems. Are external and internal auditors able to make this argument with equal ease?

3.2. Why do some auditors argue increased technical competence will increase their independence? Is there a relationship between increased technical competence and an independence in *attitude*?

3.3. Briefly explain the difference in duties between an EDP auditor who performs a staff function and an EDP auditor who performs a line function. Give two arguments for and two arguments against having EDP audit as a staff function.

3.4. Can any stronger arguments be made for having EDP audit as a staff function or a line function depending on whether the group performs external auditing or internal auditing? Explain.

3.5. Briefly explain how the nature of the business performed by an organization affects the number of EDP auditors it will need to perform the EDP audit function. What types of business activities are likely to require a greater number of EDP auditors?

3.6. What is a competency center? Give three reasons why an *external* audit organization may set up a competency center.

3.7. Give two factors that favor decentralization of EDP audit operations.

3.8. Briefly explain why system maintenance is likely to require less EDP audit effort than system development. Give an example where the reverse situation might apply.

3.9. Is it likely that external auditors or internal auditors who perform the EDP audit function will need a greater amount of ongoing training in EDP? Outline some of the factors that influence your decision.

3.10. Stanford Research Institute [1977] found that for several EDP audit techniques there was a substantial difference in the knowledge required to develop and implement the technique and the knowledge required to use the technique. Briefly explain why you think SRI obtained this finding.

3.11. Give two implications for EDP auditor training of Stanford Research Institute's finding that often the level of training needed to develop and implement an EDP audit technique was different from the level of training needed to use the technique.

3.12. Based on Perry [1977], what is the primary basis for distinguishing between an EDP auditor who has basic skills, one who has intermediate skills, and one who has advanced skills?
3.13. Outline three steps top management might take to reduce the behavioral problems caused by the introduction of an EDP audit function within the organization.
3.14. Give two characteristics of the EDP audit function that cause EDP auditors to experience problems in their interactions with data processing personnel and other audit personnel.
3.15. Briefly discuss two major problems experienced in providing a suitable career path for the EDP auditor.
3.16. Give two problems that might face a systems analyst/programmer who becomes an EDP auditor for a period of about three years and then returns to the data processing department for career advancement purposes.
3.17. Outline a career path for an external auditor who performs the EDP audit function in a staff (as opposed to a line) capacity. List some of the strengths and weaknesses of your career path.
3.18. List four characteristics of the expansion stage in the life cycle of an EDP audit group.
3.19. A "life cycle" concept implies an iterative process. What types of factors would cause a mature EDP audit group to pass once again through the three stages of initiation, expansion, and maturity?
3.20. Why is a knowledge of the life cycle of an EDP audit group useful to management?
3.21. List four "principles" of good organization and management that apply equally well to the traditional audit function and the EDP audit function.
3.22. In the long run is the EDP audit function likely to remain separate from the traditional audit function? Explain.

EXERCISES AND CASES

3.1. You are the director of internal audit for a large company. One day the president of the company calls you to inquire about the reasons for the high staff turnover in your EDP audit group. She has noted from personnel reports that on average new college graduates who enter EDP audit stay with the company for about a year only before they move to another company. She questions you about the loss of human capital that results. You respond by pointing out that the demand for EDP auditors greatly exceeds the supply so competition for EDP auditors is high.

Required: The president asks you to prepare a report for her outlining some strategies for decreasing staff turnover among the EDP audit group. You are to discuss briefly the strengths and weaknesses of each strategy and make a recommendation on which strategy the company should implement.

3.2. You are EDP manager in the internal audit department for a large retail store chain. Currently you have six EDP audit staff under you who perform a staff function in the internal audit department.

Top management of the chain has decided to change the mode of data processing used from a centralized operation to a decentralized operation. Currently each store in the chain is connected via terminals to a large computer at the head office. Over the next two years minicomputers will be installed in each store. Each store will be responsible for its own data processing and, in general, only summary information will be transmitted to the head office. A communications network will link the minicomputers in each store to the head office computer. Communications will be possible between any store though messages must be sent via the head office computer.

The data processing staff to support the new configuration will still remain centralized at the head office. Standard application system packages will be made available to each store. However, to assist in the implementation of these systems each store will have its own systems analyst/programmer.

Required: The internal audit manager has asked you to assess the impact of these changes on the organization and management of the EDP audit staff. Prepare a brief report outlining any changes you think are necessary and provide justification for the changes you recommend.

3.3. You are the internal audit manager for a small to medium sized company that has well-developed batch computer systems for all major applications. In light of recent cases of computer fraud publicized in the newspapers, management has given you permission to advertise an EDP auditor position (the first in the company) for which you will be responsible.

You receive only two applications for the position. One application is from an existing member of the internal audit staff, a college graduate hired six years ago by the company. He worked first as an accountant for the company, but because of his promise he was transferred to internal audit. He has no experience with computers except one course he took at college and as a user of the output produced by the company's computer systems. However, he has a good knowledge of the company's accounting systems and you feel his abilities and brightness would allow him to acquire the necessary computer knowledge quickly.

The other applicant is from another company with which you are familiar. She is a systems analyst/programmer for the company. Though she has been involved in the design and implementation of accounting systems, she has no formal training in accounting. Her college degree is in mathematics. After you interview her and carry out some discreet background checking with a friend you have who works with her current employer, you believe she would make a very capable employee.

Required: Prepare a brief report for management notifying them whom you have selected for the position. Provide the necessary justification for your decision. Outline what staff development you intend to take with the person you select.

REFERENCES

Arens, Alvin A., and James K. Loebbecke. *Auditing: An Integrated Approach* (Englewood Cliffs, N.J.: Prentice-Hall, Inc., 1976).

Canning, Richard G. "The Internal Auditor and the Computer," *EDP Analyzer* (March 1975), pp. 1–13.

Cutting, Richard W., Richard J. Guiltman, Fred L. Lilly, and John F. Mullarkey. "Technical Proficiency for Auditing Computer Processed Records," *Journal of Accountancy* (October 1971), pp. 74–77.

Gustafson, L. M. "Improving Relations between Audit and EDP," *EDPACS* (September 1976), pp. 1–8.

Holmes, Fenwicke. "Auditing from the EDP Manager's Viewpoint," *The Internal Auditor* (November–December 1975), pp. 29–34.

Institute of Internal Auditors. *Establishing the Internal Audit Function in EDP: Job Descriptions* (Orlando, Fla.: The Institute of Internal Auditors, Inc., 1974).

Jancura, Elise. "The Auditor's Responsibilities in Examining Computer Processed Records," *International Journal of Government Auditing* (July 1975a), pp. 13–17.

———. "Technical Proficiency Standards for Auditing Computer Processed Records," *Journal of Accountancy* (August 1975b), pp. 39–44.

Journal of Accountancy. "Demand for Graduates by Accounting Firms Up 16%," August 1977, p. 16.

Lawrence, Paul R., and Jay W. Lorsch. *Developing Organizations: Diagnosis and Action* (Reading, Mass.: Addison-Wesley Publishing Company, Inc., 1969).

Mair, William C., Donald R. Wood, and Keagle W. Davis. *Computer Control & Audit*, 2d ed. (Altamonte Springs, Fla.: The Institute of Internal Auditors, Inc., 1976).

Miller, James Grier. *Living Systems* (New York: McGraw-Hill Book Company, 1978).

Miller, J. O. "The Demand for Accountants 1978–1982: Dyall Mark II," *The Australian Accountant* (September 1978), pp. 477–482.

Mullen, Jack B. "Developing an EDP Audit Staff," *EDP Auditing* (Pennsauken, N.J.: Auerbach Publishers Inc., 1979), Portfolio 71-03-08, pp. 1–7.

Myers, Edith. "EDP Auditors: Explosive Growth," *Datamation* (August 1977), pp. 120–121, 124.

Nolan, Richard L. "Managing the Computer Resource: A Stage Hypothesis," *Communications of the ACM* (July 1973), pp. 399–405.

Perry, William E. "Career Advancement for the EDP Auditor," *EDPACS* (August 1974a), pp. 1–6.

———. "The Making of a Computer Auditor," *The Internal Auditor* (November–December 1974b), pp. 11–22.

———. "Management Support for EDP Auditing," *EDPACS* (August 1976), pp. 5–9.

———. "Skills Needed to Utilize EDP Audit Practices," *EDPACS* (November 1977), pp. 1–13.

———. "The EDP Auditor Relationship with DP Management," *EDP Auditing* (Pennsauken, N.J.: Auerbach Publishers, Inc., 1978), Portfolio 71-02-03, pp. 1–15.

———. "EDP Auditor Job Descriptions," *EDP Auditing* (Pennsauken, N.J.: Auerbach Publishers, Inc., 1979a), Portfolio 71-03-06, pp. 1–15.

———. "How to Interview an EDP Auditor Candidate," *EDP Auditing* (Pennsauken, N.J.: Auerbach Publishers, Inc., 1979b), Portfolio 71-03-07, pp. 1–12.

Rittenberg, Larry E. "The Impact of Internal Auditing during the EDP Application Design Process on Perceptions of Internal Audit Independence." Unpublished Ph.D. dissertation, University of Minnesota, Minneapolis, Minn., 1975.

———. *Auditor Independence and Systems Design* (Altamonte Springs, Fla.: The Institute of Internal Auditors, Inc., 1977).

Sawyer, Lawrence B. *The Practice of Modern Internal Auditing* (Altamonte Springs, Fla.: The Institute of Internal Auditors, Inc., 1973).

Smith, Barry W., and Barry Z. de Ferranti. *Computers and the Future of Education* (Canberra: Centre for Continuing Education, Australian National University, 1976a).

——— and ———. *The Present and Future Use of Computers in Australia, and Employment Implications* (Canberra: Australian Computer Society, Inc., 1976b).

Stanford Research Institute. *Systems Auditability and Control Study: Data Processing Audit Practices Report* (Altamonte Springs, Fla.: The Institute of Internal Auditors, Inc., 1977).

Weiss, Harold. "EDP Audit Job Descriptions," *EDPACS* (March 1974), pp. 7–11.

———. "Computer Audit Survey," *EDPACS* (September 1977), pp. 8–15.

Yasaki, Edward K. "Who Is the DP Auditor?" *Datamation* (August 1977), pp. 55–58.

PART **TWO**

THE MANAGEMENT CONTROL FRAMEWORK

The auditor's primary objective in examining the management control framework for a computer installation is to see that management manages well. A recurring theme throughout this book is that the quality of management influences the quality of controls at the detailed level and the extent to which assets are safeguarded and data integrity, system effectiveness, and system efficiency will be achieved.

Chapter	Overview of contents
4 Top Management and EDP Management	Discusses top management's and EDP management's role in planning, organizing, staffing, directing, and controlling the EDP function
5 Systems Development	Provides a normative model of the systems development process that the auditor can use for purposes of evidence collection and evidence evaluation
6 Programming Management	Provides a normative model of the programming life cycle; discusses alternate ways of organizing and managing the programming team; examines various software development aids
7 Database Administration	Discusses the functions of a database administrator; examines the control problems posed by the database administration role
8 Operations Management	Discusses the functions of operations management: computer operations, data preparation, data flow control, file library, documentation library, installation security

Examining and evaluating the management control framework is important for two major reasons. First, the auditor can use the evaluation as a basis for determining the nature and the extent of detailed testing to be carried out on individual application systems. Second, the quality of the management control framework influences the likely quality of computer data processing in the future. The auditor can form an opinion on whether application systems are likely to degrade over time.

The next five chapters present the essence of good management practices with respect to EDP. Auditors cannot evaluate management unless they know what management *should* be doing; thus, it behooves the EDP auditor to gain expertise in the management of computers.

CHAPTER 4

TOP MANAGEMENT AND EDP MANAGEMENT

CHAPTER OUTLINE

EVALUATING THE PLANNING FUNCTION
- Function of a Steering Committee in Planning
- Feasibility Study
- Changeover Plans
- Master Plan
- Project Plan
- Disaster Recovery Planning

EVALUATING THE ORGANIZING FUNCTION
- Organizational Structure Issues
- Centralization versus Decentralization
- Selecting Hardware/Software Facilities
- Methods Standards

EVALUATING THE STAFFING FUNCTION
- Personnel Acquisition
- Personnel Development
- Personnel Termination

EVALUATING THE DIRECTING FUNCTION
- Human Motivation
- Leadership
- Communications

EVALUATING THE CONTROLLING FUNCTION
  Stage Growth Hypothesis
  The Means of Control
  Controlling Users of Computer Services
SUMMARY
REVIEW QUESTIONS
EXERCISES AND CASES
REFERENCES

One finding consistently appears in empirical studies that examine why computer systems succeed or fail: the active participation of top management and the existence of high-quality EDP management are essential for the continuing successful development and implementation of computer systems.

How can the auditor evaluate top management and EDP management involvement in a computer installation? One useful way is to evaluate each of the functions management must perform: planning—determining the goals of the installation and the means of achieving these goals; organizing—providing facilities and grouping activities and personnel to accomplish required tasks; staffing—selecting and training personnel required to accomplish tasks; directing—coordinating activities, providing leadership and guidance, and motivating personnel; and controlling—comparing actual performance with budgeted performance as a basis for adjusting actions.

Each section in this chapter outlines how the auditor can evaluate these functions. It is assumed that the reader already is familiar with the fundamentals of good management (see, for example, Koontz and O'Donnell [1976]); thus, the chapter highlights those aspects of management that are somewhat different for the EDP function.

EVALUATING THE PLANNING FUNCTION

Top management and EDP management must address two fundamental planning questions. First, should the organization start to use or continue to use computers for its data processing requirements? Second, if the organization uses computers for its data processing, how should they be used?

Table 4.1 shows the major plans formulated for a computer installation, whether they are typically short run or long run, and the group responsible for their development. The various plans needed follow the life cycle of an installation. When management first contemplates using computers, a feasibility study is performed to examine the costs and benefits of the long-run use of computers in the organization. A decision to use computers results in a preinstallation plan, which is a short-run plan needed to guide the changeover process. These two plans may be needed again at a later stage in the installa-

TABLE 4.1
MAJOR PLANS NEEDED FOR A COMPUTER INSTALLATION

Plan	Brief description	Time period covered	Responsible group
Feasibility study	Investigates costs and benefits of long-run use of computers and recommends whether or not the organization should use computers	Long run	Steering committee
Changeover plan	Specifies the tasks and activities to be carried out during changeover to computer data processing, a new hardware/software configuration, or a new organization structure	Short run	Steering committee
Master plan	Strategic plan for a computer installation setting out its long-run objectives and the tasks necessary for accomplishing these objectives	Long run	Steering committee
Project plan	Forms the basis of the budget for developing a specific system and ensures the project is consistent with the goals and objectives set out in the master plan	Short run	EDP management
Disaster recovery plan	Plan needed to restore the installation's files and data processing capabilities within the required time in the event of a disaster	Short run	EDP management

tion's life when new hardware and software are purchased. The ongoing operations of the installation require a master plan to provide long-run directions and various short-run project plans to guide the development of individual systems. Finally, the installation needs a disaster recovery plan that is typically short run since it depends on the particular hardware/software configuration and the systems developed at a point in time.

Function of a Steering Committee in Planning

Top management participates in the planning function for a computer installation via a steering committee. A steering committee should be formed at the outset when an organization first contemplates using a computer for its data processing. The steering committee plays an important part in the initial feasibility study, the purchase of a computer and its setup, and later decisions on further hardware, software, and systems needed.

Strategic planning is the primary function of the steering committee. The steering committee must produce a master plan for the computer installation that guides the installation's long-run development and allows EDP management to establish short-run objectives and policies. However, Ditri et al. [1971] argue the committee has five other functions to perform:

1 Establishes the size and scope of the EDP function
2 Sets priorities within these bounds
3 Assures a viable communications system exists between EDP and its users
4 Monitors the accomplishments of the computer installation
5 Measures the results of EDP projects in terms of return on investment, etc.

A steering committee seems to work best if it comprises only a small number of members. The chairperson must be the senior organization executive ultimately responsible for the computer installation. The EDP manager should act as secretary to the committee. Other members of the committee are senior management from major user areas. At various times temporary members of the committee exist to provide specialist advice on technical matters. The committee also should have as a member the internal audit manager.

Feasibility Study

Management requires a feasibility study for any major planning decision in the life of a computer installation. For example:

1 Should a computer be used for the organization's data processing requirements?
2 Should a new application system be implemented or a major change be made to an old application system?
3 Should new hardware and software be purchased and, if so, what should be the required features of the hardware and software?
4 Would a major structural change to an organization increase its data processing capabilities?

In one sense a feasibility study is a *tool* of the planning process rather than a plan itself. In another sense it constitutes a plan since it documents the deliberations of management and provides recommendations and guidelines for implementing these recommendations.

To illustrate the process of undertaking a feasibility study, consider a decision on whether or not to use a computer. Two major steps are involved. First, a *preliminary survey* must be undertaken to determine quickly whether computer data processing may be worthwhile and whether a comprehensive feasibility study is warranted. Second, if it seems computer data processing is worthwhile, a *feasibility study proper* must be undertaken.

Carrying out a preliminary survey involves three major steps:

Major step	Examples of activities involved
Planning the Survey	Setting objectives; setting time schedules—interim and final; setting resource constraints—time, staff, financial; identifying organizational constraints; staffing the task force group
Data Gathering	Characteristics of existing systems—input and output, processing, volumes and timings of data, peakloads; strengths and weaknesses of existing systems; new systems that need developing; old systems that need modification or scrapping; potential areas of computer use; costs and benefits of computer use; resource considerations; organizational changes needed; long-run impact of computer use
Report Preparation and Recommendations	Whether or not to use computers; areas of computer use; constraints that should be applied; resources needed; basic direction to be followed for acquisition, implementation, and use; time schedule for acquisition and implementation

Management must form a task force group to perform the preliminary survey. The task force group should have well-defined terms of reference, be properly staffed and managed, and receive adequate support. It usually functions best if its size is small so group interaction problems are reduced.

If on the basis of the preliminary survey management decides to proceed to the feasibility study proper, the task force group size usually is expanded and the steps performed during the preliminary survey repeated; however, the analysis and evaluation now is more in depth and rigorous. The final report must recommend whether computer data processing should be introduced or not. If the report recommends using computers, it also should provide information on the means of computer processing to use—whether it should be in-house or provided by a service center; the computer facilities required—hardware, software, personnel, floor space, etc.; and the means of converting to computer data processing.

The description of the computer facilities required provides the basis for preparing a *manual of specifications*. The manual of specifications is a statement of requirements distributed to hardware and software vendors for use in preparing their proposals.

Perhaps the most difficult aspect of the feasibility study is deciding whether investment in computer facilities will provide an acceptable rate of return. This decision involves estimating the net cash flows from the investment over its life. Bierman and Smidt [1975] describe various techniques for appraising capital investments.

Changeover Plans

Changeover plans specify the tasks that must be accomplished, their interdependencies, and the constraints that apply when the organization undertakes some major change related to its data processing; for example, acquisition and installation of a new computer, establishing a new hardware/software configuration, or changing the organization structure. From a control viewpoint the important aspect of a changeover plan is that it forces management to articulate the necessary activities involved. Consequently, the changeover is likely to proceed in a more orderly manner. To illustrate a changeover plan, some of the typical activities included in a plan for setting up a computer installation would be:

1 Completion of hardware/software specifications
2 Evaluation and selection of hardware/software
3 Physical planning and site preparation
4 Final testing and acceptance of hardware/software
5 Delivery and installation of hardware/software
6 Design of an organization structure for the computer installation

Whereas the changeover plan budgets resources for these activities at a global level, specific project plans then have to be prepared for each activity to show how it is to be accomplished.

Master Plan

A major responsibility of the steering committee is the preparation of a master plan for the computer installation. A master plan is the rolling plan for the next several years' (two–five years) activities. It may cover a fairly long or fairly short period depending on the rate of change within the organization. Some organizations by their very nature experience frequent changes both internal and external to the organization that make long-run planning difficult; for example, research and development organizations. Other organizations are relatively stable and the task of planning is not so onerous.

The master plan focuses on whether computers should continue to be used for the organization's data processing and, if so, how they should be used. Given computers will continue to be used, the steering committee must decide on new areas of application. These new areas of application may in turn require decisions to be made on new hardware/software configurations and major structural changes within the organization.

Davis [1974] lists four major components of the master plan: (*a*) organizational goals and objectives, (*b*) inventory of current capabilities, (*c*) forecasts of developments affecting the plan, and (*d*) the specific plan. The following sections briefly review the contents of each of these components of the master plan.

Organizational Goals and Objectives For information systems development, a statement of organizational goals and objectives is important for two reasons. First, information systems must be developed to be consistent with the overall goals of the organization. Second, the organization's goals and objectives form the basis for assigning priorities to information systems development. This section of the master plan might include:

1 Statement of the organization's long-run and short-run goals
2 Description of the external environment
3 Description of the internal structure of the organization
4 Overall company policies and constraints
5 Statement of overall goals for the computer department

Current Capabilities This section of the master plan details the current resources available to the computer installation to accomplish its objectives. It enables EDP management to make two decisions. First, are the existing resource capabilities sufficient to meet short-run objectives? Second, must current capabilities be expanded or reduced to cater for future demand? The contents of this section might include:

1 Inventory: hardware and software
2 Portfolio of application systems: completed and in-progress
3 Capabilities of existing personnel: management and technical
4 Organization of the installation
5 Existence of slack resources now and in the foreseeable future
6 Historical information: strengths and weaknesses, successes and failures

Forecasted Developments An important task of the steering committee is to determine potential developments that may impact the use of computers within the organization. These developments can come from two directions. First, they may be the result of changes in the goals or structure of the organization; for example, a company may start to diversify into other areas that require different types of data processing to be carried out. Second, computer technological developments may occur that affect the way data is processed; for example, the development of database management systems changed data processing by facilitating sharing of the database among multiple users.

The Specific Plan There are usually insufficient resources to develop all the information systems an organization would like to develop. Choices must be made on the basis of cost-benefit criteria. The result is a specific plan that the computer installation will follow. This section of the master plan might include:

1 Specific application systems to be developed and an associated time schedule
2 Hardware and software acquisition schedule
3 Schedule for acquisition and development of personnel resources
4 Financial resources required
5 Structural changes needed to the computer installation or the organization

Project Plan

A project plan forms the basis of a budget for a particular project; for example, EDP management should use project plans to monitor the progress of application system development and implementation activities. System development, programming, and operations management typically perform the detailed work needed for project planning. EDP management, or in some cases the steering committee if a major project is involved, reviews and approves the final plan.

The major activities involved in project planning are:

1 Identify tasks to be performed.
2 Identify relationships between tasks.
3 Determine time constraints on project.
4 Determine resource requirements of each task.
5 Determine any other constraints applying.
6 Sequence tasks.

Several techniques have been developed to facilitate project planning activities; for example, work breakdown structure (WBS), project planning (GANTT) charts, program evaluation and review technique (PERT), critical path method (CPM), graphical evaluation and review technique (GERT), and network simulation (see, further, Cleland and King [1975]).

A project plan should be submitted to the same kind of economic analysis undertaken during feasibility studies. Management must take into account the risk of the project and use discounted cash flow procedures to determine if the return on the investment is acceptable.

Disaster Recovery Planning

A computer installation can suffer disaster for many reasons: hurricanes, sabotage, fraud, hardware failure. Management must plan for such disasters. One formal basis available for thinking about disaster recovery planning is risk management theory.

Risk management theorists divide risk into two categories: (*a*) speculative risk, and (*b*) pure risk. Speculative risk is associated with decisions made by the organization such as whether or not to expand. Pure risk is associated with events that are beyond the control of the organization. Disaster recovery planning focuses primarily on pure risk.

The following sections discuss briefly the three major activities involved in risk management: (*a*) risk identification, (*b*) risk measurement, and (*c*) risk control (see, further, FitzGerald [1978*a*, 1978*b*], Gerberick [1979], and Wong [1977]).

Risk Identification The first step in risk management is to make an inventory of potential disasters that face the organization. AFIPS [1974] lists the following categories of potential disasters:

Disaster category	Examples
Natural Disasters	Windstorm, hurricane, tornado, earthquake, fire, flood, lightning, explosion, ice and snow, rain and wind
Manmade Disasters	Fire and water, riots, strikes, industrial accidents, sabotage, loss of power or other utilities
External Threats and Financial Disasters	Legal requirements, social responsibility, libel suits, bomb threats, changes in the organization's competitive stance, changes in top management
Instability and Unreliability	Hardware, software, communications, applications, human
Hostile Action	Espionage, fraud, theft, mischief, sabotage

It is important the list of potential disasters be complete. A serious omission may mean a contingency plan to cover the situation may not be prepared.

Risk Measurement Assessing the possible loss that can occur from different disasters can be a difficult task; however, some idea of the possible loss must be obtained as a basis for determining the amount to be spent on security measures.

A coarse measurement of the risk facing a computer installation is provided by ordering possible disasters according to the likely loss that will occur. This ordering indicates the important risks and where detailed investigation and careful measurement is necessary. Another way of measuring risk is to estimate the possible losses that can occur from a disaster, the probability of each loss occurring given the disaster, and the probability of the disaster itself occurring. These estimates form the basis of calculating the expected loss from possible disasters facing an organization (see Raiffa [1968]). The expected loss from possible disasters in turn forms the basis for deciding how much to spend on risk control.

Risk Control Risks can be controlled through system design, installation of security measures, and regular security audits. However, some residual risk always will exist that cannot be covered. This residual risk can be handled in three ways (see NCC Study Group [1974]). First, the organization can bear the risk itself and treat any loss as part of normal operations. Second, the risk can be shared through a trade association or some other means; for example, an agreement among members to provide each other with backup facilities. Third, the risk can be transferred contractually by insurance (see, especially, Sleeper and Davis [1973a, 1973b, 1974]).

If a decision is made to purchase insurance, management must be careful to ensure they consider all major potential losses; the replacement cost of purchased or leased hardware must be covered, special construction relating to raised floors and air conditioning must be covered, etc. The types of insurance policies that might be obtained are:

1 Data processing policy

2 Valuable papers and records policy
3 Business interruption insurance
4 Extra expense insurance
5 Errors and omissions insurance

A final critical element in the control of risk is a disaster recovery plan for the computer installation. This plan details the procedures that should occur when disaster strikes. Adams [1974] describes a disaster recovery plan successfully used by IBM to recover from a data center fire. Its contents included:

Resource	Points considered
Programs	Inventory of programs, location of backup copies
Data	Inventory of files and storage media, schedule for preparing backup, location of backup files
Hardware	Equipment required, power and air conditioning requirements for each unit
Space	Description of current floor plan
Supplies	Inventory of supplies and associated vendors
Documentation	Inventory of documentation, location of backup copies

For each resource the plan also contained the name of the person to be contacted to obtain the backup.

A disaster recovery plan usually requires regular update to reflect the current resources within the installation. From a control perspective the auditor should check for the existence and currency of the plan.

EVALUATING THE ORGANIZING FUNCTION

The planning process establishes goals and objectives for a computer installation. The organizing process structures personnel, facilities, and information flows to enable these goals and objectives to be achieved.

On one point organization design theorists are clear. If organizations are to achieve goals effectively and efficiently, organization structures simply cannot be allowed to evolve. Organization design must be an ongoing, conscious, rational decision process within organizations.

Organizational Structure Issues

What should be the form of the organizational structure adopted within a computer installation? Traditionally, two types of hierarchical structure have been used (Figure 4.1): (*a*) a functional form—systems analysts are grouped together, programmers are grouped together, etc.; and (*b*) a project form—though some support staff may be grouped functionally, systems analysts, programmers, etc., are grouped together by application areas or specific projects.

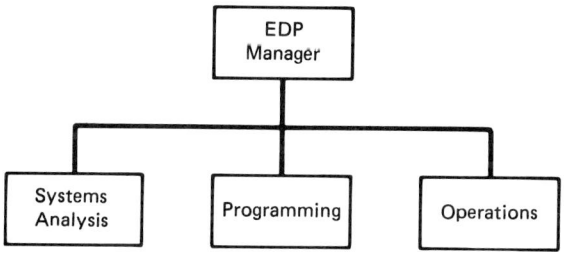

Figure 4.1a
Functional form of organization.

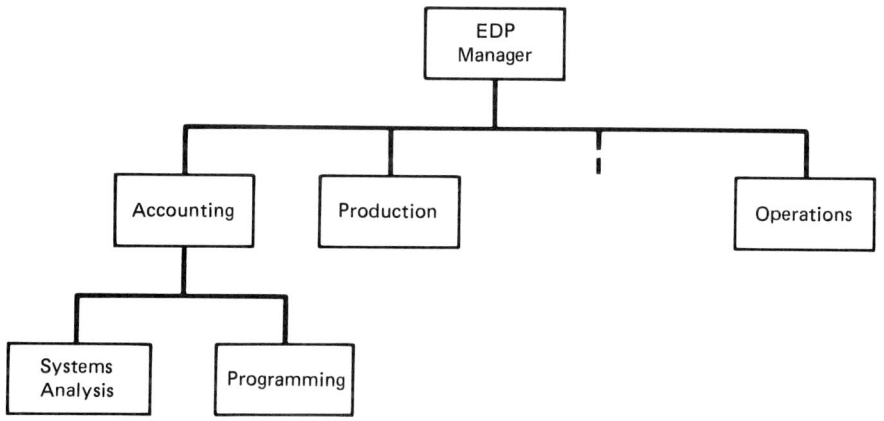

Figure 4.1b
Project form of organization.

There are various advantages and disadvantages to these structures. Using the functional form, advantages accrue through greater task specialization. Using the project form, advantages accrue because personnel are closer to the user area.

In spite of their historical prominence, however, these two hierarchical structures are not the only ways to organize a computer installation. Organization theorists argue in some cases alternate structures may be desirable; furthermore, sound theory now exists to support the choice of structures that improve the effectiveness and efficiency of organizations.

The basis for these contentions is *contingency theory*. Contingency theory evolved from empirical studies carried out on organizations over a long period of time. Based on these studies the theory states: first, there is no single best way to organize; and second, not all ways of organizing are equally effective.

The results of a number of studies show the primary variable affecting the choice of a particular organization structure is *task uncertainty*. Lawrence and Lorsch [1969] found successful organizations increasingly *differentiate* their subunits in response to higher task uncertainty, yet at the same time they *integrate* these subunits to achieve the coordination necessary for successful completion of a task. Successful organizations facing stable environments tend to have mechanistic types of organization structures with well-defined hierarchies of authority, standards, etc. Successful organizations facing unstable environments tend to have "organic" types of organization structures with delegation of decision making, less formal lines of authority and responsibility, etc.

Task uncertainty affects the amount of information an organization must process. As task uncertainty increases, the organization needs more information to cope with this uncertainty. Different organizational structures facilitate information processing in different ways. Galbraith [1977] provides a detailed discussion of how the following organization design strategies can be used to improve an organization's information processing capabilities:

Strategy	Explanation
Environmental Management	Instead of modifying its own structure, the organization attempts to modify its environment and reduce uncertainty. Strategies include cooperation, contracting, coopting, and coalescing.
Creation of Slack Resources	The organization reduces its level of performance and consequently reduces the number of exceptions occurring.
Creation of Self-Contained Tasks	Tasks are decomposed into subtasks and units are provided with all the resources necessary to accomplish the subtasks.
Investment in Vertical Information Systems	The capacity of existing communication channels is increased, new channels are created, and new decision mechanisms are introduced.
Creation of Lateral Relations	Lateral decision processes are employed to cut across lines of authority, e.g., liaison roles, task forces, teams, matrix organization.

The first two strategies are designed to reduce the need for information processing. The last three strategies are designed to increase the organization's capacity to process information. If the organization does not choose at least one strategy when faced with greater task uncertainty, reduced performance and slack resources will be created automatically.

To illustrate these concepts, consider two types of project groups that might exist within a mature EDP installation: one involved in the design and implementation of a straightforward application system, and the other involved in the initial developmental work to support the organization's move toward a distributed database system. In the former group there is low task uncertainty; thus, contingency theory predicts the group is more likely to be successful if it is organized along traditional project lines—a clear hierarchy of authority, rigorous standards, well-defined checkpoints, etc. For the latter group, however, contingency theory predicts the group will be more successful if it adopts an organic type of organization structure. For example, the group might be organized rather loosely and physically located to promote a free flow of ideas among its members. To reduce uncertainty new information channels might be established; for example, members of user groups might be coopted as members of the project group and a special committee might be established.

Contingency theory provides a framework that enables the auditor to think about how well management has chosen an organization structure for the computer installation. The auditor must attempt to gauge the task uncertainty facing the computer installation, the amount of information the organization will need to cope with this uncertainty, and whether the organization structures chosen are appropriate for the information processing needs of the computer installation.

Centralization versus Decentralization

A major organization design issue often facing top and EDP management is whether to centralize or decentralize computer facilities. The issue arises for two major reasons. First, if a centralized computer installation continues to grow, it may become awkward and unwieldy to manage. Second, top management may have made a centralization/decentralization decision for the organization as a whole. If top management decides to create divisions scattered around the country, the computer installation may have to respond by decentralizing its own facilities.

There are alternative ways of centralizing and decentralizing computer operations (see also, Davis [1974]):

Centralized functions	Decentralized functions
1 All functions	
2 Overall coordination	All other functions, i.e., development, implementation, and operations
3 Hardware/software operations	Systems development and implementation
4 Hardware/software operations, and implementation	Systems analysis
5 Systems development and implementation	Hardware/software operations

The centralization/decentralization decision can have an important impact on data integrity and system effectiveness and efficiency. Consider, for example, the following:

Organization strategy	Advantages	Disadvantages
Decentralize Systems Analysis	Better systems designed through greater awareness of user needs	Greater difficulties in standardizing and integrating systems
Centralize Programming	Economies of scale	Slower response to changes needed
Decentralize Hardware	Fewer data errors because data can be input directly from remote locations	Loss of processing power through use of smaller machines
Centralize Software	Greater standardization	Software not attuned to the needs of individual users

Miller [1978] argues that the tendency of all living systems (including organizations) is toward specialization of function and decentralization. This allows the subsystems within the system to be more robust to change; as a consequence, the system is better able to survive. If the system is not to become pathological, however, as discussed in the previous section, decentralization must be accompanied by an increase in integrating mechanisms so the system still can control its subsystems.

If Miller's theory of living systems is correct, computer systems will tend to become more decentralized. Auditors should focus on whether or not decentralization moves have been accompanied by an increase in integrating mechanisms; for example, the establishment of new information channels and increased emphasis on planning and budgeting.

Selecting Hardware/Software Facilities

Another aspect of organizing is choosing suitable hardware/software facilities. Selecting hardware/software facilities involves two major steps: first, preparing a manual of specifications for distribution to hardware/software vendors; and second, evaluating vendor proposals and selecting a final hardware/software configuration.

The manual of specifications is prepared to communicate to vendors the needs of the computer installation. It forms the basis for the vendor's proposal. From a control viewpoint the manual of specifications must: (*a*) clearly state the needs of the installation, and (*b*) act as a turnaround document to ensure uniformity in proposals tendered and thereby facilitate evaluation. Table 4.2 shows the contents of a manual of specifications.

The bases to be used for evaluating vendor proposals should be planned formally. Test data may have to be prepared. Management also must decide on the relative weightings to give different criteria in the evaluation. Chapter 21 provides an extended discussion of the different techniques that can be used for evaluating hardware and software.

TABLE 4.2
CONTENTS OF A MANUAL
OF SPECIFICATIONS

1 Description of the Organization
2 Data Processing Requirements
   a Major application systems to be developed
   b Workloads
   c Suggested processing methods
3 Hardware Requirements
   a CPU
   b Peripherals
   c Data preparation
4 Software Requirements
   a Compilers
   b Systems software
   c Generalized packages
   d Database management
5 Support Required
   a Maintenance
   b Training
   c Backup
6 Adaptability Requirements
   a Upgrading of hardware/software
   b Changeover facilities for other machines
7 Constraints
   a Processing
   b Delivery dates for hardware/software
8 Changeover Requirements
   a Test time
   b Test facilities
9 Pricing Schedule

Methods Standards

To guide and control its activities a computer installation must have: (*a*) methods standards, and (*b*) performance standards. Methods standards establish uniform practices, procedures, rules, etc., to be followed in an installation. Performance standards establish yardsticks for measuring the performance of a computer installation. Methods standards as an *organizational* technique are discussed briefly in this section. Performance standards as a *control* technique are discussed later in the chapter.

Within a computer installation, methods standards have four major purposes:

1 Facilitate communication between interdependent parties; for example, between systems analysts and programmers.

2 Reduce the effects of personnel turnover; new staff are not affected by the idiosyncracies of their predecessors.

3 Reduce the effects of technological change; for example, by facilitating hardware/software changeover.
4 Form the basis for performance standards by providing a common measurement base.

As a general rule standards should be pervasive and be formally documented in the computer installation's standards manual. Brandon [1963] provides a detailed discussion of the standards required for activities in various areas: systems analysis, programming, and operations. A major problem in formulating standards is determining their appropriate level. Very detailed standards are costly to develop and maintain and personnel made responsible for them become loathe to update them. The standards manual can become outdated quickly. Superficial standards are also useless since they provide inadequate guidance for performing tasks.

EVALUATING THE STAFFING FUNCTION

Staff are some of the critical elements in the overall computer control structure. The quality of staff directly influences the quality of systems produced by the installation.

The master plan indicates staffing needs into the future. Two factors emphasize the need for ongoing staff planning. First, historically, good computer personnel have been in short supply. This situation seems unlikely to change in the near future. Second, some staff needed in a computer installation have highly technical skills. Acquiring these staff can be very difficult. Staff planning involves taking an inventory of the current staff capabilities, determining future staff requirements, assessing the likely turnover of staff, and determining how positions will be filled.

Personnel Acquisition

To hire the right person for a job, it is important both management and the applicant for the job understand clearly the requirements of the job. For each position in the computer installation, a formal documented job specification must exist defining the nature of the job, its duties, and opportunities for advancement. The job specification forms the basis of advertising the job and evaluating applicants for the job.

Personnel can be recruited internally or externally to the organization. There are various advantages and disadvantages to each method. Internal recruitment enhances morale and captures existing experience within the organization. External recruitment may result in a better match between the job specification and the applicant's skill set. It also injects new knowledge into the organization.

Management can obtain data to evaluate applicants through interviews, aptitude tests, references, résumés, and scholastic records. Some basic control procedures that should be applied include:

1 Background checking of references, résumés, scholastic records, etc.
   2 Screening applicants for mental and physical health
   3 Bonding of key employees
   4 Explanation of organization protocol to be observed, e.g., matters not to be discussed in public
   5 General organization indoctrination

Personnel Development

Personnel development involves (a) establishing promotional and personal growth opportunities for employees, and (b) education. These activities maintain employee morale and the skill set necessary for carrying out the computer installation's tasks.

Providing promotional and personal growth opportunities can be a special problem in computer installations. On the one hand employees are often young, have experienced rapid promotion, and are quickly left with few opportunities for advancement. On the other hand the technical expertise of the "older" systems analyst or programmer makes them immobile within the organizational hierarchy. These problems have not been well-addressed.

Regular staff reviews should be carried out for three reasons: (a) to assess whether an employee warrants promotion, (b) to identify opportunities for the employee's personal growth, and (c) to identify the employee's strengths and weaknesses. Employees should understand clearly the nature of the staff review and the basis on which they will be evaluated. Management should discuss with them their overall ratings so there is scope for appeal and counsel them.

Sometimes staff reviews give insufficient emphasis to identifying opportunities for the employee's personal growth. If promotional opportunities are scarce, personal growth may be the only means of preventing high staff turnover. Management must seek more responsible and challenging positions for employees, yet at the same time determine whether employees have earned the necessary trust and have the required skill set for these positions.

Because of the high rate of obsolescence in computer technology, training and continuing education are critical for the successful ongoing operations of the computer installation. There is a tendency during high-pressure periods to forgo training. The long-run implications of this decision can be disastrous for employee morale and coping with new technology.

Training must not be haphazard. Those areas where employee expertise is lacking should be identified. Proposed coursework should be carefully evaluated. Employees attending training sessions should disseminate the knowledge acquired upon returning to the installation.

Personnel Termination

Personnel termination may be voluntary or involuntary. In either case, certain control procedures should be exercised. The severity of the procedures depends on whether the employee is disgruntled or not. Examples of these control procedures are:

1 Upon giving notice, if the employee is a key person, management should be immediately informed. The employee's supervisor should be contacted to determine reasons for leaving.

2 Upon termination, a checklist should be prepared so that: (*a*) keys and ID badges are recovered, (*b*) employee passwords are cancelled, (*c*) distribution lists are changed, (*d*) all reports, books, documentation, etc., are returned, and (*e*) any equipment issued is returned.

3 The terminating employee should provide training for the replacement employee.

4 If the employee is disgruntled, the employee should be assigned to noncritical areas.

5 Exit interviews should be given so that: (*a*) any areas of discontent are determined, (*b*) reminders are given on secrecy oaths, etc., and (*c*) potential problems are identified.

EVALUATING THE DIRECTING FUNCTION

Directing is a complex management function designed to motivate employees. Koontz and O'Donnell [1976] propose the *purpose* of directing to be achieving harmony of objectives; that is, an individual's objectives must not conflict with group objectives. The *process* of directing is based upon three major principles: first, unity of command whereby individuals should report to a single supervisor to avoid conflict in instructions and promote a greater feeling of responsibility for results achieved; second, direct supervision whereby management should supplement objective methods of supervision with direct personal contact; and third, appropriate variation of supervisory techniques to suit different people, tasks, and organizational environments.

Evaluating top management's and EDP management's ability to direct people may seem an abstruse type of activity for the EDP auditor to perform. Clearly, many EDP auditors have insufficient training in the behavioral sciences to be able to perform an in-depth evaluation. Nevertheless, EDP auditors (whether they be external or internal auditors) must still attempt to gauge (if only superficially) management's ability to direct. Ineffective directing can lead to system failure as surely as erroneous design specifications can lead to system failure: EDP staff may not understand their overall purposes, they may be poorly motivated, they may not communicate the results they achieve, etc.

How can the auditor evaluate how well top management and EDP management perform the directing function? In a few pages, this question can barely be addressed. It requires the auditor to understand areas fundamental to effective directing: how to motivate subordinates, how to give leadership, and how to communicate clearly the work requirements to subordinates.

Human Motivation

The research and writings on human motivation are immense (see, especially, Dunnette [1976]). There has been a steady progression of motivation theories advanced: Maslow's hierarchy of needs theory, Herzberg's motivator-hygiene theory, Vroom's expectancy theory. However, a contingency theory of motivation now seems to be well-accepted: there is no one best way of motivating people; the best way depends on individuals and their environment.

Consider, for example, two systems analysts in a computer installation, both of whom are well-paid. On the basis of some motivation theories, a manager may feel that it is necessary to provide "challenging" work to motivate them. However, contingency theory emphasizes that it is still necessary to take into account the individual differences of both analysts. One analyst, for example, may have a high propensity for dealing with uncertainty; the other may feel acute stress and anxiety when faced with high uncertainty. Clearly it would be unwise to assign the latter analyst to a project that involved high levels of task uncertainty, even though the project may be a challenging one. If this is done the outcome may be a poorly designed and implemented project; furthermore, an inappropriate match of tasks and personnel can mean staff turnover occurs.

The auditor usually has neither the time nor the expertise to go through a computer installation and evaluate from a motivation viewpoint the match of each individual with the jobs they perform. What the auditor can do, however, is examine variables that often indicate when motivation problems exist; for example, staff turnover statistics, frequent failure of projects to meet their budget, and absenteeism levels.

Leadership

Koontz and O'Donnell [1976] argue a manager who adopts an effective leadership style exhibits certain characteristics: awareness—they understand the essentials of motivation and leadership; empathy—they can place themselves in the position of others; objectivity—they can examine and evaluate events unemotionally; and self-knowledge—they are aware of the results their actions evoke.

Leadership styles vary along a continuum from authoritarian to democratic. As with motivation, organization theorists advocate a contingency theory of leadership: there is no one best leadership style for all people and all situations; it depends on personalities and tasks. For example, if a project team is developing a decision support system for strategic planning purposes and a high level of task uncertainty exists, a democratic style of leadership probably will be more successful than other leadership styles; in fact, at different times leadership of the group may switch to the person having most expertise with the problem being addressed at that point in time. Even within the group, some individuals require more guidance than others. They may be inexperienced or lack confidence in their abilities; thus, a more authoritarian style of leadership may be needed with these personnel.

Again, the auditor usually has neither the time nor the expertise to perform an in-depth evaluation of management's ability to choose the appropriate leadership style in a given situation. Instead, as with motivation, the auditor must be aware of indicators that suggest poor leadership: staff turnover, projects failing to meet budgets, etc.

Communications

Because so much of the work in a computer installation requires precision, effective and efficient communications between management and subordinate staff are critical. Messages must be clearly understood, the integrity of messages must be assured, and any message sent must obtain the attention of the receiver.

The auditor has both formal and informal sources of evidence for evaluating how well top and EDP management communicate with their subordinate staff. Many of the formal sources of evidence have been covered earlier in the chapter: master plans, project plans, methods standards, etc. The minutes of meetings also are an important source of formal evidence on the success or lack thereof of communications within an installation.

The informal sources of evidence include interviews with installation staff, the existence of a sense of purpose among members of a project group, general awareness by the staff of other developments within the installation even though they may not be directly involved with these developments, etc. Often the auditor assimilates this type of evidence as more formal evidence collection tasks are being performed.

EVALUATING THE CONTROLLING FUNCTION

The controlling function involves determining when the actual activities of the computer installation deviate from the planned activities. In essence the remainder of this book is concerned with how well management performs the controlling function. Nevertheless, when evaluating top and EDP management, auditors focus on only a subset of the control activities that should be performed in a computer installation; namely, those aimed at assuring the installation accomplishes its objectives at a global level.

Stage Growth Hypothesis

Chapter 3 pointed out a tendency for the growth pattern of living systems to follow an S-shaped curve. It was hypothesized that the growth pattern of an EDP audit group exhibited this shape. Nolan [1973] also hypothesizes that the growth pattern of EDP facilities within an organization follows an S shape. This pattern is traced by graphing the budget of a computer installation over time (Figure 4.2).

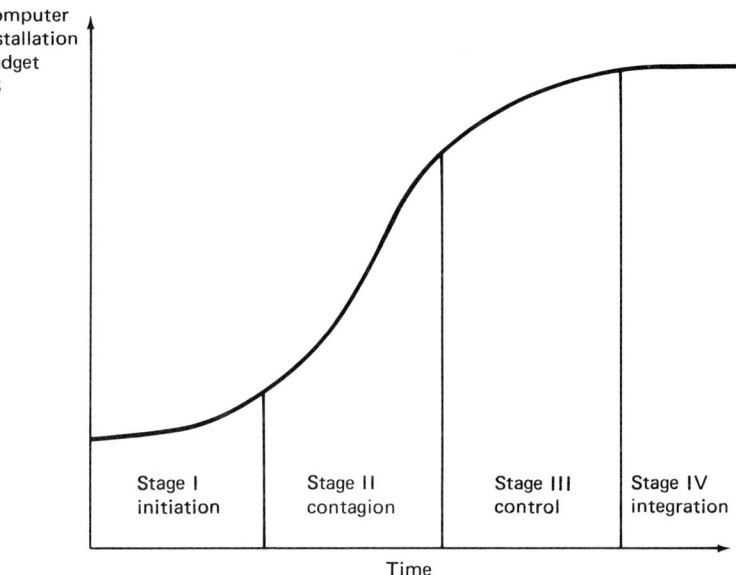

Figure 4.2
The S-shaped curve of the stage growth hypothesis *(from Nolan [1973].
Copyright 1973, Association for Computing Machinery, Inc., reprinted by
permission.)*

Nolan argues that from a control viewpoint the turning points in the S-shaped curve represent critical times in an installation's life. He identifies four stages in his stage growth model (see, also, Nolan [1979]):

Stage	Characteristics of stage
Initiation	Installation of a computer; computer often located in the primary user department; controls are lacking: only a loose budget exists, no transfer pricing scheme is used; projects are assigned priorities on a FIFO basis
Contagion	Sales-oriented management intent on showing the usefulness of the computer; higher status given to EDP manager; lax controls engender rapid applications development; few standards; informal project control and a loose budget
Control	Control-oriented management; computer moves out of primary user department; proliferation of controls to contain runaway budget; establishment of steering committee, standards, project control, post-audits; transfer pricing scheme introduced
Integration	Resource-oriented planning and control; EDP becomes a separate functional area; some decentralization of systems analysts and programmers into user areas; increasing specialization of function within computer installation; advanced systems introduced, e.g., online realtime systems; refinement of controls and transfer pricing scheme; establishment of a master plan

Lucas and Sutton [1977] conducted an empirical study that produced evidence contrary to the stage growth model. Using regression methodology they found straight-line and exponential curves provided better fits of budget data over time than an S-shaped curve. Nevertheless, they concluded the stage growth model was still useful as a means of anticipating problems that occur as an installation passes through the various stages. Rather than use the installation's budget as an indicator of the stage reached, they suggested the state of the installation's applications portfolio may be a better predictor. As the installation matures, its mix of application systems changes to include more strategic planning systems.

From an audit viewpoint Nolan's "theory" is important because it focuses on the state of controls within a computer installation as it passes through the various stages. If external auditors can determine the stage reached by an installation, they can predict the likely control problems existing in the installation. Internal auditors can use the theory as the basis for designing controls appropriate to the various stages and alerting management as to the likely problems that will exist.

The Means of Control

Management exercises control over the computer installation's activities through the normal means: plans and budgets, measuring actual performance, and determining variances from budgets. A study by McKinsey and Company [1968] demonstrates the importance of controlling computer resource usage. They found that companies which plan EDP activities and audit the results are more successful users of computers than companies which do not perform these control activities. The following sections briefly examine some essential control elements in a computer installation.

Performance Standards Together with a project plan, performance standards form the basis of constructing budgets for information system projects. Performance standards describe the resource usage that should be expected from undertaking different activities within the computer installation. Brandon [1963] provides a detailed discussion of performance standards for four major areas within a computer installation: (*a*) equipment use, (*b*) systems analysis, (*c*) programming, and (*d*) operations. Performance standards also must be formulated for other areas; for example, database administration.

Documentation Standards In an empirical study of why information system projects succeed or fail, Dickson and Powers [1973] found documentation standards to be an important factor affecting the time taken to complete a project. London [1977] argues documentation standards serve four purposes:

1 Inter-task/phase communication
2 Quality control and project control

3 Historical reference
4 Instructional reference

Management's problem is to determine the level of documentation needed in the installation. Preparing documentation is a time-consuming activity (see, also, Chapter 8). The benefits should outweigh the costs. The Canadian Institute of Chartered Accountants [1970] provides a detailed description of the types of documentation it regards as necessary within a computer installation (see also, U.S. Department of Commerce [1976, 1979]).

Postaudits Besides the audits carried out by the EDP audit group, EDP management should carry out regularly its own audits as a fundamental control procedure. The computer installation audit team has the same control objectives as the EDP audit team; however, it differs from the EDP audit team in two respects. First, it does not have to maintain independence; thus, it can be more involved in the detailed analysis, design, and implementation of a system. Second, as a corollary of the first difference, the team members can be picked specially for the audit because of their in-depth knowledge of the system to be audited.

Controlling Users of Computer Services

There are two ways of controlling users of the computer installation's services. First, some type of review committee can examine users' requests. Second, a transfer pricing or chargeout scheme can be used for computer installation services. This latter method seems preferable for several reasons. First, users understand more clearly how their use of computer services will be evaluated. Second, continuing charges for computer services should make users more aware of the costs of using their systems and motivate them to seek more effective and efficient systems. Third, even a review committee needs some basis for evaluating the costs and benefits of a system; a transfer pricing system assists with this evaluation.

The major problem with a transfer pricing scheme is determining the chargeout price that will cause managers to act optimally in terms of the overall objectives of the organization. Some transfer prices cause suboptimization because managers seeking to maximize their own profits do so by reducing the overall profit of the organization. The "theoretically correct" transfer price has been a thorny problem for researchers. Except in fairly constrained cases—for example, when perfect competition exists—the correct transfer price to use is unclear. In some cases economic theory suggests a complex system of taxes and subsidies may be needed. However, the behavioral ramifications of different transfer prices have not been researched extensively. Abdel-khalik and Lusk [1974] and Drury and Bates [1979] provide useful summaries of much of the literature.

Of direct relevance to the pricing of computer services is a study carried out by Nolan [1977]. Nolan examined the effects of different transfer pricing schemes on user/manager attitudes toward computer-based information systems. He surveyed user/manager attitudes at 13 research sites using different kinds of transfer pricing schemes and found "advanced" chargeout systems to be associated with relatively high user/manager attitudes and a marked increase in EDP usage. Interestingly, one characteristic of advanced chargeout systems was their simplicity. Users looked unfavorably upon complex transfer pricing schemes that they were unable to understand.

SUMMARY

The auditor's evaluation of top management and EDP management is a difficult task. It requires the auditor to have a sound knowledge of the principles of good management.

A useful way of evaluating top management and EDP management is to examine the various functions they perform: planning, organizing, directing, staffing, and controlling. For each of these functions normative guidelines exist that the auditor can use as a basis for evaluation.

REVIEW QUESTIONS

4.1. Why is it important the auditor be capable of evaluating the quality of top management and EDP management of an organization in relation to the computer installation?

4.2. How is the framework of managerial functions — planning, organizing, staffing, directing, and controlling — useful to the auditor?

4.3. Briefly describe each of the major plans that must be formulated for a computer installation.

4.4. What are the functions of the steering committee of a computer installation? Who should comprise the steering committee?

4.5. Briefly describe three situations in the life cycle of a computer installation when a feasibility study might be needed. What aspects of feasibility studies are of interest to the auditor? How can the auditor evaluate whether feasibility studies are carried out properly?

4.6. Briefly describe two aspects of the changeover to a new computer installation that pose major threats to an organization's data integrity. What aspects of a changeover plan would the auditor examine to determine whether these threats have been properly considered?

4.7. Innovation Inc., is a company specializing in research and development. It accepts short-term research and development projects from other companies and aims to obtain results quickly. It has been very successful in achieving this objective. (Current sales $80,000,000.)

You are a field auditor in a firm of external auditors that has just taken over the audit of Innovation. When carrying out the audit of their computer installation you find there is no master plan for the installation. This concerns you as Innovation uses computers extensively to support its activities. It has two large machines for both scientific and commercial activities. When you interview the manager of the computer installation on this problem, he informs you it is impossible to prepare a master plan for the installation because of the uncertainty surrounding Innovation's activities. How would you now proceed?

4.8. Give five reasons why project plans should be developed for computer projects. How can the auditor evaluate project planning activities within a computer installation?

4.9. Briefly describe the major activities involved in risk management. How might the internal auditor assist in the risk management of a computer installation? What role does the external auditor have with respect to risk management?

4.10. Briefly describe three major categories of disasters that can befall a computer installation. Give two characteristics of an organization that make it more amenable to disasters in one category versus another category.

4.11. How can residual risks be controlled for a computer installation? Outline a decision model you might use to choose between the various methods of controlling residual risk.

4.12. Why is the auditor interested in the organizing capabilities of management? What evidence would the auditor collect to determine whether management is competent at organizing the computer installation?

4.13. What are methods standards? What are the purposes of having methods standards in a computer installation? What is the relationship between methods standards and performance standards? Outline some methods standards you think would be needed for (a) systems analysis, and (b) programming.

4.14. Why should a computer installation have a standards manual? What impact does the absence of a standards manual have on carrying out an audit?

4.15. Give two examples of how EDP management might use lateral relations to increase the flow of information among personnel in a computer installation. (*Hint:* Read Galbraith [1977]).

4.16. When purchasing hardware and software, why is it important to prepare a manual of specifications? Outline the contents of a manual of specifications. Why should the manual of specifications be prepared to act as a turnaround document?

4.17. What evidence should the auditor seek to determine whether management of a computer installation performs the staffing function competently?

4.18. Outline the controls that should exist for personnel acquisition, development, and termination. What factors determine whether or not these controls should be applied?

4.19. What principles underlie the management function of directing? What evidence should the auditor seek to determine whether EDP management has a fundamental understanding of these principles?

4.20. How does EDP management's understanding of human motivation, theories and styles of leadership, and principles of communication impact the effectiveness and efficiency with which computer systems can be developed?

4.21. Explain Nolan's stage growth hypothesis. What is the relevance of the stage growth hypothesis to the auditor?

4.22. Explain the relationship between performance standards, budgeting, and control.

4.23. What are the purposes of documentation? Briefly describe the basic types of documentation that should exist in a computer installation. What evidence would the auditor seek to determine whether documentation standards are being applied?

4.24. Why should management periodically carry out audits of the computer installation? How are these audits different from those carried out by internal or external auditors?

4.25. What is a transfer price? How do transfer prices assist in controlling the computer installation? What does empirical evidence suggest the basic design guidelines for transfer prices should be?

EXERCISES AND CASES

4.1. Consider a medium-sized manufacturing organization that is a mature user of computers. For the organization you consider, fill in the elements of the following controls matrix where the elements represent your opinion on the likely cost-effectiveness (in general) of the various categories of controls (rows of the matrix) at achieving various control objectives (columns of the matrix). Note, assume a score of 5 means controls within a category have high cost-effectiveness and a score of 1 means controls within a category have low cost-effectiveness. Also, be sure to give a brief explanation of each of your ratings.

Controls \ Objectives	Asset safeguarding	Data integrity	System effectiveness	System efficiency
Planning				
Organizing				
Staffing				
Directing				
Controlling				

4.2. Make a list of those controls described in the chapter that would *not* be of major interest to external auditors; that is, controls that are not especially cost-effective at reducing the expected losses from lack of asset safeguarding in the computer installation or lack of data integrity. Briefly explain each of your choices.

4.3. Remote Resources Inc., is a large diversified and decentralized mining company. For some time the company has operated a bauxite mining site on the Gulf of Carpentaria in Queensland, Australia. The site is very remote. It is surrounded by tropical jungle and the road to the nearest major city, Cairns, is impassable during the wet season lasting from about December through April. The main means of access are by air—a three-hour flight from Cairns (only small aircraft can be used) — and by sea — a four-day boat trip from Cairns. However, even these means of access can't be used when cyclones are about; consequently, at times the mining site can be cut off for about a week or more.

It has become increasingly difficult to hire competent staff to perform the clerical, administrative, and accounting functions at the site. Thus, the head office of the company is contemplating installing a small computer at the site to process several accounting applications such as payroll and inventory as well as providing the mining engineers with computational support.

Required: You are on the internal audit staff of Remote Resources Inc. The internal audit manager has asked you to prepare a brief report outlining a disaster recovery plan for the proposed installation. Be sure to point out some of the major difficulties involved with disaster recovery at the mining site.

4.4. Harrison University is a large university with about 30,000 students offering a wide range of courses in the humanities and the physical, social, behavioral, health, agricultural, biological, and engineering sciences. The existing computing facilities are divided between two groups: an academic computing center and an administrative computing center. Each group has its own hardware, software, personnel, etc., and operates independently of the other group. The academic computing center services all teaching and research needs; the administrative computing center services all other computing needs — payroll, student records, budgeting, financial planning, etc.

Currently the facilities of the administrative computing center are heavily overloaded. A steering committee of the University has been formed to examine the problem. The steering committee has been given wide terms of reference. In recent years, the University has found it increasingly difficult to find sources of private funding and to obtain federal funding. The President of the University has asked the steering group to consider the possibility of amalgamating the academic and administrative computing groups, selling off the existing hardware, and purchasing a large machine that will service both groups. She feels that centralizing computer facilities may produce economies of scale. During the interim period, since the academic computer has substantial excess capacity, she also questions whether some administrative applications might not be shifted to the academic computer.

Required: You are a member of the internal audit staff of the University. The chairman of the steering committee has asked the manager of internal audit for his views on the proposed changes, and he has asked you to brief him. Prepare a memo outlining the advantages and disadvantages of the change from an internal audit viewpoint.

4.5. You are the head of internal audit for a medium-sized organization. One day you receive a memo from the controller of your organization requesting some assistance with the decision on upgrading computer facilities within your organization.

The controller's concern is that he believes the data processing manager is not giving adequate consideration to all the tenders submitted by the different vendors. Apparently she is arguing that the only tender worth considering is the one submitted by the vendor who supplies the existing hardware and software used by your organization. The reason is that she contends the changeover to another vendor would be too costly.

Required: The controller asks you to send him a brief memorandum outlining the steps you will take to investigate the issue. He also asks you to list the information you will need to be able to carry out the evaluation.

REFERENCES

Abdel-khalik, A. Rashad, and Edward J. Lusk. "Transfer Pricing—A Synthesis," *The Accounting Review* (January 1974), pp. 8–23.

Adams, Donald L. "Recovery from a Data Center Fire," *EDPACS* (April 1974), pp. 9–11.

American Federation of Information Processing Societies. *AFIPS System Review Manual on Security* (Montvale, N.J.: AFIPS Press, 1974).

Bierman, Harold, and Seymour Smidt. *The Capital Budgeting Decision*, 4th ed. (New York: Macmillan Publishing Co., Inc., 1975).

Brandon, Dick H. *Management Standards for Data Processing* (Princeton, N.J.: D. Van Nostrand Company, Inc., 1963).

Canadian Institute of Chartered Accountants. *Computer Control Guidelines* (Toronto, Canada: The Canadian Institute of Chartered Accountants, 1970).

Cleland, David, I., and William R. King. *Systems Analysis and Project Management*, 2d ed. (New York: McGraw-Hill Book Company, 1975).

Davis, Gordon B. *Management Information Systems: Conceptual Foundations, Structure, and Development* (New York: McGraw-Hill Book Company, 1974).

Dickson, Gary W., and Richard F. Powers. "MIS Project Management: Myths, Opinion and Reality," in F. Warren McFarland, Richard L. Nolan, and David P. Norton, eds., *Information Systems Administration* (New York: Holt, Rinehart and Winston, Inc., 1973), pp. 401–412.

Ditri, Arnold E., John C. Shaw, and William Atkins. *Managing the EDP Function* (New York: McGraw-Hill Book Company, 1971).

Donaldson, Haimish. *A Guide to Successful Management of Computer Projects* (New York: John Wiley and Sons, Inc., 1978).

Drury, Donald H., and John E. Bates. *Data Processing Chargeback Systems: Theory and Practice* (Hamilton, Ont.: The Society of Management Accountants of Canada, 1979).

Dunnette, Marvin D., ed. *Handbook of Industrial and Organizational Psychology* (Chicago: Rand McNally College Publishing Company, 1976).

FitzGerald, Jerry. "EDP Risk Analysis for Contingency Planning," *EDPACS* (August 1978a), pp. 1–8.

———. "Developing and Ranking Threat Scenarios," *EDPACS* (September 1978b), pp. 1–5.

Galbraith, Jay R. *Organization Design* (Reading, Mass.: Addison-Wesley Publishing Company, Inc., 1977).

Gerberick, Dahl A. "Security Risk Analysis," *EDPACS* (April 1979), pp. 1–11.

Joslin, Edward O. *Analysis, Design and Selection of Computer Systems*, 2d ed. (Arlington, Va.: College Readings, Inc., 1974).

Koontz, Harold, and Cyril O'Donnell. *Management: A Systems and Contingency Analysis of the Managerial Functions*, 6th ed. (New York: McGraw-Hill Book Company, 1976).

Krauss, Leonard I. *Administering and Controlling the Company Data Processing Function* (Englewood Cliffs, N.J.: Prentice-Hall, Inc., 1969).

Lawrence, Paul R., and Jay W. Lorsch. *Developing Organizations: Diagnosis and Action* (Reading, Mass.: Addison-Wesley Publishing Company, Inc., 1969).

London, Keith R. *Documentation Standards*, 2d ed. (New York: Petrocelli/Charter, 1977).

Lucas, Henry C., and Jimmy A. Sutton. "The Stage Hypothesis and the S-Curve: Some Contradictory Evidence," *Communications of the ACM* (April 1977), pp. 254–259.

McKinsey and Company, Inc. "Unlocking the Computer's Profit Potential," *The McKinsey Quarterly* (Fall 1968), pp. 17–31.

Miller, James Grier. *Living Systems* (New York: McGraw-Hill Book Company, 1978).

NCC Study Group. *Where Next for Computer Security?* (Manchester: The National Computing Center, 1974).

Nolan, Richard L. "Managing the Computer Resource: A Stage Hypothesis," *Communications of the ACM* (July 1973), pp. 399–405.

———. "Effects of Chargeout on User/Manager Attitudes," *Communications of the ACM* (March 1977), pp. 177–184.

———. "Managing the Crises in Data Processing," *Harvard Business Review* (March–April, 1979), pp. 115–126.

Raiffa, Howard. *Decision Analysis: Introductory Lectures on Choices Under Uncertainty* (Reading, Mass.: Addison-Wesley Publishing Company, Inc., 1968).

Sleeper, Richard C., and William P. Davis. "Data Processing Risk Insurance: Part I," *EDPACS* (November 1973a), pp. 11–14.

——— and ———. "Data Processing Risk Insurance: Part II," *EDPACS* (December 1973b), pp. 7–10.

——— and ———. "Data Processing Risk Insurance: Part III," *EDPACS* (January 1974), pp. 7–12.

U.S. Department of Commerce/National Bureau of Standards. *Guidelines for Documentation of Computer Programs and Automated Data Systems,* Federal Information Processing Standards Publication 38, Feb. 15, 1976.

———. *Guidelines for Documentation of Computer Programs and Data Systems for the Initiation Phase,* Federal Information Processing Standards Publication 64, Aug. 1, 1979.

Wong, K. K. *Computer Security Risk Analysis and Control: A Guide for the DP Manager* (Manchester: The National Computing Center, 1977).

CHAPTER 5

SYSTEMS DEVELOPMENT

CHAPTER OUTLINE

AUDITING THE SYSTEM DEVELOPMENT PROCESS
NORMATIVE MODELS OF THE SYSTEM DEVELOPMENT PROCESS
    System Development Life Cycle Approach
    Sociotechnical Design Approach
EVALUATING THE MAJOR PHASES IN THE SYSTEM DEVELOPMENT PROCESS
    Problem Recognition
    Management of the Change Process
    Entry and Feasibility Assessment
    Diagnosis and Information Analysis
    System Design
    Program Development
    Procedure and Forms Development
    Acceptance Testing
    Conversion
    Operation, Maintenance, and Audit
SUMMARY
REVIEW QUESTIONS
EXERCISES AND CASES
REFERENCES

What distinguishes a good system from a bad system? This is a question that has plagued information systems researchers for many years. In some ways the development of good systems is still an art. The formal guidelines are meager and insight and experience still play an important part in determining the quality of the resulting design.

This chapter discusses the activities that should be performed in the system development process. A normative model is described that allows the auditor to structure the evidence collection process. The model also provides the basis for evaluating how well system development activities are performed in a computer installation.

AUDITING THE SYSTEM DEVELOPMENT PROCESS

There are two ways in which the auditor may evaluate the system development process: first, as a member of the system development team (see, also, Chapter 2); and second, in an ex post review capacity when the system development process, in general, is evaluated. The objectives of the audit and the methods used to gather evidence are different for these two types of audit.

When the auditor *participates* in the system development process, the objectives are to ensure for a *specific* application system that controls are built into the system to safeguard assets, ensure data integrity, and achieve system effectiveness and efficiency. The auditor collects evidence primarily by observing the activities of the other members of the development team. This evidence then is evaluated against the auditor's normative model of the system development process.

When the auditor carries out an ex post audit, the objectives are to reduce the extent of substantive testing needed for application systems and to make recommendations for improving the system development process in general. The audit proceeds according to the general approach described in Chapter 2. First, the auditor uses interviews, observations, and a review of standards to obtain general and then detailed information on the system development process. Second, an evaluation of this information forms the basis for hypothesizing strengths and weaknesses that may exist and designing compliance tests. Third, the auditor selects a sample of application systems to determine whether the hypothesized strengths and weaknesses do, in fact, exist (see, also, Mair et al. [1976]).

NORMATIVE MODELS OF THE SYSTEM
DEVELOPMENT PROCESS

The auditor seeks answers to two basic questions when auditing the system development process. First, do system design personnel perform all the activities necessary for the design and implementation of high-quality information systems? Second, are these activities performed well? To answer these questions the auditor needs some basis for thinking about, evaluating, and approaching the audit of the system development process. System development personnel have the same problem. They need a basis, framework, or model to guide their approach to system development. The quality of the systems they design and implement depends on the adequacy of their model for *prescription* and *description* of system development activities.

System Development Life Cycle Approach

Traditionally, system development personnel have thought about the system development process in terms of a life cycle consisting of nine major phases (see, for example, Hartman et al. [1968]):

Phase	Explanation
Feasibility Study	Applying cost-benefit criteria to the proposed application
Information Analysis	Determining user information requirements
System Design	Designing files and information processing functions to be performed in the system
Program Development	Designing, coding, compiling, testing, and documenting programs
Procedures and Forms Development	Designing and documenting procedures and forms for system users
Acceptance Testing	Final testing of the system and formal approval and acceptance by management and users
Conversion	Changeover from the old system to the new system
Operation and Maintenance	Ongoing running of the system and subsequent modifications and maintenance in light of problems detected
Postaudit	Periodic review of the system

The life cycle approach does not imply all these phases must be carried out serially. Some of the phases may proceed concurrently; for example, procedure and forms development may proceed at the same time as program development occurs. Some phases may require several iterations; for example, as programs are developed the system design may have to be modified to improve processing efficiency.

The life cycle approach arose out of early efforts to apply project management techniques to the system development process. There had been a history of system failure because of massive cost overruns, inadequate economic evaluations, inadequate system design, management abdication, poor communication, inadequate direction, etc. The life cycle approach helps overcome some of these problems. By clearly defining tasks in terms of the life cycle, the project management and control techniques described in Chapter 4 can be applied. To develop high-quality systems, each phase of the life cycle should be planned and controlled, comply with developed standards, be adequately documented, be staffed by competent personnel, have project checkpoints and signoffs, etc. (see, further, Biggs et al. [1980]).

Sociotechnical Design Approach

Another set of problems motivated the sociotechnical design approach to information system development. Though the system life cycle approach might have helped alleviate the technical and managerial problems encountered with systems, behavioral problems still persist. Systems degrade through lack of use, apathy, and sometimes outright sabotage. The sociotechnical approach arose because an understanding was needed of *why* behavioral problems occur and *how* they might be remedied.

A sociotechnical system design process attempts to jointly optimize two systems: (*a*) the *technical system* where the objective is task accomplishment, and (*b*) the *social system* where the objective is to achieve a high quality of working life for the users of the system (Figure 5.1). Sociotechnical design theorists argue many of the behavioral problems arising from system implementation occur because system designers neglect the social system. Bostrom and Heinen [1977*a*] believe there are seven reasons why this is the case:

1 *System Designers' Implicit Theories* System designers make assumptions about people, organizations, and the change process that impact their modes of action. These theories are inadequate; for example, research shows

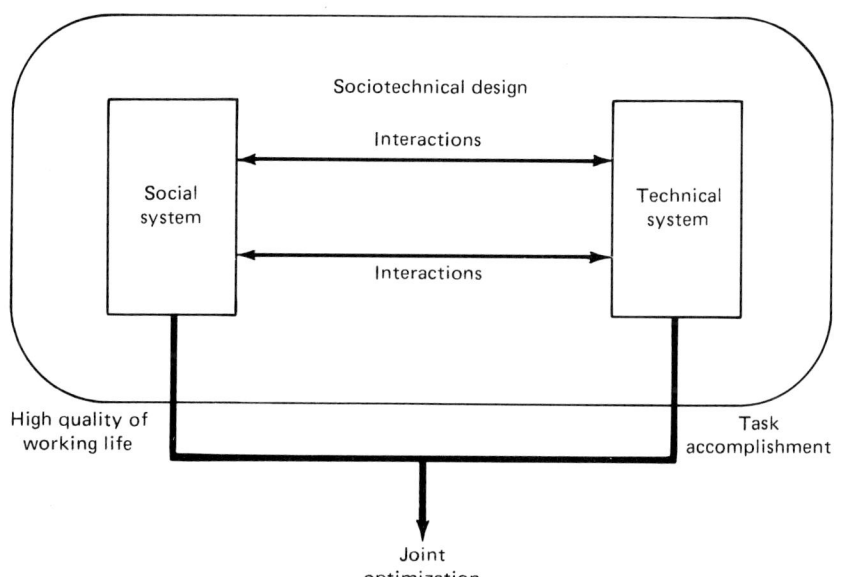

Figure 5.1
The objectives of sociotechnical design.

many system designers hold a theory X view of man, which results in them designing tightly structured job situations that lower the quality of working life of system users.

2 *System Designers' Concept of Responsibility* Research shows system designers perceive they are responsible for the system development process. Behavioral scientists argue change agents (system designers) cannot accept responsibility for another person's change; they can only facilitate or inhibit change.

3 *Limited Frameworks—Nonsystemic View* System designers have a limited view of work systems; their primary focus is the information system. There may be many secondary effects of information system development; for example, job de-enrichment.

4 *Limited Goal Orientation* System designers seek to optimize the technical system; their focus is task accomplishment and not quality of working life issues.

5 *Limited Design Referent Group* System designers have middle management as their primary design referent group. They have little concern for secondary users; for example, clerks who may be responsible for the primary input to the system.

6 *Rational/Static View of the System Development Process* Information system training emphasizes the application of formal project control techniques to a rational design process that proceeds in clearly defined steps. Behavioral scientists argue the design process should be fluid and iterative because a change process causes power shifts, conflicts, etc.

7 *Limited Change Technologies* Typically, system designers are trained in management science/operations research. They know little about behavioral science; consequently, they often know little about how to deal with social problems.

Use of a sociotechnical design approach forces system designers to take a broader and richer view of the design process than the view that Bostrom and Heinen argue designers now have of the design process. The approach consists of five major phases (Figure 5.2):

Phase	Explanation
Diagnosis and Entry	Problem identification; determining whether the organization is amenable to change; analysis of the social and technical systems and coordinating mechanisms; determining the strategic requirements of the system
Management of the Change Process	Ensuring throughout the design process that the organization is amenable to change; facilitating adaptation to change
System Design	Design of both the technical and social system

Adjustment of Coordinating Mechanisms	Changes in one subsystem may necessitate changes in another subsystem; e.g., a reward system may have to be adjusted because the information system supports a new job design
Implementation	Installation of the new sociotechnical system.

The sociotechnical design approach to the system development process does not negate the importance of project management techniques and the traditional life cycle approach. The major criticisms made are that the life cycle approach is incomplete and nonsystemic. System development is a much more comprehensive process than suggested by the life cycle approach.

EVALUATING THE MAJOR PHASES IN THE SYSTEM DEVELOPMENT PROCESS

Ultimately the auditor must choose a normative model of the system development process as a basis for structuring the evidence collection process and evaluating the activities performed in the system development process. Naumann et al. [1979] argue that different models may be appropriate at different times. If there is little uncertainty about the information requirements for a system, a straightforward linear (one-off) application of the life cycle approach may be "best." If there is a high level of uncertainty about the information requirements for a system, substantial iteration and design prototyping may be required in the system development process.

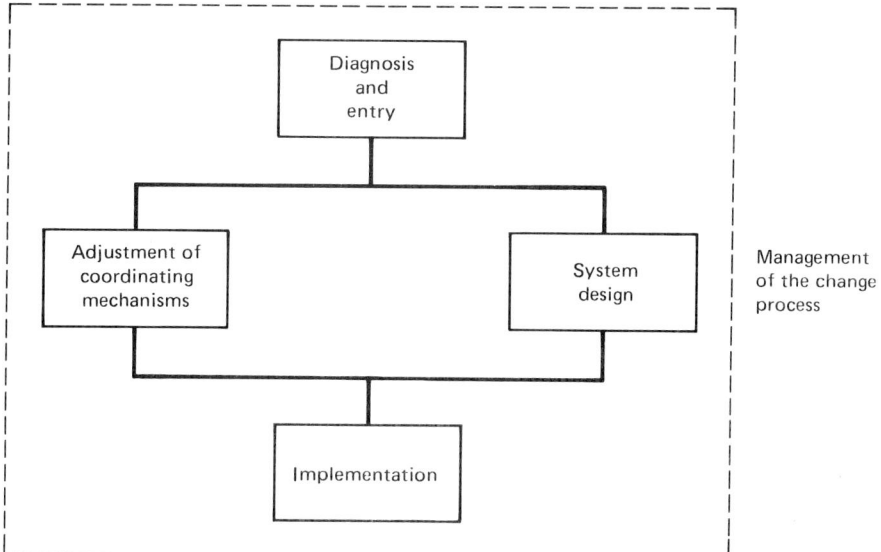

Figure 5.2
Major phases in the sociotechnical design process.

The model of the system development process proposed in this chapter is somewhat eclectic; it focuses on those aspects of the life cycle and sociotechnical approaches that are important to the auditor. However, since the life cycle approach is better documented (see the references), more emphasis has been given to explaining various aspects of sociotechnical design activities. Nevertheless, the extent to which each of these activities is performed depends on various contingencies; for example, the project size and the degree of structuredness in the decisions that the information system supports (see, further, Naumann et al. [1979]).

The normative model of the system development process advocated herein consists of 10 major phases:

1 Problem recognition
2 Management of the change process
3 Entry and feasibility assessment
4 Diagnosis and information analysis
5 System design
6 Program development
7 Procedure and forms development
8 Acceptance testing
9 Conversion
10 Operation, maintenance, and audit

Not all 10 phases of the system development process are equally important from an audit perspective. If the auditor is concerned about the effectiveness and efficiency of the system, all phases must be evaluated. However, from an attest perspective the first four phases have less importance; usually it is only when the system design phase commences that controls to ensure asset safeguarding and maintenance of data integrity assume particular importance in the system development process. Nevertheless, since an ineffective and inefficient system can lead eventually to degradation in controls that ensure asset safeguarding and maintenance of data integrity, even in an attest audit the first four phases cannot be ignored.

The following sections describe the activities that should be performed in each of the 10 phases of the system development process. If the activities are not performed or are not performed well, the auditor must evaluate the consequences for the quality of the application systems produced. In some cases compensating controls may exist to reduce the expected losses from the omission or poor performance of the activity; for example, potential weaknesses resulting from failure to provide adequate user documentation may be compensated by a thorough and extensive user training program.

Problem Recognition

The need for change may be recognized in two ways. First, management may conceive a project through the development and maintenance of a master plan for the computer installation. Second, management or system users may recognize a problem area and initiate a proposal for change. If top management gives formal approval to proceed, the system designer may "enter" the organization area where change is needed to investigate the feasibility of a new system.

To commence the entry and feasibility assessment phase, the designer needs management to provide a formal document describing (a) the definition of the problem and (b) the terms of reference. The definition of the problem outlines the problems perceived by management. The terms of reference describe the boundaries of the system to be examined, the proposed objectives of a new system, resource constraints, organizational constraints, and the formal authority for the designer to proceed with entry and feasibility assessment.

The auditor's primary concern in the problem recognition phase is the existence of documentation formally approving intervention by the system designer and setting out the terms of reference for the intervention. The auditor also should be concerned about who initiated the intervention. Fewer behavioral problems are likely to arise if the potential users of the system initiate the intervention.

Management of the Change Process

This phase in the system development process runs parallel to all other phases. The change process starts at the initial conception of the system and continues until the new system is running and the organization has adjusted to the new system. Management of the change process has two aspects: formal project control aspects and change facilitating aspects.

Chapter 4 discussed briefly the elements of project management: budgeting, exception reporting, checkpoints, user signoffs, etc. The application of formal project management techniques is critical to the successful development and implementation of systems. The auditor should examine whether these techniques have been and are being used in the system development process.

Management of the change process also involves undertaking activities that facilitate change in the organization. Sociotechnical design theorists identify three classes of activities:

Class of activities	Explanation
Unfreezing the Organization	Preparing the organization for change; providing feedback to the organization members on their attitudes and behaviors, using techniques such as education, participatory decision making, and command
Change	Changeover to the new system
Refreezing the Organization	Helping system users adapt to their new roles by providing positive feedback on their new attitudes and behaviors

Behavioral problems are likely to arise unless the designer unfreezes and refreezes the organization when a new system is implemented or an old system is modified substantially. Unfreezing activities helps avoid having to *impose* change upon organization members. Refreezing activities makes it more difficult for organization members to revert to their old attitudes and behavior patterns.

Various techniques can be used to unfreeze and refreeze an organization. Mumford and Henshall [1979] describe the techniques they used to implement a new online accounting system in Rolls-Royce Limited. To unfreeze the organization they formed a design team that included members from user departments, held workshops to educate members of the design team in techniques of analysis and design of work systems, conducted a series of extensive meetings with all staff to explain the aims of the project and the role of the design team, and solicited feedback from all organization members potentially affected by the proposed change. To refreeze the organization they set up a steering committee to provide positive support and encouragement to the design team and user departments; they also implemented the new system on a gradual basis so the benefits of the system could be documented and users' expectations, attitudes, and values could adjust to assimilate and evaluate the changes.

The auditor can obtain evidence on whether or not designers undertake unfreezing and refreezing activities by reviewing standards, examining the minutes of meetings and workshops, interviewing designers and users, determining the role of project steering committees, etc. The existence of users' own private information systems sometimes indicates refreezing activities may not have been undertaken.

Entry and Feasibility Assessment

The change process commences by the designer initiating entry to the organization area. The objective of the entry phase is to unfreeze the organization and foster among users a spirit of collaborative analysis and evaluation of the existing system. As discussed previously, the designer may use various tools such as workshops, presentations, and group meetings.

Sociotechnical theorists emphasize the importance of the entry phase and how it is carried out by the designer. Though management may want a new system, users of the system may not desire change. During entry the designer tries to show users the need for change. Unless the designer is successful, further progress cannot be made or the system must be imposed upon users. Failure to enter may result in the designer having to withdraw and the proposal for the new system having to be scrapped, at least temporarily.

If entry is successful the designer can then carry out a preliminary system study to evaluate the feasibility of a new system. There are four bases for evaluating feasibility:

Basis for evaluation	Issues
Technical Feasibility	Is the available technology sufficient to support the proposed project? Can the technology be acquired or developed?
Operational Feasibility	Can the input data be collected for the system and is the output usable?
Economic Feasibility	Does the project have a positive net present value?
Behavioral Feasibility	What impact will the system have on the users' quality of working life?

The feasibility of a system should be reassessed continuously at all stages during the system development process. As new information is gathered, the evaluation can be more complete. The initial feasibility assessment undertaken at project commencement assesses the risks involved and whether it is worthwhile proceeding further. However, for some projects it may be unnecessary or too difficult to carry out an initial feasibility assessment. If the project is small and simple, feasibility assessment may be left until the end of information analysis. If the project is very complex, feasibility assessment may be too difficult until the information analysis phase is complete.

One other factor complicates feasibility assessment at project commencement. At this stage the designer may have only a vague idea of the system design that will be used. The final design may emerge only after substantial iteration if there is high uncertainty about the job design to be used, the organization structure to be used, the information requirements, etc.

With respect to the entry and feasibility assessment phase, the auditor's primary objectives are to determine whether a new system or modification to an existing system was imposed upon users, and to ensure that an application is converted to the computer only if the benefits exceed the costs. There should be evidence in the form of reports, minutes of meetings, etc., to show that the designer successfully accomplished the unfreezing process and that a feasibility study was undertaken carefully.

Diagnosis and Information Analysis

The purpose of the diagnosis and information analysis phase is to understand the existing social and technical systems and the coordinating mechanisms, and to formulate the strategic requirements for the new system. Diagnosis forms the basis for managing the change process. For example, knowledge of the coordinating mechanisms (e.g., reward system) for the social and technical systems establishes how these mechanisms must be adjusted when a new system is implemented. Knowledge of the users' flexibility or rigidity to change impacts the rate at which change can be implemented successfully.

Determining the strategic requirements for the system establishes the goals and policies that guide the design process. The goals and policies include both task performance issues and quality of working life issues. Thus, information analysis is not confined to the information system. It involves analyzing information related to the entire sociotechnical system.

The diagnosis and information analysis phase involves four major tasks:

1 Study the present organization
2 Study the product and information flows
3 Formulate strategic requirements for the system
4 Evaluate the present system

Study the Present Organization The designer studies the present organization to gain an understanding of the existing social and technical systems and coordinating mechanisms, and the willingness of the organization to change. Table 5.1 shows the variable sets in an organization that can be manipulated to create alternate organization designs. Manipulation of one variable set may require changing another variable set if task accomplishment or the quality of working life is not to degrade.

From a design viewpoint the critical variable set is the set of coordinating mechanisms. Usually the designer can do little about the tasks that must be accomplished and the needs, values, etc., of individuals in the organization.

**TABLE 5.1
VARIABLE SETS IN THE ORGANIZATION AS A SOCIO-TECHNICAL SYSTEM**

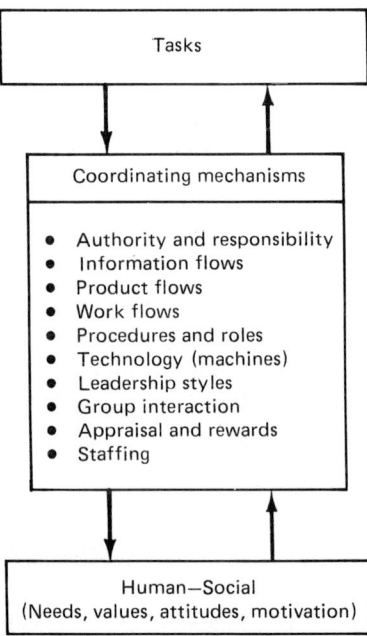

However, the set of coordinating mechanisms can be manipulated to achieve a "best" match between task accomplishment objectives and human-social objectives. Miles [1975] illustrates the choices that can be made with respect to some of the major coordinating mechanisms:

Coordinating mechanism	Example range of choices
Direction	Unilateral versus joint determination of goals and objectives; close and direct supervision versus supportive supervision allowing self-direction and control
Organizational and Job Design	Hierarchically structured, highly specialized teams versus loosely structured, self-paced heterogeneous teams; highly specialized tasks versus tasks encompassing a wide range of activities
Selection, Training, Appraisal, and Development	Selection and training focusing on traits and abilities versus the long-run needs of the organization and the individual; supervision versus joint appraisal of progress; unilateral versus joint determination of targets and objectives
Communications and Control	Vertical flows of information versus diffusing needed information directly to the decision point; transmission of information to distant points versus systems with a short feedback loop
Reward Systems	Systems based on longevity or merit alone versus systems that acknowledge both loyalty and performance; unilateral versus joint determination of the nature of rewards and the paths by which they can be attained

By studying the present organization the designer sees the design choices that have been made. This not only suggests ways of improvement but also indicates the likely impact that changing one variable set will have on another variable set.

Study the Product and Information Flows Since the information system usually is the major concern of the designer, it is important the existing information system be understood so that information needs and the strengths and weaknesses of the existing system can be determined. In some cases the information system supports a product flow. Understanding the product flow helps the designer to understand the information system and to formulate the information requirements of a new design.

Formulate Strategic Requirements The strategic requirements of a system specify the overall goals and objectives to be accomplished. Sociotechnical theorists claim that many system failures can be attributed to inadequate performance of this activity. Unfortunately, the formal guidelines available to show how this activity should be performed are scarce, somewhat abstruse, and still evolving.

Management's strategic requirements are primarily task accomplishment oriented. They may be vague; for example, increase the wealth of the shareholders. They may be more specific; for example, provide information that will allow 5% penetration of a market, or produce a product below a given cost subject to various constraints relating to the amount of pollutant emitted. The users' strategic requirements involve quality of working life issues: economic security, self-esteem, job satisfaction, control and influence, leisure. Users may be concerned with maintaining a set of flexible and differentiated tasks rather than having rigid, narrowly defined tasks. Or they may be concerned with maintaining a set of simple tasks so their work is less stressful and they have more time and energy for leisure activities. A union may be concerned with maintaining its share of power in the management of an organization.

Formulating strategic requirements at the outset gives recognition to information processing systems as neutral technology. Information systems can be designed to support various organization designs. There is not just one information system design for a given situation. There are alternate designs; and strategic requirements provide the basis for evaluating these designs. Forcing people, job designs, organization structures, etc., to fit information systems is a root cause of behavioral problems.

Evaluate the Present System In light of information obtained from the previous activities, the existing system can be evaluated. Though this activity was performed during the initial feasibility assessment phase, the gathering of more detailed information provides the basis for reassessing the proposed system. Again, the specific design that will be chosen is still unclear; however, knowledge of the strategic requirements for the system helps decide whether a new system is needed or the existing system can be modified.

System Design

Traditionally, system design has meant the design of the information processing system only. However, this concept of system design is inadequate. It has been a primary cause of system failure. The concept of system design proposed here is a full concept: it involves both the design of the social and technical aspects of the system and the set of coordinating mechanisms.

Sociotechnical system design proceeds using a methodology called *action research*. Instead of the system designer imposing a system design on users, the designer facilitates a collaborative mode whereby users jointly share the responsibility for design decisions. Design alternatives are generated, and the potential results of these designs are carefully evaluated. In this way the secondary effects of designs can be determined. Inadequate designs result in further iterations of the design process (see, for example, Mumford and Henshall [1979] and Mumford and Weir [1979]).

For the auditor acting as a participant in the system development process, the system design phase is one of major involvement. From a system effectiveness viewpoint the auditor is concerned with whether the design meets strategic requirements. From an efficiency viewpoint the auditor is concerned with the resources that will be needed to run the system. From an asset safeguarding and integrity viewpoint the auditor is concerned with the controls designed into the system.

During this phase the auditor also evaluates the ongoing auditability of the system. The auditor may deem it necessary to build certain audit capabilities into the system in the form of audit modules. These modules capture data or examine conditions of interest to the auditor concurrently with the production running of the system. Chapter 19 provides a detailed discussion of the nature and purposes of these audit modules.

If the auditor decides to build audit modules into the system, a decision must be made on who will be responsible for the detailed design, programming, and testing of the modules. This decision is based on another decision; namely, who will be allowed to use the modules? Audit modules can be a useful test vehicle for system development staff in general. Management may decide to allow system development staff to use the modules for testing purposes; consequently, system designers and programmers may assist the auditor with the development and implementation of the modules. If the auditor deems this approach to be an unacceptable loss of objectivity and surprise audit capabilities, the auditor then must take full responsibility for the development and implementation of the modules.

In the design of the system, the system designer again needs some basis (framework) for thinking about the organization and the change process to be implemented. Bostrom and Heinen [1977a] propose it is useful for the designer to think about the organization in terms of four major sets of interacting variables: (a) task, (b) technology, (c) structural, and (d) human-social. The technical system design establishes relationships within and between the first three sets of variables. The social system design establishes relationships within the human-social set. The sociotechnical system design establishes relationships within and between the four sets of variables.

Considering the design process only in terms of these four variable sets is a simplification of the problem. Other relationships are also important; for example, the relationships described in Chapter 4 between environmental uncertainty, the organization structure, and the information processing capabilities of the organization. However, the designer needs some model to form the basis for action and models are always inadequate representations of reality.

Of the coordinating mechanisms existing between the social and technical systems, information systems design tends to focus on three (see Figure 5.3):

1 Job design
2 Organization design
3 Communications and control (information processing system)

Though other coordinating mechanisms such as direction and reward systems are important, the information system designer usually does not play a major role in their design.

The following sections provide an overview of the job design, organization design, and information processing system design activities. The discussion illustrates the complexity of these design activities, the difficulties encountered by the auditor when trying to evaluate how well they are performed, and the problems of determining the implications of poor design for asset safeguarding, data integrity, and system effectiveness and efficiency objectives.

Job Design When an organization formulates its goals and objectives, one of the first steps to be undertaken is an analysis of the tasks to be performed to accomplish these goals and objectives. These tasks are structured in various ways to form a job design.

Contingency theory states there is no one best job design. Miles [1975] identifies three major types of job design, each of which may be the "best" depending on the situation:

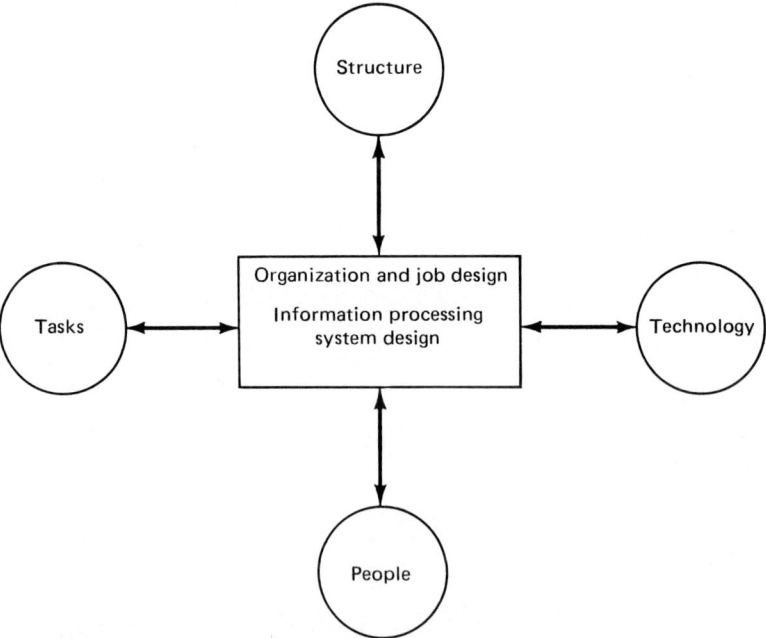

Figure 5.3
The coordinating mechanisms in the system design process.

Model of job design	Explanation
Job Design under the Traditional Model	Individuals are assumed to be more interested in what they earn rather than what they do. Jobs contain a limited number of tasks requiring similar skills and the same learning period. There is separation between thinking and doing.
Job Design under the Human Relations Model	Job prescriptions under this model are the same as for the traditional model. The difference is the focus on the context in which the job is performed, i.e., the conditions of the job. Task accomplishment is still the primary objective; however, the manager must be concerned with human needs to facilitate task accomplishment.
Job Design under the Human Resources Model	This is the most complex model. Employees accept responsibility for their own self-direction and control. The manager's role is to guide and assist employees to this position. Satisfaction is a by-product rather than a direct target of management activities.

How does the designer (and the auditor) know what job design is "right" in a given situation? Unfortunately, resolving this question still constitutes a major research area. For the same task, different employees sometimes prefer different job designs. For example, Hackman [1979b] reports the findings of a study that examined the change in job satisfaction levels of six Detroit auto workers who worked on a traditional assembly line, after they had worked for a month in the highly "enriched" team assembly jobs in a Swedish automobile plant. At the end of the month, five of the six workers stated that they preferred the traditional assembly line job design.

A useful model for considering how jobs might be designed has been proposed by Hackman [1979a]. He argues that high task accomplishment and high job satisfaction are a function of the experienced meaningfulness of work, the experienced responsibility in a job, and knowledge of results. These variables in turn are a function of five core job dimensions that can be manipulated by the designer: (a) skill variety—the extent to which the job requires different talents; (b) task identity—the extent to which an identifiable and complete job must be accomplished; (c) task significance—the extent to which the job impacts others; (d) autonomy—the extent to which the job allows freedom, independence, and discretion; and (e) feedback—the extent to which employees know the consequences of their performance.

Hackman's model, however, is not the only model of job design available. It simply illustrates some of the current thinking in the area. The difficulties involved in operationalizing any model of job design used by the designer or the auditor for design or evaluation purposes are substantial.

Organization Design Just as EDP management faces the choice of an appropriate organization structure for a computer installation, so does the system designer sometimes face the choice of an appropriate organization structure for users of a system. Chapter 4 described some of the fundamental relationships between tasks (job designs) and organization design that must be considered, especially the relationship between task uncertainty and information processing; namely, the greater the task uncertainty the greater the amount of information that must be processed. The amount of information that must be processed in turn affects the choice of an organization structure; some structures facilitate information processing better than others.

Again, contingency theory says there is no one best organization design to cover all situations and that not all ways of organizing are equally effective. For example, Woodward [1965] found that high performing firms using mass production technologies had traditional mechanistic organization designs. On the other hand high performing firms using unit process production technologies had organic, human resources forms of organization designs. Nevertheless, even within the high performing groups there were differences in the designs. There is no easy answer for the system designer (or the auditor) who must evaluate the costs and benefits of different organization structures.

Information Processing System Design Once a job design and organization design have been chosen and the information requirements determined, the information processing system can be designed. Hedberg [1975] provides two examples of how computer systems were designed to support particular job and organization designs that attempted to enrich the quality of working life without decreasing task performance. The first example is a new car assembly plant where the traditional assembly line was broken up and the logistics of the production system changed to support small semiautonomous groups of 15–20 members. Each team was responsible for one complete function of the car; for example, the electrical system. The computer system was designed to support this decentralized structure. Online terminals provided continuous quality control information back to worker groups.

The second example is a registration system for immigration authorities. The introduction of a new online registration and retrieval system foreshadowed increased task accomplishment, at least initially, but decreased quality of working life. The clerks directly involved in using the system participated in the strategic design of the system. The final design of the terminal system facilitated various forms of rotation of duties which, compared with the old system, provided a more stimulating work environment (see, also, Mumford and Weir [1979]).

The activities to be performed during information processing system design are not clear-cut. The current moves toward using structured programming methodology and the chief programmer team approach have resulted in some of the activities traditionally regarded as falling within the domain of the system designer now being regarded as the responsibility of programming staff. In the practice of design, installations fall somewhere along a continuum. Some use the more traditional approach whereby systems designers are responsible for the detailed specifications of file designs and programs. Others follow the current trend whereby designers state user-oriented specifications for input, output, and application functions, and the programming team is responsible for the detailed specification of file designs and programs. Again, a contingency theory approach to the choice of a design method may be appropriate. To the extent that high uncertainty exists about the eventual job design, organization design, etc., to be chosen, the system designer may have major responsibility for the information system design. To the extent that there is low uncertainty, the programming staff may have major responsibility for the information system design.

The next chapter describes the structured design and structured programming approaches to implementing a system. The following sections adopt a more traditional approach to describing five major information processing system design activities:

1 Design of the information flow
2 Design of the database
3 Design of the decision support system
4 Preparation of program specifications
5 Preparation of hardware/software specifications

The first three activities represent *policy* decisions made in response to the social and technical (task) system designs. The last two activities follow as *consequences* of the first three activities.

Design of the Information Flow With respect to designing the information flow, Galbraith [1977] proposes two policy decisions must be made on (*a*) the frequency and timing of the information flows to and from the decision support system, and (*b*) the extent to which the information flows will be formalized. The *frequency* and *timing* of the information flow ranges from infrequent and periodic to continuous. Galbraith [1977] argues the relationship between the timing of the information flows and the work system is as follows. The timing of the information flows affects the number of exceptions that must be referred upward in the organization hierarchy. Plans begin to decay as soon as they are conceived. As task uncertainty increases, the interval between plans must be decreased if the number of exceptions that occurs is to be stabilized. Thus, organizations facing high task uncertainty must use systems such as online realtime response systems to decrease the time interval between plans.

Formalizing the information flow reduces the number of symbols needed and the amount of resources needed to communicate information. However, formalization can be costly when personnel are needed to design and maintain the "languages" needed for communication. Also, not all information lends itself to formalization; much uncertainty may surround the variables involved, their interrelationships, and their measurement bases.

To some extent the information flow in any computer system must be formalized because programs are less flexible than humans. However, some range of choice is available. For example, a generalized interrogation language can be provided to allow ad hoc queries on the database (informal information flow); alternatively, structured fixed reports may be provided (formal information flow).

Finally, the analyst must design the flow itself: the points through which the information will pass. The flow should be kept as simple and straightforward as possible.

Design of the Database   The design of the database involves determining its *scope* (context) and *structure*. The scope of the database ranges from local to global. A major factor affecting the scope of the database is the extent of interdependence among organizational units. The greater the interdependence, the greater the need for a global database to prevent suboptimization by subunits. Organizations with highly interdependent subunits also have more incentive to share data resources; for example, by using a database management system. However, as the database becomes more global, cost increases.

Choosing the "optimal" structure for the database is an extremely complex decision. There are many interacting variables, and the problem must be solved subject to certain constraints such as the retrieval time required and the storage space available. Some of the major design considerations are:

1 Response time required
2 Frequency of record addition, deletion, and modification
3 Storage space required—primary versus secondary
4 Ease of programming
5 Data integrity constraints
6 Data redundancy permissible

The structural design of the database involves three decisions:

Decision	Explanation
Choice of the Data Structure	Choice of the items, groups, and relationships between groups to be established; choice of a structure, e.g., flat file, tree, network, relational
Choice of the Storage Structure	How to linearize and partition the data structure; choice of external access paths, e.g., direct addressing, indexing, and hashing; and internal access paths, e.g., sequential search and binary search; choice of a structure, e.g., chain, multilist, inverted list, B-tree
Choice of the Physical Representation	How to represent the storage structure on the physical media, e.g., across tracks, cylinders, disks

Various attempts have been made to develop formal mathematical tools to aid this design process. Senko [1977] provides a review of much of the relevant research (see, also, Severance and Merten [1972], Severance and Carlis [1977], Severance and Duhné [1976], and Severance [1974a, 1974b]).

Design of the Decision Support System The decision support system assists the decision maker to process information and to select alternatives (see, further, Keen and Scott Morton [1978]). The design process must identify the type of decision support system that a user of the system needs. Davis [1974] provides one way of viewing this design decision in terms of the user activities the system must support:

Activity	Information system support
Strategic Planning	Intelligence support through search for opportunities or problems; design support to structure the problem, generate possible solutions, and test the feasibility of solutions; choice support through providing decision models
Management Control	Planning support through forecasting models; control support through exception reporting
Operational Control	Processing support for transaction data; control support through exception reporting and automatic correction of deviations

The type of decision support system needed also depends on the decisions made on the frequency and formalization of the information flow and the scope of the database. For example, on the one hand decision support systems for strategic planning may use informal, infrequent, and global information. On the other hand, decision support systems for operational control may use formal, frequent, and local information.

Preparation of Program Specifications This activity involves grouping the functions to be performed within the system into logical subunits. Substantial progress has been made at both a theoretical and practical level on how functions should be grouped (see Chapter 6). Basically the method of grouping functions attempts to maximize the cohesiveness of functions in a subunit and to minimize the interdependencies between subunits.

When evaluating program specifications the auditor should check to see that they include:

1 A clear statement of purpose
2 Input/output file layouts
3 Functions to be performed
4 Computer language to be used
5 Peripheral and core storage limitations

6 Efficiency to be attained
7 Coding discipline to be exercised
8 Documentation to be provided
9 Testing requirements

Prepare Hardware/Software Specifications If the system requires hardware and system software not currently available in the installation, hardware and software specifications must be prepared for the additional resources required. The specifications and feasibility analysis follow the same format described in Chapter 4.

Program Development

After the system design phase is complete, the next phase in the system development process is program development. Program development involves various activities: (*a*) design, (*b*) flowcharting, (*c*) coding, (*d*) compiling, (*e*) testing, and (*f*) documenting. Chapter 6 discusses these activities in detail.

The audit staff may be involved in program development themselves if they have sole responsibility for any audit modules to be embedded in the system. If these modules are to be made generally available to system development staff, the auditor must carefully review any programming work performed by nonaudit staff.

Procedure and Forms Development

Decisions made on the types of procedures and forms to use in a system depend on organization design, job design, and information system design decisions. For example, if online entry of data is required at the work site, the number of forms required may be minimum; however, the procedures for entering the data may need to be explicit.

Procedure and forms development involves four major activities:

Activity	Explanation
Design of Procedures	To the extent that procedures must be specified, they must be matched with the job/task design. What triggers the tasks and the task input and output must be identified.
Design of Forms	Considerations include specifications of content, demands of appearance and readability, type of handling, storage, size, machine readability.
Testing Procedures and Forms	User involvement in test running the procedures and forms.
Preparation of User Manuals	Documentation of forms and procedures and set up of a change procedure for documentation.

Sociotechnical theorists emphasize the importance of minimum specification of how a task is to be accomplished. What needs to be done should be clearly specified. Where possible, how it should be done should be left to the person responsible for the task. To the extent possible, procedures and forms should be straightforward and clear without enforcing rigidity in task performance.

Acceptance Testing

The purpose of acceptance testing is to identify as many errors and deficiencies in the system as possible prior to its implementation. Besides testing normal processing, attempts should be made to "crash" the system to determine its tolerance to errors and ability to respond to exceptional circumstances.

The design of test data can be a difficult and expensive task, particularly where programs are large and complex, variable length records are used, data structures are complex, and a large number of different types of transactions exist. Moreover, testing can be a boring and irksome task and, as a consequence, subject to error.

Several tools have been developed to assist the testing task; for example, test data generators. Later chapters discuss these tools. Nevertheless, even with the assistance of these tools, for two reasons it is normally impossible to test all aspects of the system. First, it is difficult to conceive every logic path through a system of moderate complexity. Second, the costs of testing may outweigh the benefits obtained.

There are three major types of acceptance testing:

Type of testing	Explanation
Program Testing	Programmers who develop individual programs must test the processing accuracy and efficiency of their programs.
System Testing	Testing the overall information processing system with emphasis on the interfaces between programs within the system.
User Testing	Testing the *total* system including the job design, organizational design, forms, procedures, programs, etc. Provides the basis for management and users signing off on the final system.

From an audit viewpoint an important aspect of testing is the planning and design of test data and the documentation of test results. Careful planning and design is necessary since resources for testing are not unlimited, and the objective is to obtain the maximum benefits possible. The auditor should check that test documentation shows:

1 How the testing process was planned
2 How test data was designed and developed

3 What test data was used
4 What results were obtained
5 Action taken as a result of errors identified
6 Subsequent modifications to test data

One of the outcomes of the testing phase should be a test bed of data for individual programs and the overall system that should be properly documented and maintained. A test bed facilitates later testing of modifications and maintenance to the system by making available a standard set of test data with known, documented results.

Conversion

Conversion to a new system can occur in one of three ways. First, the old system may be totally stopped and the new system takes over immediately. Second, both systems may run in parallel for a period (but performing different functions) with output from both systems being used. Third, both systems may run in parallel (performing the same functions) with the old system output being used. In this last case, parallel running provides the basis for validating the design and implementation of the new system.

Changeover to a new system involves four activities:

Activity	Explanation
Personnel Training	Primary and secondary users of the system need training. For example, primary users such as management need training in the use of system output. Secondary users such as clerks need training in the preparation of input. Operators and programmers need training if new hardware and software has been purchased.
Install New Hardware and Software	If new hardware and software has been purchased, it must be installed.
Conversion of Files and Programs	This can be a complex and lengthy process, particularly when there is a changeover from a manual system. Taking up manual system files may involve several months of work. Maintaining two systems in parallel may place substantial strain on the users of the system.
Scheduling of Operations and Test Running	Scheduling involves timing of input, processing, and output. The schedules should be tested for a period and any needed adjustments made before the final schedule is frozen and documented.

The auditor is especially concerned with maintaining data integrity during the conversion process. Tradeoffs sometimes must be made between the integrity of data taken up on the system and the need to get the system running; for example, data validation criteria must be relaxed because of the large number of errors identified. Later correction of data is then essential. Nevertheless, when data is converted from one storage medium or one data structure to another, control totals must be developed to help identify any data corruption that occurs during the changeover process, or any errors that exist in the data already.

Operation, Maintenance, and Audit

During the operation of a system, three types of changes may be needed. First, processing errors may be discovered that require correction. Second, changes in the system (user) environment may necessitate system modification. Third, changes may be made to improve processing efficiency. The auditor's concern is that a formal change process exists to authorize and control needed changes to the system.

The system also should be reviewed on a regular basis by a team consisting of management, users, and auditors. The purpose of the review is to obtain answers to such questions as:

1 How has the system impacted task accomplishment and the quality of working life of the users?

2 Do the benefits of the system exceed the costs?

3 Are there any major problem areas with the system?

4 Can modifications be made to improve effectiveness, efficiency, and data integrity?

5 What has been learned from the system so that the system development process can be improved?

The postaudit is the basic means of ensuring that an application system adapts to organizational and user changes. It provides the auditor with evidence on how responsive the computer installation is to stresses in its environment.

SUMMARY

The auditor can be involved in the system development process in two ways. First, in a participative capacity the auditor evaluates the quality of the system development process for a particular system, ensures needed controls are built into the system, and implements any audit modules required to monitor the system. Second, in a review capacity the auditor evaluates, in general, the quality of the overall system development process. This review allows judgments to be made on the likely quality of individual application systems developed and the extent of substantive testing of application systems that will be needed.

Both activities require the auditor to have a thorough knowledge of the system development process. The auditor needs to know what activities should be performed, how they should be performed, and when they should be performed if the resultant system is to safeguard assets, maintain data integrity, and be effective and efficient. The auditor also must recognize the system development process is a sociotechnical design process and that joint optimization of task accomplishment and the quality of working life are necessary if implementation of the system is to be successful. The past emphasis on project management techniques has resulted in well-defined methodologies for planning and controlling resource usage during system development. However, this is not the only area of concern for the auditor. The history of system failure shows neither the system designer nor the auditor can ignore the behavioral side of information systems.

REVIEW QUESTIONS

5.1. What are the two ways in which the auditor may become involved with the system development process? How do the audit objectives of the two methods of audit involvement differ? How do the evidence collection methods differ?

5.2. Why does the auditor need a normative model of the system development process? How might the adequacy of normative models of the system development process be evaluated?

5.3. Two ways of thinking about the system development process are the life cycle approach and the sociotechnical system design approach. What are the major *differences* between the two approaches? What are the major *similarities* between the two approaches? Can the two approaches be reconciled?

5.4. What is meant by middle management being the primary design referent group for system designers? Why do Bostrom and Heinen [1977a] claim this "condition" has been one of the primary reasons for behavioral problems in information system development?

5.5. The sociotechnical design approach negates almost every major feature of the traditional life cycle approach to system development. Comment.

5.6. Why might different normative models of the system development process be appropriate for the auditor to use at different times? Give an example to help your explanation.

5.7. The primary concern of the auditor when evaluating the system development process is the application of the appropriate methodology to the design and implementation of application systems. Why is it difficult for the auditor to sort out what aspects of system development methodology deal with data integrity objectives, what aspects deal with system effectiveness objectives, and what aspects deal with system efficiency objectives? How do these difficulties in being able to differentiate the objectives of activities carried out during system development impact the audit?

5.8. How might the need for a new system be recognized? What control techniques would the auditor look for when examining the ways in which system development projects are initiated?

5.9. Briefly explain the impact the following may have on the quality of the system development process:

a. standards
b. documentation
c. quality of the system development staff
d. checkpoints and signoffs

5.10. If the system development staff does not unfreeze and refreeze the organization when developing and implementing a new system, what are the possible implications for data integrity in the new system? How might an audit be carried out on the way in which the change process is managed?

5.11. What are the bases on which the feasibility of a system should be assessed? Which bases are the most important from an audit perspective?

5.12. As the partner-in-charge of the external audit of a company, you are reviewing the work of one of the junior auditors who has carried out a review of the standards manual of the computer installation of the company. The junior auditor has found the standards manual emphasizes the need for system users to participate in the system design process. On this basis the junior auditor recommends limiting the extent of substantive testing needed on individual application systems. What is your decision?

5.13. Why is it important for the system designer to study the present organization before commencing the system design phase? What are some of the important aspects of the organization that the designer should study?

5.14. Briefly explain the nature of a coordinating mechanism in an organization. Why are coordinating mechanisms of primary interest to the system designer and the auditor?

5.15. What is meant by the strategic design of a system? What is the relationship between system effectiveness and the strategic design of a system? How would an auditor carry out an ex post review audit of the strategic design phase of the system development process?

5.16. In what ways might the auditor fruitfully participate during the system design phase? Give special attention to the way in which the auditor might be involved in the adjustment of coordinating mechanisms between the social and technical systems.

5.17. What relevance has contingency theory for the auditor trying to evaluate a job design, an organization design, and the impact of these designs on system effectiveness and efficiency? How would an auditor carry out an ex post audit of the job and organization design phases in the system development process?

5.18. Briefly explain the effects of increasing task uncertainty on the frequency and timing of information flows and the extent to which the information flow is formalized. How might information systems be designed to respond to these effects?

5.19. Briefly outline the audit steps that might be followed to evaluate the adequacy of standards for database design in the system development process.

5.20. Give two attributes of a decision support system that are of audit interest. Briefly explain why they are of audit interest.

5.21. What aspects of procedure and forms design activities impact the extent to which an application system maintains data integrity?

5.22. Briefly describe the major activities in acceptance testing. Why is documentation an important part of acceptance testing? What should be documented during acceptance testing?

5.23. What is meant by a "test bed" of data? How is a test bed created and maintained? List the advantages and disadvantages of a test bed.

124 PART 2: THE MANAGEMENT CONTROL FRAMEWORK

5.24. Why must data validation procedures sometimes be relaxed during system changeover? If validation procedures are relaxed, what procedures should the auditor follow?

5.25. What are the purposes of a postaudit of an operational system? Why should the auditor who participated in the system development process not participate in the postaudit of the system?

EXERCISES AND CASES

5.1. Repeat Exercise 4.1 where the elements of the controls matrix constitute *proper performance* of the activities within each phase of the system development process. In other words, you are to rate how important it is (in general) to properly perform the activities in each phase of the system development process if the four control objectives (columns of the matrix) are to be achieved.

Controls \ Objectives	Asset safeguarding	Data integrity	System effectiveness	System efficiency
Problem recognition				
Management of the change process				
Entry and feasibility assessment				
Diagnosis and information analysis				
System design				
Program development				
Procedure and forms development				
Acceptance testing				
Conversion				
Operation, maintenance, and audit				

5.2. The vice-president of production has requested top management to have the information systems department investigate the feasibility of a computer system to improve the scheduling of production. She is convinced that though her production managers are extremely competent, they do not always make the best production scheduling decisions. One of the system designers from the information system department starts the process of entry by requesting the production managers participate in a series of workshops that will examine the strengths and weaknesses of the total scheduling system. Even though attendance at the workshop is voluntary, most of the production managers still attend. After six workshops over a period of four months, the system designer reports to management that the production managers are convinced a computer system will solve many of their problems. The vice-president of production is convinced the project should go ahead. However, because top management is uncertain about the eventual success of the system, they come to you as the internal audit manager to ask your advice. They value your independence.

Required: Prepare a brief report advising top management on how they should proceed.

5.3. Sunmatics started out as a small manufacturing firm producing solar energy equipment. With the impending shortage of energy, demand for its production has grown and the company has trebled in size over a period of five years. As a result of problems experienced with inventory control, a computer system has been designed to assist reordering and keeping control over inventory. There are about 800 components used in the various solar energy equipment manufactured. Currently, inventory records are maintained on bin cards. Inventory levels constantly change as production workers obtain components for their needs.

Required: The system development team is meeting to consider changeover procedures for the inventory file. You are the internal auditor participating in the system development effort. How would you recommend the file changeover be accomplished? What controls would you recommend being set up to maintain data integrity during changeover?

5.4. Finerfoods, Inc., is a large decentralized and diversified organization that primarily manufactures and sells grocery items. Various divisions of the company are widely dispersed geographically. In the past, divisions have been responsible for all aspects of their data processing operations. Recently, top management has questioned whether or not it would be more efficient to have a centralized group of analysts and programmers develop and implement standard systems that could be distributed and used by all divisions within the company. The vice-president of information systems is strongly objecting to the proposed change. He argues that the primary reason information systems in the company have been so successful is that they have been designed not only to accomplish task objectives but also to achieve a high quality of working life for users of the system. He contends that data processing departments in the division should be left to develop and implement their own systems since they are best able to develop systems that will support the organization and job design of their users. However, top management is questioning whether the costs of having individual divisions develop their own systems can be justified.

Required: As the manager of internal audit for the company, the president of the company asks you to prepare a report outlining your thoughts on the costs and benefits of the proposed change. He asks you to give him your opinion on the validity of the arguments made by the vice-president for information systems.

REFERENCES

Awad, Elias M. *System Analysis and Design* (Homewood, Ill.: Richard D. Irwin, Inc., 1979).
Biggs, Charles L., Evan G. Birks, and William Atkins. *Managing the Systems Development Process* (Englewood Cliffs, N.J.: Prentice-Hall, Inc., 1980).
Bostrom, Robert P., and J. Stephen Heinen. "MIS Problems and Failures: A Socio-Technical Perspective — Part I: The Causes," *Management Information Systems Quarterly* (September 1977a), pp. 17-32.
_____ and _____. "MIS Problems and Failures: A Socio-Technical Perspective — Part II: The Application of Socio-Technical Theory," *Management Information Systems Quarterly* (December 1977b), pp. 11-28.
Cherns, Albert. "Principles of Sociotechnical Design," *Human Relations*, vol. 29, no. 8, pp. 783-792.
Cleland, David I., and William R. King. *Systems Analysis and Project Management*, 2d ed. (New York: McGraw-Hill Book Company, 1975).
CODASYL Development Committee. "An Information Algebra Phase I Report," *Communications of the ACM* (April 1962), pp. 190-204.
Condon, Robert V. *Data Processing Systems Analysis and Design* (Reston, Va.: Reston Publishing Company, Inc., 1975).
Couger, J. Daniel, and Robert W. Knapp, eds. *System Analysis Techniques* (New York: John Wiley and Sons, Inc., 1974).
Daniels, Alan, and Donald Yeates. *Systems Analysis* (Palo Alto, Calif.: Science Research Associates, Inc., 1971).
Davis, Gordon B. *Management Information Systems: Conceptual Foundations, Structure, and Development* (New York: McGraw-Hill Book Company, 1974).
Eliason, Alan L., and Kent D. Kitts. *Business Computer Systems and Applications* (Chicago: Science Research Associates, Inc., 1974).
Fitzgerald, John M., and Ardra F. Fitzgerald. *Fundamentals of Systems Analysis* (New York: John Wiley and Sons, Inc., 1973).
Galbraith, Jay R. *Organization Design* (Reading, Mass.: Addison-Wesley Publishing Company, Inc., 1977).
Gore, Marvin, and John Stubbe. *Elements of Systems Analysis for Business Data Processing* (Dubuque, Iowa: Wm. C. Brown Company Publishers, 1975).
Hackman, J. Richard. "Work Design," in Richard M. Steers and Lyman W. Porter, *Motivation and Work Behavior*, 2d ed. (New York: McGraw-Hill Book Company, 1979a), pp. 399-426.
_____. "The Design of Work in the 1980's," in Richard M. Steers and Lyman W. Porter, *Motivation and Work Behavior*, 2d ed. (New York: McGraw-Hill Book Company, 1979b), pp. 458-573.
Hartman, W., H. Matthes, and A. Proeme. *Management Information Systems Handbook: Analysis, Requirements Determination, Design and Development, Implementation and Evaluation* (New York: McGraw-Hill Book Company, 1968).
Hedberg, Bo. "Computer Systems to Support Industrial Democracy," in Enid Mumford and Harold Sackman, eds., *Human Choice of Computers* (New York: American Elsevier Publishing Company, 1975).
Hopwood, Anthony. *Accounting and Human Behavior* (London: Haymarket Publishing Ltd., 1974).

Keen, Peter G. W., and Michael S. Scott Morton. *Decision Support Systems: An Organizational Perspective* (Reading, Mass.: Addison-Wesley Publishing Company, Inc., 1978).

Langefors, Börje. *Theoretical Analysis of Information Systems, Vols. I and II* (Sweden: Studentlitteratur, Lund, 1970).

Macy, Barry A., and Philip H. Mirvis. "A Methodology for Assessment of Quality of Work Life and Organizational Effectiveness in Behavioral Economic Terms," *Administrative Science Quarterly* (June 1976), pp. 212–226.

Mair, William C., Donald R. Wood, and Keagle W. Davis. *Computer Control and Audit*, 2d ed. (Altamonte Springs, Fla.: The Institute of Internal Auditors, Inc., 1976).

Miles, Raymond E. *Theories of Management: Implications for Organizational Behavior and Development* (New York: McGraw-Hill Book Company, 1975).

Mumford, Enid, and Don Henshall. *A Participative Approach to Computer Systems Design* (New York: John Wiley and Sons, Inc., 1979).

———, and Mary Weir. *Computer Systems in Work Design—the ETHICS Method* (New York: John Wiley and Sons, Inc., 1979).

Naumann, J. David, Gordon B. Davis, and James D. McKeen. "Determining Information Requirements: A Contingency Method for Selection of a Requirements Assurance Strategy," Management Information Systems Research Center Working Paper WP-80-02, University of Minnesota, Minneapolis, Minn., 1979.

Nunamaker, J. F., Benn R. Konsynski, Thomas Ho, and Carl Singer. "Computer-Aided Analysis and Design of Information Systems," *Communications of the ACM* (December 1976), pp. 674–687.

Rittenberg, Larry E. *Auditor Independence and Systems Design* (Altamonte Springs, Fla.: The Institute of Internal Auditors, Inc., 1977).

Senko, Michael E. "Data Structures and Data Accessing in Data Base Systems: Past, Present, Future," *IBM Systems Journal* (July 1977), pp. 208–257.

Severance, Dennis G. "The Evaluation of Data Structures in a Data Base System Design," *Proceedings of the 1974 IEEE International Conference* (March 1974a), pp. 1–6.

———. "Identifier Search Mechanisms: A Survey and Generalized Model," *Computing Surveys* (September 1974b), pp. 175–194.

———, and A. G. Merten. "Performance Evaluation of File Organizations through Modeling," *Proceedings of the 1972 ACM Conference* (August 1972), pp. 1061–1072.

———, and Ricardo Duhne. "A Practitioner's Guide to Addressing Algorithms," *Communications of the ACM* (June 1976), pp. 319–326.

———, and John V. Carlis. "A Practical Approach to Selecting Record Access Paths," *Computing Surveys* (December 1977), pp. 259–272.

Woodward, Joan. *Industrial Organization: Theory and Practice* (Oxford: Oxford University Press, 1965).

———. *Industrial Organization: Behavior and Control* (Oxford: Oxford University Press, 1970).

CHAPTER 6

PROGRAMMING MANAGEMENT

CHAPTER OUTLINE

THE PROGRAM LIFE CYCLE
- Analysis and Design
- Coding
- Testing
- Operation and Maintenance

ORGANIZING THE PROGRAMMING TEAM
- Traditional Organization Structures
- Chief Programmer Teams
- Adaptive Teams

MANAGING THE SYSTEM PROGRAMMING GROUP
- Control Problems
- Control Measures

SOFTWARE DEVELOPMENT AIDS
- Coding Aids
- Debugging/Testing Aids
- Execution Aids

SUMMARY

REVIEW QUESTIONS

EXERCISES AND CASES

REFERENCES

Recently many researchers have investigated how software might be "engineered" to improve its quality and lower its costs. There have been three major motivating factors. First, the demand for software exceeds its supply. Boehm [1976] estimates the demand for software is growing at 21-23% per year; this growth rate will exceed the growth rate of available software even given increased programmer productivity. Second, the ratio of software costs to hardware costs is increasing; some predict it will grow as high as 9:1 (see McGowan and Kelly [1975]). Third, the growth of new software is inhibited by the extent of the effort that must be spent on maintaining existing software. Various researchers report 50-80% of software costs involve maintenance activities (see, for example, Mills [1976], Elshoff [1976], Lientz and Swanson [1978], and Canning [1978b]).

As a result of the research undertaken, improved methodologies now exist for the development and maintenance of software and the overall management of the programming process. From an audit viewpoint these advances have produced two major benefits. First, the availability of a more refined normative model of the programming process enables the auditor to perform a better evaluation of the process. Second, the existence of higher quality software enables the auditor to employ evidence collection techniques that previously were very difficult and costly to use. For example, the new programming methodologies result in more readable programs; thus, the auditor is better able to carry out a review of program code as a means of evidence collection or design test data to validate logic paths in the program.

This chapter discusses those practices that result in high-quality programs being produced. The first section of the chapter provides an overview of the program life cycle. It focuses on normative methodologies for developing and maintaining programs. The second section examines alternative ways of organizing and managing the programming team. It highlights the advantages and disadvantages of the different organization and management structures that can be used. The third section discusses the special control problems associated with managing a system programming group and some ways in which these control problems can be overcome. Finally, several software development aids are reviewed with special attention being given to some control problems associated with the use of these aids.

THE PROGRAM LIFE CYCLE

As discussed in Chapter 5, program development is a major phase in the system development life cycle. However, the phase itself also can be considered to have a life cycle. The four major phases in the program life cycle are:

1 Analysis and design
2 Coding
3 Testing
4 Operation and maintenance

If each phase in the program cycle is well managed, high-quality programs should be produced. Yourdon [1975] discusses seven characteristics of a high-quality program:

1 The program works.
2 The design is simple.
3 Development costs are minimal.
4 Testing costs are minimal.
5 Maintenance costs are minimal.
6 The program should be amenable to change.
7 The program should run efficiently.

The following sections examine each of the four phases in the program life cycle. They discuss those activities that should be carried out within each phase; thus, they provide a normative model that the auditor can use to evaluate the overall programming process in an installation.

Analysis and Design

The program analysis and design phase has two objectives: (*a*) to define a set of programs that will fulfill a set of user requirements, and (*b*) to provide specifications for each program showing how the program is to be constructed. To some extent program analysis and design is still a heuristic process. However, some progress has been made on formalizing the process. The following sections discuss the theory underlying the approach currently advocated for program analysis and design, the objectives and methodology of the approach, and some tools developed to facilitate the approach.

A Formalized Approach to Analysis and Design Program analysis and design is a process of organizing complexity. It should not be surprising that some techniques for organizing complexity learned in other disciplines are also relevant for the analysis and design of programs.

One of the first researchers who attempted to provide a general theory of complexity was Simon [1969]. In his analysis he noted two characteristics of complex systems that *survive*. First, he observed these systems take on a hierarchical structure of subsystems. Second, he observed that two "laws" seem to govern the way in which their subsystems form: (*a*) only highly interdependent elements of the system will form into a subsystem, and (*b*) each subsystem will seek to minimize its dependence on other subsystems (see, also, Alexander [1964]).

The formal approach currently advocated for program analysis and design aims at producing programs that have these two characteristics. The approach goes under various names: top-down design, structured design, composite design, stepwise refinement, the levels of abstraction approach. Whatever the name given, the approach seeks to fulfill certain objectives: these objectives are discussed in the next section.

Analysis and Design Objectives The top-down approach to program design emphasizes six objectives:

1 Break each system down into a hierarchical structure of modules.
2 For each module focus on "what" is to be done rather than "how" it is to be done.
3 Limit attention to three to six modules at any one time.
4 Maximize module strength.
5 Minimize module coupling.
6 Analyze functions and data simultaneously.

The output of the system analysis phase is a set of functional (user) requirements that a set of programs must fulfill. Top-down design proceeds by successively breaking down these functions into more detailed functions, each function constituting a module within a hierarchy. From the broadest to finest level of detail, three categories of functional module result: (a) system modules, (b) program modules, and (c) subprogram modules.

Consider, for example, a general ledger system. Using the top-down approach the highest level function "Update general ledger" might be subdivided into three lower level functions (Figure 6.1a). Each of these functions is subdivided again into lower level functions. For example, "Validate journal entries" might be broken up into a function to validate manually coded entries (adjustments) and a function to validate journal entries provided as the output of other application systems such as accounts receivable, accounts payable, payroll, cash receipts, etc. (Figure 6.1b). Further subdivision then occurs (Figure 6.1c).

There are several guidelines for the designer to follow when performing the decomposition process. The designer should focus on *what* function a module will perform rather than *how* it will perform the function. Myers [1975] argues the function description for a module must contain a verb; thus, "retrieve master record" is a valid description but "master record routine" is not.

The description of a module also involves defining its data input and data output. A top-down approach should be used to design data for the system. Experience with top-down design shows the functions that a module performs and the data on which it operates should be considered jointly in the design process. The data structure design should be deferred as long as possible until the program procedures are defined; otherwise, the programmer may be forced to write poor code (see, also, Canning [1974c]). Thus, in the general ledger system example discussed above, a top-level data description might be "journal entry." As the lower level functional modules are defined, the data elements needed in the journal entry and the relationships that will exist among those data elements also are defined.

At each level in the hierarchy the designer should focus only on a small number of elements or modules. This guideline recognizes the limited capacities of humans to process information (see, also, Chapter 9). By disregarding other levels, modules, and elements in the hierarchy, the designer is better

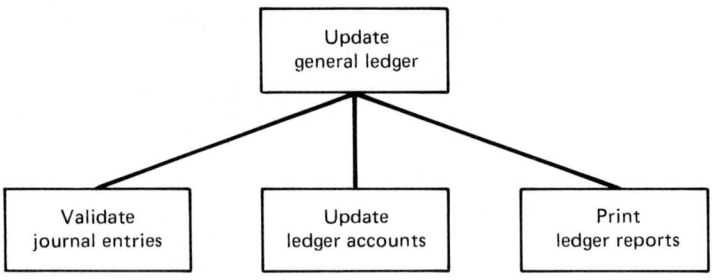

Figure 6.1a
System level functional modules.

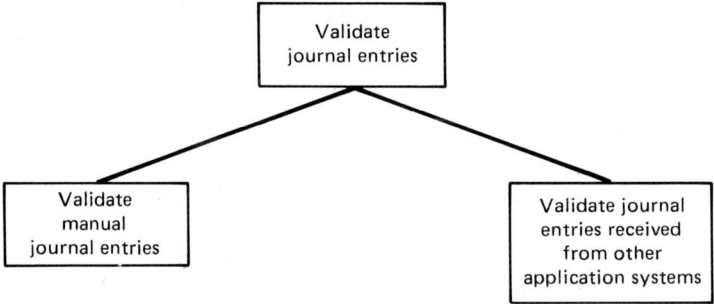

Figure 6.1b
Program level functional modules.

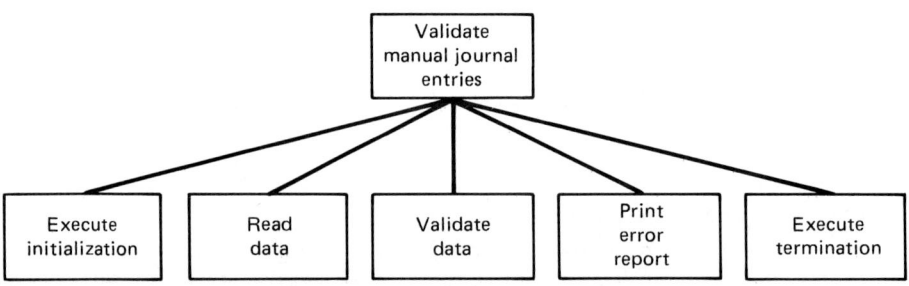

Figure 6.1c
Subprogram level functional modules.

able to define the functions and data of the small set of modules under consideration. If possible that part of the design under consideration should fit on a single page.

One of the primary difficulties in the decomposition process is identifying what functions should be performed within a module and what functions should be excluded; and, similarly, what data should be processed by the module and what data should be excluded. It is the design problem of identifying the boundaries of a module: its "bounded context."

Two guidelines exist for defining the boundaries of a module. First, the designer should attempt to maximize the *strength* of a module (Figure 6.2a). Second, the designer should attempt to minimize the *coupling* between modules (Figure 6.2b). Both guidelines seek to give modules the characteristics of systems that survive.

To achieve module strength the interdependencies between elements within a module should be maximized. Myers [1975] identifies seven types of interdependencies that can exist between the elements of a module, and rates them according to their ability to maximize module strength. From highest strength to lowest strength they are:

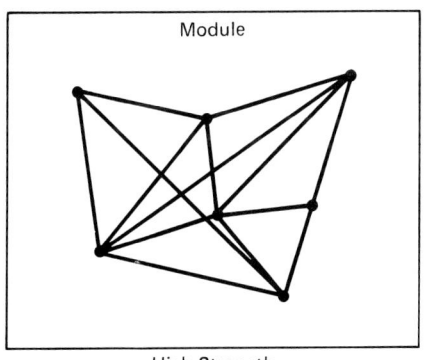
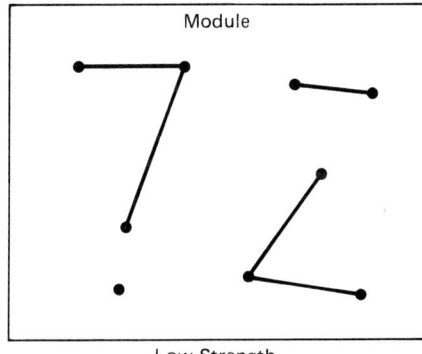

Figure 6.2a
Module strength.

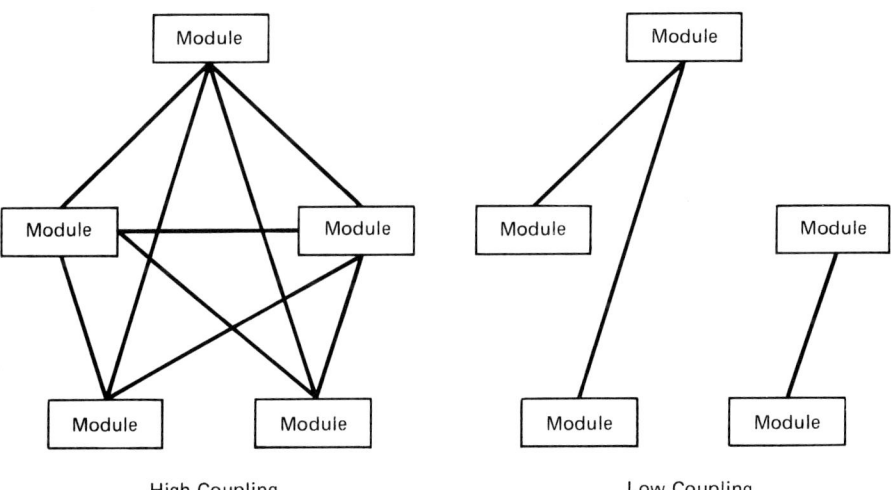

Figure 6.2b
Module coupling.

Interdependency	Explanation
Functional	All elements in the module perform only a single function.
Informational	Elements in the module perform multiple functions but only on a single data structure.
Communicational	Elements in the module reference the same data set or pass data among themselves.
Procedural	Elements in the module perform different functions but the functions are related via a common procedure.
Classical	Elements in the module perform a class of functions that are related in time.
Logical	Elements in the module perform a class of functions.
Coincidental	No meaningful relationships exist between the elements in the module.

The process of decomposition involves increasing the strength of modules. The elements of high-level modules have only weak interdependencies; for example, classical or logical interdependencies. The elements of the lowest level of modules should have only functional interdependencies.

Minimizing module coupling involves reducing the interdependencies between modules. If modules are only loosely coupled, a modification to one module has little impact on other modules. Again, the extent of coupling is a function of the nature of the interdependency that exists between modules. Myers [1975] identifies six types of interdependency. Ranked according to their ability to reduce coupling between modules they are:

Interdependency	Explanation
Data Coupling	Only data *elements* are passed as arguments between modules.
Stamp Coupling	A data *structure* is passed as an argument between modules.
Control Coupling	Control elements (flags, switches) are passed as arguments between modules.
External Coupling	Modules access the same data *elements* that exist in a shared storage area.
Common Coupling	Modules access the same data *structure* that exists in a shared storage area.
Content Coupling	One module directly references the contents of another module.

Analysis and Design Aids Several aids have been proposed to facilitate the top-down design process (see Canning [1979a]). However, all these aids have a common characteristic: the use of graphic notation to represent the decomposition process.

Perhaps the best known of the top-down analysis and design aids is IBM's HIPO (hierarchical plus input-process-output) chart (see Stay [1976]). Figure 6.3 shows an example of a HIPO chart for a payroll application system. The

CHAPTER 6: PROGRAMMING MANAGEMENT **135**

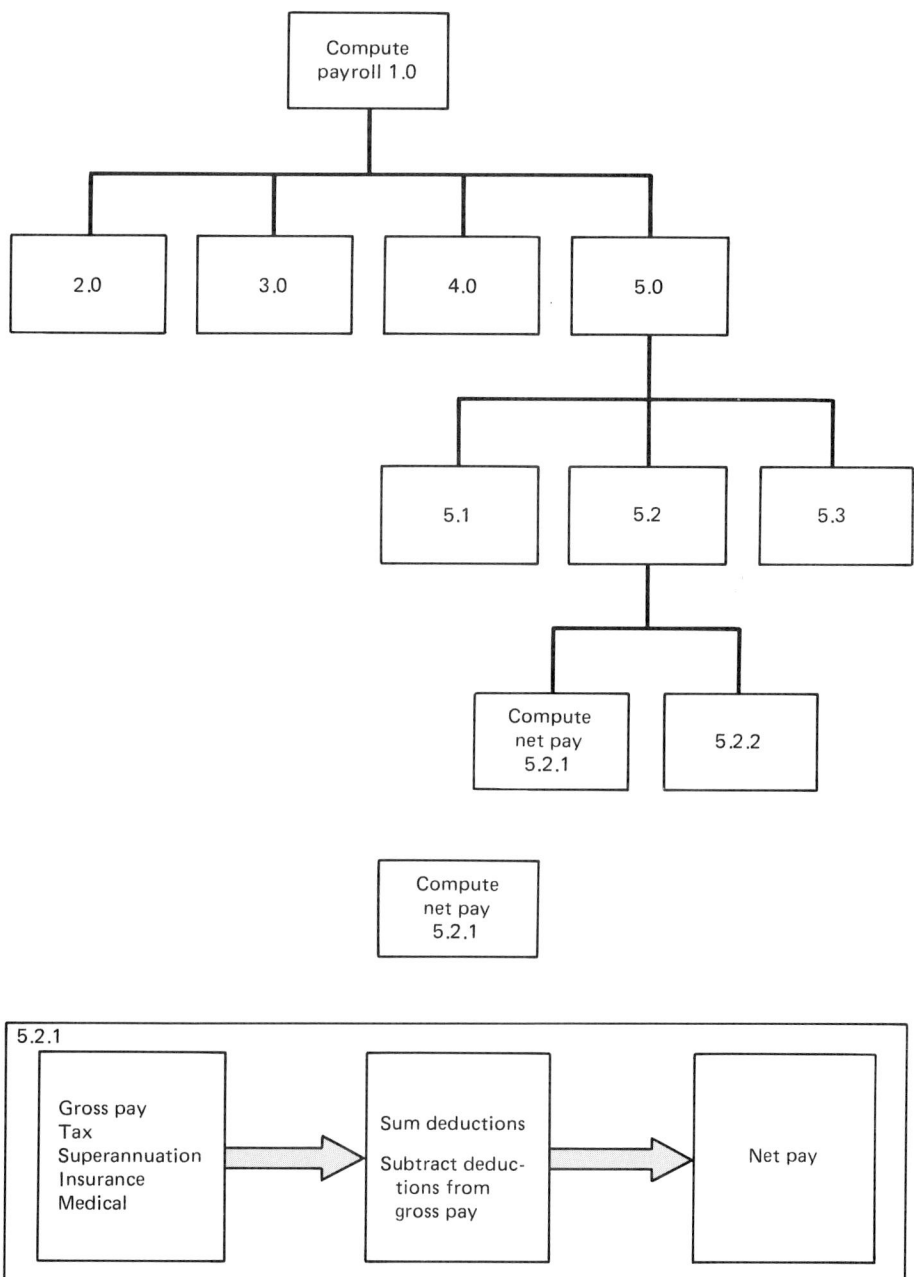

Figure 6.3
HIPO chart.

chart has two components: (*a*) a hierarchy chart that shows how functional modules are decomposed into lower level functional modules; and (*b*) for each module an input-process-output chart that shows the input, processing, and output for each function. Figure 6.3 also shows the numbering system used to assign identifiers to each diagram.

Besides the use of graphics and a numbering system, Canning [1979*a*] lists six other desirable characteristics of a top-down analysis and design aid:

1 Simple for users to grasp
2 Easy to change
3 Defined procedure for use
4 Adequate training material available
5 Frequent inspections
6 Leads into the design method

He criticizes the HIPO chart on two of these characteristics. First, he argues HIPO really does not lead into the design method. It does not have data analysis proceeding concurrently with the function analysis. It has the designer considering only one module at a time rather than the recommended three to six modules. Second, the charts are not compact. They are wordy and somewhat difficult to redraw. Top-down design is not a oneoff process from top to bottom. It is an iterative process, higher level designs being revised in light of discoveries at lower levels of the design.

The development of suitable aids for top-down analysis and design is still a research area. Progress is being made (see, for example, Combelic [1978]). However, the auditor is unlikely to find any particular aid receiving widespread use.

Coding

Developments in the way programs should be coded have paralleled developments in the way programs should be designed. The theoretical work on complex systems again underlies the work on how programs should be coded.

Top-Down Coding Even given a top-down program design approach, there is some dispute over whether or not the coding of programs also should follow a top-down philosophy. In its "pure" form, top-down coding means each module is coded immediately after it is designed. Thus, higher levels in the hierarchy of modules will be coded before the lower levels even are designed.

Opponents of the pure top-down coding approach argue that because the programmer is working with incompletely defined lower level modules, it is inevitable design revisions will be necessary for higher level modules. As such the initial code will be invalidated. Moreover, with current programming languages it is difficult, if not impossible, to incrementally compile and test modules one at a time as they are designed and coded (see, also, Canning [1974*c*]).

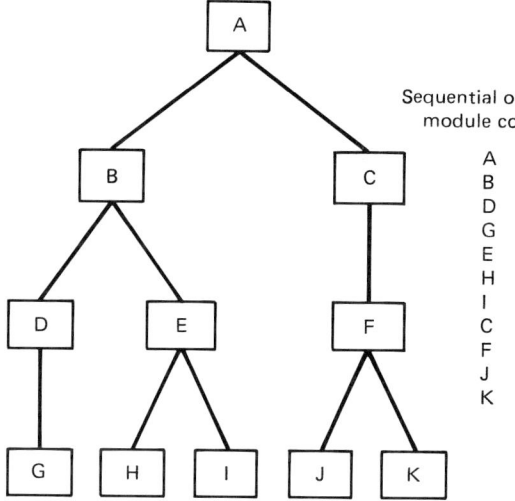

Figure 6.4
Preorder traversal of program design hierarchy for sequential coding of modules. (Adapted from Yourdon [1975]; by permission of Prentice-Hall, Inc.)

A less extreme form of top-down coding has the programmer proceeding down the hierarchy in some order and coding the modules at each level. However, program design is complete before coding commences. The installation should adopt a standard for traversing the design hierarchy; for example, Yourdon [1975] suggests a preorder traversal might be used for sequential coding of the modules (Figure 6.4).

Structured Programming Irrespective of the method used to traverse the design hierarchy or the time at which coding commences, all code should be prepared according to a particular discipline. This discipline is characterized by its prohibition of the use of the "GO TO" statement. The discipline is called "structured programming" and sometimes "GO-TO-LESS" programming.

The theory supporting structured programming derives from the work of researchers such as Dijkstra [1972] and Böhm and Jacopini [1966]. In a fundamental paper, Böhm and Jacopini demonstrated that all programs could be constructed from three basic control structures, none of which required a "GO TO" mechanism (Figure 6.5):

1 Simple sequence (SEQUENCE)
2 Selection based on a test (IF-THEN-ELSE)
3 Conditional repetition (DO-WHILE)

Currently, none of the widely used programming languages have implemented these control structures in a rigorous manner. For example, COBOL implements the structures in the following ways:

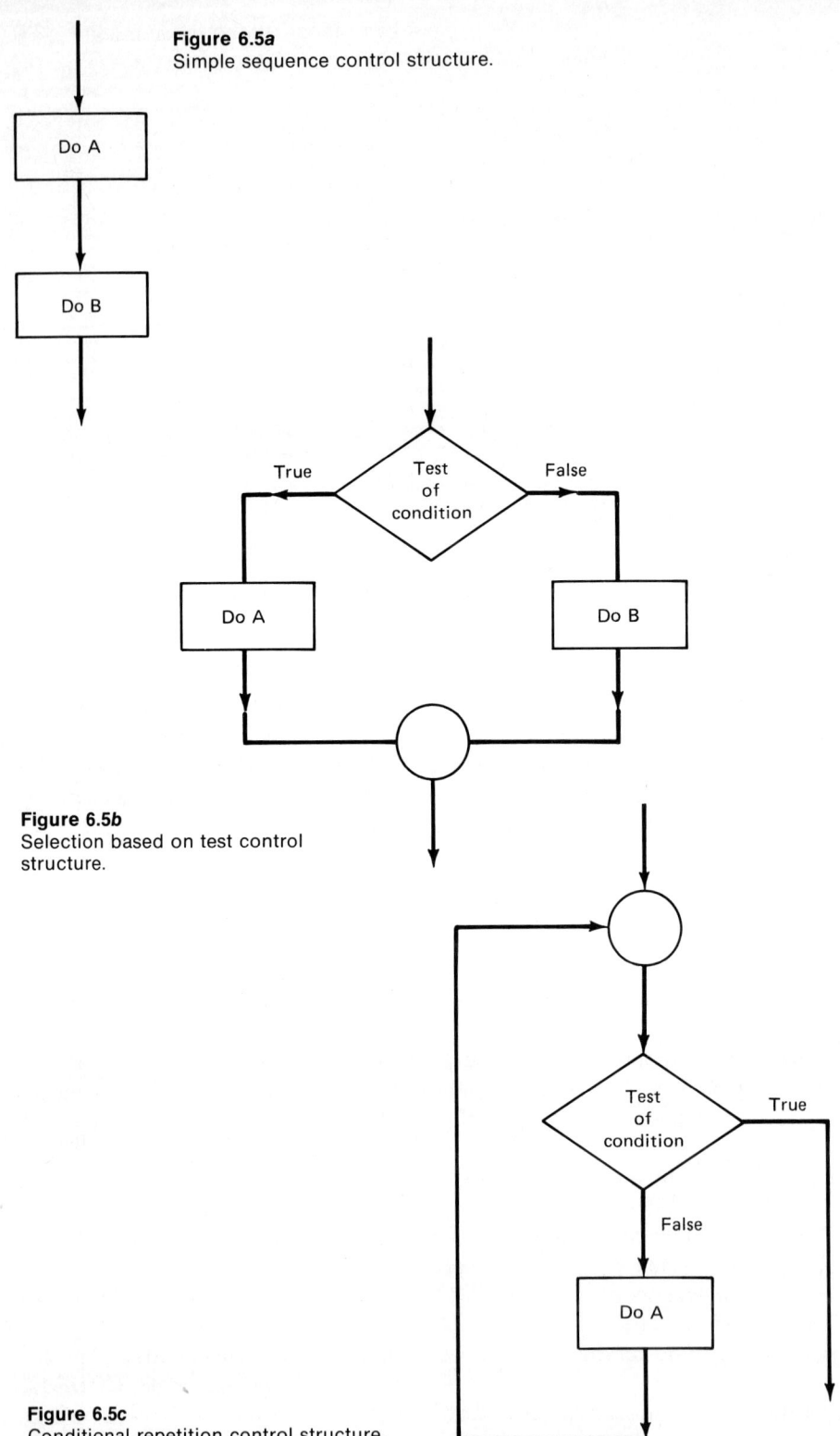

Figure 6.5a
Simple sequence control structure.

Figure 6.5b
Selection based on test control structure.

Figure 6.5c
Conditional repetition control structure.

1 Simple Sequence
  Examples: a MOVE ZEROS TO AMOUNT.
           b MULTIPLY HOURS BY RATE GIVING PAY.
2 Selection Based on a Test
  Examples: a IF HOURS GREATER THAN 50 MOVE 'ERROR'
                TO ERROR MESSAGE
              ELSE
                MOVE ZEROS TO AMOUNT.
           b GO TO
                SALES-A
                SALES-B
                SALES-C
              DEPENDING ON SALES-TYPE.
3 Conditional Repetition
  Examples: a PERFORM READ-JOURNAL UNTIL REC-TYPE
              EQUALS 99.
           b PERFORM ADD-ROUTINE UNTIL TOTAL-VALUE
              GREATER THAN 1000.

However, the implementations violate some of the "principles" of structured programming. One version of the IF-THEN-ELSE control structure uses a GO TO clause. For the DO-WHILE control structure the PERFORM clause does not pass the data to be operated upon as arguments to the module to be performed. Myers [1976] discusses the deficiencies of PL/1, FORTRAN, COBOL, APL, RPG, and ALGOL in more depth.

Pseudocode A major argument advanced (discussed further below) for adopting the pure form of top-down coding is that it facilitates carrying out top-down testing of a design. As the top levels in the hierarchy are coded the design can be inspected for errors.

Unfortunately it is generally impossible to express the top levels of the design in code that would be compilable in any of the currently available programming languages. For example, some high-level functions in a job costing program might be:

1 Accumulate job costs for each engineer.
2 Accumulate job costs for each project.
3 Accumulate job costs for each district.

These functions could not be expressed concisely in a language such as COBOL.

To help overcome this problem some organizations use a pseudocode to express these high-level functions (see, for example, Van Leer [1976]). A pseudocode or metacode is simply an informal language used to express a program design.

However, not just any language should be used for a pseudocode. If an organization uses a pseudocode to aid its program design process it should be careful to specify the syntactic and semantic rules of the pseudocode. For example, a quality pseudocode would permit only the control structures allowed in structured programming and use an indented format to show the flow of control. It should be easy to translate the pseudocode into compilable code.

Some Structured Programming Conventions In the past, flowcharts have constituted a major part of the documentation of a program. Structured programming tends to deemphasize flowcharts as a documentation tool and requires the program code to be self-documenting. Flowcharts still are used but primarily as a development tool when the code initially is being written. They are discarded when the program is released into production. Whereas programmers can forget to update flowcharts, they cannot avoid updating code when program modifications take place. Providing programmers follow certain coding conventions, structured programs are meant to be readable and understandable without flowcharts. The self-documenting features of structured programs arise because (see, also, Davis et al. [1977]):

1 The program is constructed as a hierarchy of modules with higher level modules calling or performing lower level modules.
2 Each module has only one entry point and one exit point.
3 Each module is limited to about 50–100 source statements.
4 There is no use or very restricted use of the GO TO statement.
5 Meaningful data names are used.
6 Comments are used liberally to document the functions of a module and the nature of its interface.
7 Line indentation follows rules; for example:
a. Each sentence begins on a new line.
b. Subsequent lines belonging to a sentence are indented.
c. Statements following conditional tests, such as the DO part of the DO-WHILE control structure and the THEN and ELSE parts of the IF-THEN-ELSE control structure, are indented.

Testing

The objective of program testing is to validate the logic paths within a program. In a program of moderate size (say, 3000 source statements long), carrying out a test of every logic path through the program would be enormously time consuming and very costly. At best, tests can be performed only on a sample of logic paths through the program; hopefully, the more important logic paths. Even so, Canning [1974b] reports that testing and debugging usually takes from 40–70% of the initial program development time.

Much of the stimulus for top-down design and programming has come from researchers who are concerned with developing formal proofs of program correctness. If it is possible to prove a program is correct in the same way it is possible to prove a theorem in mathematics, then brute force approaches (test data) to validating logic paths would no longer be necessary. Further, as Dijkstra [1972] has pointed out, testing can show only the presence of bugs; it cannot show their absence.

Unfortunately, the practical application of proofs of program correctness is still some time off. However, substantial insights have been gained into how the program testing process should be carried out. The following sections outline the newer approaches to testing programs. To provide the auditor with a normative basis for evaluating programming management, the focus is on the philosophies underlying the approaches. Chapter 18 discusses the more procedural aspects of testing: the design of test data, use of test data generators, etc.

Top-Down Testing Historically, programmers have used a bottom-up approach to testing. First, modules in a program are tested; then the program is tested; finally the system is tested. Even the modular approach to programming uses a bottom-up testing procedure (see Canning [1974a]). Programmers test modules; then combine modules and test the interfaces between modules.

The primary motivation for adopting a top-down testing approach is the recognition that the most critical errors in a program are those that occur in the interfaces between modules. Errors in the interfaces affect at least two modules. Errors internal to a module are localized. Top-down testing involves testing the interfaces between modules first; then the modules themselves are tested.

The pure form of top-down testing has testing in progress at the same time top-down design and top-down coding are in progress. At first glance it is difficult to see how testing can commence when the top-level modules—the system level modules—are being designed and coded. For example, in a simple system the first level of modules might be:

1 Validate and edit data
2 Update master files
3 Print reports

The corresponding pseudocode in the mainline control module might be:
CALL VALIDATION AND EDIT ROUTINE.
CALL MASTER FILE UPDATE ROUTINE.
CALL REPORT ROUTINE.
When coding is complete, each of these routines may constitute programs or even multiple programs. However, if testing commences at this stage of design and coding, these lower level modules have not even been developed; that is, there is no logic for the test data to traverse.

To overcome this problem the top-down testing technique uses dummy modules or program "stubs." For example, the "VALIDATION AND EDIT ROUTINE" may contain one command only: "EXIT." Alternatively, the module may print some message to indicate it has been called satisfactorily, or perform some simple transformation on data passed as arguments to the module.

Carrying out a test when even the first-level modules exist as stubs may seem ludicrous. However, Yourdon [1975] argues a test at this time at least allows the job control commands for the system to be validated. For some systems correctly formulating these commands may not be easy. In any case the top-down testing approach is not meant to be rigid. Programmers should exercise their intuition and experience to determine at what levels in the hierarchy of modules tests are worthwhile.

Structured Walk-Throughs The proponents of top-down design, top-down coding, and top-down testing argue programmers should not perform these tasks in isolation. Their designs, code, and tests should be reviewed by peer groups, especially at the planning stage.

One technique used for review purposes is a structured walk-through. Structured walk-throughs involve programmers responsible for the design, code, or test plan leading a group of about six other programmers, who usually are on the project team, through the work they have performed. The review group focuses on detecting design flaws, coding errors, or test plan deficiencies. The product of the review process is a list of errors to be corrected, and not a list detailing how the errors are to be corrected. Often a program librarian takes responsibility for preparing formal notes and disseminating information on the errors detected to project team members.

Design and Code Inspections Structured walk-throughs are simply an extension of the desk-checking approach used by programmers to detect errors in their program logic. Still a further formalization of structured walk-throughs is a design and code inspection.

Design and code inspections consist of five steps (see Fagan [1976]):

Inspection step	Explanation
Overview	The designer or programmer who performed the work to be inspected provides the review team with an overview of what has been done.
Preparation	Individual review team members study the documentation for the design or program so they understand in detail the work performed.
Inspection	The review team gathers together to find errors in the work done. A "moderator" (usually a person from an unrelated project) guides the review process and prepares a written report on the inspection and its findings.
Rework	The person who performed the work must resolve all the errors identified.
Follow-up	The moderator performs a follow-up to check the errors identified have been corrected. If major rework is involved, the moderator may reconvene the review team to inspect the changes made.

The major difference between structured walk-throughs and design and code inspections is the level of formality involved in carrying out the review process. In a structured walk-through, the conduct of the inspection primarily is left up to the review team members. In a design and code inspection, prescribed procedures must be followed. At a more detailed level, further differences are (see, also, Fagan [1976]):

1 Whereas the designer or programmer responsible for the work being reviewed leads a structured walk-through, a trained moderator leads a design and code inspection team.
2 There are defined participant rules for each review team member in a design and code inspection; in a structured walk-through this is not the case.
3 Design and code inspections make use of formal tools to guide the inspection process; for example, checklists for "how to find errors" and ranked distributions of error types for error-prone modules.
4 Design and code inspections use preprinted forms for documenting the results of a review team meeting. These forms also provide the basis for follow-up to determine whether or not rework has been carried out correctly.
5 Typically, structured walk-throughs occur only at three stages in the development of a system: (*a*) after preliminary design of the module hierarchy, (*b*) after detailed design of individual modules, and (*c*) after coding (but prior to compilation) of the modules. Design and code inspections occur at every stage in the program development process where it is possible to define a checkpoint; that is, a point where specific exit (output) criteria can be specified.
6 Structured walk-throughs have little or no follow-up procedures; the follow-up procedures in design and code inspections are extensive.

In general, it seems that the more formal the inspection process, the more likely it is to be successful. However, inspections add overheads to the programming process; thus, their benefits and costs should be carefully evaluated.

Operation and Maintenance

When a program is released into production it is modified and maintained until redesign and reprogramming is necessary. Management must decide when cost-effective modifications and maintenance still can be carried out and when the program must be scrapped and the development process restarted.

Unfortunately, there are few formal guidelines that programming management can use to decide when systems and programs must be reworked. They must rely primarily on their intuition and experience. However, some research has been carried out on the dynamics of program evolution that at least suggests the sorts of things on which programming management should focus in making this decision.

Belady and Lehman [1976] studied the evolutionary dynamics of several operating systems. One of their objectives was to derive some measure of system complexity that could be used by programming management to decide when complete structural redesign of a program was necessary. Though their research involved only very large programs, they found several general patterns existing in the evolutionary process (see, also, Canning [1978b]):

Evolutionary pattern	Explanation
Smooth Growth in Size	With each new release of the operating systems, the rate of growth in size (measured by the change in the number of new modules added to the system) was constant.
Exponential Growth in Complexity	Complexity (measured by the fraction of modules handled) increased exponentially at each release.
Decreasing Growth Rate with Age	System size (measured by number of modules) increases at a decreasing rate over time.
Exponential Growth in Release Intervals	The time between successive releases of the operating systems increased exponentially.

The research cannot give a definite answer on when structural redesign is necessary; however, the research suggests some useful variables which management can monitor as indicators of when structural redesign should be considered, namely:

1 Age of the program
2 Size of the program
3 Interval between production releases
4 Extent of change to program at each release

Since the research indicates these variables tend to exhibit different types of smooth relationships with one another, any marked deviation from these predetermined relationships may mean structural redesign is necessary.

ORGANIZING THE PROGRAMMING TEAM

In 1971 IBM completed a project for *The New York Times*. The system designed and implemented was an online retrieval system for the newspaper's file of clippings. Throughout the project IBM used a programming team organized on radically different lines to the traditional ways programming teams are organized. For the size of the project—about 83,000 lines of source code—the results were impressive (see Baker [1972]):

1 The system was delivered on time after 22 elapsed months and 11 worker-years of effort.
2 Only 21 errors were found in the five weeks of acceptance testing allowed for the system. Each error could be fixed within a single day. Most of the errors occurred in the lower level modules which had been written during the last two months of the project.

3 Only a further 25 errors were found during the system's first year of operation.

4 Each principal programmer on the project averaged one detected error and 25,000 lines of source code per worker-year.

5 Approximately half of the subprograms consisting of about 200–400 lines of source code were correct at the first compilation.

6 One week after coding was complete the file maintenance subsystem was delivered. It operated for 20 months before any errors were discovered.

The success of this project and other similar projects highlights the importance of the organization structure adopted for a programming team as a factor affecting programmer productivity and the quality of systems designed and implemented. The following sections examine the different types of organization structures proposed for programmers and their strengths and weaknesses. Again, the objective is to provide the auditor with a basis for evaluating these structures in terms of how well they facilitate the design and implementation of high-quality programs.

Traditional Organization Structures

Chapter 4 discussed the traditional organization structures used within an EDP installation, which also are applied to programmers: function-based structures and project-based structures. Programmers may be members of a central pool of programmers. The programming manager simply assigns work to individual programmers as it becomes available. Alternatively, programmers may be members of a project team; they work for some time on a suite of programs needed for an application. Often, they also are responsible for maintaining the programs in the application system.

As discussed in Chapter 4, modern organization theory focuses on task uncertainty as the primary factor affecting the choice of an organization structure. Task uncertainty in turn affects the amount of information the organization must process. If the organization needs to process only small amounts of information to accomplish its tasks, in general, a mechanistic organization structure will suffice. Alternatively, if an organization faces high task uncertainty and must process large amounts of information, in general, an organic organization structure will be needed.

Function-based organization structures tend to be more mechanistic than project-based organization structures. If the computer installation has its programmers organized along functional lines, the auditor should question whether or not the task uncertainty faced by programmers is low. Programmers must be given a precise set of program specifications. Further, the specifications must comply with well-defined standards. The programmer also must produce a program that meets well-defined standards. If programmers have to rely on substantial interaction with other personnel to accomplish their tasks, it is unlikely a functional organization structure will be successful. However, if programming tasks are small or well-defined, a functional organization structure imposes few overhead costs, since programmers do not have to interact with other personnel.

Several benefits accrue from organizing programmers along project lines. First, the programmers develop expertise in an application area, so there are few startup costs when new programs must be developed or old programs must be maintained. In some cases the application area requires the programmer to have expert knowledge in the area anyway. Second, having programmers identify themselves with projects encourages a commitment to the project. Third, project teams can be organized to facilitate communication among members of the team (see Chapter 4). This is especially important if there is high task uncertainty. Nevertheless, project-based organizations typically are more loosely structured than function-based organizations; thus, they often are more costly to control.

Chief Programmer Teams

The particular organization structure used by IBM on *The New York Times* project is known as a chief programmer team. A chief programmer team is simply a specific form of a project-based organization structure.

Figure 6.6 shows the structure of a chief programmer team. The functions of the various personnel who are members of the team are:

Team member	Functions
Chief Programmer	Ultimately responsible for the system on which the team works; must be an expert, highly productive programmer; responsible for designing, coding, and integrating the critical parts of the system; assigns work to the backup and support programmers
Backup Programmer	A senior programmer responsible for providing full support to the chief programmer; must be capable of assuming the chief programmer's duties at any time
Support Programmer	Needed for large projects that could not be handled by the chief programmer and backup programmer alone; provides specialist support and assists in the coding and testing of lower level modules
Librarian	Responsible for maintaining the program production library (discussed below); submits input and collects output for programmers; files output from compilations and tests; keeps source code and object code libraries up to date

Underlying the choice of the chief programmer team structure is a major assumption; namely, that programmers face a high level of task uncertainty. The chief programmer team structure is designed to reduce the need for information processing among its members and to increase their capacities to process information. It achieves these objectives in three ways:

1 Reduces the number of communications channels needed among team members
2 Allows task specialization
3 Provides a lateral coordinating role

A chief programmer team structure reduces the number of communications channels needed among team members by minimizing the number of personnel on the team. However, as a consequence the structure places more onerous productivity requirements on each team member to compensate for the loss of worker resources.

Each member of the chief programmer team performs specialized tasks. The chief programmer primarily is responsible for designing, coding, and testing the system. The backup programmer and support programmers provide specialized support; for example, they may advise the chief programmer on the intricacies of the operating system. The librarian relieves the chief programmer, backup programmer, and support programmers of the routine, clerical duties associated with the system. Thus, the structure aims at improving productivity by having team members do what they do best.

The team's capacity to process information is increased by having the librarian perform a lateral coordinating role. Central to this role is a program production library consisting of two parts: an internal part and an external part (see, also, McGowan and Kelly [1975]). The internal part consists of source code, object code, linkage commands, job control statements, etc. It is maintained solely by the librarian, not the programmers. The external part consists of folders containing compilation results, test results, and other supporting documentation. The programmers work only with the external library, making whatever changes they need on program listings or coding sheets, and the librarian implements these changes. Each team member has access to the external library; thus, code, test results, etc., are public. Programmers are encouraged to examine each other's work so errors or potential interface problems are identified.

The success of the chief programmer team structure suggests programmers often face high task uncertainty. Perhaps this task uncertainty arises because

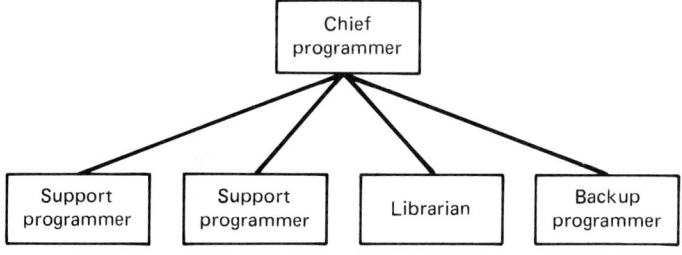

Figure 6.6
Chief programmer team organization structure.

they need such a precise specification of what must be done. Consequently, they must work within an organizational structure that facilitates the flow of information necessary to reduce this uncertainty.

Adaptive Teams

Weinberg [1971] proposes another type of team structure for programmers: an adaptive team. Like chief programmer teams, adaptive teams consist of only a small number of individuals, say, 6–10 programmers. The structure of the team is meant to cater for two sets of needs: (*a*) the organization's requirements for quality programs to be produced, and (*b*) the social/psychological needs of each programmer in the team.

Adaptive teams differ from chief programmer teams in three ways. First, adaptive teams have no hierarchy of authority. The leadership of the team rotates among its members. The person having greatest skill with the activity undertaken at a point in time usually assumes the leadership for the duration of that activity. Second, in an adaptive team, tasks are assigned to members of the team rather than defined positions. When assigning tasks the objective is to exploit the strengths and avoid the weaknesses of a particular team member. Thus, there is no notion of a chief programmer with a defined role, a backup programmer with a defined role, etc.; an adaptive team is self-organizing. Third, an adaptive team has no formal librarian role to perform a lateral coordinating function. Instead, team members are responsible for carefully examining and evaluating one another's work. The intent is to foster a feeling of joint responsibility for the quality of the programming product. At the same time team members cannot have an ego attachment to the work they perform if open evaluation is to exist; hence, this type of programming is sometimes called "egoless" programming.

An adaptive team gives recognition to the fact that substantial individual differences exist among programmers in their abilities to perform various types of programming tasks (see, for example, Sackman et al. [1968]). It also is structured to allow the free flow of information among team members. Thus, adaptive teams are suited to programming tasks where a high level of uncertainty exists. However, currently few organizations use adaptive teams so there is little empirical evidence on the relative strengths and weaknesses of adaptive teams versus chief programmer teams. Further, Yourdon [1975] suggests adaptive teams may produce various psychological problems in team members. Programmers who lack confidence and self-esteem may suffer if intense design and code reviews end up being destructive in nature rather than constructive.

MANAGING THE SYSTEM PROGRAMMING GROUP

There are two types of programmers in a computer installation: application programmers and system programmers. The former are responsible for developing and maintaining programs for application systems. The latter develop and maintain system software; that is, software that provides general functions useful to a wide range of application software (see, also, Chapter 12).

Control Problems

The existence of a system programming group poses a number of difficult control problems in an installation. First, since system software is a shared resource, it is critical the software is reliable if errors are not to permeate application system processing. Management must seek to ensure system software is free of errors. Second, because system software is a shared resource and it sometimes must run in privileged mode, it provides system programmers with a means of perpetrating frauds. Third, system programmers are highly skilled personnel; it is sometimes difficult to evaluate their work from asset safeguarding, data integrity, effectiveness, and efficiency viewpoints. Fourth, system programming groups often are small; consequently, it is difficult to exercise traditional management controls such as separation of duties and independent checks on performance.

Control Measures

In many installations there has been a tendency to regard the system programming group as uncontrollable. Moreover, there has been a belief that the imposition of controls over system programmers would cause their work to deteriorate; they are sensitive, creative, often erratic individuals who do not take kindly to restrictions.

Auditors should be skeptical of these claims. Organizations that use them run the risk of losing their assets. Well-controlled system programming groups *do* exist. These groups experience neither high staff turnover nor low-quality work being produced.

Though it may be difficult to exercise strong and varied controls over system programmers, several control measures still can be instituted. First, management should ensure they hire only quality system programming staff. More in-depth background checking and interviewing might be undertaken for system programmers compared with application programmers. Second, careful thought should be given to the duties of system programmers within the installation and the ways in which performance of these duties will be evaluated. Both methods and performance standards must be established and documented. Third, to the extent that it is possible the duties of system programmers should be separated and independent checks on performance used. For example, if the installation has two system programmers, one might design and code a program and the other test the program. Fourth, the powers given to system programmers should be restricted. They must not be allowed to "tinker" with the operating system during production time. System software that operates in a privileged mode should be developed only during special test periods. During production periods system programmers should be given only the same powers allocated to application programmers. Fifth, both a manual and machine log should be kept of system programmer activities. Periodically this log should be scrutinized. Sixth, from time to time consultants might be employed to evaluate the work of system programmers.

Application programmers often can exercise control over the activities of a system programmer. Some application programmers are capable of understanding system software code, though they are not capable of efficiently designing and coding system software. These application programmers may be able to intelligently appraise a system programmer's work.

SOFTWARE DEVELOPMENT AIDS

The reliability of programs and the productivity of programmers can be increased through the use of various software development aids that are available. When evaluating programming management the auditor can check to see the extent to which these aids are used as an indicator of the likely quality of programs produced by the programming group. The following sections provide an overview of these aids. The discussion highlights how these aids facilitate the program development process and some of the control problems experienced in using these aids. Naftaly et al. [1972] examine many of the aids available for COBOL; they also provide the names and addresses of vendors (see, also, Canning [1972a]).

Coding Aids

Coding aids have five purposes:

1 Reduce the effort required to code a program
2 Speed up the coding process
3 Increase the documentation content of program code
4 Increase the amount of standardized code used
5 Improve the accuracy of coding

The following sections review seven types of coding aids that currently are available.

Shorthand Preprocessors Languages such as COBOL are verbose. Shorthand preprocessors allow the programmer to write an abbreviated form of code; they then translate this abbreviated form into the full language syntax. For example, a COBOL shorthand preprocessor might allow the programmer to use "P" for "PERFORM" and "M" for "MOVE." Besides a set of predefined abbreviations, users can define their own abbreviations; for example, for data names "GP" might be used for "GROSS-PAY."

Some shorthand preprocessors perform other functions. If the installation uses only a subset of a language (see below), they will ensure programmers adhere to this subset. Some check syntax and automatically correct certain types of errors; for example, punctuation errors. Some format code to enhance its readability. The shorthand preprocessor is sometimes part of a librarian package (see Chapter 8).

Macro/Subroutine Facility A macro or subroutine facility allows users to have a standard set of code inserted in their programs by writing a single instruction. For example, the instruction "DO N-P" might insert a subroutine in a program that calculates net pay, given a standard argument list consisting of gross pay and various deductions. Modern compilers provide macro/subroutine facilities. However, some shorthand translators also provide this facility in association with the facility that allows abbreviated commands to be used.

Decision-Table Preprocessors Decision-table preprocessors convert decision tables inserted in the code of a program into the source code of the compiler language in which the program is written. The characteristics of decision-table preprocessors vary. Beside limited entry tables, some allow extended entry tables to be used (see, further, Naftaly et al. [1972]). Often the decision table is included in the source code generated as a note or comment to aid documentation (Figure 6.7). Some preprocessors check for redundancy and contradiction in the table.

Providing the programmer codes the decision table correctly, the source code generated by the preprocessor will be correct. The code generated may be somewhat inefficient, but most preprocessors attempt to optimize the code they generate. For an experienced user of decision tables, in general, it is faster to code a decision table than the associated source code. Further, the code generated is standardized, readable, and maintainable through changes to the decision table.

Copy Facility A copy facility allows large sections of code to be copied from a library into a program. For example, coding the DATA DIVISION of a COBOL program can be very laborious. Using the COPY facility, only one programmer needs to code the DATA DIVISION. It then can be stored on a library and other programmers can copy those sections of the DATA DIVISION needed in their program. COPY facilities exist in most modern compilers, librarian packages, and shorthand preprocessor packages.

Online Coding Facility An online coding facility allows programmers to code and compile programs while working in an interactive mode with a computer. The facility provides appropriate instructions for entering, modifying, and deleting code, storing source and object programs, listing programs, etc. Some facilities compile source code on a line by line basis; thus, the programmer has almost immediate feedback on any syntax errors made.

152 PART 2: THE MANAGEMENT CONTROL FRAMEWORK

```
PROGRAM NAME :-           TSAR
TABLE NAME :-             J0000
NUMBER OF CONDITIONS :-   002
NUMBER OF ACTIONS :-      005
NUMBER OF RULES :-        007
IDENTIFICATION :-
FIRST SEQUENCE NUMBER :-  029300

    029300  J0000.
    029310         NOTE
    029320 1                             1    2    3    4    5    6    E    E
    029330  CONT-WD1A =                  W10AW10AW10BW10BW10CW10C
    029340  W04RG-END = 1                Y    N    Y    N    Y    N
    029350 9
    029360  PERFORM T1000                X    X    X    X    X    X
    029370  PERFORM T0810 THRU T0-EXIT   X    X
    029380  PERFORM T0820 THRU T0-EXIT             X    X
    029390  PERFORM T0830 THRU T0-EXIT                       X    X
    029400  GO TO J0000                       X         X         X
    029410 E     .
    029420  J00000.
    029430         IF CONT-WD1A = W10A NEXT SENTENCE ELSE GO TO J00001.
    029440         IF W04RG-END = 1 GO TO J00900.
    029450  J00001.
    029460         IF CONT-WD1A = W10A NEXT SENTENCE ELSE GO TO J00002.
    029470         IF W04RG-END = 1 NEXT SENTENCE ELSE GO TO J00901.
    029480  J00002.
    029490         IF CONT-WD1A = W10B NEXT SENTENCE ELSE GO TO J00003.
    029500         IF W04RG-END = 1 GO TO J00902.
    029510  J00003.
```

Figure 6.7
Extended entry decision table inserted by preprocessor as note in program.

There is some debate over the benefits and costs of using an online coding facility (see Canning [1972b]). In general, an online coding facility allows faster development of programs. Further, because turnaround is faster, programmers are better able to maintain their momentum. This may improve their problem-solving abilities. However, online coding can lead to sloppy programming. Programmers may not take sufficient time to think out their program design and structure their code.

A primary concern for the auditor should be the access controls instituted in an online coding facility (see, also, Adams and Perry [1976a, 1976b]). Since programmers can retrieve programs, modify them, and restore them, scope exists for unauthorized modification of programs. The auditor should check to see that programmers cannot obtain unauthorized access to production programs or programs being developed. Chapter 10 discusses access controls in more detail.

Text Editors Text editors allow parameter-specified modifications of source code. For example, a programmer may wish to change a data name from "G-PAY" to "GROSS-PAY." By using a text editor command such as C/G-PAY/GROSS-PAY/, all instances of G-PAY in the source code will be changed to GROSS-PAY. The text editor also can be used to print out where G-PAY occurs in the program. Thus, changes can be made quickly and accurately.

Tidy Facility A tidy facility can be used to "clean up" the source code of a program. For example, by specifying the appropriate parameter values, all "IF" statements in a program can be indented to make the code more readable. Similarly, nested "DO" or "PERFORM" statements can be indented to show more clearly the various levels.

Debugging/Testing Aids

In any computer installation the auditor should expect to see at least two basic debugging/testing aids in use: (a) core dumps, and (b) traces. Core dumps show the state of core at a point in time. When chasing a program bug, a programmer may need to examine the contents of a particular register or field at some point in the program's execution; for example, when the program references a location outside its assigned boundaries. Traces show the status of memory locations at various stages throughout a program's execution; for example, as a counter is incremented by the program. Typically, the machine vendor supplies software for core dumps and traces. For example, different packages will be available to format core dumps for programs written in different languages. Special verbs such as "TRACE" or "MONITOR" may be included in a compiler to perform a trace function.

There are two major reasons why debugging and testing aids should be used during the program life cycle. First, program testing and debugging is an extremely time-consuming and difficult task. Brooks [1971] argues that debugging and testing problems are major causes of software being late. He estimates testing and debugging time normally take about 50% of program development time. Second, testing and debugging aids facilitate correct program maintenance. Boehm [1973] estimates programmers have only a 50% chance of correctly changing 10 source statements in a program; if 50 source statements are changed the probability of success is only 20%.

The following sections discuss eight types of debugging and testing aids that are available. Chapter 18 also discusses some of these aids, as they are useful to the auditor when designing test data for audit evidence collection. The aids have several purposes:

1 Facilitate understanding of program logic
2 Assist test data development
3 Assess accuracy of test results
4 Ensure comprehensive testing of logic paths
5 Aid identification of logic errors
6 Handle the mechanics of program testing
7 Provide documentation of the testing process

Cross-Reference Listers Cross-reference listers show where in a program or set of programs a data name, procedure name, or literal is used. Programmers making changes to programs can determine quickly what parts of a program the change affects without having to perform a serial search of the program code. The lister associates with each named item the line numbers where it appears in a program. The cross-reference list may be ordered alphabetically by item name and appear at the end of the source code listing. Alternatively, it may be embedded in the source code listing so that line numbers appear by the item name where it is defined in the program. Beside each line number some cross-reference listers also print the operation performed on the item; for example, the symbol "M" to indicate a MOVE and the symbol "P" to indicate a PERFORM.

Traces/Monitors Naftaly et al. [1972] identify two types of traces: intraprogram traces and extraprogram traces. Intraprogram traces are extensions to the source language; for example, the TRACE and MONITOR commands discussed previously. Extraprogram traces are separate object programs that must be link-edited to the object programs they monitor. Extraprogram traces are activated by a hardware interrupt. The trace takes a snapshot of the state of core when an interrupt occurs so the programmer can identify whether an invalid instruction or invalid data caused the interrupt. The trace then attempts to correct the instruction or data that caused the interrupt so the program can proceed.

Test Data Generators Test data generators perform three major functions: (*a*) automatic generation of data items having certain attributes, (*b*) automatic creation of records for these data items, and (*c*) automatic creation of data (file) structures for these records. By specifying the appropriate parameter values, the programmer can have data generated in several ways; for example (see, also, Adams [1973]):

Data generation method	Explanation
Constants	The data item has a constant value in all records containing the item.
Range	Instances of the data item have values generated within a range.
Random	Random values are assigned to the data item.
Computation	The value of a data item is an arithmetic function of other data item values generated.
Logical	The value of a data item depends on whether a test carried out on other data items produces a true or false result.
List	Data item values are selected from a list.

Again, by specifying the appropriate parameter values the programmer can select either fixed length or variable length records for the data items and have the records structured as a sequential file, indexed sequential file, etc.

Flowcharters Flowcharters use as input the source code of a program and produce as output a flowchart for the program (Figure 6.8). The value of the flowchart produced depends both on how well the program is documented and the capabilities of the flowcharter. The flowcharter simply transcribes the data names and procedure names used in a program onto the flowchart it produces. If meaningful data names and procedure names are not used, the flowchart produced also will be less useful as an aid to understanding the program's logic. Flowcharters differ on the basis of a number of attributes; for example, whether or not they use ANSI symbols, how they paginate, how they group source statements together, how they handle GO TO's or PERFORM's, how they cross-reference the flowchart to the source listing.

Output Analyzers Output analyzers check the accuracy of the results produced by a test run. There are three types of checks that an output analyzer can perform. First, if a standard set of test data and test results exists for a program, the output of a test run after program maintenance can be compared with the set of results that should be produced. Second, as programmers prepare test data and calculate the expected results, these results can be stored on a file and the output analyzer compares the actual results of a test run with the expected results. Third, the output analyzer can act as a query language; it accepts queries about whether certain relationships exist in the file of output results and reports compliance or noncompliance.

Online Debugging Facility An online debugging facility allows programmers to monitor the status of their programs while the programs are executing. Programmers type in commands to the facility at a terminal and receive responses as the program executes.

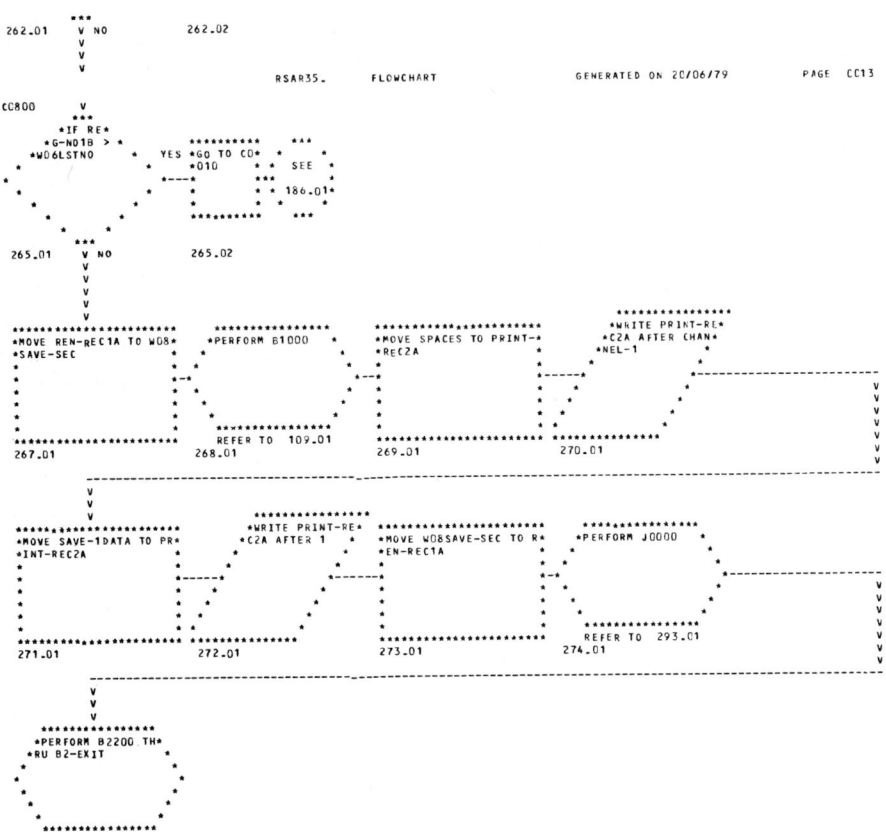

Figure 6.8
Output of automatic flowcharter (U.S. Navy).

The facility provides four major functions (see, also, Yourdon [1972]). First, programmers can examine memory locations in their programs. If the memory location is a data field that changes as the program executes, the changing status is printed out. Second, programmers can change the contents of a memory location; a data field or instruction can be modified while the program is executing. Third, control points can be set in the program. When the program reaches a control point, it either stops and awaits further instructions or indicates the particular control point reached. Fourth, programmers can have memory locations searched for particular values.

While an online debugging facility is a very powerful and useful tool, it also presents some major control problems (see, also, Perry [1975]). It is critical the facility is used only for programs that are being developed or maintained. If it is used on production programs, unauthorized code can be inserted in the program or unauthorized modification of data can take place. Further, the change may be temporary; only while the core resident version of the program executes a particular instruction at a point in time. Access controls must exist to restrict the computing resources on which the facility can operate, and an audit trail must be kept of all uses of the facility (see, also, Chapters 10 and 14).

Logic Path Monitors A logic path monitor detects whether or not logic paths in a program have been traversed by test data designed by the programmer (see, also, Adams [1975]). The monitor reads a source program and inserts flags at all branch points within the program. The modified program then is compiled and the test run carried out. If a logic path is tested the flag for that path is set. When testing is complete the logic path monitor provides a report on all unset flags; that is, it shows those paths within the program that were not traversed by the test data (Figure 6.9). The programmer then can design further test data to traverse these paths.

Test Managers A test manager is a control program that calls and executes the resources needed to carry out test runs for a program or set of programs and manages the production of the output test results. For example, for a single program the test manager might retrieve stored test input data, call the program to be tested, call and execute a logic path monitor, execute the program to be tested, simulate the operation of various input devices such as online enquiry terminals, capture and secure output, call and execute an output analyzer, and order and print output test results. Thus, a test manager performs many functions that otherwise would have to be performed by a computer operator.

Execution Aids

Execution aids improve the run-time efficiency of programs. There are two types of execution aids: (*a*) language subsets, and (*b*) code optimizers.

PROGRAM TSAR   TEST DATA VALIDATION REPORT   PAGE NO. 1   29/06/79

SEQ NO.	TRUE PATH	FALSE PATH	SEQ NO.	TRUE PATH	FALSE PATH	SEQ NO.	TRUE PATH	FALSE PATH
008400	0 **	2	011200	0 **	12	012000	8	0 **
012800	12	0 **	013600	12	0 **	014400	12	0 **
015200	12	0 **	016000	12	0 **	016800	12	0 **
018900	0 **	2	020000	33	3	020300	0 **	3
020700	0 **	3	020900	1	2	022000	0 **	2
022800	0 **	34	024000	1	1	025300	0 **	0 **
025900	0 **	3	026300	0 **	3	026600	1	2
027700	0 **	2	029430	(101)	135	029440	(0) **	101
029460	101	135	029470	0 **	101	029490	37	98
029500	0 **	37	029520	37	98	029530	0 **	37
029550	14	84	029560	0 **	14	029580	14	84
029590	0 **	14						

Number of Tests of Path   Path Not Tested

**** END OF REPORT

Figure 6.9
Output of logic path monitor (Main Roads Department).

Language Subsets Compiler languages provide a very general set of instructions. Depending on the way in which these instructions are implemented and the characteristics of the machine on which the compiler operates, some of these instructions may execute inefficiently. For example, for some COBOL compilers the COMPUTE verb takes substantial time to execute.

There are two objectives of preparing a subset of a compiler language for use in an installation: (*a*) to identify a set of instructions that execute efficiently, and (*b*) to identify a set of instructions that are sufficient to construct any program. Coding flexibility is traded off for improved efficiency. To prevent programmers using instructions other than those in the subset, a shorthand preprocessor can be used.

Code Optimizers Code optimizers operate on either the source code or object code of a program to remove inefficient code without changing the intent of the program. In the case of source code optimizers a diagnostic report sometimes is prepared showing the nature of the inefficiencies. Code optimizers typically reduce both the core requirements of a program and execution time.

SUMMARY

Recent advances in software engineering have provided the auditor with normative models that can be used to evaluate the program development process. These models involve top-down analysis and design, structured coding, and top-down testing. They are based on a theory of complexity: a theory that identifies the characteristics of complex systems that survive.

Associated with software engineering advances have been attempts to find better organization and management structures for programming teams. One particular organization structure, the chief programmer team, seems to have been especially successful in allowing programmers to produce high-quality software. By reducing the need for information, yet at the same time increasing the ability of the team to process information, the structure allows the team to cope with the uncertainty surrounding the programming task.

A major problem in programming management is controlling the activities of system programmers. The nature of system programming is such that many opportunities exist to perpetrate frauds. Ultimately, controls over system programming can be exercised only through a sound system of management controls.

When evaluating the programming process the auditor should determine whether or not various program development aids are being used. These aids allow programmers to develop high-quality software. There are three types of program development aids: coding aids, testing and debugging aids, and execution aids. The use of some of these aids must be controlled since they provide opportunities to breach data integrity.

REVIEW QUESTIONS

6.1. What are the major phases in the program life cycle? What events indicate the termination of each phase? Why can the program development process be called a life cycle?

6.2. Give three attributes of a high-quality program. From an audit viewpoint what is meant by a "high-quality" program?

6.3. How is a theory of complexity relevant to the program development process? What insights were gained from the theory of complexity proposed by Simon [1969]?

6.4. Briefly explain the concepts of module strength and module coupling. When evaluating a program, how can the auditor gauge the extent of its module strength and the extent of its module coupling?

6.5. Why do programming researchers currently advocate a top-down approach to program analysis and design? Give two advantages that a top-down approach has over a bottom-up approach. Can you think of a disadvantage?

6.6. Why in the analysis and design process should the designer focus only on a small number of modules? How can the auditor determine whether this design principle is being followed in an installation?

6.7. When evaluating an installation's documentation standards for the program analysis and design phase, on what attributes of a documentation standard should the auditor focus? In terms of a top-down approach to analysis and design, does a flowchart have desirable or undesirable characteristics as a documentation standard?

6.8. There is no difference between modular programming and structured programming. Comment.

6.9. What impact does the "GO TO" statement have on the module strength and module coupling of a program? Why is it unnecessary ever to use a "GO TO" statement in a program?

6.10. What is the purpose of a pseudocode in the coding phase of the program life cycle? Give two desirable attributes of a pseudocode.

6.11. Is adherence to the three control structures of structured programming a sufficient condition for well-documented code in a program? If not, explain.

6.12. Why have programming researchers been concerned with developing formal proofs of program correctness as opposed to developing better ways of testing programs? What is meant by the statement: "Testing can only show the presence of bugs; it cannot show their absence"?

6.13. What is the basic difference between the top-down approach to testing and the bottom-up approach to testing? How is the top-down testing approach based on a theory of complexity?

6.14. Briefly discuss the relationship between desk checking, structured walk-throughs, and design and code inspections. Briefly explain why it appears structured walk-throughs have been more successful at finding design flaws and program bugs than desk checking, and why design and code inspections appear to be more successful than structured walk-throughs.

6.15. What relevance does the research on the dynamics of program evolution have for management of the operation and maintenance phase of the program life cycle? Why is it important to know when a program should be scrapped and redesigned and when it should be modified and maintained?

6.16. Why has there been heightened interest in the way programming teams should be organized? Are the organization structures currently proposed using a functional approach or a project team approach? Explain why you think this is the case.

6.17. Give three advantages that a chief programmer team structure has over traditional organization structures for programming teams. Give one potential disadvantage of the chief programmer team approach.

6.18. Briefly explain the role of the librarian in a chief programmer team. What duties does the librarian have with respect to the program production library? How does the librarian role inhibit unauthorized program modification?

6.19. Give two motivations for organizing programmers as an adaptive team. What are the differences between a chief programmer team and an adaptive team? Give an example of a programming project where you think an adaptive team might be more successful than a chief programmer team.

6.20. Give a specific example of how a system programmer might use system software to perpetrate a fraud.

6.21. What types of system software is a system programmer likely to use to perpetrate a fraud? Briefly explain your choices.

6.22. How might application programmers assist in controlling system programmers?

6.23. How can a shorthand preprocessor be used to enforce a coding standard prohibiting use of the "GO TO"? What other types of coding standards can a shorthand preprocessor be used to enforce?

6.24. What control problems arise when online coding and debugging facilities are used? Outline the objectives and the major steps in the audit of an online coding and debugging facility. (*Hint:* See Adams and Perry [1976*b*].)

6.25. Briefly explain the limitations of flowcharters as an aid to testing and debugging programs. What aspects of the testing and debugging process does a flowcharter facilitate?

6.26. Briefly explain how a test data generator and a logic path monitor can be used in conjunction with one another. Is a logic path monitor likely to identify a section of unauthorized code in an object program?

6.27. Briefly explain the functions a test manager might perform when tests on a *set* of programs are carried out.

6.28. How useful are execution aids for monitoring data integrity within an installation? How useful are they for ensuring programs are effective; that is, programs achieve their objectives?

EXERCISES AND CASES

6.1. Construct a controls matrix where the columns show "what can go wrong" in the programming process and the rows show the controls that can be exercised over the programming process. In each element of the matrix, rate how cost-effective you think each control would be at reducing the expected losses from each cause of the loss. Use a 5-point scale where a score of 5 represents high cost-effectiveness and a score of 1 represents low cost-effectiveness.

6.2. You are the manager of internal audit of Coverit Corporation, a large insurance company. One day you receive an urgent letter from the controller expressing his concerns about some organizational changes that are about to occur in the data processing department. He has received a memorandum from the manager of data processing explaining that in future all new information system projects will be designed and implemented using the chief programmer team approach. The controller is concerned that the organization structure of the chief programmer team violates a fundamental internal control principle; namely, effective separation of duties. He asks you to evaluate the chief programmer team approach with respect to the basic internal control principles that he believes must be maintained.

Required: Prepare a brief report that provides the analysis requested and give a recommendation as to whether you think the organizational change proposed should be allowed to proceed.

6.3. Since program development and implementation is a major phase in the system development process, the auditor may carry out an evaluation as a member of the design team or in an ex post review capacity (refer back to Chapter 5). For *each* of these types of audit evaluation, make up a list showing the major sources of audit evidence on the overall quality of the program development and implementation process.

6.4. The chief programmer team or the adaptive team are not always the most effective and efficient ways to organize programmers. These structures should be used only when there is a high level of uncertainty surrounding the programming task. If the programming task is straightforward and well-defined, traditional organization structures should be used. Comment.

6.5. Make a list of those activities in the program development and implementation phase that directly impact the asset safeguarding and data integrity objectives. As an external auditor, briefly outline how you would evaluate each of these activities.

REFERENCES

Adams, Donald L. "A Survey of Test Data Generators," *EDPACS* (April 1973), pp. 5-9.

———. "COMBI as an Audit Tool," *EDPACS* (April 1975), pp. 7-8.

———, and William E. Perry, "The Audit and Control of TSO-Part I," *EDPACS* (March 1976a), pp. 1-11.

———, and ———. "The Audit and Control of TSO-Part II," *EDPACS* (April 1976b), pp. 1-4.

Alexander, Christopher. *Notes on the Synthesis of Form* (Cambridge, Mass.: Harvard University Press, 1964).

Aron, J. D. *The Program Development Process: Part 1: The Individual Programmer* (Reading, Mass.: Addison-Wesley Publishing Company, Inc., 1974).

Baker, F. T. "Chief Programming Team Management of Production Programming," *IBM Systems Journal*, vol. 11, no. 1, 1972, pp. 56-73.

Belady, L. A., and M. M. Lehman. "A Model of Large Program Development," *IBM Systems Journal*, vol. 15, no. 3, 1976, pp. 225-252.

Boehm, Barry W. "Software and Its Impact: A Quantitative Study," *Datamation* (May 1973), pp. 48-59.

———. "Software Engineering," *IEEE Transactions on Computers* (December 1976), pp. 1226-1241.

Böhm, C., and G. Jacopini. "Flow Diagrams, Turing Machines, and Languages with Only Two Formulation Rules," *Communications of the ACM* (May 1966), pp. 366-371.

Brooks, Frederick P., Jr. "Why Is the Software Late?" *Data Management* (August 1971), pp. 18–21.
Canning, Richard G. "COBOL Aid Packages," *EDP Analyzer* (May 1972a), pp. 1–14.
_____. "On-Line Development of COBOL Programs," *EDP Analyzer* (June 1972b), pp. 1–15.
_____. "Modular COBOL Programming," *EDP Analyzer* (July, 1972c), pp. 1–14.
_____. "That Maintenance 'Iceberg'," *EDP Analyzer* (October 1972d), pp. 1–14.
_____. "Issues in Programming Management," *EDP Analyzer* (April 1974a), pp. 1–14.
_____. "The Search for Software Reliability," *EDP Analyzer* (May 1974b), pp. 1–14.
_____. "The Advent of Structured Programming," *EDP Analyzer* (June 1974c), pp. 1–14.
_____. "Progress Toward Easier Programming," *EDP Analyzer* (September 1975), pp. 1–14.
_____. "Progress in Software Engineering: Part 1," *EDP Analyzer* (February 1978a), pp. 1–13.
_____. "Progress in Software Engineering: Part 2," *EDP Analyzer* (March 1978b), pp. 1–13.
_____. "The Analysis of User Needs," *EDP Analyzer* (January 1979a), pp. 1–13.
_____. "The Production of Better Software," *EDP Analyzer* (February 1979b), pp. 1–13.
Chrysler, Earl. "Some Basic Determinants of Computer Programming Productivity," *Communications of the ACM* (June 1978), pp. 472–483.
Combelic, Donn. "Experiences with SADT," *Proceedings of the 1978 National Computer Conference* (Montvale, N.J.: AFIPS Press, 1978), pp. 631–633.
Constantine, L. L., G. J. Myers, and W. P. Stevens. "Structured Design," *IBM Systems Journal*, vol. 13, no. 2, 1974, pp. 115–139.
Davis, Gordon B., Margrethe H. Olson, and Charles R. Litecky. *Elementary Structured COBOL: A Step by Step Approach* (New York: McGraw-Hill Book Company, 1977).
de Freitas, S. L., and P. J. Lavelle. "A Method for the Time Analysis of Programs," *IBM Systems Journal*, vol. 17, no. 1, 1978, pp. 26–38.
Dijkstra, Edsger W. "The Humble Programmer," *Communications of the ACM* (October 1972), pp. 859–866.
Duke, M. O. "Testing in a Complex Systems Environment," *IBM System Journal*, vol. 14, no. 4, 1975, pp. 353–365.
Elshoff, James L. "An Analysis of Some Commercial PL/1 Programs," *IEEE Transactions on Software Engineering* (June 1976), pp. 113–120.
Fagan, M. E. "Design and Code Inspections to Reduce Errors in Program Development," *IBM Systems Journal*, vol. 15, no. 3, 1976, pp. 182–211.
Fosdick, Lloyd D., and Leon J. Osterweil. "Data Flow Analysis in Software Reliability," *Computing Surveys* (September 1976), pp. 305–330.
Hantler, Sidney L., and James C. King. "An Introduction to Proving the Correctness of Programs," *Computing Surveys* (September 1976), pp. 331–353.
Ivie, Evan L. "The Programmer's Workbench—A Machine for Software Development," *Communications of the ACM* (October 1977), pp. 746–753.
Jones, T. C. "Measuring Programming Quality and Productivity," *IBM Systems Journal*, vol. 17, no. 1, 1978, pp. 39–63.

Lientz, B. P., and F. B. Swanson. "Characteristics of Application Software Maintenance," *Communications of the ACM* (June 1978), pp. 466–471.

McCue, Gerald M. "IBM's Santa Teresa Laboratory—Architectural Design for Program Development," *IBM Systems Journal*, vol. 17, no. 1, 1978, pp. 4–25.

McGowan, Clement L., and John R. Kelly. *Top-Down Structured Programming Techniques* (New York: Petrocelli/Charter, 1975).

McNurlin, Barbara C. "Using Some New Programming Techniques," *EDP Analyzer* (November 1977), pp. 1–13.

_____. "Program Design Techniques," *EDP Analyzer* (March 1979), pp. 1–13.

Mills, H. D. "Software Development," *IEEE Transactions on Software Engineering* (December 1976), pp. 265–273.

Myers, G. J. *Reliable Software through Composite Design* (New York: Petrocelli/Charter, 1975).

_____. "Composite Design Facilities of Six Programming Languages," *IBM Systems Journal*, vol. 15, no. 3, 1976, pp. 212–224.

_____. *Composite/Structured Design* (New York: Van Nostrand Reinhold Company, 1978).

Naftaly, Stanley M., Michael C. Cohen, and Bruce G. Johnson. *COBOL Support Packages: Programming and Productivity Aids* (New York: John Wiley & Sons, Inc., 1972).

Perry, William E. "Control of SUPER-ZAP," *EDPACS* (July 1975), pp. 1–7.

Rogers, J. G. "Structured Programming for Virtual Storage Systems," *IBM Systems Journal*, vol. 14, no. 4, 1975, pp. 385–406.

Sackman, H., W. J. Erickson, and E. E. Grant. "Exploratory Studies Comparing Online and Offline Programming Performance," *Communications of the ACM* (January 1968), pp. 3–11.

Scott, Randall F., and Dick B. Simmons. "Predicting Programming Group Productivity—A Communications Model," *IEEE Transactions on Software Engineering* (December 1975), pp. 411–414.

Simon, Herbert A. *The Sciences of the Artificial* (Cambridge, Mass.: The M.I.T. Press, 1969).

Stay, J. F. "HIPO and Integrated Program Design," *IBM Systems Journal*, vol. 15, no. 2, 1976, pp. 143–154.

Van Leer, P. "Top-Down Development Using a Program Design Language," *IBM Systems Journal*, vol. 15, no. 2, 1976, pp. 155–170.

Walson, C. E., and C. P. Felix. "A Method of Programming Measurement and Estimation," *IBM Systems Journal*, vol. 16, no. 1, 1977, pp. 54–73.

Weinberg, Gerald M. *The Psychology of Computer Programming* (New York: Van Nostrand Reinhold Co., 1971).

Yourdon, Edward. *Design of On-Line Computer Systems* (Englewood Cliffs, N.J.: Prentice-Hall, Inc., 1972).

_____. *Techniques of Program Structure and Design* (Englewood Cliffs, N.J.: Prentice-Hall, Inc., 1975).

_____, and Larry L. Constantine. *Structured Design: Fundamentals of a Discipline of Computer Program and Systems Design* (Englewood Cliffs, N.J.: Prentice-Hall, Inc., 1979).

CHAPTER 7

DATABASE ADMINISTRATION

CHAPTER OUTLINE

MOTIVATIONS TOWARD A DATABASE ADMINISTRATION ROLE
SOME AUDIT CONSIDERATIONS
FUNCTIONS OF THE DATABASE ADMINISTRATOR
    Defining, Creating, and Retiring Data
    Making the Database Available to Users
    Informing and Servicing Users
    Maintaining Database Integrity
    Monitoring Operations
ORGANIZATIONAL CONSIDERATIONS
DATA DICTIONARY
    Elements of a Data Dictionary System
    Audit Aspects of a Data Dictionary
CONTROL OVER THE DATABASE ADMINISTRATOR
    Control Weaknesses
    Remedial Measures
SUMMARY
REVIEW QUESTIONS
EXERCISES AND CASES
REFERENCES

The database administrator is a human agent who is responsible for the management of an organization's database; that is, its control and use. The evolution of a distinct database administration role as an integral part of the management control framework of a computer installation is fairly recent. Historically, the functions of a database administrator have been dispersed across the various users of data, though partial recognition was given to the need for a database administrator through the formation of a file librarian role. The existence of a full database administration role reflects the growing recognition that data is a critical *resource* of an organization and the effective management of data is necessary for its ongoing existence.

This chapter discusses the motivations for creating a database administration role and the functions that should be performed by the database administrator. Several factors that determine the effectiveness and efficiency of the role are examined, especially the database administrator's position within the organization hierarchy and the availability of tools to assist the role. Finally, the chapter discusses several control problems posed by the role and some remedial measures.

MOTIVATIONS TOWARD A DATABASE ADMINISTRATION ROLE

It is not necessary for a computer installation to be using a database management system to institute a database administration role. The term "database" simply implies a centrally *planned* and *controlled* collection of mechanized data. The need for a database administration role arises when an organization makes a commitment to the centralized planning and control of data rather than allowing its planning and control to be dispersed across a number of users of data.

Centralized planning and control does not necessarily mean *physically* centralized planning and control nor a *physically* centralized database. It is quite possible planning and control will be delegated and decentralized in the normal manner. Similarly, it is quite possible a distributed database may be a more effective and efficient way of processing data within the organization. Centralized planning and control simply implies ultimate responsibility for the database is vested in a single organization role—the database administrator.

For management to commit an organization to centralized planning and control of data and for users to relinquish control over data to a central authority on an ongoing basis, certain objectives must be accomplished in managing the database (see Everest [1982]):

Objective	Explanation
Sharability	A fundamental objective of database management is that the database be shared. This means multiple users of the database with different processes should have access to the same data at virtually the same time.

Availability	Availability means the database should be available to users when it is needed, where it is needed, and in the form it is needed. This implies diverse languages and usage modes should be available to satisfy diverse user needs.
Evolvability	Evolvability means the database must be able to change in response to changing needs. It implies not only the ability to expand but also the ability to contract.
Database Integrity	Database integrity means the data in the database must be unimpaired, complete, pure, etc. Maintenance of database integrity is especially critical in a shared data environment. An error in data affects all users.

One means to achieving these objectives is a database management system. Another means is the database administrator.

Consider some of the problems that arise through attempting to achieve the objectives of database management. Sharing data among various users inevitably means conflict will arise among these users. For example, one user may need a data structure that facilitates fast batch processing. Another user may need a data structure that facilitates fast online access to data. The data structure each user needs may be unsatisfactory from the viewpoint of the other user. Users cannot pursue their individual goals oblivious to the needs of other users; otherwise, suboptimization of the organization's overall goals may result. In the event of conflict, compromise must take place. The database administrator performs a mediating function to help achieve this compromise (Figure 7.1).

Achieving the other objectives of managing the database requires someone to have a global knowledge of organization requirements. Maintaining the availability of the database means user requirements for education, documentation, and access tools must be examined continuously. Presumably not all needs can be satisfied. Choices must be made subject to resource constraints. Achieving evolvability means current requirements for database use must be tempered by future requirements. For example, a suboptimal data structure may have to be designed for current use to avoid costly restructuring in the future as the number of users expands and different needs have to be satisfied. Data integrity controls must be built that satisfy the requirements of future users of the data as well as current users. It is the database administrator's responsibility to adopt the global perspective of organization needs required to achieve these objectives.

SOME AUDIT CONSIDERATIONS

If an organization has made a commitment to centralized planning and control of data and has instituted a database administration role within its management control framework, the audit function is impacted in three ways. First, since much of the communications within a database environment is chan-

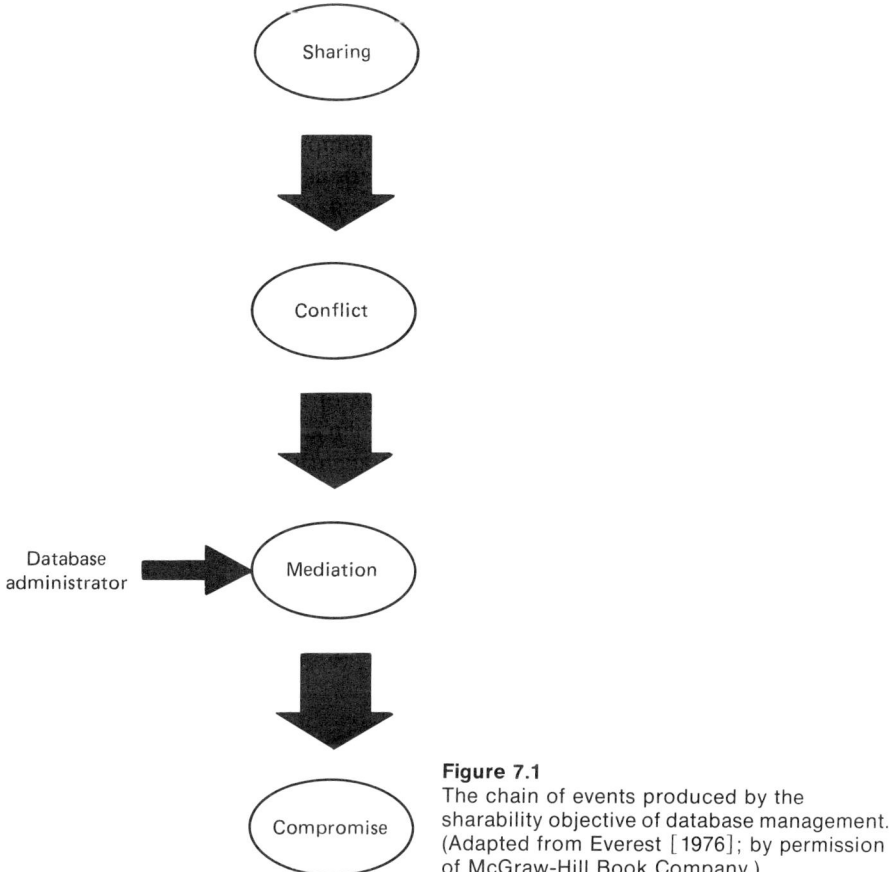

Figure 7.1
The chain of events produced by the sharability objective of database management. (Adapted from Everest [1976]; by permission of McGraw-Hill Book Company.)

neled through the database administrator, the database administrator is an important source of information on strengths and weaknesses within the environment. Second, the database administrator provides technical and administrative information that the auditor needs to know and in some cases database tools that the auditor needs to use. For example, the database administrator may make available to the auditor documentation describing the data structures in the database and software that will extract data from the database. Third, since the ongoing existence of a database environment is directly dependent on the quality of its database administrator, the auditor must have a sound knowledge of the functions that should be performed by the database administrator so the performance of these functions can be evaluated.

FUNCTIONS OF THE DATABASE ADMINISTRATOR

Database administration involves five major functions (see Everest and Weber [1979] and Lyon [1976]):

1 Defining, creating, and retiring data
2 Making the database available to users
3 Informing and servicing users
4 Maintaining database integrity
5 Monitoring operations and performance

Since the creation of a database administration role often occurs when an installation purchases a database management system, the following discussion assumes the existence of a database management system to aid the database administrator perform the various functions required by the role. If a database management system is unavailable, the tasks of the database administrator will be more difficult to perform. Nevertheless, they can be accomplished partially at least.

Defining, Creating, and Retiring Data

When a user requires data that does not currently exist, the life cycle of data commences. The first step is the design of a logical structure that mirrors the user's "real world" view of the structure naturally inherent in the data. During this initial definition stage, compromise may be involved. Different users may perceive data differently, and it may be impossible to incorporate every perception in the database. The database administrator must determine a structure that satisfies the needs of all users.

Once a data structure has been determined, the new structure is introduced formally into the database management system through the data definition language of the system. Again, compromise may be involved. Each database management system permits only certain kinds of data structures to be defined, and so the initial data structure may have to be modified to make it acceptable to the system. For example, the user may view the data as a network. However, the database management system may not provide for a network structure within its data structure class. Thus, the initial data structure may have to be modified into a tree structure or some other type of data structure.

Once the logical definition process is complete, the database administrator must determine how the data structure will be defined physically on the storage media used. During this stage the layout of the data on storage, indexes to be used, orderings, access paths, etc., are specified. Since resources typically are not unlimited, compromise is again a facet of the physical design process. For example, the database administrator may be unable to create an index allowing fast access to the data because of storage constraints.

When the new data definition has been established, the database then must be populated with the data according to that definition. The database administrator is responsible for specifying the methods to be used in capturing the data and populating the database. Typically, intensive validation and editing procedures are needed during this phase to ensure the quality of the data obtained.

As user needs change, so do the existing data structures undergo modification. A major problem that occurs when data redefinition must be undertaken is determining the impact of the redefinition on the database environment. The redefinition may affect some or all existing programs and users. The database administrator is responsible for determining the effects of a redefinition and then establishing how the changes can be accomplished.

As the usefulness of data declines it must be retired. Management policies must be established to provide guidelines for data retention. The database administrator is responsible for executing these policies.

Making the Database Available to Users

Users of the database need various tools to interrogate and update the database. These tools have to be purchased or developed. Since user needs change over time, the database administrator is responsible for monitoring these changes and ensuring the required tools are available on a timely basis. Where possible the tools, whether they be purchased or developed, should have generalized capabilities so they adapt better to changes in user needs. Any new tool placed into production must be comprehensively tested by the database administrator.

Informing and Servicing Users

As the focal point in a database environment, the database administrator is responsible for informing and assisting users, and educating and training users. These activities are accomplished in the normal ways.

Users must know the current status of the database and any changes made to supporting systems. For example, they need to know if a portion of the database has been damaged or a new availability tool has been purchased or developed.

To inform and service users the database administrator must establish a viable communication system. There are a number of means; for example, documentation, memoranda, and system messages. Some typical examples of documentation needed are:

1 A dictionary of data names, cross-referenced to associated data names
2 Semantic descriptions of data elements
3 Physical storage information to aid efficient use of data
4 Data retention information
5 Reference and user manuals

A memorandum system must inform users on such matters as:

1 Potential hazards or loss of integrity of the database
2 New standards implemented
3 New user tools available
4 Training courses to be given

Maintaining Database Integrity

To maintain the integrity of the database, the database administrator must undertake six control measures: (*a*) definition control, (*b*) existence control, (*c*) access control, (*d*) update control, (*e*) concurrency control, and (*f*) quality control (see, further, Everest [1982]).

Definition Control Definition controls seek to establish correspondence between the database and its definition at all times. The database administrator must ensure neither a program nor a procedure could destroy this correspondence. For example, application system programs should not be permitted to manipulate pointers in the database in case a defined access path is destroyed.

Existence Control The database administrator protects the existence of the database by establishing suitable backup and recovery procedures. Chapter 15 provides an extensive discussion of these procedures.

Access Control Access controls prevent inadvertent or unauthorized disclosure of data in the database. Access controls take many forms: passwords, physical locks on terminals, voice prints, etc. Various levels of access controls are needed for data items, groups, and files. Someone other than the database administrator should be responsible for assigning users a level of access authorization. However, the database administrator should implement the required access controls and provide advice on the level of access authorization a user should have assigned. By separating duties in this way there is less scope for improper access authorizations to be established.

Update Control Update controls restrict update of the database to authorized users. Update authorization takes two forms. The first form permits only addition of data to the database. The second form allows a user to change or delete existing data. Various refinements on these update forms exist. For example, a user may only be permitted to add data to the end of a file. The database administrator must establish the level of update authorization appropriate for each user.

Concurrency Control Data integrity problems arise when two update processes are allowed access to the same data item at the same time. The database may end up in an inconsistent state. The database administrator must establish controls to ensure this situation does not arise. Chapter 12 provides an extensive discussion of these issues.

Quality Control Quality controls ensure the accuracy, completeness, and consistency of data maintained on the database. Included within this set of controls are traditional measures such as program validation of input data and batch controls over data transit through the organization. The database administrator is responsible for ensuring that user-specified validation procedures are complete and consistent.

Monitoring Operations

Finally, the database administrator must monitor operations and performance within the database management system. Since the price of generality within a database management system usually is increased processing overhead, this function is important if overall system degradation is to be prevented.

To accomplish this task the database administrator uses various monitors to gather performance statistics. For example, the database administrator may monitor the types and frequency of user requests against the database with a view to designing a more efficient logical or physical structure. Response time statistics indicate when reorganization of the database might be necessary. Other statistics indicate the need for increased access controls, existence controls, or quality controls.

In part, the integrity of the database is dependent on users being able to use the database efficiently. A typical response to processing inefficiencies is decreased control requirements. Furthermore, the future integrity of the database is dependent on the ability of the system to respond in time to changing user needs. Perceiving the required changes necessitates monitoring the database environment on a timely basis.

ORGANIZATIONAL CONSIDERATIONS

The functions of the database administrator dictate a position of importance within the organization hierarchy of the computer installation. The extent of the responsibilities vested in the database administrator position requires the position has substantial authority.

Figure 7.2 shows a possible organization chart where the installation is organized on a functional basis. If the database administrator is to be capable of

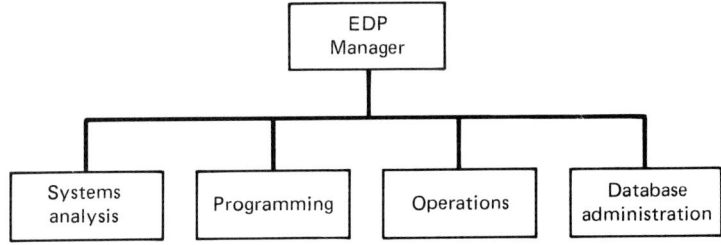

Figure 7.2
Possible position of the database administrator within the computer installation's organizational hierarchy.

performing a mediation function, the position cannot be subordinate to any functional or project group. This would destroy the database administrator's position of independence. Users of the database would lose confidence in the database administrator's ability to act in an unbiased manner. The database administrator must report directly to the EDP manager if a position of independence is to be maintained.

If a computer installation has a database administrator, the auditor should check the organizational position has authority commensurate with the responsibilities assigned the position. The responsibilities of the position would depend upon the organization's commitment to database management and how far the organization has moved toward a full database management system environment.

DATA DICTIONARY

A major tool available to assist the database administrator is the data dictionary. The data dictionary should provide definitional information on all the data contained in the database.

Unfortunately, the current implementations of many data dictionaries are incomplete. The designers of these data dictionaries have taken only a limited view of the information needed to fully define data within a database environment. Plagman and Altshuler [1972] argue a database management system needs a single, complete data definition. This definition must serve both people and processes. The current data dictionaries are oriented toward serving people. They do not provide the information needed by processes (programs) that operate on the database.

Elements of a Data Dictionary System

Everest [1982] describes three major elements needed to completely define a database:

Element	Description
Structural Information: Items, Groups, Relations	A data structure is built upon items, groups of items, and relations between items and groups. Structural elements have names for external human use and internal process use. Synonyms for structural elements may exist. A value set describes the allowable values for a data item. The value set may be defined in terms of a value class: numeric, string, alphabetical, etc. A data item has a defined length. It may be fixed or variable. Groups are collections of data items or other groups and may be repeating or nonrepeating, depending on whether there are multiple instances of the group. Relations may be hierarchical or associative.

Storage and Access Information	Structural information is oriented primarily toward the user. It does not provide sufficient information for system processes to store and access the data. Storage and access information defines how the data structure is mapped onto storage devices. It describes how the data structure is linearized and partitioned for physical mapping purposes, how item values and group instances are delimited, the bases used for access paths, and the allocation of physical storage to the data.
Nonstructural Information	Nonstructural information provides additional information primarily for the users of the database. It includes report formats, validation criteria, source documents used to create the data, programs referencing the data items, person responsible for the data, etc. Adams [1976] provides an extensive description of nonstructural information that can be included in a data dictionary.

If a data dictionary does not contain all these elements, it will be inadequate to meet all the needs of users and processes. Since many of the current data dictionaries contain incomplete data definitions for processes, additional data definitions must be constructed to supplement the data dictionary. The inevitable problems arise when two separate definitions of the same data exist. The update task is more onerous and inconsistencies will occur between the definitions. What is needed is a single, complete definition. In this sense the term "data dictionary" is unfortunate since it implies only a partial user-oriented definition of the database. The more comprehensive term "database definition" should be used.

Taking an inventory of all data is extremely costly. Particularly with respect to nonstructural information, the database administrator should weigh the costs and benefits of collecting and maintaining the information. If the installation is not using a database management system or the database management system being used has incomplete facilities for data definition, a number of software packages are available to assist the database administrator with the task of data definition. Adams [1976] provides a description of several of these packages. They provide the normal facilities for creation, update, and retrieval of data from the data dictionary. Figure 7.3 illustrates the major facilities available to the user. Alternatively, the installation may write specific software if packages are unsuitable.

Audit Aspects of a Data Dictionary

There are two implications for the auditor when an installation uses a data dictionary. First, the data dictionary assists the installation achieve asset safeguarding, data integrity, and system efficiency. Second, the existence of a data dictionary facilitates the audit process.

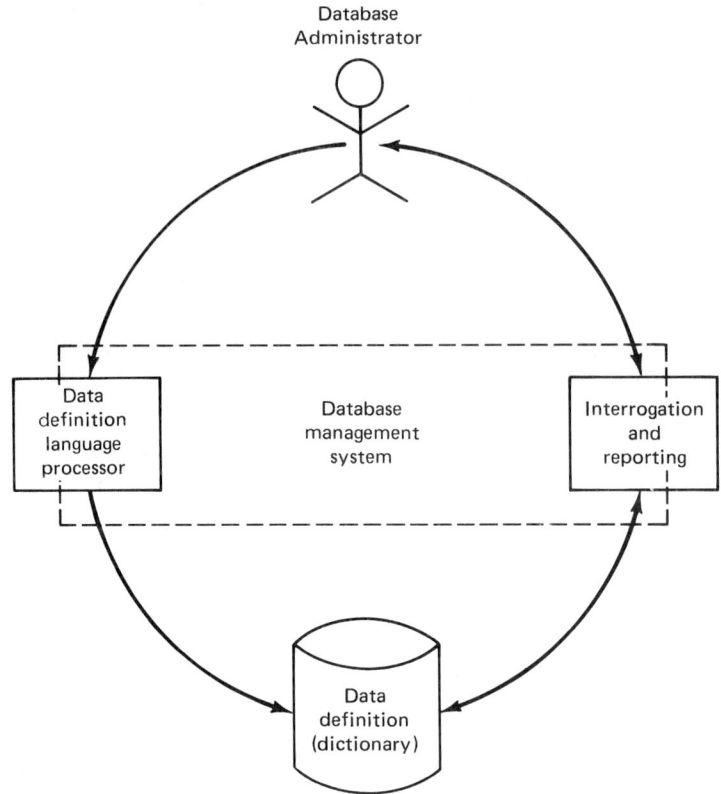

Figure 7.3
Major user facilities in a data dictionary package.

Control Aspects The data dictionary is a critical master file within the installation and it should be subject to various security, backup, and recovery controls. Loss or destruction of the data dictionary would severely impair the operations of the installation. A duplicate copy of the data dictionary should be stored at off-site premises. The privacy of data in the data dictionary is also important. Since the data dictionary contains detailed information supporting all systems within the installation, access controls must be established to prevent unauthorized use of this information.

If an organization commits itself to establishing a database and using a data dictionary to support the database, the auditor has to ensure this commitment extends to all users of the database. A data dictionary can be maintained only if it has the active support of all users of the database. A data dictionary imposes constraints on database users. Naming and numbering conventions must be established. Creation, update, and retirement of any element in the data dictionary requires the approval of the database administrator. From a user's viewpoint, complying with these requirements can be irksome. However, unless the administrative support system functions correctly, the data dictionary will decline in usefulness.

Usage Aspects The auditor is also a user of the data dictionary. It provides structural information that the auditor needs to be able to use software for evidence collection purposes. The nonstructural information provided by the data dictionary is also useful. For example, the auditor can examine the adequacy of the validation criteria applied to various data elements if this information is contained in the data dictionary. If the auditor wishes to trace a data item's path through an application system, the data dictionary provides information on the programs that use the data item, the files where the data item is stored, and the reports where the data item is printed.

CONTROL OVER THE DATABASE ADMINISTRATOR

Even a cursory examination of the functions that should be performed by the database administrator shows this role provides a position of unique power within a database environment. This power can be used to the organization's advantage or it can be abused. On the one hand, centralizing certain functions to be performed in a database environment improves communication, coordination, and control. On the other hand, vesting substantial power in a single organization position runs contrary to the fundamental principles of sound internal control. The auditor must be aware of the control weaknesses resulting when a database administration position exists and remedial measures that are available to reduce the potential effects of these weaknesses.

Control Weaknesses

Besides the control problems that can result from improper role performance by the database administrator, two other aspects of the database administrator's position represent direct threats to data integrity. First, the existence of the database administration role at least partially violates the traditional control principle of separation of duties. Second, the database administrator has available tools, which though necessary for the performance of various functions, also can be used to override established controls.

Inadequate Separation of Duties Traditionally, separation of duties has been used as an internal control method to prevent any one individual from having sufficient power to perpetrate a fraud, or as a check on the correct performance of one person's duties by other personnel. For simple systems having well-defined processes and few interfaces with other systems, this fundamental principle of internal control causes few problems. However, as systems become more complex, the number of interfaces among subsystems increases, the risk of error in the communication process increases, and separation of duties can cause rather than prevent control problems. Control is increased in complex systems by simplifying processes and decreasing the number of interfaces existing among subsystems.

The concept of a database administrator arose in response to the problems presented by the complexity of a database environment. A database administration position reduces the number of interfaces needed among the users of a database by channeling communications through a single point, thereby increasing control. A tradeoff must be made with the decreased control caused by vesting substantial power in a single position.

Availability of Tools to Override Database Integrity Since the database administrator has available tools to set up many of the controls needed over the database, the corresponding power exists to override these controls. For example, tools exist to establish various levels of access and update authorization, find out user passwords, restructure the database, etc. The database administrator can assign a program a level of access and update authorization that will override all other controls. Confidential data can be examined by finding out a user's password. Access paths can be eliminated to remove records from an audit trail. Database tools must be used only for their intended purposes.

Remedial Measures

Control over the database administrator presents many of the same problems that arise with controlling any senior position within the organization. Primary emphasis must be placed on administrative controls, though a set of technical controls are available, depending on the sophistication of the hardware and software used within the database environment. The extent of the controls used depends on cost-benefit considerations.

Assign Appropriate Seniority to the Position As discussed previously, to be able to function effectively and efficiently the database administrator must hold a senior position within the computer installation's organization hierarchy. Individuals who attain the position must be considered trustworthy and have been subject to the scrutiny that all senior personnel should undergo. Standard control procedures should be applied such as background checking, interviewing, and bonding. Further, the position should be reviewed regularly and the person holding the position evaluated.

Separate Duties to the Extent Possible Careful thought should be given to how the duties of the database administrator can be separated without unduly impairing the functions of the role. If a database administration *group* exists rather than a single database administrator, different functions may be assigned different members of the group. For example, different personnel might be responsible for monitoring, data retirement, design of access controls, establishment of access controls, etc.

TABLE 7.1
POSSIBLE BREAKDOWN OF AUTHORITY AND RESPONSIBILITY OVER DATABASE SERVICING TOOLS

Function	Person responsible
Storage of source code, listings, and documentation	Installation librarian
Object code	Program librarian
Use of database tools	Database administrator
Log of uses of database tools	Operations manager
Update and maintenance	Programming manager

Another basis for separating duties is to separate authority to use a database servicing tool from the authority to store and maintain the tool. Table 7.1 presents a possible breakdown of authority and responsibility over database servicing tools. The installation librarian has responsibility for safeguarding the source code and documentation for the tools. Only the programming manager can gain access to this source code and documentation for update and maintenance purposes. Source code may not be available if the tool has been supplied by a database management system vendor. The program librarian exercises control over the object code. Release of the object code for use might require the joint authority of the operations manager and the database administrator. The operations manager should have responsibility for safeguarding any machine logs maintained on activities related to database servicing tools.

Maintain Logs Two types of logs can be kept to record the activities of the database administrator: (*a*) manual logs and (*b*) machine logs. Manual logs record such activities as the database administrator's requests for access to the database, the use of servicing tools, the database administrator's and operations manager's requests for object code from the program librarian, the programming manager's requests for source code listings and documentation from the installation librarian, and the return of source code listings and documentation to the installation librarian. Where possible, machine logs should record similar activities to provide an independent check on the manual logs. For example, the operating system should keep a log of the database administrator's accesses to the database.

Periodically the auditor should check the correspondence between the two logs and attempt to detect any unauthorized activity. For example, when the database administrator uses a servicing tool, the auditor should check to see an unauthorized copy of the object code was not made. Similarly, if a maintenance programmer retrieves a copy of source code from a program file, the auditor should check to see no other copies were made.

Training and Rotation of Duties If the size of the installation warrants a database administration group rather than a single database administrator, control can also be exercised through training and rotation of duties. Training gives several personnel the capabilities needed to perform a required task, thereby allowing duties to be rotated among the members of the database administration group.

SUMMARY

A key element in the management control framework of a computer installation is the database administrator. Organizations establish a database administration position when they give full recognition to data as an important resource and make a commitment to centralized planning and control of data.

A database administration position impacts the audit in several ways. First, the database administrator provides the auditor with information on strengths and weaknesses within the database environment. Second, the database administrator provides the auditor with administrative and technical information necessary for the auditor to be able to carry out the evidence collection and evaluation functions. Third, since proper performance of the database administration role is critical to maintaining asset safeguarding, data integrity, effectiveness, and efficiency in a database environment, the auditor must know what functions the database administrator should perform as a basis for evaluating the role.

The database administrator performs five major functions: (*a*) defining, creating, and retiring data, (*b*) making the database available to users, (*c*) informing and servicing users, (*d*) maintaining database integrity, and (*e*) monitoring operations and performance. The database administrator acts as a mediator when the sharing of data produces conflict among users which requires compromise. This mediation role necessitates a position of independence. Thus, the database administrator should report directly to the EDP manager and not be responsible to any functional or project group within the installation.

The position of power held by the database administrator and the availability of servicing tools needed to perform database administration functions create special control problems. Several remedial steps can be undertaken to increase control; for example, separating duties to the extent possible with the position and maintaining logs to record activities relating to the database administration role.

REVIEW QUESTIONS

7.1. What are the objectives of database management? Why is a database administrator needed to help accomplish these objectives?

7.2. Is it necessary for a computer installation to be using a database management system before it institutes a database administration role? Support your answer.

7.3. Sharing of data among multiple users inevitably produces conflict among those users. What part does the database administrator play when conflict arises?

7.4. What are the database administrator's responsibilities with respect to the definition of data?

7.5. What is meant by populating the database? What steps should the database administrator undertake to preserve data integrity when the database is being populated?

7.6. What is the difference between database restructuring and database reorganization? What are the implications of database restructuring and database reorganization for:

  a. data integrity
  b. system effectiveness
  c. system efficiency

  In each case give an example of the impact of restructuring and reorganization.

7.7. How can the database administrator "comprehensively test" a new availability tool acquired for database users?

7.8. Why should the database administrator be responsible for informing and servicing users and not someone else be responsible for this function within a database environment?

7.9. Briefly explain the database administrator's responsibilities with respect to:

  a. definition control
  b. existence control
  c. access control
  d. update control
  e. concurrency control
  f. quality control

7.10. Give three performance statistics that the database administrator might collect to improve performance within the database environment.

7.11. To maintain independence the database administrator must hold a senior position within the organization hierarchy of the computer installation. Explain.

7.12. What is a data dictionary? Explain the relationship between a data dictionary and the database definition.

7.13. Briefly describe the major elements of a database definition and give examples of each. What are the possible outcomes if a data dictionary does not contain each of these elements?

7.14. Why is it important to exercise control over the data dictionary? Give three control procedures which should be used.

7.15. Why is obtaining support for a data dictionary from programmers and systems analysts sometimes difficult? Why is it important to obtain this support? Give some ways in which this support might be obtained.

7.16. How is the auditor a user of the data dictionary? How might the auditor's use of the data dictionary give insights into the problems of other users?

7.17. Explain how the position of the database administrator both strengthens and weakens control. Briefly describe the nature of the tradeoffs involved.

7.18. Give three examples of tools the database administrator needs to perform his/her functions and which also can be used to override database integrity.

7.19. There are two types of remedial measures that can be used to increase control over the database administrator: (*a*) administrative controls and (*b*) technical controls. Explain the nature of each set of controls and give an example of each. Which set of controls do you think will be the more effective, and why?

7.20. Explain how separation of duties can be used to increase control over the database administrator.

7.21. What types of logs should be kept on activities relating to the database administrator? How does the operating system assist in maintaining logs? What alternatives are available to the auditor if the operating system does not maintain logs?

7.22. How can the auditor use logs to examine the activities of the database administrator?

7.23. Why is the database administrator a key element in the audit of a database? Why is it important the auditor has a sound understanding of the functions that should be performed by the database administrator?

7.24. Is there likely to be some relationship between the existence of a database administration role in a computer installation and the overall quality of the management control framework? Explain.

EXERCISES AND CASES

7.1. You are the external auditor for Dumpadollar National Bank, a large bank within the metropolitan area. Dumpadollar has an extensive online realtime update database system.

One of the controls exercised by the data processing management of Dumpadollar is to print out each day a listing of all sensitive utility programs used. This data is obtained from the operating system log. The listing is checked to detect any unauthorized use of these utility programs.

During a review of this log, you notice that Delores Sleek, Dumpadollar's database administrator, had used a pointer maintenance utility on the database. This utility is capable of adding, deleting, or modifying the pointers that establish the logical relationships between records on the database.

You are concerned about unauthorized use of this utility and you express your concern to Harry Thompson, the data processing manager. He explains that sometimes a pointer in the database is corrupted and that Delores is the only person with sufficient knowledge of the database to be able to correct the pointer. When you ask how often a corrupted pointer occurs, Harry informs you that Delores reports the occurrence of one about once a week. When you ask why a corrupted pointer occurs, Harry says he does not know and that you will have to talk with Delores.

Required: Write a brief report to your supervisor documenting why you are concerned about the current situation and informing her what action you now intend to take.

7.2. Some organizations are now moving toward the establishment of a *quality assurance function*. This function has responsibility for the overall integrity of data (and systems) within the organization.

A major reason for setting up this function often is the use of a database management system. In a database environment the traditional "ownership" of data by particular users diminishes or is lost. Data is shared and joint responsibility exists for the integrity of a data item. Unfortunately, one user of a data item may not recognize the integrity requirements of another user; for example, whereas personnel files are notorious for being out of date, it is rare to find a payroll file out of date. Often a payroll section demands a higher level of data integrity in its files than a personnel section. When personnel data is shared, the integrity of the data must meet the minimum level of integrity demanded by the user with the most stringent requirements.

Required: Write a brief report outlining the nature of the interface you think will occur between the quality assurance function and the database administration function in an organization.

7.3. To improve access times to its database, an organization purchases higher density disks. The database administrator is given the responsibility of converting the database from the old disk packs to the new disk packs.

Required: As the internal auditor for the organization, what items would you look for in the conversion plan proposed by the database administrator? Highlight any differences between the conversion plan for the database and the conversion plan that should have been prepared if the organization was converting traditional application system files to higher density disks.

7.4. Wowem Corporation manufactures a wide range of clothing apparel. Wowem is a decentralized organization where different divisions have responsibility for the manufacture and distribution of major product lines.

The corporation uses a database management system for its data processing. The DBMS allows a tree data structure to be created. Wowem's responsibility accounting system has been set up using the DBMS so it has the following tree data structure:

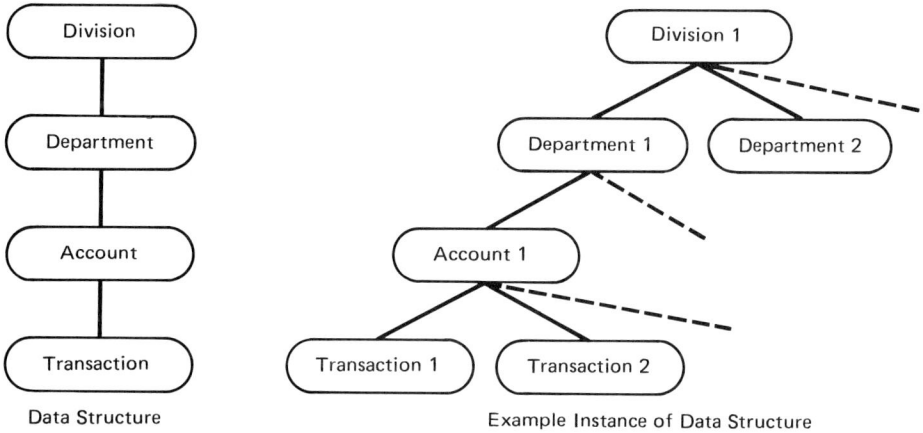

In a major effort to arrest its declining profitability, Wowem undertakes an extensive reorganization of its divisions. Existing product lines are assigned to different divisions, and different departments are assigned to different divisions. As a consequence of this reorganization, the database has to be reorganized.

Required: Wowem's database administrator is responsible for the reorganization of the database to reflect the new lines of responsibility. As the internal auditor for Wowem, you have been asked to review and evaluate the reorganization plan prepared by the database administrator. Make a list of the major items you think should exist in the plan if data integrity is to be preserved during the reorganization process.

REFERENCES

Adams, Donald L. "System and Audit Aspects of a Data Dictionary," *EDPACS* (May 1976), pp. 1-14.

Canning, Richard G. "The 'Data Administrator' Function," *EDP Analyzer* (November 1972), pp. 1-14.

CODASYL Programming Language Committee. *Data Base Task Group Report* (New York: Association for Computing Machinery, 1971).

Everest, Gordon G. "Database Management Systems Tutorial," in Gordon B. Davis and Gordon C. Everest, eds., *Readings in Management Information Systems* (New York: McGraw-Hill Book Company, 1976), pp. 164-187.

———. *Database Management: Objectives, System Functions, and Administration* (New York: McGraw-Hill Book Company, 1982).

———, and Ron Weber. "Database Administration: Functional, Organizational, and Control Perspectives," *EDPACS* (January 1979), pp. 1-10.

GUIDE-SHARE Data Base Requirements Group. *Data Base Management System Requirements* (New York: SHARE, Inc., 1970).

Kroenke, David. *Database Processing* (Chicago, Ill.: Science Research Associates, Inc., 1977).

Lyon, John K. *The Database Administrator* (New York: John Wiley & Sons, Inc., 1976).

Plagman, Bernard K., and Gene P. Altshuler. "A Data Dictionary/Directory System within the Context of an Integrated Corporate Data Base," *AFIPS Fall Joint Computer Conference* (Montvale, N.J.: AFIPS Press, 1972), pp. 1133-1140.

Weber, Ron. "Review of John K. Lyons, 'The Database Administrator'," *EDPACS* (February 1978), pp. 9-17.

Wiederhold, Gio. *Database Design* (New York: McGraw-Hill Book Company, 1977).

CHAPTER 8

OPERATIONS MANAGEMENT

CHAPTER OUTLINE

OVERVIEW OF OPERATIONS MANAGEMENT
COMPUTER OPERATIONS
    Operator Protocols
    Machine Utilization
    Maintenance
DATA PREPARATION
CONTROL SECTION
FILE LIBRARY
    Use of Files
    Maintenance of Files
DOCUMENTATION LIBRARY
SECURITY SECTION
    Responsibilities of the Security Administrator
    Security Threats and Remedial Measures
SUMMARY
REVIEW QUESTIONS
EXERCISES AND CASES
REFERENCES

Ultimately, programs run on a machine. Well-designed program controls can be compromised if an operator alters the state of core at a console. Well-designed program code will execute inefficiently if there is an undesirable job mix in the machine. Preventing these events occurring is the concern of operations management. This chapter examines the functions that operations management should perform. It focuses on the ways in which operations management contributes to asset safeguarding, maintaining data integrity, and achieving system effectiveness and efficiency.

OVERVIEW OF OPERATIONS MANAGEMENT

The primary concern of operations management is the daily running of systems. However, this does not mean that operations management purely has a short-term perspective. When making their decisions on the resources needed to support the future operations of a computer installation, top and EDP management seek the advice of operations management.

Though there are some variations across installations, Figure 8.1 shows operations management often has responsibility for six major functions (see, also, Chapter 4):

1 Computer operations
2 Data preparation
3 Production work flow control
4 File library
5 Documentation library
6 Installation security

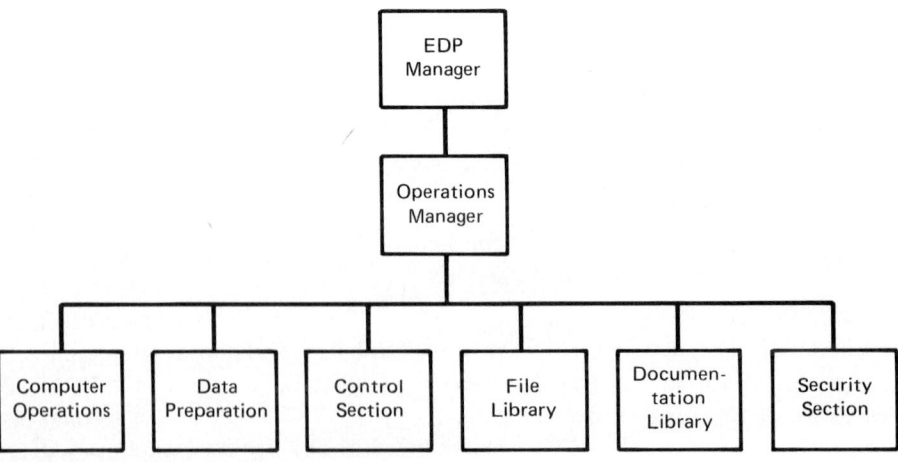

Figure 8.1
Organization chart for the operations management function.

In some ways these functions appear routine and mundane. However, if they are not carried out properly, some serious consequences can occur. For example, poorly trained operators can degrade machine throughput. A disgruntled operations employee can severely damage or destroy the assets of an installation. In one case a file librarian sent out blank tapes for backup and gave operators the installation's master files as scratch files. Thus, the auditor should examine carefully the functions of operations management for potential areas of exposure. The remaining sections of the chapter discuss in more detail each of the functions of operations management.

COMPUTER OPERATIONS

Controls over computer operations govern the ways in which activities are carried out in the computer room. Three sets of controls must exist: (*a*) those that prescribe the functions computer operators should perform; (*b*) those that prescribe how hardware and software is to be utilized; and (*c*) those that prescribe how hardware is to be maintained.

Operator Protocols

A well-managed computer room provides two sources of information on the protocols operators should follow. First, a standards manual details both methods and performance standards for computer operators. The contents of the manual include, for example, procedures for starting up and closing down the machine, actions to be taken upon a system crash, disaster procedures, standard times for mounting and dismounting storage media, prescribed work flow patterns, and descriptions of prohibited activities. Second, application system run manuals detail the procedures to be followed during production running of each system and the resource consumption that can be expected if the system is operating normally. Thus, the standards manual prescribes procedures common across application systems; run manuals prescribe procedures specific to an application system.

From an audit viewpoint a major concern is the existence and enforcement of standards that prevent computer operators from carrying out unauthorized modifications to programs or data. Traditional internal control procedures still apply: rotation of operator duties, use of two or more operators on a shift, compulsory vacations, proper training. However, several other steps can be taken to safeguard assets and protect data integrity. First, operators can be prevented from having free access to file and documentation libraries. The less an operator knows about the detailed logic in a system, the more difficult it is to carry out an unauthorized modification to that system. Similarly, if operators can gain access to program and data files only for production purposes, it becomes more difficult to carry out an unauthorized modification to these files. Second, under normal circumstances operators should be prohibited from using system resources that enable direct "fixes" to be carried out to programs or data; that is, alterations that are not part of the normal production maintenance or modification processes. System resources that allow direct fixes take various forms: instructions that can be entered at the console or programs that operate in privileged mode. Third, the duties of operators should be restricted purely to the running of systems. They should not be responsible for attempting to correct programs or data when an application system fails; this is the responsibility of the project manager for the application. Their knowledge of programming should be sufficiently limited so they cannot easily carry out modifications to program code. From a control viewpoint, career paths that allow an operator to receive programming training while still acting as an operator are suspect.

The record of operator activities is the operating system log (see, also, Chapter 14). Periodically the log can be examined by the operations manager to check operator compliance with standards. Thus, it is important that the operator cannot compromise data recorded on the log. Alterations to the log must not be permitted. If the log is disabled, management must determine whether unauthorized activities have occurred. In some installations where security is highly critical, the log might be maintained on a storage device located at a different site from the computer room.

Machine Utilization

Controls over machine utilization seek to ensure that the computer is used only for authorized purposes and that consumption of system resources is efficient. Production systems should run according to a predetermined schedule set up by applications project managers and the operations manager. Thus, a substantial part of the consumption of system resources can be authorized in advance. Provision must be made in the daily run schedule for other types of activities: system reruns, system crashes, program development activities. Nevertheless, it is usually possible to determine deviations from normal operations. Various daily routine reports should be prepared by operators for the operations manager; for example, reports on completed and uncompleted jobs, a report on downtime, a report on unused machine time. These reports usually can be prepared from data on the machine log (see Chapter 14). The operations manager can examine these reports for exception conditions.

To ensure system resources are used only for the purposes intended, authority must be given for all program runs. In the case of production systems operating on a regular schedule, the computer operations manager can authorize their running; for example, by signing a prepared schedule for the day. In the case of programs being developed, the programmer responsible for the program can authorize compilation and test runs, though the operations manager must authorize whether development and testing is to be carried out during a time block allocated for development and testing or in background mode while production systems are running.

The most difficult authorization problems arise when systems or programs must be rerun because some type of problem has occurred. In general, it is undesirable to allow operators to authorize reruns. The project manager responsible for the system should investigate why the rerun is needed before the rerun takes place. However, in some cases the run may be outside normal working hours, and deadlines may have to be met. The operator in charge of a shift then may have to authorize the rerun. The project manager should undertake follow-up the next day on the reasons for the rerun.

Efficient use of system resources requires decisions to be made on the mix of jobs to be run in the machine at any one time. The objective is to have programs in the mix that do not conflict with each other in terms of the resources they request. For example, it is preferable to run a processor-bound program with an input/output-bound program rather than assign two input/output-bound programs to the machine. Similarly, programs that use files on the same storage device may conflict with each other over the use of a channel if they are run concurrently. The operations manager is responsible for determining a mix of jobs that attempts to maximize the throughput of the machine. This is a difficult task. It highlights a benefit of prior scheduling of production system runs and adhering to that schedule to the extent possible.

Maintenance

Maintenance of computer hardware is either preventive or remedial in nature. Preventive maintenance occurs on a regular basis and includes routine tests and inspections as well as replacement of components. Remedial (repair) maintenance occurs on demand when a machine component fails.

Maintenance typically is performed by an outside vendor. Generally the hardware vendor recommends a maintenance schedule; however, the relative amounts of preventive and remedial maintenance always can be traded off with each other. More frequent preventive maintenance usually means less frequent repair maintenance. Management's problem is to minimize the total cost of both preventive and remedial maintenance (Figure 8.2).

An important factor affecting the frequency with which preventive maintenance is carried out is the location of the computer installation. For example, the computer installation may be at some remote mining site. Repair maintenance may involve several days of waiting while an engineer is flown to the site. The downtime may be intolerable. Thus, more frequent preventive maintenance may be carried out to reduce the likelihood of repair maintenance being needed. Conversely, if the computer installation exists in a large city with ready access to engineers, management may undertake less preventive maintenance and bear the costs of repair maintenance if and when it is needed.

As a basic control, the operations manager should review periodically various maintenance reports prepared by the maintenance engineer and operators; for example, the amount of downtime that has occurred, the amount of time consumed by preventive and repair maintenance, and the amount of main-

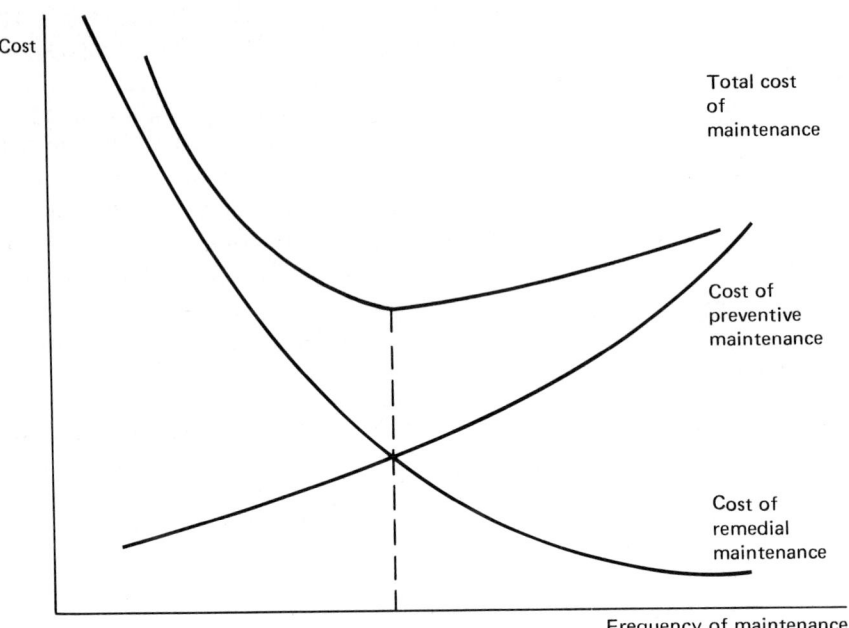

Figure 8.2
Tradeoff between preventive and remedial maintenance.

tenance incurred by each hardware unit. This information is important for replacement decisions and identifying abnormal maintenance cost deviations.

Like system programmers, maintenance engineers cause some difficult control problems for management. Engineers have available to them special hardware and software tools that allow them to bypass the various controls implemented in hardware and software. The tools are necessary if maintenance is to be carried out effectively and efficiently. However, their misuse may mean integrity violations occur. Pinchuk [1974] describes the engineering tools available for one hardware/software system configuration and the ways in which these tools can be used to breach data integrity.

It is difficult to know how much effort should be expended on controlling engineers and what types of controls should be instituted over their activities. There is little empirical evidence showing whether or not engineers are a major source of integrity violations in computer systems. Perhaps this is because the technical expertise required to detect any integrity violation is high. Perhaps it is because the number of violations is small. What is clear, however, is that a high potential exists for engineers to perpetrate an integrity violation.

Unless another engineer is employed to check the work of the maintenance engineer, management must rely on some basic internal control procedures. If possible, engineers should be rotated. Unfortunately this usually causes high maintenance costs as it takes some time to know the idiosyncracies of a particular machine; however, it ensures a backup engineer exists if the regular engineer is unavailable. Periodically a consultant engineer might be employed to check the work of the maintenance engineer.

If the engineer carries out concurrent maintenance, that is, maintenance during normal production running, if possible, sensitive programs and data should be unloaded. This inhibits any attempt to violate the privacy of data. The engineer also might be required to sign a "nondisclosure" agreement in case sensitive data is exposed in the normal course of duties. With each change of engineer, management should carry out some background checking to assess the likely integrity of the engineer.

DATA PREPARATION

Cardenas [1973] argues that data preparation often is the major bottleneck in the work flow of a computer installation. Moreover, it is a major cost area, often taking about 30–50% of the data processing budget.

Chapter 9 discusses several management decisions that have an important impact on how accurately and efficiently data is converted into machine-readable form: the choice of appropriate data preparation equipment, the choice of the data preparation machine room layout, how jobs should be assigned to keypunch operators, and what training is required for data preparation personnel. The smooth, ongoing daily operations of the data preparation section require several other management decisions to be made.

As with the hardware in the computer room, a regular maintenance schedule must be set up for data preparation equipment. The equipment vendor typically recommends a schedule; management must ensure compliance with this schedule. Any abnormal problems that are experienced with particular equipment can be identified if regular maintenance is carried out and reports are prepared.

The data preparation section often accepts responsibility for storing the data files submitted as input to the computer. Source documents are returned to the user after they have been keypunched; the cards, paper tape, or magnetic tape on which the source data has been keypunched are returned to the data preparation section. The keypunched data constitutes backup in case input files are corrupted or lost so it must be stored securely. Decisions also must be made by the operations manager and applications project manager on how long the data will be retained. Once the retention period has expired, the data must be destroyed in a secure manner; for example, punch cards and paper tape should be shredded. Input data can be just as valuable as a master file to a competitor or a person wanting to perpetrate a fraud.

Management must ensure backup exists for the data preparation equipment. Often the focus is on ensuring backup exists for the hardware and software in the computer room. However, these resources will stand idle if they have no input data to process. Usually it is easy to find suitable backup for data preparation equipment. Nevertheless, if the equipment has its own programmed data validation capabilities (e.g. as with key-to-disk), operations management must ensure that backup copies of the data validation software also exist.

CONTROL SECTION

The control section in a computer installation manages the flow of data between users and the installation and between data preparation and the computer room (Figure 8.3). There are four major reasons for setting up a control section within a computer installation. First, it facilitates the orderly flow of work to and from the computer installation and within the computer installation. Second, it assigns the responsibility for this work flow to some group. Thus, the control section becomes the focal point for queries about the work flow. For users, the control section also becomes the focal point for queries about the quality of work performed. Third, setting up a control section applies the traditional control principle of separation of duties. It becomes more difficult for operators and data preparation personnel to collude and perpetrate a fraud; for example, by altering input data. Fourth, the control section often detects simple errors made during data processing.

The control section performs several major functions. First, it receives input from users. This input is checked to see that it is in order by scanning it for reasonableness and completeness and checking control totals; then it is entered in a log. Second, the input is dispatched either to the computer room or data preparation. In some cases the data already may be in machine-readable

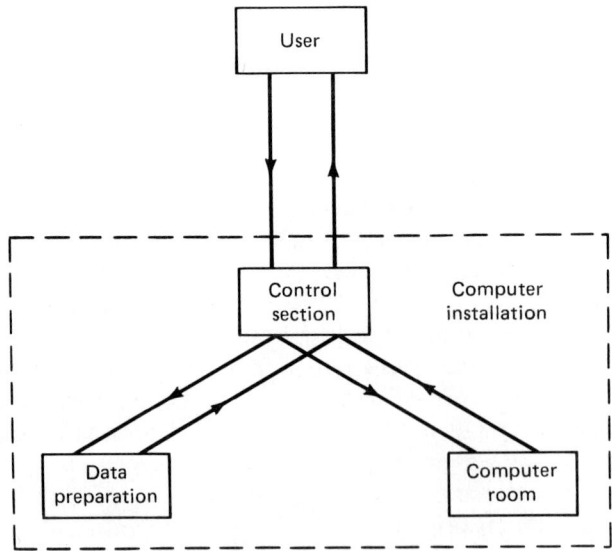

Figure 8.3
Control section as the focal point for data flow in computer data processing.

form; for example, it can be read by an optical character recognition device. Otherwise, it must be keypunched. Third, after data preparation is complete, the control section collects the source data and machine-readable data and checks to see all data needed for the production run has been prepared. It then dispatches the machine-readable data to the computer room. Fourth, after the production run, the control section collects the output and machine-readable data from the computer room. It scans the output for completeness and any obvious errors. Finally, the system output and source data are returned to users, and the machine-readable input is returned to the data preparation section.

Often the control section performs other functions. If the installation uses a transfer pricing system (see Chapter 4), the control section may have responsibility for billing users, collecting receipts, and follow-up on unpaid accounts. It may be responsible for ordering all supplies—cards, tapes, disks, paper, forms, etc.—for the installation. Typically, it is the first point of contact for inquiries directed to the computer installation; for example, a query about missing output or the availability of consulting advice.

FILE LIBRARY

The file library section is responsible for maintaining the installation's library of machine-readable files. The section has two major functions. First, it attempts to ensure files are used only for the purposes intended. Control must be exercised over two types of files: program files and data files. Second, it maintains (in correct working order) the storage media used for files.

Use of Files

A large computer installation may have several thousand files. It is a substantial management problem to ensure correct control and use of these files. A basic prerequisite for effective and efficient management is an orderly filing system. The filing system must encompass procedures for storing and retrieving the files and storage media and maintaining records of events that occur to the files and the storage media.

Files should be stored in a secure room adjacent to or near the computer room to facilitate the issue of files for processing and their return upon completion of processing. Like the computer room, the file storage room must have a stable environment: constant temperature, dust free, etc. Many types of cabinets are available for secure storage of files.

To keep a record of all events that occur to files, a log must be maintained. The log contains information such as:

1 Name of file
2 Programs that access the file
3 Persons authorized to use the file
4 Person ultimately responsible for the file

5 Version number of the file
6 Creation date
7 Scratch date
8 Serial number of storage medium, e.g., tape number
9 Backup requirements
10 Place where backup stored
11 History of uses—date issued, to whom, for what purpose, date returned

The log serves two purposes. First, it facilitates routine, daily operations. For example, if a file is requested for production purposes, it must be retrieved from its storage location and several checks performed: the person requesting the file is authorized to use it, the file is to be used for an allowed purpose, there are no special "hold" instructions on the file. Second, the log provides the basic source data for management reports on file use. Periodically, various exception reports might be prepared; for example, issues of files to persons other than those listed as authorized to use the file.

A librarian package can be used to facilitate control and use of *program* files. These packages have several types of functional capabilities (see, also, Adams [1973, 1974]):

Functional capabilities	Examples
Update Capabilities	Addition, modification, deletion of program source code; institution of temporary changes to source code; resequencing of source code; editing capabilities, e.g., global change of a particular character string; insertion of special documentation records
Integrity Capabilities	Access control over programs through the use of passwords; each source program assigned a modification number and version number; each source statement has an associated creation date; encryption and data compaction facilities; automatic creation of backup
Report Capabilities	Listing of additions, deletions, modifications; index of programs and their attributes, e.g., programmer, size, purpose; report on storage space utilization by library

For data files a large installation typically requires a computer system to maintain its file library records and prepare reports. Manually searching the records to find out what files can be scratched or what files are stored on a particular disk pack may require inordinate amounts of time.

Care must be taken when the retention dates of files expire and they are issued as scratch files. In some computer systems, scratching simply means the header information for the file is changed; however, the data in the file is not overwritten. Thus, the program that next uses the file simply can read the data and the privacy of the data is violated.

For some peripheral devices a scratch command causes the device's control unit to disconnect the device from the channel and under microprogram control overwrite data on the file. If the device does not undertake this action, sensitive data should be destroyed before the file is issued as a scratch file. Magnetic tape files can be demagnetized (*degaussed*). Disk and drum files can be *sanitized;* that is, the data on the disk file can be overwritten (see, further, Short [1974]).

The placement of multiple files on a single storage medium can cause control problems. The system must ensure that a program reading one file cannot backspace itself into another file and read sensitive data. Thus, the placement of files on storage media should be managed carefully. Sensitive files might be allocated sole use of a storage medium if there is some risk of a program reading outside file boundaries.

Maintenance of Files

Magnetic storage media periodically require cleaning and recertification. A log must be kept on each storage medium containing:

1 Serial number of the storage medium
2 Location
3 Files stored on the medium
4 Maintenance instructions
5 History of failures – read/write errors
6 Maintenance record – cleaning, recertification
7 History of uses – date issued, to whom, for what purpose, date returned

If tapes and disks are sent outside the organization for cleaning and recertification, care must be taken to erase any sensitive data contained on the media. If the worn ends of magnetic tapes are to be clipped, degaussing should be undertaken first in case the clippings contain sensitive information. An unauthorized person may retrieve the clippings from a trash can and examine the data recorded on the clippings. As a further protective measure the clippings can be destroyed.

Various file management reports can be prepared from the maintenance log; for example:

1 Listing of media requiring maintenance
2 Media experiencing an abnormal number of read/write errors
3 Media that should be retired from use

On the basis of these reports, management may decide to move files from one storage medium to another. For example, critical master files might be stored only on new disk packs. If a disk pack starts to experience an abnormal number of read/write errors, files on the disk may be moved to another disk. Older storage media might be used for backup purposes only.

Again, requirements for cross-referencing data – for example, files with storage media – highlight the need for a computer system to support file library functions. The system needed is relatively simple; however, the volume of data on file usage that must be processed in even a moderate-sized installation makes computer support almost a necessity.

DOCUMENTATION LIBRARY

The documentation library contains the documentation supporting all systems run by the installation: system documentation, program documentation, operator run manuals, and user manuals. The documentation library also may be the site where the installation's standard manual is kept and maintained, records of installation memoranda are kept, and books and journals are kept.

The documentation librarian has three major functions: (*a*) ensuring documentation is stored securely, (*b*) issuing documentation to authorized personnel only, and (*c*) maintaining adequate backup for documentation. Secure storage can be achieved by having documentation stored in cabinets in a separate room. A log of issues and returns of documentation should be kept. Special authority might be needed to obtain some documentation; for example, the programming manager's authority to obtain program documentation and a project manager's authority to obtain system documentation.

Providing adequate backup for documentation can be a difficult task. It is easy to copy a magnetic file for backup. It is also relatively easy to make additional copies of initial documentation for backup. However, keeping backup documentation up to date in light of changes can be an onerous task, simply because it is often awkward and inconvenient to amend program listings, flowcharts, textual descriptions, etc. It is not uncommon to find good backup for files on magnetic media and poor backup for documentation.

One solution to the problem of maintaining up-to-date backup for documentation is to store documentation on magnetic media. The widespread availability of word processing equipment and computer text processors makes this means of backup for documentation available to many computer installations (see McNurlin [1978*a*, 1978*b*]). When documentation is altered, the master cassette, diskette, etc., is updated and a copy made for backup purposes. Maintaining documentation on magnetic media also has other advantages:

1 Facilitates amendments and production of revised hard copy documentation; consequently the time needed and labor costs incurred to carry out amendments should be reduced.

2 If documentation is maintained online, provides increased accessibility to information. The auditor must then assess whether or not adequate access controls have been installed (see Chapter 10).

3 If the word processing system is connected to a communications network, facilitates distribution of documentation (e.g. user manuals) and amendments to authorized users. The auditor must then assess whether or not adequate communications controls have been installed (see Chapter 10).

4 An audit trail of accesses to the documentation can be maintained by the system that manages use and control of the documentation.

5 Allows automation of controls over documentation; thus, the documentation is less susceptible to corruption through human error.

Another solution to the problem of backup of documentation is to microfilm the documentation. However, this can be a time-consuming process. It is not likely to be cost-effective to produce new microfilm every time documentation is changed. Thus, the backup usually will be somewhat out of date.

SECURITY SECTION

The security administrator in a computer installation reports to the operations manager on matters of *physical* security affecting the installation. In some very sensitive installations the security section may exist as an organizational entity separate from operations. However, in general, there is usually insufficient ongoing work to justify this separation, and security falls within the ambit of operations responsibilities.

Responsibilities of the Security Administrator

Security administration involves two major functions. First, the security administrator advises top and EDP management during the formulation of the disaster recovery plan for the installation (see Chapter 4). This advice takes several forms: a listing of potential threats to the installation, an assessment of their importance, a listing of both preventive and detective measures and the associated costs of these measures, and recommendations as to what security measures should be implemented (see, for example, Courtney [1977] and FitzGerald [1978b, 1978c]).

Second, the security administrator is responsible for implementing the security measures chosen by top and EDP management and ensuring that the disaster recovery plan is operable. This involves the acquisition of security devices, formulation of security procedures, training of personnel, regular carrying out of drills, and regular security audits.

Security Threats and Remedial Measures

The major problem for the security administrator is assessing the likely security threats to the installation and cost-effective remedial measures that can be undertaken. Computer centers have been destroyed by aircraft crashes and mobile shovels toppling through walls. It is possible to protect a center from these events; however, it may be very costly. Further, the probability of these events occurring is small.

The following sections discuss various security threats to an installation and some protective measures that can be undertaken. The subject of physical security is complex and somewhat situation specific. AFIPS [1974], Fitz-Gerald [1978a], and Martin [1973] provide extensive checklists for assessing physical security within an installation. As always, the most effective security measures are usually the most costly. The security administrator is responsible for balancing the benefits and costs of the various security measures.

Fire Damage Fire is often the major threat to the physical security of a computer installation. Loss from fire can be substantial. A fire in the Pentagon destroyed $6.7 million worth of hardware and over 7000 magnetic tapes. A fire in First Data Corporation's computer installation in New York City destroyed over $2 million worth of hardware.

Some countries have various public service and government organizations that provide advice on fire protection measures. However, the implementation of a specific system usually requires specialist advice. Some major features of a well-designed fire protection system are:

1 Both automatic and manual fire alarms are placed at strategic locations throughout the installation.

2 An automatic extinguisher system exists that dispenses the appropriate suppressant: water, carbon dioxide, halon.

3 The appropriate types of manual fire extinguishers exist at strategic locations throughout the installation.

4 A control panel shows where in the installation an automatic or manual alarm has been triggered.

5 Beside the control panel, master switches exist for power (including air conditioning) and the automatic extinguisher system.

6 The building has been constructed from fire resistant materials and it is structurally stable when fire damage occurs.

7 Fire extinguishers and fire exits are marked clearly.

8 When a fire alarm is activated a signal is sent automatically to a permanently manned station.

The security officer should arrange regular inspections of all fire protection systems. Proper use of these systems requires staff training and periodic drills. The procedures to be followed during an emergency should be documented.

Water Damage Water damage to a computer installation can be the outcome of a fire; the specific system sprays water that enters hardware, or water pipes may burst. However, water damage results from other sources: cyclones, tornadoes, ice. In 1974 the city of Brisbane experienced freak flooding as the Brisbane River burst its banks. Several computer installations were submerged completely.

Some of the major ways of protecting the installation against water damage are:

1 Where possible have waterproof ceilings, walls, and floors.
2 Ensure an adequate drainage system exists.
3 Install alarms at strategic points within the installation.
4 In flood areas have the installation above the high water level.
5 Have a master switch for all water mains.
6 Use a dry pipe automatic sprinkler system that is charged by an alarm and activated by the fire.
7 Cover hardware with a protective fabric when it is not in use.

Again, regular inspections and regular drills are essential if the disaster plan is to be operational when a situation of potential water damage arises.

Energy Variations Energy variations take the form of increases in power (spikes), decreases in power (brownouts), or loss of power (blackouts). Voltage regulators protect hardware against temporary increases in power; circuit breakers protect the hardware against sustained increases. Batteries will provide power if a temporary loss occurs; however, a generation plant is needed for sustained losses in power. The level of protection needed depends on the utility company's ability to maintain an uninterrupted power source and the likelihood of other disasters occurring (e.g. earthquake) that would destroy the power source.

Power is needed not only to keep the hardware running but also to maintain an acceptable environment for the hardware; that is, an environment that is dust free and relatively constant with respect to temperature and humidity. Thus, careful assessment of the likelihood of unacceptable energy variations is essential to the ongoing operations of the installation.

The security officer has two major responsibilities relating to the maintenance of the energy source for the installation. First, the availability of power should be monitored on an ongoing basis. Abnormal power fluctuations may mean the reliability of the power source has to be reassessed. Second, the impact of any new energy consumer (e.g. new hardware) on the existing power supply must be assessed. The resulting energy drain may mean the existing power source is inadequate and alternative sources have to be considered.

The design of security for the installation must provide for the possibility of total loss of power. For example, certain controls such as doors may failsafe on a power loss. It must be possible to manually deactivate these controls. To the extent that other safeguards such as alarms and extinguisher systems do not have their own independent power source, the security of the installation is weakened.

Structural Damage Structural damage to the installation can occur in several ways: earthquake, wind, mud, snow, avalanche. It may be an outcome of some other disaster; for example, fire. Some installations are more prone to structural damage than others; for example, those situated in an earthquake region.

Preventing disaster occurring because of structural damage is primarily an engineering problem. In the design of a building, the structural stresses that might be placed on a building are considered. However, if a computer is to be housed in the building, the design engineers should be notified so they can provide for any special structural requirements.

If there is some choice on where the computer is to be housed, the site chosen should be the least prone to structural damage; for example, away from a flood plain or an earthquake region. Similarly, it is better to house the computer on an upper floor of a building. It is less susceptible to damage by floods. It also makes unauthorized intrusion more difficult.

Within the installation, hardware and storage cabinets should be secured so they will not tip easily if structural stress is placed on the building; for example, when vibrations occur during an earthquake. If a disk storage cabinet falls, the damage to a disk can be sufficient to make its contents unreadable.

Pollution The ongoing operations of a computer depend upon a pollution-free environment. The major pollutant is dust. Dust arises if there is inadequate filtering of air passing through the air conditioning system or if it is allowed to accumulate on equipment, floors, etc. However, there are some more subtle forms of pollution. Extensive damage to a central processor resulted when a cheese sandwich was left on the unit. It melted with the heat generated by the unit and the cheese seeped onto the electronics.

Several steps can be taken to avoid polluting the installation. Regular cleaning of ceilings, walls, floors, storage cabinets, and equipment is necessary. Vacuuming is especially important, particularly in areas where dust collects; for example, under raised floors. Dust-collecting rugs can be placed at entrances. Floors can be treated with special antistatic compounds. Dust generating activities, for example, paper shredding, decollation, or bursting, should be carried out well away from the computer room. Foodstuffs can be prohibited in certain areas such as the computer room. Regular emptying of wastepaper baskets prevents dust collecting.

In general, pollution is minimized by having good housekeeping procedures. Good househeeping procedures also facilitate the orderly running of the installation. Some are essential if disaster procedures are to be carried out effectively and efficiently. For example, if exits are blocked, personnel may be unable to evacuate the installation quickly enough when a fire occurs.

Unauthorized Intrusion Unauthorized intrusion takes two forms. The intruder physically may enter the installation to steal assets or carry out sabotage. Alternatively, the intruder may eavesdrop on the installation by wiretapping, installing an electronic bug, or using a receiver that picks up electromagnetic signals. One other form of eavesdropping is visual eavesdropping. The intruder may photograph sensitive information or use a telescope to view the information.

Physical intrusion can be inhibited or prevented by erecting various barriers. The building that houses the computer may be protected by a wall or fence. Doors and windows of the building should be secured. Sometimes air conditioning ducts allow unauthorized entry to the building. The intruder simply has to gain access to the roof of the building (perhaps via the fire escape) and crawl through the ducts. The security administrator must ensure these are not potential sources of exposure for the installation.

Alarms and guards can be used to detect an unauthorized intruder. Martin [1973] discusses various types of security devices and systems that signal the presence of an intruder. However, ultimately these defenses may be compromised: a guard may be bribed or a security device deactivated. The last lines of protection are the safes, vaults, or filing cabinets used to store the installation's assets; for example, the program and data files. Even these may not withstand the threats posed by a saboteur intent on destruction.

An intruder also may attempt entrance to the installation using the normal means. A receptionist placed at the entry to the installation can challenge unidentified visitors and provide advance warning of unauthorized intrusion. A badge system can be used to identify the status of personnel within the installation: permanent staff or visitors. All visitors should be escorted by a permanent staff member. Unescorted visitors or persons without a badge should be questioned as to their presence in the installation. A security check might be performed before a visitor is issued a badge.

Eavesdropping breaches the privacy of data. It may be used by an intruder to obtain a password. It may be used to obtain the signals transmitted to an output device. Sometimes these signals can be deciphered to obtain sensitive sales information, geological survey information, engineering design information, etc. Short [1974] reports a case where a van with equipment for receiving and processing electromagnetic signals was parked next to an unshielded computer center. The printer in the van produced the same output as the installation's printer.

Various devices are available to detect the presence of bugs. The security administrator periodically may employ a security firm that possesses these devices to examine the installation.

In a communications network the points most likely to be wiretapped are the junction boxes and the private branch exchange. It is very difficult to wiretap a communications line once it leaves the building in which the computer is housed. The line may be underground, signals may be sent via microwave, several thousand channels may be multiplexed together (see, further, Martin [1973]). Thus, the security administrator should ensure the junction boxes and private branch exchange are secure.

The covers on hardware inhibit much electromagnetic emission. In general, most emission occurs with peripherals; for example, printers and terminals. Some vendors now specifically design their hardware to minimize electromagnetic emission. Shields can be placed around peripherals to further inhibit emission. It is best to keep equipment with high emission levels away from the walls of a building.

Visual eavesdropping can be prevented in several ways. Cameras should not be allowed in the installation. Some installations have no windows; however, staff may object to the absence of natural light. If windows do exist they can be shielded by blinds or curtains. Visual display units and printers can be placed strategically so it is impossible for an intruder outside the building with a telescope or a camera with a telescopic lens to view or photograph output.

SUMMARY

The primary responsibility of operations management is the daily running of systems. However, operations management also advises top and EDP management on the resources that will be needed to support the future operations of the computer installation.

Typically, operations management has responsibility for six functions within the installation: (*a*) computer operations, (*b*) data preparation, (*c*) production work flow control, (*d*) the file library, (*e*) the documentation library, and (*f*) the physical security of the installation. The operations manager must ensure methods and performance standards exist for each function, quality personnel are hired for each function, and the personnel comply with the standards established.

REVIEW QUESTIONS

8.1. What is the role of operations management with respect to long-run planning within the installation? What expertise qualifies them to play this role?

8.2. Give two items in the computer room standards manual and two items in an application system run manual that an auditor may examine from a control viewpoint. Briefly explain why these items are of interest.

8.3. Give a *specific* example of how a direct "fix" made at the console by an operator may compromise controls within an application system. What controls can be used to prevent direct fixes occurring and to detect them when they do occur?

8.4. You are the external auditor for a small–medium size company that uses the computer extensively for its data processing. There is sufficient work for the computer to operate on a six day per week 24 hour a day basis. When you examine the assignment of operators to shifts, you note that only one operator is present for the late night and early morning shifts.

When you raise the potential control problems which result from this action with the operations manager and the EDP manager, they argue one operator can easily run the machine during these periods and they see no reason why they should incur the expense of having another operator present during these shifts.

Required: List the control weaknesses you pointed out to the operations manager and the EDP manager. How will you respond to their argument for using only one operator?

8.5. Briefly explain why it is undesirable to allow operators to authorize reruns of application systems.

8.6. The mix of jobs in a machine usually is chosen to minimize resource contention among the programs running. Is there any reason a mix of jobs might be chosen from the viewpoint of maintaining data integrity?

8.7. Briefly explain the difference between preventive and repair maintenance. Why might an EDP manager decide to increase the amount of preventive maintenance undertaken on a machine?

8.8. Give two routine decisions that management should make on the basis of data contained in the maintenance log.

8.9. Briefly describe two ways in which an engineer might violate data integrity within a computer installation. List some controls that might be exercised over the engineer to inhibit or prevent the integrity violations you describe.

8.10. Disaster recovery planning for data preparation involves ensuring not only backup exists for machines but also backup exists for programs. Explain.

8.11. Briefly explain the control section's responsibilities with respect to source documents for an application system. Why does the control section have these responsibilities?

8.12. When considering the purchase of supplies from different vendors, what factor(s) must be considered from a backup perspective?

8.13. Briefly explain why operators should not take responsibility for the file library. In a small installation where there is insufficient work for a separate file librarian position, who might take responsibility for the file library?

8.14. Briefly explain the two major purposes of the file library log. Why is it sometimes advantageous to have a computer system to support the maintenance of this log?

8.15. From a control perspective list four benefits of using a librarian package for maintenance of program files.

8.16. What is meant by degaussing and sanitization? Briefly explain the purposes of degaussing and sanitization as control procedures.

8.17. Briefly explain the purposes of maintaining a history of read/write errors for magnetic storage media.

8.18. What is the purpose of preventing *operators* from having access to program documentation? To what extent should *programmers* be prevented from obtaining access to program documentation? Why should management periodically review the log showing accesses to documentation?

8.19. Why is it generally more difficult to provide backup for documentation as compared to files? Give two strategies for facilitating the backup process for documentation.

8.20. Briefly describe the major functions of the security administrator within a computer installation.

8.21. As the auditor of a computer installation, you decide to check the adequacy of hand-held fire extinguishers within the installation. List the major points you would cover in your review.

8.22. What is the purpose of covering hardware with protective fabric when it is not in use?

8.23. Briefly discuss the responsibilities of the security officer with respect to ensuring maintenance of the energy supply within a computer installation. Why is it im-

portant a master switch exists that can terminate supply of energy to all facilities (including the air conditioning) within the installation?
- 8.24. Outline the steps an auditor might take to determine whether an installation can withstand structural damage.
- 8.25. Briefly describe two problems that can be caused by the presence of dust within the computer installation.
- 8.26. From a security viewpoint what advantages accrue from having no windows in the computer installation, providing only one entrance, and placing the installation on an upper floor of the building?
- 8.27. Briefly describe two ways in which data integrity may be violated using an electronic bug. Where in a computer installation are bugs most likely to be placed?
- 8.28. What are the most vulnerable points in a data communications network with respect to wiretapping? What actions can the security administrator take to prevent or inhibit wiretapping?

EXERCISES AND CASES

- 8.1. You are on the internal audit staff of Brownem, Inc., a large producer of suntanning oils and creams and other health and beauty products. Your organization's main computer installation has a file library consisting of 5000 reels of tape and 1000 disk packs.

    Required: The internal audit manager asks you to help formulate an audit plan for the file library. He asks you to prepare a memorandum outlining:
    1. The objectives of the audit
    2. The major controls to be examined and evaluated and how they relate to the audit objectives
    3. The means of evidence collection to be used

- 8.2. Light-a-Lamp, Inc., is a wholesaler of electrical fittings, electric appliances, lights, etc. It has offices in the major cities and towns scattered throughout Western Australia. The company's management is considering purchasing for each office a desk-top minicomputer to aid its offices with their data processing; for example, maintain records of their customer accounts, inventory, accounts payable. Before going ahead with the purchase, management has asked you, as the partner in charge of the external audit of the company, for some advice. They are concerned about physical security and backup for the minicomputers and their diskette files. Some of their offices are located in remote towns.

    Required: Prepare a brief report for the management of Light-a-Lamp identifying the control objectives for physical security and backup of the hardware, software, and data files at the minicomputer sites. For each of these control objectives, list some possible controls that might achieve these objectives. Be sure that the controls are likely to be feasible to implement.

- 8.3. Banksystems, Inc., is a large data processing service bureau for 300 participant banks in the midwest of the United States. Banksystems provides a wide variety of data processing facilities for the banks, including online banking systems. The management of Banksystems regards business interruption as their major exposure; consequently, they have implemented many controls to prevent business interruption occurring.

The company has just opened a second data center in the country outside a metropolitan area. This data center duplicates the facilities in the primary data center located in the downtown area. During normal operations the two centers share the workload.

You are a member of the external audit team evaluating the physical security measures undertaken by Banksystems. Your responsibility is to examine the disaster recovery plan dealing with power loss. When you interview the operations manager at the downtown computer center, she informs you that, in the event of power loss, the hardware provides a sufficient reservoir of power for orderly shutdown of operations. The second computer center in the country then takes over all data processing, since it operates on a different power grid to the downtown computer center. Similarly, the reverse procedure applies if the computer center in the country suffers a power loss.

Required: Prepare a brief report for your audit manager outlining any concerns you have about disaster procedures if a power loss occurs. In your report, outline what steps you will take now to evaluate the adequacy of the disaster recovery provisions.

8.4. Recently, the computer installation in your organization has purchased a word processing system to facilitate update and maintenance of program, system, and user documentation. Master copies of documentation will be stored on diskette. A single hard copy report of the latest version of the documentation also will be maintained for day-to-day use by authorized installation staff.

Required: As a member of the EDP audit staff of your organization, the EDP audit manager asks you to consider the consequences of the change from a *data integrity* viewpoint. He asks you to prepare a brief report that considers:

a. whether or not anything could go wrong with the new documentation system that eventually could lead to corruption of data integrity in the organization's database;

b. if so, what controls could be implemented in the new system to reduce the expected loss from the cause of loss.

8.5. Assemblit, Inc., is a medium-size parts manufacturing company based in London with distribution outlets in the major cities throughout Great Britain. As a member of the external audit team of the company, you have gathered the following information on the company's operations:

1. All the company's major application systems are computerized; some are online realtime update and some are batch.

2. The company uses a database management system. The DBMS was purchased initially to aid bill-of-materials processing (online realtime update system), but now it is used extensively with other applications.

3. All the company's sales outlets have online access to the head office machine, and source data is captured at the terminals in each sales outlet.

4. The computer runs six days a week, two shifts a day. Sunday and the third shift are available for "hands on" development and testing by programmers and analysts; however, during normal operations only the operators and the system programmer have access to the computer room. Access is controlled using a card lock system.

5. Assemblit's computer is located in the basement of its head office. A floor plan is attached.

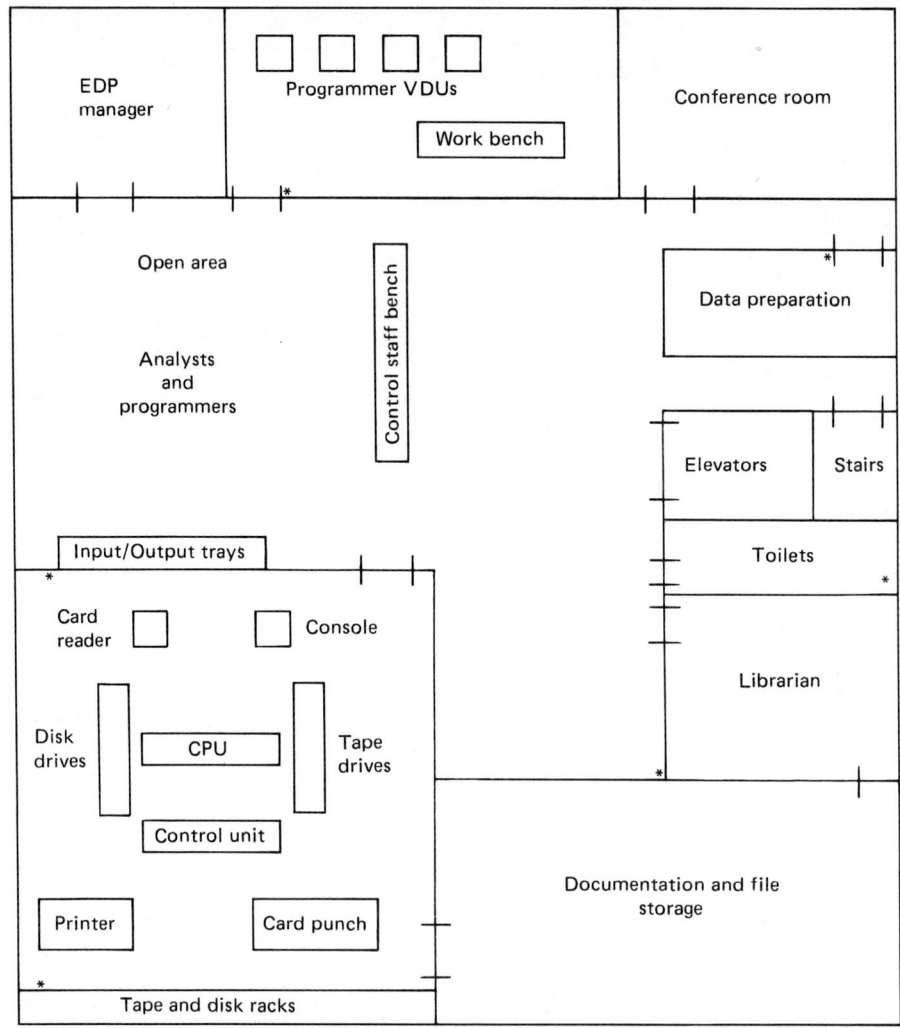

Floor Plan — Assemblit Computer Installation

*Fire extinguishers

6. The following DP staff are employed:
   a. DP manager
   b. eight analysts
   c. 15 programmers
   d. seven operators (three–four per shift; shifts rotated)
   e. four control clerks (day and evening shifts only)
   f. one system programmer
   g. one librarian (day shift only)
   h. three key-to-disk operators
7. Control clerks and analysts set up daily processing schedules a day in advance.

8. During the week, programmers and analysts use visual display units for development and maintenance work. The company has purchased powerful software to support online programming work.
9. Program development and maintenance work must be authorized by the analyst in charge of an application system.
10. Copies of all tape files and disk files are taken twice a week for backup purposes. The backup files are stored on site in a special fire resistant vault room.
11. The vendor has promised to provide backup hardware within a few days if an emergency occurs.
12. Input/output is placed in trays just outside the computer room. The operators collect input periodically. Every hour the control clerks pick up output and forward it to users. Users reconcile input to output and notify a control clerk if there are discrepancies.

Required: On the basis of the information you have so far, write a short report for your manager indicating suspected control weaknesses.

REFERENCES

Adams, Donald L. "A Survey of Library System Packages," *EDPACS* (July 1973), pp. 4–8.
_____. "Library System Packages – Revisited," *EDPACS* (February 1974), pp. 7–10.
American Federation of Information Processing Societies. *AFIPS System Review Manual on Security* (Montvale, N.J.: AFIPS Press, 1974).
American Institute of Certified Public Accountants. *Controls Over Using and Changing Computer Programs* (New York: American Institute of Certified Public Accountants, 1979).
Butler, Johnny. "Computer Operations Audit – Some New Areas," *EDPACS* (June 1974), pp. 5–8.
Canning, Richard G. "Protecting Valuable Data – Part 1," *EDP Analyzer* (December 1973), pp. 1–13.
_____. "Protecting Valuable Data – Part 2," *EDP Analyzer* (January 1974), pp. 1–14.
_____. "The Upgrading of Computer Operators," *EDP Analyzer* (September 1974), 1–13.
Cardenas, Alfonso F. "Data Entry: A Giant Cost," *Journal of Systems Management* (August 1973), pp. 35–42.
Courtney, Robert H., Jr. "Security Risk Assessment in Electronic Data Processing Systems," *Proceedings of the 1977 National Computer Conference* (Montvale, N.J.: AFIPS Press, 1977), pp. 97–104.
FitzGerald, Jerry. *Internal Controls for Computerized Systems* (San Leandro, Calif.: E. M. Underwood, 1978*a*).
_____. "EDP Risk Analysis for Contingency Planning," *EDPACS* (August 1978*b*), pp. 1–8.
_____. "Developing and Ranking Threat Scenarios," *EDPACS* (September 1978*c*), pp. 1–5.
Gross, Steven E. "Data Center Security," *EDP Auditing* (Pennsauken, N.J.: Auerbach Publishers, Inc., 1978), Portfolio 72-03-03, pp. 1–20.
Jarocki, Stanley R., and Erick J. Novotny. "Data Security/Privacy Requirements in Federal Bureaus," *The EDP Auditor* (Summer 1979), pp. 35–66.

Krauss, Leonard I. *Administering and Controlling the Company Data Processing Function* (Englewood Cliffs, N.J.: Prentice-Hall, Inc., 1969).
Kuong, Javier F. *Computer Security, Auditing and Controls* (Wellesley Hills, Mass.: Management Advisory Publications, 1974).
McNurlin, Barbara C. "The Automated Office: Part 1," *EDP Analyzer* (September 1978a), pp. 1-13.
_____. "The Automated Office: Part 2," *EDP Analyzer* (October 1978b), pp. 1-13.
Madnick, Stuart E. *Computer Security* (New York: Academic Press, 1979).
Mair, William C., Donald R. Wood, and Keagle W. Davis. *Computer Control & Audit*, 2d ed. (Altamonte Springs, Fla.: The Institute of Internal Auditors, Inc., 1976).
Martin, James. *Security, Accuracy, and Privacy in Computer Systems* (Englewood Cliffs, N.J.: Prentice-Hall, Inc., 1973).
Moore, Richard A., Benjamin F. Rose, and Thomas J. Koger. "Computer Generated Documentation," *Journal of Accountancy* (June 1975), pp. 82-86.
Pinchuk, P. L. "TRW Evaluation of a Secure Operating System," *Data Security and Data Processing Volume 6 Evaluations and Installation Experiences: Resource Security System* (New York: IBM Corporation, 1974), pp. 39-121.
Ruder, Brian, and J. D. Madden. *An Analysis of Computer Security Safeguards for Detecting and Preventing Intentional Computer Misuse.* (Washington, D.C.: Institute for Computer Sciences and Technology, National Bureau of Standards, 1978), Report No. C13.10:500-25.
Scherf, John Arthur. "Computer and Data Security: A Comprehensive Annotated Bibliography," *Data Security and Data Processing Volume 4 Study Results: Massachusetts Institute of Technology* (New York: IBM Corporation, 1974), pp. 223-300.
Short, G. E. "Threats and Vulnerabilities in a Computer System," *Data Security and Data Processing Volume 5 Study Results: TRW Systems, Inc.* (New York: IBM Corporation, 1974), pp. 25-73.
State of Illinois. "Recommended Security Practices," *Data Security and Data Processing Volume 3 Part 2 Study Results: State of Illinois* (New York: IBM Corporation, 1974), pp. 245-380.
Weston, Stephen S. "Program Library Control and Security," *EDPACS* (September 1979), pp. 1-9.
Van Tassel, Dennis. *Computer Security Management* (Englewood Cliffs, N.J.: Prentice-Hall, Inc., 1972).

PART **THREE**

THE APPLICATION CONTROL FRAMEWORK

Application system controls seek to ensure that individual application systems safeguard assets, maintain data integrity, achieve their objectives, and process data efficiently. Application system controls differ from management controls in four ways. First, hardware and software usually exercise them rather than people. Second, they apply to data and the processing of data rather than the system development, modification, and maintenance processes. Third, their existence in *each* application system is a cost-benefit question. The existence of management controls, on the other hand, depends on cost-benefit questions relating to the *whole* set of application systems. Fourth, they tend to focus on safeguarding assets (reducing expected losses from unauthorized or inadvertent removal or destruction of assets) and maintaining data integrity (ensuring data is authorized, complete, and accurate). Nevertheless, systems effectiveness and efficiency are also their objectives; for example, an output distribution control may exist so an application system meets a timeliness requirement, and an audit trail control may exist to provide data on resource consumption by an application system.

On the basis of the evaluation of the management control framework, the auditor may decide to evaluate application controls for two reasons. First, the auditor may hypothesize that control weaknesses exist in a specific application system. For example, it may be that certain management controls were not applied in the development of an accounts payable system. Second, the auditor may wish to test a hypothesis about weaknesses in specific types of controls within application systems. For example, system testing standards for communications controls may be considered to be deficient. Thus, the auditor examines a sample of application systems having communications facilities to test this hypothesis.

The next seven chapters examine in detail the application control framework. The chapters follow a natural sequence: the flow of data from its source through processing to its eventual storage for archival purposes.

Chapter	Overview of contents
9 Data Capture, Data Preparation, and Data Entry Controls	Overview and evaluation of data capture, preparation, and entry methods; source document design; interactive language design; data code controls; check digits; batch controls
10 Access and Communications Controls	Access control mechanism; user identification and authentication; sources of network failure; improving network reliability; cryptography
11 Input Controls	Field, record, batch, and file validation checks; design of input programs; control over submission and transmission of input; generalized input system
12 Processing Controls	Validation checks; concurrency and deadlock; hardware and system software controls; checkpoint/restart controls
13 Output Controls	Controls over preparation, distribution, use, and retention of output; interrogation languages and output response errors; designing effective and efficient output
14 Audit Trail Controls	The accounting audit/management trail; the operations audit/management trail
15 Backup and Recovery Controls	Need for backup and recovery; backup and recovery strategies; administrative aspects

CHAPTER 9

DATA CAPTURE, PREPARATION, AND ENTRY CONTROLS

CHAPTER OUTLINE

OVERVIEW OF DATA CAPTURE, PREPARATION, AND ENTRY

EVALUATION OF DATA CAPTURE METHODS
- Document-Based Data Capture
- Direct Entry Data Capture
- Hybrid Methods of Data Capture

EVALUATION OF DATA PREPARATION/ENTRY METHODS
- Keypunch Methods
- By-Product Methods
- Turnaround Documents
- Pattern Recognition Methods
- Terminals
- Point-of-Sale Terminals
- Other Data Input Devices

SOURCE DOCUMENT DESIGN
- Choice of Medium
- Choice of Makeup
- Choice of Layout and Style

INTERACTIVE LANGUAGE DESIGN
- Design Dimensions
- Design Process

DATA CODE CONTROLS
   Design Requirements
   Data Coding Errors
   Types of Codes
CHECK DIGITS
   Calculating Check Digits
   Efficiency of Check Digit Methods
   When to Use Check Digits
BATCH CONTROLS
   Controls over Batches
   Batch Design
OTHER DATA CAPTURE AND PREPARATION CONTROLS
   Procedures Controls
   Procedural Review
   Verification
   Design of Keying Tasks/Environment
   Personnel Training
SUMMARY
REVIEW QUESTIONS
EXERCISES AND CASES
REFERENCES

Input of data into a computer involves three steps: (*a*) data capture, (*b*) data preparation, and (*c*) data entry. *Data capture* is the process of identifying and recording real world events relevant to the ongoing operations of an organization. *Data preparation* is the process of converting data that has been captured into machine-readable form. *Data entry* is the process of reading the data into the computer.

   This chapter discusses the sets of controls that should exist over the data capture, data preparation, and data entry processes. Once the data is in machine-readable form, hardware/software controls (discussed in Chapter 12) ensure the data converts correctly into electronic signals and the computer's internal code. Thus, data entry controls are rarely a concern for the auditor since they are machine-based. However, data capture and preparation controls are especially important for two reasons. First, the data capture and data preparation processes involve substantial amounts of routine, sometimes monotonous, human intervention and, as such, are error-prone. Second, these processes often are the target of fraud. Allen [1977] studied 156 cases of computer fraud and found 108 of these cases involved addition, deletion, or alteration of an input transaction.

OVERVIEW OF DATA CAPTURE, PREPARATION, AND ENTRY

Table 9.1 presents the variety of ways in which data can be captured, prepared, and entered into the computer. Three methods of capturing data exist:

TABLE 9.1
THE INPUT PROCESS: DATA CAPTURE, DATA PREPARATION, AND DATA ENTRY METHODS

Data capture method	Data preparation method/device	Data entry method/device
Documents	Keypunched	
	Card	Card reader
	Paper tape	Paper tape reader
	Magnetic tape	Magnetic tape unit
	Magnetic disk	
	Cassette	
	Diskette	
	By-product	
	Card	Card reader
	Paper tape	Paper tape reader
	Journal tape	Optical character recognition
	Magnetic tape	
	Cassette	Magnetic tape unit
	Diskette	
	Turnaround	
	Tags	Tag reader
	Cards	Card reader
	Documents	Pattern recognition
	Encoded	Pattern recognition
	Typewritten	Magnetic ink character recognition (MICR)
	Preprinted	
	Handwritten	Optical character recognition (OCR)
		Optical mark sensing
	Photographed	Computer input microfilm
	Keyed	Terminals
Direct Entry	Keyed	Terminals
		Keyboard terminals
		Visual display units (VDU)
		Special purpose
	Speech	Voice recognition units
	Physical measurement	Process control devices
Hybrid	Encoded	Point-of-sale terminals (POS)
	Preprinted	
	Keyed	Touch-Tone
		Teller terminals
		Badge readers

(*a*) documents, (*b*) direct entry, and (*c*) a hybrid approach. *Document-based data capture* involves recording events on paper or some related medium such as tags or cards. For example, a clerk transcribes data onto a source document or detaches a Kimball tag from a clothing item that has been sold. *Direct entry data capture* involves immediate recording of an event as a digital signal. The time lag between identification of the event and recording is very small; transcription of the event to a document is not an intermediate step. For example, a customer requests a seat on a flight and an airline reservations clerk immediately keys in the booking using an online terminal. *Hybrid methods* are some combination of document-based and direct entry data capture. For example, a production worker uses a badge (document) to transmit to a computer constant data that has been prerecorded on the badge and keys in variable data about the time taken to complete a job.

Data preparation occurs in a variety of ways and at a variety of times. In the usual case it takes place after data capture (Figure 9.1*a*). Data is captured on a source document, keypunched or keyed in at an online terminal, and then read by an input device or transmitted to the computer. Sometimes data preparation occurs before data capture. For example, tags, turnaround documents, and badges require some data preparation prior to their distribution. They are encoded, preprinted, premarked, or prepunched. Upon data capture it may be possible to enter them immediately into the computer (Figure 9.1*b*), or some further data preparation may be necessary. If a hybrid method of data capture is used, data preparation occurs before and after data capture (Figure 9.1*c*). For example, for a badge reader the badge is prepared, an event occurs, and further data is keyed into the computer. For a point-of-sale device, the product code must be printed on the container. Upon sale of the product the code is read using a scanner with further data being keyed in at the point-of-sale terminal.

Data entry devices may be offline or online to the computer. A card reader, optical reader, or terminal may provide input directly into the central processing unit. Alternatively, an optical reader may write data to a magnetic tape for later processing, or a terminal may store data temporarily on a disk.

Table 9.2 presents an overview of the major sets of controls applicable to the data capture and data preparation processes. The system designer's (and auditor's) major problem is to choose a combination of data capture, data preparation, data entry methods, and specific controls applicable to these methods, that best meets the needs of system effectiveness, system efficiency, asset safeguarding, and maintenance of data integrity. The remainder of the chapter explores this problem further.

EVALUATION OF DATA CAPTURE METHODS

Historically, document-based data capture has been the major form of data capture because the data preparation and entry devices necessary to support direct entry and hybrid methods of data capture have been costly. Recently,

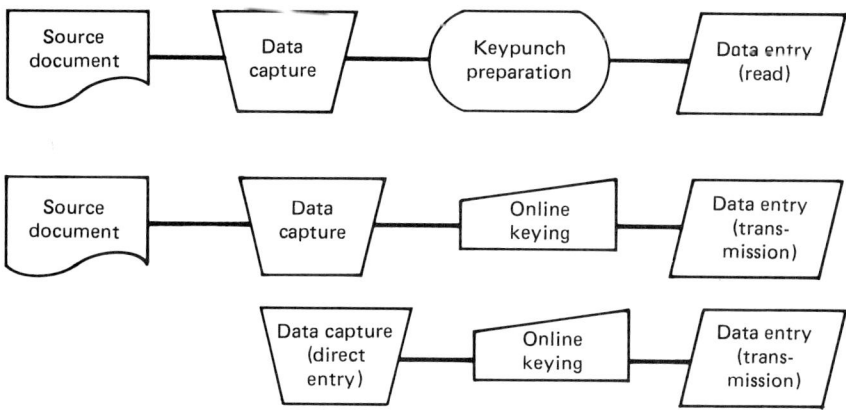

Figure 9.1a
Input sequence: data capture, preparation, entry.

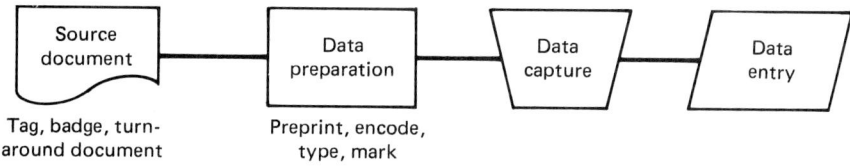

Tag, badge, turn-around document   Preprint, encode, type, mark

Figure 9.1b
Input sequence: data preparation, capture, entry.

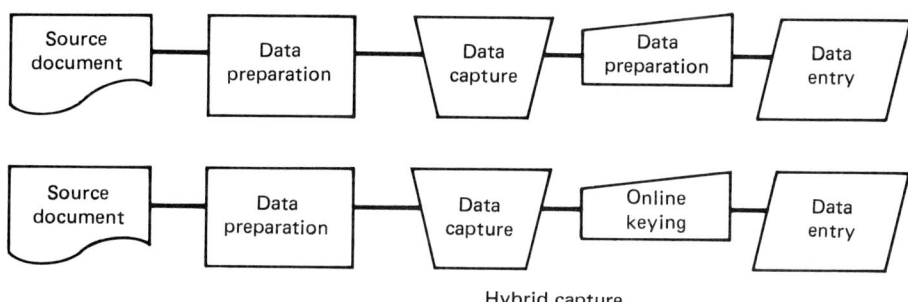

Hybrid capture

Figure 9.1c
Input sequence: data preparation, capture, preparation, entry.

the technology supporting direct entry and hybrid methods of data capture (e.g., microcomputers) has advanced rapidly and they are now being used more extensively.

Document-Based Data Capture

Document-based data capture methods have two major advantages: (*a*) simplicity, and (*b*) flexibility. Document-based data capture simply requires pre-

TABLE 9.2
OVERVIEW OF MAJOR CONTROLS IN THE DATA CAPTURE AND DATA PREPARATION PROCESSES

Control	Nature	Where applied	Effects
Source document design	Preventive	Data capture	Reduces recording errors, speeds up data capture
		Data preparation	Reduces keying errors, speeds up data preparation
Interactive language design	Preventive	Data capture	Reduces recording errors, speeds up data capture
		Data preparation	Reduces keying errors, speeds up data preparation
Data code design	Preventive	Data capture	Reduces coding errors, speeds up data capture
		Data preparation	Reduces keying errors, speeds up data preparation
Check digits	Detective	Data preparation	Detects coding and keypunch errors
Batch controls	Detective	Data capture	Detects batches missing or modified in transit
		Data preparation	Detects additions, deletions, alterations to data
Procedures controls	Preventive	Data capture	Reduces recording errors, speeds up data capture
		Data preparation	Reduces keying errors, speeds up data preparation
Procedural review	Detective	Data capture	Detects recording errors
Verification	Detective	Data preparation	Detects keying errors
Design of keying tasks/environment	Preventive	Data preparation	Reduces keying errors, speeds up data preparation
Personnel training	Preventive	Data capture	Reduces recording errors, speeds up data capture
		Data preparation	Reduces keying errors, speeds up data preparation

paring source documents that are preprinted, premarked, prenumbered, etc., and training clerks to prepare these documents as events occur. Expensive data preparation and entry devices are not needed at the points of data capture. Data can be collected easily close to the source of the data. For many data capture tasks, clerks often require little training.

Document-based data capture methods have a major disadvantage: they require greater effort for data preparation and entry than direct entry and hybrid methods. Often document-based methods involve large amounts of human intervention in data preparation and entry, sometimes making these methods costly and error-prone.

Direct Entry Data Capture

Direct entry data capture reduces the amount of human intervention in the overall input process, thereby reducing labor costs and the likelihood of clerical or operator error. Compared to document-based data capture the training costs for direct entry data capture are usually higher; however, the difference may be small. The hardware and software to support direct entry data capture has been designed to facilitate its use; for example, input instructions can be displayed on a screen at a lower light intensity than the data keyed in by the operator.

The major disadvantage of direct entry data capture is the cost of the hardware and software necessary to support its use. If a large number of data capture points exists, it may be too costly to provide direct entry facilities at all these points. If data capture points are dispersed physically, communications hardware and software also may be necessary.

Hybrid Methods of Data Capture

Hybrid data capture methods have some of the advantages of both document-based and direct entry methods. By preprinting, premarking, or prepunching constant information on a tag, card, badge, packet, container, etc., and reading this information directly (e.g., using an optical reader), human intervention in the data capture process is reduced. Thus, labor costs and the risk of errors being made during data input are reduced. Variable information about an event can be keyed in directly to the computer. For example, with a point-of-sale device, a wand scanner can be used to read a bar code to identify a product type, and the keyboard used to enter information about the tender offered— cash, checks, or coupons.

The major disadvantage of hybrid data capture methods is the cost of the support hardware and software needed. However, as with direct entry techniques the technology is advancing quickly, and labor cost savings may soon outstrip extra hardware and software costs.

EVALUATION OF DATA PREPARATION/ENTRY METHODS

Separating a discussion on the relative advantages and disadvantages of various data preparation and data entry methods results in large overlap. Data preparation is tied closely to the method of data entry, and vice versa. Consequently, the following discussion is an integrated approach. It assumes basic familiarity with the various devices used for data preparation and entry (see Clifton [1978] and Wooldridge [1974]). However, those features of the devices salient to a discussion of asset safeguarding, data integrity, system effectiveness, and system efficiency are described briefly.

Keypunch Methods

Key-based data preparation methods are still the dominant methods of preparing data for input to the computer. However, there has been a shift away from using cards as the storage medium to using magnetic storage such as tapes and disks.

Cards Some modifications have been made to the traditional keypunch (key-to-card) and verifier machines to improve efficiency and assist in maintaining data integrity. An important innovation is the buffered combination keypunch/verifier known as a card data recorder. Buffering permits data to be stored until keying of a card is complete. The data then is punched automatically as the operator commences to key data for a new card.

Buffered keypunch/verifiers offer several advantages:

1 Fast correction of conscious keying errors. About 80% of all keying errors made are conscious errors; that is, the keypunch operator is aware of the error as soon as it is made.
2 About a 25–30% faster keying rate than unbuffered keypunch/verifiers.
3 Card layout can differ from the source document layout to facilitate data capture by the user and data preparation by the operator.

In addition to the advantages obtained through buffering, the following features improve keying efficiency and help maintain data integrity:

1 Automatic creation and checking of check digits
2 Automatic preparation of control totals for designated fields to allow batch control checking
3 Programming capability to allow automatic selection of different card formats, automatic insertion of constant data, zero and blank filling of fields, left or right justification of data punched in fields, and high-speed skipping over blank columns
4 Preparation of statistics on number of cards punched, keystrokes made, and errors corrected

As an input medium, cards have as their major advantages ease of handling and visibility of the data stored. They have several disadvantages:

1 Cards damage easily through mishandling or improper storage.
2 Compared to other data preparation methods, cards are slow because they are labor intensive and use mechanical rather than electronic equipment.
3 Cards are bulky, heavy, and their storage sometimes difficult.
4 Cards are not a reusable storage medium.

Paper Tape For most applications, other storage mediums have superseded paper tape. However, in some areas it is still useful; for example, data input from a typewriter terminal.

Compared to cards, paper tape is lighter, less bulky, and sometimes faster to prepare and read. However, it has the same disadvantages as cards. In addition, correction of keypunch errors is more difficult because paper tape is a continuous medium. Corrections are made in several ways. The tape can be spliced, but this is time-consuming and causes jams in paper tape readers. Some keypunch machines produce an error punch over the character in error. The paper tape reader ignores characters having an error punch. Paper tape verifiers output a new reel of tape containing correct data from the original reel used as input and new data where an error on the original reel has been identified.

Magnetic Tape Key-to-tape devices allow source data to be keyed directly to a magnetic tape that can be read by a computer. Both stand-alone and clustered devices exist. A stand-alone device has its own tape recording unit. A clustered device has several keyboards with a multiplexor reading alternately from each keyboard. Clustered devices are less expensive than stand-alone devices, but before they can be justified they require applications where large amounts of the same type of data are being keyed.

Since key-to-tape devices are buffered, they offer all the usual advantages: fast and easy correction of conscious errors, automatic skipping of columns, zero or blank filling, left and right justification of data entered into certain fields. When a device writes a buffer to tape, it performs checks to ensure the buffer has been written correctly; for example, a parity check and a read-after-write check. Verification simply involves switching the device to verification mode. Correction of errors occurs immediately by overwriting the character in error.

Key-to-tape devices have several different and optional characteristics. Some provide a display showing the last character entered. Others provide a full display of the record entered. A printer can be attached to the device to provide hard copy output. Records can be retrieved using a search facility. Check digit verification can be carried out. The devices also will gather various statistics: number of keystrokes, number of errors made. Various offline devices exist to support key-to-tape devices; for example, a tape pooler and a communications controller so data can be sent over long distances.

Key-to-tape devices offer several advantages over traditional keypunch equipment: records are not restricted to 80 characters, less mechanical movement, less operator intervention as cards do not have to be loaded and unloaded, faster input to the computer. Though key-to-tape devices are more expensive than key-to-card devices, they allow faster data preparation and data entry. Currently, as a rule of thumb, about three key-to-tape devices replace four key-to-card devices.

There are few disadvantages to using key-to-tape equipment, though they are being superseded by key-to-disk equipment. Sometimes operators resist a changeover from traditional keypunch equipment. A few machine compatibility problems also have existed, but these are disappearing.

Magnetic Disk The natural extension of key-to-tape devices is key-to-disk devices. Key-to-disk devices feature: (*a*) multiple keystations attached to a single processor, (*b*) validation and editing capabilities performed by the processor, (*c*) a supervisor's control station, and (*d*) a magnetic tape unit for output of data that has been keyed, edited, and validated.

The number of keystations available with a key-to-disk device varies; small systems have about eight keystations and large systems have in excess of 60 keystations. A keystation consists of a keyboard and a panel display or visual display. The display shows the data entered, and a cursor or light indicates any data identified as being in error. A keystation can be used for initial input of data or verification. One keystation can perform verification while another performs input, providing some time lag exists between entry and verification.

Data validation and editing is performed by a program stored in the processor. The system vendor usually supplies generalized software for validation and editing, but users also can write their own routines. Validation and edit capabilities are fairly comprehensive (see, also, Chapter 11), but the available core sometimes imposes limitations so that some validation and editing still must be carried out by the input program in the mainframe. When the validation and edit program identifies an error, it locks the keyboard, sounds an alarm, and indicates the field or character in error on the display.

The supervisor's control station controls data input to the system and data output from disk storage to magnetic tape for input to the mainframe. The supervisor assigns buffer storage to keystations, allocates areas on disk, assigns batch numbers, monitors system statistics, and determines when data should be dumped from disk to tape.

Key-to-disk devices offer the same advantages as key-to-tape devices. The major additional advantage is the validation and editing capabilities provided by the processor. If communications facilities are attached to a key-to-disk system, in effect the system constitutes a frontend terminal that can be placed at some remote location. Data can be captured and entered close to its source, thereby enabling timely identification and fast correction of errors made.

The major disadvantages of key-to-disk equipment relate to the consequences of device failure. Not just one but several keystations become inoperable. Data that has been already keyed may be lost. Key-to-disk systems are also costly. However, cost is decreasing; key-to-disk is now a strong competitor with key-to-card and key-to-tape systems.

Cassette A variation on key-to-tape devices is key-to-cassette devices. The major advantage of cassettes over tape is ease of handling. Spooling and tape loading are unnecessary with cassettes. Because cassettes are much smaller in size than tapes, they also can be transported readily or sent through the mail. They are easier and more economical to store than magnetic tapes.

Diskette Diskettes (floppy disks) are replacing cassettes as a data storage medium. Their major advantage over cassettes is that they allow fast direct access to data. There are no significant cost differences. However, one disadvantage of diskettes is low reliability. Because the read/write heads make contact with the diskette surface, compared to a conventional magnetic disk, recording errors are more likely to occur.

By-Product Methods

Data can be prepared as a by-product of other activities; for example, cash registers produce paper tape or journal tape suitable as input to an optical character reader, accounting machines produce paper tape or magnetic tape, electric typewriters produce punched cards or cassette tape.

There are several advantages to producing data in machine-readable form as a by-product of other processes. First, no special operator training is necessary for data preparation equipment. Second, by-product data preparation reduces further data preparation activities. For example, if data entered onto a source document is typewritten, keypunching of data from the source document is unnecessary. Third, in the absence of machine failure, there is exact correspondence between data on the sales invoice or ledger card and data in machine-readable form. However, most by-product methods of data preparation are being superseded. For example, cheap minicomputers have replaced many accounting machines. Many documents previously typewritten now are produced by the computer.

Turnaround Documents

Turnaround documents reduce the time and effort needed for data capture, preparation, and entry and the risk of errors being made throughout the input process. They take three forms: (*a*) tags, (*b*) cards, and (*c*) documents.

Tags are used primarily in retail stores where they are attached to the item to be sold. Information about the item, price, style, department, and supplier, is printed, prepunched, or premarked on the tag so the tag provides information to potential customers and salespersons as well as being in machine-readable form. Tags are prepared in different ways: using a special device that is online to the computer, a special keypunch, or a special device that uses magnetic tape as input. Multipart tags are used sometimes. The return of one part denotes receipt of an item; another part the sale of an item. Tags are read using a special online device or a special offline device that produces magnetic tape or some other input medium.

Cards are prepunched or premarked prior to their distribution as a turnaround document. If additional data is captured, further punching or marking must take place. The cards are read using a mark sensing device or a card reader. There are numerous applications of punched cards as turnaround documents. For example, in a payroll system a punched card can be produced for each employee. The foreperson fills in details and returns the card for further data preparation and entry to the computer.

Documents are more flexible than tags or cards as turnaround documents. Data is preprinted or premarked (typewritten or computer-produced) and the document distributed. If further information is captured, it is marked, handwritten, or typewritten, and the document then is read using an optical recognition device. For example, sales invoices can be produced by the computer, returned by the customer with payment, payment details added to the document, and the document then read into the computer.

The major disadvantage of turnaround documents is their susceptibility to damage. Even though they reduce data capture and preparation errors through minimizing human intervention, they must be robust to withstand extra handling. Also, they can be maliciously damaged.

Pattern Recognition Methods

Pattern recognition devices read and evaluate characters or marks on a document based on the presence or absence of a magnetic flux or a light pattern formed. These devices usually are more expensive than keypunch equipment. However, they eliminate a substantial part of data preparation through being able to read data directly from a source document. They may be online to the computer or offline producing magnetic tape for later input.

Magnetic Ink Character Recognition (MICR) The popularity of MICR arises from its extensive use by the banking industry for processing checks. MICR requires characters to be encoded on a document using a special type font and special magnetic ink. Reading takes place by the device sensing the presence or absence of magnetic ink in a character matrix. The character is identified by the pattern formed in the matrix. In some cases a character passing under the read head may be slightly out of position and a "folded" character is sensed. The reader shifts a folded character vertically and attempts to identify it as a member of the valid set of patterns.

MICR offers several advantages:

1 High reading rates (up to 1600 documents per minute), and low error rates for documents of varying size, thickness, and condition.
2 Documents can be sorted at the time of reading; for example, by account number within bank number.
3 Some devices permit some input validation to be carried out; for example, sequence checking, accumulating, and printing batch totals.
4 The MICR type font can be read easily by humans.

There are two major disadvantages to using MICR. First, it is time-consuming to correct rejected or damaged documents. Second, low error and rejection rates require high-quality printing and ink. The magnetic ink loses much of its magnetism soon after encoding. To minimize read errors and rejections, documents must be handled infrequently.

Optical Character Recognition (OCR) Three types of OCR devices are available: (*a*) document readers, (*b*) page readers, and (*c*) journal tape readers. The primary difference between a document reader and page reader is the size of the document that can be read; document readers accept smaller size documents than page readers. Journal tape readers accept narrow rolls of paper usually produced by a cash register.

Data for input to an OCR device can be prepared in a variety of ways: typewritten, offset, printed by computer, handwritten. A multitude of type fonts is acceptable. However, in general, the less expensive the OCR device, the fewer the number of fonts it can read. Handwritten characters must be printed carefully and conform to a certain style. Flexibility in the types of fonts and handwriting styles that can be read is not always desirable. Besides being less costly, an OCR device that accepts only one type font and a restricted handwriting style generally has a lower error and rejection rate.

OCR input offers several advantages. First, the fonts that OCR devices read are read easily by humans. Second, to aid data capture and preparation, instructions can be printed on the source document in a drop-out color that cannot be read by an OCR device. Third, by minimizing data capture and preparation, OCR is useful for high-volume input. Document readers can process about 400 documents per minute; page readers are slower. Wu [1975] reports the use of OCR for credit card billing by one U.S. oil company resulted in an increased cash flow of $25,000,000 during the first six months of operation.

However, the success of OCR has been limited. OCR devices are still relatively expensive and their reliability lower than other input devices. A major factor determining the success or failure of OCR is the quality of the input system design. A simple switch from keypunches to OCR often is unsuccessful. Using OCR to full advantage may require complete redesign of the input system.

Optical Mark Sensing Optical mark sensing devices read marks instead of alphanumeric characters. As with OCR equipment, the marks may be preprinted, typewritten, handwritten, or computer-produced. The position of the marks on the document or card indicates their alphabetic or numeric value.

In spite of the greater flexibility and sophistication of OCR devices, optical mark sensing still has its place. It is especially useful for low-volume, exception data entry. For example, a salesperson marks an order form to indicate the number of items ordered; an employee marks a timesheet to indicate normal and overtime hours worked. In both cases constant information is preprinted on the document in a drop-out color. Providing the data captured is straightforward, data preparation usually is easy and few errors are made after a little practice.

If the data to be captured is diverse and volatile, optical mark sensing generally is unsuitable as an input method. Since data must be coded as a pattern of marks, diverse data requires many different codes. This increases the risk of clerical error and slows the data capture and preparation processes. If data is volatile, frequent changes to preprinted forms may be necessary. For example, if product lines are preprinted on a sales order form and these lines are volatile, the forms must be changed constantly. Again, the risk of clerical error increases.

Terminals

There are two types of terminals: (*a*) keyboard, and (*b*) visual display units (VDUs). Keyboard terminals provide only hard copy printed output. VDUs provide visual output on a display screen. In addition, they have various other features and options; for example, paging and scrolling capabilities, detachable printers, light pens, joysticks for moving graphic displays in any direction, unpluggable keyboards so different keyboards can be attached.

The keyboard terminal was the first major step toward online use of the computer. It provides several advantages. First, it allows data upon capture to be immediately available for processing. Second, it reduces the effort involved in capturing, preparing, and entering data. Third, in many cases it decreases the input error rate. Less scope exists for clerical error because human intervention is reduced. Data can be validated upon entry and feedback immediately provided to the operator so errors can be corrected. Verification of data is rarely necessary. The computer can be used to guide the terminal operator during data entry by providing instructions and answering queries.

VDUs provide additional advantages to those listed above for keyboard terminals. The absence of mechanical movement with a VDU results in faster and quieter keying of data. The display assists the operator reduce data capture and preparation errors in several ways. Source documents used for data capture can be displayed at low light intensity as background data. Data entered by the operator can be displayed at a high light intensity (double brightness) as foreground data. A cursor (moveable dot, upward arrow, dash) indicates the next character to be entered so the operator clearly sees what point has been reached in the input task. The cursor also can be repositioned to insert, delete, or change data, or made to blink to indicate a character or field in error.

VDUs became "intelligent terminals" when they have minicomputers or microprocessors attached that provide validation, editing, and storage capabilities independent of the main computer. Thus, a VDU can be offline but the user has the same facilities as if the VDU were online. Data that has been validated and edited can be stored (e.g., on cassette tape) and forwarded to the mainframe during quiet periods.

The major disadvantage of terminals is their expense in terms of both hardware and software; however, costs are decreasing rapidly.

Point-of-Sale Terminals

Productivity and data integrity in supermarkets and retail stores has been considerably enhanced by point-of-sale data input devices. In the case of supermarkets the technology permitting these advances is a fixed laser checkout scanner capable of reading premarked codes on an item for sale. In the case of retail stores it is a handheld wand. The wand either reads codes optically or it reads magnetically encoded tickets.

The nature of supermarket and retail store selling operations is different. The salesclerk in a supermarket spends most time at the point-of-sale, whereas the salesclerk in a retail store spends most time selling rather than checking items out. Another difference is the complexity of the transactions that occur. In a supermarket environment transactions are relatively straightforward: an exchange of tender for the total cost of the items purchased. In a retail environment a large number of different types of transactions exist. Antonelli [1975] reports some retail stores have over 600 combinations of sales transactions; for example, discount, COD, layaway, partial payment, multiple charge plans. Correct recording of a retail store transaction is confounded by the fact that most sales occur during a two-month period of the year when large numbers of temporary staff are employed. The cost of training is significant and the risk of error high. Thus, a point-of-sale terminal for supermarkets differs from a point-of-sale terminal for retail operations.

Compared with cash registers, the major advantages of using supermarket point-of-sale devices are:

1 Optical scanning of a premarked code, for example, the universal product code (UPC), enables faster throughput of items.

2 Increased accuracy in pricing items since a minicomputer retrieves prices from a price file based on an item's unique code.

3 Reduced price marking upon receipt of an item and upon change of the item's price; the price need only be marked on the shelf and not on the item itself.

4 Improved customer satisfaction since a display shows the item and its price as it is checked out; a more detailed customer receipt is printed automatically.

5 Improved control over tender since the terminal controls the cash drawer, automatically dispenses change and stamps, and handles any type of tender—cash, checks, coupons, or food stamps.

6 Automatic check authorization.

7 Better inventory control and shelf allocation through more timely information on item sales.

8 Better information on item advertising effectiveness, the performance of new items, and customer preferences for different brand names.

Retail store point-of-sale terminals have similar advantages. However, an important function of a retail store terminal is to display instructions to salesclerks to guide them through the variety of transaction types that can occur.

Point-of-sale devices present problems when hardware failure occurs. The terminals typically are connected to a store controller that, in turn, is connected to a host computer. Hippert et al. [1975] describe various methods of increasing the reliability and availability of the terminals. If failure occurs the terminal usually can act as a stand-alone register.

Other Data Input Devices

Table 9.1 lists several other input devices that have not been discussed: computer input microfilm, voice recognition units, process control devices, Touch-Tone devices, teller terminals, badge readers. They are left for further study (see Wooldridge [1974]). From an audit viewpoint, so far they are either relatively unimportant, their use is not widespread because the technology is still evolving, or they are variations on a device discussed already.

SOURCE DOCUMENT DESIGN

Source documents are the forms used to record data that has been captured. A source document may be a piece of paper, a turnaround document such as a punched card, or an image displayed on a VDU for online input of data.

Source document design can be a complex matter. For example, in the case of documents to be read by a pattern recognition device, the design depends on technical characteristics of the device such as its trim and skew tolerance. However, the auditor must understand the fundamentals of good source document design. As a basic data input control, a well-designed source document achieves several purposes:

1 Increases the speed and accuracy with which data can be recorded
2 Controls the work flow

3 Facilitates preparation of the data in machine-readable form
4 For pattern recognition devices, increases the speed and accuracy with which data can be read
5 Facilitates subsequent reference checking

Source document design occurs after carrying out source document analysis. Source document analysis determines what data will be captured, how the data will be captured, who will capture the data, how the data will be prepared and read into the machine, and how the document will be handled, stored, and filed. Once these requirements have been determined, three decisions can be made: (*a*) the medium to be used for the source document, (*b*) the makeup of the source document, and (*c*) its style and layout.

Choice of Medium

The medium used for source documents usually is paper. Other media such as cards may be used. The following choices must be made:

Choice	Considerations
Length and Width	Amount of data to be captured; compliance with organization standards; processes and devices that use the form, e.g., typewriters, mailing in window envelopes, file storage
Grade and Weight	Amount of handling; retention period; where, when, and by whom the document will be completed, e.g., truck drivers at a loading bay versus clerks in an office

Choice of the wrong length and width or grade and weight can cause a variety of problems; for example, inability to manipulate the document in a typewriter, fast deterioration of the document in storage, frequent tearing of the document when being completed.

Choice of Makeup

The choice of makeup depends on the number of copies of the form required and how it will be completed. There are four types of makeup: (*a*) padding, (*b*) multipart sets, (*c*) continuous forms, and (*d*) snap-apart sets. Wooldridge [1974] discusses in detail the relative advantages and disadvantages of the different types of makeups. Choice of the wrong makeup results in input errors occurring through documents tearing, and data being too lightly written to be read.

Choice of Layout and Style

The layout and style of a source document probably is the most important factor affecting the number of data capture and preparation errors made. Some general design guidelines follow:

1 *Preprint Wherever Possible* Preprint all constant information on a source document. If only a limited number of responses is appropriate to a question, preprint the responses and have the user tick the correct responses or delete those that are inappropriate.

2 *Provide Titles, Headings, Notes, and Instructions* A title clearly identifies the purpose of the source document. Headings break up the document into logical sections. Notes and instructions assist the user to complete the document. Where codes are used, preprint their meaning on the form so the user does not have to rely on memory or waste time referencing manuals.

3 *Use Techniques for Emphasis and to Highlight Differences* Different-type fonts such as italics and boldface give emphasis to different parts of the form. Heavy thick lines or hatching highlight important fields. Different colors facilitate distribution of different copies of the form. Background colors emphasize special sections of the document; for example, those for office use only.

4 *Arrange Fields for Ease of Use* Design the document to be completed in a natural sequence from left to right, top to bottom. Group related items together. The sequence of fields should follow the work flow; the most used fields on the left of the document, those usually used in the center, and those seldom used on the right.

5 *Where Possible Provide Multiple-Choice Answers to Questions to Avoid Omissions* Figure 9.2a shows how this technique can be used. Instead of asking users to remember all the business subjects they studied, provide a list they can check.

6 *Use Boxes to Identify Field Size Errors* Figure 9.2b shows how this technique highlights field overflow or underflow.

7 *Combine Instructions with Questions* Figure 9.2c shows how this technique overcomes possible confusion.

8 *Space Items Appropriately on Forms* Correct spacing of fields on forms is particularly important if responses are to be typewritten. Incorrect spacing results in manual shifting of the document in the machine and too many tab stops.

9 *Design for Ease of Keypunching* Have the order of punching fields follow the order of field placement. Figure 9.2c shows how column numbers can be preprinted with a field to show operators the punch positions of characters.

10 *Prenumber Source Documents* Prenumber source documents so it is possible to account for every document. If each document has a unique serial number, input transactions can be sorted by serial number and breaks in the sequence of numbers identified.

Good	Bad
Check the business subjects you have studied	List the business subjects you have studied
☐ Accounting ☐ Management	_____
☐ Data Processing ☐ Business and Society	_____
☐ Commercial Law ☐ Management Science	_____
☐ Taxation ☐ Marketing	_____
☐ Microeconomics ☐ Industrial Relations	_____

Figure 9.2a
Using multiple choice to prevent omissions.

Good	Bad
Social Security Number ☐☐☐ – ☐☐ – ☐☐☐☐	Social Security Number _____

Figure 9.2b
Using boxes to prevent field size errors.

Good	Bad
4 9	
Date: ☐☐☐☐☐☐	Date: _____
Y Y M M D D	

Figure 9.2c
Combining instructions with questions.

11 *Conform to Organization's Standards* An organization should have a forms control section responsible for overall forms design standards; for example, numbering and color conventions, placement of the organization's logos, retention requirements, ordering and stockkeeping requirements. Ensure the source document design conforms to these standards.

INTERACTIVE LANGUAGE DESIGN

Stanford Research Institute [1977] reports that in the United States in 1970 the number of general-purpose computers having communications terminals was 25%; by 1975, 54% had terminals. Furthermore, the number of terminals used is growing exponentially. By 1980 SRI estimated 3,000,000 terminals would be installed in the United States.

As terminals are used increasingly as a means of data input, the importance of high-quality interactive language design grows as a basic control in computer systems. The quality of interactive language design affects both input and output processes. On the input side, poor-quality designs inhibit accurate, complete, and efficient data capture and preparation. On the output side, poor-quality designs result in misspecification of user queries and poor presentation of data needed for decision making.

The following sections focus on interactive language design from an input perspective. Much of the discussion, however, is also relevant to the design of interactive languages from an output perspective. For the auditor involved in evaluating the quality of an interactive language design, Martin [1973] provides an extensive introduction to the topic.

Design Dimensions

Three major factors affect the design of an interactive language: (*a*) characteristics of the task to be performed, (*b*) characteristics of the task environment, and (*c*) user (operator) characteristics. Unfortunately, the language attributes required to satisfy these factors are sometimes conflicting and mutually exclusive. The designer's problem is to achieve a global optimum.

Characteristics of the Task The frequency and complexity of a task affect the amount of feedback an interactive language must provide a user. The less frequent the task, the greater the need for the interactive language to provide guidance to the user. Tasks may be simple: operators using an online terminal as if it were a keypunch, continuously entering data from source documents. The interactive language needs to provide only minimum instructions to the operator. Tasks may be complex: a salesclerk entering transactions for an extensive range of products where complex combinations of credit and discount are allowed. The interactive language may need to provide extensive guidance to the salesclerk.

Characteristics of the Task Environment Consider an airline reservations clerk under duress as a flight is about to close with a queue of anxious and impatient customers waiting, some of whom are becoming abusive. The reservations task is complex; customers cancel bookings, require information on alternate flight plans. request different flights. The task environment is hectic and pressured. There are conflicting requirements for the design of the interactive language. To handle the task complexity the interactive language should provide extensive guidance to the clerk. However, if the clerk is under duress, the language must provide fast responses and allow fast data input. In practice, usually the pressures of the task environment primarily influence the design. Most interactive languages for airline reservations provide cryptic, mnemonic output and allow concise data input.

Characteristics of the User Unfortunately, little research has been undertaken on the ways in which user characteristics affect effective and efficient use of an interactive language. However, the importance of user characteristics can be observed readily; for example:

Psychological/demographic characteristics	Effects on language design
Experience	Naïve users need frequent access to "help" routines. Experienced users become frustrated if they cannot proceed quickly through a task.
Computer Knowledge	More sophisticated instructions can be provided to users having extensive computer knowledge.
Tolerance for Ambiguity	Users having low tolerance for ambiguity require more extensive guidance and feedback.

User psychological attributes also affect the amount of information that should be displayed at a terminal, the amount of data that should be requested as input, and the response time that should be provided. If too much information is provided or requested at the one time, information overload occurs. However, information can be displayed and requested at too slow a rate. Users become bored and make data errors through losing concentration. Miller [1968] argues humans expect a response time of about 2 seconds unless a condition called task closure occurs; that is, the user considers all steps in a task to be complete.

On the basis of these psychological considerations, Martin [1973] argues a number of "principles" should be followed in the design of interactive languages:

1 Display only a small amount of information at one time.
2 Have only one idea per display.
3 Require only a short user response.
4 Always give a response after operator action.
5 Use clearly formatted displays.
6 Adopt similar formats for different displays.
7 Avoid difficult words and characters.
8 Permit easy correction of a mistake.
9 Highlight user instructions.
10 Clean up the display screen as dialog progresses.
11 Always provide a "help" facility.

These "principles" allow person–machine dialogs to proceed faster, reduce the number of input errors the terminal user is likely to make, and reduce traffic on communications lines.

Design Process

A high-quality interactive language design is the product of a design process that is structured and controlled. In summary form the process consists of the following steps:

Design step	Explanation
Determine the Purposes of the Language	The purposes of the language may differ from the wider objectives of the overall system.
Identify the Types of Users	Consider the effects of various user psychological and demographic characteristics. Users may not interact directly with the language. A specialist operator may perform an intermediary function.
Determine the Characteristics of the Language to Be Used	Based on the purposes of the language and the characteristics of the user, the broad structure of the language syntax and semantics can be designed.
Determine Hardware/Software Requirements	Response time requirements and the characteristics of the language indicate the types of hardware/software support necessary.
Detailed Design of Language	The detailed design of the language is an iterative process. Before programming, test a design in a simulated situation (discussed below) and modify it in light of the findings.
Programming	Once a final design has been determined, programming can take place using a conventional language or a dialog generator.
Testing	Upon completion of programming, the language must be tested to see if an irrational user can "crash" the language in any way.

It is especially important that a design be tested before programming commences. Preliminary testing of the design may result in the whole structure of the language being altered, a move that may be too costly if the language already has been implemented.

There are several ways of carrying out preliminary testing. Martin [1973] describes a transaction simulator system that allows the designer to create terminal displays with limited branching logic establishing relationships between the displays. User responses to the displays can be tested in a laboratory setting. A simple method of preliminary testing is to write the various displays on cards, have the designer and a prospective user sit on opposite sides of a table, and the dialog proceed by the designer presenting a card and the user responding. This testing procedure can be programmed so prospective users are sitting at one terminal and their responses are displayed on the designer's terminal. Based on the user's response the designer selects a new display from a file of stored displays.

Errors in the programming process are reduced if a dialog generator can be used instead of a conventional language such as COBOL or FORTRAN. These higher-level dialog generators also speed up the programming process. Unfortunately, only a limited number of dialog generators exist, some having been designed for specific purposes such as computer-assisted instruction; thus, their use is not widespread.

DATA CODE CONTROLS

Data codes have two purposes in computer systems. First, they uniquely identify an entity or identify an entity as a member of a group or set. Textual or narrative description does not always uniquely identify an entity; for example, two people may have the same name. Second, for identification purposes, codes often are more efficient than textual or narrative description, since they require a smaller number of characters to carry a given amount of information.

Design Requirements

Badly designed codes affect the input process in two ways. First, they are error-prone. Second, they cause data recording and keypunching processes to be slow and inefficient. A well-designed coding system achieves certain objectives:

Objective	Explanation
Flexibility	Easy addition of new items or categories.
Meaningfulness	Where possible, a code should indicate the values of the attributes of the entity.
Compactness	Maximum information conveyed with a minimum number of characters.
Convenience	A code should be easy to assign, encode, decode, and keypunch.
Evolvability	Where possible, a code can be adapted to changing user requirements.

Data Coding Errors

Data coding errors are one of six types:

 1 *Addition*   An extra character is added, e.g., 87942 coded as 879142.

 2 *Truncation*   A character is omitted, e.g., 87942 coded as 8792.

 3 *Transcription*   A wrong character is recorded, e.g., 87942 coded as 81942.

 4 *Transposition*   Adjacent characters are reversed, e.g., 87942 coded as 78942.

 5 *Double Transposition*   Characters separated by more than one character are reversed, e.g., 87942 coded as 84972.

 6 *Random*   Some combination of the above, e.g., 87942 coded as A7492.

Research shows two attributes of a code are important determinants of the number of errors made with the code: (*a*) its length, and (*b*) its alphabetic-numeric mix.

The notion that length may be important derives from the work of Miller [1956] who argues humans can hold in short-term memory only about five to nine (average seven) "chunks" of information and process them effectively. This theory has been supported by many empirical studies on coding systems (see, for example, Conrad [1959] and Chapdelaine [1963]). In general, the idea of breaking up long codes into chunks by using hyphens or slashes is well-accepted as a means of reducing coding errors.

If alphabetic and numeric characters are to be mixed in a code, the error rate is lower if the alphabetics are grouped together and the numerics are grouped together (see Owsowitz and Sweetland [1965]). Thus, a code such as ABN653 is less prone to error than a code of A6B53N. From the viewpoint of keypunching, the former code is better also. The latter code breaks the rhythm of keying by interchanging alphabetics and numerics. The alphabetic characters I, J, O, Q, and Z also should be avoided since often they are misread.

Types of Codes

Even given the general design guidelines specified above, the choice of a coding system for an application system is not always clear-cut. The following sections briefly discuss the various coding systems available and their relative advantages and disadvantages.

Serial Codes Serial coding systems assign consecutive numbers (or alphabetics) to an entity irrespective of the attributes of the entity. Thus, a serial code uniquely identifies an entity; however, the code indicates nothing further about the entity; for example, the category of items in which it belongs. The major advantages of a serial code are the ease with which a new item can be added and conciseness. The code presents problems when the file of items is volatile; that is, significant numbers of additions and deletions occur. Deleted items must have their codes reassigned to new items; otherwise, significant gaps in the sequence occur and the code is no longer concise.

As another disadvantage, a serial code often conveys no information about the characteristics of the entity to which it is assigned. However, in some ways this is also an advantage. Consider a database management system environment where there is sharing of data and the number and types of users and their needs are in a state of flux. Different users may wish to view data differently. A code that presumes one view of data may be inappropriate for certain users. Thus, a serial coding system may contribute better to the evolvability of the system.

Block Sequence Codes Block sequence codes assign blocks of numbers to particular categories of an entity. The primary attribute on which entities are to be categorized must be chosen, and blocks of numbers assigned for each value of the attribute. For example, if account numbers are assigned to customers on the basis of the discount allowed each customer, a block sequence code would be:

101 R. Allen
102 J. Smith   } 3% discount allowed
103 M. Clarke

.
.
.

201 S. Elders } 3½% discount allowed
202 M. Ball

.
.
.

301 K. Kline
302 G. Brown } 4% discount allowed
303 F. Water

Block sequence codes have the advantage of giving some mnemonic value to the code. Nevertheless, there are problems in choosing the size of the block needed (and the remedy if overflow occurs) and ensuring blocks are not too large so wasted characters occur and the code is no longer concise.

Hierarchical Codes Hierarchical codes require selection of the set of attributes of the entity to be coded and their ordering in terms of importance. The value of the code for the entity is a combination of the values of the codes for each attribute of the entity. For example, the following hierarchical code for an account breaks up into three components (expenditure within departments within divisions):

C65 / 423 / 3956
Division Department Type of
number   number   expenditure

Hierarchical codes usually are more meaningful to their users than are serial or block sequence codes. They also carry more information about the entity to which they are assigned. Nevertheless, sometimes they present problems when change occurs. For example, if in the example given above a change to the organizational structure occurred and department 423 was assigned to a different division C25, new codes would have to be learned and the master file altered and resequenced.

Association Codes Association codes go by a variety of names: significant digit codes, mnemonic codes, alphabetic derivation codes (see, for example, Gore and Stubbe [1975]). With an association code the attributes of the entity to be coded are selected and unique codes assigned each attribute value. The codes may be numeric, alphabetic, or alphanumeric. The code for the entity is simply a linear combination of the different codes assigned the attributes of the entity. Unlike an hierarchical code, the order in which the codes for the attributes occur in the overall code does not necessarily imply some type of hierarchical relationship. The following is an example of an association code assigned a shirt:

    SHM32DRCOT
where SH = shirt
    M = male
    32 = 32 centimeters, the neck size
    DR = dress shirt
    COT = cotton fabric

Association codes have high mnemonic value; they carry substantial information about the entity they represent. However, they quickly become long. Since often a full set of characters is not used for each character position, they are not concise.

CHECK DIGITS

In some cases errors made in transcribing or keying data can have serious consequences. For example, punching the wrong account number for a creditor may result in a payment being made to someone who has no legal claim on the assets of the organization. Keying a wrong part number may result in a large quantity of incorrect parts being sent to a job. One control used to guard against these types of errors is a check digit.

Calculating Check Digits

A check digit is a redundant digit(s) added to a data code that enables the accuracy of other characters in the code to be checked. The check digit may act as a prefix character, a suffix character, or it may be placed somewhere in the middle of the code. The last alternative is sometimes used for credit cards so that if a blank plastic card is stolen, it is difficult for a forger to work out a valid account number.

 There are many ways of calculating check digits. A simple way is to add up the digits in a number and assign the result as a suffix character. For example, if the code is 2148, the check digit is $2 + 1 + 4 + 8 = 15$. Dropping the tens digit, the check digit will be 5 and the code 21485. However, this check digit does not detect a very common kind of coding error, namely, a transposition error. The incorrect code 2814 still produces the correct check digit.

 To overcome this problem a different method of calculating a check digit can be used. Given, again, the code 2148, the steps are:

 1 Multiply each digit by a weight. In this case the weight used will be 5-4-3-2; that is, 2 for the units digit, 3 for the tens digit, 4 for the hundreds digit, and 5 for the thousands digit, viz:

$$8 \times 2 = 16$$
$$4 \times 3 = 12$$
$$1 \times 4 = 4$$
$$2 \times 5 = 10$$

2 Sum the products = 42.

3 Divide by a modulus. In this case the modulus 11 is chosen.

$$\frac{42}{11} = 3 \text{ with remainder } 9$$

4 Subtract the remainder from the modulus and the result constitutes the check digit.

$$11 - 9 = 2$$

5 Add the check digit to the code as a suffix. The result is 21482.

The check digit can be recalculated upon keypunching to detect a coding or keypunch error, or upon reading the data into the computer. The recalculation for the above code proceeds as follows:

1 Multiply each digit by its corresponding weight. The check digit takes a weight of 1.

$$2 \times 1 = 2$$
$$8 \times 2 = 16$$
$$4 \times 3 = 12$$
$$1 \times 4 = 4$$
$$2 \times 5 = 10$$

2 Sum the products = 44.
3 Divide by the modulus

$$\frac{44}{11} = 4$$

4 If the remainder is zero, there is a high probability the code is correct.

If the code contains alphabetics, a check digit can still be calculated. Each alphabetic must be assigned a number according to some rule.

Efficiency of Check Digit Methods

Table 9.3 shows the relative efficiency of various check digit methods. Anderson et al. [1974] provide further information on the relative efficiency of some of the methods based on whether they generate a distribution that is skewed; that is, some check digits occurring more often than others.

TABLE 9.3
EFFICIENCY OF DIFFERENT MODULI FOR CHECK DIGITS

Modulus	Range weights that may be used	Max. length of number without repeating weight	Weights used	Percentage errors detected				
				Tran-scription	Single trans-position	Double trans-position	Other trans-position	Random
10	1–9	8	1-2-1-2-1	100	97.8	Nil	48.9	90.0
			1-3-1-3-1	100	88.9	Nil	44.5	90.0
			7-6-5-4-3-2	87.0	100	88.9	88.9	90.0
			9-8-7-4-3-2	94.4	100	88.9	74.1	90.0
			1-3-7-1-3-7	100	88.9	88.9	44.4	90.0
11	1–10	9	10-9-8.....2	100	100	100	100	90.9
			1-2-4-8-16, etc.	100	100	100	100	90.9
13	1–12	11	Any	100	100	100	100	92.3
17	1–16	15	Any	100	100	100	100	94.1
19	1–18	17	Any	100	100	100	100	94.7
23	1–22	21	Any	100	100	100	100	95.6
27	1–26	25	Any	100	100	100	100	96.3
31	1–30	29	Any	100	100	100	100	96.8
37	1–36	35	Any	100	100	100	100	97.3

Source: Daniels and Yeates [1971]. Used by permission. The National Computing Center.

Note from Table 9.3 that modulus 37 detects the greatest percentage of errors. However, in practice modulus 11 is more commonly used because modulus 37 requires two check digits instead of one. Admittedly modulus 11 produces a remainder of 1, which means a check digit of 10; but some convention can be used to code a check digit of 10 as some other character—for example, zero or an alphabetic. With the most common types of errors—transcription and transposition errors—modulus 11 and modulus 37 are equally efficient. Since random errors occur very infrequently, the overhead of using two character check digits instead of one usually is considered to be unacceptable. For example, if many thousands of cards have to be keypunched, an extra digit may add hours to keypunch time.

When to Use Check Digits

Check digits involve overhead in terms of a redundant character carried at least partially through the system and extra computation needed to calculate and check the check digit. Therefore, use of check digits should be limited to critical fields.

Manual calculation or checking of check digits should be avoided. The process is time-consuming and error-prone. For new codes the check digit should be precalculated and assigned as part of the code. Where possible, the computer should assign new codes with their check digits.

Checking of check digits should take place only by machine; for example, during keypunching or by an input program. To save storage space the check digit can be dropped once it has been read into the machine and recalculated upon output. The tradeoff here is storage space versus processing time.

BATCH CONTROLS

Some of the simplest and most effective controls over data capture, preparation, and entry processes are batch controls. Batching is the process of grouping together transactions bearing some type of relationship to each other. Various controls then can be exercised over the batch to prevent or detect errors.

There are two types of batches: physical batches and logical batches. Physical batches are groups of transactions that constitute a physical unit. For example, source documents can be spiked and tied together. Logical batches are groups of transactions bound together on some logical basis, rather than being physically contiguous. For example, different clerks may enter transactions into a system using an online terminal. Each clerk keeps control totals of the transactions that she/he has entered. The input program logically groups transactions entered on the basis of the clerk's identification number, and after some period has elapsed, prepares control totals for reconciliation with the clerk's control totals.

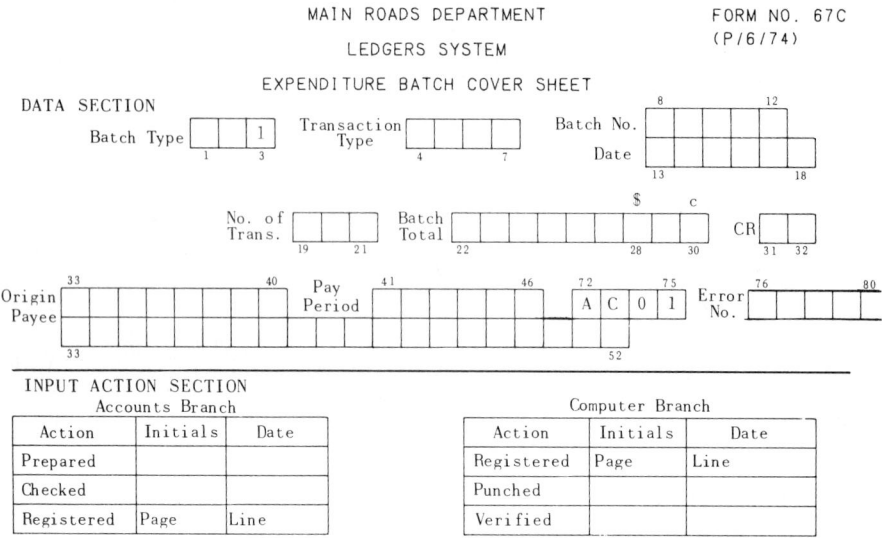

Figure 9.3
Batch cover sheet (Main Roads Department, Queensland, Australia).

Controls over Batches

Controls over batches have two purposes: (*a*) to ensure the accuracy and completeness of their content, and (*b*) to ensure they are not lost during transportation. Two documents are needed to help achieve these purposes: a batch cover sheet and a batch control register.

A batch cover sheet (Figure 9.3) for a physical batch contains some or all of the following information:

1 A unique batch number
2 Control totals for the batch
3 Data common to the various transactions in the batch, e.g., transaction type
4 Date when the batch was prepared
5 Information on errors detected in the batch
6 Space for signatures of personnel who have dealt with the batch, e.g., the person who prepared the batch, the person who checked the batch, the person who keypunched the batch, the person who filed the batch

For a logical batch, only some of this information may be recorded. For example, a clerk simply may keep a record of the transaction amounts entered into the system over the time period during which batch control totals are computed.

Control totals calculated for a batch are one of three types:

Control total type	Explanation
Financial Totals	Grand totals calculated for each field containing dollar amounts
Hash Totals	Grand totals calculated for any code on a document in the batch; e.g., the source document serial numbers can be totalled
Document/Record Counts	Grand totals for the number of documents or records in the batch

To check control totals, either the input validation program, or in some cases the data entry device, recomputes the total. Discrepancies arise through incorrect calculation of a control total, insertion or removal of documents, changes made to fields, or incorrect keypunching.

A batch control register (Figure 9.4) records the transit of physical batches between various sections or departments within an organization. Each person responsible for handling batches has a batch register. The register is signed each time a batch is received or dispatched. The person who brings the batch or takes the batch away countersigns the register. In some cases the person taking over responsibility for the batch also checks its contents; however, this procedure is costly.

Batch Design

Batch design involves choosing the size and nature of the batches to be used. Three major design guidelines should be followed:

1 Have the batch small enough to facilitate locating errors if batch controls do not balance.

2 The batch should be large enough to constitute a reasonably sized unit of work.

3 The batch should constitute a logical unit; for example, a group of documents all containing a single transaction type.

OTHER DATA CAPTURE AND PREPARATION CONTROLS

Table 9.2 lists several other controls that are important in the data input process. Since these controls are either well-known in manual systems or relatively straightforward, the following sections provide only brief overviews.

Procedures Controls

Procedures controls ensure work follows established patterns. Written procedures should clearly document the tasks that must be done. This helps

MAIN ROADS DEPARTMENT
LEDGER SYSTEM
BATCH CONTROL REGISTER

FORM 67A
(P/1/75)

DATE _____

PAGE _____

LINE	ACCOUNTS BRANCH TIME DESPATCHED............							COMPUTER TIME RECEIVED............			
	IDENTIFICATION			CONTROL		VALIDATION RESULTS			G.C.S. BATCH No.	VERIFIED	TRANSFER TAPE No.	ERASE DATE
	TYPE	BATCH No.	DATE	No.	AMOUNT	No.	AMOUNT	DATE				
1						A R						
2						A R						
3						A R						
4						A R						
5						A R						
6						A R						
7						A R						
8						A R						
9						A R						
10						A R						
11						A R						
12						A R						
13						A R						
14						A R						
15						A R						
16						A R						
17						A R						
18						A R						
19						A R						
20						A R						

Figure 9.4
Batch control register (Main Roads Department, Queensland, Australia).

achieve: (*a*) accurate and complete data capture, preparation, and entry, (*b*) improved efficiency through task standardization, and (*c*) decreased personnel training costs. Procedures manuals should be written according to some discipline; for example, a PLAYSCRIPT style (see Shultis [1964]).

Procedural Review

Procedural review simply involves scanning input data to detect obvious errors. The clerk performing the review may detect fields on a source document that have not been completed, or fields containing data clearly in error.

Verification

Verification is a duplicate process whereby data already keyed is rekeyed to check the accuracy of the initial keying. It is a costly control because it duplicates work, and it should be used only for critical fields where errors are difficult to detect using an input validation program.

Design of Keying Tasks/Environment

Two important factors affecting the speed and accuracy of keying are the design of keying tasks and the design of the keying environment.

In general, to relieve operator boredom, keying tasks should take no longer than an hour. Operators also must be able to perceive an end to a task. If source documents continue to arrive, the operator gets further behind, and frustration and loss of confidence cause inaccuracies and decreased keying speed.

Three aspects of the task environment affect keying speed and accuracy: (*a*) lighting, (*b*) acoustics, and (*c*) layout. Lighting must be adequate without causing glare. Acoustically the environment can be too noisy or too quiet. Carpets, panelling, screens, and proper flooring reduce noise levels. Key-to-tape and key-to-disk devices now make an audible click to break the silence so the operator can maintain a keying rhythm. Layout considerations include space, amenities, and position of keying devices.

Personnel Training

Management sometimes has the impression that data capture and preparation tasks are easy and require little training. In some cases this is a reasonable assumption. However, often proper training improves the speed and accuracy of data capture and preparation. Experienced clerks can disseminate their knowledge on how tasks should be performed. Proper performance of data preparation tasks is not simply a matter of providing good typists with a new device. Utilizing the full capabilities of a data preparation device requires training. Furthermore, today many organizations are involved in teaching keying skills and experimenting with new keying techniques and keyboard formats, some of which seem capable of improving keying speed and accuracy.

SUMMARY

Data capture and preparation controls are especially important to the auditor for two reasons. First, data capture and preparation tasks involve large amounts of human intervention, are often routine, monotonous, and error-prone. Second, research suggests the data capture and data preparation processes often are used to perpetrate a fraud.

Evaluating controls over data capture and data preparation is a complex problem for the auditor. A large number of different combinations of data capture, data preparation, and data entry methods exist. Each of these combinations has different strengths and weaknesses. The auditor must have a good understanding of the different methods to be able to evaluate the decisions made by a system designer.

Once a data capture and data preparation method has been chosen, other controls must be instituted. These controls include good source document design, good interactive language design, selection of an appropriate data coding method, choice of a check digit method for key fields, use of batch controls and procedural review, verification of critical fields, adequate training of personnel, provision of procedural reference manuals, and good design of keying tasks and a keying environment.

REVIEW QUESTIONS

9.1. Briefly distinguish between data capture, data preparation, and data entry. Why are data capture and data preparation controls especially important to the auditor?

9.2. Classify each of the following types of data capture as either document-based, direct entry, or a hybrid approach:
   a. a salesperson uses a card dialer Touch-Tone device to input data from a remote location about a sale to a customer
   b. a manager makes alterations with a light pen to a cost-volume-profit graph displayed on a VDU
   c. an investment analyst receives a magnetic tape containing stock prices from the stock exchange for input to her financial modelling package
   d. a warehouse receiving clerk speaks into a voice recognition device to update a file containing information on the state of various inventory bins
   e. a salesclerk removes a punched card attached to a product to designate sale of the product
   f. various patents are microfilmed for input to the computer using computer input microfilm

9.3. Briefly describe the different times at which data preparation can occur during the input process. In each case give an example.

9.4. Compare the relative advantages and disadvantages of direct entry and hybrid data capture methods.

9.5. American Telephone and Telegraph Company bills its customers using punch cards as turnaround documents. As described in the chapter, the oil companies bill customers using documents (to be input to OCR devices) as turnaround documents. Suggest why these alternate approaches may have been chosen.

9.6. From a data integrity perspective, what advantages does a VDU offer over an ordinary typewriter terminal?

9.7. List the major types of data capture and data preparation errors that may be made by: (*a*) a checkout clerk in a supermarket, and (*b*) a sales clerk in a retail store. Which of these errors might be prevented using point-of-sale devices?

9.8. Briefly discuss how user (operator) characteristics affect the design of an interactive language for capturing source data.

9.9. Why is it important that the receipt of all data sent by a user at an online terminal be acknowledged by the computer?

9.10. Briefly describe some techniques for testing the quality of the design of an interactive language before it is placed in production.

9.11. What attributes of a data code affect the likelihood of a recording error being made by a user of the code? Briefly outline some strategies to reduce error rates that occur with data codes.

9.12. List the four types of data codes—serial, block sequence, hierarchical, and associative—in increasing order of: (*a*) mnemonic value, (*b*) compactness, and (*c*) flexibility for expansion.

9.13. Briefly discuss the distinction between a physical batch and a logical batch. Are there any differences in the controls that can be exercised over physical and logical batches?

9.14. Why should information that is common to all the transactions in a batch be coded on the batch cover sheet?

9.15. Briefly explain why it is best not to have different transaction types within the same batch.

9.16. Briefly explain the difference between the following batch control totals: (*a*) document count, (*b*) hash total, and (*c*) financial total. For each control total, give an example where the application of the control total to a batch would *not* be useful or appropriate.

9.17. Distinguish between procedural controls and procedural review. In general, which of these controls is likely to be more powerful? Which of these controls is a preventive control and which is a detective control?

9.18. Briefly explain the advantages of writing a procedures manual according to a certain style. (*Hint:* Refer to Shultis [1964] or Haga [1968]).

9.19. Outline some of the factors to be considered in the design of keying tasks and the work environment in a keypunch preparation area.

9.20. List three differences between the keying tasks performed by a typist and a keypunch operator. What training implications do these differences have?

EXERCISES AND CASES

9.1. Consider a medium-size insurance company. Fill in the elements of the following controls matrix for the company where the elements represent the cost-effectiveness of the controls at reducing the expected losses from the causes of loss. Assume a score of 5 represents high cost-effectiveness and a score of 1 represents low cost-effectiveness. Justify your rating for any score above 3.

Controls \ Cause of loss	Removal of assets	Destruction of assets	Unauthorized data	Incomplete data	Ineffective systems	Inefficient systems
Appropriate data capture method						
Appropriate data preparation method						
Appropriate data entry method						
Good source document design						
Good interactive language design						
Good data code design						
Check digits						
Batch controls						

9.2. Buildit Corporation is a construction engineering firm with offices scattered throughout Australia in the capital cities and major country cities and towns. Engineers on a job complete source documents to record various information about the job; for example, direct material and direct labor costs, overhead, progress made, and deviations from plans. These source documents then are batched in the various offices and sent to the head office in Sydney for processing.

When the source documents arrive in Sydney they are keypunched on cards. Currently a high keypunching error rate exists. Because the source documents are completed under adverse conditions, keypunch operators often find them illegible. The problem of errors is confounded further because error reports must be sent back to the respective offices for correction. By the time an office tracks down the responsible engineer, the time delay between completion of the source document and error notification may be several weeks. Often the engineer has difficulties in remembering the circumstances surrounding the data.

Required: The problem has grown to sufficient proportions that Buildit's management has formed a task force group to develop possible solutions. As the manager of internal audit they have asked you to participate as a member of the task force group. Prepare a report outlining some alternative recommendations that may be acceptable. Briefly describe the relative advantages and disadvantages of your proposed solutions. You should at least consider the possibility of redesigning the source documents or having data prepared in the various offices. In the latter case, most district offices could support about three card keypunches on a full-time basis. Note, also, that data communications costs in Australia are high.

9.3. Your company has just installed five key-to-disk devices. Each of these devices has 30 keystations attached to each processor. The key-to-disk devices will be used in the conventional way: punching batches of source documents. The data processing manager is concerned about a device failure since all 30 keystations will be affected and data previously punched may be lost. He has asked the internal audit manager to examine the problem and she has asked you to prepare a report. Outline a scheme(s) for backup and recovery after device failure. Be sure to describe any advantages or disadvantages of your scheme(s).

9.4. Design an order form that can be used by a wholesaler as a turnaround document and input to an optical mark sensing device. The wholesaler distributes these forms each month to its retail customers. The order form must provide for the following fields:

Field	Picture	Comments
Customer account no.	9(6)	Binary marks preprinted by computer
Customer name and address	X(80)	Four lines of X(20), preprinted by the computer for display in a window envelope
Month number	9(4)	Binary marks preprinted by computer
Product description	X(30)	Preprinted by the computer; some products change from month to month; allow for up to 50 products
Order quantities	9(2)	Marks to be made by hand by the customer; up to 99 units of a product can be ordered
Comments	X(100)	Information for the customer preprinted by the computer; e.g., availability of new products, special discounts available

Briefly indicate any data integrity problems you think may result with your design.

9.5. A supermarket chain in a large city is considering the installation of point-of-sale equipment. One of management's concerns is backup and recovery if hardware or software failure occurs. The chain has 20 supermarkets in the city. The proposed hardware configuration is to have the terminals in a store (normally about 10 checkout lanes) connected to a store controller, which in turn is connected to a host processor at the chain's head office. As the manager of internal audit for the chain, management has asked you to prepare a brief report outlining some possible backup and recovery strategies that can be used in the event of hardware/software failure (*Hint:* Refer to Hippert et al. [1975]).

9.6. For each of the following cases, choose a medium and makeup for the source document to be completed so as to minimize keypunch errors caused by illegible writing, a torn form, etc.:

246 PART 3: THE APPLICATION CONTROL FRAMEWORK

    a. a traveling salesperson completes orders in the field and mails the orders to head office for keypunching and input to an invoicing system
    b. a foreperson on a production floor completes employee time sheets for keypunching and input to the payroll system
    c. truck drivers provide data on deliveries made to customers for keypunching and input to an invoicing system
    d. a clerk at the front desk of an insurance company provides data on claims made by customers for keypunching and input to a claims system

9.7. Suggest some ways in which the following source document, an employee timesheet for a job costing system, might be improved to reduce data capture and preparation errors:

Produceit Company   ℗   Daily Time Sheet   Form No: 4SP-66

Employee Name: _____

Employee Number: _____   Date: _____

Hours		Job Number	Machine		Stage of Completion	Comments
Regular	Overtime		Number	Hours		

Foreperson's Signature _____

9.8. Comment on the quality of the following display. Clerks provide data for an invoicing system describing where orders are to be sent.

#87AB649531G

INVOICE TO: SHIP TO:

WEIRDO T-SHIRTS, INC.   WEIRDO T-SHIRTS, INC.
895 COLLING STREET   895 COLLING STREET
MELBOURNE. VIC. 3743   MELBOURNE. VIC. 3743

IS THE ABOVE INFORMATION CORRECT AND, IF SO, IS SHIPMENT REQUIRED IN < 10 DAYS?

9.9. Calculate check digits for the following:

Code	Modulus	Weight
753642	10	1-2-1-2-1
43196	11	6-5-4-3-2
841975	37	1-3-7-1-3-7

How would you have calculated the check digits if each of the above codes had contained some alphabetic characters?

9.10. The following journal entry transaction card is keypunched for input into a general ledgers system. Indicate, with reasons why, those fields where you would use a check digit and those fields you would verify:

Record type
Account number
Transaction code
Description
Amount
Source document number

REFERENCES

Akresh, Abraham D., and Michael Goldstein. "Point-of-Sale Accounting Systems: Some Implications for the Auditor," *Journal of Accountancy* (December 1978), pp. 68–74.

Allen, Brandt. "The Biggest Computer Frauds: Lessons for CPAs," *Journal of Accountancy* (May 1977), pp. 52–62.

Anderson, Lane K., Raymond A. Hendershot, and Robert C. Shoonmaker. "Self-Checking Digit Concepts," *Journal of Systems Management* (September 1974), pp. 36–42.

Antonelli, D. C. "The Role of the Operator in the Supermarket and Retail Store Systems," *IBM Systems Journal*, vol. 14, no. 1, 1975, pp. 34–45.

Berk, M. A., C. W. Dunbar, and G. C. Hobson. "Design and Performance Considerations for the Retail Store System," *IBM Systems Journal*, vol. 14, no. 1, 1975, pp. 64–80.

Carey, L. Chester. "The Quality Form," *Journal of Systems Management* (June 1972), pp. 28–30.

Chapdelaine, P. A. *Accuracy Control in Source Data Collection* (Ohio: Headquarters, Air Force Logistics Command, Wright-Patterson Air Force Base, 1963).

Clifton, H. D. *Business Data Systems: A Practical Guide to Systems Analysis and Data Processing* (London: Prentice-Hall International, Inc., 1978).

Conrad, R. "Errors of Immediate Memory," *The British Journal of Psychology* (November 1959), pp. 349–359.

Coughlin, Clifford W. "The Need for Good Procedures," *Journal of Systems Management* (June 1974), pp. 30–33.

Crannell, C. W., and J. M. Parrish. "A Comparison of Immediate Memory Span for Digits, Letters, and Words," *The Journal of Psychology* (October 1957), pp. 319–327.

Daniels, Alan, and Donald Yeates. *Systems Analysis* (Palo Alto: Science Research Associates, Inc., 1971).

Davis, Gordon B. *Management Information Systems: Conceptual Foundations, Structure, and Development* (New York: McGraw-Hill Book Company, 1974).

Evans, Hugh S. "Where to Use Optical Mark Systems," *Journal of Systems Management* (March 1973), pp. 8–13.

Gore, Marvin, and John Stubbe. *Elements of Systems Analysis for Business Data Processing* (Dubuque, Iowa: Wm. C. Brown Company Publishers, 1975).

Haga, Clifford I. "Procedures Manuals," *Ideas for Management* (Cleveland: Systems and Procedures Association, 1968), pp. 127–154.

Hartman, W., H. Matthes, and A. Proeme. *Management Information Systems Handbook: Analysis, Requirements Determination, Design and Development, Implementation and Evaluation* (New York: McGraw-Hill Book Company, 1968).

Hauck, Edward J. "Be Kind to Your Data Codes," *Journal of Systems Management* (December 1972), pp. 8–12.

Hippert, R. O., L. R. Palounek, J. Provetero, and R. O. Skatrud. "Reliability, Availability, and Serviceability Design Considerations for the Supermarket and Retail Store Systems," *IBM Systems Journal*, vol. 14, no. 1, 1975, pp. 81–95.

McEnroe, P. V., H. T. Huth, E. A. Moore, and W. W. Morris. "Overview of the Supermarket System and the Retail Store System," *IBM Systems Journal*, vol. 14, no. 1, 1975, pp. 3–15.

Martin, James. *Design of Man-Computer Dialogues* (Englewood Cliffs, N.J.: Prentice-Hall, Inc., 1973).

Mason, John O., and William E. Connelly. "The Application and Reliability of the Self-Checking Digit Technique," *Management Advisor* (September–October 1971), pp. 27–34.

Metz, W. C., and D. Savir. "Store Performance Studies for the Supermarket System," *IBM Systems Journal*, vol. 14, no. 1, 1975, pp. 46–63.

Miller, George A. "The Magical Number Seven, Plus or Minus Two: Some Limits on Our Capability for Processing Information," *The Psychological Review* (March 1956), pp. 81–97.

Miller, Robert B. "Response Time in Man-Computer Conversational Transactions," *Proceedings of the 1968 AFIPS Fall Joint Computer Conference* (Washington: The Thompson Book Company, 1968), pp. 267–278.

Owsowitz, S., and A. Sweetland. *Factors Affecting Coding Errors* (Santa Monica, Calif.: The Rand Corporation, 1965). Rand Memorandum RM-4346-PR.

Rocke, Merle G. "The Need for Data Code Control," *Datamation* (September 1973), pp. 105–108.

Savir, D., and G. J. Laurer. "The Characteristics and Decodability of the Universal Product Code," *IBM Systems Journal*, vol. 14, no. 1, 1975, pp. 16–34.

Shultis, Robert L. " 'Playscript'—A New Tool Accountants Need," *NAA Bulletin* (August 1964), pp. 3–10.

Staggs, Earl W. "Maybe It's Your Forms," *Journal of Systems Management* (March 1972), pp. 8–12.

Stanford Research Institute. *Systems Auditability and Control Study: Data Processing Control Practices Report* (Altamonte Springs, Fla.: The Institute of Internal Auditors, Inc., 1977).

Wooldridge, Susan. *Computer Input Design* (New York: Petrocelli Books, 1974).

Wu, Margaret. *An Introduction to Computer Data Processing* (New York: Harcourt Brace Jovanovich, Inc., 1975).

CHAPTER 10

ACCESS AND COMMUNICATIONS CONTROLS

CHAPTER OUTLINE

ACCESS CONTROLS
    Functions of an Access Control Mechanism
    Implementing an Access Control Mechanism
COMMUNICATIONS CONTROLS
    Sources of Network Failure
    Treatment of Line Errors
    Improving Network Reliability
CRYPTOGRAPHY
    Cryptographic Techniques
    Choosing a Cipher System
    Key Management
    Cryptography for Databases
SUMMARY
REVIEW QUESTIONS
EXERCISES AND CASES
REFERENCES

Access controls seek to prevent the unauthorized use of computing resources. *Communications controls* seek to maintain the integrity of data transmitted over communications lines. For a long time both these sets of controls were neglected aspects of computer technology. However, recently there has been substantial stimulus for research in both these areas. As computing resources are shared increasingly, access controls become more important. Data communications traffic is experiencing explosive growth. Withington [1975] estimates the current growth rate of 35% per annum will continue through 1985; the average reduction in communications line costs through 1985 should be about 50% overall.

Besides the above trends, two other factors heighten the auditor's interest in access and communications controls. First, the use of electronic funds transfer (EFT) systems for exchange of monies is increasing (see Dolan et al. [1976] and Schaller [1978]). Since these systems are communications network-based systems, access and communications controls are especially important to safeguarding assets and maintaining data integrity. Second, for those organizations that use service bureaus to carry out their data processing, access and communications controls are fundamental to preventing unauthorized use of resources by other customers of the service bureau (see, for background, American Institute of Certified Public Accountants [1974] and Roussey [1978]).

ACCESS CONTROLS

Access controls usually are a minor problem when only one person uses the resources of a computing system (providing separation of duties exists). Access control simply amounts to excluding anyone else from using the system; for example, by physically barring access to the system. There may be cases where the computing resources used are so critical that they justify this form of access control. Certain defense installations fall into this category. However, given the processing power of current computing systems, typically a single person can use only a small proportion of the available capabilities. Absolute access control of the type described above is an expensive strategy.

The trend in current computing technology is toward increased sharing of resources. This is achieved by having a single computer simulate the operations of several computers. Each of the simulated computers is called a virtual machine. Virtual machines allow more efficient use of resources through decreasing a single computer's idle capacity. In a virtual machine environment, however, it is a major design problem to ensure each virtual machine operates as though it were completely unaware of the operations of other virtual machines. Increased scope exists for unintentional or malicious damage. A design flaw may result in one virtual machine unintentionally violating the integrity of processes and data belonging to another virtual machine. Furthermore, because it is difficult to completely isolate virtual machines from each other, one virtual machine may be used *intentionally* to attempt unauthorized access to another virtual machine.

In a shared resource environment the auditor has two concerns about access controls. First, the auditor must determine whether or not the access control mechanism used within the computer installation is capable of preventing unauthorized access to and use of resources. Since the access control mechanism normally is embedded within the operating system or the database management system, assessing the capabilities of the access control mechanism can be a complex task (see, also, Chapter 12). Second, given the capabilities of the access control mechanism, for any particular application system the auditor must determine whether or not the access controls chosen for that system suffice. Since the sufficiency of the application system access controls depends directly on the capabilities of the access control mechanism, the following sections discuss the major features that should exist in an access control mechanism.

Functions of an Access Control Mechanism

An access control mechanism associates with identified, authorized users the resources they are permitted to access and the action privileges they have with respect to those resources. The mechanism processes users' requests for resources in three steps (Figure 10.1). First, users identify themselves to the mechanism, thereby indicating their intent to request use of system resources. Second, users must authenticate themselves, and the mechanism must authenticate itself. Authentication is a two-way process. Not only must the mechanism be sure it has a valid user, users also must be sure they have a valid mechanism. This matter is discussed in more detail later in the chapter. Third, users request specific resources and specify the actions they intend to undertake with the resources. The mechanism accesses previously stored information about users, the resources they can access, and the action privileges they have with respect to those resources, and permits or denies the request.

Identification and Authentication Users identify themselves to the access control mechanism by providing information such as a name or account number. This identification information enables the mechanism to select from its file of authentication information the entry corresponding to the user. The authentication process then proceeds on the basis of the information contained in the entry, the user having to indicate prior knowledge of this information.

Everest [1982] lists four classes of authentication information provided by users:

Class	Examples
Remembered Information	Name, account number, passwords
Possessed Objects	Badge, plastic card, key
Personal Characteristics	Fingerprint, voiceprint, hand size, signature
Dialog	Through/around the computer

Each authentication class has its inherent weaknesses; any particular authentication scheme may use several methods to counteract some of these weaknesses; for example, a user may need a key to a terminal and also have to provide a password.

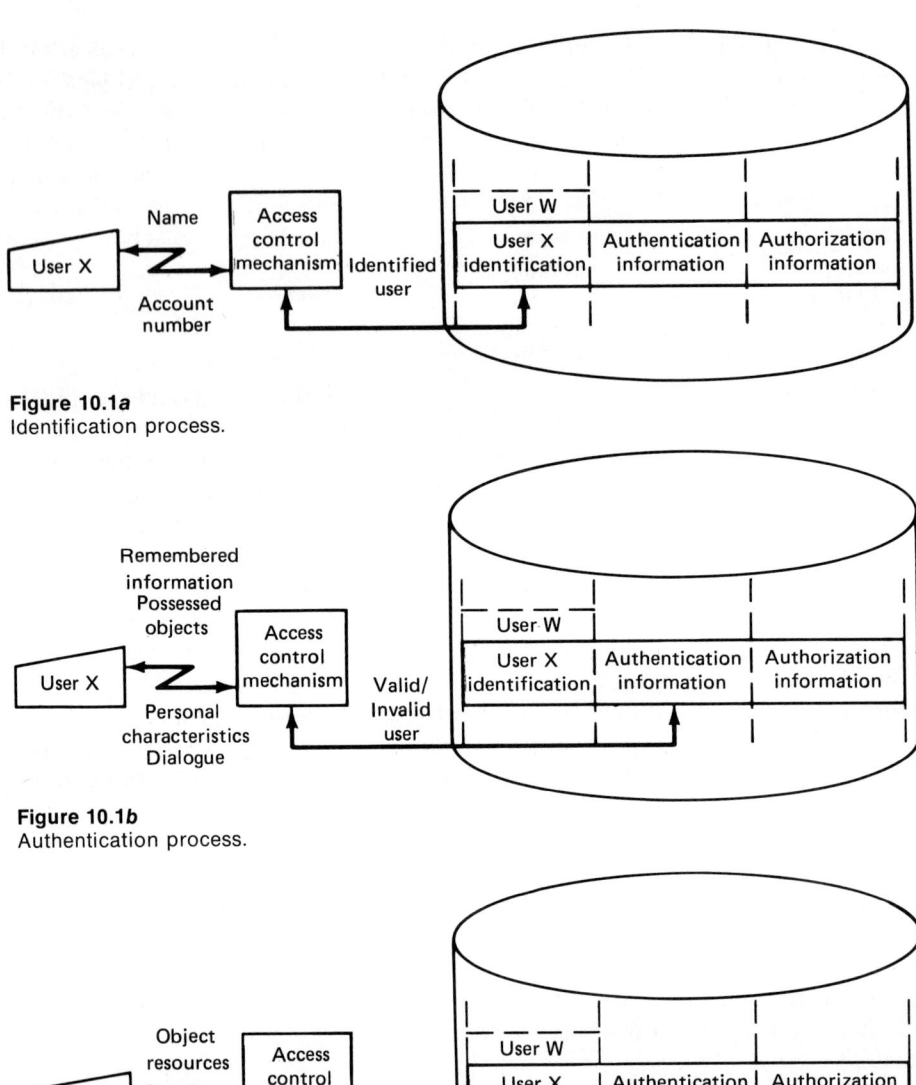

Figure 10.1a
Identification process.

Figure 10.1b
Authentication process.

Figure 10.1c
Authorization process.

The primary problem with *remembered information* as an authentication method is that it can be forgotten. A password is probably the most common method used to authenticate users yet it is a good example of an authentication scheme fraught with problems.

The first major defect of passwords is that users tend to choose passwords that are easy to remember. Saltzer and Schroeder [1975] report that a study of 300 self-chosen passwords for a typical time-sharing system showed over 50% of the passwords were short enough to guess by exhaustion, or they could be derived from some attribute of the user; for example, the user's name or birth date. Various schemes have been proposed to overcome this difficulty. Everest [1982] suggests using a mathematical function known to both the user and the system; for example, $z = 4x + 3y + 7$. When the user signs on to the system, the access mechanism supplies the exogenous values, say, $x = 3$ and $y = 6$. The user must respond with the correct value for the endogenous variable; in this case 37. Saltzer [1974] suggests having the access mechanism generate random passwords that are pronounceable so there is less temptation for the user to write them down.

The second major defect of passwords is that many access mechanisms associate passwords with resources instead of associating them with users. Consequently, instead of users having to remember just a single password, they must remember every password associated with each resource they wish to use. This strategy causes several problems. First, since most users will have to remember several passwords (some perhaps even hundreds of passwords), a strong incentive exists for users to record the passwords somewhere, thereby increasing the risk of exposure. Second, in general, the access mechanism can exercise only a coarse level of access authorization. For example, if a database administrator wished to exercise access control in a database at the data item level, in some cases this may involve users of the database having to know several hundred passwords. Consequently, access control probably would have to be exercised at a higher level; for example, a user does or does not have access to a file in the database. Third, administrative procedures for an access control scheme where passwords are associated with resources are awkward and unwieldy. If the administrator responsible for assigning passwords suspects a password is no longer secure, a new password must be assigned and all users of the existing password notified. This may be a very time-consuming process, especially if a password must be changed often.

An alternative scheme is to associate passwords with users rather than resources. Each user has a single password and associated with each password is a list of entries showing the resources that the user is permitted to access and the action privileges that the user has with respect to these resources. With this scheme, users can change their passwords as frequently as they desire without affecting other users. The access control mechanism must perform more functions since it must couple passwords with access control lists. However, passwords are more secure since a user has only one to remember, and the password can be changed easily when it is suspected to be no longer secure.

The primary problem with *possessed objects* as a means of authentication is that they can be lost or stolen. However, aside from the inconvenience caused, the access control mechanism readily should be able to handle lost or stolen possessed objects. Providing the user immediately notifies the administrator responsible for access controls that the object has been lost or stolen, the access control mechanism can be instructed to reject all further requests for resources made using the object. Further, it should log any attempts made to use the object, sound an alarm, and perhaps refuse to eject the object from the reading device.

So far the primary problem with using *personal characteristics* as a means of authentication is that the mechanisms used to read personal characteristics still make errors: they may accept an unauthorized user or reject a legitimate user. The reliability of the devices is improving. Adams [1977a, 1977b] describes several commercially available devices capable of reading personal characteristics. However, the technology in this area is still evolving (see, further, Everest [1982]).

Passwords, possessed objects, and personal characteristics all have a further weakness. The authentication information eventually is reduced to a bit stream and transmitted to the computer. A would-be penetrator simply has to intercept the bit stream to break security (Figure 10.2). Thus, it is critical for communication lines to be secure if the integrity of authentication information is to be preserved.

To some extent the above problem can be overcome by using *dialog* as a means of authentication. If dialog *through* the computer is used, the user first stores a set of personal characteristics; for example, spouse's name, birth date. When the user signs on, the access control mechanism randomly selects several characteristics from the set of stored characteristics and questions the user about their values. A would-be penetrator has to intercept dialogs over a period and try to construct the set of stored characteristics. Dialog *around* the computer simply involves a security officer asking the questions rather than an access control mechanism.

In all cases users must be sure they are not providing authentication information to a foreign access control mechanism. A penetrator can masquerade

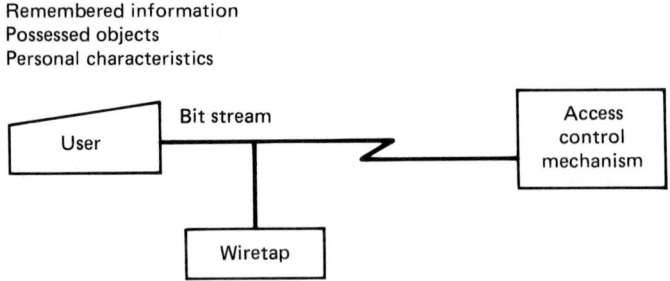

Figure 10.2
Using a wiretap to violate the integrity of authentication information.

as a system's access control mechanism, capture a user password, simulate a system crash, and then ask the user to sign on again, this time to the valid access control mechanism.

Saltzer and Schroeder [1975] describe one method for preventing masquerading (Figure 10.3). It requires a terminal be equipped with enciphering

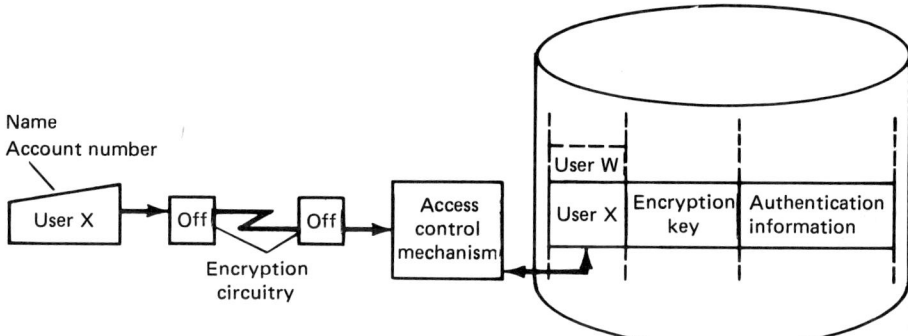

Figure 10.3a
User identification in a two-way authentication process.

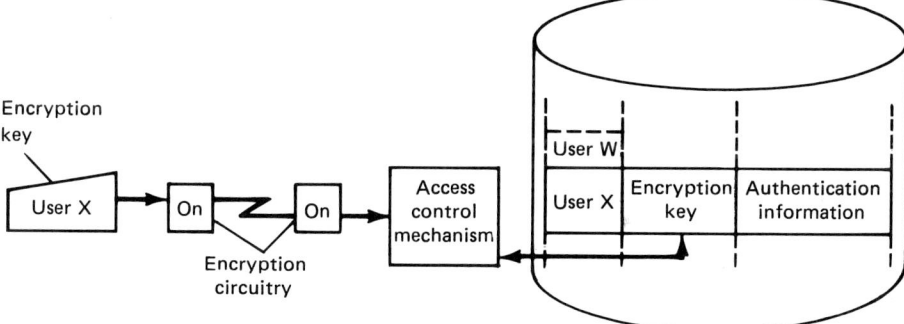

Figure 10.3b
Activation of encryption circuitry and load of encryption key by both user and access control mechanism in a two-way authentication process.

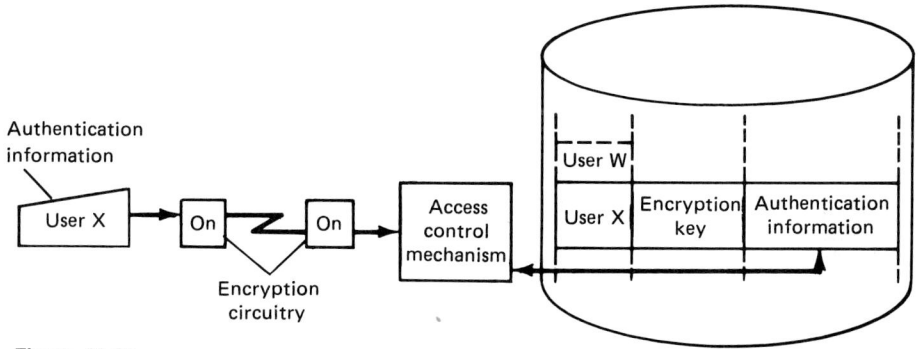

Figure 10.3c
Encrypted dialog in a two-way authentication process.

circuitry. The terminal user first signs on, bypasses the circuitry, and supplies identification information. The access control mechanism uses the identification information to look up a secured encryption key assigned the user. The access control mechanism then loads the key into its encryption device and starts dialog with the user. In the meantime the user has loaded the encryption key at the terminal, activated the enciphering circuitry, and stands ready for the first response from the access control mechanism. If both the user and the access control mechanism hold the same key, some form of dialog can proceed; otherwise, the user receives an unintelligible bit stream.

Object Resources In a generalized access control mechanism all resources must be named since the mechanism must couple users with the resources they are permitted to use. Resources can be classified into four types:

Resource classification	Example
Hardware	Terminals, printers, processors, disks
Software	Application system programs, generalized system software
Commodities	Processor time, storage space
Data	Files, groups, data items

Action Privileges The action privileges assigned a user depend on the user's authority level and the type of resource requested for use. In most cases a user is or is not permitted to use a *hardware* device. There are some refinements. A user may be permitted to use a terminal only in display mode; or the user may not be able to use the light pen attached to the terminal.

Similarly, a user may or may not be able to use a *software* resource. Again, various refinements exist. Some users may be permitted to make copies of the source or object code of a program. Some may only be permitted to view the source code at a terminal. Others may only be allowed to activate the program.

Commodity resources are measured quantitatively. If a user has permission to use a commodity, the amount of the commodity that the user can consume must be specified. Thus, a user is assigned so many seconds of processor time, so many tracks of disk space, a certain number of input/output channels that can be used at one time, etc.

The most complex action privileges relate to the use of *data* resources. Some of the action privileges needed are:

1 Read
 • direct read
 • statistical or aggregate data only
2 Add
 • insert
 • append
3 Modify (Write)

These action privileges should apply at an aggregate level and a detailed level. For example, they may apply at the level of a file so that all the contents of the file are subject to the action privileges assigned the file. Alternatively, they may apply to data items (fields) within a file, different data items within the file having different action privileges assigned.

Conway et al. [1972] also point out the need to distinguish between data independent and data dependent action privileges. Data independent action privileges do not depend on the content of the object data; for example, a user is given or denied access to a salary field in a payroll record. Data dependent action privileges are conditional on the content of the object data; for example, a user only has access to a salary field if the salary field is under $15,000 per year.

The notion of conditional action privileges applies more generally than just data resources. For example, users may be authorized to use greater than two tape units only if the core storage consumed by their program is less than 10,000 words.

Still another variation on conditional action privileges relates to output. Users may not be permitted access to data depending on the results of a query they specify. This type of control is especially important in maintaining the privacy of individuals' data where statistical databases are used.

Consider, for example, a database containing information about individuals — name, address, birth date, birth place, education, credit information. A user formulates a query to obtain the average credit rating of all those people born at Biloela, Queensland, Australia, who received undergraduate education at the University of Queensland, postgraduate education at the University of Minnesota, currently reside in Brisbane, and are academics by occupation. It is highly likely the average credit rating would be calculated on a population of one individual — the author of this book! Hansen [1971] provides other examples showing how queries can be specified on statistical databases to obtain information about individuals. He also provides some recommendations to prevent unwanted disclosure.

Implementing an Access Control Mechanism

The previous sections have outlined the major elements of an access control mechanism. Given the current state of technology, however, a full implementation of this model is extremely costly. In practice, some tradeoffs must be made; overall control must be decreased to reduce costs. For any particular computer installation, the auditor's problem is to evaluate whether the tradeoffs made in the access control mechanism used by the installation are reasonable, given the overall control requirements of the installation. To aid this evaluation, the following sections discuss some of the problems encountered in implementing an access control mechanism.

Approaches to Authorization There are two approaches to implementing the authorization module in an access control mechanism: (*a*) a "list-oriented" approach, and (*b*) a "ticket-oriented" approach. In the list-oriented approach a list of resource objects and action privileges is associated with the unique identifier of each user. When the user requests a resource the mechanism examines the list for the appropriate authorization. In the ticket-oriented approach, the user is assigned a ticket for an object resource. To obtain the resource the user must present the correct ticket to the access mechanism.

Each approach has its advantages and disadvantages. With the list-oriented approach, users have to remember only their unique identifiers to obtain access to resources. Further, the access mechanism always knows who is accessing a resource via the unique identifier in the access list. The approach has two major disadvantages. First, it consumes substantial processor time since the access mechanism must reference the list each time a resource is requested. Second, the access lists may require substantial storage space. If the access lists are conceived as rows in a matrix (Figure 10.4) where each row is the triple (user unique identifier, object resource, action privileges), for 100 users and 100 resources the matrix would contain 30,000 elements. If access control is exercised over data resources at the data item level, the matrix would be considerably larger. Admittedly, in many cases the matrix would be sparse; usually most entries should be a denial of access to a resource (a null value in the matrix). Efficient algorithms exist for storing sparse matrices (see Knuth [1973]). Users also could be classified into homogeneous groups and access lists assigned to a group identifier (see Gladney [1978]). Conway et al. [1972] discuss other methods for reducing the size of the authorization matrix.

The ticket-oriented approach reduces the processor time required to authorize access to a resource. The access control mechanism simply compares the ticket presented by the user with the ticket necessary to gain access to the

User \ Resource	File X	Editor	File Y	Program 5
User A	Read	Enter		
User B	Statistical Read Only	Enter		Enter
User C		Enter	Append Only	
User D		Enter		Read Source Code Only

Figure 10.4
Authorization matrix in an access control mechanism.

resource. It is the user's responsibility to present the correct ticket. The approach has two major disadvantages. First, it is difficult to ensure tickets remain secure. All the problems of having passwords associated with resources instead of users arise. Second, the access control mechanism cannot identify who has presented the ticket. Thus, there is no accountability. The mechanism simply assumes a valid ticket is presented by a valid user. Further, since the mechanism has no means of identifying who presents an invalid ticket, it cannot keep a log of attempted resource accesses that failed.

In practice, some combination of the list-oriented and ticket-oriented approaches often is used to implement access authorization. For example, when interacting with users, the access control mechanism adopts a list-oriented approach. Once users have presented their unique identifiers, they are assigned temporary tickets that are then used to make further decisions on whether or not the user should be allowed access to a resource.

Conditional Action Privileges Conditional action privileges can be implemented using special run-time fetch and store functions. Conway et al. [1972] define four sets of functions needed within an access control mechanism:

F_t translation time fetch function
S_t translation time store function
F_r run-time fetch function
S_r run-time store function

The functions F_t and S_t are used for unconditional action privileges and can be generated as object code at compile time. The functions F_r and S_r are used for conditional action privileges. They are called at execution time and apply a Boolean test to determine whether or not action privileges will be granted for the input resources, or in the case of statistical databases, the output results.

Dynamics of Authorization Some difficult implementation problems arise in the area of authorization dynamics. Saltzer and Schroeder [1975] present two cases. First, consider the question of whether user A can access resource Z. A simple check of an entry in the authorization matrix is insufficient. It may show user A has no action privileges with respect to resource Z. However, a further question must be asked: Does user B have action privileges with respect to resource Z, and can user A request user B to assign these action privileges to user A? Further, is the assignment temporary (perhaps leaving no audit trail) or permanent? More complex chains of authorization can be illustrated. Second, what should happen if user B revokes user A's action privileges with respect to resource Z while A is using the resource? If user A is allowed to continue, an integrity violation may occur. If user A is aborted, it may cause substantial disruption. Both these cases demonstrate the need for an external agent, for example, a database administrator, who has a global view of the access authorization needs of the installation, and who can perform a mediating function when conflict arises.

COMMUNICATIONS CONTROLS

If application systems use a communications network for transmission of data between points, the auditor needs to evaluate the capabilities of the network for asset safeguarding, preserving data integrity, and allowing the application systems to achieve their objectives effectively and efficiently. The design of networks cannot be left to chance. Asset safeguarding, data integrity, system effectiveness, and system efficiency considerations dictate careful planning of networks.

The following sections examine some of the major design decisions that must be made with respect to controls in communications networks. The focus is on asset safeguarding and preserving data integrity, though some questions of effectiveness and efficiency are considered in passing. These latter questions can be considered only superficially because they are complex and warrant separate volumes (see, further, Martin [1972], Kimbleton and Schneider [1975], Cypser [1978], and Doll [1978]).

The discussion assumes basic familarity with the terms (concepts) used in teleprocessing though, where necessary, for review purposes they are defined. The reader should be familar with such terms as bauds; amplitude, frequency, and phase modulation; time division and frequency division multiplexing; concentrators; multidrop lines; simplex, half-duplex, and full-duplex transmission; private and public lines; packet switching; roll-call and hub polling. Awad [1977], Bohl [1976], and Watson [1970] provide introductions to the area.

Sources of Network Failure

Three types of failure can occur in a network: (*a*) line errors caused by noise, (*b*) hardware faults, and (*c*) software faults. Noise is the random electrical signals that occur in communications lines causing degraded performance. There are two types of noise: white and impulse. White noise occurs through the motion of electrons. It increases as a function of absolute temperature. Impulse noise occurs for a variety of reasons: atmospheric conditions, faulty switching gear, poor contacts. Noise increases as users transmit more data over communications lines. If the public telephone exchange network is used for data transmission, line errors increase during peak periods of use because of the additional noise produced.

Hardware and software failures in a communications network may be temporary or permanent and localized or global. An intermittent failure in a modem (data set) may corrupt a bit pattern transmitted over a communications line. An operating system may crash for some unknown reason but the operator is able to achieve restart within seconds. Terminal failure may affect only the user of the terminal. Failure in a concentrator, however, affects all users connected to the concentrator.

Treatment of Line Errors

Since a bit pattern can be corrupted during transmission through noise occurring, an important design decision is the way in which line errors will be detected and corrected. Cypser [1978] reports data from four surveys carried out in the United States and the United Kingdom to determine transmission error performance. Bit error rates spanned a range from 1 in 1000 to 1 in 1,000,000. Particularly when public lines are used for data transmission, the designer should assume a wide range of line error rates will be encountered.

The effects of line errors can be catastrophic. Martin [1972] uses the following example to show how a database can be corrupted quickly through line errors occurring. Consider an online database where transactions arrive with one bit in every 100,000 bits in error. Assume a record is updated 100 times a month, and if one of 20 five-bit characters is in error an update error occurs. After six months, approximately 4500 records will be in error. Certain line errors may have more serious effects than others. For example, if a transaction-type code field is corrupted, erroneous shipments of inventory may be made or a record deleted from the database by mistake.

Error Detection Line errors can be detected through using either a loop (echo) check or building some form of redundancy into the message transmitted. Thus, the quality of data transmitted increases at the cost of reduced throughput over the communications line. The design problem is to balance the cost of reduced throughput with the costs of undetected errors.

A *loop check* involves the receiver of a message sending back the message received to the sender. The sender checks the message received by the receiver is correct by comparing it with a stored copy of the message sent. If there is a difference, the message is retransmitted with suitable line protocol data to indicate the previous message received was in error. In fact, the message received may have been correct; the receiver's retransmission of the message back to the sender may have been corrupted.

Since a loop check at least halves the throughput on communications lines, normally it is used on full-duplex (simultaneous two-way communication) lines or where communications lines are short. If lines are short, the high protection afforded data transmission using a loop check may justify the costs of the extra channel capacity needed. On full-duplex lines the return path is often underutilized anyway so it can be used for error detection purposes.

Redundancy takes the form of error detecting codes. Three major types of codes exist: (*a*) parity checking codes, (*b*) M-out-of-N codes, and (*c*) cyclic codes.

Both vertical and horizontal *parity checks* can be used: a vertical parity check applies to a character, and a horizontal parity check applies to a string of characters. It is dangerous to use only vertical or horizontal parity checking. Martin [1970] quotes figures from an International Telegraph and Telephone Consultative Committee (CCITT) Study on the lengths of bursts of noise. The figures show a high probability (40–50%) that a burst of noise will corrupt more than one bit in a character. Thus, a single parity check (vertical or horizontal) will not detect an error if the corrupted bits compensate. There is about a 30% chance a single parity check will fail. A combination of vertical and horizontal parity checking affords greater protection against line errors.

In *M-out-of-N* codes characters must be represented by a fixed number of 1 and 0 bits in a character. For example, if a 4-out-of-8 code is used, the bit string for a character must consist of four 1 bits and four 0 bits. If the bit string received does not conform to this requirement, a line error has occurred. Martin [1970] argues an M-out-of-N code offers only a marginal improvement over a single parity check. Unfortunately, bursts of noise often oscillate, thereby causing one bit to change in one direction and a nearby bit to change in the opposite direction. Thus, a string 10 may change to a string 01 and the M-out-of-N code would fail to detect the error. Experiments carried out within IBM show the percentage of undetected errors with a single parity check to be about 1.9 times greater than an M-out-of-N code. However, the M-out-of-N code has more redundancy. A 4-out-of-8 code allows 70 characters to be represented, whereas 128 characters are possible when only one bit is used as a parity check.

Cyclic codes or polynomial codes are more complex than parity checking codes or M-out-of-N codes, but they offer a higher degree of protection against line errors. Peterson and Brown [1961] provide a detailed explanation of how to calculate cyclic codes. The way in which cyclic codes are generated can be chosen to minimize the number of undetected errors, given the characteristics of the particular communications line used. Even though cyclic codes are more complex than parity or M-out-of-N codes, the circuitry needed for decoding and encoding is simple.

Correction of Errors Once line errors have been detected they then must be corrected. There are two methods used to correct errors: (*a*) error correcting codes, and (*b*) retransmission of data in error.

Error correcting codes enable line errors to be detected and corrected at the receiving station. However, in general, to be able to carry out error correction, large amounts of redundancy are required in the messages transmitted. There is also a danger the attempted correction of an error will be carried out incorrectly. For these reasons, detection of errors and retransmission usually is chosen as the error correction strategy in preference to error correcting codes.

If retransmission is used to correct errors, a decision must be made on how much data is to be retransmitted. It may be as small as a character or as large as a batch of several records. Retransmission of a small quantity of data has two advantages. First, it is faster to retransmit a small amount of data than a large amount. Second, the buffer storage required to hold the message until correct transmission has occurred is small. The major disadvantages of using small amounts of data for retransmission arise because error detecting codes are less efficient for small amounts of data (greater amounts of redundancy are required) and more line control characters are needed.

Error correction through retransmission requires special logic (line protocols) to indicate the correct or incorrect receipt of a message. The ASCII ACK-NAK logic is an example. An ACK signal is transmitted by the receiver if the message received is correct. A NAK signal is transmitted by the receiver if the message is incorrect. The sender waits for either an ACK or NAK signal before transmitting the next message.

Noise also may corrupt the control characters used for retransmission in an error detection and correction system. An odd-even record count enables such errors to be detected. For example, consider the situation where control characters are corrupted and two messages appear to the receiver to be a single message. Assume the control character for the first message was odd. The control character for the second message, an even number, has been corrupted. Thus, when the receiver identifies a third message having an odd-numbered control character, it will recognize a message is missing and an error has occurred.

Improving Network Reliability

Besides using hardware and software to detect and correct line errors, a communications network can be designed to reduce the likelihood of line errors and system failure occurring and to minimize the effects of line errors and system failure when they do occur. The following sections discuss how the choice of modems, communications lines, and network topology affect overall network reliability.

Choice of a Modem In general, computer hardware uses and generates discrete, direct current (dc) binary signals. These signals can be transmitted over wires up to about 5–6 kilometers in length. However, if transmission occurs over a longer distance, the signals become so distorted they cannot be decoded. Communications lines that allow digital transmission of binary signals over much longer distances have been developed and are being used increasingly. However, most data transmission still occurs through converting digital signals to continuous analog signals (Figure 10.5). The device that accomplishes this conversion is called a modem or data set.

Modems have two major purposes: (*a*) to reduce line errors caused by noise, and (*b*) to increase the speed of data transmission. A tradeoff must be made in accomplishing both objectives: faster data transmission means a greater number of line errors occur.

Modems work by varying either the amplitude, frequency, or phase of an

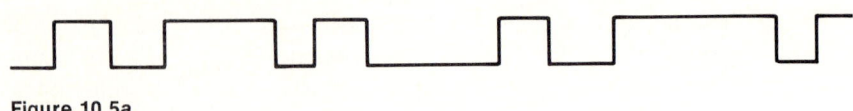

Figure 10.5a
Digital signal.

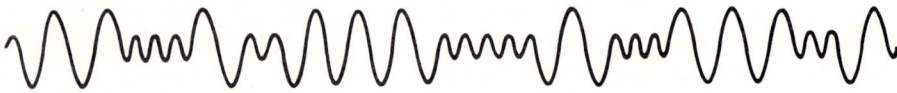

Figure 10.5b
Analog signal.

analog signal to represent a digital signal (Figure 10.6). Noise affects the performance of the three modulation methods differently. Both theoretical and empirical research results show phase modulation outperforms frequency modulation and frequency modulation outperforms amplitude modulation in terms of the number of line errors that occur. Further, if the analog waveform is generated having more than two states so that dibits or tribits are encoded for faster throughput, phase modulation typically is used since it withstands noise better than the other forms of modulation. Unfortunately, phase modulation costs more than either frequency or amplitude modulation.

Beside noise, line errors are caused also through the presence of distortion. Two forms of distortion exist. *Attenuation distortion* is the unwanted change in waveform that results through decreases in the magnitude of current, voltage, or power in a signal being transmitted. *Delay distortion* occurs when different waveform frequencies are delayed by different amounts. There are two ways of controlling distortion: (*a*) line conditioning, and (*b*) modem equalization. Line conditioning is the process by which a carrier makes a communications line conform to certain quality characteristics. It is discussed in the next section. Modem equalization is the process by which a modem compensates for distortion.

Modem equalization is especially important in controlling line errors when public lines are used for data transmission. Since in the public network any line might be chosen for transmission, the user has no prior knowledge of the specific characteristics of the line. The line cannot be conditioned. However, modems for public lines can be purchased with circuitry for dynamic equalization, a process that measures the characteristics of the line in use and performs automatic adjustment for attenuation and delay distortion.

For control of line errors it is also an advantage if a modem can transmit at different speeds. As transmission speeds increase the effects of noise are more pronounced. A modem with different speeds can recognize when high levels of noise occur and transmit at a slower rate to reduce the effects of this noise.

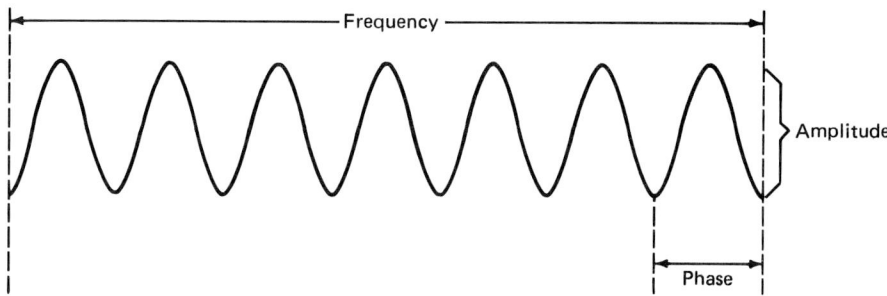

Figure 10.6a
Wave form characteristics.

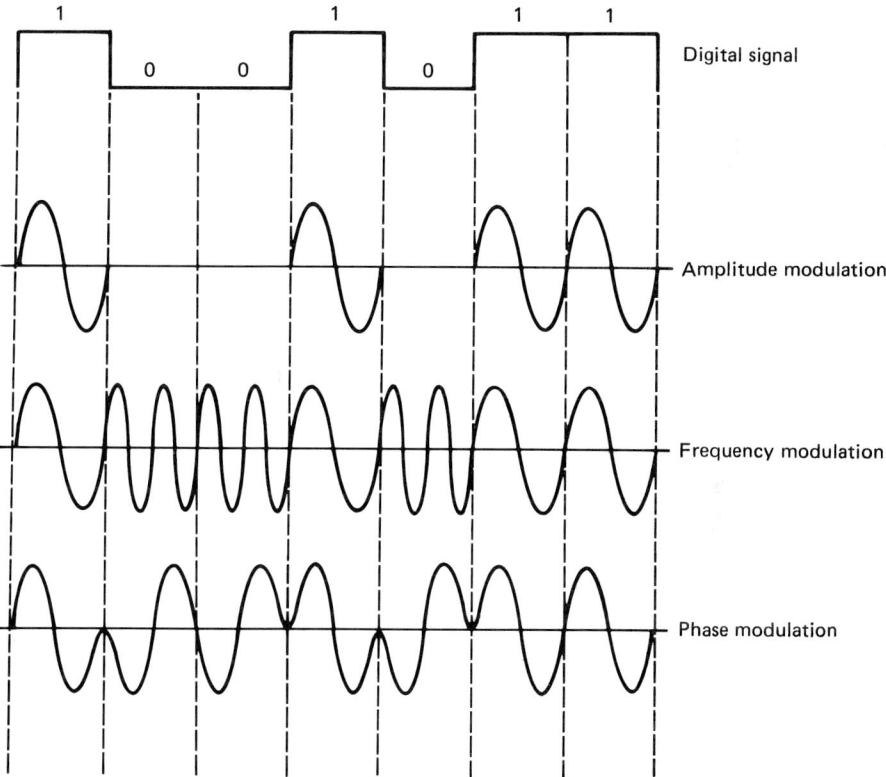

Figure 10.6b
Modulation techniques.

If a private line is used for data transmission, where possible, modems that have automatic or semiautomatic dial-up capabilities should be used. Thus, if the private line fails the modem will transfer automatically data transmission over to the public network.

Choice of a Communications Line A major factor affecting the reliability of data transmission is whether the communications line chosen is a public line or a private line. Public lines use the normal public switching exchange facilities. Users either have none or only partial control over the lines allocated to them for data transmission. In some cases users can specify the characteristics of the lines they require, and the switching center will allocate a line having those characteristics. Private lines are lines that are dedicated to service a particular user. For small amounts of data transmission (generally, less than a few hours per day), public lines are cheaper than private lines. However, as usage increases, private lines become cheaper than public lines.

Private lines have two other major advantages. First, in general, they allow higher rates of data transmission. Second, private lines can be conditioned; that is, the carrier ensures the line has certain quality attributes.

The network designer also should consider whether or not digital transmission should be used instead of analog transmission. Digital lines are not as widely available as analog lines; however, available services are increasing. Digital transmission is more reliable than analog transmission. Analog lines require linear amplifiers that amplify both the signal and any noise present on the line. Digital lines use nonlinear repeaters that do not pass on certain types of noise. Since noise levels are lower, faster data transmission also can be accomplished.

Other technologies that offer increased speed and higher reliability are becoming increasingly available; for example, satellite transmission and optical fiber (laser) transmission. Optical fibers have a major advantage in that they preclude the possibility of wiretapping. There is no technology available for tapping light waves; furthermore, splicing cables and making connections to the glass strands used in optical fiber transmission is difficult. However, optical fiber transmission can be used only over short distances since the light loss that occurs when signals are transmitted through glass is high.

Choice of Network Topology In simple terms, a network topology specifies the location of nodes within a network, the ways in which these nodes will be linked, and the data transmission capabilities of the links between the nodes. Specifying the optimum topology for a network is a problem of immense complexity.

Consider some of the design constraints that apply to the choice of a network topology (see, also, Kimbleton and Schneider [1975]). First, an overall cost constraint exists. There is usually a maximum limit specified for the cost per bit of information transmitted. Second, throughput and response time constraints exist. Communication of messages between different points in the network must be achieved within a certain time. Third, availability and reliability constraints exist. The network must be available for use at any one time by a given number of users. If a component of the network fails, alternate routing of messages or alternate hardware and software may be needed. The problem of determining an optimum topology is the subject of current research. Computationally feasible algorithms for determining an optimum are still evolving. Because of the complexity of the problem, the approach so far is still heuristic.

Figure 10.7 shows some of the possible topologies (configurations) for a network linking seven terminals to a host computer. Figure 10.7a is one extreme. It achieves high reliability since any one terminal is not dependent on the functioning of another terminal or a communications link other than the one that links it to the host computer. However, line costs are high because of the total length of line needed.

Figure 10.7b is another extreme. Here a multidrop line has been used to reduce line costs. However, the network is extremely sensitive to failure in a component of the network. For example, failure in a line segment affects all terminals further down the line.

Figure 10.7c is an intermediate case. Here a communications controller and a concentrator have been used. Line costs are lower than the first extreme but higher than the second extreme. However, the communications controller and the concentrator add to the cost of the overall network. Presumably they have been used to reduce the load on the host computer and improve line utilization, thereby permitting faster throughput, response time, and availability. Network reliability is lower than the first extreme but higher than the second extreme. Failure in the controller or concentrator affects all terminals connected to the controller or concentrator. Failure in the line segment linking the controller or concentrator to the host computer does more damage than failure in a line segment linking a terminal to the controller or concentrator.

In light of the above considerations relating to line costs and reliability, several common types of network topology have emerged, each giving higher priority to different objectives. Again, two polar extremes exist: (a) a ring network, and (b) a completely connected network. A third topology, the intermediate case, is a star network.

Figure 10.8a shows a ring network. In this case communications lines link a number of host computers. These host computers may be small front-end machines, major processors, communications controllers, etc. The ring network minimizes line costs by providing only the minimum number of links required to allow communications between any pair of host computers. To reduce costs further, communications are unidirectional (simplex). However, a ring network has low reliability since failure in a host or a communications link may prevent communications between any two host computers. To some extent this problem can be overcome by allowing communications to be bidirectional (half-duplex or duplex).

Figure 10.8b shows a completely connected network. It maximizes network reliability by providing a direct link between any two host machines. Failure in a communications link or host simply means messages have to be rerouted. However, compared to a ring network, line costs are high and more complex message switching facilities are needed.

268   PART 3: THE APPLICATION CONTROL FRAMEWORK

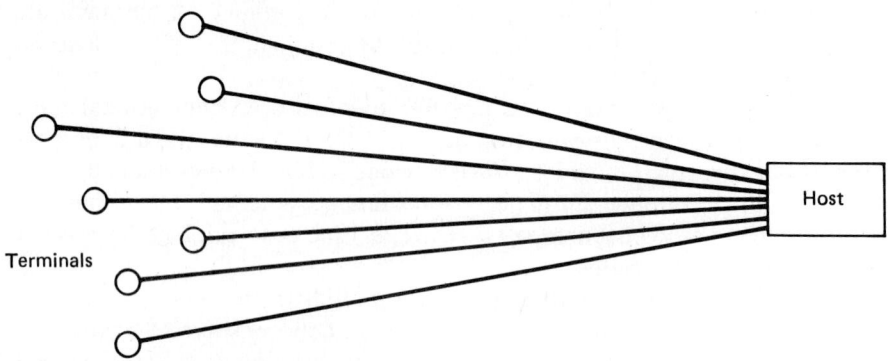

Figure 10.7a
Network using point-to-point lines.

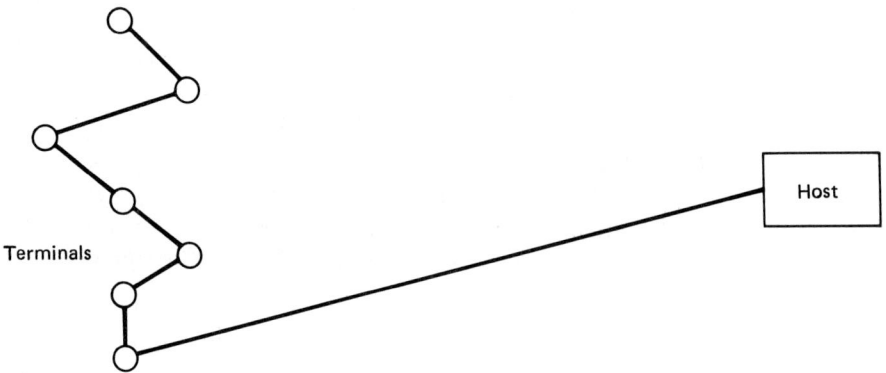

Figure 10.7b
Network using a multidrop line.

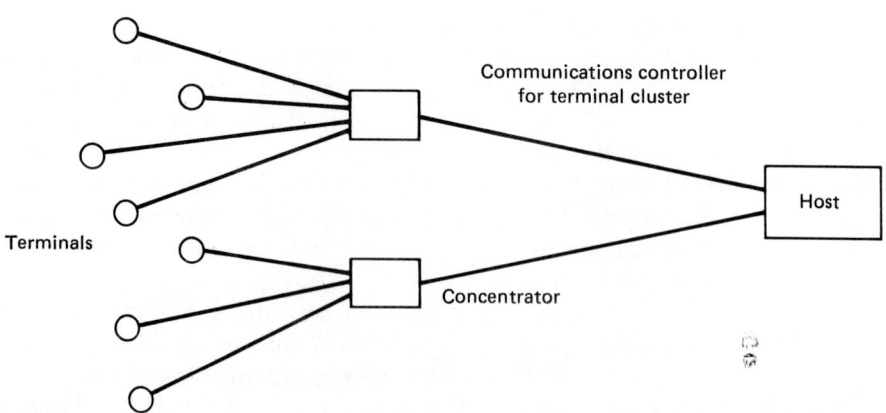

Figure 10.7c
Network using communications controller and concentrator.

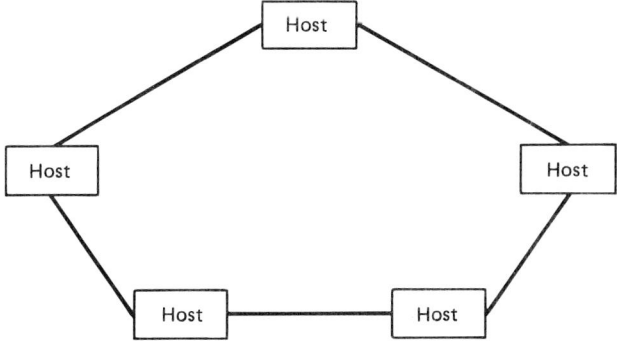

Figure 10.8a
Ring network.

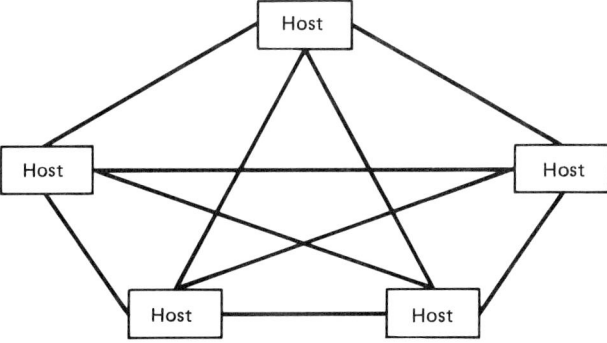

Figure 10.8b
Completely connected network.

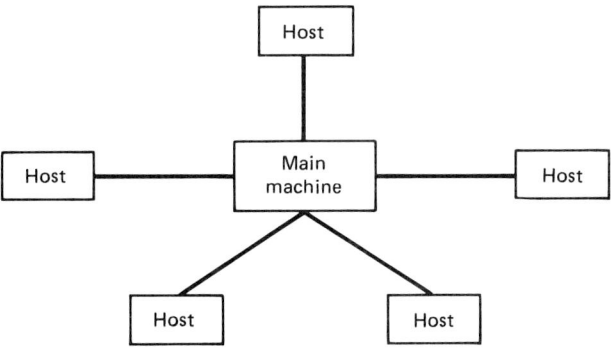

Figure 10.8c
Star network.

Figure 10.8c shows a star network. Each host is linked directly to a main machine. The main machine performs message switching functions. Thus, line costs are lower than those for a completely connected network, and communications between two hosts are more direct than communications in a ring network. Compared to a ring network, failure in a host or communications link is less critical. However, failure in the main machine is disastrous.

In all cases network reliability is increased by providing alternate routes for messages through using either a greater number of lines or instituting more complex switching devices. If message switching is used to increase network reliability, several controls must exist to ensure a message that must be switched is not lost. First, it is important that the message switching device has a store and forward capability in case the receiving station is busy and the message must be transmitted at a later time. Second, all messages must have a unique identifier—a message number, an originating terminal number, a user number or password. Third, messages should be transmitted promptly to reduce the risk of loss. Thus, fast throughput in a message switching system is critical from a control viewpoint.

CRYPTOGRAPHY

Cryptology is the science of secret codes. It incorporates the study of cryptography and cryptanalysis. *Cryptography* deals with systems for transforming data into codes (cryptograms) that are meaningless to anyone who does not possess the system for recovering the initial data. *Cryptanalysis* deals with techniques for illegitimately recovering the critical data from cryptograms. The person who designs a cryptographic system (*cryptosystem*) is called a *cryptographer*. A *cryptanalyst* is the antagonist or opponent of a cryptographer.

Cryptography protects the privacy of data. Access and communications controls fail for a variety of reasons: an operating system flaw, a hardware or software fault, misrouting of transmitted data, masquerading, wiretapping. If unauthorized access to data occurs, cryptography renders the data useless.

Cryptographic Techniques

A cryptographic technique transforms (encrypts) data (known as *plaintext*) into cryptograms (known as *ciphertext*). The strength of a cryptographic technique is measured in terms of its *work factor*; that is, the time and cost needed for a cryptanalyst to decipher the ciphertext.

There are three classes of techniques for enciphering plaintext: (*a*) transposition ciphers, (*b*) substitution ciphers, and (*c*) product ciphers. The following sections provide brief introductions to these techniques. Kahn [1967] and Sinkov [1968] give more comprehensive treatments.

Transposition Ciphers Transposition ciphers use some rule to permute the order of characters within a string of data. For example, a simple transposition rule is to swap the position of characters in consecutive pairs. Thus the message:

PEACE IS OUR OBJECTIVE

would be coded as:

EPCA ESIO RUO JBCEITEV

Note that spaces have been counted within a character pair.

Even the more complex transposition ciphers are an easy target for the cryptanalyst. They protect the privacy of data only against the casual browser. When the privacy of data is critical, transposition methods should not be used.

Substitution Ciphers   Substitution ciphers retain the position of characters within a message and hide the identity of the characters by replacing them with other characters according to some rule. The key-word Caesar alphabet is an example of a substitution cipher. Using this cipher a key first must be chosen, say, UNCOPYRIGHTABLE (see Van Tassel [1972]). Given the 26 letters of the alphabet, the ciphertext for each letter is derived in the following manner. The first 15 letters of the alphabet are replaced by the key letters. The remaining 11 letters are replaced by those letters not contained in the key, proceeding from the beginning of the alphabet to the end. Thus, the alphabet and its corresponding ciphertext are:

Plaintext: A B C D E F G H I J K L M N O P Q R S T U V W X Y Z
Ciphertext: U N C O P Y R I G H T A B L E D F J K M Q S V W X Z

The message:

PEACE IS OUR OBJECTIVE

would be coded as:

DPUCP GK EQJ ENHPCMGSP

Again, this type of encryption method could be broken easily by a cryptanalyst.

There are many other substitution ciphers including the much stronger vigenére and Vernam systems that were widely used before the advent of computers (see Kahn [1967]). However, these systems can be broken fairly easily using a computer and again would be of use only for preventing the casual browser from violating the privacy of data.

Product Ciphers   Product ciphers use a combination of transposition and substitution methods. Research has shown product ciphers are strong; that is, they are resistant to cryptanalysis. Today, product ciphers are the major method of encryption used. The remaining discussion deals only with this class of ciphers.

Choosing a Cipher System

A cipher system has two components: (*a*) an encipherment method or algorithm that constitutes the basic cryptographic technique, and (*b*) a cryptographic key upon which the algorithm operates in conjunction with plaintext to produce ciphertext. Shannon [1949] lists five desirable properties of a cipher system:

Property	Explanation
High Work Factor	The cipher should be difficult for the cryptanalyst to break.
Small Key	The cryptographic key should be small so it can be changed frequently and easily.
Simplicity	Complex cipher systems can be costly.
Low Error Propagation	Some types of ciphertext depend on previous ciphertext generated for a message. If a chained encryption method is used, corruption of a single bit of ciphertext will cause subsequent decryption to be in error (see Ehrsam et al. [1978]).
Little Expansion of Message Size	Some cipher systems introduce noise into a message to hinder use of statistical techniques to break a code. These techniques examine single-letter frequencies, double-letter frequencies, etc.

Shannon shows these properties cannot all be achieved simultaneously when encrypting natural language. Computer cryptographic methods have traded off either smallness in the key or simplicity in the algorithm. Those cipher systems that use a simple algorithm and a long key are called long key systems; those that rely on a known algorithm for their strength are called strong algorithm systems.

In effect the system designer's choice of a cipher system has now been abrogated. During 1977 the National Bureau of Standards (NBS) in the United States accepted as a standard an algorithm developed by IBM. This algorithm is known as the Data Encryption Standard (DES). Both software and hardware implementations of the algorithm exist (see Bright and Enison [1976] and Lennon [1978]). It is simply a matter of time before further implementations are widespread.

The DES is a strong algorithm cipher system. Long key systems cannot be broken by a cryptanalyst if the key is random and equal in length to the number of characters in the message to be encrypted. However, in most commercial data processing systems a long key approach is impractical because of the volume of data traffic that occurs. Keys need to be relatively short, fixed length, and capable of repeated use. For these reasons the NBS chose the strong algorithm approach. The DES uses a 64 bit key: the algorithm uses 56 bits and 8 bits are parity. The algorithm converts a 64 bit (8 character) block into a 64 bit block of ciphertext by passing through 16 rounds of encipherment.

Key Management

In both strong algorithm and long key systems, maintaining the secrecy of the cryptographic key is of paramount importance. It cannot be assumed the algorithm will remain secure. In the case of the DES, the algorithm is publicly known.

To ensure the secrecy of the keys used in cryptography, a system for managing the keys must be established. Key management involves three functions: (*a*) key generation, (*b*) key distribution, and (*c*) key installation. From an audit viewpoint, evaluating key management is the most critical aspect in assessing the reliability of a cryptosystem.

Key Generation Management of the key generation function involves addressing two questions. First, what keys must be generated? Second, how should these keys be generated? These are relatively complex questions to answer. The following paragraphs provide only a brief introduction to the topic (see, further, Ehrsam et al. [1978] and Matyas and Meyer [1978]).

To examine the question of what keys must be generated, consider a data processing system having a shared database and teleprocessing facilities. At one extreme only one cryptographic key might be used within the system. All data passes through a cryptographic facility, and system users need not concern themselves with encryption processes. This approach has the advantage of simplicity. However, it has several disadvantages. First, the approach only protects the privacy of data against unauthorized parties external to the system. If internal users gain unauthorized access to another user's data, since they have access to the cryptographic key, they can decipher the ciphertext. Second, the approach is susceptible to attack by a cryptanalyst. If the cryptanalyst somehow can submit plaintext to the system (perhaps through illegally obtaining a valid password), and then obtain the corresponding ciphertext (perhaps through wiretapping), the probability of discovering the key is high. Since the key is not specific to a particular terminal session or file, once it is discovered all other users are exposed. Third, the approach does not guard against hardware or software faults such as misrouting a message during data transmission.

To overcome these problems Ehrsam et al. [1978] suggest another approach that uses multiple keys. They define two classes of keys: (*a*) key encrypting keys (used to encipher other keys) that remain relatively stable over long periods, and (*b*) data encrypting keys (used to encipher data) that are time varying and dynamically changing. The latter class of keys remain in existence only as long as the data they protect.

To illustrate the use of a multiple-key cryptosystem, consider a communications session between a host computer and a terminal. Two key encrypting keys are needed: a host master key and a terminal master key. Only a single data encrypting key, a session key, is needed.

The cryptographic protocol for the communications session proceeds as follows. The host master key and the cryptographic algorithm reside in a cryptographic facility that is inaccessible except for encryption/decryption purposes. The host master key exists in the clear (in plaintext); for protection, keys outside the facility are encrypted using the host master key. A copy of the terminal master key exists at the host and the terminal. At the host the terminal master key is encrypted under the host master key. When a session commences, a session key is generated dynamically. The host first decrypts the terminal master key and then encrypts the session key under the terminal master key. The session key encrypted under the master key is then sent to the terminal where it is decrypted. Communications with data encrypted under the session key can then proceed.

The above protocol, in fact, contains a cryptographic weakness that can be overcome through the use of multiple host master keys. The protocol can be modified easily to handle the storage and retrieval of data in a database and communications between two host computers. These matters are left for further study (see Ehrsam et al. [1978], Lempel [1979], Merkle [1978], Popek and Kline [1979], and Simmons [1979]).

Once a decision has been made on what keys must be generated, a decision then can be made on how the keys will be generated. In the case of a multiple-key cryptosystem, Matyas and Meyer [1978] suggest generating the host master key by throwing dice or tossing a coin. It is critical this key be generated by a completely random process. All other keys can be generated using a pseudorandom number generator.

Key Distribution The method used to distribute keys throughout the cryptosystem depends on the type of key that must be distributed. Since data encrypting keys are encrypted under key encrypting keys, they can be transmitted through the system over the normal communications paths. Even if they are intercepted by an unauthorized person, they are useless to the person because they are in encrypted form.

Different methods must be used to distribute key encrypting keys throughout the system as they are not protected by encryption. Any of the normal external channels can be used: courier, registered mail, telephone. The key might be fragmented and the different fragments sent over different paths so it would require collusion before a key is compromised. Whatever the method chosen it must be reliable; maintaining the secrecy of key encrypting keys is essential to maintaining the overall secrecy of the cryptosystem.

Key Installation If a key is not generated internally to the cryptosystem, it must be installed physically at the relevant node; for example, a host master key at the host computer and a terminal master key at the associated terminal.

The method used to install the key depends on the hardware/software architecture of the cryptographic facility used. If hard-wired entry of the key to the cryptographic facility is possible, it will be entered by setting switches or dials. If only indirect entry is possible, the key first must be read into memory and a special command then invoked to load it into the cryptographic facility.

Since the cryptographic facility should prevent direct reading of a key once it has been loaded, tests must be undertaken to ensure the key residing in the facility is the one intended. In the case of a host master key, an encrypted value under the key can be computed externally to the system and compared with the result obtained internally to the system using the encrypt function. In the case of terminal master keys, it is important both the host and the terminal have identical versions of the key installed. Some type of handshaking procedure can be designed whereby the host expects a certain value to be transmitted from the terminal that can only be transmitted if the host and terminal have identical keys.

Cryptography for Databases

So far the major work undertaken on cryptography relates to its use in data communications. Its use in databases is less evolved. However, the auditor should be aware that some special considerations relate to the use of cryptography for databases.

Not all types of encryption can be used for databases. Since chained encryption creates interbit dependence, the addition, deletion, or modification of data in a database would make the plaintext irrecoverable. Thus, the added strength of chained encryption is lost. However, to compensate in part for this lost strength, only critical data in the database should be encrypted so a cryptanalyst who gains unauthorized access to the database has less data with which to work.

If a multiple-key cryptosystem is used, keys relating to data have a longer life than keys relating to communications sessions. The cryptographer must be careful to ensure that a change in a key encrypting key does not make the plaintext irrecoverable. For example, if a file key is encrypted under a host master key and the host master key is changed, all file keys must be decrypted and then encrypted under the new master key. This particular protocol is unwieldy. Ehrsam et al. [1978] present another protocol for handling such changes.

SUMMARY

Access and communications controls are becoming increasingly important with greater sharing of data and more use of teleprocessing. The current growth rate of 35% per annum in data communications traffic still should continue into the mid to late 1980s.

Access controls seek to prevent the unauthorized use of computing resources. They are implemented through an access control mechanism that resides in the operating system or database management system. An access control mechanism must identify and authenticate users, permit or deny access to resources users request, and permit or deny actions that they wish to undertake with respect to those resources.

Communications controls seek to preserve the integrity of data passing over communications lines. Communications errors occur through noise being present on a line or failure in hardware and software. The auditor should evaluate the design decisions taken to achieve network reliability. These design decisions include how line errors will be detected and corrected, what types of modems will be used, whether public or private lines will be used, what transmission medium will be used, and what network topology will be used.

Even with extensive controls, unauthorized access to data can still occur through hardware or software fault, wiretapping, masquerading, etc. Cryptography can be used to render the data useless to anyone who does not possess the cipher and key used to encrypt the data. With the acceptance by the National Bureau of Standards of a Data Encryption Standard based on a strong algorithm approach to encryption, the auditor's main concern is with cryptographic key management. The auditor must evaluate how keys are generated, distributed, and installed in a cryptosystem.

REVIEW QUESTIONS

10.1. What is meant by access control? Why are access controls necessary in most computer systems?

10.2. What functions should an access control mechanism perform? Why might the auditor examine the access control mechanism in an operating system or a database management system?

10.3. Outline the advantages and disadvantages of associating passwords with resources rather than users.

10.4. Distinguish between identification and authentication. Is there a relationship between the two? In setting up an authentication scheme, what would be the major factor(s) influencing you to choose personal characteristics in preference to possessed objects as a means of authentication?

10.5. Explain why authentication should be a two-way process: the computer authenticating itself and users authenticating themselves.

10.6. To gain unauthorized access to a file, you decide to carry out a masquerading scheme. Why is it important the terminal user not know you have carried out the masquerading?

10.7. Why do statistical databases still pose a problem for the privacy of an individual's data? Outline some controls you could institute to ensure the privacy of an individual's data in a statistical database is not violated.

10.8. Briefly explain the difference between conditional and unconditional action privileges. Give two examples of fields in an accounts receivable file where conditional action privileges may be required.

10.9. Briefly explain the major differences between a "ticket-oriented approach" and a "list-oriented approach" to access authorization. Outline the relative advantages and disadvantages of each approach.

10.10. What is meant by noise in a communications line? What factors affect the amount of noise which exists on a line? What are the effects of noise?

10.11. Explain the difference between a loop check and redundancy as means of error detection in communications lines. What are the relative advantages and disadvantages of each approach?

10.12. If redundancy is used as a means of error detection, what factors would you investigate to assess the reliability of error detection in a communications line?

10.13. Give an example of where error correcting codes might be chosen in preference to retransmission as a means of error correction.

10.14. Noise on a communications line may corrupt the special control characters needed for transmission and retransmission of data. Briefly describe a method which can be used to detect errors in control characters.

10.15. Why is the choice of a modem an important consideration in the design of a reliable network? Outline some desirable control features of a modem used on a private line.

10.16. Briefly explain what is meant by line conditioning. Why are public lines not conditioned?

10.17. Briefly explain what is meant by the topology of a network. List five factors you would consider as a designer in choosing a network topology.

10.18. The map below (drawn to scale) shows the physical locations of nine terminals and a host computer.

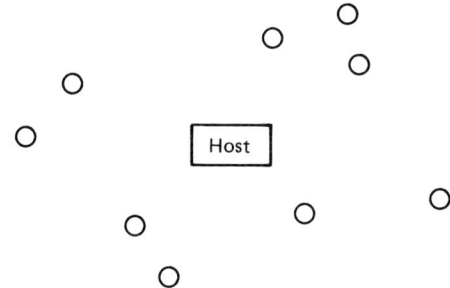

Required: Draw three topologies, one minimizing line costs, one maximizing reliability, and the other representing a compromise between line costs and reliability.

10.19. Give three desirable features of a communications network that increase the reliability of message switching activities.

10.20. Why is cryptography an important control protecting the integrity of data passing over public lines? Is cryptography also a useful control for data passing over private lines?

10.21. For computer cryptography, why have product ciphers been chosen in preference to transposition and substitution ciphers?

10.22. Briefly explain the difference between a strong algorithm cryptosystem and a long key cryptosystem. Why did the National Bureau of Standards choose a strong algorithm cryptosystem for the Data Encryption Standard?

10.23. What functions must be carried out in cryptographic key management? Why is the evaluation of key management probably the most important aspect of evaluating a computer installation's use of cryptography?

278 PART 3: THE APPLICATION CONTROL FRAMEWORK

10.24. Briefly explain the relative advantages and disadvantages of generating and using a single key versus multiple keys in a cryptosystem.
10.25. How does the architecture of a cryptographic facility affect the method used to install cryptographic keys?
10.26. Outline any differences in the methods used to distribute key encrypting keys and data encrypting keys.
10.27. What special considerations apply to the use of cryptography for stored data?

EXERCISES AND CASES

10.1. You are the manager of the internal audit of a savings and loan association that has decided to install a bill payment by telephone system for its customers. The system will allow customers to telephone a number to enter the system, record bill payment transactions that they wish to make within the next 30 days, and transfer funds between savings and checking accounts. A voice feedback system instructs customers on how to complete each step of a transaction; for example, record the date of a payment and the amount to be paid. Note, all data is entered using a Touch-Tone telephone.

Required: The data processing manager has asked you to advise her on the access controls you think should exist in the system. Prepare a brief report with your recommendations. Be sure to consider how the system will ensure:
a. it is dealing with a valid customer
b. it is allowing customers to transfer funds to or from authorized accounts only
c. customers do not overdraw accounts
d. payments are made only to creditors that the customer has authorized

10.2. Global Airways is a major airline company based in Los Angeles. It has a computer system dedicated to reservations and ticketing operations. Over 1000 terminals scattered throughout the United States are connected to the computer in the company's head office.

You are a member of the external audit team examining access and communications controls within the reservation and ticketing system. You are amazed to find the system does not use passwords as an access control. When you question the data processing manager why this is the case, he informs you that passwords are unnecessary. He explains that each terminal connected to the computer is given a unique identification number. This number is stored in a table within a secure area of the operating system. A terminal must supply this identification number with each message it sends and the system will respond only to a valid identification number. The identification number is sent automatically by a terminal since it is hard-wired in the terminal.

He further explains that a password system had been tried previously and abandoned. Each reservation and ticketing clerk had been given a unique password. However, since multiple clerks often used a single terminal, the system was too awkward and unwieldy as clerks had to continuously sign on and sign off. The system caused major problems during rush periods.

Required: Write a brief report identifying what could go wrong, if anything, with the current system that would result in the company losing assets or violation of data integrity in the system occurring.

10.3. First International Bankco of Illinois is a large Chicago-based bank. As the manager of internal audit, you are called one day to a meeting with the controller.

The bank has operated for some time now automatic teller machines (ATMs). However, several major problems have arisen with customers' use of the ATMs. The controller outlines the following difficulties:

a. Currently the bank issues each customer a plastic card containing the customer's account number (magnetically encoded) and a personal identification number (PIN). Unfortunately, customers have been writing their PINs on their cards; consequently, when customers have lost their cards or their cards have been stolen, unauthorized withdrawals of funds have occurred. The number of unauthorized withdrawals is increasing.

b. The ATMs allow a customer three attempts to enter the current PIN; then they lock the card in the machine. Many customers seem to forget their PINs. Recently, an irate customer tried to retrieve his card using a crowbar.

c. The bank currently mails cards and PINs to new customers. Recently, mail has been stolen and unauthorized withdrawals of funds have occurred.

Required: The controller asks you to consider the problems and propose some solutions. Write a brief report outlining your recommendations.

10.4. You are the partner-in-charge of EDP auditing for a large public accounting firm. One of your clients is a major insurance company that is a mature user of data processing. The company is based in Minneapolis, but it has offices scattered throughout the United States. You receive an invitation from the chairman of the company's audit committee to participate in a meeting on the company's proposed move to a distributed system. The company is contemplating distributing both its database and its processing.

The primary reason for the meeting is a debate that has arisen between the vice-president of internal audit and the vice-president of data processing about whether or not the move to distributed processing is beneficial from a control perspective. The vice-president of data processing argues that the major security problem facing the company is the risk of wiretapping by unknown parties. Substantial information is sent via satellite from terminals located in the company's offices. He argues that a distributed system will minimize the amount of information that has to be communicated, thereby reducing the expected losses from data integrity violations. The vice-president of internal audit argues, on the other hand, that the primary security problems arise from within the company in the form of unauthorized actions by employees. He argues a single centralized site is much easier to control.

Required: The chairman of the audit committee asks you to prepare for her a report outlining your own feelings on this matter. She also asks you to identify the types of information that the committee would have to obtain to try and resolve the debate.

REFERENCES

Adams, Donald L. "Computer Security Hardware Devices and Services—I," *EDPACS* (March 1977*a*), pp. 1–10.

———. "Computer Security Hardware Devices and Services—II," *EDPACS* (July 1977*b*), pp. 10–16.

American Institute of Certified Public Accountants, *Audits of Service-Center-Produced Records* (New York: American Institute of Certified Public Accountants, 1974).

_____. *Audit Considerations in Electronic Funds Transfer Systems* (New York: American Institute of Certified Public Accountants, 1979).

Awad, Elias M. *Introduction to Computers in Business* (Englewood Cliffs, N.J.: Prentice-Hall, Inc., 1977).

Azzarone, Stephanie. "Safety Pin: Can It Keep Card Systems Secure?" *Bank Systems and Equipment* (November 1978), pp. 40–49.

Blackman, Maurice. *The Design of Real Time Applications* (New York: John Wiley and Sons, Inc., 1975).

Bohl, Marilyn. *Information Processing*, 2d ed. (Chicago: Science Research Associates, Inc., 1976).

Branscomb, L. M. "Computing and Communications—A Perspective of the Evolving Environment," *IBM Systems Journal*, vol. 18, no. 2, 1979, pp. 189–201.

Bright, Herbert S., and R. L. Enison. "Cryptography Using Modular Software Elements," *Proceedings of the 1976 National Computer Conference* (Montvale, N.J.: AFIPS Press, 1976), pp. 113–123.

_____, and William E. Perry. "Computational Cryptography and Security," *EDPACS* (September 1977), pp. 1–8.

Browne, Peter S., and Dennis D. Steinauer. "A Model for Access Control," in E. F. Codd and A. L. Dean, eds., *Proceedings of the 1971 ACM-SIGFIDET Workshop: Data Description, Access and Control* (New York: Association for Computing Machinery, Inc., 1971), pp. 241–262.

Bryant, P., F. W. Giesen, and R. M. Hayes. "Experiments in Line Quality Monitoring," *IBM Systems Journal*, vol. 15, no. 2, 1976, pp. 124–142.

Canning, Richard G. "Data Encryption: Is It for You?" *EDP Analyzer* (December 1978), pp. 1–13.

Champine, George A. *Distributed Computer Systems* (Amsterdam, The Netherlands: North-Holland Publishing Co., 1980).

Conway, R. W., W. L. Maxwell, and H. L. Morgan, "On the Implementation of Security Measures in Information Systems," *Communications of the ACM* (April 1972), pp. 211–220.

Cypser, R. J. *Communications Architecture for Distributed Systems* (Reading, Mass.: Addison-Wesley Publishing Company, 1978).

Davies, D. W., D. L. A. Barber, W. L. Price, and C. M. Solomonides. *Computer Networks and Their Protocols* (New York: John Wiley and Sons, Inc., 1979).

Dolan, William J., Don L. Sneary, and Ray M. Whitworth, "Planning for the Impact of EFT Systems on Internal Controls and Audits," *Arthur Andersen Chronicle* (April 1976), pp. 48–59.

Doll, Dixon R. *Data Communications: Facilities, Networks, and System Design* (New York: John Wiley and Sons, Inc., 1978).

Donaldson, Hamish. *Designing a Distributed Processing System* (New York: John Wiley and Sons, Inc., 1979).

Ehrsam, W. F., S. M. Matyas, C. H. Meyer, and W. L. Tuchman. "A Cryptographic Key Management Scheme for Implementing the Data Encryption Standard," *IBM Systems Journal*, vol. 17, no. 2, 1978, pp. 106–125.

Everest, Gordon C. *Database Management: Objectives, System Functions, and Administration* (New York: McGraw-Hill Book Company, 1982).

FitzGerald, Jerry, and Tom Eason. *Fundamentals of Data Communications* (New York: John Wiley and Sons, Inc., 1978).

Ford, J. B. "Enhanced Problem Determination Capability for Teleprocessing," *IBM Systems Journal*, vol. 17, no. 3, 1978, pp. 276-289.
Frazer, W. D. "Potential Technology Implications for Computers and Telecommunications in the 1980's." *IBM Systems Journal*, vol. 18, no. 2, 1979, pp. 333-347.
Gladney, H. M. "Administrative Control of Computing Service," *IBM Systems Journal*, vol. 17, no. 2, 1978, pp. 151-178.
_____, E. L. Worley, and J. J. Myers. "An Access Control Mechanism for Computing Resources," *IBM Systems Journal*, vol. 14, no. 3, 1975, pp. 212-228.
Hansen, Morris H. "Insuring Confidentiality of Individual Records in Data Storage and Retrieval for Statistical Purposes." *Proceedings of the AFIPS 1971 Fall Joint Computer Conference* (Montvale, N.J.: AFIPS Press, 1971), pp. 579-585.
Hecht, H. "Fault-Tolerant Software for Real-Time Applications," *Computing Surveys* (December 1976), pp. 391-407.
Hoffman, Lance J. "The Formulary Model for Flexible Privacy and Access Controls," *Proceedings of the AFIPS 1971 Fall Joint Computer Conference* (Montvale, N.J.: AFIPS Press, 1971), pp. 587-601.
Hubbert, James F. "An Audit of a Realtime System—A Case Study," *EDPACS* (December 1979), pp. 1-8.
Kahn, David. *The Codebreakers* (New York: The Macmillan Company, 1967).
Kimbleton, Stephen R., and G. Michael Schneider. "Computer Communication Networks: Approaches, Objectives, and Performance Considerations," *Computing Surveys* (September 1975), pp. 129-173.
Knuth, Donald E. *The Art of Computer Programming, Vol. 1: Fundamental Algorithms*, 2d ed. (Reading, Mass.: Addison-Wesley Publishing Company, 1973).
Lee, Gerald W. "Re-Thinking Terminal Security Requirements," *EDPACS* (October 1978), pp. 138-150.
Lempel, Abraham. "Cryptology in Transition," *Computing Surveys* (December 1979), pp. 285-303.
Lennon, R. E. "Cryptography Architecture for Information Security," *IBM Systems Journal*, vol. 17, no. 2, 1978, pp. 138-150.
Lorin, H. "Distributed Processing: An Assessment," *IBM Systems Journal*, vol. 18, no. 4, 1979, pp. 582-603.
Louderback, Peter D. "Electronic Funds Transfer Systems," *World* (Spring 1975), pp. 9-14.
Lyons, Norman R. "Segregation of Functions in EFTS," *Journal of Accountancy* (October 1978), pp. 89-92.
McGlynn, Daniel R. *Distributed Processing and Data Communications* (New York: John Wiley and Sons, Inc., 1978).
Martin, James. *Design of Real-Time Computer Systems* (Englewood Cliffs, N.J.: Prentice-Hall, Inc., 1967).
_____. *Teleprocessing Network Organization* (Englewood Cliffs, N.J.: Prentice-Hall, Inc., 1970).
_____. *Systems Analysis for Data Transmission* (Englewood Cliffs, N.J.: Prentice-Hall, Inc., 1972).
_____. *Security, Accuracy, and Privacy in Computer Systems* (Englewood Cliffs, N.J.: Prentice-Hall, Inc., 1973).
Matyas, S. M., and C. H. Meyer. "Generation, Distribution, and Installation of Cryptographic Keys," *IBM Systems Journal*, vol. 17, no. 2, 1978, pp. 126-137.

Merkle, Ralph C. "Secure Communications Over Insecure Channels," *Communications of the ACM* (April 1978), pp. 294–299.

Minsky, Naftaly. "Intentional Resolution of Privacy Protection in Database Systems," *Communications of the ACM* (March 1976), pp. 149–159.

Needham, Roger M., and Michael D. Schroeder. "Using Encryption for Authentication in Large Networks of Computers," *Communications of the ACM* (December 1978), pp. 993–999.

Peterson, W., and D. Brown. "Cyclic Codes for Error Detection," *Proceedings of the IRE* (January 1961), pp. 228–235.

Popek, Gerald J., and Charles S. Kline. "Encryption and Secure Computer Networks," *Computing Surveys* (December 1979), pp. 331–356.

Richardson, Dana R. "Auditing EFTS," *Journal of Accountancy* (October 1978), pp. 81–87.

Rivest, R. L., A. Shamir, and L. Adleman. "A Method for Obtaining Digital Signatures and Public Key Cryptosystems," *Communications of the ACM* (February 1978), pp. 120–126.

Roussey, Robert S. "Third-Party Review of the Computer Service Center," *Journal of Accountancy* (August 1978), pp. 78–82.

Saltzer, Jerome H. "Protection and Control of Information Sharing in Multics," *Communications of the ACM* (July 1974), pp. 388–402.

_____, and M. D. Schroeder. "The Protection of Information in Computer Systems," *Proceedings of the IEEE* (September 1975), pp. 1278–1308.

Schaller, Carol A. "The Revolution of EFTS," *Journal of Accountancy* (October 1978), pp. 74–80.

Shannon, Claude E. "Communication Theory of Secrecy Systems," *Bell System Technical Journal* (October 1949), pp. 656–715.

Simmons, Gustavus J. "Symmetric and Asymmetric Encryption," *Computing Surveys* (December 1979), pp. 305–330.

Sinkov, A. *Elementary Cryptanalysis: A Mathematical Approach* (New York: Random House, 1968).

Sykes, David J. "Protecting Data by Encryption," *Datamation* (August 1976), pp. 81, 84–85.

Van Tassel, Dennis. *Computer Security Management* (Englewood Cliffs, N.J.: Prentice-Hall, Inc., 1972).

Watson, Richard W. *Timesharing System Design Concepts* (New York: McGraw-Hill Book Company, 1970).

Withington, Frederick G. "Beyond 1984: A Technology Forecast," *Datamation* (January 1975), pp. 54–73.

CHAPTER 11

INPUT CONTROLS

CHAPTER OUTLINE

INPUT VALIDATION CHECKS
    Field Checks
    Record Checks
    Batch Checks
    File Checks

DESIGN OF THE INPUT PROGRAM
    Data Validation
    Handling of Errors
    Reporting of Errors

CONTROL OVER INPUT

A GENERALIZED INPUT SYSTEM
    Generalized Validation Module
    Input/Output Pool
    Error File
    Generalized Reporting Module
    Archival System

SUMMARY

REVIEW QUESTIONS

EXERCISES AND CASES

REFERENCES

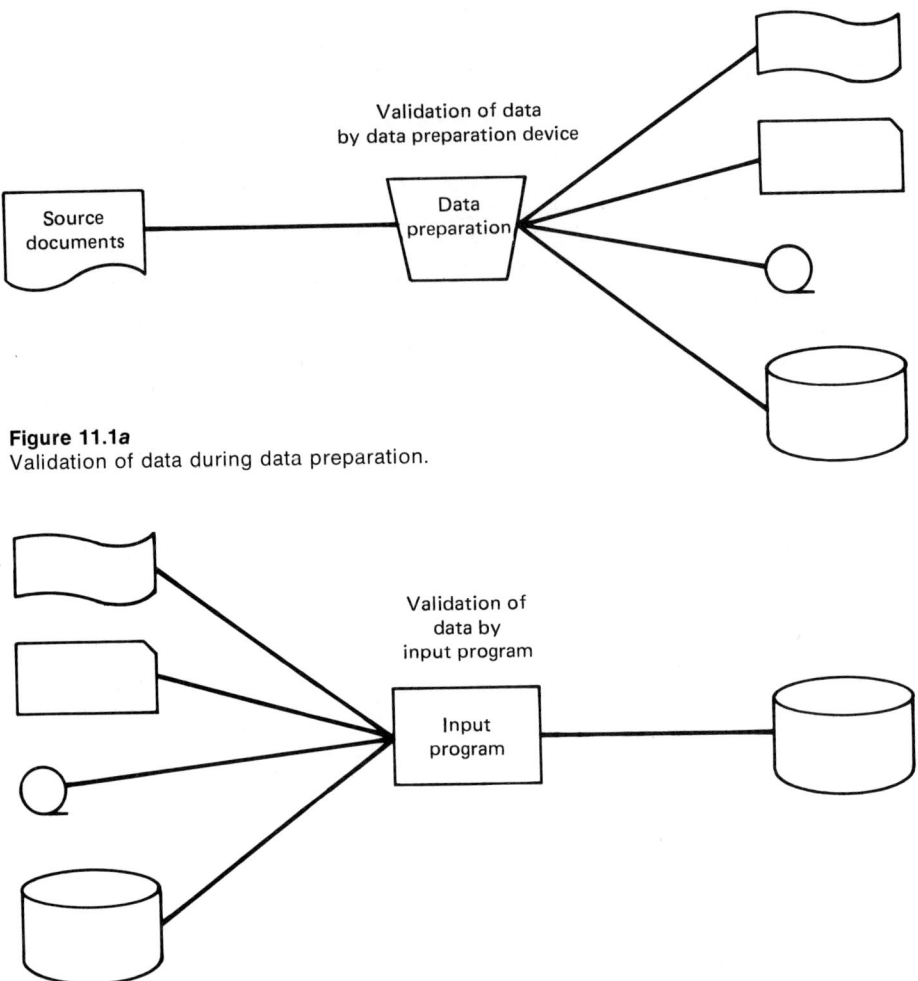

Figure 11.1a
Validation of data during data preparation.

Figure 11.1b
Validation of data by input program.

Input controls are designed to detect errors in data entered into a computer system. They can be exercised at various stages in the flow of data through an application system: during data preparation if the data preparation device provides programmed data validation capabilities; during input when data is read by a card reader, paper tape reader, etc.; during direct entry of data at a terminal if the terminal is intelligent or it is online to a computer (Figure 11.1).

In general, data should be validated as soon as possible after it has been captured and as close as possible to the source of the data. There may be occasions when, from a cost or efficiency viewpoint, validation should be delayed. For example, validating some fields requires referencing a master file.

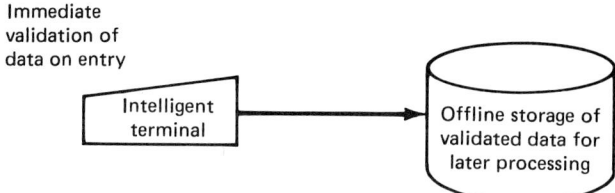

Figure 11.1c
Use of an intelligent terminal for offline validation and storage of data.

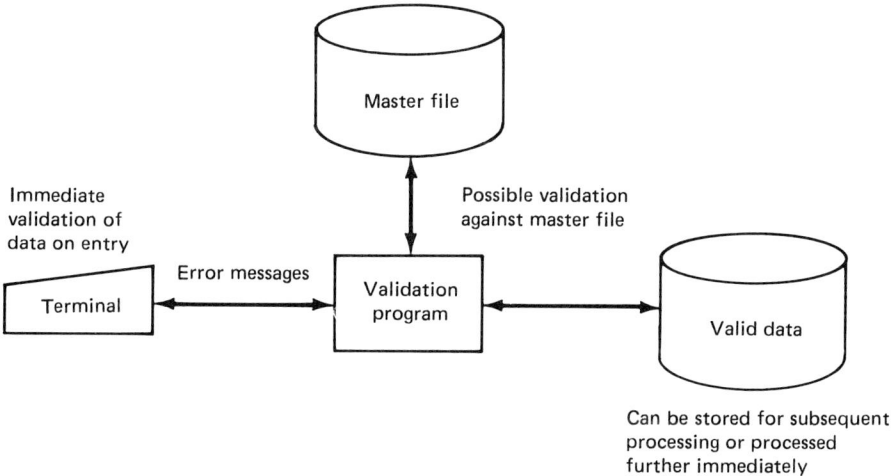

Figure 11.1d
Use of an online terminal for data validation.

If the master file is stored as a sequential file, this validation check is difficult to perform unless data is entered or sorted in the same sequence as the master file. Nevertheless, to the extent that the time lag between data capture and data validation can be reduced, the easier it is for personnel who capture and prepare data to correct errors. The circumstances surrounding the data are still fresh in their minds and the effort required to correct the data is minimal. Where data first must be prepared in machine-readable form, the trend is to install data validation capabilities in the data preparation device rather than wait for the input program to validate the data (see, further, Chapter 9).

INPUT VALIDATION CHECKS

Controls to check the validity of input data can be exercised at four levels:

1 Field checks

2 Record checks
3 Batch checks
4 File checks

Field Checks

With a field check the validation logic applied to the field in the input validation program does not depend on other fields within the record or other records within the batch. The following field checks can be applied:

Field check	Explanation
Missing Data/Blanks	Is there any missing data in the field? For example, if a code should contain two hyphens, though they may be in a variable position, can only one be detected? Does the field contain blanks when data always should be present?
Alphabetics/Numerics	Does a field that should only contain alphabetics or numerics contain alphanumeric characters?
Range	Does the data for a field fall within its allowable value range?
Set Membership	If a permissible set of values is defined for a field, is the data in the field one of these values; for example, one of the valid transaction types for a record?
Check Digit	Is the check digit valid for the value in the field (see, also, Chapter 9)?
Master Reference	If the master file can be referenced at the same time input data is read, is there a master file match for the key field?
Size	If variable length fields are used and a set of permissible sizes is defined, does the field delimiter show the field to be one of these sizes? If fixed length fields are used and spaces are defined between fields, do the spaces contain blanks?

Record Checks

With a record check the validation logic applied to a field depends on the field's logical interrelationships with other fields in a record. The following record checks can be applied:

Record check	Explanation
Reasonableness	Even though a field may pass a range check, the contents of another field may determine what is a reasonable value for the field. For example, $35,000 may fall within the range of salaries paid but it is not a reasonable salary for lower level managers.
Valid Sign—Numerics	The contents of one field may determine which sign is valid for a numeric field. For example, a cash payment transaction should always have a negative sign for the amount field.

Size	If variable length records are used, the size of the record is a function of the sizes of the variable length fields. The permissible size of variable and fixed length records also may depend on a field indicating the record type.
Sequence Check	If during input logical records require more than one physical record and a sequence number is punched in each physical record, do the physical records follow the required order?

Batch Checks

Batch checks apply validation logic to fields and records based on their interrelationships with controls established for the batch. Whereas field and record checks can always be undertaken, batch checks are not always possible. For example, in an online system, clerks may enter single transactions as they occur rather than accumulate them in batches of the same type and enter them at a later stage. If single transactions are entered, the only type of batch checking that can occur is logical batch checking; that is, where the computer sorts the transactions entered by the clerk over the processing period and prepares control totals for each transaction type. At the end of the processing period these totals are reconciled with the clerk's control totals. On the other hand, if data is entered as a batch with a batch header record containing certain control information, the following types of checks can be performed:

Batch check	Explanation
Control Totals	Does the accumulation of a field reconcile with a financial total or hash total specified on the batch header? Does the number of records in the batch agree with the number specified on the batch header?
Transaction Type	If the batch transaction type is punched on the follower records, does it agree with the transaction type specified on the batch header?
Batch Serial Number	If the batch serial number is punched on the follower records, does it agree with the batch serial number on the batch header?
Sequence Check	If a sequence number is punched on follower records, do the follower records occur in the required order?
Size	If there is an absolute limit to the number of follower records in the batch, is this limit exceeded?

File Checks

File checks ensure correct files are input to a production run of an application system. These checks are especially important for master files where reconstruction may be difficult and costly. The following types of file checks can be applied:

File check	Explanation
Internal Label	Is the name of the file correct?
Generation Number	Is the correct generation of the file being used?
Retention Date	Has the retention date on the file expired?
Control Totals	A record within the file may contain control totals that can be checked. This record is updated at the end of each run and the control totals reported. On the next run users supply a parameter value to the update program to check the control totals on the file.

DESIGN OF THE INPUT PROGRAM

A well-designed input program ensures that the quality of data entering an application system is high, and it facilitates correction and resubmission of errors. If extensive validation, editing, formatting, and encoding must be performed, good design is essential if the program is to be efficient. If large volumes of input data must be processed, efficiency considerations may be paramount.

The auditor is especially interested in three aspects of the design of the input program:

1 How is data validated?
2 How are errors handled?
3 How are errors reported?

Data Validation

Experience and ingenuity play a large part in being able to specify all the kinds of errors that are likely to occur in input data. The system specifications usually give a programmer some indication of errors to be expected. However, other errors the programmer anticipates through experience; for example, checking the sequence of records that will "always" be in sequence.

It is sometimes easiest to start the design of the validation routines by specifying what should be correct and then identifying deviations that may occur. This activity also aids the program design process since logic that should be grouped in modules can be identified (see, also, Chapter 6). This aspect of the design process should be documented for later use by maintenance programmers and auditors.

Errors should be ordered by their likelihood of occurrence. Ideally, the input program checks for all possible errors. However, hopefully not all code needs to be executed during production running. It is inefficient to check for rare errors first. The cost of comprehensive validation routines should be storage space and not processing efficiency; that is, though program logic always consumes core, it need not be executed always if the program is well-designed.

Valid codes or values should be stored in tables in the program and not exist as literals in the procedural section of the program. This facilitates changing the program when codes or values change. The procedure section should reference only variable names.

The input program must identify as many errors as possible in a record or batch. It is frustrating for users to correct one error only to find that another exists. Even when an error has been identified, the program must continue to search for other errors.

There should be no closed routines in an input program. A closed routine exists when a program assumes the existence of a condition if other conditions do not exist. For example, if a program checks for five possible values in a field, a closed routine exists when the program checks for four values and assumes the existence of the fifth value when the other tests fail. Thus, a sixth value is not anticipated. The program should check all possible values and invoke a general error routine if a value other than those permitted is found.

One of the more onerous requirements in writing an input program is ensuring its ability to recover when errors occur. If the program gets "out of step," it may start to read valid records as errors. For example, if the program assumes 50 records follow a batch header record, and in a particular batch read by the program only 49 exist, it should not read the 50th record—a new batch header—as a follower record, signify the current batch is in error, and then process further batches in error because they have no batch header. The program must recognize the 50th record as a new batch header, signify the current batch is in error, and recommence validation for the new batch.

Where possible the input program should correct errors automatically. If an error has to be corrected manually, the likelihood of a further error being made is increased. Processing is delayed also while the error is corrected. If the input program can correct the error, the chance of further errors is reduced and processing can continue without interruption.

Documentation of the input program is essential. It takes two forms. First, external documentation must exist providing detail about the program. Second, comments must occur liberally throughout the program explaining what each validation routine accomplishes. A decision-table preprocessor is especially helpful in documenting the program. Often the validation routines are amenable to coding as decision tables. The decision-table preprocessor ensures correct generation of processing logic and provides useful documentation of the logic involved in the validation routines by automatically inserting comments in the form of decision tables throughout the program (see, further, Chapter 6).

Handling of Errors

Once errors have been identified in the input data, the program must report the errors and write them to an error file. It is insufficient only to report errors. Errors also must be stored on a file to await correction (Figure 11.2); other-

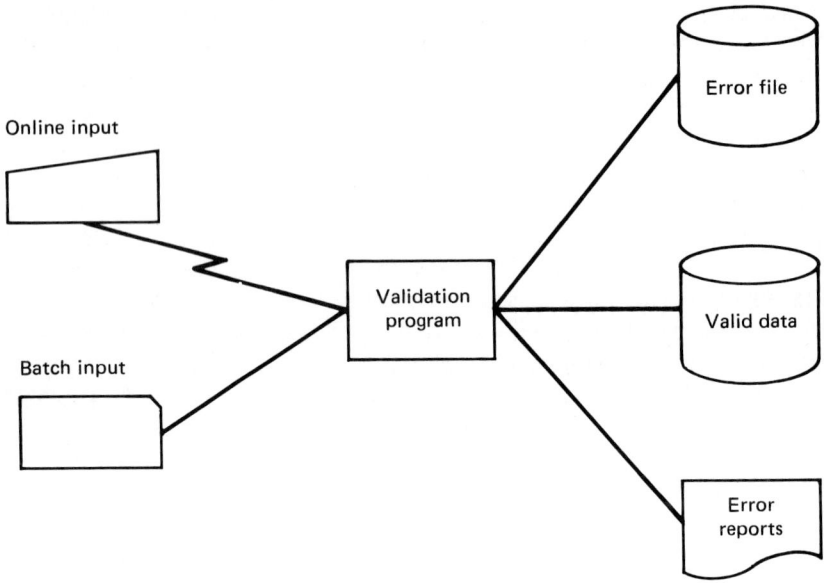

Figure 11.2
Use of an error file for data validation.

wise, the data may be lost through failure to resubmit the errors in corrected form.

Updating and maintaining an error file can involve some reasonably difficult programming. Each error on the file must be given a unique identification number. Problems arise because the start error number for a new validation run is dependent on the last error number used in the previous validation run. With a direct access error file a special record can be placed in a unique physical position (e.g., the first record in the file), and the update program can directly access this record at the start and end of processing. At the start of processing the program obtains the start error number; at the end of processing the program stores the last error number used.

Magnetic tape error files present more difficult problems because records cannot be accessed directly. The file can be read only sequentially. Several methods are available for keeping a record of error numbers used. First, if the record containing the last error number used is stored at the beginning of the file, upon completion of the run the file can be closed and rewound and the first record read again and updated. Hopefully the error file is small so this strategy does not take undue amounts of time. Second, the user can be made responsible for supplying the start error number as a parameter for a validation run. At the conclusion of the run the last error number used is printed out so it can be supplied as the start error number for the next run. Third, some type of coding strategy may be used that depends on the date and time of the validation run. For example, the day's errors may start at one and be prefixed by the number of the day of the year; the errors on January 4 would start 004001 if no greater than 999 errors are expected in a day. If there is more than one validation run in a day, the error number might be prefixed by time; for example, the error run at 10:30 p.m. on January 4 would start 0042230001.

Magnetic tape error files also present problems for the order in which errors are resubmitted after correction. Since the error file typically is maintained in sequential order by error number, the corrected errors must be resubmitted in that order. Also, corrected errors must be processed before new data so that the order of the file is preserved. One strategy is to allow corrected errors to be placed anywhere and in any order in the input file. The input file must be sorted prior to processing so the corrected errors sort to the front of the input file. Alternatively, the user has to place corrected errors at the front of the input file. The input program first reads the corrected errors, sorts the errors into order by using, for example, the COBOL SORT verb, processes the errors, and then reads the new input data for validation.

For direct access error files the corrected errors need not be resubmitted in order. An index can be maintained or hashing algorithm used to access existing errors or store new errors on the file.

Depending on the type of errors identified, a single record or entire batch must be written onto the error file. If an error is identified at the field or record level, only the record need be written onto the error file. If an error is identified at the batch level, the entire batch must be written onto the error file. The input program must recognize whether the correction submitted is a record or batch correction. Perhaps the simplest way to handle batch corrections is to require resubmission of the entire batch rather than allow selected correction of fields or records in the batch on the error file.

The user must decide on the number and types of errors that determine when further processing of data through the system should be stopped. If the input program identifies too many errors, it may not be worthwhile updating the master file. Some types of errors are critical since the validity of other processing depends on their correction. For example, for the master file supplying the information on social security payments, it is essential all errors in notifications to cease payment be corrected before the update and check printing runs take place. Otherwise, social security recipients will be overpaid. The input program must print a message to stop further processing if it identifies too many errors that are critical. A major advantage of using an error file is that data can be submitted and corrected several times before further system processing occurs. Thus, the error file can be "cleaned off" before the update program is run.

Reporting of Errors

Errors must be reported by the input program in a manner that facilitates fast and accurate correction of the errors. The program must identify clearly the cause of the error and provide adequate cross-references to permit retrieval of source documents if they are needed.

In some cases it may be necessary to sort the errors prior to reporting them. For example, all errors of a certain transaction type might be sorted together to facilitate correction. If different user sections correct different errors, the errors for each user section must be sorted together so the error report can be separated and distributed to the different users. Sorting also may be needed for filing purposes.

The report should clearly identify the field in error by printing indicators such as upward arrows or asterisks under the field (Figure 11.3). In some cases it may be worthwhile printing a blown-up version of the record so the field in error can be identified easily.

Space should exist on the error report for the signature of the person correcting the error, the date of correction of the error, and the number of the batch in which the corrected version of the transaction has been resubmitted. This helps ensure all errors are corrected, corrections are not duplicated, and an audit trail exists for corrected errors.

Where possible the error report should be designed to act as a turnaround document for resubmitting corrected errors. For example, a monetary transaction may not have a match for its account number on the master file. Rather

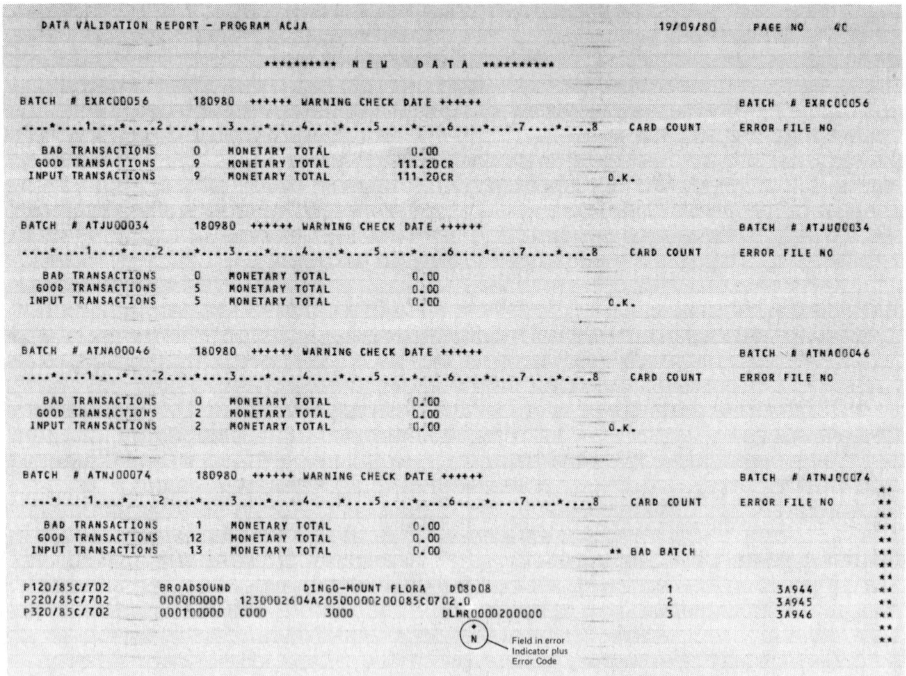

```
   DATA VALIDATION REPORT - PROGRAM ACJA                                   19/09/80    PAGE NO    4C

                          ********** N E W   D A T A **********

BATCH  # EXRC00056     180980  ++++++ WARNING CHECK DATE ++++++                      BATCH  # EXRC00056

....*....1....*....2....*....3....*....4....*....5....*....6....*....7....*....8   CARD COUNT   ERROR FILE NO

  BAD TRANSACTIONS     0   MONETARY TOTAL         0.00
 GOOD TRANSACTIONS     9   MONETARY TOTAL       111.20CR
INPUT TRANSACTIONS     9   MONETARY TOTAL       111.20CR             O.K.

BATCH  # ATJU00034     180980  ++++++ WARNING CHECK DATE ++++++                      BATCH  # ATJU00034

....*....1....*....2....*....3....*....4....*....5....*....6....*....7....*....8   CARD COUNT   ERROR FILE NO

  BAD TRANSACTIONS     0   MONETARY TOTAL         0.00
 GOOD TRANSACTIONS     5   MONETARY TOTAL         0.00
INPUT TRANSACTIONS     5   MONETARY TOTAL         0.00               O.K.

BATCH  # ATNA00046     180980  ++++++ WARNING CHECK DATE ++++++                      BATCH  # ATNA00046

....*....1....*....2....*....3....*....4....*....5....*....6....*....7....*....8   CARD COUNT   ERROR FILE NO

  BAD TRANSACTIONS     0   MONETARY TOTAL         0.00
 GOOD TRANSACTIONS     2   MONETARY TOTAL         0.00
INPUT TRANSACTIONS     2   MONETARY TOTAL         0.00               O.K.

BATCH  # ATNJ00074     180980  ++++++ WARNING CHECK DATE ++++++                      BATCH  # ATNJ00074
                                                                                                         **
....*....1....*....2....*....3....*....4....*....5....*....6....*....7....*....8   CARD COUNT   ERROR FILE NO   **
                                                                                                         **
  BAD TRANSACTIONS     1   MONETARY TOTAL         0.00                                                   **
 GOOD TRANSACTIONS    12   MONETARY TOTAL         0.00                                                   **
INPUT TRANSACTIONS    13   MONETARY TOTAL         0.00               ** BAD BATCH                        **
                                                                                                         **
                                                                                                         **
P120/85C/702      BROADSOUND          DINGO-MOUNT FLORA   D08D08              1            3A944         **
P220/85C/702      000000000  1230002604A205000002000085C0702.0                2            3A945         **
P320/85C/702      000100000  C000          3000          DLMR000200000        3            3A946         **
                                                          *                                              **
                                                          N                                              **
```


Figure 11.3
Input validation report (Main Roads Department).

PROGRAM ACBB			NON-MATCHING RECORDS REPORT					21/06/78		
								PAGE 2		
TYPE BATCH ORIG	DOCUMENT	JOB NUMBER	* CD *TYP *1-2	JOB NUMBER 3-19	TRANSN CR AMOUNT INDIC 20-28 29-30	DOC NO 31-38	RESUB FROM 39-48	* TRAN ERR RECOV * DATE DATEBATCH		
TRMS 1169 8183	287435	MRD13640	NO DIGIT*	B1 MRD 13640 -8	000001400	287435		*21/06/78		
TSWS 1175 1A/6/78	305854	MRD13945-3	INVALID*	B1 MRD 13945-8	000001370	305854		*21/06/78		
EXSV 73716 00000000		PM10808	NO DIGIT*	B1 PM 10808 -0	000010500	EX73716		*21/06/78		
TSWS 1196 M2208	T291909	PM11600-2	INVALID*	B1 PM 11600 -8	000043219	T291909		*21/06/78		
CLDO 2221 6M181C		PM11650-9	INVALID*	B1 PM 11605 -9	000123600	6M181C		*21/06/78		
CLDO 2211 M0306		PM11863-1	INVALID*	B1 PM 11863 -9	000004674	M0306		*21/06/78		
EXSV 73713 00000000		PM11937-1	INVALID*	B1 PM 11937 -6	000000420	EX73713		*21/06/78		
TSDI 1153 R328	150672	PM12379-7	INVALID*	B1 PM 12379 -9	000025571	150672		*21/06/78		
EXSV 73716 00000000		PM12463-8	INVALID*	B1 PM 12463 -9	000021527	EX73716		*21/06/78		
TSWS 1176 5/6/78	292850	PM13394-5	INVALID*	B1 PM 13394 -8	000042750	292850		*21/06/78		
CLDO 2206 CY4715		PM13449-5	INVALID*	B1 PM 13499 -5	000000737	CY4715		*21/06/78		
TSWS 1176 5/6/78	292850	PM13544-0	INVALID*	B1 PM 13544 -4	000000950	292850		*21/06/78		
TRMS 1184 B6520	273109	PM13590-9	INVALID*	B1 PM 13590 -8	000006300	273109		*21/06/78		
TRMS 1186 B28/78	T289827	PM13824-5	INVALID*	B1 PM 13824 -9	000008550	T289827		*21/06/78		
TRMS 1190 R355	T265166	PM9005-4	INVALID*	B1 PM 90005-4	000001350	T265166		*21/06/78		
		Corrected Field		B1 C601/3085/1	000292918 CR	CS558				

Field in Error → (pointing to INVALID column)
Field to be Repunched

	NUMBER	TOTAL TRANSACTION AMOUNT
MATCHING RECORDS	3966	1920660.02
NON-MATCHING RECORDS	40	14437.92
COMPUTER SUSPENSE A/C	40	14437.92
NON MONETARY TRANSACTIONS	72	

THIS IS THE END OF THE REPORT

Figure 11.4
Validation report for use as turnaround document. (Main Roads Department).

than have the person responsible for correcting the error recopy the correct information onto a new source document, thereby increasing the risk of transcription errors occurring, space can be provided on the error report for inserting the corrected account number (Figure 11.4). However, this method of resubmitting corrected errors can be awkward for keypunch operators. Clear punching instructions must be printed on the report. For example, card column numbers for each field can be printed as a heading on the top of the report.

Using the error report as a turnaround document for resubmission of errors is especially useful if large volumes of errors occur and the personnel responsible for correcting errors are under heavy workload pressures. This situation often arises during conversion from a manual system to a computer system (see, also, Chapter 5). The manual system records may contain many errors and a backlog of errors requiring correction and resubmission develops. Using the error report as a turnaround document reduces workloads and the probability of new errors arising.

It is important that the error messages printed clearly state the nature of the errors. Where possible, printing error codes instead of error messages should be avoided. Users may incorrectly interpret a code, or if the documentation of codes is out of date, users may waste time looking for errors that do not exist. Wooldridge [1974] suggests printing a detailed key to the codes at the end of an error report if codes are used instead of error messages. This also simplifies the change procedure needed when a code is altered or a new error type is added. User manuals do not have to be changed; only the input program needs to be modified.

At the end of the error report, summary statistics should be printed for the transactions processed and the different types of errors identified. Control totals should show the total number of transactions processed and any monetary amounts involved. The frequency of each error type also should be printed. This allows the control section to check all data has been processed and to identify abnormal numbers of errors.

CONTROL OVER INPUT

Careful control must be exercised over input to ensure: (*a*) all data is entered into the system, (*b*) all errors are corrected, (*c*) errors are not corrected more than once, (*d*) changes in the pattern of errors are identified, and (*e*) backup for input data and errors exists. These duties are the responsibility of user departments and the computer installation's control section (see, also, Chapter 8).

Registers and control totals are the means of ensuring all data enters the system. The input program must print a report showing all batches processed; this report can be checked against the register of batches submitted to the system. The control totals for valid data and total errors should be reconciled with the control total for all data submitted to the system.

To ensure all errors are corrected and errors are not resubmitted to the system more than once, corrected errors should be initialed on the error reports and the source documents containing the corrected errors should be stamped when they have been punched. If an attempt to correct an error fails, the error must be printed out again with a cross-reference to the previous error report. The input program must not add a second error to the error file.

Statistics on the frequency of different errors are useful for three reasons. First, they may indicate the need for training in the user area responsible for submitting the data. Second, they may indicate the need for redesign of the input system. Third, they may enable the input program to be rewritten to be more effective and efficient. For example, it may be possible to correct more errors automatically, or the tests for errors may be reordered so more frequent errors are recognized first.

Procedures must exist for backup and recovery of input data. Input data may have to be reprocessed to recover a destroyed master file. It should be stored for a period until it is no longer needed for recovery. The error file is subject to the same backup and recovery procedures used for any master file. Chapter 15 discusses these procedures in detail. Error reports should be properly filed since their loss may make correction of errors difficult.

A GENERALIZED INPUT SYSTEM

To enhance control over input, some organizations have developed a generalized input system. A generalized input system provides centralized management of the data validation processes needed for the installation's portfolio of application systems.

Several factors motivate the use of a generalized input system. First, much commonality exists across application systems in the functions needed for processing and validating input. Rather than continue to rewrite these processes for each new application system, a generalized system providing parameter-driven processes can cater for the specific requirements of each application system. Second, a generalized input system allows the development and modification of input validation routines for application systems to be accomplished quickly. However, generality incurs a cost in terms of processing overheads. Third, use of a generalized input system ensures a consistent standard is achieved for the input validation processes used in individual application systems. Fourth, having a single system maintain files of valid data and errors increases control within the installation.

A generalized input system consists of five major components (Figure 11.5):

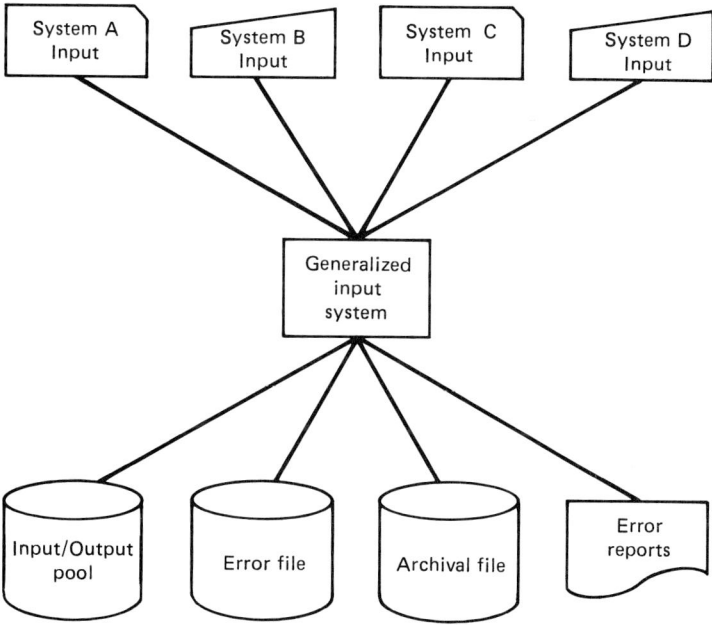

Figure 11.5
Using a generalized input system for validation of data.

1 Generalized validation module
2 Input/Output pool
3 Error file
4 Generalized reporting module
5 Archival file

All components of a generalized input system are shared resources. The system must permit simultaneous input and validation of data by multiple application systems. Similarly, the files and reporting system must be available simultaneously to multiple application systems.

Generalized Validation Module

Because many of the validation processes needed in application systems are common across application systems, it is possible to write generalized programming code for these processes. These processes are then invoked via parameters that specify the specific validation needs of a particular application system. For example, a parameter may specify that a range check is needed for field GROSS-PAY and that the limits are $500 and $3000. The range check is a generalized routine; the limits are parameter-supplied values.

Besides providing generalized validation processes, the generalized validation module must permit specific validation processes to be written. Some validation processes involve complex logic that cannot be handled using generalized code. In other cases the generalized module performs validation too inefficiently. The generalized validation module must allow user-written routines to be stored and these routines to be invoked at run time.

Input/Output Pool

The generalized input system dumps valid data into an input/output pool. The file is called a "pool" because it is periodically filled with data, and at various times the "plug" is pulled to remove some or all of the data. The pool file holds valid data temporarily until the data is selected for application system processing.

When an application system is to be run, the generalized input system's retrieval routines select data from the pool and funnel it off to the application system. Data for the application system can be selected on several bases: all data, data up to a certain date, or by transaction type. If the application system's processing follows a definite schedule, this schedule may be stored in the generalized input system and the system programmed to call and activate automatically the application system according to this schedule.

Error File

A generalized input system's error file stores all errors detected by the validation module. As with the pool, all errors (transactions) are given a unique application system identifier. Resubmissions of corrected errors are validated, and successful resubmissions are cleared off the error file. The input system recognizes an unsuccessful resubmission, leaves the old error on the error file, and prints a message denoting the failed transaction as an unsuccessful resubmission and the reasons for failure.

A major advantage of the error file relates to the issue of reminders if errors are not cleared off the file. The generalized input system checks how long an error has remained on the error file and reminds the user it needs correction if it has been on the file for longer than a specified period. Thus, errors are not lost through failure to resubmit corrections.

Generalized Reporting Module

The format of error reports is common across most application systems. Similarly, the error messages needed are common. Variable information can be obtained from the parameter values supplied to the generalized input system by the user. For example, if an error message states a range test has been violated, the upper and lower limits can be printed from the parameter values supplied. Other information is standard on all error reports. For example, control totals that enable input to be reconciled with the data processed should always be provided.

Because of these commonalities, a generalized input system can also provide a generalized reporting module. Using the module means the installation must establish standards for reporting errors. This is desirable from a control perspective. However, the generalized reporting module should also allow user-written report modules to be supplied when the generalized module cannot cater for the reports needed.

Reports need not be generated for every validation run. They can be stored and a number of reports combined or generated separately in a single run. Thus, data might be validated and submitted to the generalized input system throughout a day. Reports generated are stored and printed during the night shift for use the following day. This function also can be performed by spooling software. Report files generated may be kept for a short period as backup for hard copy reports.

Archival System

When data on the pool has been used by all application systems that need the data, it must be written to an archival file. The archival system contains routines for retiring data and retrieving data. Data may be retrieved for all application systems, a specific application system, a certain time period, or a specific application system run. Retrieval from the archival file may be needed for backup and recovery purposes.

There are two major advantages of having a single archival file for the installation. First, instead of having to provide backup for each application system's input data, only the archival file needs to be backed up since it contains all the input data for each application system. Second, the archival file provides data that enables historical trends to be analyzed. For example, the growth in volume of a particular type of transaction might be examined to determine whether a new method of input may be more efficient.

SUMMARY

Input controls can be applied at four levels: (*a*) fields, (*b*) records, (*c*) batches, and (*d*) files. Field validation logic assesses the integrity of data within individual fields. Record validation logic uses logical interrelationships among fields in a record to assess the integrity of data within a record. Batch validation logic uses batch controls supplied on a batch header record to assess the integrity of data within a batch. File validation logic attempts to ensure the correct file is used for production running of an application system.

The design of the input program involves three major decisions: (*a*) how data will be validated, (*b*) how errors will be handled, and (*c*) how errors will be reported. As long as benefits exceed costs, the input program should detect as many errors as possible. These errors must be written onto an error file so they are not lost through system users failing to correct them. Error reports must explain clearly the nature of errors detected and provide control totals for checking whether all data has been processed.

Control over input is the responsibility of both the system users and the computer installation's control section. Both groups must ensure all data enters the system, errors are corrected, and data is entered only once. Periodic analysis of errors should take place to determine whether: (*a*) users are continually making the same error, and (*b*) the effectiveness and efficiency of the input program can be improved.

To enhance control over input an installation can use a generalized input system. A generalized input system provides a generalized module for validating data, an input/output pool for storing valid data, an error file, a generalized reporting system, and an archival file.

REVIEW QUESTIONS

11.1. Unfortunately the input program is sometimes called the input *edit* program. Why is this a misnomer? Distinguish between the functions of validating, editing, and formatting data.

11.2. As a general rule, data should be validated as soon as possible and as close as possible to the source of the data. Briefly discuss the rationale behind this rule. Give one exception to the rule.

11.3. Briefly describe the *nature* of (without giving examples):
   a. field checks
   b. record checks
   c. batch checks
   d. file checks

11.4. Distinguish between a range check and a reasonableness check. Why is a reasonableness check not a field level check?

11.5. Once the check digit for an input field has been read and validated, from a control perspective should the check digit be carried through the system with the field? Discuss the advantages and disadvantages of carrying a check digit through the system.

11.6. From a control perspective, variable length fields represent a data integrity threat because of their added processing complexity. Briefly describe the circumstances when variable length fields for input data *should* be used.

11.7. What problems does a master reference field check normally pose for input validation? Briefly discuss the variables that would influence your decision to include or not include a master reference check in an input program.

11.8. Why is the check of a valid sign for a numeric field not a field level check?

11.9. Distinguish between a logical batch and a physical batch. For online data entry, are there any situations where it would be impossible to exercise control through using a logical batch?

11.10. For a magnetic tape file, briefly explain any difficulties surrounding the use of control totals as a *file* check.

11.11. Briefly explain why knowledge of the frequency of possible errors is important to the programmer writing the input program.

11.12. What is meant by a "closed routine" in program logic? Briefly explain the problems that can arise if closed routines exist in an input program.

11.13. An input program should identify as many errors in a record as possible and not terminate validation of the record after only one error has been discovered. Why?

11.14. Briefly explain how a program can get "out of step." Write a short algorithm (use any language) that would not get out of step for an input program that expects 25 follower cards after a batch header.

11.15. Briefly explain the advantages and disadvantages of using decision tables and a decision-table preprocessor in writing an input validation program.

11.16. Briefly explain the importance of an error file. Outline some of the difficulties encountered in using magnetic tape error files.

11.17. Give two examples where a large number of errors or certain types of errors in the input data may necessitate further processing through the application system be stopped.

11.18. Suggest two techniques that can be used in the design of error reports to prevent errors being corrected and resubmitted more than once.

11.19. Briefly explain the advantages of printing the key to all error codes used in an error report at the end of the error report.

11.20. Why should control totals and summary statistics for the different types of errors be printed at the end of an error report?

11.21. In an input system, why is it possible errors may be resubmitted more than once? How does an error file assist in preventing errors that may arise from duplicate resubmission of errors?

11.22. Briefly explain the features of the validation module in a generalized input system. Why is it necessary to permit user-written subroutines to be invoked within the module?

11.23. Briefly explain how the input/output pool and the error file facilitate continuous submission of data to an application system.

11.24. How does the "reminder" system function for an error file? Should resubmitted errors that again fail validation tests be written onto the error file? Explain.

11.25. Briefly explain the advantages of having a single input/output pool file, an error file, and an archival file for an installation. What are the disadvantages? Should all systems in a computer installation use the generalized system?

11.26. Briefly explain the features of the reporting module in a generalized input system. If spooling software is available, would it be necessary to provide a system that stores reports for later printing?

EXERCISES AND CASES

11.1. You are an internal auditor participating in the design phase of a new order filling system. The programmer responsible for the design of the input validation program asks your opinion on whether or not the input validation tests proposed for customer orders are satisfactory. Customer orders are batched and keypunched. The validation tests proposed are:

Field	Missing data	Must be numeric	Must be alphabetic	Valid range	Check digit	Valid code	Valid sign	Valid batch number
Card code						X		
Customer number		X		X	X			
Salesperson number		X				X		
Purchase order number	X							
Part number	X				X			
Quantity ordered	X	X					X	
Price instructions			X			X		
Batch number		X						X

The following data on the fields is relevant to your decision:

Field	Description
Card Code	Must be the value "04"
Customer Number	Numeric value that must range between 01000 and 90000
Salesperson Number	Must be one of 50 numeric values

Purchase Order Number	Five character field; first character is alphabetic, last four are numeric
Part Number	Alphanumeric field
Quantity Ordered	Four character numeric
Price Instructions	Alphabetic; only four codes are valid
Batch Number	Four character numeric

Required: Write the programmer a brief report with your comments on the validation tests.

11.2. Huymans & Co. is a Dutch civil engineering firm based in Amsterdam. It performs construction work throughout Western Europe. The firm employs 2000 people at various offices and construction sites.

As an internal auditor for the firm, you are investigating controls over personnel change of status processing in the computer payroll system.

The various offices and sites send personnel change of status information to the personnel department in head office. Change of status source documents are prepared after the supporting documentation has been checked. The source documents are batched and two control totals are calculated: a hash total of the employee numbers in the batch and a document count. Periodically a clerk collects the batches and takes them to data processing for keypunching.

When the control section in data processing receives the batches, each batch is logged in a register. The batches are then keypunched, verified, and submitted for processing.

The input program performs a comprehensive set of validation checks and prints a report showing the rejected batches. This report, together with the batches, is returned to the personnel department. A clerk in the personnel department checks to see all batches have been stamped as keypunched, and gives the rejected batches report to another clerk who is responsible for correcting and resubmitting the batches. As each batch is corrected and resubmitted, the clerk initials the batch entry on the rejected batches report. Periodically the personnel manager reviews the rejected batch reports.

Required: Prepare your working papers and indicate:
a. any control weaknesses that exist
b. the possible consequences of these control weaknesses
c. some remedial measures

11.3. Refer to case 10.1. Using the bill payment by telephone system, customers enter the following data:
a. customer number
b. account number
c. creditor number
d. amount to be paid creditor in cents
e. date when amount is to be paid

An automated teller requests each data item on a step-by-step basis. After the date when amount is to be paid has been entered, the teller asks for a new creditor number. Note, creditor numbers must be authorized for customers. They must write or telephone the savings and loan association at a prior time and new creditor numbers for the customer will be entered into the system. Customers

also have special instructions that they can enter using the Touch-Tone telephone, for example:
a. by entering #9# when a creditor number is requested, the customer terminates data entry
b. by entering #8# they can obtain their account balance
c. by entering #4# the automated teller will repeat the last transaction entered

Required: Identify the types of data entry errors that a customer could make. What controls could be used to detect these data entry errors?

11.4. The following card provides input from employee timecards to a payroll system:

Field	Picture
Employee number	9(6)
Regular hours	9(2)
Overtime hours	9(2)
Expenses/commissions	9(4).9(2)
Sick time	9(2)
Vacation time	9(2)

What field and record validation checks do you suggest should be performed on the card? Make up any parameter values you need for your tests but make sure they are reasonable. All fields are fixed length.

11.5. The following batch card and follower card are used to update the master file for a job costing system. The master file contains accounts that are the responsibility of each manager of a job:

a. Batch Card

Field	Picture
Record type	A(1)
Batch number	9(4)
Transaction type	X(4)
Number of records in batch	9(2)
Financial control total	9(6).9(2)
Date of preparation	9(6)

b. Follower Card

Field	Picture
Record type	A(1)
Transaction type	X(4)
Account number	X(12)
Amount	9(4).9(2)
Transaction date	9(6)

Suggest any validation checks you think appropriate. Make up any parameter values you need for your tests but make sure they are reasonable. All fields are fixed length.

REFERENCES

American Federation of Information Processing Societies. *AFIPS System Review Manual on Security* (Montvale, N.J.: AFIPS Press, 1974).
Canadian Institute of Chartered Accountants. *Computer Control Guidelines* (Toronto, Canada: The Canadian Institute of Chartered Accountants, 1970).
_____. *Computer Audit Guidelines* (Toronto, Canada: The Canadian Institute of Chartered Accountants, 1975).
Davis, Gordon B. *Auditing and EDP* (New York: American Institute of Certified Public Accountants, 1968).
EDP Auditors Association, Inc. *Control Objectives* (Hanover Park, Ill.: EDP Auditors Association, 1975).
Jancura, Elise G. *Audit and Control of Computer Systems* (New York: Petrocelli/Charter, 1974).
_____, ed. *Computers: Auditing and Control*, 2d ed. (New York: Petrocelli/Charter, 1977).
Mair, William C., Donald R. Wood, and Keagle W. Davis. *Computer Control and Audit*, 2d ed. (Altamonte Springs, Fla.: The Institute of Internal Auditors, Inc., 1976).
Porter, W. Thomas, and William E. Perry. *EDP Controls and Auditing*, 2d ed. (Belmont, Calif.: Wadsworth Publishing Company, Inc., 1977).
Wooldridge, Susan. *Computer Input Design* (New York: Petrocelli Books, 1974).

CHAPTER 12

PROCESSING CONTROLS

CHAPTER OUTLINE

VALIDATION CHECKS
SOME MATTERS OF PROGRAMMING STYLE
   Sequence Check Master and Transaction Files
   Ensure All Records on Files Are Processed
   Process Master File Changes before Updates
   Handle Rounding Correctly
   Maintain a Suspense Account
   Print Run-to-Run Control Totals
   Print Control Data for Internal Tables (Standing Data)
   Minimize Operator Intervention
   Avoid Closed Routines
CONCURRENCY CONTROL
   The Problem of Deadlock
   Solutions to Deadlock
   Preventing Deadlock
SYSTEM SOFTWARE INTEGRITY
   Operating System Integrity
   Auditing System Software
CONTROL OVER HARDWARE MALFUNCTIONS
CHECKPOINT/RESTART CONTROLS
SUMMARY
REVIEW QUESTIONS

EXERCISES AND CASES
REFERENCES

Processing controls safeguard assets and maintain data integrity during the time period after the data has been read and validated until it has been output on some device. Providing data read into the computer is authorized, accurate, and complete, processing errors may occur for two major reasons. First, the application system program processing the data may contain unauthorized or erroneous logic. Second, a hardware fault or system software fault may cause data to be processed incorrectly.

This chapter describes the various types of validation checks that application programs should perform and the control information that they should report to ensure processing of data is authorized, accurate, and complete. Various techniques for preventing, detecting, and correcting hardware or system software errors are discussed. As a matter of convenience, the chapter also describes the hardware and system software controls that exist in computer systems. Strictly speaking some of these controls apply to input and output functions. However, because substantial overlap exists between the hardware/software system controls for input, processing, and output, their grouping here allows a tidier discussion.

VALIDATION CHECKS

Processing validation checks primarily ensure computations performed on *numeric* fields are authorized, accurate, and complete. The processing involved with alphabetic or alphanumeric fields typically is minimal: an existing field value is replaced or data is inserted in a field when a new record is created. Because the types of processing performed on data vary considerably, it is difficult to describe generally the validation checks that should be applied. Nevertheless, the following are common:

Level of check	Type of check	Explanation
Field	Overflow	Overflow may occur if a computational field (perhaps in working storage) is not zeroized initially. In COBOL, for example, a special overflow clause is available.
	Range	An allowable value range may apply to the field.
Record	Reasonableness	The contents of one field may determine the allowable value for another. For example, after an employee's allowable deductions have been calculated for payroll, they may be checked to see if they fall within a valid range of values, given the employee's position within the organization.

	Sign	The contents of one field, for example, the record type field, may determine which sign is valid for a numeric field.
File	Crossfooting	Separate control totals can be developed for related fields and crossfooted at the end of a run. For example, for payroll, control totals can be calculated for gross pay, deductions, and net pay. At the end of processing, net pay should equal gross pay less deductions.
	Control Totals	Run-to-run control totals can be developed and compared with the results of a run. For example, if the current balance of an accounts receivable file is $100,000 and the incoming transactions consist of $10,000 debit and $8,000 credit, the new balance of the file should be $102,000. The last record on the transaction file used as input to the master file update program may be a control record showing the totals for the debit and credit entries. The master file update program can use these control totals to check the accuracy of its computations.

As always, the costs of performing a validation check should be compared with the benefits derived. For example, if a payroll program computes individual pays correctly, it is difficult to conceive how a crossfooting error can occur. Nevertheless, the computer used may be an old machine that occasionally suffers undetected memory or parity errors, thereby resulting in a corrupted field.

SOME MATTERS OF PROGRAMMING STYLE

The auditor should be aware of some traps for the unwary or inexperienced programmer that can result in incomplete or inaccurate processing of data. These traps can be avoided through good programming style. The experienced analyst and programmer specifically designs test data to create the underlying conditions for these traps and to check that the program handles these conditions correctly. The following sections describe some elements of good programming style that help avoid these traps and ensure authorized, accurate, and complete processing of data.

Sequence Check Master and Transaction Files

In a typical batch update run the transaction file is sorted just prior to the update of the master file. It seems superfluous, therefore, for the master file update program then to check the sequence of the master file and transaction file during processing. Nevertheless, several conditions may cause the master file or transaction file to get out of sequence. First, some "patching" of a master file or transaction file may occur because of an update error. If a data or program error exists, rather than reprocess all the data, a utility program may be used to correct the error existing on the master file or transaction file. Patching often occurs during the changeover from one system to another when data has to be cleaned up. If patching occurs incorrectly, files can get out of sequence. Second, an erroneous update program may insert records in incorrect sequence on the master file. Third, on rare occasions a sort utility package processes erroneously (perhaps after modification) or a hardware/system software error goes undetected.

Ensure All Records on Files Are Processed

If correct end-of-file protocols are not followed in a program, records may be lost from either a master file or transaction file. A common error is to close the transaction file upon reaching the end of the master file, and, less frequently, to close the master file upon reaching the end of the transaction file. In the former case there may be new records for insertion after the last record on the old master file. In the latter case, if a new physical version of the file is to be created (e.g., as with a magnetic tape file), existing master file records are lost. Correct end-of-file protocols can be complex if multiple transaction files and master files are processed concurrently.

Process Master File Changes before Updates

Multiple transactions may occur for a single master file record; for example, several monetary transactions for an accounts receivable record plus a change of address transaction. It is important that any master file record insertions, deletions, or changes be made before other types of transactions are processed. Otherwise, several types of errors can occur; for example, billing a customer at a wrong address, continuing to pay an employee after termination, or failing to pay an employee who has just been hired. The system should be designed so transaction codes cause changes to a record to sort before other types of transactions, such as monetary updates.

Handle Rounding Correctly

Rounding problems occur when the level of precision required for an arithmetic calculation is less than the level of precision actually calculated. For example, the interest on a bank account may be calculated to five decimal digits. However, only two are required to record the lowest monetary amount; that is, a cent. If the remaining three decimal digits simply are dropped, an interest calculation made on the grand total of account balances may not agree with the sum of the individual interest calculations. Thus, uncertainty sur-

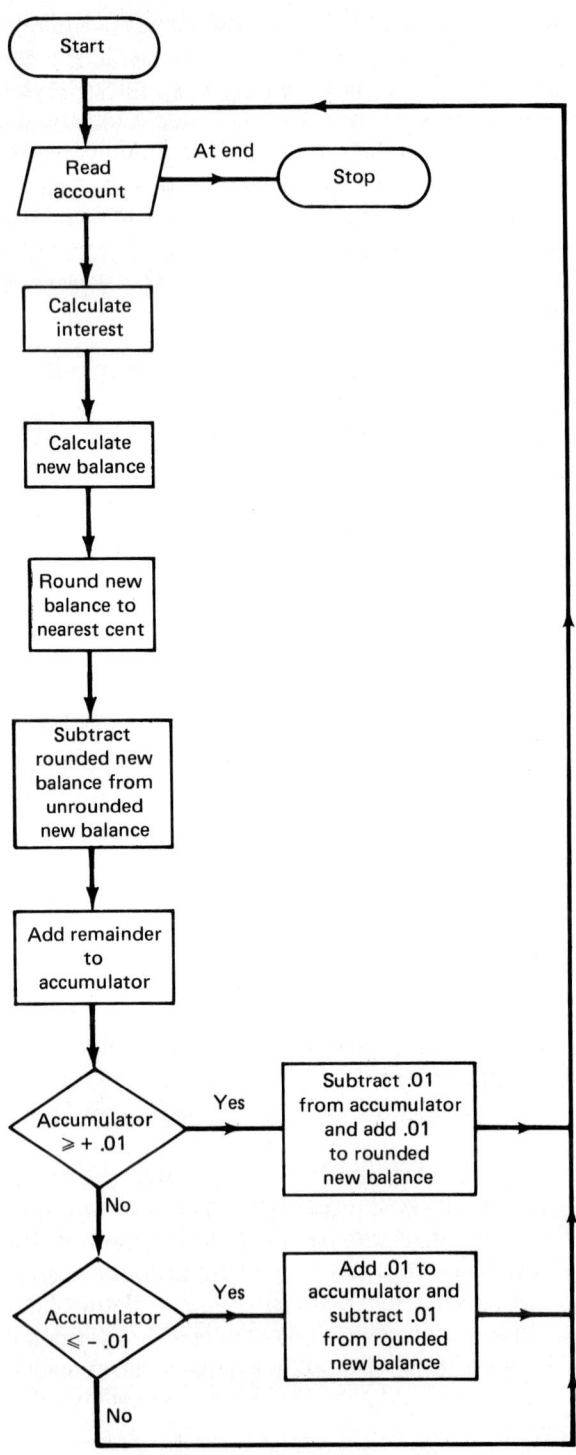

Figure 12.1
Algorithm for interest rounding calculations.

rounds the accuracy of the processing performed by the interest calculation routine.

An algorithm for handling this problem is well-known. The auditor should check to see the algorithm has been used for two reasons. First, it may not be known by the inexperienced programmer. Second, a minor modification to the algorithm provides an easy means to perpetrate a fraud. Figure 12.1 shows the algorithm for handling the rounding problem. Consider the following three examples of how the algorithm works for an interest rate of 3.25%:

1	Existing accumulator balance	$-.00815$
	Old account balance	1,351.62
	Interest calculated	43.92765
	New account balance	1,395.54765
	Rounded account balance	1,395.55
	New accumulator balance	$-.0105$ $(-.00235 - .00815)$
	Final account balance	1,395.54
	Final accumulator balance	$-.0005$
2	Existing accumulator balance	.00917
	Old account balance	650.23
	Interest calculated	21.13248
	New account balance	671.36248
	Rounded account balance	671.36
	New accumulator balance	.01165 $(.00248 + .00917)$
	Final account balance	671.37
	Final accumulator balance	.00165
3	Existing accumulator balance	.00002
	Old account balance	2,911.20
	Interest calculated	94.614
	New account balance	3,005.814
	Rounded account balance	3,005.81
	New accumulator balance	.00402 $(.004 + .00002)$
	Final account balance	3,005.81
	Final accumulator balance	.00402

Depending on the balance in the accumulator, some accounts are rounded up and others are rounded down. By using this method, the interest calculated on the grand total of the old account balances plus the grand total of the old account balances will equal the sum of the new account balances.

To perpetrate a fraud a programmer simply modifies the algorithm so that when the condition occurs to add a cent to the rounded new account balance (i.e., accumulator $\geq + .01$), this cent is added to another accumulator. After processing is complete this second accumulator then is added to an account specially created by the programmer. Though the amounts are small, if several hundred thousand accounts exist, over a year the fraud can amount to a reasonable sum.

Maintain a Suspense Account

Whenever monetary transactions are involved, the master file update program should maintain a suspense account—generally the last account on the master file. The suspense account is the repository for monetary transactions that mismatch the master file. These mismatches occur for several reasons; for example, an account number may be coded incorrectly or a new account may not be inserted on the master file correctly. If monetary items are not charged to a suspense account, they may be lost because someone fails to correct the mismatch. The master file update program must accumulate the monetary effects of mismatches throughout processing and charge the net amount to the suspense account at the end of processing. A suspense account report should be produced showing which transactions were posted to this account. The mismatches also must be written to an error file and removed as they are corrected. Reminders should be issued if they are not removed promptly (see, also, Chapter 11).

Print Run-to-Run Control Totals

At each stage during the processing of data, a program should print control totals. These control totals provide evidence that the program processed all the input data and that it processed the data correctly. For example, an accounts receivable master file update program should show the total value of input transactions, the total value of accounts on the input master file, and the total value of accounts on the output master file. These control totals can be checked against user-prepared control totals to see whether the correct files were used as input, whether all data entered the program, etc. Sometimes control totals are supplied as input parameters to a program; for example, the current value of the accounts on the master file may be input so the program can check whether it read the correct input master file.

Print Control Data for Internal Tables (Standing Data)

Many programs have internal tables that they use to perform various functions: for example, a payroll program may have an internal table of pay rates; a billing program may have an internal table of prices. Maintaining the integrity of these tables is critical since the effects of an error can be substantial. For example, an error in a table of prices may mean several thousand customers are underbilled for merchandise. It may be too costly to recover the monies lost; furthermore, the organization may not want the error to be known publicly because of an adverse reaction by shareholders, creditors, etc.

Any changes to internal tables (e.g., updating a pay rate) should be checked carefully for accuracy and completeness. The program should print out the table after the changes have been made so a user can validate the changes made.

Even if no changes to an internal table are made, if the table is small, it can be printed out after each program run so users can check that no unauthorized changes have occurred to the standing data (table values). If the table is large and a decision is made not to print the table, the program at least should calculate some control total (e.g., a hash total) for the values in the table. Users then can check this control total to determine whether unauthorized changes have occurred.

Minimize Operator Intervention

As a general rule, programs that minimize operator intervention are less prone to processing errors. Operators always can make mistakes when providing input for a program such as a parameter value or an alternate start point. Sometimes it is impossible to avoid some level of operator intervention; for example, the program may have to be activated at a different start point depending on whether it is performing end-of-month or end-of-quarter procedures. In these cases the program must provide clear instructions and clear feedback to the operator. Where possible, it also should check the validity of the operator's actions.

Avoid Closed Routines

As discussed in Chapter 11, closed routines should not exist in programs. The program must check for all possible values in a field, rather than assume the existence of a particular value if all other tests fail.

CONCURRENCY CONTROL

Problems arise for maintaining the integrity of data processing when several programs (processes) access a file or database concurrently. Traditionally, different application systems maintained their own files, even though substantial duplication of data resulted. Inevitably inconsistencies arose when different versions of the same data existed. With the development of database management systems, the notion of multiple users sharing the same data has become better accepted.

The following example illustrates a problem that can arise when several programs are allowed to access the same data concurrently. Consider an inventory application where a salesclerk and a receiving clerk are online to the inventory master file. Moreover, they are allowed concurrent access to the file. Figure 12.2 shows a time sequence of events that can occur whereby data integrity is violated. A supplier delivers 100 units of good XYZ and the receiving clerk accesses the inventory master file to update the record for XYZ. Input/output routines copy an image of the existing record into the receiving program's buffer, and the program commences to update the image of the record. At the same time a customer places an order for 175 units of XYZ

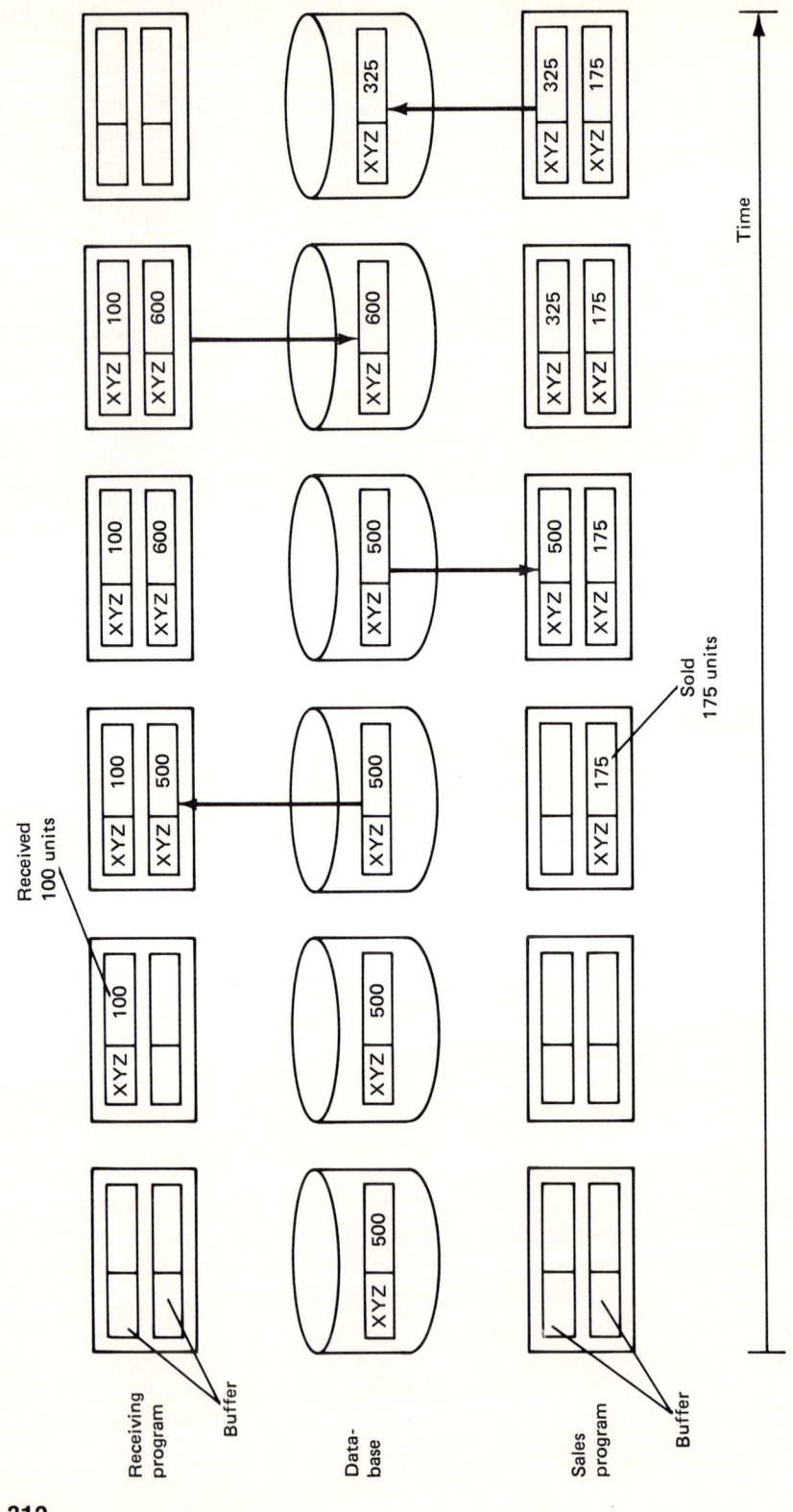

Figure 12.2 Concurrent processes as a threat to data integrity.

and the salesclerk accesses the inventory master file to update the record for XYZ. Input/output routines copy an image of the record into the program's buffer. In the meantime the receiving program completes its update and returns the buffer image of the record to the master file. The sales program carries out its update and returns the buffer image to the master file. Instead of the inventory record showing 425 units, it shows only 325 units. Thus, the record understates the true value of inventory on hand. This may lead to excessive inventory ordering and extra costs of storage space, obsolescence, lost interest, etc.

Data integrity problems caused by concurrent processes are not confined to update programs. Read-only programs can produce erroneous results if they operate concurrently with an update program. For example, a read-only program may be producing a trial balance for an accounts master file. If an update process is concurrently posting debit and credit entries to the accounts, only one side (e.g., the debit) of a double-entry transaction may be posted prior to the read-only program accessing the records to be updated. Thus, the trial balance will not balance.

The obvious solution to data integrity problems caused by concurrent processes is to lock out one process from a data resource while the resource is being used by another process. However, this solution can cause a system to come to a halt because of a situation called deadlock or the "deadly embrace."

The Problem of Deadlock

Figure 12.3 shows the problems that can arise when one process is allowed to lock out another process from a resource. At time t process P acquires exclusive control of data resource 1 and process Q acquires exclusive control of data resource 2. At time $t + 1$ process P makes an additional request for data resource 2 and process Q makes an additional request for data resource 1. Neither process can continue until one process releases control of the data resource that it acquired at time t. A deadlock situation results.

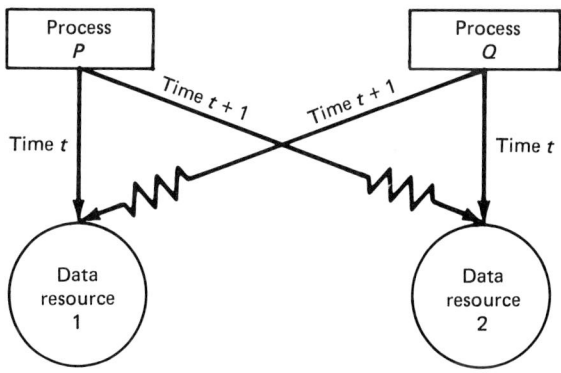

Figure 12.3
A deadlock situation.

Everest [1974] describes the necessary and sufficient conditions for deadlock to occur:

Condition	Explanation
Lockout	A process can exclude another process from using a resource. Note, a read-only process may not wish to exclude other read-only processes, only update processes.
Concurrency	Two or more processes can compete concurrently for exclusive control of two or more resources.
Additional Request	While holding exclusive control of a resource, a process can request exclusive control of another resource.
No Preemption	One process cannot force another process to release a resource prior to the process finishing with the resource.
Circular Wait	A circular chain of processes exists, each process in the chain holding a resource needed by the next process in the chain.

Solutions to Deadlock

How can a deadlock situation be resolved? At first thought the situation in Figure 12.3 might be resolved by simply forcing either process P or process Q to release the data resource over which it has exclusive control. In some cases this indeed may be a solution to the problem. In other cases, however, it may not be a solution.

Consider the following simple example. Salesperson 1 receives a request from a customer for a certain set of parts. The customer is unwilling to take the order unless all the parts requested can be supplied. Salesperson 2 receives a similar request from another customer. Both salespersons make an initial inquiry of the database to determine whether sufficient inventory exists for all the parts requested (a read-only process). Recognizing that inventory may be depleted in the meantime because of other orders, they both commence to place their orders. Figure 12.4 shows the situation that may result. Assume part A and part B are required in both salesperson's orders. Salesperson 1 acquires exclusive control of part A's record first and decreases the existing stock of 100 units by 80 units. At the same time salesperson 2 acquires exclusive control of part B's record and decreases the existing stock of 150 units by 100 units. At time $t + 1$ a deadlock situation results. Consider what would happen if salesperson 1's program was allowed to preempt salesperson 2's program. After accessing part B's record, salesperson 1's program would find only 50 units (150 − 100) of part B available since salesperson 2's program already had updated part B's record. Thus, salesperson 1's order would have to be cancelled in its entirety since 90 units of part B are required.

The same situation results if salesperson 2's program was allowed to preempt salesperson 1's program. Unless the updates of one program are undone before the other program continues, both customer orders are lost, whereas

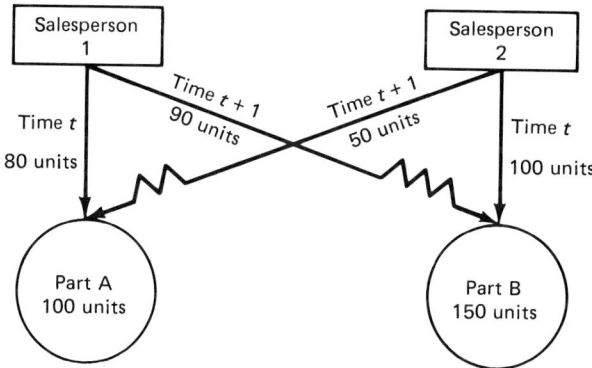

Figure 12.4
Inventory example of a deadlock situation.

only one order need be lost. The problem arises because the database is in an inconsistent state when the preemption occurs.

Rolling back the changes made by one program can be difficult. Shipping notices, invoices, etc., may have been prepared by the program that is preempted, and these messages have to be cancelled. The degree of complexity is affected by how far the program needs to be rolled back. Further, there is the question of which program should be preempted. Different criteria for making this choice may be used (see, for example, Fossum [1974] and McGee [1977]).

Preventing Deadlock

Recognizing a deadlock situation and recovering from a deadlock situation may consume substantial system resources. A more desirable strategy is to prevent deadlock occurring. Prevention of deadlock can be accomplished in four ways (see, further, Everest [1974]):

Strategy	Explanation
Presequence Processes	For those processes where a deadlock situation may result, an external administrator must presequence them to prevent their running concurrently.
Preempt Resources	One process may force another process to give up control of a data resource.
Preorder Resources	To prevent a circular chain of requests, data resources are preordered. Resource requests made by a process must follow this preorder.
Preclaim Resources	A process must obtain exclusive control over all resources that it needs before using them.

None of these strategies is entirely satisfactory for preventing deadlock. In an online realtime environment, presequencing resources may be impossible and result in the database being unavailable on a timely basis for users. The problems of rolling back changes to the database under a preemption strategy already have been discussed. Preordering data resources may be extremely difficult, if not impossible. A process may require data resources in an order that violates the preorder, or forcing programs to request data resources according to the preorder may degrade system performance substantially. Under a preclaim strategy a process may be blocked indefinitely from proceeding because it is unable to acquire all the resources it needs. Currently it is impossible with existing hardware to lock all the resources needed simultaneously. Thus, a process must lock needed resources sequentially. If the process fails on the first attempt because a resource is locked already, it must be backed out and the locking process attempted again. To prevent an "accordion effect" occurring indefinitely, a single locking mechanism for all processes is needed, and a process must acquire higher locking priority each time it fails to lock needed resources.

In many cases deadlock situations will be infrequent (see, for example, Munz and Krenz [1977]). As the sharing of data among multiple users increases, however, the likelihood of deadlock arising also increases. Whenever system resources are shared, the auditor may have to evaluate the operating system or database management system used to see how well it handles deadlock.

SYSTEM SOFTWARE INTEGRITY

When an application program processes data, it is not just dependent on itself for maintaining the integrity of data; it relies, also, on other resources it must use: the system software and hardware needed to support its functioning. Hardware controls are examined later in the chapter. The following discussion relates to system software.

The term "system software" is imprecise. It generally refers to software developed to perform functions needed by *several* application systems. The focus is on performing "system" rather than "application" functions. Thus, system software includes operating systems, compilers, file utilities, report generators, statistical packages, etc.

The subject of system software integrity has not been well-addressed by auditors for two major reasons. First, system software is normally very reliable software. Since it is often used by multiple users with diverse needs over long periods of time, most errors in the software are discovered quickly and corrected. Because of its high reliability, auditors have tended to regard system software as a low-risk area. As the auditor faces time constraints, the question of audit priorities must be addressed; consequently, system software has been neglected. Second, the technical knowledge often required to audit system software is high. Most auditors currently do not have this knowledge.

The knowledge resides with system software vendors or the system programmers in the computer installation. To carry out a system software audit the auditor may have to rely on others. Questions of audit independence then arise.

For several reasons auditors must increase their awareness of the issues involved in system software integrity. First, the number of documented cases where data integrity has been violated by breaching system software integrity is growing. Second, installation modification of vendor-supplied system software seems to be an ongoing problem. The risk of errors occurring in system software thereby increases. Third, as discussed in Chapters 6 and 8, system programmers and field engineers have available special tools that can be used to violate data integrity. Thus, periodic review of system software must be included in the overall EDP audit plan.

Operating System Integrity

Perhaps the most critical system software from an audit perspective is the operating system. The operating system is the master program responsible for sharing resources within a computer system: processor time, memory, secondary storage, channels, compilers, etc. Violating the integrity of the operating system means resources may be allocated in an uncontrolled manner; for example, a file may be assigned to an unauthorized user.

Designing, implementing, and testing secure operating systems is a complex topic—the subject of some of the frontier research in computer science. Further, the knowledge obtained in this area is not always disseminated. The following statement indicates one group of researcher's attitude toward publishing information on operating system security (Abbott et al. [1976], italics added):

> The authors of this document have attempted to write it in a way that provides as much information as possible to those responsible for system security while at the same time minimizing its potential usefulness to someone who might misuse the information. It is generally acknowledged that the security provisions of most current operating systems can be broken by an experienced programmer who has spent much time working with the system and has a very detailed understanding of its inner workings. The guidance used in the preparation of this document was that it should not increase the number of people who know all the details needed to effect a security penetration. *Many details about specific security flaws have not been included in this report either because there is no reasonable enhancement to correct the flaw or because exploitation of the flaw could be carried out by someone with relatively little additional detailed information about the system.* (Quoted by permission, the National Bureau of Standards. *Note:* The quote does not represent necessarily the position of the U.S. government.)

Thus, for the auditor who must be concerned with operating system integrity or system software integrity generally, it will be difficult, if not impossible, to go to books, journals, and reports to acquire the needed information.

Operating System Integrity Threats Operating system integrity threats may occur accidentally or be deliberate in nature. Accidental threats include hardware or software failures that cause the system to crash or process erroneously. A user also may undertake some unexpected procedure that the operating system cannot handle or handles incorrectly. These failures breach data integrity by corrupting data or violating the privacy of data. A system crash may result in sections of memory being dumped on various output devices in an uncontrolled manner. As a consequence, user passwords may be exposed.

Deliberate threats to operating system integrity usually aim at unauthorized removal of assets or breaching data integrity by violating data privacy. Deliberate threats occur in various ways. First, privileged personnel abuse their powers. For example, field engineers or system programmers use the special utilities provided them to examine system directories and user files. Second, special devices are used to detect electromechanical radiation or wiretap communications lines. Third, a would-be penetrator actively interacts with the operating system to determine and exploit a flaw in the system.

Some of the major known methods of penetrating operating systems follow:

Penetration technique	Explanation
Browsing	Involves searching residue to gain unauthorized access to information. The residue may be magnetic media such as core or disk storage, or wastebaskets containing discarded printouts, printer ribbons, etc. In these ways passwords and other sensitive information are obtained.
Masquerading	Involves carrying out unauthorized activities by impersonating a legitimate user of the system or impersonating the system itself. In the latter case the penetrator sends a message to an operator that looks like a system-generated message. The operator undertakes some action that results in a penetration.
Piggybacking	Involves intercepting communications between the operating system and the user and modifying them or substituting new messages. A special terminal is tapped into a communications line.
Between Lines Entry	A penetrator takes advantage of the time during which a legitimate user still is connected to the system but is inactive. As with piggybacking, the penetrator connects a special terminal to a communications line.
Spoofing	A penetrator fools the user into thinking he/she is interacting with the operating system. For example, a penetrator duplicates the logon procedure, captures a user's password, simulates a system crash, and requests the user to repeat the logon procedure. The second time the user actually logs on to the operating system.
Trojan Horse	Can be accomplished by a "system hacker" providing a utility for use by all other users. When the utility is executed by a program in privileged mode, it assigns the hacker's password the highest privilege level available on the system (see, further, Parker, [1976]).

Operating System Integrity Flaws Operating system penetrations result because integrity flaws exist in operating systems. Abbott et al. [1976] describe seven major integrity flaws often found in current operating systems (see, also, Short [1974]):

Integrity flaw	Explanation
Incomplete Parameter Validation	The system does not check the validity of all attributes of a user's request. For example, the user requests an address outside the area allocated to the user's program and the system fails to reject the request.
Inconsistent Parameter Validation	The system applies different validation criteria to the same construct within the system. For example, the user is able to create a password containing blanks but is unable to change or delete the password because the system regards it as illegitimate.
Implicit Sharing of Data	Part of the operating system's work space is a subset of the space allocated to the user program. The operating system reads in other user's passwords to this space that can be accessed by the user program.
Asynchronous Validation	If the operating system permits asynchronous processes, the user takes advantage of timing inadequacies to violate integrity. For example, a user requests an I/O operation and the operating system validates the user parameters. The system finds the channel needed is busy and issues an interrupt. The user then changes the address for the I/O operation to an address outside the valid work space. The system returns control to an illegal address.
Inadequate Access Control	The operating system performs incomplete checking, or one part of the system assumes another part has performed the checking. For example, a user loads a program with the same name as a system routine and the operating system does not check to see the program is from the system library. Thus, a user routine supplants a system routine.
Violable Limits	System documentation states limits, e.g., the maximum size of a buffer. However, the system does not check to see if these limits are exceeded and runs erroneously when they are exceeded.
Exploitable Logic Error	A system bug is discovered which can be exploited to place the user in privileged mode.

Requirements of a Secure Operating System A secure operating system safeguards assets and prevents corruption of data integrity; for example, it prevents an unauthorized person obtaining an illicit copy of a proprietary program or examining confidential data on someone else's religious beliefs.

For the system to be secure, however, Stepczyk [1974] identifies five goals that must be attained. First, the system must be protected from user processes.

A user process must not be able to halt system running, destroy essential information, take control of the system, or change the system in any way. Second, users must be protected from each other; one user must not be able to corrupt another user's process or data. Third, users must be protected from themselves. A user process may consist of a number of distinct modules, each with its own memory area and files. One module should not be able to corrupt another module. Fourth, the system must be protected from itself. Since the operating system also consists of a number of distinct modules, one module should not be able to corrupt another module. Fifth, the system must be protected from its environment. In the event of environmental failure (power, flood, etc.), where possible, the system should bring operations to an orderly halt to enable recovery at a later stage.

A fundamental way of achieving these goals is through the principle of isolation. Isolation simply means that system resources should be separated from each other whenever it is possible. If system resources cannot be separated from each other, they should have only limited access to each other.

A primary form of isolation used is isolation by function. Isolation by function means that two processes performing different functions are separated from each other. Isolation by function can be achieved using (*a*) the principle of least privilege, and (*b*) an access monitor security kernel. The *principle of least privilege* simply means the operating system grants to a user process only the minimum authority needed to carry out a function. This reduces the risks of a process using system resources when it is not authorized to do so. An *access monitor security kernel* is a system element that provides a single door for all user processes to system resources. For example, in a database management system, the database manager—the hardware/software component that controls all accesses to the database—is the access monitor security kernel.

Still other forms of isolation exist (see Stepczyk [1974]): isolation by obfuscation—system elements can be encrypted; isolation by context—a translator or compiler limits access to system resources by not providing the necessary syntactic or semantic capabilities; physical isolation—a physical interface does not exist between two system resources; and isolation in time—two processes are prevented from running concurrently.

Besides isolation there are other ways of achieving the goals of a secure operating system. Chapter 10 discussed the generalized access control mechanism that should be provided by the operating system. The system also should provide a surveillance and detection element that scans the various elements of the operating system, detects integrity violations, logs them, and corrects them if possible (see, further, Chapter 14).

Auditing System Software

The audit of system software requires substantially more advance preparation than the audit of application software. Before an audit can be commenced, four major steps must be undertaken:

1 *Determine the Criticality of System Software for Overall Data Integrity*
The different types of system software within the installation can be ranked according to their criticality. Certain types of software always will be critical; for example, operating systems and database management systems. Other types of system software will be less critical; for example, sort packages and report generators.

2 *Determine the Required Frequency of System Software Audits* Criticality is an important factor affecting the frequency with which system software should be audited. Other factors affecting audit frequency are the frequency with which modifications are made to the software and whether or not the software is vendor-supplied or developed in-house. Usually vendor-supplied software is less likely to contain errors because it has been tested by a greater number of users.

3 *Obtain the Relevant Expertise* Effective audits of system software require a high level of expertise. The EDP audit team must decide whether to develop this expertise itself or employ consultants. Even if consultants are employed, members of the EDP audit team still must have sufficient knowledge of the area to be able to communicate with the consultants.

4 *Establish an Audit Program* The audit program for system software should be an integral part of the overall audit program for the installation with defined objectives, review procedures, responsibilities, and reporting requirements (see, further, Linde [1975] and Weber [1975]).

It is especially important to focus only on those control attributes of system software that affect asset safeguarding and data integrity for the application systems used by the installation being audited. Since system software is generalized software, some control attributes may not be relevant for a specific installation's application systems.

CONTROL OVER HARDWARE MALFUNCTIONS

A hardware malfunction can affect not only the integrity of data that is processed but also the integrity of data that is input, output, or transmitted across communications lines. Except under unusual circumstances, or unless the auditor confronts an old machine, controls over hardware functions are rarely a concern. The technology for achieving reliable hardware is well-developed, and current machines rarely have undetected errors. In most cases the machine also corrects any error it discovers. However, errors are inevitable: hardware errors do occur.

Hardware failures result from (*a*) deterioration in system components, (*b*) hardware design and implementation errors, (*c*) power surges or transients, (*d*) environmental failures (dust, heat, humidity), and (*e*) operator error such as the failure to switch a memory module from test to online mode. Four types of malfunction may occur:

Malfunction	Explanation
Processor Error	The processor fails to execute instructions correctly. This type of error is rare; it is most likely to occur in very new or very old machines.
Memory Error	For some reason data in memory is corrupted. Memory failures are detected through parity checks.
Input/Output Device Error	Because of the electromechanical nature of input/output devices, they are prone to failure. Failures take various forms, e.g., a disk head crash, timing failures, or malfunctions in the read/write units.
Input/Output Interface Error	Failures may occur in a channel or various elements in a communications network, e.g., a multiplexor, a communications line, or a modem.

Most hardware malfunctions are detected and corrected automatically. Detection and correction facilities are implemented through hardware, firmware, or software. These facilities typically depend on some form of redundancy checking. Though the types of error detection and correction facilities and the ways in which these facilities are implemented vary across machines and manufacturers, the following checks are common to many machines:

Check	Explanation
Parity Checking	A redundant bit is stored for the group of bits representing a character (vertical parity) or for the group of bits in a channel for a record (longitudinal parity). For odd parity checking the parity bit causes the sum of the bits to be an odd number. The converse applies for even parity checking. Parity checking is used to check the validity of data in main memory or secondary memory or data sent across communications lines.
Valid Operation Code/Address	The processor checks to see if the instruction it is attempting to execute is one of a valid set and the memory address supplied is within a valid range.
Valid Character Check	There are more combinations of bits (punch holes) in a frame (vertical column) than needed to represent the valid character set of the machine. The bit combination is checked to see it is a member of the valid set. Used for card readers, printers, data communications.
Dual Read/Write, Read-After-Write	A second read or write station compares the results of the read or write with the data that has been read or written by the first station. Used with input/output equipment, e.g., card readers and punches.
Echo Check	The processor sends an activation signal to an input/output device. The input/output device returns a signal showing the mechanism (e.g., punch or print mechanism) was activated.

Equipment Check	Input/output devices are activated prior to a read/write operation to check their correct functioning, e.g., the photocells on a card reader are tested prior to data input.
File Protection Ring	A ring must be inserted into a magnetic tape before a write operation can be undertaken.

The auditor obtains information on the reliability of hardware by examining operating and maintenance reports. Continuing failure in a hardware component may indicate improper maintenance procedures are being undertaken. If this is the case, the auditor can check to see the hardware device has not been used for critical operations; for example, the use of a faulty disk pack to store a master file.

CHECKPOINT/RESTART CONTROLS

An important processing control that should be used with programs that consume substantial resources is a checkpoint/restart facility. Even though a program fails, some of the processing carried out by the program may be accurate and complete. It is desirable not to have to repeat this valid processing during the recovery process. A checkpoint/restart facility allows an operator to restore a program to some prior valid intermediate point in its processing and restart the program from that point.

For some types of program failure, completely redoing the processing run may be the only means of recovery. For example, if the program contains a serious logic error, the logic has to be corrected and all processing redone. However, the following three examples show where a checkpoint/restart facility is useful as a means of recovering from localized damaged or abnormal termination of the program. First, a hardware error may occur that is not expected to recur if processing is repeated. For example, a processor error may be corrected by replacing circuitry and the program restarted at a previous checkpoint. Second, an operator error may mean partial reprocessing of transactions is necessary. For example, with a multireel file the operator may load the incorrect version of the third reel. Thus, the first two reels have been processed correctly, and the error can be corrected by restarting processing at the beginning of the third reel. Third, a program may have to be abnormally terminated for some reason. For example, it may have to be rolled out to allow a higher priority program to operate, or it may be terminated because the operator recognizes an impending hardware failure.

A checkpoint is taken when the contents of memory are dumped onto a log file. The contents of control registers, buffers, working storage, etc., must be flushed and written to the file. The positions of all active files also must be recorded so these files can be repositioned on their respective devices if program restart is needed. For example, the current block number of an input tape file must be recorded if the tape is to be repositioned correctly when the program is restarted at the checkpoint.

An effective and efficient checkpoint/restart system must fulfill several requirements (see, also, Crook et al. [1969]). First, the system must set checkpoints at high speed and be capable of recovering and restarting at high speeds. Reentrant programs facilitate checkpoint/restart systems. Multiple copies of the program need not be kept in memory and only the variable section of the program specific to each application program need be written onto the log file at checkpoint time. Second, the system must be flexible from the viewpoint of both operators and programmers. The programmer must be able to initiate a checkpoint in several ways; for example, by transaction count or elapsed time. The operator should be able to accomplish easily a return to a checkpoint and a restart from that checkpoint. Third, the system must ensure the integrity of the recovery process. For example, if different files must be mounted on a tape or disk device, the system should check the files mounted are correct. Fourth, programmers and operators should have minimal responsibilities for checkpoint/restart processes. Programmers should be able to initiate checkpoints through simple commands; for example, a call statement to a system utility. Operators should have available system utilities that perform as many of the restart activities needed as possible.

An important form of checkpoint/restart relates to preserving the contents of memory when the computer system crashes. For example, an online system may "hang up" or a disk head may drop onto a disk platter. If the contents of memory can be preserved at the point of crash, this constitutes a checkpoint.

The auditor needs to perform four checks on an installation's checkpoint/restart facilities. First, the checkpoint/restart facilities available should be adequate for the installation's needs. These needs vary depending on such factors as the length of processing runs and whether the system is online or simple batch. Second, the auditor must check to see checkpoint/restart facilities are implemented in those programs where they are needed. Third, documentation on the checkpoint/restart facilities should exist. Fourth, checkpoint/restart facilities should be tested periodically to determine whether or not they work.

SUMMARY

Processing controls detect errors that occur in data after it has been read and validated until the time when it has been output on some device. Processing errors occur because erroneous application program logic exists or hardware/system software errors occur.

The risk of application program processing errors can be reduced by incorporating certain validation checks in a program and ensuring the program conforms to good programming style. Detecting and correcting errors in system software is more complex. Difficulties arise because of the magnitude and complexity of certain system software — for example, the operating system — and the complexity of the situations that the system software has to handle — for example, concurrency and deadlock situations.

Today, hardware problems are rare since the reliability of hardware is high. Most problems will be experienced with very new or very old machines. However, the auditor should examine operating and maintenance reports for evidence of any problems.

If processing errors do occur and substantial resources have already been consumed up to the point of error, where possible, returning to the start of program processing should be avoided. If some of the processing is correct, checkpoint/restart procedures can be used to restart the program at some valid interim point in its processing prior to the point of error.

REVIEW QUESTIONS

12.1. Briefly describe the nature of processing controls. In general, what are the major sources of processing errors?
12.2. Give two types of errors that run-to-run control totals may identify.
12.3. How is it possible for a master file to get out of sequence? If a transaction file is sorted prior to a master file update, why is it necessary to check the sequence of this transaction file in the master file update program?
12.4. Flowchart the end-of-file protocols for an update program that has two transaction files and one master file as input. Assume the transaction files contain the same types of data and are supplied from different divisions within the organization.
12.5. The record type for an accounts receivable transaction file is four characters long. Give transaction codes for debtors master file record insertions, deletions, modifications (e.g. address changes), and monetary transaction updates so the transactions will sort in correct order for master file updating.
12.6. Flowchart the algorithm you could use to perpetrate a fraud using the round down technique for interest calculations on a bank accounts master file.
12.7. Monetary transactions that mismatch the master file accounts should be posted to a suspense account and an error file. Describe how the suspense account should be cleared. If the error file for mismatches is on magnetic tape, describe how the error file can be maintained.
 (*Hints:* There must be an input error file and output error file. A unique identification number must be assigned each mismatch.)
12.8. Give two examples where operator intervention may be necessary in an application system. Why is it desirable to minimize operator intervention?
12.9. Briefly explain the data integrity problems that can be caused by concurrent update processes? Why might a read-only process want to exclude a concurrent update process?
12.10. How can lockout lead to deadlock? What problems can arise if preemption is used to break deadlock without rolling back the preempted processes?
12.11. Briefly describe the necessary and sufficient conditions for deadlock, and the nature, advantages, and disadvantages of the strategies that can be used to prevent deadlock.
12.12. Why may it be necessary for the auditor to examine the integrity of system software? How frequently should the auditor examine system software?
12.13. Briefly describe how you could write a COBOL program to "browse" core.
 (*Hint:* Set up a program with a large working storage section.)
12.14. Briefly describe how you could set up a Trojan Horse with a utility program.

Describe two ways in which you could perpetrate a fraud using the Trojan Horse technique. Remember, you must be able to remove the organization's assets illegally.

12.15. As an auditor, how could you check for the occurrence of spoofing? What control procedures would you need to be able to check spoofing?

12.16. Briefly describe three major integrity flaws often found in current operating systems. How would you go about determining whether these flaws exist in an operating system you are auditing?

12.17. Briefly explain the principle of isolation in operating systems, and discuss two ways in which the principle can be implemented. What are the relationships between the principle of isolation, the principle of least privilege, and the access monitor security kernel?

12.18. From a control perspective, list four types of system software that are likely to be important and four types that are likely to be unimportant. What are the bases an auditor can use to determine whether system software will be important from an audit perspective?

12.19. Discuss the arguments for and against developing expertise to audit system software within the EDP audit team. What do you think the major factors will be in deciding whether to obtain the expertise from outside consultants or develop the expertise in-house?

12.20. What are the major components of a computer system in which hardware malfunctions occur? Briefly describe possible causes for these malfunctions. How can the auditor determine whether hardware malfunctions are a problem within the installation being audited?

12.21. What types of errors would *not* be detected by (*a*) an echo check, (*b*) a valid character check, and (*c*) an equipment check?

12.22. Briefly explain the purpose of checkpoint/restart controls. What situations may arise where checkpoint/restart controls are needed?

12.23. How is a program checkpoint accomplished? Why is it necessary to know the position of all files being used by the program when a checkpoint is taken? When restarting the program, how is a repositioning of files accomplished?

12.24. From an audit perspective, what are the important requirements of a checkpoint/restart system? How can the auditor determine the adequacy of checkpoint/restart facilities?

EXERCISES AND CASES

12.1. The dollar control totals for a master file update run are correct for the input transaction file and the input master file; however, the output master file control total is incorrect. List the possible reasons why the control total may be incorrect. Further, explain how you would check to see whether the reasons you advance are the cause of the error. Since your time as an auditor is a scarce resource, you also should list the reasons according to their probability of being the cause of the error.

12.2. As the manager of internal audit for Streaker Products, a manufacturer of running shoes and related athletic goods, you are called one day to a meeting with the controller, the data processing manager, and the accounts branch manager. The data processing manager is furious. He explains that the accounts receivable master file update program has been dropping records from the master file progressively over the last six months. The error has only just been discovered. He complains that reconstructing the master file is going to be costly; furthermore, the company has lost revenue because the accounts receivable records have been lost. He is upset because the accounts branch has failed to check the control totals reported by the program. If this had occurred, the error would have been discovered earlier.

The accounts branch manager is equally upset. She complains that her branch is understaffed and her clerks have had little time to check anything. Furthermore, she argues that the error occurred because a change to the update program was not tested properly. This is the data processing manager's fault, not hers!

Required: The controller asks you to write a brief report for her explaining:
a. how the master file might be reconstructed
b. how the revenue lost from failure to bill customers might be recovered
c. how this event can be prevented in the future

12.3. Consider the following controls evaluation table where the columns represent control objectives for the processing phase and the rows represent controls that can be exercised to attain these objectives.

Controls (good programming practices)	Authorized processing only	Complete processing	Accurate processing
Master/transaction file sequence check			
Correct end-of-file protocols			
Process master file changes before updates			
Handle rounding correctly			
Maintain a suspense account			
Print run-to-run control totals			
Print control data for internal tables			
Minimize operator intervention			
Avoid closed routines			

Required: Fill in the elements of the table where each element represents your opinion on the cost-effectiveness, in general, of each control with respect to each control objective. Assume a score of 5 represents high cost-effectiveness and a score of 1 represents low cost-effectiveness.

12.4. Pieces and Parts, Ltd., is a diversified manufacturing company based in New York. However, it has manufacturing facilities throughout the country. The company is contemplating changing its centralized data processing operations to distributed data processing operations. The plants will operate more effectively and efficiently if each has its own data processing facilities.

A major question to be answered if the company uses distributed processing is whether or not the company's database should be partitioned and the different partitions allocated to the plants most likely to use them, or whether or not replicated copies of the entire database should be sent periodically to each plant.

Required: As the head of the internal audit department, management has asked you to identify the advantages and disadvantages of partitioning versus replicating the database from the viewpoint of ensuring accurate and complete processing of data.

REFERENCES

Abbott, R. P., J. S. Chin, J. E. Donnelley, W. L. Konigsford, S. Tokubo, and D. G. Webb. *Security Analysis and Enhancements of Computer Operating Systems* (Washington, D.C.: Institute for Computer Sciences and Technology, National Bureau of Standards, 1976), Report No. NBSIR-76-1041.

American Federation of Information Processing Societies. *AFIPS System Review Manual on Security* (Montvale, N.J.: AFIPS Press, 1974).

Attanasio, C. R., P. W. Markstein, and R. J. Phillips. "Penetrating an Operating System: A Study of VM/370 Integrity," *IBM Systems Journal*, vol. 15, no. 1, 1976, pp. 102–116.

Canadian Institute of Chartered Accountants. *Computer Control Guidelines* (Toronto, Canada: The Canadian Institute of Chartered Accountants, 1970).

————. *Computer Audit Guidelines* (Toronto, Canada: The Canadian Institute of Chartered Accountants, 1975).

Crook, B. H., A. P. Smithies, and J. H. Raeburn. "Program Rerun Facilities in Magnetic Tape Systems," *Proceedings of the Fourth Australian Computer Conference* (Adelaide: Australian Computer Society, 1969).

Davies, C. T. "Data Processing Spheres of Control," *IBM Systems Journal*, vol. 17, no. 2, 1978, pp. 179–198.

Davis, Gordon B. *Auditing and EDP* (New York: American Institute of Certified Public Accountants, 1968).

Denning, P. J. "Fault-Tolerant Operating Systems," *Computing Surveys* (December 1976), pp. 359–390.

Donovan, J. J., and S. E. Madnick. "Hierarchical Approach to Computer System Integrity," *IBM Systems Journal*, vol. 14, no. 2, 1975, pp. 188–202.

EDP Auditors Association, Inc. *Control Objectives* (Hanover Park, Ill.: EDP Auditors Association, 1975).

Everest, Gordon C. "Concurrent Update Control and Database Integrity," in J. W. Klimbie and K. L. Koffeman, eds., *Data Base Management* (Amsterdam: North-Holland Publishing Company, 1974), pp. 241–270.

Fossum, Barbara M. "Database Integrity as Provided for by a Particular Data Base Management System," in J. W. Klimbie and K. L. Koffeman, eds., *Data Base Management* (Amsterdam: North-Holland Publishing Company, 1974), pp. 271–288.

Jancura, Elise G. *Audit and Control of Computer Systems* (New York: Petrocelli/Charter, 1977).

———, ed. *Computers: Auditing and Control*, 2d ed. (New York: Petrocelli/Charter, 1977).

Linde, Richard R. "Operating System Penetration," *Proceedings of the National Computer Conference, 1975* (Montvale, N.J.: AFIPS Press, 1975), pp. 361-368.

Linden, Theodore A. "Operating System Structures to Support Security and Reliable Software," *Computing Surveys* (December 1976), pp. 410-445.

McGee, W. C. "The Information Management System IMS/VS Part V: Transaction Processing Facilities," *IBM Systems Journal*, vol. 16, no. 2, 1977, pp. 148-168.

Mair, William C., Donald R. Wood, and Keagle W. Davis. *Computer Control and Audit*, 2d ed. (Altamonte Springs, Fla.: The Institute of Internal Auditors, Inc., 1976).

Munz, R., and G. Krenz. "Concurrency in Database Systems—A Simulation Study," in D. C. P. Smith, ed., *Proceedings of the SIGMOD International Conference on Management of Data* (New York: Association for Computing Machinery, Inc., 1977), pp. 111-120.

Parker, Donn B. *Crime by Computer* (New York: Charles Scribner's Sons, 1976).

Porter, W. Thomas, and William E. Perry. *EDP Controls and Auditing*, 2d ed. (Belmont, Calif.: Wadsworth Publishing Company Inc., 1977).

Short, G. E. "Threats and Vulnerabilities in a Computer System," *Data Security and Data Processing Volume 5 Study Results: TRW Systems, Inc.* (New York: IBM Corporation, 1974), pp. 25-73.

Stepczyk, F. M. "Requirements for Secure Operating Systems," *Data Security and Data Processing Volume 5 Study Results: TRW Systems, Inc.* (New York: IBM Corporation, 1974), pp. 75-205.

Weber, Ron. "An Audit Perspective of Operating System Security," *Journal of Accountancy*, 140 (September 1975), pp. 97-100.

CHAPTER **13**

OUTPUT CONTROLS

CHAPTER OUTLINE

CONTROLS OVER REPORTS
    Controlling Batch Output
    Controlling Online Output
INTERROGATION LANGUAGES AND OUTPUT RESPONSE ERRORS
    Syntactic Considerations
    Semantic Considerations
CONTROLS OVER FILES
SOME OUTPUT EFFECTIVENESS/EFFICIENCY CONSIDERATIONS
    Effectiveness Issues
    Efficiency Issues
SUMMARY
REVIEW QUESTIONS
EXERCISES AND CASES
REFERENCES

Output controls have two major purposes. First, they seek to preserve the integrity of data: (*a*) produced and transmitted or distributed in report form to a user, and (*b*) produced and stored (typically on a magnetic file) for later use within an application system. Second, they seek to ensure the efficient production and effective use of application system reports.

This chapter first examines output controls that should be applied to the reporting process, distinguishing between controls needed for reports produced by a batch system and controls needed for reports produced by an online system. It then examines those attributes of interrogation languages that affect a user's ability to specify queries correctly and to obtain the desired output. The controls needed to maintain the integrity of data produced for later use within an application system are discussed next. Finally, the chapter examines some efficiency and effectiveness considerations in the production and use of reports.

CONTROLS OVER REPORTS

Interestingly, there are few reported cases of fraud perpetrated through breaching output controls over reports (see Parker [1976] and Allen [1977]). The primary purpose of output controls over reports is to protect the privacy of data contained in the reports. By violating the privacy of data contained in reports, an organization can be made to suffer losses in several ways. First, the reports may contain data that enables unauthorized access to the organization's computing resources. Jerry Schneider used this technique to gain access to Pacific Telephone's computer system. He sifted through trash cans and retrieved discarded output that provided him with the data necessary to penetrate the system (see Chapter 1). Second, the data contained in reports may be sold to a competitor. Trade secrets, patents, marketing data, credit information, etc., would all be valuable to a competitor. Third, the data contained in reports may be used to blackmail an organization.

Two factors affect the choice of output controls needed over reports: (*a*) the sensitivity of the data reported, and (*b*) whether the reports are produced by a batch system or an online system. The first factor determines how much should be spent on controls over output. The second factor determines the number and types of controls needed.

In general, a batch system requires more output controls over reports than an online system. Batch system reports involve hard copy output. More intermediaries are needed between the production of a batch report and its eventual receipt by a user. For example, operators are responsible for loading the relevant programs and files, loading the stationery needed for the report, and printing the report. Clerical staff are responsible for decollating, bursting, collating, and distributing reports.

In an online system, reports are printed or displayed at a terminal. The terminal user directly interacts with the machine to obtain the output required. No intermediaries are needed. From a control viewpoint the major concerns are preventing an unauthorized person from intercepting the transmission of data from the machine to the user and viewing output displayed at a terminal.

Controlling Batch Output

Controls can be exercised over batch output through carefully designing reports and carefully managing the reports throughout all aspects of their creation, distribution, and use. Good report design facilitates the orderly flow of reports through the output process. Good management ensures adherence to the control procedures laid down for the output process.

Table 13.1 shows the information that should be included in a well-designed

TABLE 13.1
CONTROL INFORMATION TO BE INCLUDED IN A WELL-DESIGNED REPORT

Control information	Position in report	Purposes
Report name	Title page	Permits immediate identification of report.
Time and date of production	Title page, detail pages	Prevents confusion if report produced several times per day or if for some reason the report has to be produced again, e.g., an error in a program.
Distribution list (includes number of copies)	Title page	Allows operator to check correct multipart stationery has been used. Facilitates distribution of report by control section.
Processing period covered	Title page	User can see what data has been included in the report. Control section can check against data submitted.
Program producing the report	Title page	Permits immediate identification of originating system/program.
Security classification	Title page	Alerts operators/control section as to sensitivity of data contained in report.
Retention date	Title page	Indicates date before which the report should not be destroyed.
Method of destruction	Title page	Indicates if special procedures to be followed for disposal of report.
Page heading	Detail pages	Shows content of report pages.
Page number	Detail pages	Prevents undetected removal of a report page.
End-of-job marker	Immediately after last entry, last page of report	Prevents undetected removal of last page of report.

CHAPTER 13: OUTPUT CONTROLS **333**

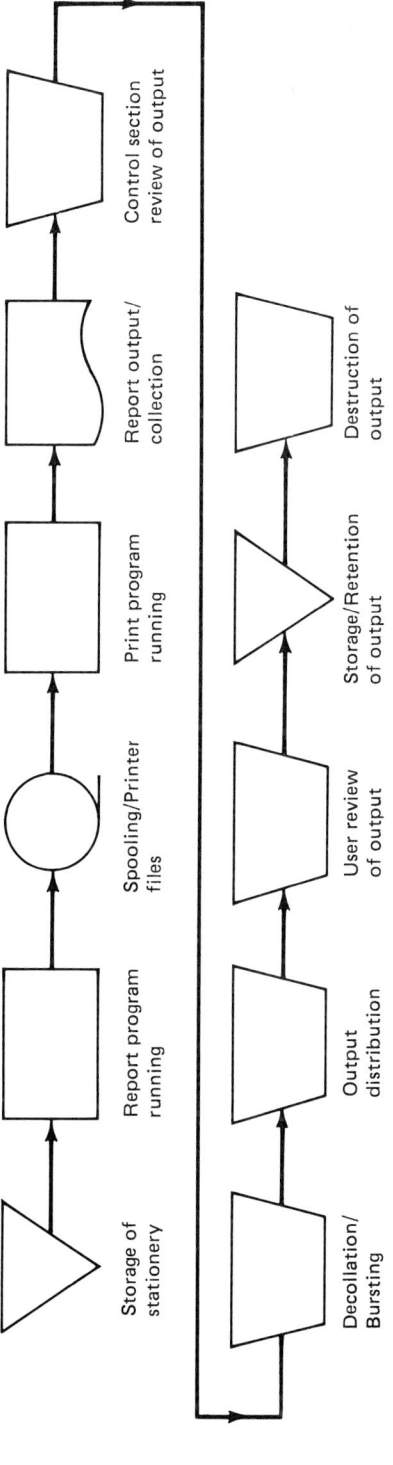

Figure 13.1
Stages in the output process for batch reports where controls can be applied.

report to facilitate its flow through the output process. The title page contains information that assists operators and control section personnel perform their work. In an environment where large numbers of reports are produced, this information is especially important. If the same report is produced several times a day, or a report program has to be rerun for some reason, confusion can arise if each instance of a report is not identified uniquely.

The information on the detail pages of a report prevents the unauthorized removal of data from the report. A person wishing to prevent a fraud from being discovered may remove a page containing exception information. Certain pages of a report may be especially valuable to a competitor. Page numbering and end-of-job markers prevent the undetected removal of a page. Even if the report is split because the printer runs out of paper, the user still can determine if pages were removed by checking page numbers are continuous.

Figure 13.1 shows all the possible stages through which a batch report may pass during the output process. All reports may not pass through every stage; for example, a report may be printed directly rather than spooled, a single copy report does not need decollating, some reports may not need bursting. However, identifying all the stages through which a report may pass provides a basis for logically grouping the controls that should be applied to the output process.

The following sections examine the controls that should exist at each output stage. Whether or not a control is implemented, however, depends, as always, on cost-benefit considerations. The full set of controls may be implemented only for reports containing very sensitive data.

Controls Over Stationery Supplies Computer installations use a wide variety of stationery types; for example, plain stationery for management reports, preprinted invoice stationery for billing customers, preprinted check stationery for employee and creditor payment. Careful control must be exercised over all stationery supplies; however, control of preprinted stationery is especially important. Preprinted stationery can be used to remove assets from an organization or cause the organization considerable embarrassment. For example, check stationery can be used to write unauthorized checks. To destroy an organization's goodwill among its customers, invoice stationery can be used to bill its customers for goods they did not purchase. The following controls help prevent unauthorized use of stationery:

Control	Explanation
Maintain an Inventory System for Stationery	Helps account for all purchasing, receipt, and use of stationery.
Store Stationery in a Secure Location	Prevents unauthorized destruction/removal of stationery.
Control Access to Stationery Supplies	To prevent unauthorized use of stationery, operators should not be able to gain direct access to stationery supplies.

Where Possible Use Preprinted Stationery	Preprinted stationery makes it more difficult to forge reports, notices, checks, etc.
Prenumber Preprinted Stationery	Facilitates control over use of preprinted stationery.
Store Signature Stamps at Different Physical Location to Stationery Inventory	Prevents unauthorized use of signature stamps, e.g., use on stolen checks.

Controls Over Report Program Running Auditors have three concerns when they examine controls over production running of a report program. First, they must ensure the correct version of the program has been loaded and activated. They should have formed an opinion on the likelihood of this happening when they examined management controls over program libraries. Second, auditors must ensure operators have not used the console to make direct alterations to the program residing in core. Third, large report programs should have checkpoint/restart facilities; auditors must ensure these facilities have not been misused. For example, by restarting at a checkpoint, an operator may have obtained duplicate copies of a section of a report. Evidence on these questions can be obtained by examining the console log. Chapter 14 discusses these matters further.

Controls Over Spooling/Printer Files If a report program cannot write directly to a printer, the output is spooled and a printer file is created; that is, system software causes the report program to "think" it is writing to the printer when actually it is writing to magnetic tape or disk storage. When the printer becomes available, spooling software reads the file and produces the report.

The presence of an intermediate file in the printing process causes several control problems. Printer files provide opportunities for unauthorized modification and copying of reports. Software can be used to change the value of a field in the printer file. The printer file can be copied. Some copies may be authorized for backup and recovery purposes; others may be unauthorized. Spooling software facilities may be abused. For example, spooling software allows the operator to return to a prior point on the printer file and restart printing should the printer malfunction. Some spooling software allows the operator to request a different number of copies of a report than the number specified by the programmer. Both these facilities can be used to obtain unauthorized copies of a report. The auditor must ensure:

1 The contents of printer files cannot be altered.
2 Unauthorized copies of printer files are not made.
3 Printer files are printed only once.
4 If copies of printer files are kept for backup and recovery purposes, they are not used to make unauthorized copies of reports.

Control also can be enhanced by using the input/output pool for temporary

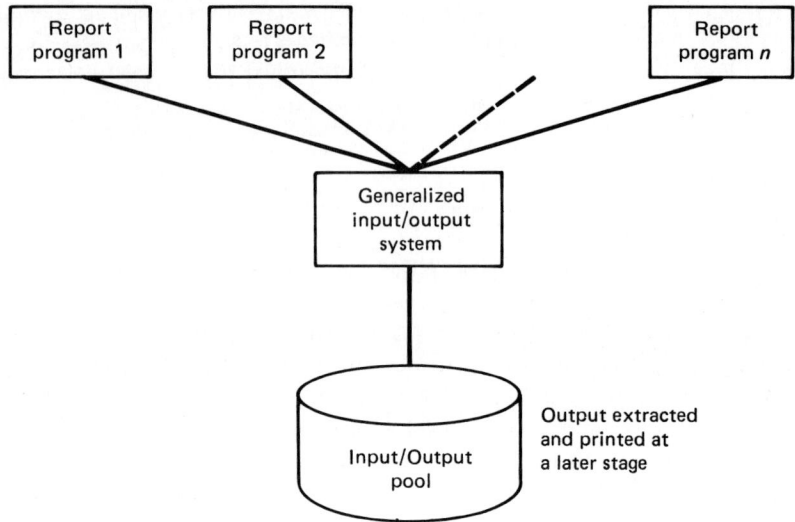

Figure 13.2
Use of the input/output pool for temporary storage of output.

storage of output (see Chapter 11). Spooling software can write printer files to the pool, or application system programs can invoke the facilities of the generalized input/output system to write output to the pool (Figure 13.2). Output can be printed at a later time when a printer is available or a report is required. Instead of having to exercise controls over multiple files, only use of the input/output pool needs to be controlled.

Controls Over Printing Controls over printing have two purposes: (*a*) to ensure only the required number of copies of reports are made, and (*b*) to prevent operators scanning sensitive data printed on reports.

Various steps can be taken to control the number of copies of a report printed. To avoid having to dispose of extra copies of a report made through operator error, the operator's manual for an application system should state clearly the number of copies of a report required. In some cases the report program may print a console message specifying what stationery should be loaded, halt temporarily while the operator checks the printer, and reactivate upon an operator command.

To prevent unauthorized copies of reports being made, the issue of stationery to operators should be controlled. The number of pages in a report usually varies from run to run; however, over a period of time the average number of pages produced can be determined. The clerk in charge of the stationery inventory can estimate the amounts of the different types of stationery needed for a period (say, an operator shift) and issue only the amount required. Actual usage can be checked against budgeted usage. In the case of preprinted, prenumbered forms the report program can provide a control total of the number of pages of output, which can be reconciled against the difference in the beginning and ending number on the forms.

New printer ribbons are also a means of obtaining copies of at least sections of a report. On its first cycle a printer ribbon contains a clear imprint of the pages printed. As with stationery the distribution of printer ribbons should be controlled. Further, operators should be prevented from bringing their own stationery and printer ribbons into the computer room.

Often operators see at least sections of a report. Operators check paper alignment, head of form positioning, etc. They may scan the first few pages of a report to check all is well. In the case of sensitive data it may be necessary to prevent operators seeing any report contents. This can be accomplished in several ways. The report can be printed at a remote printer. A security officer can stand by the printer while the report is printed. The report program can print several covering pages to allow operators to perform printer housekeeping functions before the contents of the report are printed. However, sufficient stationery must be loaded so these housekeeping functions do not have to be performed again at some intermediate stage during report printing when the report contents would be visible to the operator. Special multipart stationery can be purchased with the top copy colored black so printing cannot be read. For example, pay advice slips can be printed in this way to preserve the privacy of payroll data. Employees simply tear off the unreadable top copy of the pay slip and the duplicate copy contains the readable pay details (Figure 13.3). Wooldridge [1975] suggests completely filling a print line with characters so the report user has to apply a template to a page to detect report characters from characters used to camouflage the report contents. This technique protects the privacy of report contents against casual perusal by an unauthorized party but would not prevent a determined attempt to violate data integrity.

Report Collection Controls Once reports have been printed they should be collected promptly by control section staff. All output can be placed in a locker and collected periodically. Reports should not be left to accumulate in the computer room where they may be lost or their contents perused by an unauthorized person.

The computer operations manager may prepare a list of all reports to be produced during an operator shift. Control section staff can use this list to determine whether any reports are missing when they collect output from the computer room.

Control Section Output Review Controls Unless a report contains highly sensitive data that only users are allowed to read, the computer installation's control section should perform two checks on output reports produced. First, the control section should scan reports for obvious errors; for example, fields containing unreasonable values, format errors, missing data. These errors may have been caused by a report program bug or a hardware error such as a

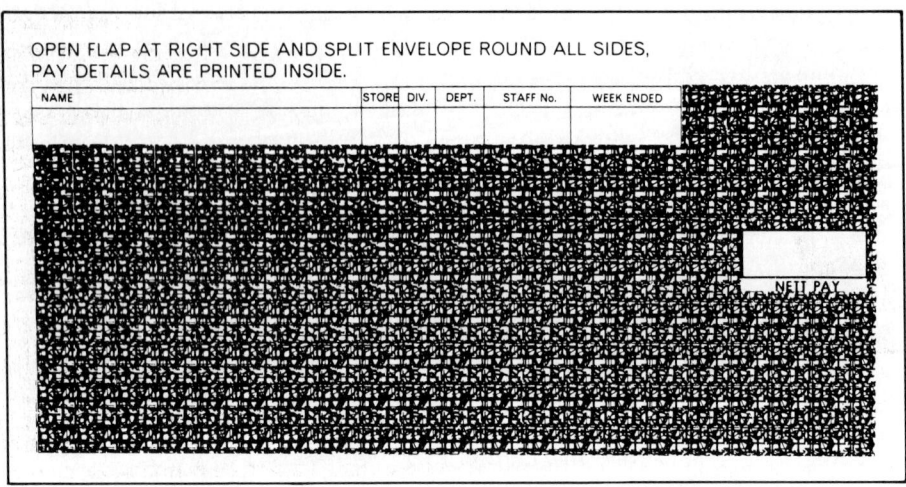

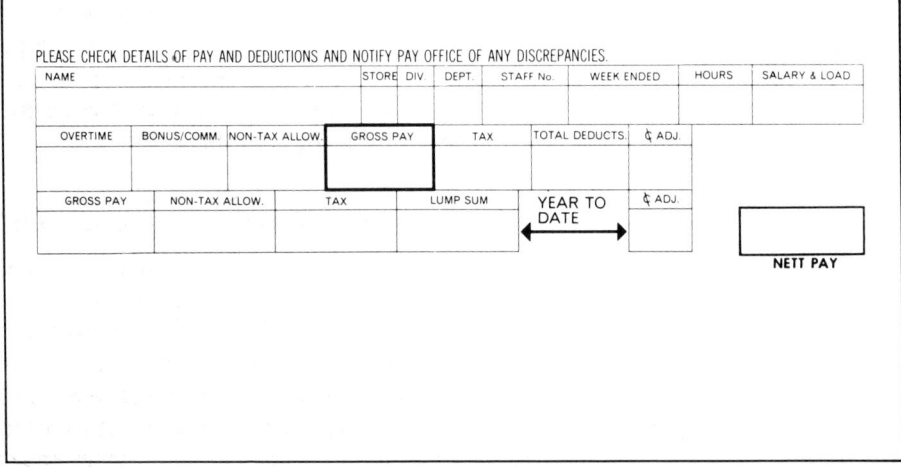

Figure 13.3
Protecting data privacy with multipart forms (Moore Paragon Australia Ltd.).

missing print position. Second, periodically on a random basis the control section should check thoroughly the output on a report. The control section may not exercise this control if the report is not critical or the review is performed by users (see, also, Chapter 8).

Decollation/Bursting Controls Though the decollation and bursting processes for reports are straightforward clerical activities, the personnel involved must be trustworthy. When performing the processes, clerks have opportunities to peruse the contents of reports. For highly sensitive data, decollation and bursting might be performed by the report users.

There must be no opportunities for clerks performing decollation and bursting to make photocopies of reports or remove pages from reports. Reports should be transported directly to and from the decollation and bursting facilities. Upon return of the reports, the control section should check to see the reports are still complete.

It is important to dispose of the carbon paper removed from multipart reports in a secure manner. The carbon paper contains an imprint of the report contents and can be read easily.

Report Distribution Controls After decollation and bursting, reports can be distributed to users. There are various ways to ensure only authorized users obtain the reports. Control section staff can deliver the reports directly to users. Reports can be placed in lockers, only authorized users having keys to the lockers. A courier service can be used to deliver reports to remote locations. For highly sensitive reports, users may have to pick them up in person and sign for them.

Special care must be taken where a large number of copies of a report must be produced and distributed. Often a user name and address file is maintained, and to facilitate distribution of the report the file is printed on gummed labels that are attached to individual copies of the report. Because of changes in the user population the number of copies of the report required may vary from run to run. In these cases maintaining the integrity of the name and address file is critical. If an unauthorized party inserts a name and address record on a file, a gummed label will be produced and a copy of the report distributed.

User Output Review Controls Users should perform reviews of output similar to those carried out by the control section to detect errors in reports. However, because users are more familiar with the application area, they are better able to detect errors. Users also should provide feedback to the computer installation on ways in which reports could be made more effective.

Output Storage/Retention Controls When reports are no longer useful they should be destroyed. They still may contain information valuable to a competitor. As with magnetic files, a retention date must be determined for each report. Various factors affect the retention date assigned; for example, the need for archival reference of the report, taxation legislation specifying a minimum retention time for the report, privacy legislation specifying a maximum retention time for the report. Until the retention date has expired, reports should be filed and stored in a secure location.

Output Destruction Controls Report destruction can be accomplished easily using a paper shredder. As retention dates expire, reports should be transported in a secure manner to the shredding facility. Aborted report runs and discarded stationery also should be shredded to prevent any unauthorized use.

340   PART 3: THE APPLICATION CONTROL FRAMEWORK

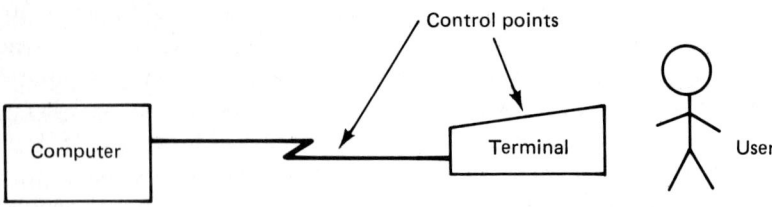

Figure 13.4
Control points for online output.

Controlling Online Output

Figure 13.4 shows the two areas where controls must be exercised over online output. An unauthorized person can intercept either report data being transmitted over a communications line to a terminal or view a report being displayed or printed at a terminal.

Chapter 10 described the controls necessary to prevent an unauthorized person gaining access to and using data transmitted over communications lines. The line can be made physically secure so wiretapping cannot be carried out. However, if data is transmitted over a public line it is impossible to make the line physically secure. Encryption then can be used to render the data useless to anyone without the cryptographic key who gains access to the data.

Unauthorized viewing of data can be prevented in several ways; for example, placing each terminal in a separate room, using hoods on terminals, displaying reports at a low light intensity, positioning terminals so users sit with their backs to a wall. For the novice terminal user, these measures also reduce the "fishbowl effect"; that is, the tendency for these users to feel their inadequacies in interacting with the system are being viewed publicly (see Lancaster and Fayen [1973]).

If the system crashes, users should be asked to sign on again if the system is unavailable for some time. Users may leave a terminal if they have to wait too long for the system to come up again. If when the system comes up it continues to print the report being displayed at the time of the crash, the person then sitting at the terminal may be unauthorized to view the report.

INTERROGATION LANGUAGES AND OUTPUT RESPONSE ERRORS

Interrogating a database involves two processes: formulating a query and obtaining a response. It is only recently that researchers have realized certain attributes of interrogation languages have important effects on a user's ability to formulate queries correctly so the desired response is obtained.

Chapter 11 focused on interactive languages from an input perspective. The intent there was to show how various attributes of an interactive language affected a user's ability to provide correct transaction data input to an application system. Here the focus is on output. Admittedly, a user's inability to obtain a correct response because of a query misspecification is really an input error. Assuming the software processes correctly, erroneous output means the user has provided incorrect parameter values to the language. However, it seems more natural to think of the controls that should be exercised to prevent the user misspecifying queries and obtaining incorrect responses as output controls.

Preventing query misspecification involves applying two basic controls: (a) choosing an interrogation language that best meets user needs, and (b) providing adequate training in the use of that language. Since little can be said about the latter control, the following sections discuss only the former control. Specifically, they examine two attributes of interrogation languages that have a major impact on the choice process: the syntax of the interrogation language and the semantics of the interrogation language. Unfortunately, the discussion is somewhat superficial. The research on this choice process is still meager and the findings tentative. Nevertheless, the discussion illustrates some dimensions of the choice problem (see, also, Shneiderman [1978]).

Syntactic Considerations

The syntax of an interrogation language is the set of rules governing the combination of words or terms within the language. The syntax of interrogation languages varies from formal non-English like syntax to syntax approaching natural language. Compare, for example, the syntax of two interrogation languages SQUARE and SEQUEL when operating on an accounts receivable file stored as a relational data structure (see, further, Weber [1977]).

Query:
   Print the customer numbers of those customers who had more than 10 transactions over $200.

SQUARE Solution:

$$\chi_{\text{CUSTNO}} \in \text{TRANS} : \text{COUNT} (\text{TRANS}'_{\text{CUSTNO AMOUNT}} (> (200), \chi_{\text{CUSTNO}})) > 10$$

SEQUEL Solution:

```
SELECT      CUSTNO
FROM        TRANS
WHERE       AMOUNT > '200'
GROUP BY    CUSTNO
HAVING COUNT (*) > '10'
```

Intuitively, which syntax is more likely to cause users to misspecify a query and get erroneous output? Probably most people would answer the SEQUEL syntax is less likely to cause problems, particularly for users having little experience with computers. Can we generalize then to say that interrogation languages having English like syntax cause fewer query misspecifications than those having non-English like syntax? Unfortunately, at this stage the answer is not clear-cut. There is at least some tentative evidence to suggest a certain degree of formalism in syntax assists users to specify queries correctly (see Thomas and Gould [1975]). Natural language is fraught with redundancy and ambiguity. Perhaps there are fundamental differences between human communication and querying databases that cause natural language syntax for interrogation languages not to be the desired goal.

It may be, also, that the syntax which minimizes query misspecifications is conditional upon other factors; for example, the nature of the task and task environment and user psychological and demographic variables (see, also, Chapter 9). In the absence of further research, all the designer can do is identify those factors likely to affect a user's ability to specify queries correctly using the syntax of an interrogation language, and then make a judgment on which language best matches the user's needs.

Semantic Considerations

The semantics of an interrogation language ascribe meanings to the words or terms and legitimate combinations thereof included in the language. The designer attempts to choose an interrogation language having semantics that minimize incorrect output caused by query misspecification. Three aspects of a language's semantics affect this choice: (*a*) the functions included in the language, (*b*) the terminology or words used to express these functions, and (*c*) the semantic model or data structure on which the functions operate. Again, these matters are complex and the subject of current research; thus, the discussion below is brief and serves only to illustrate the problems involved.

Conceptually, there is some set of atomic functions that allows all operations to be performed on data. To reduce a user's workload, interrogation languages combine these functions in various ways to provide high level, more general functions. For example, the function implied by the syntax COUNT < data item > can be broken up into other functions: selection of the data item named, establishment of a counter, zeroizing the counter, an addition operation, etc.

A term (word) and combination of terms must be chosen to describe the function. For example, should COUNT or ADD be chosen to describe an addition operation? Unfortunately, many of the terms used in the computer domain are ambiguous; this ambiguity carries over into the semantics chosen for interrogation languages.

When interrogating data, the user has to think of the data in terms of some structure. In some cases the structure used may be constrained by the way in which data is structured in the database. For example, the user may think about the data in terms of a hierarchy, but it is structured in the database as a flat file. This may force the user to express queries in a particular way. In other cases the interrogation language may permit or force a mapping between one data structure and another.

Again, without further research, all the designer can do is make a judgment on what type(s) of semantics will minimize query misspecification. The objective is to choose the language having the functions, the terminology, and the data structures that the user can most easily understand and use. Similarly, all the auditor can do is determine whether the designer has considered all the relevant factors in choosing a language and judge the quality of the choice made.

CONTROLS OVER FILES

Output controls over files seek to ensure the contents of files are not overwritten or erased before the end of their useful life. These controls take the form of special data written into the header label or trailer label of a file which enables a program intending to use the file to determine whether or not the file can be used. The following control data, discussed previously in Chapter 11, can be written on the file:

1 Internal label
2 File generation number
3 Retention date
4 File control totals

In some cases the operating system will supply default values; for example, a retention date 30 days from when the file was written. However, since the output control needs of each application system vary, a design decision should be made for each magnetic file in each application system.

SOME OUTPUT EFFECTIVENESS/EFFICIENCY CONSIDERATIONS

Output effectiveness and efficiency concern the auditor for three reasons. First, today, output is an area where major cost savings can be obtained through improved efficiency. Paper is a high-cost resource. Second, the quality of decision making (problem solving) depends on the quality of output reports produced; in turn, the profitability of an organization depends on the quality of decisions made. Third, poor output quality can lead to errors being introduced into an application system; for example, a cluttered display may cause a clerk entering input data to miss an error message.

Effectiveness Issues

Effective reporting facilitates decision making; it enables good decisions to be made on a timely basis. Effective reporting depends on three factors: (a) the quality of the information presented, (b) the method of presentation, and (c) in interactive systems, the response time for presentation.

Quality of Information Adams [1973] studied the attitude of 75 managers toward information. The managers rated information quality and quantity as having an equal impact on job performance. However, 90% of the managers preferred improved quality of information over an increased quantity of information.

The auditor can use four attributes of information to assess its quality:

Attribute	Impact on information quality
Accuracy	Quality decreases with decreasing accuracy. Accuracy implies a known, accepted measurement scale; either a nominal, ordinal, interval, or ratio scale (see, especially, Mock [1976]).
Age	Age is a function of: (a) the information interval, defined as the interval between reports, and (b) the reporting delay, defined as the delay between the end of the information interval and the issuance of a report. Information quality decreases with age.
Relevance	Quality increases with increasing relevance. Relevance is defined in terms of the decision which the information supports. More relevant information is also more informative (see, also, Feltham [1972]).
Compactness	Information should be coded as efficiently as possible to minimize storage space needed, prevent information overload, reduce data transmission loads, etc. However, humans have psychological needs for feedback and redundancy in information (see Davis [1974]).

Information quality requirements of accuracy, age, relevance, and compactness vary across application systems. Improved quality usually means increased costs. Further, tradeoffs sometimes must be made. For example, in a strategic planning system the decision maker may be willing to trade off accuracy against age. Up to a certain level, timeliness may be more important than accuracy.

Method of Presentation Four factors must be considered when choosing a method of presenting output results: (a) the medium to be used, (b) the method of formatting results, (c) the layout of the report, and (d) the language style to be used for communicating the results.

The *medium* used for presentation of output usually is either paper or a visual display. If the decision task requires the user to flip back and forth through a report, perhaps for cross referencing purposes or to gain a total "picture" of the problem, printed reports often are more easily used than a visual display. Scanning a visual display report in a disjointed manner requires the user to input some instruction to obtain the relevant page. Users sometimes experience a "peephole" effect; that is, they start to feel the contents of the database can be reviewed only in very small pieces (see Lancaster and Fayen [1973]). However, if users proceed through a report in an orderly fashion or examine several different short reports, perhaps as they work with the computer in an interactive problem-solving mode, visual displays may be preferred because they are faster and quieter and allow the user to maintain continuity in thought.

A report can be *formatted* either as a table or a graph. Tables classify and order data for reference purposes. Graphs indicate trends or patterns in data. The research on which format is more effective for decision making is meager. Gerrity [1971] and Morton [1971] found decision makers preferred graphical reports. In a particular decision setting, Benbasat and Schroeder [1974] found graphical reports increased the effectiveness of decision making.

The *layout* of a report determines how much data will be placed on a page and where the data will be placed. If the user simply references a report and makes a decision, if possible, all data relevant to the decision should be placed on a single page. If the user is working in an interactive mode and sequentially making a series of decisions, only data relevant to a specific decision or a single idea should be displayed. Miller and Thomas [1977] also suggest it may be worthwhile partitioning the display into several fixed areas; for example, a main work area (about two lines), a diagnostic area (about one line), a fixed response area (about four lines).

Two major factors affecting the choice of *language style* used for a report are the user's experience with the report and the maximum reporting delay that can be tolerated. If users have extensive experience with a report, a formal, cryptic language might be used. If users must make decisions quickly and they require a fast response from the computer, again, a formal, cryptic language might be used to reduce the number of characters that must be displayed or printed.

Response Time In an interactive system the quality of decisions made depends heavily on the output response time. Miller [1968] identifies two psychological needs that dictate certain response-time requirements for interactive systems. First, humans expect a response to a communication within two to four seconds, even if the response is simply to acknowledge receipt of the message. Second, humans cluster their activities into logical groups and become frustrated if they are delayed in completing a cluster of activities. Psychological closure occurs upon terminating a cluster of activities, and a delay is then more likely to be tolerated. Further, sudden drops in problem-solving ability occur as response delays exceed a given point. Except when psychological closure occurs, response times should be no longer than about two seconds if the thinking continuity necessary to sustain problem solving is to be maintained (see, also, Chapter 9).

Response times, however, can be too fast. Decision makers may feel pressured to make fast decisions to the detriment of overall problem-solving effectiveness. Lancaster and Fayen [1973] argue for forced temporal spacing between responses.

Efficiency Issues

Recently, we have confronted severe paper shortages and rising stationery costs. Paper is no longer a cheap, plentiful resource. Wooldridge [1975] reports that 75% of paper usage in Europe and North America is computer stationery. Axelrod [1977] points out that many large computer installations spend several hundred thousand dollars a year on paper. Various benefits accrue from reducing the quantity of printed output; for example, possible elimination of a printer, faster turnaround, reduced stationery costs, improved online response performance.

There are two ways of reducing output print time. First, data in a report can be eliminated or compressed so fewer pages are needed for the report. Figure 13.5b shows a revised version of Figure 13.5a; it is more difficult to

EQUIPMENT UTILIZATION REPORT			MONTH	APRIL	PAGE 36 of 94
EQUIPMENT NO.	765A				
DESCRIPTION:	BULLDOZER 124 HP				

JOB NO	HOURLY RATE	HRS WORKED	DATE	DOLLAR CHARGE	TOTAL CHARGE
113	35.00	3	0401	105.00	
113	35.00	2	0404	70.00	
113	35.00	4	0405	140.00	315.00
261	35.00	4	0402	140.00	
261	35.00	1	0404	35.00	
261	35.00	1	0405	35.00	
261	35.00	5	0408	175.00	385.00
—					
421	35.00	5	0415	175.00	455.00
				EQUIPMENT TOTAL	4065.00

Figure 13.5a
Equipment utilization report with high readability.

```
        EQUIPMENT UTILIZATION REPORT    MONTH   APRIL   PAGE 36 of 94

EQUIPMENT NO.  765A   DESCRIPTION: BULLDOZER 124 HP   HOURLY RATE  35.00


JOB          HRS           DATE           $ CHARGE            TOTAL
NO           WORKED

113           3            0401           105.00
113           2            0404            70.00
113           4            0405           140.00              315.00
261           4            0402           140.00
261           1            0404            35.00
261           1            0405            35.00
261           5            0408           175.00              385.00
___
___
421           5            0415           175.00              455.00
                                    EQUIPMENT TOTAL          4065.00



EQUIPMENT NO. 9421C   DESCRIPTION: BACKHOE     HOURLY RATE 10.00


—
—
—
```

Figure 13.5b
Equipment utilization report redesigned to improve print time.

read but more efficient in terms of printer time required. Second, the layout of a report can be changed to take advantage of the way in which printers skip lines. The greater the number of lines to be skipped, the lower the average time per line for skipping. Printers take several lines to accelerate to their maximum speed. Thus, it is more efficient to skip several lines at a time than skip a single line. Figure 13.6a shows an accounts receivable statement with a sales message positioned to have more visual impact than the same message in Figure 13.6b; however, Figure 13.6b is more efficient in terms of print time. Preprinting data on forms also may allow the printer to skip a greater number of lines.

Periodically, the reports produced by a computer installation should be reviewed. Axelrod [1977] suggests four questions should be asked:

1 Is the report used?
2 Is all the information on the report required?
3 Can the number of lines printed be reduced?
4 Can the spacing between printed lines and between pages be reduced?

\	MOONSHINE, Inc. P. O. Box 261 HAPPYVILLE, Q. 40612.					
Please change address below if incorrect		Account No.	Month Ending	Past Due	This Month	Amount Due
Mr. H. S. Smithies 16 Uranda St. The Range Q. 45617		49-1253	791130	61.00	201.00	201.00
		Please write in amount of payment enclosed →				
Please pay by due date Terms: 30 days					Detach and enclose top portion with payment	

Date	Invoice No.	Details	Debit	Credit
		Opening Balance	61.00	
791102	41724	4 CASES JONATHON WHISKEY	40.00	
791104	53219	8 CASES XXXX BEER	56.00	
791115	53240	2 CASES OBLITERATION GIN	18.00	
791121	76431	2 CASES RITEOFF RUM	22.00	
791126	76478	5 CASES TORTURE TEQUILA	65.00	
791126	30872	PAYMENT – THANK YOU		61.00
		XMAS SPECIAL – 10% DISCOUNT ON BEER		
Month Ending	791130	Your Ref: Payment Made	Amount Due	201.00

Figure 13.6a
Accounts receivable statement with sales message positioned to achieve effect.

Records can be kept to aid assessing output efficiency. Control section (see Chapter 8) can keep count of the number of pages produced in a report. The stationery clerk can keep count of the amounts purchased of the different types of stationery. Any major change in these figures indicates an investigation may be needed.

SUMMARY

Output controls seek (a) to safeguard reports and preserve the integrity of data produced as reports or stored on files for later use, and (b) to help achieve efficient production and effective use of reports.

The major purposes of output controls over reports is to protect the privacy of data contained in the reports. Batch reports usually present more output control problems than online reports since they require greater numbers of people to be involved in their production and distribution.

The major purpose of output controls over files is to ensure the contents of the files are not overwritten or erased before the end of their useful life.

		MOONSHINE, INC. P. O. Box 261 HAPPYVILLE, Q. 40612				

Please change address below if incorrect	Account No.	Month Ending	Past Due	This Month	Amount Due
Mr. H. S. Smithies 16 Uranda St. The Range. Q. 45617	49-1253	791130	61.00	201.00	201.00
		Please write in amount of payment enclosed →			

Please pay by due date
Terms: 30 days

Detach and enclose top portion with payment

Date	Invoice No.	Details	Debit	Credit
		Opening Balance	61.00	
791102	41724	4 CASES JONATHON WHISKEY	40.00	
791104	53219	8 CASES XXXX BEER	56.00	
791115	53240	2 CASES OBLITERATION GIN	18.00	
791121	76431	2 CASES RITEOFF RUM	22.00	
791126	76478	5 CASES TORTURE TEQUILA	65.00	
791126	30872	PAYMENT – THANK YOU XMAS SPECIAL – 10% DISCOUNT ON BEER		61.00
Month Ending	791130	Your Ref: Payment Made	Amount Due	201.00

Figure 13.6*b*
Accounts receivable statement with sales message repositioned to improve print time.

This can be achieved by writing special control information into the header or trailer label of a file, which will be checked by any program intending to write new data on the file.

Three factors affect how well a report aids decision making: (*a*) the quality of the information presented, (*b*) the method chosen to present the information, and (*c*) in interactive systems, the response time taken to present the results. Efficient reporting requires careful control be kept over the volume of output produced. Periodically, output reports should be examined to see whether they can be made more effective and more efficient.

REVIEW QUESTIONS

13.1. What are the major purposes of output controls? Describe two ways in which an organization can be made to suffer losses by breaching output controls.

13.2. Why does a batch reporting system usually require more controls than an online reporting system?

13.3. Why is it important for each page in a report to have a heading and a page number? What is the purpose of printing an end-of-job marker immediately after the last entry on a report?

13.4. Briefly describe the major elements of an inventory system for computer stationery. Give three advantages that will accrue from having the inventory system you describe. Are there any disadvantages?

13.5. List some of the advantages and disadvantages of using preprinted stationery in a computer system instead of simply having the computer print constant data on plain stationery.

13.6. Briefly explain how checkpoint/restart facilities in a report program can be used to obtain unauthorized copies of a report. Suggest a method for detecting the unauthorized use of checkpoint facilities.

13.7. Outline some controls that could be instituted to prevent alteration of fields on a printer file produced as a result of spooling. What controls could be used to ensure a printer file is printed only once?

13.8. Why do printer ribbons and carbon paper present output control problems? Suggest ways in which the problems presented can be overcome.

13.9. Briefly describe four techniques that can be used to prevent an operator perusing the contents of a report during the printing process. For each technique give an example report where the technique might be applied.

13.10. Briefly explain the difference between decollation and bursting. What control problems do the decollation and bursting activities pose for output?

13.11. Why should the control section of a computer installation review output before its distribution to users? List three problems that the control section may identify with output.

13.12. Outline some of the controls that should exist over a user name and address file from which gummed labels are printed and attached to reports to facilitate distribution. Assume the reports contain sensitive data that should not fall into the hands of unauthorized parties.

13.13. List three factors that may affect retention requirements for reports. What should be done with reports once their retention date expires?

13.14. Are there any differences in the controls needed for an output process where batch reports are (a) printed on paper, and (b) written on microfilm? List the differences you identify.

13.15. From an output control perspective, briefly explain why it is sometimes necessary to require a user to sign on again when an online system crashes. When would it not be necessary to repeat the signon procedure after a system crash?

13.16. When choosing an interrogation language so as to minimize output response errors caused through query misspecification, is it always desirable to obtain a language having syntax close to natural language syntax? Briefly explain.

13.17. Briefly explain how the choice of terms (words) to describe functions in an interrogation language can affect the number of query misspecifications made.

13.18. Briefly explain how each of the following can be used to prevent a magnetic disk file being overwritten or erased:
   a. internal label
   b. file generation number
   c. retention date
   d. file control totals

13.19. What is meant by an effective report? Give three problems that can arise when a report is not effective.

13.20. What is meant by quality decision making or problem solving? List three attributes of a quality decision. Briefly describe how an effective report may help ensure these attributes are present during problem solving.

13.21. Decisions sometimes are classified into two types: (*a*) programmed, routine decisions, and (*b*) nonprogrammed, nonroutine decisions. Would you expect to see any differences in the way reports are designed (including their content) to support these two categories of decisions? Support your answer.

13.22. If i is the information interval and d is the reporting delay, give formulas for the maximum, minimum, and average age of information of the following:
  a. an accounts receivable balance
  b. daily sales over a month for a new product
Are there any differences in the formulas for these two examples? If so, explain why (*Hint:* As a last resort, see Davis [1974]).

13.23. What is meant by the relevance of information? When assessing the effectiveness of a report, how can the auditor measure the relevance of the information contained in the report?

13.24. When using a visual display to output information, what is meant by the "peephole" effect? How does the peephole effect impact the quality of decision making? Suggest some ways of overcoming the peephole effect.

13.25. For visual display output of reports, what factors determine the amount of information that should be output on a single display?

13.26. What characteristics of a user's task impact the choice of language style used to communicate information in reports output on a visual display?

13.27. Briefly explain how the following conditions may impact the quality of decisions made by a user working at an online terminal:
  a. a very fast response time
  b. a very slow response time
  c. a response time subject to large variations

13.28. Reducing output print time sometimes means reducing the readability of reports. Explain.

EXERCISES AND CASES

13.1. Ubend, Inc., is a large wholesaler of plumbing parts based in Sydney with outlets in the major cities and towns in New South Wales. Each outlet sends all its transactions to the head office for computer data processing, and the head office returns to the outlet summary hard copy reports plus microfiche reports on all the transactions processed. The outlet uses these microfiche reports to answer customer queries on charges to the accounts, determine whether vendors have been paid, etc.

You are a member of the external audit team examining controls over output with the head office computer system. Your manager-in-charge has listed, among others, the following objectives for the audit:
  a. Ensure report data cannot be lost.
  b. Ensure report data cannot be stolen.
  c. Ensure unauthorized access to report data cannot occur.
  d. Ensure report data is retained for seven years to fulfill statutory requirements relating to tax.

Required: Your manager-in-charge asks you to brief him on any *differences* in controls you think would be needed for the hard copy versus microfiche reports so the control objectives will be achieved.

13.2. First South Australian State Bank recently has installed a new network for teller operations in its 500 branches throughout the state. Teller machines in each branch are connected to a branch controller, and the controllers are connected to the head office machine. While some processing has been distributed to the controllers, the customer account master file still remains centralized.

Unfortunately, the network is unreliable. Furthermore, the problems are not being solved quickly since the bank data processing staff are blaming the machine vendor and the machine vendor is blaming the bank data processing staff.

One consequence of the unreliable network is the submission of duplicate transactions by tellers. The network often goes down for only a few minutes. Tellers are supposed to check whether the last transaction they submitted was posted to the account by submitting an inquiry when the network comes up. Unfortunately, customer lines are long because of the network unreliability and tellers often simply resubmit the last transaction to save time rather than initiate an inquiry. Thus, the same transaction sometimes is processed twice.

Required: Assuming the unreliability of the network continues, what controls would you implement to prevent duplicate transaction processing?

13.3. Rosendale Savings and Loan has recently installed a management information system to support its loan officers. When a customer makes application for a loan, the loan officer uses a terminal to inquire about the customer's financial status based on information in the association's database. The association purchased color-graphic terminals to use with the new system. The color capabilities of the terminal are used to highlight various information: for example, the loan officer detects a credit balance in an account because it is printed in red, and a debit balance is printed in green; colored bar charts are used to show the trend in account balances over the last five years.

Required: Some major errors have resulted in making loan decisions based on information provided by the system. The system has been checked carefully and no errors have been detected in the processing logic. The data processing manager is perplexed. Have you any suggestions to make on what might be wrong and what actions might be undertaken to correct the problems occurring?

13.4. Savecents Ltd., is a major retailing company with stores scattered throughout the United States. Each month the company's head office mails to all stores sales information that management considers to be highly confidential. Store managers are responsible for the reports. They must follow prescribed procedures for preserving the privacy of the information contained in the reports; for example, when a new report is received, the old report must be shredded.

As the manager of internal audit for the company, the controller has expressed some concerns to you about whether store managers are following carefully the procedures defined to preserve the privacy of the reports. She asks you whether it is possible to gain some assurance that the procedures are being followed. Furthermore, she asks you whether any control procedures might be installed to detect any deviation from the procedures.

Required: Write a memorandum to the controller advising her how you intend to obtain assurance that the managers are following the procedures. You also should advise her on any extra control measures that might be implemented to ensure the managers comply with the privacy procedures. (*Note:* Savecents has a communications network linking all its stores, but many reports are mailed to the stores to save communications costs and reduce the risks of privacy violations occurring during data transmission.)

REFERENCES

Adams, Carl R. "Attitudes of Top Management Users Toward Information Systems and Computers," Working Paper MISRC-WP-73-07, Management Information Systems Research Center, University of Minnesota, Minneapolis, Minn., 1973.

Allen, Brandt. "The Biggest Computer Frauds: Lessons for CPAs," *Journal of Accountancy* (May 1977), pp. 52–62.

Axelrod, C. Warren. "Reduce Computer Printing Costs," *Journal of Systems Management* (December 1977), pp. 30–33.

Benbasat, Izak, and Roger G. Schroeder. "An Experimental Investigation of Some MIS Design Variables," Working Paper MISRC-WP-75-01, Management Information Systems Research Center, University of Minnesota, Minneapolis, Minn., 1974.

Caldwell, John. "The Effective Reports Crisis," *Journal of Systems Management* (June 1975), pp. 7–12.

Davis, Gordon B. *Management Information Systems: Conceptual Foundations, Structure, and Development* (New York: McGraw-Hill Book Company, 1974).

Feltham, Gerald A. *Information Evaluation* (Sarasota, Fla.: American Accounting Association, 1972).

FitzGerald, Jerry. *Internal Controls for Computerized Systems* (San Leandro, Calif.: E. M. Underwood, 1978).

Gerrity, T. P. "Design of Man-Machine Decision Systems: An Application to Portfolio Management," *Sloan Management Review* (Winter 1971), pp. 59–71.

Lancaster, F. W. *Information Retrieval Systems: Characteristics, Testing and Evaluation*, 2d ed. (New York: John Wiley & Sons, Inc., 1979).

———, and E. G. Fayen. *Information Retrieval On-Line* (Los Angeles, Calif.: Melville Publishing Company, 1973).

Martin, James. *Design of Man-Computer Dialogues* (Englewood Cliffs, N. J.: Prentice-Hall, Inc., 1973).

Miller, Lance A., and John C. Thomas, Jr. "Behavioral Issues in the Use of Interactive Systems," *International Journal of Man-Machine Studies* (September 1977), pp. 509–536.

Miller, Robert B. "Response Time in Man-Computer Conversational Transactions," *Proceedings of the 1968 AFIPS Fall Joint Computer Conference* (Washington: The Thompson Book Company, 1968), pp. 267–278.

Mock, Theodore Jaye. *Measurement and Accounting Information Criteria* (Sarasota, Fla.: American Accounting Association, 1976).

Morton, M. S. *Management Decision Systems* (Boston, Mass.: Division of Research, Graduate School of Business Administration, Harvard University, 1971).

Parker, Donn B. *Crime by Computer* (New York: Charles Scribner's Sons, 1976).

Rouse, William B. "Design of Man-Computer Interfaces for On-Line Interactive Systems," *Proceedings of the IEEE* (June 1975), pp. 847–857.

Shneiderman, Ben. "Improving the Human Factors Aspect of Database Interactions," *ACM Transactions on Database Systems* (December 1978), pp. 417–439.

Thomas, John C., and John D. Gould. "A Psychological Study of 'Query by Example,'" *Proceedings of the 1975 National Computer Conference* (Montvale, N. J.: AFIPS Press, 1975), pp. 439–445.

Weber, Ron. "Implications of Database Management Systems for Auditing Research," in Barry E. Cushing and Jack L. Krogstad, eds., *Frontiers of Auditing Research* (Austin, Texas: The University of Texas at Austin, Bureau of Business Research, 1977).

Wilkinson, Bryan. "Controlling Output Distribution," *EDP Auditing* (Pennsauken, N. J.: Auerbach Publishers, Inc., 1978), Portfolio 74-02-01, pp. 1–12.

Wooldridge, Susan. *Computer Output Design* (New York: Petrocelli/Charter, 1975).

CHAPTER **14**

AUDIT TRAIL CONTROLS

CHAPTER OUTLINE

THE ACCOUNTING AUDIT TRAIL
  Nature of the Accounting Audit Trail
  Need for an Accounting Audit Trail
  Operational Requirements for the Accounting Audit Trail
  Some Problems of Change
  Some Further Design Considerations
THE OPERATIONS AUDIT TRAIL
  Nature of the Operations Audit Trail
  Types of Operations Data Collected and Its Uses
  Interrogating the Operations Audit Trail
  Some Control Issues
SUMMARY
REVIEW QUESTIONS
EXERCISES AND CASES
REFERENCES

An audit trail is a chronological list of events that have occurred to an entity. There are two types of audit trail in computer systems. The *accounting audit trail* shows operations upon data items within the database; for example, postings of monetary transactions to an account, modification of a name and address record, an inquiry upon a data item's value. The *operations audit trail* shows the series of events surrounding test or production running of an application system; for example, the load of an update program, the abnormal termination of a validation program, the occurrence of an attempt to gain unauthorized access to data.

This chapter examines the nature of both the accounting and operations audit trails. It discusses why the audit trail is a necessary control within a computer environment and the ways in which the audit trail can be used. Some problems confronting the design and implementation of audit trails are examined; the consequent design tradeoffs that must be made also are discussed briefly.

THE ACCOUNTING AUDIT TRAIL

The accounting audit trail is not a concept peculiar to computer systems. The notion of an accounting audit trail as a basic control in application systems was well-evolved in manual systems long before the advent of the computer.

Nature of the Accounting Audit Trail

An accounting audit trail achieves two purposes. First, it permits a transaction to be traced from its source through to the data item upon which it operates — the *implosion* purpose (Figure 14.1a). Second, it permits reconstruction of the time series of operations upon the data item — the *explosion* purpose (Figure 14.1b).

To achieve the implosion purpose, two pieces of information must be stored with transactions: (a) a source identifier, and (b) a destination identifier. The source identifier enables the origin of the transaction to be traced unambiguously. The destination identifier enables the data item that will be affected by the transaction to be identified unambiguously. For example, in a simple batch accounts receivable system the source identifier might be a unique document number; the destination identifier might be the unique customer number stored in the accounts receivable record. In an online inventory system the source identifier might be a unique terminal user number; the destination identifier might be the unique inventory item number of the inventory record to be updated.

The explosion purpose requires a further piece of information to be stored with a transaction: a unique time stamp indicating when the transaction operated upon the record. By sorting the time stamp within the destination identifier, the chronological sequence of operations on a data item can be reconstructed.

Need for an Accounting Audit Trail

In the past, many prophets of doom have forecasted the disappearance of the accounting audit trail with the introduction of computers. Some auditors feared

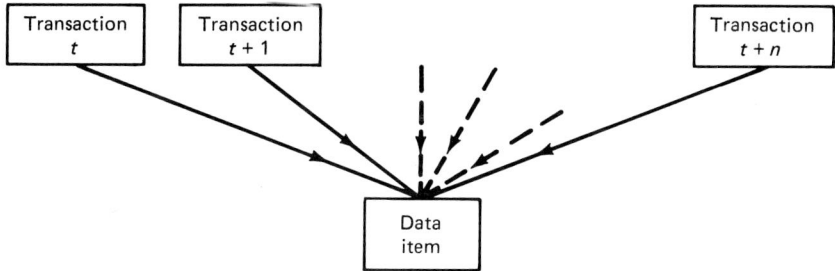

Figure 14.1a
Implosion purpose of an accounting audit trail.

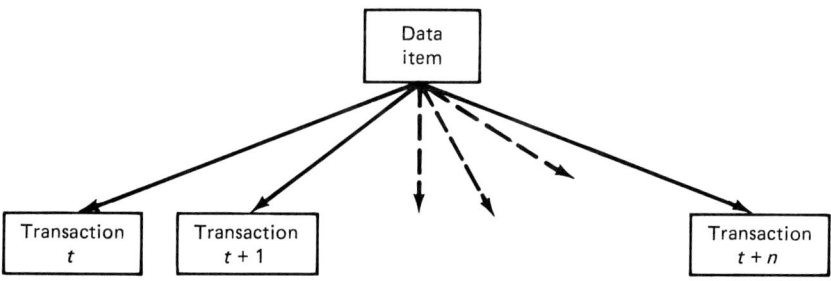

Figure 14.1b
Explosion purpose of an accounting audit trail.

audit trails would not exist in computer systems because many of the documents and associated clerical activities carried out in manual systems would no longer be necessary.

These fears were ill-founded. McHugh [1978] reports the results of his empirical study in Australia: "Traditional audit trails are alive and well." Audit trails have not disappeared. Admittedly, their form has changed. Instead of audit trail data existing on documents, journals, ledgers, worksheets, etc., the data now is stored on magnetic media. However, usually it can be readily accessed with a software package (see Chapters 16 and 17).

There are six major reasons why an accounting audit trail must be maintained for a computer system:

1 *Query Answering* Queries often arise as to the status of a data item; for example, customers may question charges made to their accounts, management may ask for detailed information relating to a variance investigation, a salesperson may want to know whether or not an order has been processed. The accounting audit trail provides the data necessary to answer these queries. In this sense the accounting audit trail might better be called a *management trail*.

2 *Statutory Requirements* The accounting audit trail may be needed to fulfill certain statutory requirements. For example, in the United States, the Internal Revenue Service (IRS) has issued Revenue Ruling 71-20 and Revenue Procedure 64-12 which state, in effect, that accounting transactions maintained on machine-sensible media constitute records for IRS purposes and a suitable audit trail must be maintained (see, further, Greenwald and Oberlander [1975]).

3 *Monitoring Purposes* The accounting audit trail provides a means of monitoring an application system. Periodically, transactions may be traced through the system to determine if all processes are functioning correctly.

4 *Deterrent to Fraud* The presence of an audit trail reduces the probability of a fraud going undetected. The perpetrator knows the events surrounding the fraud will be recorded. Steps must be taken to either inhibit this recording or destroy the audit trail.

5 *Detecting Consequences of Error* If a past state of the database is discovered to be in error, it may be necessary to obtain information to determine the effects of this error; for example, who accessed the data, who made decisions based on the data, and whether the error had significant consequences for the decisions made. The audit trail allows the effects of an error to be traced.

6 *Backup and Recovery* Some of the data stored in the accounting audit trail also is useful for backup and recovery purposes. For example, transaction data may need to be reprocessed against a record. If the initial input data no longer exists, the data may have to be extracted from the audit trail. Chapter 15 provides a detailed treatment of the data and operations needed for backup and recovery purposes.

Operational Requirements for the Accounting Audit Trail

Software must exist to provide four types of operation on an accounting audit trail: (*a*) creation, (*b*) modification, (*c*) deletion, and (*d*) retrieval. Since these operational requirements are common across application systems, often generalized software can be used to support the audit trail. In some cases, however, specialized software may be needed where generalized software cannot handle a specific audit trail requirement or it is too inefficient at handling the requirement. Whether generalized or specialized software is used, the auditor must check that the operational support exists for the accounting audit trail requirements of each application system.

Creation The capabilities should exist to create two types of audit trail record: (*a*) a permanent record, and (*b*) a temporary record. A permanent record always is created as necessary data for the ongoing operations of the application system. For example, a monetary transaction that updates an account record must be maintained as a permanent audit trail record. A temporary record is created on demand. For example, auditors may decide they wish to monitor a specific type of transaction over a certain time period, say, a few days. A temporary audit trail record is produced containing specific data the auditor wishes to examine only for that time period.

Temporary audit trail records often are more costly to create than permanent audit trail records. Permanent records usually contain data satisfying relatively static audit trail needs. A decision already has been made on *what* data will be collected and *where* it will be collected within the application system. Thus, the logic necessary to create the record is built into the application system during the initial implementation, and the data is collected on an ongoing basis.

Temporary records usually are created in response to changing audit needs. For example, a problem occurs within an application system and the auditor needs data not collected already by the system as part of the audit trail, or the auditor decides to carry out random tests on various aspects of an application system and the necessary audit trail data does not exist. New logic must be embedded in an existing application system to collect the required data. Ex post modification of application systems to satisfy audit trail requirements usually is more costly than including the necessary logic during the initial design and implementation stages.

Sometimes temporary records provide data for static audit trail requirements. For cost-benefit reasons audit trail records are not produced on an ongoing basis. Instead, the auditor invokes logic already embedded in the application system when the temporary audit trail records are needed. This may be accomplished by setting a program switch. Chapter 19 discusses these matters in more detail.

Modification Usually an accounting audit trail record does not have to be modified; it is meant to be a true history of what happened to the database. However, two situations can arise where modifications to the audit trail may be necessary. First, the application system processes erroneously so the audit trail is a history of incorrect operations on the database. Unfortunately, someone accessing the audit trail may make incorrect decisions on the basis of this information; for example, sue a customer for supposedly unpaid amounts. Second, the subroutines that create the audit trail may be in error. In this case the audit trail is not a true history of what happened to the database. Again, incorrect decisions may be made on the basis of an erroneous audit trail. In both cases, once the error is identified, it may be desirable to modify the audit trail so later decisions made on the basis of data contained in the audit trail are not affected by the erroneous data.

If it becomes necessary to modify the audit trail, a decision then must be made on how the audit trail will be modified. This decision depends on whether or not a history of modifications to the audit trail should be kept; in essence, an audit trail for an audit trail. On the one hand some users of the audit trail may be unconcerned about modifications to erroneous data in the audit trail providing the data they retrieve is correct; for example, clerks using the audit trail to respond to customer queries. On the other hand some users may be concerned with how the audit trail was modified; for example, auditors checking that modifications to the audit trail were authorized and performed correctly.

Modifications to the audit trail present some difficult design problems. To illustrate some of the complexities involved, consider Figure 14.2. Figure 14.2a shows an audit trail of transactions for data item D1. Assume that D1 had an initial value of 40; there were three update transactions T1, T2, and T3, which reduced the value of D1 by 5, 15, and 10 respectively. Between transactions T2 and T3 occurring, a user retrieved the value existing in D1, the current value at that time being 20 (40 − 5 − 15).

Figure 14.2b shows a subsequent inquiry made upon the audit trail. A user enquired about the value of transaction T2. Thus the chain of transactions attached to T2, in this case the single transaction R2, is a second-level audit trail—an audit trail for another audit trail (see, also, Bjork [1975]).

Assume shortly after R2 occurred, T2 was discovered to be in error because of erroneous logic in a program. T2 should have been 20. There are several consequences: (a) D1 is now in error, (b) R1 is now in error, and (c) R2 is now in error. Unfortunately, in the case of R1 and R2, decisions may have been made that now cannot be reversed.

Figure 14.2c shows one possible way of carrying out corrective action on the data item and its associated audit trail. Assume transaction T2 should have had a value of 20 instead of a value of 15. The program carrying out the correction first accesses the data item and adjusts it to the correct value. It then searches down the first-level audit trail until it finds the transaction in error. Upon identifying T2, it adjusts it to its correct value. It then checks to see if any retrieval transactions have occurred for T2. The second-level audit trail indicates a transaction R2 has occurred. Since a user has accessed T2 and relied upon incorrect data, some action must be taken at this point to notify the user an error exists. The program then inserts T4 in the audit trail for T2 as a record of the modification made.

Next the program searches down the first-level audit trail for any retrieval transactions that have occurred subsequent to T2. In this case a user has accessed D1 via R1 and obtained an incorrect value; that is, the user would have obtained the value 20 instead of 15. Again, some action must be taken to notify the user of the incorrect data retrieved.

Consider, now, the problems that arise if T4 is carried out in error. Users who have accessed D1 or T2 again must be notified of the error that exists. To confound the problem even further, a user (an auditor) may have accessed T4 and relied upon the erroneous data. Thus, a third-level audit trail, that is, an audit trail for T4, must be kept.

The above design strategy has two advantages. First, a user who is unconcerned about corrective modifications to the audit trail simply has to follow the first-level audit trail. Second, for users who are concerned with these modifications, the relevant transactions are chained to the first-level audit trail as a hierarchy of lower-level audit trails.

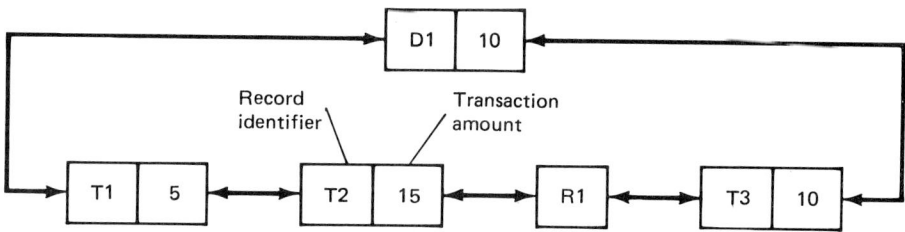

Figure 14.2a
Audit trail transactions for a data item.

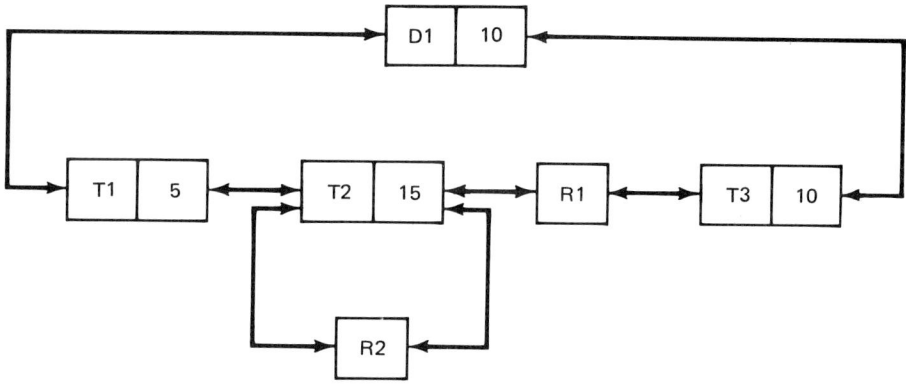

Figure 14.2b
Enquiry upon the audit trail.

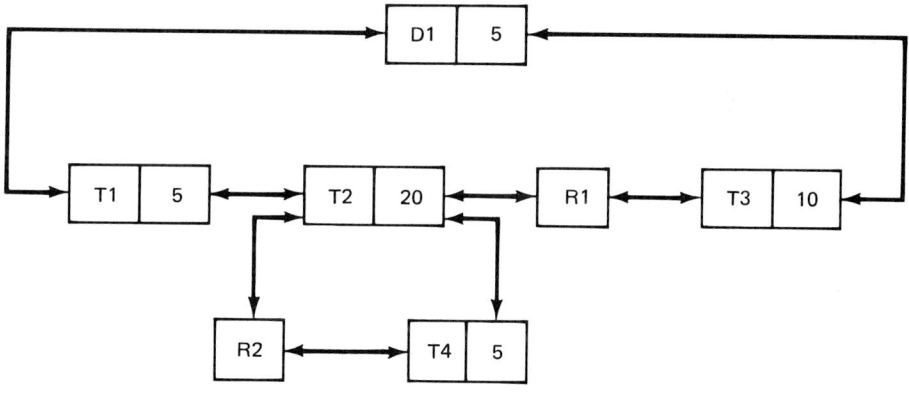

Figure 14.2c
Modifications to correct error in the audit trail.

The disadvantage of the strategy is its complexity. If modifications to the audit trail are rare, a simpler design strategy may suffice. For example, if modifications must be made to the first-level audit trail, rather than build lower-level audit trails, an error flag might be set in the transaction in error and

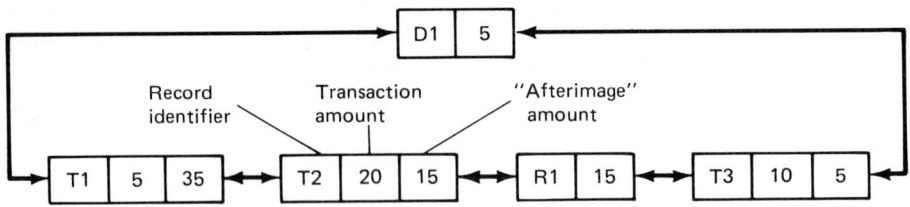

Figure 14.3
Audit trail with "afterimage" data.

a field used to store a cross-reference to manual documentation explaining the change. The reader should consider other possible design strategies.

Note, also, two other complexities that arise when modifications to the audit trail must be made. First, consider what actions must be taken when users have accessed either data item D1 or audit trail transaction T2 when they were in error. Other than notifying the user that the data was in error, can anything else be done? What happens if the "user" accessing D1 was not a person but a process; for example, an inventory reorder program checking the quantity on hand of an inventory item? These matters are left for further study.

Second, modifications are more complex if the audit trail transactions contain data that is a function of the changes made; for example, the value of D1 after an update, or the value presented to the user when a retrieval on D1 occurred. Figure 14.3 shows a design where the audit trail record contains the "afterimage" of D1 as well as the transaction amounts. Now if T2 is identified as being in error, must all the afterimage data contained in R1 and T3 be corrected? Again, these matters are left for further study.

Deletion Periodically the audit trail must be purged of records which are no longer useful; otherwise, if a high volume of transactions occurs the database becomes very large.

The software that carries out the deletion function must permit selective purging on several bases. For example, monetary transactions that update a data item may have to be kept for several years to fulfil statutory requirements; however, transactions that simply inquire as to the status of a data item perhaps can be deleted within several days. The nature of the data item for which the audit trail must be kept also affects when audit trail records can be deleted. For example, transactions that update monetary items usually have to be kept longer than transactions that update a name and address file.

Retrieval In general, retrieval operations on the audit trail are no different from retrieval operations on any other data items. In some cases, however, the user must specify the actions to be undertaken by the retrieval program should an audit trail record be accessed that has been identified as being in error. If the user requires only the correct version of the audit trail record, the retrieval program automatically should take into account any modifications made to correct errors in the audit trail. If the user wants to see the history of modifications made and this data is stored in the audit trail, the program automatically should present this information whenever an audit trail record that has been modified is retrieved. Hopefully, the retrieval software will permit the user to make this choice simply through setting a program switch.

The usual order for presentation of results is time stamp within destination identifier. The user wants to see the sequence of events that led to a data item having a certain value. Often a single audit trail record also will be retrieved to answer queries about a particular transaction that updated the database.

Some Problems of Change

Most application systems are not constant; they evolve over time. Some of these changes have implications for the audit trail. Consider, for example, the following changes that can occur within an application system:

1 A new data item is defined in the database definition and data collected to populate the database.

2 An existing data item is deleted from the database definition and data no longer collected for that data item.

3 The name used for a data item is changed.

4 A change of measurement scale occurs for a data item; for example, conversion from pounds to kilograms.

5 The coding system used for a data item changes; for example, conversion from a numeric to an alphanumeric code.

6 The key used to encrypt a data item is changed.

All these changes affect the various operations that have to be performed on the audit trail. The addition or deletion of data items from the database definition may mean the data structure and the storage structure used for the audit trail have to be changed. Problems arise when a user wants to retrieve data from the audit trail for a time period during which some change has occurred that has affected the audit trail. For example, suppose a user wishes to examine all transactions that have updated an account during a particular financial period, but the code used for that account has changed during the period. If the user is unaware of the change of code for the account, only a subset of transactions for the account may be retrieved. Ideally, the system that supports the audit trail automatically will identify that a change has occurred and provide users with the full set of transactions; or at least alert users to the change that has invalidated their query specification.

The problems posed by system change are general problems. They are the motivation for research in areas such as database management systems. Various solutions have been proposed, all having their advantages and disadvantages. For example, as discussed in Chapter 7, one solution is to separate the definition of data from the processes that access the data. Using this

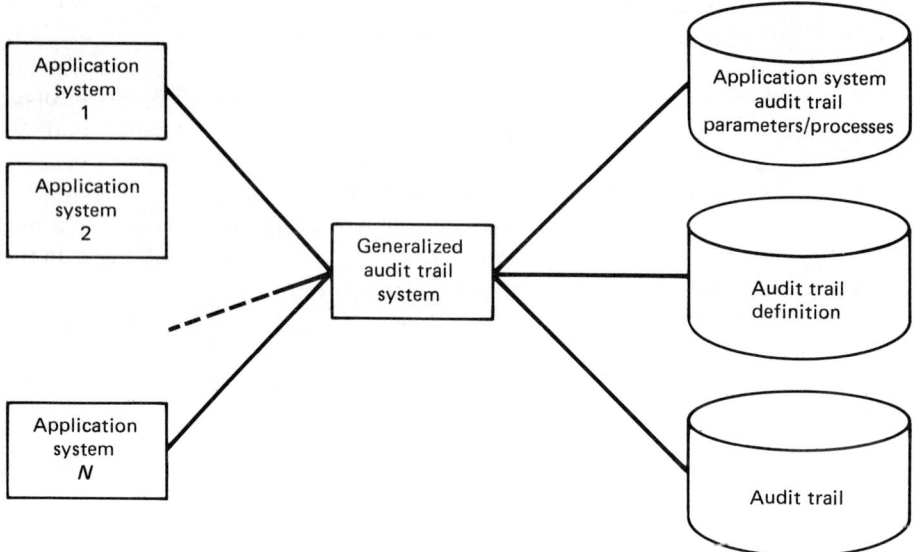

Figure 14.4
Generalized audit trail system.

technique the processes are more robust to changes in the data structure or storage structure of the database. Binding the data definition to the process occurs at some point prior to accessing the database (see Everest [1982]).

Figure 14.4 illustrates this technique applied to the audit trail. A generalized audit trail system accepts output from the various application systems within the computer installation. This output might be dumped in an input/output pool and selectively retrieved periodically by the generalized audit trail system. The definition of the audit trail is separate from the processes that access the audit trail. The audit trail definition maintains the history of definitions for data existing in the audit trail. When a process requires access to the audit trail, the generalized audit trail system binds the audit trail definition to the process. In some cases more than one definition may be bound to the process. For example, if a retrieval process requests data for a period during which the audit trail definition has changed, the generalized audit trail system will change the definition bound to the process when the process accesses data created under the changed definition.

Some Further Design Considerations

Since the audit trail often grows to be extremely large, the designer usually faces some difficult decisions on how to best satisfy logical requirements with the available physical resources. The following sections illustrate some of the design decisions that must be made with respect to the data structure and storage structure chosen for the audit trail.

Data Structure Decisions Data structure design for the audit trail involves specifying the data items to be included in the audit trail, how these data items will be grouped, and the relationships among groups of data items.

Since the major purpose of the audit trail is to permit a history of activities to be traced, there is an incentive to maintain as many data items as possible in the audit trail describing the events that occurred to other data items in the database. Some or all of the following data items might be kept in an audit trail entry (see, also, Bjork [1975]):

Data item	Explanation
Transaction Amount	Value of change to be made to data item in the database
Beforeimage	Prior value of data item in the database to be updated
Afterimage	New value of updated data item in the database
Type of Event	Operation causing the audit trail entry: retrieval, insertion, deletion, modification
Time Stamp	Unique indication of when transaction updated a data item in the database
Transaction Identifier	Unique identifier of transaction
User Identifier	Unique identifier of user who initiated the transaction
Terminal Identifier	Unique identifier of hardware device where transaction read
Process Identifier/Version	Unique identifier of program and version of program that used the transaction to operate upon the database
Status Flags	Can be used to indicate: (a) data logically deleted, (b) doubts exist as to the validity of the data, (c) audit trail entry superseded
Purge Parameters	Information used by the purge routine to determine whether or not the audit trail entry should be deleted

As discussed previously, having "derived" data items in the audit trail such as afterimages and beforeimages can cause problems if modifications must be made to the audit trail to correct data that is in error. For example, if a transaction amount is in error, all beforeimages and afterimages stored after the transaction occurred may have to be corrected. The designer must trade off the costs of recomputing these derived values if they are needed but not stored with the costs of carrying out any corrections needed if they are stored.

In general, the decisions on how to group data items in the audit trail and the relationships that should be established between groups of items in the audit trail are relatively straightforward. All the data items describing the characteristics of an event (operation) usually are grouped together. The relationships established are those previously discussed: a two-way relationship between the transaction and the data item on which it operates, and any relationships needed as a result of modifications made to data items in the audit trail.

Storage Structure Decisions Storage structure decisions require the designer to specify how the data structure chosen for the audit trail is to be linearized and partitioned so it can be mapped onto the storage medium to be used.

Here some difficult design decisions can arise. On the one hand the designer wants to provide fast access to the audit trail. For example, an organization's goodwill may depend in part on a clerk being able to provide fast answers to customers' telephone queries about charges to their accounts. An online inquiry system requiring direct access storage may be necessary. On the other hand the organization may generate a huge volume of audit trail entries. It may be very costly to store these entries on direct access storage, and magnetic tape may have to be considered.

Decisions also must be made on what access paths will be established within the storage structure chosen for the audit trail, and how they will be implemented. Indexes or hashing algorithms may be chosen to provide external access paths to the audit trail. Internal access paths may be established via pointers. If magnetic tape is used as the storage medium, a decision must be made on the primary relationship between groups of items to be used and the file ordered on the basis of that relationship.

The designer also may decide to distribute the audit trail rather than have one centralized audit trail. This involves making decisions on how the audit trail will be partitioned, and how the audit trail will be synchronized when operations on the audit trail cut across partitions.

THE OPERATIONS AUDIT TRAIL

For a long time the operations audit trail was a neglected audit resource. Many auditors found the nature of the trail was unclear, the uses to which it could be put were unclear, and the level of technical skill needed to create and access the trail was too high. To a large extent these obstacles now have disappeared. The auditor's EDP skills have improved. The nature of the trail and its audit uses are better known. Generalized software is available to provide access to and allow use of the trail.

Nature of the Operations Audit Trail

Most operating systems provide a facility to create a comprehensive log of events that occur during the running of the system. Before its auditing uses were perceived, the log was intended as a resource that enabled better management of computer operations. For example, it permitted users to be billed for use of resources, resource consumption patterns to be identified, and impending hardware malfunctions to be detected.

Maintaining an operations audit trail adds overhead to system running. The benefits of maintaining the trail must be traded off against these extra costs. Further, the value of these benefits and costs depends on factors peculiar to the computer installation and the application systems that run within the computer installation. For example, a service bureau may maintain a more comprehensive operations audit trail than its customers would if they used their own machines. The service bureau may fear loss of customer goodwill if it is unable to recover quickly from a system failure or charge equitably for resource consumption. Thus, a comprehensive operations audit trail may be necessary. If customers used their own machines, they may tolerate slower recovery or a coarser chargeout scheme rather than maintain a comprehensive operations audit trail. Similarly, an online inquiry system often needs a more comprehensive operations audit trail than a simple batch system because faster recovery is necessary in the event of failure.

To cater for these varying needs, the operations audit trail logging facilities in operating systems often are parameter-driven. The user specifies what data should be logged for each application system, stores these requirements as operating system parameters, and the operating system invokes the necessary logging facilities for each application system depending on the value of these parameters (Figure 14.5).

Types of Operations Data Collected and Its Uses

The facilities available for collecting operations data usually are very flexible. There is a temptation to log too much data. The system overhead incurred can be high—up to about a 20% increase. Even with careful logging, Schaller [1976] reports common increases in system overhead of between 2% and 5%.

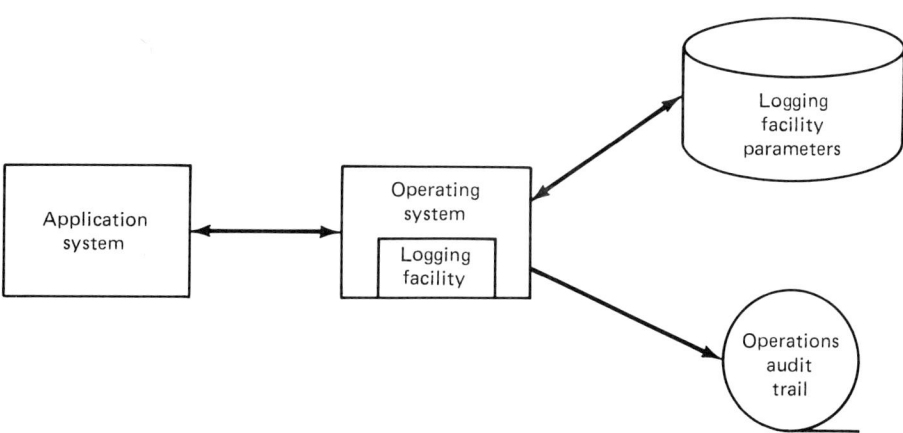

Figure 14.5
Parameter-driven operating system logging facility for operations audit trail.

In general, the logging facilities enable operations data to be collected on four types of events:

1 Resource consumption
2 Attempted integrity violations
3 Hardware malfunctions
4 User-specified events

The following sections describe in more detail the nature of this data and the types of uses, both management and audit, to which it can be put (see, also, Perry [1975a, 1975b, 1976]).

Resource Consumption This data identifies who consumed a resource, what process was used to consume the resource, and when the resource was consumed. The following types of resource consumption are monitored:

Resource category	Examples
Hardware	CPU time used, peripherals used, main memory used, secondary storage space used
Software	Compilers used, subroutine libraries used, file management facilities used
Data	Files accessed, frequency of access to data items, way in which data used, i.e., deleted, inserted, modified
Personnel	Number of tapes/disks mounted and unmounted, number of operator program starts

Typically, users can specify whether they want this data collected at the level of application system running, program running, subroutine running, or sometimes even program step running. Obviously, the lower the level specified for collection of the data, the more data generated and the more overhead added to system running.

Resource consumption data can be used for many management and audit purposes, for example:

1 *Billing* The data provides the basis for charging users for the resources they consume (see, further, Schaller [1974]). The data also may form the basis for the installation's lease or rental payments on some resources. Auditors can use the data to check whether correct billings, lease, or rental payments are made.

2 *Performance Evaluation* The extent to which resources are used efficiently can be examined. The time required for an application program, subroutine, or system software program to process one transaction can be calculated. This may suggest the logic in the program or subroutine needs to be restructured, or more efficient system software needs to be purchased. Hard-

ware utilization can be examined. A particular input/output channel may be the cause of a bottleneck. Program mixes in a multiprogramming environment may have to be changed to eliminate the bottleneck. Some devices may be underutilized. Chapter 21 discusses these matters in more detail.

3 *Potential Integrity Breaches* Certain resource consumption data indicates potential system integrity violations. For example, checks can be made on when a program was run, how many times a program was run, the duration of program running, who initiated the program run. Any variations in the norms for these factors may indicate unauthorized activities are being carried out. Data also can be extracted on who accessed files, who copied files, who renamed files, etc., to determine whether the users and activities are authorized. Files used over a period can be checked against the installation's authorized list of files to see whether any foreign files exist. Any process that was terminated abnormally also can be investigated to determine the reasons why.

Attempted Integrity Violations The logging facility creates audit trail entries for all attempts to use resources that failed. For example, if a terminal user supplies the wrong password, the logging facility records this event. These entries can be extracted from the log to see if an abnormal number exists.

Hardware Malfunctions The logging facility can be used to record data that indicates potential problems with hardware. For example, read/write errors for magnetic media are recorded. An abnormal number of errors may mean a tape or disk needs to be cleaned or replaced.

User-Specified Events Often the logging facilities will permit users to write their own subroutines to collect operations data. The logging facility will invoke this subroutine when a user-specified event occurs; for example, the completion of a program step or the occurrence of a particular transaction type. This capability permits the user to collect data useful for audit purposes at the same time as application systems are processing. Thus, the logging facility provides the auditor with powerful evidence collection capabilities that can be used concurrently with application system processing. Chapter 19 discusses these matters in detail.

Interrogating the Operations Audit Trail

Interrogating the operations audit trail involves four major steps (Figure 14.6):

1 Specifying audit objectives
2 Extracting data from the operations audit trail necessary to meet these objectives
3 Sorting the data into the required order
4 Formatting and presenting the results

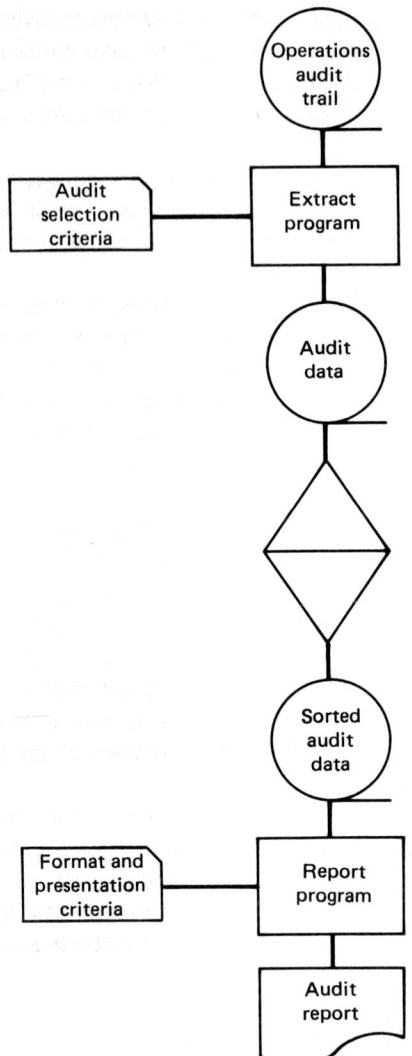

Figure 14.6
Interrogating the operations audit trail.

In the past, auditors often have experienced some difficulty in interrogating the operations audit trail. The log may contain a multitude of data items and record types, voluminous data spanning several tapes or disks, data that has been encoded and compacted to reduce storage space requirements, data requiring some editing before it is in a form suitable for use, etc.

To help overcome these problems a number of vendors have developed generalized packages that can be used by both management and auditors to interrogate the operations audit trail (see, further, Adams [1977]). These packages produce a set of standard reports using the operations audit trail data. Management or the auditor simply has to specify as parameters to the program what reports they require. The packages then extract the necessary data, sort the data in the required order, and format and present the results. Typical reports that the users of these packages can obtain automatically are:

1 System user billing report
2 Hardware utilization report
3 Program resource consumption report
4 Hardware malfunction report
5 Program run schedule report
6 Programmer resource consumption report
7 Report on programs abnormally terminated

Even if generalized software is not available for the operations audit trail of a particular machine or operating system, to some extent the auditor can overcome the problems of interrogating the operations audit trail by using generalized audit software (see Chapter 16).

Some Control Issues

The existence of software that records data for the operations audit trail sometimes poses control problems for the auditor. The software may permit the user to modify or delete records accessed by an application system during production running, or modify or delete records written to the operations audit trail (see, also, Perry and Adams [1974]). For example, if the software allows the user to declare a run-time exit so a user subroutine can be invoked, this subroutine may be able to carry out unauthorized activities on data, especially if the subroutine can run in the operating system's privileged mode.

There are various ways of detecting and preventing unauthorized use of the logging software. For example, users may be prevented from writing their own subroutines without special authority. Use of user subroutines can be monitored with the logging software to detect any unauthorized activity.

SUMMARY

Two types of audit trail should exist within computer systems: (*a*) an accounting audit trail that shows operations on data items in the database, and (*b*) an operations audit trail that shows the series of events surrounding test or production running of an application system. The accounting audit trail serves six purposes: (*a*) query answering, (*b*) statutory requirements, (*c*) application system monitoring, (*d*) fraud deterrent, (*e*) detecting the consequences of error, and (*f*) backup and recovery. The operations audit trail also serves many purposes; for example, user billing, performance monitoring, detecting hardware malfunctions, and detecting attempted security violations.

The software maintaining the accounting audit trail must permit the normal operations of insertion, modification, deletion, and retrieval. Many problems arise when an audit trail must be modified because it is in error. An error in one audit trail entry may have ramifications for other audit trail entries. Multiple levels of audit trails may have to be maintained to record the complete history of the changes made.

A major problem in maintaining an operations audit trail is deciding what data should be collected. System overhead can increase dramatically if control is not kept over the types of data to be written to the operations audit trail. Both management and the auditor must give careful thought to how the operations audit trail will be used.

REVIEW QUESTIONS

14.1. Define what is meant by an audit trail. Distinguish between the accounting audit trail and the operations audit trail.

14.2. Why did the accounting audit trail exist even in manual systems? Is it likely an operations audit trail existed in manual systems, also? Briefly explain.

14.3. Distinguish between the implosion and explosion purposes of an accounting audit trail. Use an accounts payable system to illustrate your answer.

14.4. Describe in some detail the technique you would use to place a unique time stamp in each transaction that operates upon a ledger account record.

14.5. Briefly explain how the accounting audit trail can be used to detect the consequences of an error in application system logic.

14.6. Briefly explain the difference between a permanent audit trail record and a temporary audit trail record. Give an example of a data item that most likely would be stored in a temporary record.

14.7. Why are modifications to the audit trail sometimes necessary? Be sure to explain how errors in the audit trail can occur and why it is necessary to correct these errors.

14.8. Why is it sometimes necessary to maintain multiple levels of audit trails? Give two factors that affect the decision on whether or not to maintain multiple-level audit trails.

14.9. Briefly explain some of the problems that can arise when beforeimage and afterimage data is maintained in an audit trail record.

14.10. Give two attributes of a data item that most likely would affect the decision on when it should be deleted from the accounting audit trail.

14.11. Are there any differences between retrieval operations for the accounting audit trail and retrieval operations for an application system file within the database? Briefly explain your answer.

14.12. Briefly describe how separating the definition of data in the audit trail from the data itself makes the audit trail more robust to either logical or physical changes that occur.

14.13. Assume that so many audit trail entries are generated for a ledgers system that magnetic tape must be used for the storage medium. Would you have the audit trail records on the tape ordered differently if explosion was the primary retrieval requirement rather than implosion? Explain.

14.14. List the four categories of events that are recorded on the operations audit trail. Which category is likely to have more entries? Briefly explain why.

14.15. What interest does the auditor have in the way in which resource consumption data is used to bill system users?

14.16. For the following types of audits, list the data items the auditor would need to extract from the operations audit trail and outline the way in which the data would be presented on the audit report:
   a. program run frequency – to check for possible integrity problems
   b. invalid passwords – to check for an abnormal number
   c. abnormal job termination – to check whether problems are being experienced in running particular jobs
   d. processing time per transaction – to check how efficiently a program processes data
14.17. List two types of events the auditor may wish to monitor using the exit facilities in the operations audit trail logging facility. Briefly explain why these events are of interest to the auditor.
14.18. Briefly explain why generalized software is useful in assisting the auditor retrieve data from the operations audit trail. What factors might influence the auditor not to use generalized software for at least some retrieval operations?
14.19. Outline the control problems posed by the existence of an operations audit trail logging facility that allows user exits. Give two strategies for overcoming these control problems.
14.20. Is it likely the same data items would be collected in the accounting audit trail and the operations audit trail for all types of application systems? If not, identify some attributes of application systems that would cause differences to exist.
14.21. Briefly explain why some people regard the term "audit trail" to be a misnomer. What other terms might be used?
14.22. Does there appear to be any truth to the assertion that computer systems are causing the accounting audit trail to disappear? Justify your answer. Are computer systems having any type of effect on the audit trail?
14.23. What impact do advanced systems, such as online realtime systems, have on the accounting and operations audit trails? Are the audit trails maintained for these systems different from those maintained for simple batch systems?
14.24. Briefly discuss the likely impact, if any, that the increased use of minicomputers and microcomputers will have on the maintenance of the accounting and operations audit trails (see Kirschner [1978]).

EXERCISES AND CASES

14.1. The unique code for a ledger account is 6/35/321 where:
   6 = division number
   35 = department number
   321 = expenditure item
   Suppose a major reorganization occurs and department 35 is assigned to division 2. Thus, the ledger account code now is 2/35/321. Because of the nature of the data, an audit trail of transactions operating on the ledger account must be kept for six years. During that time it is possible clerks and internal auditors may access the audit trail.
   Required: Briefly describe two ways of alerting users of the audit trail to the change that has occurred if they retrieve data that spans the change. List the advantages and disadvantages of each method you propose.
14.2. Sun Belt Savings and Loan is based in Atlanta, Georgia. The Association oper-

ates a large number of automatic teller machines (ATMs) to provide a 24-hour service for its customers.

As the manager of internal audit for Sun Belt, one morning you are called to the controller's office to examine a problem that has occurred. During the previous night, 50 customer accounts had been overdrawn by $199. In a strange sequence of events, each of the accounts had been reduced to a $1 balance in the last half hour that the association was open the previous day. Unfortunately, these transactions had occurred just after a copy of the accounts master file had been taken for the night ATM operations. Note, at night the ATMs are online to a small computer system. The Association considers it to be too costly to keep its main machine operating to support the small workload generated by ATM operations. Consequently, a copy of the accounts master file is taken just prior to the close of operations each day, and this copy is used by the small computer system at night to authorize ATM transactions. The controller is perplexed. She always has recognized this area as a control problem. Nevertheless, she thought that imposing a withdrawal limit of $200 per account using an ATM would limit losses. Fifty overdrawn accounts in one night, however, is a cause for concern.

Required: Identify those data items in the audit trail that would allow you to track down who initiated the transactions that ultimately resulted in the overdrawn accounts. Be sure to explain how you would use these data items.

14.3. You are an internal auditor participating in the design phase of a new online accounts receivable system. Customer accounts will be updated automatically with data captured using point-of-sale devices. The customer service department will have terminals to create new accounts, debit customer accounts, inquire upon the status of accounts, and make alterations to adjust any errors identified in accounts.

When you receive the design of the audit trail, you notice that the system designer has not provided for storing before- and afterimages of the account balance with transaction records. When you ask him about this omission, he explains that he has made this choice to save storage space, since the manager of data processing has expressed concerns about the effects on the availability of mass storage that the system will have.

You explain to the designer that the customer service department will need to know the status of an account balance at various points in time to answer customer queries. He answers that all transactions for an account are chained to the account, and that obtaining an account balance is simply a matter of adding up all transactions after the transaction that is subject to the inquiry and subtracting this amount from the current account balance. He explains that this algorithm will be in the retrieval program.

Required: Evaluate the designer's answer from an audit viewpoint. Can you think of any reasons why before- and afterimages still should be stored with the transaction in spite of the storage constraint problem?

14.4. Greatgoodies Ltd., is a supermarket chain based in Chicago with stores scattered all over the country. Each store uses point-of-sale equipment. The store controller is connected to a district office computer that in turn is connected to the head office computer. The point-of-sale devices, store controllers, district office computers, and head office computer form a complex nationwide communications network.

Recently the company has been experiencing reliability problems with its network. Transactions, and even batches of transactions, have been lost in the network. The problem is that the data processing staff is unable to trace *where* the transactions have been lost. Data may take any one of a number of routes, depending upon data traffic or the availability of particular communications lines.

Required: Outline the nature of the audit trail that should exist so the company can trace where the data is being lost in the network.

REFERENCES

Adams, Donald L. "Audit Uses of SMF Reporting and Analysis Software," *EDPACS* (April 1977), pp. 1-11, 16.

Bjork, L. A., Jr. "Generalized Audit Trail Requirements and Concepts for Data Base Applications," *IBM Systems Journal*, vol. 14, no. 3, 1975, pp. 229-245.

Burch, John G., Jr., and Joseph L. Sardinas, Jr. *Computer Control and Audit: A Total Systems Approach* (New York: John Wiley & Sons, Inc., 1978).

Davis, Gordon B. *Auditing and EDP* (New York: American Institute of Certified Public Accountants, 1968).

Everest, Gordon C. *Database Management: Objectives, System Functions, and Administration* (New York: McGraw-Hill Book Company, 1982).

Greenwald, Bruce M., and Gary Oberlander. "IRS Audits of EDP Systems," *Management Accounting* (April 1975), pp. 13-15.

Jancura, Elise G. *Audit and Control of Computer Systems* (New York: Petrocelli/Charter, 1974).

Kirschner, Leslie S. "Auditing in a Minicomputer Environment," *EDPACS* (June 1978), pp. 1-8.

McHugh, Arthur J. "EDP and the Audit Function," *Accounting Education* (November 1978), pp. 34-54.

Perry, William E. "Using SMF as an Audit Tool—Accounting Information," *EDPACS* (January 1975a), pp. 1-9.

———. "Using SMF as an Audit Tool—Performance," *EDPACS* (December 1975b), pp. 1-7.

———. "Using SMF as an Audit Tool—Security," *EDPACS* (January 1976), pp. 1-8.

———, and Donald L. Adams. "SMF—An Untapped Audit Resource," *EDPACS* (September 1974), pp. 1-8.

Schaller, Carol A. "A Survey of Cost Allocation Techniques," *Journal of Accountancy* (June 1974), pp. 41-46.

———. "Auditing and Job Accounting Data," *Journal of Accountancy* (May 1976), pp. 36-42.

CHAPTER 15

BACKUP AND RECOVERY CONTROLS

CHAPTER OUTLINE

NEED FOR BACKUP AND RECOVERY

BACKUP AND RECOVERY STRATEGIES

    Grandfather, Father, Son
    Dual Recording
    Dumping
    Logging
    Residual Dumping
    Differential Files

SOME ADMINISTRATIVE ASPECTS

SUMMARY

REVIEW QUESTIONS

EXERCISES AND CASES

REFERENCES

Backup and recovery controls are needed to reestablish the physical existence of a database in the event of loss. Loss may be localized or total: a file or portion of a file may be lost or the entire database may be destroyed.

A major factor affecting the form of the backup and recovery method used is whether or not the input file to an update process remains intact and a completely new version of the file is produced. This occurs with magnetic tape files where both unchanged records and changed records must be written onto the new output tape. In this case it is always possible to recover from failure by reprocessing the input transactions against the old version of the master file. If a file exists on direct access storage media and update occurs in place, an old version of the file does not exist. To effect recovery, dumps of the database must be taken periodically and logs of transactions or changes to the database must be maintained.

Backup and recovery operations take two basic forms. First, the *current* state of the database may have to be restored if the entire database or a portion of the database is lost; for example, through failure of a physical device. This involves a *rollforward* operation using a prior dump of the database and a log of transactions or changes since that dump. Second, a *prior* state of the database may have to be restored because the current state of the database is invalid; for example, an erroneous program has updated the database incorrectly. This involves a *rollback* operation to undo the damage. The current state of the database and a log of transactions or changes are used to restore the database to a previous state.

This chapter discusses the need for backup and recovery, the types of backup and recovery strategies available and their advantages and disadvantages, and the various considerations involved in choosing a backup and recovery strategy. Throughout the chapter the term "database" is used to mean the installation's total collection of files. These files may or may not be shared among users. Though the extent of sharing can affect the choice of a backup and recovery strategy, the forms of the strategies are independent of whether or not the database is shared.

NEED FOR BACKUP AND RECOVERY

Loss of the database occurs through five types of failure:

1 Program error
2 System software error
3 Hardware failure
4 Procedural error
5 Environmental failure

Program errors occur because of an undiscovered bug or failure to allow for some processing condition. Program errors usually cause only localized damage to the database specific to the file the program is updating. However, more widespread damage may result if the program starts to process pointers incorrectly, reads records from other files, and attempts to update these records. The program should be written to recognize this situation quickly and halt processing. Since program errors usually cause localized damage, if update occurs in place a rollback procedure enables the database to be restored to a correct prior state.

System software is supplied by a vendor or developed within the installation. Even though it may be extensively tested, program bugs still can be present. An operating system, database management system, file copy utility, etc., may contain dormant errors. The extent of damage that results depends on the nature of the system software and the way in which it is used. For example, an error in an operating system can cause damage to the whole database since the operating system services all programs. An error in a utility program may cause damage only to the file on which it is used. However, the extent of damage also depends on whether the utility is used on a small section or a large section of the database and how often it is used by different application systems.

In spite of the high reliability of *hardware,* failure still occurs. A processor or memory error sometimes happens. A communications network fails because of a faulty terminal, a dataset generating spurious interrupts, or a multiplexor getting into a continuously busy state. An arm drops onto a disk surface, perhaps through a power failure, and scores a concentric circle, thereby destroying file control tables, indexes, etc. An input/output channel starts to write blocks incorrectly. Whether damage is total or localized is situation specific.

There are many forms of *procedural* errors that damage a database. An operator can load an incorrect version of a program or mount an incorrect file. Programs can be run out of sequence. A user may supply an incorrect parameter for an update run. A master file may be incorrectly scratched. Again, whether damage is total or localized is situation specific.

Finally, *environmental* failure can occur. The installation may be flooded, sabotaged, or destroyed by fire. Environmental failure typically results in extensive damage to the database. Off-site storage of files is essential for recovery from environmental failure.

Often the cause of system failure is unknown. Most terminal users know the frustrations of the system "hanging up" or crashing and active programs and files being lost. If the operator accidently zeroizes memory before it is dumped, the problem may never be found. Yourdon [1972] provides an extensive discussion of system failure in an online environment.

BACKUP AND RECOVERY STRATEGIES

All forms of backup and recovery involve using some version of the database at a point in time and a log of transactions or changes to the database. If the update program creates a new physical version of the file, the previous version can be used for backup purposes and the file of transactions used for recovery. If update occurs in place, decisions must be made on the frequency with which dumps will be taken and the form of the log that will be maintained. Backup and recovery strategies differ on the basis of their frequency and comprehensiveness of dumping versus their frequency and comprehensiveness of logging. Frequent dumping permits fast recovery of the database. However, logging normally incurs less system overhead. As always, tradeoffs must be made.

The following sections discuss the traditional forms of backup and recovery. In addition, some of the newer more promising backup and recovery strategies are described, even though their use is not widespread. The discussion highlights the relative advantages and disadvantages of each strategy.

Grandfather, Father, Son

The grandfather, father, son strategy involves using the previous version of a master file and the update transactions used to create the current file to recreate the current master file if it becomes damaged. There are two requirements for using the strategy. First, the input master file to an update run must be kept physically intact; that is, both changed and unchanged records must be written onto a new file. Second, the transaction file from the update run must be kept. Re-creation simply involves redoing the update run.

The current version of the master file is called the son; the previous version the father (Figure 15.1). The grandfather file is the input file to the run that created the father. The grandfather is kept as backup for the father. If for any reason the father cannot be read—for example, it has been acciden-

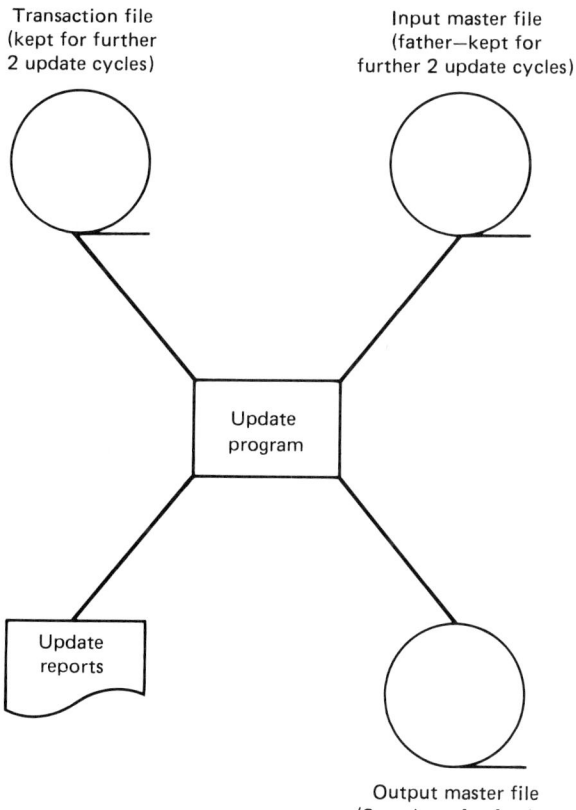

Figure 15.1 Father and son in a grandfather, father, son backup strategy.

tally destroyed or a parity error has occurred—the update run to create the father must be reprocessed. Thus, the strategy involves keeping three generations of the master file and the previous and current versions of the transaction file. It is critical that the different files be stored in different places so that all files are not lost if environmental failure occurs.

The major advantage of this strategy is its simplicity. There are four disadvantages: (*a*) it precludes update in place, (*b*) the file is not available to other processes during recovery, (*c*) concurrent processes cannot update the file, and (*d*) if the update process consumes substantial resources and damage is localized, recovery is expensive. Thus, the strategy is most useful for batch sequential systems.

Dual Recording

Dual recording involves keeping two completely separate copies of the database and updating both simultaneously (Figure 15.2). The two copies should not be maintained at the one physical location. One copy of the database must be stored remotely to protect against environmental failure. To protect against hardware failure, a second processor has to be used. If failure occurs, switches

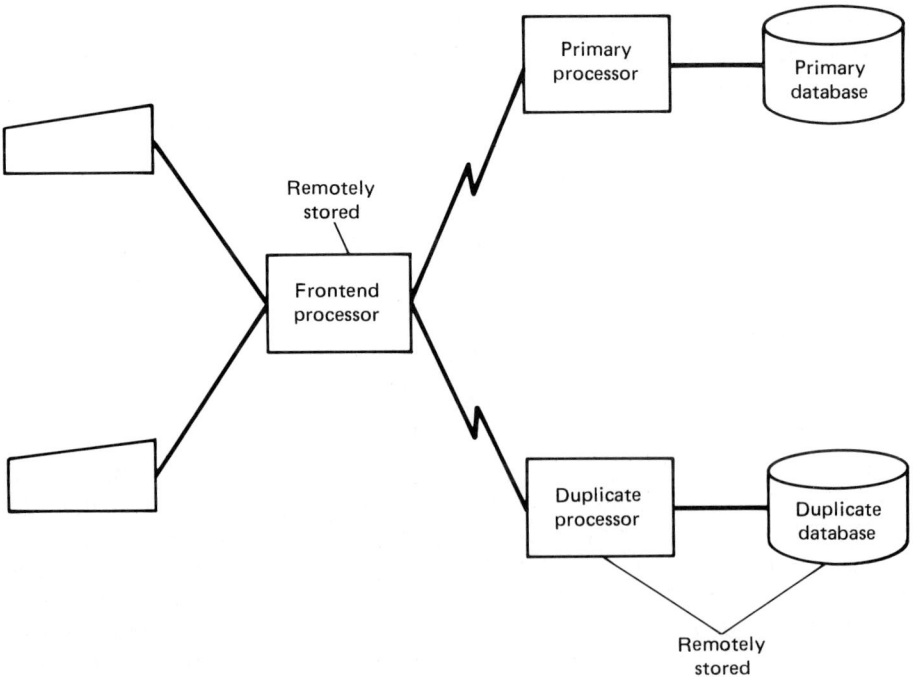

Figure 15.2
Dual recording strategy with remote storage of frontend processor, primary processor and primary database, and duplicate processor and duplicate database.

are set and the second database (and processor) becomes the primary database.

This strategy must be used if it is critical that the database be continuously available as, for example, in an online reservations system. In these cases the losses resulting from the unavailability of the database exceed the costs of maintaining duplicate resources.

Dual recording affords little protection against a procedural error, a system software error, or an application program error. These errors corrupt both databases. Thus, a second backup and recovery strategy must be used to recover from these types of errors. The dual recording strategy assumes procedural and software errors will not occur. In some cases this is a reasonable assumption. For example, in an online reservations system the software often has been extensively tested and widely used so that it is "error-free." Further, procedures are well-defined and also have been extensively tested and widely used. Constancy is a feature of these systems. New processes and procedures are introduced with much caution.

Recovering a database after hardware or environmental failure may or may not be difficult depending on (a) the length of time during which the database is unavailable, and (b) the number of update transactions that have occurred during that period. Two recovery strategies can be used. First, at a convenient time a copy of the intact database can be taken, which becomes the secondary database. Update processes must be denied access to the database during the copy, so it must be performed in an off-peak period. Second, a log of transactions being processed against the intact database can be kept and processed against a previous dump of the damaged database. This strategy is used if it is important to recover the damaged database quickly and it will be some time before an off-peak period is available to undertake a copy of the intact database. Update transactions are copied onto the log concurrently with it being processed against the damaged database. For the damaged database to be able to catch up to the intact database, processing of the log must be faster than the rate at which transactions are written to the log.

Dumping

Dumping involves copying the whole or a portion of the database to some backup medium—typically, magnetic tape. Recovery involves rewriting the dump back onto the primary storage medium and reprocessing transactions since the dump was taken. Users may be responsible for resubmitting transactions from the time of the dump. Alternatively, a log of transactions may be kept between dumps. If users are responsible for resubmitting transactions, they must know at what time each dump is taken, or they must be informed of the time of the last dump taken prior to the failure of the database.

Either a physical dump or a logical dump may be taken. A *physical dump* involves reading and copying the database in the serial order of the physical records; for example, track by track. In some cases physical boundaries define the space occupied by a file and dumping may be selective. In other cases the physical location of a file is unknown. If the installation uses a database management system and the data is shared, records in a file may be intermingled with records from other files in any particular physical area. In this case, selective recovery of a file may be impossible.

Logical dumping involves reading and copying the database in the serial order of the logical records in a file. When recovering the database it is not necessary to rewrite the records back into their previous physical locations. Instead, the storage space occupied by the damaged file is freed up, and the dump can be written onto the database wherever available space exists.

Logical dumping becomes complex if data is shared and records are members of several files. Consider, for example, the problems posed by a multilist file organization. In Figure 15.3, record AB is a member of two lists, A and B. Assume an erroneous program updates list A and damages record AB. Recovering AB using only a logical dump of list A is insufficient unless record AB is written back into its previous physical location. Otherwise, list B contains a corrupted record, and furthermore, two copies of record AB now exist on the database. For logical dumping purposes, the two lists must be considered as a single file.

Physical dumping is faster than logical dumping. However, whether recovery is faster from a physical dump or logical dump depends on the nature

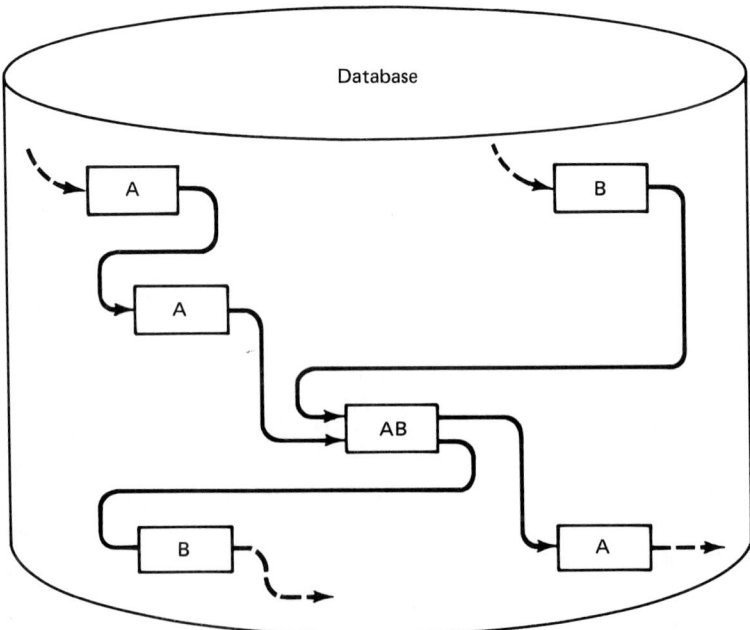

Figure 15.3
Multilist to illustrate some problems with a logical dump backup strategy.

of the damage. Physical dumping facilitates global recovery of the database. It is useful in the event of environmental failure or the failure of a physical device. Logical dumping facilitates selective recovery of the database. It is useful in the event of damage to the database by an erroneous update program or erroneous system software.

If physical dumping is used as a backup strategy, physical reorganization of the database cannot occur between dumps unless the whole database is reorganized and recovered. Partial reorganization means that pointers in a file or on another device may be invalid if, for example, a disk has to be recovered because of physical failure.

Dumping is only a partial backup strategy. It restores the database to a valid state prior to the time of failure. However, the effects of transactions after the dump up to the point of failure still must be recovered through users resubmitting data or the system maintaining a log of transactions or changed images of records on the database. Recovery can be complex when several different update programs are authorized to update the record. Recovering the record if failure occurs means transactions from multiple sources must be recaptured or several programs have to be rerun to restore the database.

Dumping can consume substantial resources. Large databases may take hours, even days, to dump (see, for example, Severance and Lohman [1976]). For some computer installations the time required to take a full dump of the database may be intolerable.

Logging

Logging involves recording a transaction that changes the database, an image of the record changed by the update action, or the change parameters resulting from the update action. Requiring users to resubmit transactions to recover the database may not be a viable strategy for several reasons. First, the downtime required for users to resubmit all transactions may be unacceptable. Second, recovering the database may require transactions to be resubmitted in a specified order. For example, if a bank account fluctuates between a debit and a credit balance and interest is charged on debit balances, the time sequence for the resubmission of transactions to the account is important. If users have not recorded transactions in a time sequence or there are multiple sources of input, obtaining the required time sequence for resubmission of transactions may be impossible. Third, transaction data may not be received directly from a user. It may be generated automatically by a program or received from another computer (perhaps another organization's computer). In these cases some form of logging must occur.

There are four basic types of logging strategies:

1 Logging input transactions
2 Logging beforeimages of the record changed
3 Logging afterimages of the record changed
4 Logging change parameters

Each logging strategy has different advantages and disadvantages and the strategy or combination of strategies chosen depends on the requirements of the application. Whatever logging strategy is chosen, the log file must never be buffered or blocked. If the system crashes and the contents of memory are lost, the log file is not current if the contents of the buffer have not been written to the log.

Logging Input Transactions Using this strategy for recovery involves reprocessing update transactions from the time of the last dump up until the time the database was damaged. To be able to select the relevant transactions from the log, a time and date-of-processing identifier must be stored with each transaction. If selective recovery of the database is to be attempted, a file and program identifier also may be needed for the transaction.

A major problem with this strategy is determining how the input transactions should be reprocessed. One method is to have a special recovery update program that reads the log and updates the database in the same way the various application programs perform updates. This program would be stripped of much of the logic contained in the application update programs. For example, it would not need logic to generate reports or handle transactions that did not change the database. The recovery update program would be very large if a large number of application update programs exists in the installation. As a further disadvantage, someone must ensure correspondence always exists between the recovery and application update programs. All modifications to application update programs must be incorporated in the recovery update program.

A second method of recovery is to read the log and have a master program call each application update program as a transaction for that application program is read. This involves storing a program identifier with each transaction on the log. Everest [1982] suggests a recovery flag be used to modify the normal operations of the application update programs. The recovery flag inhibits the regeneration of reports, error messages, etc. Instead, special control total reports can be produced for verifying the accuracy and completeness of the recovery process.

In some cases recovery is speeded up by sorting like transactions together. For example, all the transactions for a particular application update program can be sorted together or all the transactions for a particular record can be sorted together, their effects summed, and a single update processed against the database. A tradeoff must be made between the costs of sorting and summing the effects of the transactions and the cost of reprocessing all the transactions. Sorting the transactions also may reduce update time through minimizing disk head movement. However, sorting cannot be undertaken if a particular time sequence of transactions is important to database integrity; for example, as with the interest calculation on a bank account in the example previously discussed.

If a user is submitting transactions from an online terminal, a message

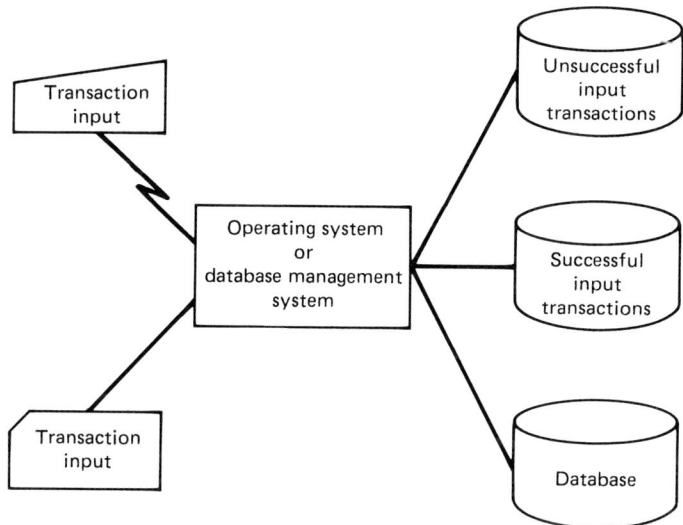

Figure 15.4
Separate logging of successful and unsuccessful input transactions for recovery and audit purposes.

must be printed to tell the user the last successful transaction processed and perhaps the time at which the transaction was processed. This is especially important if the user has to resubmit transactions because only partial recovery can be accomplished using a transaction log. It is also helpful if the system prints the user a message when a transaction has been processed unsuccessfully. In this way the user knows when the transaction has been logged successfully and when the master file has been updated successfully.

A decision must be made on when to log transactions. All transactions input to the system may be logged or only those transactions processed successfully may be logged. If the first alternative is adopted, the effects of unsuccessful transactions (for example, those that fail a validation test) must be inhibited or the user warned when a recovery process is to be undertaken. Otherwise, duplicate error messages for unsuccessful transactions can be confusing. These problems do not arise if only successful transactions are logged. However, as Everest [1982] points out, this strategy is deficient in providing a complete audit trail (see, also, Chapter 14). One solution is to log successful and unsuccessful transactions on separate files and process only the file containing the successful transactions during recovery (Figure 15.4).

Logging Beforeimages Logging beforeimages of the database is a strategy designed to facilitate rollback of the database. Each time a record is to be updated its image before the update is logged. If an erroneous program updates the database, rollback occurs to the point where the erroneous program commenced processing. The log is read backwards and the beforeimages are used

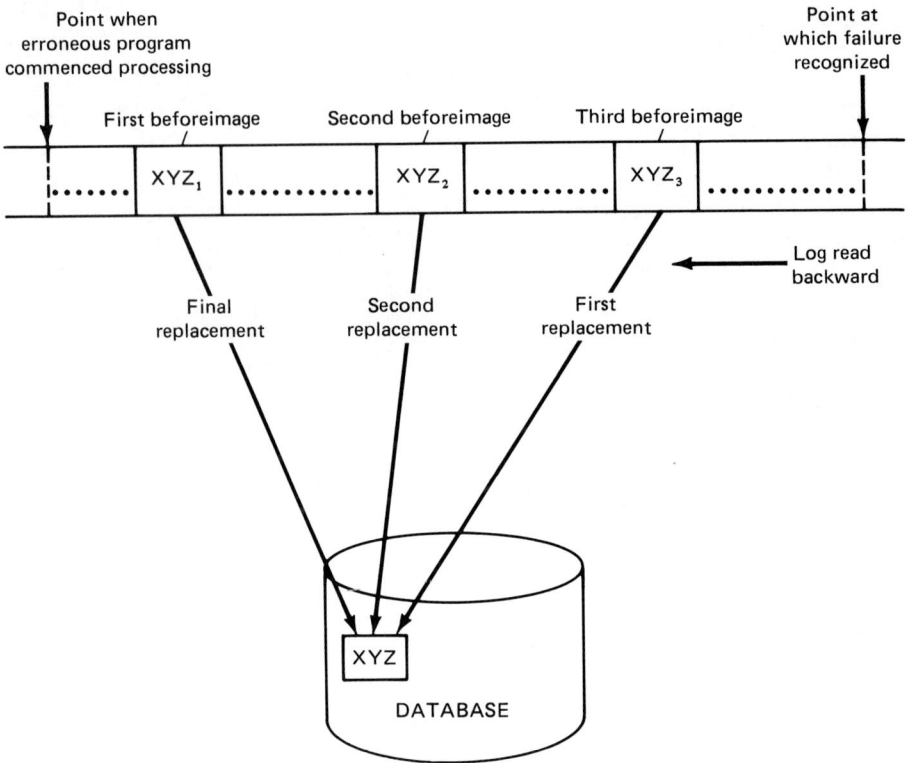

Figure 15.5
Removing the effects of an erroneous program using beforeimages.

to replace the existing records on the database. As the log is read backward, the last beforeimage read for a record up to the point where the erroneous program commenced processing is the state of the record just prior to the program commencing processing (Figure 15.5).

Beforeimages also can be used for rollforward by applying them to a previous dump of the database. For those records that have been changed since the dump, their status is recovered up to the point where the last transaction for these records has not been processed. This is usually an unacceptable loss of data integrity for most financial information systems.

It is beneficial to log the transaction for the record with its beforeimage. Since the erroneous program must be corrected and the transaction reprocessed, logging the transaction with the beforeimages facilitates recovery.

Adding or deleting records on the database can cause several beforeimages to be taken and logged. If a record is chained to other records, the addition or deletion of the record involves updating pointers in other records within the chain. For example, Figure 15.6 shows a multilist file where one record within the multilist is to be deleted. This record is a member of three lists: A, B, and C. The pointers in the lists go in only one direction. Deleting the record means a beforeimage of the deleted record must be taken. Also, beforeimages of the records that point to the deleted record must be taken since the pointer addresses in these records must be updated. Four beforeimages are needed.

Adding or deleting records also may cause some reorganization of a file; for example, moving an overflow record to the home address if the record occupying the home address is deleted. Again, multiple beforeimages must be taken for all records changed. Similarly, if indexes have to be updated through addition or deletion of a record or a changed value in the field of a record, multiple beforeimages will be needed.

If some time passes before it is recognized an erroneous program has entered the system, rollback is often difficult. Other processes may have updated the damaged records in the interim period and the effects of their changes must be preserved. Some actions also may have been taken on the basis of the contents of the damaged records; for example, inventory may have been reordered. It can be difficult, if not impossible, to determine the extent of the damage that has resulted. Recovery may involve a systems programmer directly altering the contents of the damaged records rather than using a rollback procedure for recovery.

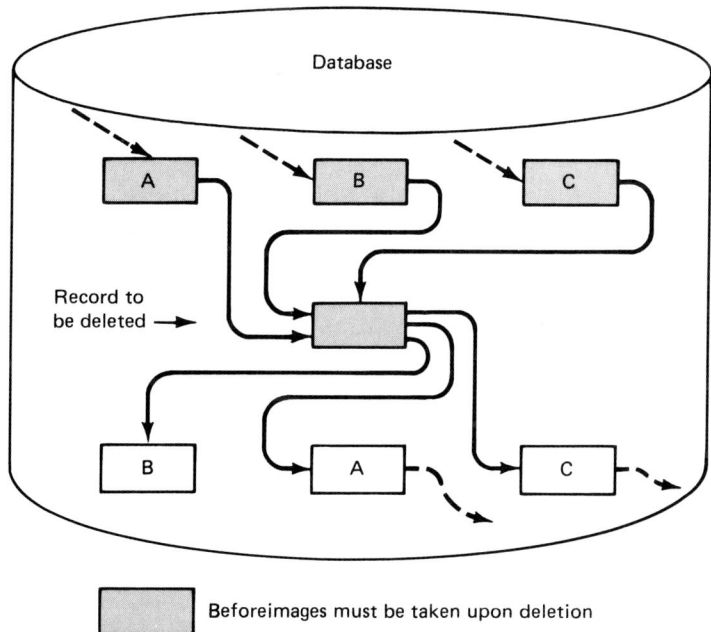

Figure 15.6
Example where multiple beforeimages must be logged upon update.

Concurrent processes present further problems for rollback. Even if it is recognized that a program is in error while it is running, the program may not have locked out other processes from the file it is updating. Consequently, other processes may have read or updated records already processed by the erroneous program. Thus, programs concurrently reading the data will produce erroneous results. Programs concurrently updating the data will operate on incorrect data item values. As soon as an error is recognized in a program, other processes must be locked out from the data that has been damaged. Someone (the database administrator) must be responsible for determining the extent of the damage and the likely effects of the damage. Other users of the database have to be warned of the condition that exists in case they have accessed the damaged records. A decision then must be made on whether rollback can be accomplished. If too many updates have occurred since the erroneous update, other means of restoring database integrity may have to be used.

Logging Afterimages Logging afterimages of the database is a strategy designed to facilitate rollforward of the database. After a record has been updated by a transaction, its image is copied onto the log. If, for example, a physical device fails, recovery is accomplished by rolling forward using the latest dump of the database and replacing the dump version of the record with afterimage versions from the log. The log is read forward and the latest afterimage version read for a record constitutes the status of the record before the database was damaged. As with beforeimages, the unique location of each record must be stored with its afterimage on the log so that replacement of the dump version can be accomplished.

Recovering the database to the point of damage is useless unless the programs operating on the database at the point of failure also can be restarted. It may be difficult to determine what updates have been accomplished. If pointers have to be updated, not all the maintenance may have been undertaken at the point of failure. Unless the system can store the status of registers, buffers, etc., at the time of failure, restarting the programs may be impossible. Recovery then has to occur to a point where programs can be restarted — for example, a checkpoint — and transactions have to be reprocessed.

Additions or deletions of records on the database can cause several afterimages to be written to the log. As with beforeimage logging, this occurs when pointers must be updated, indexes must be maintained, or the database undergoes reorganization.

If an erroneous program updates the database, rollback also can be accomplished, though the logic involved can be complex. The log must be read backward and the afterimages used to replace the database version of the record. If a record has been updated several times, more than one afterimage will exist. The afterimage for a record addition will have no previous version on the database. This presents no problems as the afterimage is written to an address and the previous contents of the address are irrelevant (it should be free space). The complexity arises when the point where the erroneous program entered the system is reached. One more afterimage of each record damaged must still be obtained prior to this point. The recovery program must continue to read the log backward and flag the database record when it is replaced by one more afterimage to prevent any further replacements. The problem is to determine when all the required afterimages have been obtained. The log can be read back until a dump is reached, and providing the recovery program can determine which records still require an afterimage (e.g., by maintaining a table or searching for unflagged records), the dump version of the record can be used to obtain the afterimage. Further complexities surround record deletes. There will be no afterimage for a deleted record. The recovery program can identify a delete if an update occurred to the record after the dump and prior to the delete. However, if no update occurred, the dump version of the record is the required version. The recovery program somehow must identify this situation. In general, because of the complexities involved, using afterimages for rollback should be avoided.

Logging Change Parameters Frequent reorganization and update activity involving a high number of record additions and deletions may mean heavy logging overheads. If records in the database are linked by pointers, multiple beforeimages and afterimages must be taken. The log quickly becomes very large and the processing overheads become very high. One strategy used to help overcome these problems is to log the parameters of the change. Consider, for example, a record in which only the pointer field is to be updated. Rather than copy the whole image of the record, only the unique identifier of the record and the pointer field to be changed might be copied. Information showing the position of the pointer field in the record must also be copied; for example, its start character position. The recovery process is slightly more complex but less storage space is consumed on the log.

Residual Dumping

As an alternative to logging and taking a periodic full dump of the database, Everest [1975] suggests a backup strategy that he calls residual dumping. The primary motivation for residual dumping is the overhead involved in taking a full dump of the database. A log is insufficient for complete backup protection. If only a log is available for recovery, the possibility exists of having to examine all the entries on the log since the creation of the database. A dump avoids this problem by making it unnecessary to look back at the log prior to the dump. Nevertheless, dumps are costly in three ways: (*a*) they may take substantial time to accomplish, (*b*) the database is unavailable during the dump, and (*c*) dumps waste resources in that they are not selective. A record may be logged and dumped within a short period resulting in redundant backup.

Residual dumping involves logging records that have *not* been changed since the last residual dump. Thus, records that have not been subject to an

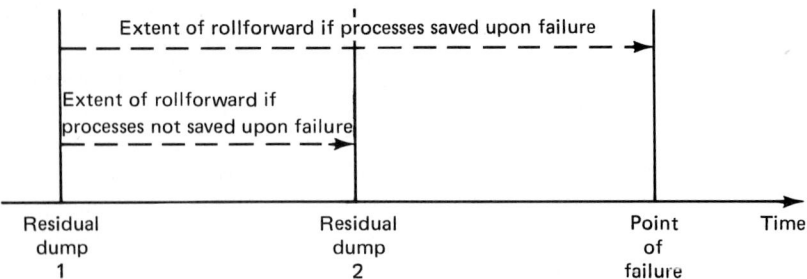

Figure 15.7
Rollforward recovery for a residual dump backup strategy.

update action (and thereby logged) since the last residual dump are logged. Residual dumping is used in conjunction with a beforeimage and afterimage logging strategy. Residual dump records are flagged to show their beforeimage and afterimage are the same.

If a rollforward operation is required, recovery involves going back to (but not including) the second last residual dump taken. The recovery operation starts with an empty database and progressively fills the database by writing afterimages to the database. How far the database must be rolled forward depends on whether or not the status of all the various processes could be saved at the point of failure. Consider Figure 15.7. If at the point of failure the status of all processes could be saved, recovery starts immediately after residual dump 1 and continues up to the point of failure. Between residual dump 1 and residual dump 2, the database is populated with the afterimages of all changes made to the database during this period. Just prior to residual dump 2, the database contains the latest state of all records that have been changed during the period (some of the records may have been changed multiple times). The "empty slots" still remaining in the database because some records have not been changed are then filled with residual dump 2. After residual dump 2 has been read and the dump records written to the database, a complete copy of the database exists. If the status of processes could not be saved at the point of failure, once residual dump 2 has been written back to the database a checkpoint exists at which all processes can be restarted. If the status of all processes could be saved at the point of failure, the rollforward operation continues up to the point of failure.

Residual dumping has no impact on a rollback operation. Beforeimages are utilized in the normal way to effect recovery. Residual dump records are ignored.

Rather than lock out concurrent update processes while residual dumping takes place, a residual dump can be undertaken as a background activity. Thus, residual dumping takes place over an interval while concurrent update processes are running. Again, a rollback operation is no different. However, what now constitutes the backup interval for a rollforward operation? Consider Figure 15.8. If the first residual dump extends over time period R_1 to S_1, when the second residual dump commences at R_2, should records not changed since R_1 or S_1 be logged? Both strategies are viable. With strategy 1, if records older than S_1 are logged, the backup interval is from S_1 to S_2. With strategy 2, if records older than R_1 are logged, the backup interval is from R_1 to S_2. Note that for strategy 2 the backup interval is longer but fewer records are dumped. With strategy 1 a record that has not been updated between the two residual dumps still will be dumped again during the second residual dump, thereby resulting in duplicate backup. With strategy 2 a record that has not been updated between residual dumps will not be dumped again during the second residual dump. Thus, inactive records will be dumped every alternate residual dump. Again, the frequency of dumping is related inversely to recovery time.

If residual dumping occurs as a background operation and other processes are not excluded from updating the database, it is critical that checkpoints of all programs be taken at the end of a residual dump. If a rollforward operation is required and checkpoints cannot be taken when the database is damaged, it may be impossible to recover. There is no synchronization point for the database and the processes operating on the database. If checkpoints of programs cannot be taken at the time of damage, recovery involves rolling forward to the end of the last residual dump and reestablishing the status of programs in progress at that point in time. Transactions then must be reprocessed up to the time of failure.

Everest [1975] discusses five advantages of a residual dump strategy compared with a traditional dump and log strategy. First, concurrent update processes are not excluded from the database during residual dumping. For large databases that take several days to dump, residual dumping may be the only feasible backup strategy. Second, residual dumping results in less duplicate backup, since a record will be logged only once unless it has been updated more than once. Third, residual dumping offers greater flexibility in leveling

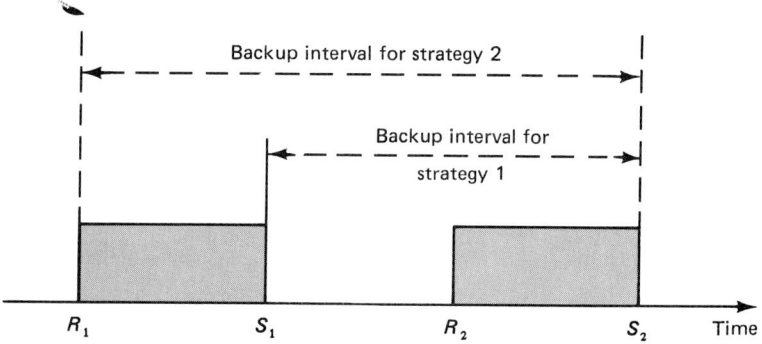

Figure 15.8
Residual dumping as a background operation.

system workloads. Residual dumping can take place as a background operation and be assigned a low priority. Further, the time and period of residual dumping can be varied. Fourth, residual dumping simplifies the recovery process, since only a single log file is needed. A dump file is not needed. Fifth, if residual dumping occurs on a logical basis, reorganization of the database can occur without having to take physical dumps before and after the reorganization.

Differential Files

Severance and Lohman [1976] have suggested using a differential file technique to facilitate backup and recovery operations. A differential file is a file of changes made to the database. Rather than apply the changes to the database, the database is left intact and updates are stored on a differential file. Access times increase but update costs decrease as changes to records (treated as new record additions) do not have to be written back onto the master file. The differential file is stored on a separate device and channel so that instruction overlap occurs to the maximum extent possible and access times are minimized (Figure 15.9). In due course as the size of the differential file grows, the changes are applied to the database because the overheads of maintaining and accessing the file become excessive. There are several advantages of a differential file, some of which relate to backup and recovery:

Advantage	Explanation
Reduces Database Dumping Costs	Since the primary file remains unchanged, only the differential file need be dumped.
Facilitates Incremental Dumping	If additions to the differential file can be allocated sequential addresses on secondary memory and still be accessed (e.g., via an index or hashing algorithm), only the physical section of the device containing these changes to the differential file need be dumped for backup.
Permits Realtime Dumping and Reorganization with Concurrent Updates	By building a differential-differential file (i.e., a second differential file), dumping the first differential file, or reorganization of the primary file and first differential file, can occur concurrently with update. The differential-differential file can be held in main memory if the time for dumping is short.
Facilitates Rollback	The primary file constitutes beforeimage versions of updated records.
Facilitates Rollforward	More frequent dumping can be undertaken since it is inexpensive to dump a differential file.
Reduces the Risk of Serious Data Loss	The small critical area of the differential file can be stored on a highly reliable device or duplexed.

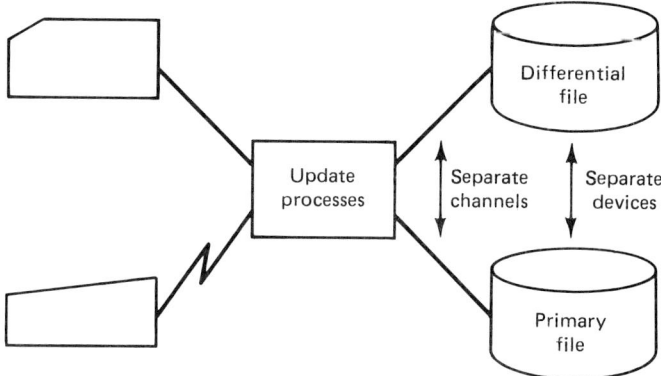

Figure 15.9
Differential file technique for backup and recovery.

SOME ADMINISTRATIVE ASPECTS

There are some administrative aspects of backup and recovery with which the auditor should be concerned. These include: (a) the need to make someone ultimately responsible for backup and recovery operations in an installation, (b) the formal planning and documenting of backup and recovery strategies to be used, and (c) the periodic testing of backup and recovery operations for the installation.

In a database management system environment, the person who should be responsible for backup and recovery is the database administrator (see, also, Chapter 7). Only the database administrator has sufficient global knowledge of the community of users of the database to be capable of determining suitable backup and recovery strategies for the database. If a database management system is not being used, the various application project managers are probably in the best position to make a decision on a backup and recovery strategy for their application files. However, this decision may need to be made in consultation with the operations manager, systems manager, and programming manager.

Since the decision on a suitable backup and recovery operation for an application can be complex, it should be formally considered, planned, and documented. Periodically, the decision should be reviewed, perhaps in light of changing circumstances or experience with the strategy. For example, because of increased use of the system, tolerable downtime may decrease.

Periodically, backup and recovery strategies should be tested to see if they work both technically and administratively. For large databases, testing may be extremely expensive. However, after the database has been lost it is too late to find out the backup and recovery strategy does not work. Vital information also may be obtained from measuring the values of those variables that affect the choice of a strategy; for example, recovery time.

SUMMARY

Backup and recovery operations restore the physical existence of a database when it is lost or damaged. Loss or damage occurs in a variety of ways: (a) program error, (b) system software error, (c) operating system failure, (d) hardware failure, (e) procedural error, and (f) environmental failure. Loss or damage to the database may be localized or complete.

All forms of backup and recovery involve using some version of the database at a point in time and a log of transactions or past states of records on the database. Two forms of recovery must be available. First, the current state of the database may be lost, and recovery involves a rollforward operation using a past version (dump or generation) of the database and a log of transactions or afterimages of records that have been changed on the database. Second, the current state of the database may be invalid, and the erroneous effects that caused the invalid state must be undone. This involves a rollback operation using the current state of the database and beforeimage versions of the records that have been changed.

Many variables affect the choice of a backup and recovery strategy; for example, the size and volatility of the database, the required uptime of the database, the tolerable downtime, the time required for dumping versus logging, the availability of backup hardware and software, and the extent to which physical separation of resources is possible. Someone should be ultimately responsible for backup and recovery operations within an installation. Further, backup and recovery needs to be planned formally, decisions documented, and the strategies periodically tested and evaluated.

REVIEW QUESTIONS

15.1. Briefly discuss the purpose of backup and recovery. Distinguish between a rollforward operation and a rollback operation. For each type of operation give two examples of failures that would necessitate the operation be undertaken.

15.2. What conditions must exist before a grandfather, father, son backup strategy can be used? Briefly discuss the advantages and disadvantages of the strategy.

15.3. The dual recording backup strategy does not allow recovery from all kinds of failure. Briefly describe the situations where recovery cannot be accomplished.

15.4. With a dual recording strategy, explain the various methods available for "catching up" the primary copy of the database if it fails and the secondary copy must be used. Discuss the advantages and disadvantages of each strategy.

15.5. A backup and recovery strategy cannot be considered in isolation from a checkpoint and restart strategy. Explain.

15.6. Explain the differences between logical dumping and physical dumping. What are the relative advantages and disadvantages of each method of dumping? Explain how a logical dump of a hashed (random) file would be undertaken.

15.7. Consider a file that consists of simple lists; that is, records that are chained to only one head-of-list record. If the pointer from the head-of-list record to the first record in the list is corrupted, what implications will this have for a logical dump backup strategy? What implications will it have for a physical dump backup strategy?

15.8. Why is dumping only a partial backup strategy?

15.9. Briefly explain the various kinds of logs that can be used for recovery purposes. Why might a combination of logging strategies be used for recovery purposes?

15.10. Discuss the various tradeoffs made between more frequent dumping versus more frequent logging.

15.11. What are the differences (if any) between a grandfather, father, son backup and recovery strategy and a dump and log backup and recovery strategy?

15.12. If beforeimages and afterimages are stored on a log file, apart from audit trail considerations, why might transactions still be logged?

15.13. Briefly discuss the various methods of reprocessing input transactions for recovery purposes. Outline the problems that arise when data is shared and multiple processes concurrently update the database.

15.14. Explain why it may be important to preserve a time sequence of transactions when recovering a database rather than sort the transactions into an order that speeds recovery.

15.15. When logging input transactions, why is it necessary to distinguish between transactions that have been processed successfully and those that are in error? If this distinction is not made, during the recovery process what actions must be taken?

15.16. Briefly explain the process of rolling back the database using beforeimages of the records on the database. Why is it necessary to take beforeimages of records in a list file that are moved because of physical reorganization?

15.17. Discuss the various situations that complicate a rollback recovery operation and make recovering the integrity of the database difficult, if not impossible. What actions can be taken to restore the database in these situations?

15.18. Explain the problems of using afterimages to roll back the database. Why might a decision have been made not to log beforeimages, even though the problems of rolling back the database were recognized?

15.19. Briefly explain the rationale behind logging change parameters rather than beforeimages and afterimages.

15.20. Briefly explain the residual dumping backup and recovery strategy. Is it necessary to log both beforeimages and afterimages of records changed using a residual dumping strategy?

15.21. Explain how rollforward operations and rollback operations are accomplished using residual dumping.

15.22. If residual dumping occurs as a concurrent process with update processes, why is it necessary to periodically take checkpoints of the status of processes in operation?

15.23. What would be the backup interval if residual dumping occurs on a continuous basis; that is, a new residual dump starts immediately on completion of the current residual dump?

15.24. If the database is recovered from a residual dump using a rollforward operation, what date of last change should be given to the records on the database? Discuss what will happen when the first residual dump is taken after the recovery.

15.25. Briefly explain the concept of a differential file. What advantages does a differential file have for backup and recovery purposes?

15.26. Discuss some of the administrative aspects of backup and recovery that should be the concern of the auditor.

15.27. Are audit trail controls and backup and recovery controls necessarily the same? Are they related? Explain.

15.28. Why is it important a log file not be buffered or blocked?

EXERCISES AND CASES

15.1. Feetfirst Inc., is a major manufacturer of boots and shoes. It has diverse types of data processing systems including straightforward batch systems, online realtime update systems, and some application systems (some of which are also online realtime update) that use a database management system. The company does not use telecommunications; all terminals are located at the head office.

The internal audit manager is concerned that an audit has never been conducted to evaluate the adequacy of the company's backup and recovery procedures. As a member of the internal audit staff, he asks you to prepare an audit plan so an evaluation can be undertaken.

Required: Outline an audit plan for evaluating Feetfirst's backup and recovery operations. Your plan should include: (*a*) a statement of audit objectives; (*b*) an outline of compliance testing procedures; (*c*) an outline of substantive testing procedures.

15.2. You are the head of a consulting firm that specializes in EDP audit and control. One day you are approached by a representative of the shareholder group of an organization that has recently gone bankrupt. The reason for the bankruptcy was a fire that destroyed the organization's data processing installation. The backup and recovery procedures for the installation were inadequate; consequently, the organization could not reestablish its critical data files. The representative explains that the shareholders are contemplating legal action against the external auditors of the organization. The shareholders feel that it was the responsibility of the external audit firm to identify the inadequacy of backup and recovery. The shareholders are concerned, however, that the external audit firm has made it clear that the evaluation of backup and recovery procedures was not necessary to assess the adequacy of the financial statements and, as such, was not the responsibility of the external auditor. Thus, the shareholders seek your advice on the wisdom of pursuing legal action.

Required: Write a brief report for the shareholders advising them on the course of action they should take and whether or not their lawsuit is likely to be successful.

15.3. The Convict Savings Bank is a large bank based in Sydney with branches scattered throughout Australia. The bank uses an online realtime update system for its customer accounts system. The branches are connected via a telecommunications network to a centralized database in the head office. The bank uses a database management system for its database.

As a member of the external audit firm of the bank, you are reviewing the adequacy of backup and recovery procedures for the online realtime update system. During an interview with the database administrator, she explains to you that when a system crash occurs, the computer operators attempt to restart the system immediately because downtime is intolerable with the system. Since the database management system used by the bank establishes relationships between entities via pointers, you express your concern to her about the possibility of pointers in the database not having been updated (that is, an update is in progress) when the crash occurs and the database being in an inconsistent state. The database administrator concedes this point. Nevertheless, she argues that it is a relatively minor problem. When the system is restarted, tellers are supposed to check whether the last transaction they submitted was posted. If it was not posted, they resubmit the transaction. An inquiry transaction also will identify inconsistent or corrupted pointers. If the database is in an inconsistent state, since it is unlikely another transaction will occur for the customer's account during that day, backup and recovery is left until the night shift.

Required: Write a brief report for your manager commenting on the adequacy of backup and recovery procedures for the online system. Make any suggestions that you feel would improve the adequacy of backup and recovery procedures for the system.

15.4. Bits-and-Pieces Inc., is a parts retailing firm that has an online realtime update system for its sales system. Clerical staff enter sales transactions and the customer accounts file and parts inventory file are updated immediately.

As the manager of internal audit for Bits-and-Pieces, one day you are called to a meeting with the controller and data processing manager. The controller explains that during the previous day a system crash occurred at 3 p.m. Recovery was started immediately; however, during the recovery process, for the first time ever, a log tape error was encountered. The result was that transactions up to 11 a.m. only could be recovered. Clerical staff were asked to resubmit their transactions from 11 a.m. onward. Unfortunately, new transactions (those that occurred after 3 p.m.) also were submitted because the downtime required for resubmission of old transactions was intolerable. As a consequence, new transactions depleted some stock items to a zero balance before old sales transactions on those stock items were reposted. Thus, sales had been made of inventory where stockouts existed.

Required: The controller is concerned about the loss of customer goodwill that may occur. At this time the cause of the log tape error is unknown. However, he asks you to prepare a brief report outlining your thoughts on how a similar disaster might be prevented in the future. Of course, a log tape error is always possible, though it is usually a rare occurrence.

REFERENCES

American Federation of Information Processing Societies. *AFIPS System Review Manual on Security* (Montvale, N.J.: AFIPS Press, 1974).

Canning, Richard G. "Recovery in Data Base Systems," *EDP Analyzer* (November 1976), pp. 1-11.

Chandy, K. Mani, James C. Browne, Charles W. Dissly, and Werner R. Uhrig. "Analytic Models for Rollback and Recovery Strategies in Data Base Systems," *IEEE Transactions on Software Engineering* (March 1975), pp. 100-110.

Drake, R. W., and J. L. Smith. "Some Techniques for File Recovery," *The Australian Computer Journal* (November 1971), pp. 162-170.

Everest, Gordon C. "Residual Dump Backup Strategy for Large Databases," Working Paper MISRC-WP-76-04, Management Information Systems Research Center, University of Minnesota, Minneapolis, Minn., 1975.

———. *Database Management: Objectives, System Functions, and Administration* (New York: McGraw-Hill Book Company, 1982).

LeGore, Laurence B. "Smoothing Data Base Recovery," *Datamation* (January 1979), pp. 177–180.

Lohman, Guy M., and John A. Muckstadt. "Optimal Policy for Batch Operations: Backup, Checkpointing, Reorganization, and Updating," *ACM Transactions on Database Systems* (September 1977), pp. 209–222.

Sayani, Hasan H. "Restart and Recovery in a Transaction-Oriented Information Processing System," in Randall Rustin, ed., *ACM SIGMOD Workshop on Data Description, Access and Control* (New York: Association for Computing Machinery, 1974), pp. 351–366.

Severance, Dennis G., and Guy M. Lohman. "Differential Files: Their Application to the Maintenance of Large Databases," *ACM Transactions on Database Systems* (September 1976), pp. 256–267.

Verhofstad, J. S. M. "Recovery Techniques for Database Systems," *Computing Surveys* (June 1978), pp. 167–195.

Yourdon, Edward. *Design of On-Line Computer Systems* (Englewood Cliffs, N.J.: Prentice-Hall, Inc., 1972).

PART

EVIDENCE COLLECTION

To evaluate the quality of an application system the auditor needs to collect evidence. Various techniques and tools have been developed to aid this evidence collection function. Some primarily gather data on how well assets are safeguarded; some on a system's ability to maintain data integrity; others are useful for collecting data on system effectiveness; still others gauge processing efficiency; and even some have eclectic capabilities. The auditor's problem is not a shortage of evidence collection techniques to use. Rather, it is knowing what technique or set of techniques is best to use for a given system or program.

The next six chapters describe the various evidence collection tools and techniques developed to gather data on whether systems safeguard assets, maintain data integrity, achieve their objectives effectively, and process data efficiently. The focus is on the nature of the tools and techniques, methodologies for using the tools and techniques, and the relative advantages and disadvantages of the tools and techniques.

Chapter	Overview of contents
16 Generalized Audit Software	Functional capabilities and limitations of generalized audit software; audit tasks that can be accomplished; managing an audit software application; accessing complex data structures; purchasing audit software
17 System Software and Specialized Audit Software	Types of system software useful to the auditor; need for specialized audit software; developing and implementing specialized audit software

18 Code Review, Test Data, and Code Comparison	Methodology of program source code review; designing, creating, and using test data; source and object code comparison
19 Concurrent Auditing Techniques	Nature of concurrent auditing techniques; types of concurrent auditing techniques; design and implementation; advantages and disadvantages
20 Interviews, Questionnaires, and Control Flowcharts	Designing, conducting, and analyzing an interview; design and use of questionnaires; questionnaire reliability and validity; constructing a control flowchart; advantages and disadvantages of control flowcharts
21 Performance Monitoring Tools	Objects of measurement; general characteristics of performance monitoring tools; types of tools available; data integrity issues

CHAPTER 16

GENERALIZED AUDIT SOFTWARE

CHAPTER OUTLINE

MOTIVATIONS FOR GENERALIZED AUDIT SOFTWARE DEVELOPMENT

FUNCTIONAL CAPABILITIES
  File Access
  File Reorganization
  Selection
  Statistical
  Arithmetic
  Stratification and Frequency Analysis
  File Creation and Updating
  Reporting

AUDIT TASKS THAT CAN BE ACCOMPLISHED
  Examine the Quality of Data
  Examine the Quality of System Processes
  Examine the Existence of the Entities the Data Purports to
    Represent
  Undertake Analytical Review

FUNCTIONAL LIMITATIONS
  Ex Post Auditing Only
  Limited Ability to Verify Processing Logic
  Limited Ability to Determine Propensity for Error

INSTALLATION/AUDIT GROUP MATURITY ISSUES
   Impact of the Installation Life Cycle
   Impact of the Audit Group Life Cycle

MANAGING A GENERALIZED AUDIT SOFTWARE APPLICATION
   Feasibility Analysis and Planning
   Application Design
   Coding and Testing
   Operation
   Evaluation and Documentation of Results

ACCESSING COMPLEX DATA STRUCTURES
   Accessing Methods: Advantages and Limitations
   Auditor Independence Issues

PURCHASING AUDIT SOFTWARE
   Major Differences Among Audit Software
   Selecting a Package

SUMMARY

REVIEW QUESTIONS

EXERCISES AND CASES

REFERENCES

A major tool available to the auditor for collecting evidence on the quality of an application system is generalized audit software. Generalized audit software provides a means to gain access to and manipulate data maintained on computer media. The auditor obtains evidence directly on the quality of the records produced and maintained by the application system. In turn the quality of the records reflects the quality of the system processing these records.

This chapter discusses why generalized audit software was developed, the major functional capabilities and limitations of audit software, and those factors that over time affect the usefulness of audit software. The bases for managing an audit software project are discussed. Techniques for accessing complex data structures are described and evaluated. Finally, the chapter discusses an approach to acquiring audit software.

MOTIVATIONS FOR GENERALIZED AUDIT SOFTWARE DEVELOPMENT

A generalized audit software package is a program providing powerful data retrieval, data manipulation, and reporting capabilities specifically oriented to the needs of auditors. The primary motivation for developing this software is the set of problems caused by the diversity of computerized information processing environments that confront the auditor.

In a manual system important sources of audit evidence are the records showing the various transactions undertaken by the organization and their resulting effects on the organization. This hard-copy evidence can be examined readily by the auditor. In a computer system this evidence exists on magnetic media and can only be examined using a program to extract or dump the contents of files. The problem is that external auditors (if not internal auditors) must deal with systems having diverse characteristics: different hardware and software environments, different data structures, different record formats, different processing functions. With resource constraints it is often impossible to develop specific programs for every system that will extract, manipulate, and report data required for audit purposes. For this reason generalized software has been developed that is capable of handling a wide variety of different systems. The tradeoff made is processing efficiency for the ability to develop quickly a program capable of accomplishing audit objectives in a new environment. In many cases the loss in processing efficiency is more than compensated by savings in labor hours required for developing audit software capabilities for specific computer systems.

A second major motivation for developing audit software is the need to develop quickly an audit capability in light of changing audit objectives. Both external auditors and internal auditors face situations where new audit objectives must be developed or existing audit objectives change. Generalized audit software facilitates adaptation by the auditor when these changes occur.

A third major motivation for developing audit software is the need to provide audit capabilities to auditors relatively unskilled in the use of computers. In the past many auditors have had little training in computers. Most generalized audit software packages can be used by auditors who are not computer audit specialists, thereby extending the computer audit capabilities of these auditors.

FUNCTIONAL CAPABILITIES

Generalized audit software allows the auditor to use a high-level, problem-oriented language to invoke functions to be performed on computer files. The auditor must comply with the various syntactic and semantic rules of the language; that is, rules governing the combination of words or terms that can be used in the language, and rules governing the meanings ascribed to the words and legitimate combinations thereof included in the language. Typically, pre-printed input specification sheets are supplied with the software package, and the auditor completes these specification sheets for keypunching and input to the software. Some packages allow the auditor to provide terminal input. The

TABLE 16.1
MAJOR SETS OF FUNCTIONS GENERALLY AVAILABLE
IN GENERALIZED AUDIT SOFTWARE

Set of functions	Examples
File Access	Capabilities to read different record formats and different file structures, especially sequential, index sequential, and random; multiple files can be read simultaneously
File Reorganization	Sorting and merging files
Selection	Boolean and relational operators available, e.g., A AND (B OR C); A EQ 2500; A GT 3000
Statistical	Varies from sampling every nth item to capabilities supporting attributes and variables sampling
Arithmetic	Full set available: addition, subtraction, multiplication, division
Stratification and Frequency Analysis	Capabilities to classify data according to certain criteria
File Creation and Updating	Capabilities to create and update work files based on the installation's files
Reporting	Editing and formating of output

package examines input for syntax and semantic errors but, as with programming language compilers, certain logic errors cannot be recognized. After errors identified have been corrected, the package attempts to carry out the functions invoked. Table 16.1 shows the major functions included in generalized audit software packages. The following sections provide a brief description of these functions.

File Access

The file access functions enable files having different record formats and file structures to be read. Records may have fixed or variable formats. Typically, the file structures that can be read are sequential, index sequential, and random, although some packages now provide access to more complex structures such as trees and networks. Several files usually can be read simultaneously by generalized audit software.

File Reorganization

The file reorganization functions allow data to be sorted into different orders and data from different files to be merged onto one file. Sorting capabilities are necessary for a variety of purposes; for example, reporting data in a specified order or comparing data on two files. Merging capabilities are needed if data from separate files is to be combined on a separate work file.

Selection

Generalized audit software provides powerful selection capabilities for extracting data that satisfies certain tests. Typically, the Boolean operators AND, OR are provided as well as the relational operators EQ, GT, LT, NE, GE, LE; that is, equal to, greater than, less than, not equal to, greater than or equal to, and less than or equal to. Complex queries containing nested tests can be formulated. Brackets establish precedence. For example, the query (PAY GT 12000 AND (OVERTIME GE 2000 OR ALLOWANCES EQ 6)) would extract employee records where pay is greater than $12000 per year and overtime is greater than or equal to $2000 per year, or employee records where pay is greater than $12000 and the allowances classification is category 6.

Statistical

The statistical capabilities of generalized audit software vary from primitive to sophisticated. At a basic level every nth record can be selected. However, several packages provide comprehensive attributes and variables sampling capabilities. In some cases functions exist supporting financial analysis; for example, regression and financial ratio analysis. Alternatively, the audit software may be designed to provide input to separate statistical and financial modeling software.

Arithmetic

Generalized audit software provides the full set of arithmetic operators enabling work fields to be computed, the arithmetic accuracy of data to be checked, control totals to be produced, etc. For example, net pay calculations for a payroll file can be recomputed or files can be crossfooted.

Stratification and Frequency Analysis

The software provides varying capabilities with respect to stratification and frequency analysis. If stratification and frequency analysis capabilities are provided, frequency tables and bar charts (histograms) can be produced. For example, the frequency of accounts receivable balances in certain classes can be determined: $0–$200, $200.01–$400, $400.01–$600, etc. The distribution of accounts receivables balances is an important determinant of the type of sampling method chosen.

File Creation and Updating

Some generalized audit software packages allow work files to be created and updated. The auditor uses the software to extract the data needed for audit purposes from the application system files. By using the work file for audit purposes, the auditor causes minimum interference to normal application system processing.

Reporting

Finally, the software can produce reports containing information useful to the auditor. These reports can be formatted in different ways. Edit criteria can be applied; for example, zero suppression and addition of dollar signs.

AUDIT TASKS THAT CAN BE ACCOMPLISHED

The functional capabilities of generalized audit software can be combined in different ways to accomplish several audit tasks:

1 Examine the quality of data
2 Examine the quality of system processes
3 Examine the existence of the entities the data purports to represent
4 Undertake analytical review

The following sections examine the ways in which these tasks can be accomplished.

Examine the Quality of Data

The auditor can use the functional capabilities of generalized audit software to examine the existence, accuracy, completeness, and consistency of data maintained on files. Some examples follow. Records for various fixed assets can be retrieved to see if, in fact, the records exist. The calculation of sales discounts can be checked for accuracy. The address field in an accounts receivable file can be examined to see if it contains blanks. Records on the personnel file and payroll file can be compared for consistency.

The auditor examines the quality of data maintained on application system files for two reasons. First, the quality of the data reflects the quality of the application system that processes the data. For example, if the address fields in debtors' records contain blanks, the auditor must question the adequacy of the validation processes contained in the system. Second, the quality of data reflects the quality of the personnel who developed and maintain the application system, and the quality of the personnel who use the system. If the data is low in quality, the application system processing the data may be poorly designed, poorly implemented, or poorly maintained. If this situation has been allowed to continue, the quality of the personnel who use the system must be questioned. Also, it is possible that even though the system is well-designed, implemented, and maintained, the data supplied by users is low in quality.

Examine the Quality of System Processes

Besides the methods described above, the auditor can examine more directly the quality of both the manual and computer system processes in other ways. Even though the quality of system data is high, the quality of system processes may be low from the viewpoint of achieving the objectives of the organization. For example, upon using generalized audit software to age an accounts receivable file, the auditor may find substantial numbers of overdue accounts. This attribute of the data reflects adversely on both the computer system and the manual system. The computer system may not be producing timely information for control over debtors. The manual system may have inadequate debt collection facilities.

Similarly, the auditor may use generalized audit software to prepare inventory turnover statistics for obsolescence analysis. This analysis highlights inadequate management of inventory and enables the auditor to prepare recommendations for improvement. Generalized audit software provides powerful capabilities for producing management reports useful for various kinds of analyses that reflect on the quality of system processes.

Mair [1975] describes another way of using generalized audit software to examine the quality of system processes via the *parallel simulation* technique. Parallel simulation involves the auditor writing a program to replicate those application processes that are critical to an audit opinion and using this program to reprocess application system data. The results produced are compared with the results produced by the application system and any discrepancies identified. For example, Figure 16.1 shows a parallel simulation program reprocessing transaction data against a master file and producing a new master file. Generalized audit software then compares the master file produced by the parallel simulation program with the master file produced by the application system and generates a report of discrepancies.

The parallel simulation program can be written in any programming language; however, because generalized audit software is a high-level, problem-oriented language, it allows fast development of a program that will accomplish the audit functions required. Since parallel simulation runs are often one-off runs, processing efficiency usually is not a major consideration.

There are several steps involved in constructing a parallel simulation program. First, the auditor must obtain an understanding of the functions performed by the application system. Second, the auditor must identify those functions where reliability is critical to an audit opinion. Third, the auditor constructs a parallel simulation program. Fourth, the auditor runs the program. Finally, the auditor evaluates the results produced. Discrepancies indicate a flaw in either the simulation program or the application system processes.

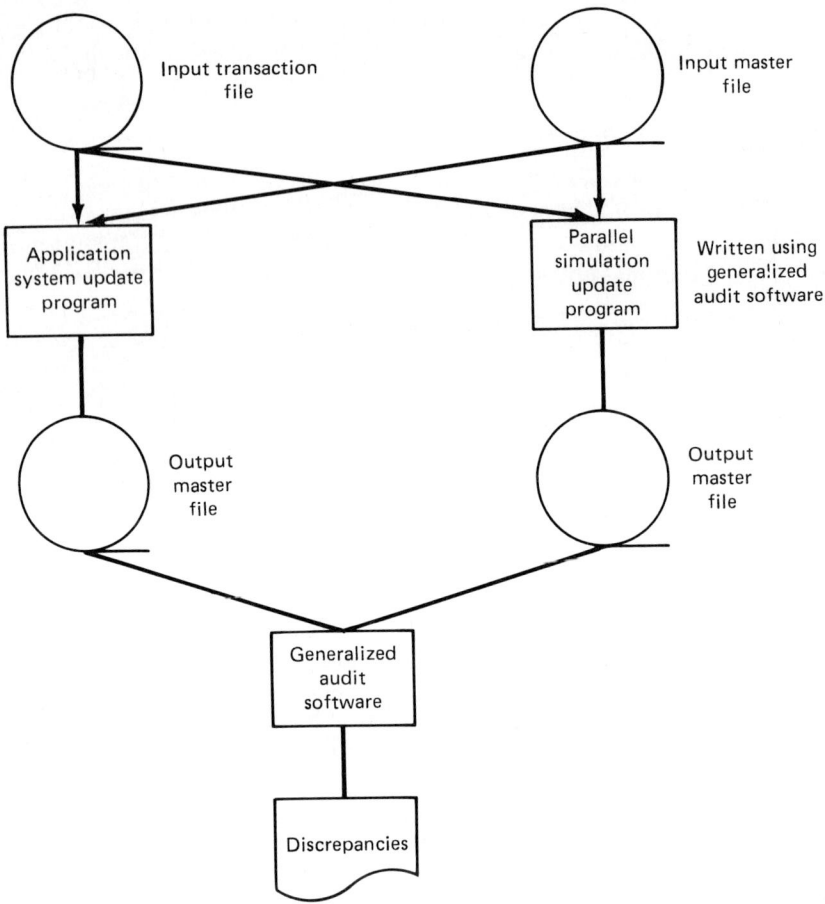

Figure 16.1
Example use of the parallel simulation technique.

Examine the Existence of the Entities the Data Purports to Represent

Data may exist, be accurate, complete, and consistent; however, it may have no real world correspondence. It may represent a bogus insurance policy or an inventory item that no longer exists. The auditor must determine the existence of entities that the data purports to describe.

The statistical sampling capabilities of audit software allow the auditor to investigate the existence of the entities described by the data. The auditor can use the software to automatically generate confirmation notices for accounts receivable, select inventory for observation, circularize creditors for accounts payable, etc. Further, the software can print reports to facilitate the sampling process; for example, for observation purposes sort inventory items selected in the sample by their physical location. The statistical sampling capabilities of audit software allow the auditor to make a probabilistic statement about the existence of the assets and equities that the data describes.

Undertake Analytical Review

Analytical review is the process of obtaining key ratios and totals from an organization's data for comparison with previous years' ratios and totals or industrywide ratios and totals. The information obtained from analytical review is used to support or question preliminary audit conclusions based on system reviews and other substantive tests.

Generalized audit software supports analytical review in several ways. It can be used to extract data required for analytical review and prepare various ratios and totals. If the package provides regression analysis capabilities, it can be used to examine firm and industry trends. It can be used to extract and prepare information in suitable form for input into other financial analysis and modeling packages.

FUNCTIONAL LIMITATIONS

To use generalized audit software effectively and efficiently, the auditor must understand both the capabilities and the limitations of the software. The following sections examine three limitations of generalized audit software that cause it to be only a partial solution to the auditor's problems with evidence collection for computer systems. These deficiencies are:

1 Generalized audit software permits only ex post auditing and not concurrent auditing.

2 Only limited capabilities exist for verifying processing logic.

3 It is difficult to determine the application system's propensity for error using generalized audit software.

Ex Post Auditing Only

Generalized audit software enables evidence to be collected only on the state of an application system after the fact. The software examines the quality of data after it has been processed. Even if the auditor uses parallel simulation, the results produced by the parallel simulation program are checked against a set of existing results produced by the application system. Thus, some time lag exists between an application system error occurring and its identification. In some cases this elapsed time may be substantial if the application system is not audited on a regular basis.

For some types of systems the timely identification of errors may be critical. Consider, for example, a situation where multiple online users access a shared database. Unless an error in a data item is discovered quickly, it may permeate the database and cause several incorrect decisions to be made. It is important to quickly identify and correct the error. Chapter 19 discusses the use of concurrent auditing techniques that permit evidence to be collected, and sometimes evaluated, at the same time as system processing occurs. The auditor must use specialized audit software rather than generalized audit software to implement these techniques.

Limited Ability to Verify Processing Logic

In general, the tests performed with generalized audit software involve "live" data; that is, data captured and processed by the application system. The limitations of using live data for testing application systems are well-known. The data may not test the exceptional condition that occurs. It is important to know whether the application system will handle this condition. To overcome this problem, parallel simulation can be used with test data as input to both the application system and the parallel simulation program. Chapter 18 further discusses these matters.

Limited Ability to Determine Propensity for Error

Systems can be designed and implemented in a manner that allows them, at least to some extent, to cope with change. Alternatively, they can be designed and implemented so they are inflexible and degenerate quickly when change occurs. For example, writing programs using a structured programming discipline permits programs to be modified quickly in light of change. The ability of the system to cope with change is a concern of the auditor. The auditor can obtain little evidence on this issue by using generalized audit software. The evidence must be obtained in other ways: reviewing the management control framework, examining system designs and program code, etc.

INSTALLATION/AUDIT GROUP MATURITY ISSUES

There is some constancy in the usefulness of generalized audit software for the external auditor. The external auditor continually confronts different information processing environments where a need exists for software having generalized capabilities to cope with these different environments. For the internal auditor, however, the usefulness of generalized audit software may change over time. Audit needs may not remain constant for two reasons. First, the computer installation's life cycle imposes changes on the means of achieving audit objectives for the installation. Second, the internal EDP audit group itself experiences a life cycle throughout which the needs and capabilities of the group change.

Impact of the Installation Life Cycle

Chapter 4 discussed the phases in the life cycle of a computer installation: initiation, expansion, formalization, and maturity. Two aspects of the life cycle impact the audit group's tasks and the usefulness of generalized audit software: (a) the changing types of systems developed by the installation throughout its life cycle, and (b) the changing levels of control exercised by management over the activities of the installation.

As the installation matures, the systems it develops and maintains change in two ways. First, the systems tend to stabilize. Second, there is a tendency to move toward more complex systems: database management systems, online realtime systems, data communications systems. As systems stabilize, there are fewer problems for the auditor in coping with changed file structures, record formats, etc., and the audit objectives for the systems also stabilize. This increased stability may motivate the auditor to develop specialized audit software so the overheads incurred by the installation because of the audit function are reduced. As a further motivation toward using specialized audit software, the usefulness of ex post auditing declines in more complex information processing environments. There is a greater need for concurrent auditing to identify errors on a timely basis.

Maturity also means control objectives for systems stabilize. During the formalization phase, the controls absent from application systems during the expansion phase are built into systems. The auditor has increasing involvement in the system development life cycle to provide guidance on the design of controls. Thus, the auditor has more scope for designing controls and performing novel tests on these controls.

Impact of the Audit Group Life Cycle

As discussed in Chapter 3, the audit group also experiences a life cycle consisting of three phases: initiation, expansion, and maturity. Two aspects of this life cycle impact the usefulness of audit software: (a) the increasing stability of control objectives for application systems, and (b) the growing capabilities of the EDP audit group.

Generalized audit software is most useful during the early stages of the group's life cycle. At this time, control objectives for application systems are unclear and the group's computer or audit expertise may be low. The group may be subject to pressures to institute EDP audit procedures quickly. In the past it has been common for management to respond to crisis situations by setting up an EDP audit group. Generalized audit software provides a means for the audit group to respond quickly to demands for application system audits. The group can gain access quickly to data and change audit programs in light of experience or changing audit objectives.

However, when the audit group matures, its tasks, objectives, standards, and expertise have stabilized. The group may be carrying out efficiency auditing as well as effectiveness auditing. Application system audits are conducted on a regular basis. The group seeks to reduce the overhead costs caused by auditing so it develops specialized audit software to take over the functions previously performed by generalized audit software.

MANAGING A GENERALIZED AUDIT SOFTWARE APPLICATION

Managing a generalized audit software application closely follows the steps needed for properly managing the development of any software project. Since these steps have been discussed extensively in Chapter 6, the following sections provide only a brief discussion of their applicability to the management of an audit software application.

There are five steps involved in managing an audit software application:

1 Feasibility analysis and planning
2 Application design
3 Coding and testing
4 Operation
5 Evaluation and documentation of results

Feasibility Analysis and Planning

When an auditor recognizes a potential opportunity for using audit software, feasibility analysis should be undertaken to see if the likely benefits will exceed the costs. The likely benefits depend on the audit objectives that the audit software application will help achieve. For example, audit software may be used to extract a statistical sample for substantive testing. The value of the substantive test in part depends on the assessed reliability of the internal control system. If the internal control system is weak, the value of the substantive test is higher than if the internal control system is very strong.

When considering the costs of an audit software application, some of the factors to be considered are:

Cost factor	Explanation
Adequacy of Installation Documentation	Substantial costs can be incurred through the installation having incomplete or inaccurate documentation of its systems and files. The auditor may code up an audit software program incorrectly, undertake useless runs because record formats have been changed, etc.
Complexity of Application System and Files	If the application system is complex, coding up a parallel simulation program using audit software may be costly. Some complex file structures or record formats present access problems for audit software. These problems may take substantial time to overcome.
Labor Costs for Auditor	These costs are for the auditor's time expended through all stages of the audit software application.
Technical and Administrative Advice	Besides the auditor, other personnel may expend time on the application. The auditor may need technical or administrative advice from installation personnel.
Computing Costs	These costs include testing and operating costs, running dump utilities to examine the format of records on a file, etc.

Supplies	These costs include punch cards, tapes, stationery such as confirmation forms, and forms for documenting the application.

Once estimates of costs and benefits have been obtained, a budget and a timetable should be prepared. Decisions then can be made on whether the application should proceed and whether resource deficiencies exist.

Application Design

This stage involves the detailed design of the audit software application. The major steps are:

Design step	Explanation
Obtain Detailed Understanding of Installation Application System	This understanding can be obtained through reviewing the application system documentation, flowcharting the application system, preparing decision tables, etc.
Design Output Reports Required	The output reports constitute some of the working papers for the audit. It is critical to see all the information required for the audit is output in a convenient form.
Prepare File Definitions	The files to be accessed and any work files to be created must be defined.
Define the Logic of the Audit Software Program	The logic should be flowcharted or described in decision tables.
Define Supplementary Data Needed	Reference (look-up) tables for the audit software may have to be designed.
Prepare a Test Plan	Testing may be undertaken using a test deck or live data. Chapter 18 discusses the various techniques for testing programs.
Desk Check Logic	When the logic of the audit software application has been designed, it should be desk-checked to see if audit objectives are met.

Once the design has been prepared, it should be reviewed and evaluated against the budget and timetable prepared during the feasibility analysis stage.

Coding and Testing

After the design has been prepared, the preprinted generalized audit software specification sheets are completed. On these sheets the auditor describes the commands necessary to invoke the functions provided in the software. Any data (constants) the software needs for processing also must be described. Before keypunching the sheets, they should be desk-checked to see they comply with the design specifications.

After the specification sheets have been punched, they are input to the audit software package, which checks the accuracy of syntax and certain semantics. The package produces an error and diagnostics report, and the auditor must correct the problems identified before proceeding. When the package produces no further diagnostics, the auditor can undertake test runs to check the accuracy of the processing logic specified. Logic errors then must be corrected.

Operation

Once the coding and testing stage is complete, the auditor should make a final check to see no changes have been made to the application system that would impact the audit software program; for example, a change to a record format. The processing time schedule then must be confirmed with the operations manager of the installation and the audit software application run.

Evaluation and Documentation of Results

Upon obtaining the audit software reports, the output should be reviewed to check for any errors and determine whether audit objectives have been attained. Respecification and rerunning of the program may be necessary.

The documentation and results must be incorporated into the audit work papers along with any suggestions for improvements in future runs. The costs and benefits of the application should be compared with the budget. Finally, any files created that may be needed for future use should be secured.

ACCESSING COMPLEX DATA STRUCTURES

Recently, one of the problems confronting the auditor using generalized audit software is gaining access to more complex data structures than sequential, index sequential, and random structures. Typically, this problem has arisen when the auditor must gain access to the data maintained by a database management system. Database management systems use a variety of data structures, some of which are complex: tree, network, inverted list, and multilist (for a discussion of these structures, see Martin [1975]).

Accessing Methods: Advantages and Limitations

Litecky and Weber [1974] identify three methods of using generalized audit software to access complex data structures, especially those maintained by a database management system:

1 Extract a sequential file for use with generalized audit software.
2 Use generalized interface routines to map the more complex data structures into the simpler data structures used by generalized audit software.
3 Include specialized access routines in generalized audit software that can handle complex data structures.

These solutions also can be applied to situations where the complex data structures are maintained by a procedure-oriented language such as COBOL. An installation does not always use the facilities of a database management system.

Extracting a Sequential File Rather than directly access complex data structures, the auditor can have an intermediate file prepared for use with generalized audit software. The facilities of the database management system or a file utility can be used to restructure data in a complex data structure as a flat file (Figure 16.2). Records on the file contain only data relevant for the auditor's purposes.

The primary advantage of this approach is its simplicity. Further, it may be the only viable approach for an external auditor to use when the generalized audit software package will not operate on a client's hardware/software configuration. This is a problem as several database management systems oper-

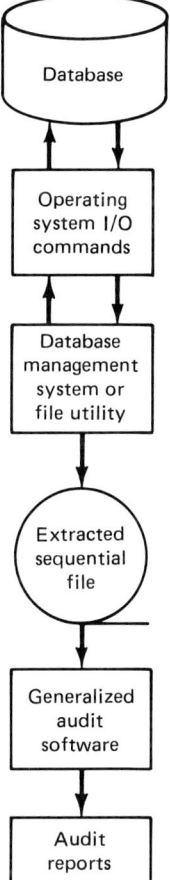

Figure 16.2
Extracting a sequential file from complex data structures for use by generalized audit software.

ate on a wider variety of hardware/software configurations than many generalized audit software packages.

The approach has several disadvantages. First, unless the auditor develops the routine for extracting the sequential file, there is a risk the integrity of data on the file has been violated. For example, generalized audit software might be used to prepare confirmations from the file. Asset records purposely not included on the file would not be confirmed. Second, the auditor does not take advantage of processing efficiencies offered by the data structures; for example, faster access to records through indexes and pointers. Third, the auditor loses a means of obtaining a deeper understanding of the installation's database management system and its application systems. By dealing directly with complex data structures, the auditor obtains a better appreciation of the problems posed for data integrity by the structures and the problems faced by the user in accessing and maintaining the structures.

Using Generalized Interface Routines One means commonly used to access complex data structures maintained by some database management systems is generalized interface routines. These routines are called host language extensions and have been built to obviate the need for programmers to write the programming code necessary to access and maintain complex data structures. To access a data structure, the program calls the routine, supplies record identification and access parameters, and the routine simply "presents" the program with the retrieved record. For addition, modification, or deletion activities, the program again supplies the change parameters to the routine, and the routine carries out the required maintenance to the data structure. The most commonly used database management systems, TOTAL, IMS, SYSTEM 2000, ADABAS, and IDMS, all provide host language extension facilities for programming languages such as COBOL and FORTRAN. Several audit software packages now have "libraries" of host language extensions for the major database management systems. These libraries are maintained by the audit software vendor. Figure 16.3 shows the overall approach.

Even if a database management system is not used, providing the installation develops and uses standard sets of access routines across application systems, these routines can be used by generalized audit software to access complex data structures. It is only when different application systems have their own specialized access routines that problems arise for the auditor who uses audit software.

The primary advantage of this approach is that the auditor through the host language extensions gains direct access to the database. An intermediate file does not have to be created. The auditor gains a better appreciation of integrity and usage problems experienced with the data structures.

The primary disadvantage surrounds some awkward and unwieldy query processing that can result with tree and network data structures. For generalized audit software to be capable of performing queries on trees and networks, these structures must be flattened. The method to be used for flattening

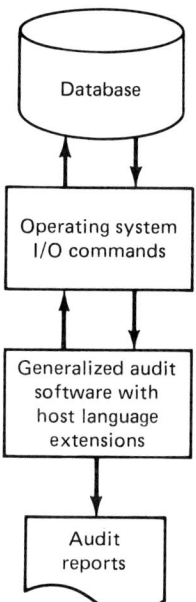

Figure 16.3
Including host language extensions in generalized audit software to access complex data structures.

the structure and specifying the query on the flattened structure can be a difficult problem. The whole issue of the relationship between the data structure and the query language that operates on the data structure is a complex issue and it is left for further study. Weber [1977] provides an extended discussion of this issue in an audit context.

Using Specialized Access Routines In some cases, for the auditor to be able to use generalized audit software to directly access complex data structures, specialized access routines have to be included in the audit software package. This occurs under two situations. First, the installation does not use a standard set of access routines or a database management system to maintain the data structures. Specialized access routines are embedded in the application system. For example, a COBOL program maintains its own indexes and pointers for the multilist file that it updates. Second, the database management system being used by the installation is a self-contained database management system; that is, a system that does not provide host language (programmer) facilities, only nonprogramming generalized facilities. Thus, the access routines are built into the database management system, often regarded as proprietary by the system vendor, and generally unavailable for use. Everest and Weber [1977] discuss these systems more fully and provide a list of available systems.

Figure 16.4 shows this solution method for accessing complex data structures. Its primary advantage is processing efficiency. If the auditor frequently audits critical application systems containing specialized access routines, the audit software vendor may be requested to incorporate these access routines

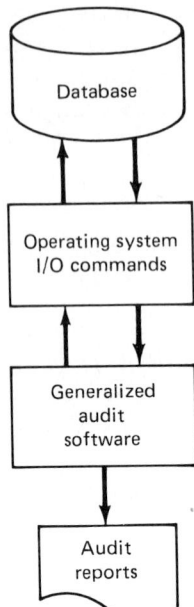

Figure 16.4
Including specialized access routines in generalized audit software to access complex data structures.

into the software. Alternatively, if the audit software package provides a user own-coding routine call facility, the access routines may be invoked using this facility.

There are several disadvantages of using this method. First, in the case of self-contained database management systems, the vendor may not supply the information necessary for the modifications. Second, the modifications may be costly and perhaps only relevant to a single application system. Third, the auditor is responsible for ensuring the access routines are updated if they are changed.

Other alternatives for accessing the data should be considered. The sequential file approach can be used. In the case of self-contained database management systems, many of the functions required by the auditor are available in the system's generalized retrieval language (see, further, Weber [1975]). The auditor should consider using the database management system itself rather than generalized audit software for evidence collection purposes.

Auditor Independence Issues

When the auditor does not use an independently controlled generalized audit software package to directly access complex data structures, but instead has a sequential file extracted or uses database management software for evidence collection purposes, questions sometimes are raised about whether the auditor maintains independence. Some would argue the auditor compromises independence by relying on the installation's software. This software may have been modified so the auditor can no longer rely on the integrity of the data obtained using the software.

This argument is false for two reasons. First, independence is well-accepted as a "state of mind." It is an independence in attitude that is required. Second, even if the auditor uses generalized audit software with host language extensions, or generalized audit software with embedded access routines to access the database, reliance still is placed on certain of the installation's software; namely, the integrity of the host language extensions and the integrity of the operating system input/output routines. In the end, to ensure the integrity of the evidence collection process, the auditor would have to stop and restart the hardware, load an independently controlled operating system, an independently controlled generalized audit software package, and perhaps an independently controlled database management system. Even this is not an inviolable process. The microcode of the machine could have undergone unauthorized modifications.

Jenkins and Weber [1976] suggest three methods that can be used to determine whether critical installation software has been modified:

Method	Explanation
Blueprint Approach	Obtain from the vendor a copy of the installation's operating system and database management system object code, and compare this with the version used by the client to determine discrepancies. Some are unwilling to supply such "blueprints."
Hash Total Approach	The auditor obtains a hash total of the object code of the installation's critical software and rechecks this total each time the software is used.
Test Data Approach	Test data is developed to test the critical modules in the database management system or operating system to see if their integrity has been violated.

These approaches are not trouble-free. The installation may make legitimate modifications to an operating system or database management system to improve efficiency or provide facilities not existing in the software. Thus, blueprints and hash totals must be updated and test data must be modified.

In deciding which approach to adopt to access complex data structures, the auditor should consider the costs and benefits of each approach. All have their various advantages and disadvantages. Different approaches may be appropriate at different times.

PURCHASING AUDIT SOFTWARE

The purchase cost of most audit software packages is not very high. A basic package costs as low as $5,000. However, optional modules may be available with the purchase; for example, interfaces to different database management

TABLE 16.2
SOME MAJOR GENERALIZED AUDIT SOFTWARE PACKAGES AND THEIR VENDORS

Package	Vendor	Package	Vendor
ASI-ST	Applications Software, Inc. 21515 Hawthorne Boulevard Torrance, Calif. 90503	AUDITPAK II	Coopers & Lybrand 1251 Avenue of the Americas New York, N. Y. 10020
ASK-360	Whinney Murray 57 Chiswell Street London, ED1 4SY, England	AUDIT REPORTER	Burroughs Corporation World Headquarters 1 Burroughs Place P.O. Box 418 Detroit, Mich. 48232
AUDASSIST	Alexander Grant & Co. One First National Plaza Chicago, Ill. 60670	(AUTRONIC-16 (AUTRONIC-32	Ernst & Whinney 1300 Union Commerce Building Cleveland, Ohio 44115
(AUDEX (AUDEX 100	Arthur Andersen & Co. 69 West Washington Street Chicago, Ill. 60602	BASE	Computrol, Inc. 10820 Sunset Office Drive St. Louis, Mo. 63127
AUDIT	U.S. Department of Commerce Springfield, Va. 22151	CARS	Cullinane Corporation Wellesley Office Park 20 William Street Wellesley, Mass. 02181
AUDITAID	Seymour Schneidman & Associates 405 Park Avenue New York, N. Y. 10022	COMPUTER FILE ANALYZER	Price Waterhouse & Co. 1251 Avenue of the Americas New York, N. Y. 10020
AUDITAPE	Deloitte, Haskins & Sells 1114 Avenue of the Americas New York, N. Y. 10036	DYL-AUDIT	Dylakor Software Systems, Inc. 16255 Ventura Boulevard Encino, Calif. 91436
AUDITEC	Carleton Corporation 44 Bromfield Street Boston, Mass. 02108	EDP-AUDITOR	Cullinane Corporation Wellesley Office Park 20 William Street Wellesley, Mass. 02181
AUDITFIND	Dataskil Reading Bridge House Reading, England		

CHAPTER 16: GENERALIZED AUDIT SOFTWARE **421**

Package	Vendor	Package	Vendor
EDP-Auditor/3	Cullinane Corporation Wellesley Office Park 20 William St. Wellesley, Mass. 02181	SCORE-AUDIT	Programming Methods, Inc. 1301 Avenue of the Americas New York, N. Y. 10019
HEWCAS	Department of Health, Education & Welfare Audit Office of the Assistant Secretary, Comptroller 330 Independence Avenue Washington, D.C. 20201	STRATA	Touche Ross & Co. 1633 Broadway New York, N. Y. 10019
		S/2190	Peat, Marwick, Mitchell & Co. 345 Park Avenue New York, N. Y. 10022
MARK IV AUDIT	Informatics, Inc. 21050 Vanowen Street Canoga Park, Calif. 91303	THE AUDIT ANALYZER	Program Products, Inc. 95 Chestnut Ridge Road Montvale, N. J. 07645
PANAUDIT	Pansophic Systems, Inc. 709 Enterprise Drive Oak Brook, Ill. 60521		
PROBE	Computer Resources Co. 23 Leroy Avenue Darien, Conn. 06820		

systems. These options usually cost extra. The final cost of a package can range up to about $30,000.

Because of the relatively low cost of purchasing an audit software package, there is a temptation to regard the purchase as an unimportant matter. However, the purchase cost is not the only cost of using audit software. If the "best" audit software package has not been acquired, there are the ongoing opportunity costs of not having acquired an audit software package that allows the most effective and efficient auditing. Further, some audit groups have found they need to purchase more than one audit software package to accomplish their audit objectives. The level of effort devoted to the evaluation and acquisition of an audit software package should be appropriate for the expected costs, both purchase and opportunity costs.

A large number of generalized software packages is available for purchase by the auditor for use as audit software. Some of these packages were developed specifically as audit software. Others are generalized retrieval packages that auditors have found useful for audit purposes. Table 16.2 lists some of the packages available. The following sections discuss the major differences existing among the packages and describe the steps that should be undertaken when purchasing the software (see, also, Wilkinson [1978]).

Major Differences among Audit Software

Audit software packages differ on three bases: (*a*) semantics, (*b*) syntax, and (*c*) operating environment. The semantics of the software are the functions that the software can perform. The syntax of the software is the set of rules governing the combination of words or terms used to activate the software. The operating environment is the hardware/software configuration on which the software will run.

Semantics There is a large number of functions common across audit software packages. However, two areas of differences exist. First, some software provide generalized functions tailored for specific industries; for example, banking or insurance. Second, some software provide capabilities for accessing complex data structures.

Industry specific audit software is now starting to emerge. It takes the form of a generalized audit software package modified to better suit the industry or an audit software package specifically written for the industry. For example, one audit software package written specifically for the banking industry provides generalized functions that check for a low or zero interest rate in an account record, overdrawn accounts, dormant accounts, incorrect loan payment schedules, and suspected kiting. (Kiting involves a customer drawing a check against uncollected funds in an account.) The auditor simply activates these functions by supplying parameter values; for example, the number of months of inactivity required before an account is considered dormant.

Some of the optional modules that can be acquired with generalized audit software packages are interfaces to database management systems and interfaces to other special purpose packages that use complex file structures. For example, some audit software packages provide interfaces to bill-of-materials packages used for manufacturing applications. Bill-of-materials packages typically use complex data structures such as networks.

Syntax The syntax of audit software takes two basic forms (see, also, Adams and Mullarkey [1972]). First, it may require the auditor simply to answer a set of questions in checklist form. Second, to accomplish a task it may require the auditor to undertake some coding in the audit software language.

The first syntax form is the higher level syntax form and the easiest to use. It may involve the auditor giving a yes or no response to a question; for example, should a field be totaled? It may involve the auditor supplying parameter values for a predefined function; for example, defining the class intervals for frequency analysis. Three examples of this syntax form are:

1 SORT REQUIRED (Y OR N) ☐
    35

(Explanation: The auditor inserts a Y or N in the box and this value will be punched in column 35 of a card.)

2 POPULATION SIZE ☐☐☐☐☐☐☐☐☐☐
                  41   50

SAMPLE SIZE ☐☐☐☐☐☐☐☐
             51   58

(Explanation: For a statistical sampling routine, the auditor supplies the population size and sample size required.)

3 CONFIRMATIONS (Circle One)

| A | Positive Reply |
| B | Negative Reply |

36

(Explanation: The auditor chooses whether the confirmation notices should be printed in positive form or negative form.)

The second syntax form is a lower level syntax and more difficult to use. However, it provides greater flexibility in allowing different audit tasks to be accomplished. It is used, typically, to specify selection expressions in terms of Boolean and relational operators and for arithmetic expressions. Two examples of this syntax are:

1 | W | 0 | 4 | M | U | L | W | 0 | 5 | W | 0 | 6 |
  | 1 | | 3 | 4 | | | 6 | 7 | | 9 | 10| | 12

(Explanation: Field W04 is multiplied by field W05 and the result is placed in a work field labeled W06.)

2 SELECT: PAY.GT.'15000'.AND.STATUS.EQ.'MGR'
(Explanation: This is a free format selection expression containing Boolean and relational operators.)

Typically, audit software packages use both forms of syntax. If the package is intended for use by the auditor with little computer knowledge, it will contain more of the first syntax form. Conversely, if the package is intended for use by a computer audit specialist, it will contain more of the second syntax form. The second syntax form allows more audit tasks to be performed. Also, it usually permits greater processing efficiencies to be attained. However, this is not always the case. An industry-specific audit software package may process more efficiently because unneeded functions have been eliminated. It may also use mainly the first syntax form because flexibility is not a major requirement.

Operating Environment In general, the greater the variety of hardware/software configurations on which an audit software package will run, the greater will be its processing inefficiencies. Vendors of audit software have made one of two design choices. Some have designed and implemented their packages to run on only a few makes of machines; namely, those makes most often used for accounting applications—IBM, Burroughs. To attain processing efficiency, they have written their packages in the assembly code of these machines. Other vendors have designed and implemented their packages to run on a wide variety of configurations. Consequently, they have written their packages in a high-level language—ANS COBOL. The tradeoff is portability versus efficiency. Whether or not portability is a critical requirement depends on the needs of the audit group. Internal auditors may be concerned only with having a package that will operate on their particular hardware/software configuration. External auditors need packages that will operate on diverse configurations.

Selecting a Package

The steps that should be followed in selecting an audit software package are the same as those that should be followed in selecting any software package. Wooldridge [1973] provides an extensive discussion of the methodology. There are two major steps involved: (*a*) evaluation, and (*b*) acquisition. The depth in which these steps are carried out depends on the likely benefits and costs of using the software. The selection process itself can be costly. It must be tempered by cost-benefit considerations.

Evaluation The objective of the evaluation stage is to select a generalized audit software package that best meets the needs of the audit group. The following steps should be undertaken:

1 *Plan and Initiate the Project* This step involves setting up the project team to undertake the information gathering and information evaluation phases and preparing a budget for the project—required completion date, labor, overheads, etc.

2 *Determine Audit Needs* The project group must determine the needs of the audit group that the package must satisfy; for example, functions required, hardware/software configurations on which the package must operate, complexity of language syntax permitted.

3 *Determine Constraints* Constraints take several forms; for example, the dollar amount available for purchase, limitations on the amount of core and the number of peripherals that the package can use, training time permitted.

4 *Collect and Evaluate Information on Available Packages* The purpose of this step is to select from the list of packages that may satisfy the needs and constraints, those that will be subject to an in-depth evaluation. Information on packages can be obtained from vendors. At various times surveys of audit software are published (see, for example, Neumann [1977]). Different software information houses (e.g., Auerbach and Datapro) provide feature analyses and user survey reports on some audit software packages. Existing users of a package should be consulted. A feature comparison checklist must be prepared and a set of feasible alternatives selected.

5 *In-Depth Study* The in-depth study determines in detail a package's strengths and weaknesses. Detailed information on a package must be gathered and evaluated. A technical evaluation must be carried out. Benchmark tests may be necessary. Proposed contract terms must be understood and evaluated.

6 *Cost-Benefit Analysis* After the in-depth study, the costs and benefits of the packages can be evaluated and a final selection made.

Acquisition Acquisition of an audit software package involves two steps: (*a*) negotiating a contract with the vendor, and (*b*) final acceptance testing. The contract is a critical element in the final purchase decision. It must specify agreements on prices, payments, delivery, installation, modifications, maintenance, improvements, training, use, penalties, liabilities, termination, etc. Legal advice should be sought if necessary.

In some cases an acceptance test is not necessary. Satisfactory benchmark tests may have been carried out. A free-trial period may be available or a short-term lease/rental contract has been negotiated. If there are any major doubts still remaining about the performance of the package, an acceptance test provides a means of confirming or dispelling these doubts.

SUMMARY

Generalized audit software provides an important means for the auditor to gain access to data maintained on computer media. However, the effective and efficient use of audit software requires an understanding of both its capabilities and limitations. The benefits and costs of using audit software depend in part on the maturity of the audit group and the maturity of the computer installation being audited. The benefits and costs also depend on how well an audit software project is managed.

Accessing complex data structures may present some problems for using generalized audit software. However, alternative methods for accessing these structures have been developed. The choice of a method is situation dependent.

When purchasing generalized audit software the audit group should follow the standard procedures that are now well-established for purchasing any software package. Though the different audit software packages have many common features, there are sufficient differences to warrant careful evaluation before a purchase decision is made.

REVIEW QUESTIONS

16.1. Briefly discuss the motivations for developing generalized software specifically for audit purposes. Even though generalized retrieval software already existed before audit software was developed, why did auditors prefer to develop their own software packages?

16.2. What is a generalized audit software package?

16.3. Without using the examples in the chapter, give two examples of how each of the following functional capabilities of audit software might be used by the auditor:
  a. file reorganization
  b. statistical
  c. arithmetic
  d. stratification and frequency analysis

16.4. Briefly explain the difference between a Boolean operator and a relational (conditional) operator used in a selection expression for generalized audit software. Be sure to explain their different purposes from an audit perspective.

16.5. What are the auditor's purposes in using generalized audit software to examine the quality of data maintained on application system files?

16.6. Briefly explain the parallel simulation technique. What is the purpose of using parallel simulation? Outline some of the advantages and disadvantages of using this technique for audit purposes.

16.7. If the auditor confronts a hardware/software configuration on which available generalized audit software will not run, how can the activities normally carried out with audit software be accomplished?

16.8. Why does generalized audit software have only limited capabilities for verifying the processing logic of an application system and the propensity of the application system for error?

16.9. Discuss the advantages of using generalized audit software when an organization first forms an EDP audit group. What factors may cause a decline in the usefulness of generalized audit software as the audit group matures?

16.10. Briefly discuss the impact that complex systems have on the usefulness of generalized audit software.

16.11. When using audit software, why is it important that the installation personnel responsible for the application system being audited be consulted and their cooperation solicited?

16.12. Briefly outline the contents of the audit work papers for an audit software application. Why is it important that the application be documented properly?

16.13. As the manager of an audit software application, what factors would you look for as warnings that the costs of completing the application may exceed the benefits and/or the budget?

16.14. When might it be necessary to keep the files created during an audit software application for a future period's work? Give an example.

16.15. Briefly explain what is meant by the host language extensions of a database management system. How can host language extensions be used in generalized audit software to gain access to complex data structures such as trees and network?

16.16. When confronted with the problem of using generalized audit software to access complex data structures, for each of the following solutions give an example of where you would choose the solution in preference to the two others:
   a. extract a sequential file
   b. use generalized interface routines
   c. use specialized access routines
   Briefly justify your selection.

16.17. Some auditors claim that to maintain independence an auditor must always use an independently controlled audit software package to access a database. Why is this a moot point?

16.18. Audit software must interface with other software, for example, the operating system, to carry out its functions. Briefly describe some techniques the auditor can use to determine whether unauthorized modifications have been made to this software. Outline the advantages and disadvantages of each technique.

16.19. Even though audit software may be relatively inexpensive to purchase, why is it important that alternative packages be evaluated carefully before a purchase decision is made?

16.20. Select two currently available audit software packages and list their differences on the basis of:
   a. syntax
   b. semantics
   c. operating environment

16.21. Find an industry-specific audit software package and list those functions included in the package that are not available in a generalized audit software package.

16.22. Select a generalized audit software package and try to find information that describes the advantages and limitations of the package.

16.23. Briefly describe the activities you would carry out during the in-depth study of an audit software package that you are considering for purchase.

EXERCISES AND CASES

16.1. Livalife Insurance is a large insurance company with offices scattered throughout the United States and over 1000 independent agents. As a member of the external audit team, during the year-end work you are called to a meeting with your manager. He explains that he is concerned about the activities of one agent who seems to have submitted an abnormal number of change of address forms for her clients. All the change of address forms give a single new address; namely, the agent's home address. On many of the policies taken out by the agent's clients, personal loans have been obtained. Your manager explains that he is concerned that the agent may be illegally obtaining policy loans on her clients' policies, unbeknown to her clients.

Required: Explain how you could use generalized audit software to find out whether the agent has been illegally taking out policy loans on her clients' policies. Assuming the agent has been acting illegally, what controls would you recommend instituting to prevent this type of fraud happening again?

16.2. For the following inventory file, list the audit objectives that you could accomplish using generalized audit software:
  part number
  part name
  part description
  bin location
  unit price
  unit cost
  unit measure
  quantity on hand
  quantity on order
  item activity
  special prices allowed

16.3. For the following fixed assets file, list the audit objectives that you could accomplish using generalized audit software:
  fixed asset number
  fixed asset description
  fixed asset classification
  location
  responsible manager
  maintenance schedule
  purchase price
  purchase data
  vendor information
  depreciation method
  current depreciated value
  salvage value
  depreciation account
  taxable value
  insured value
  insurance vendor

16.4. The following payroll input detail file has been obtained from time card data. List the audit objectives you could accomplish using generalized audit software:

employee number
regular hours
overtime hours
expenses
commission payments
sick time
vacation time
leave time without pay

16.5. Suppose accounting data for a project is maintained in a tree structure of the following form (*Note:* there can be multiple projects, jobs, and transactions):

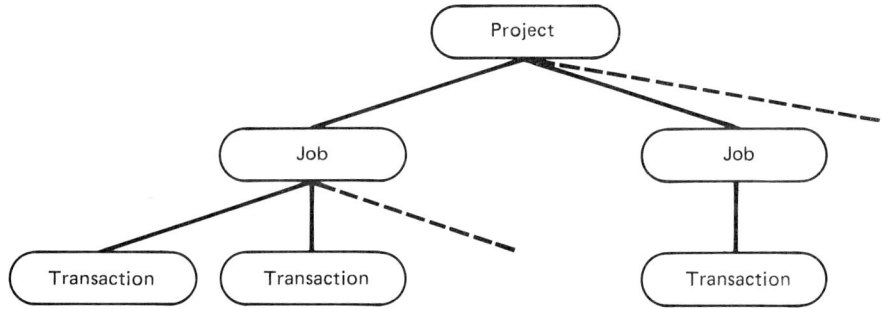

Find a currently available audit software package which will allow access to a tree structure and code up the following query. For project number BC6493, print out any inventory transactions that are less than $50 or greater than $1000 for any jobs numbered between A100 and A199.

16.6. For the previous question, how would you extract a sequential file containing the data you need for your query on the tree structure? Using the audit software package you have selected previously, code up the query again, this time applied to the sequential file you have extracted.

16.7. For the previous two questions, briefly discuss any problems you had in formulating the query under both approaches. Discuss the advantages and disadvantages of each approach.

REFERENCES

Adams, Donald L., and John F. Mullarkey. "A Survey of Audit Software," *Journal of Accountancy* (September 1972), pp. 39–66.

Everest, Gordon C., and Ron Weber. "Data Base Supported Systems and the Auditing Function," *Auerbach Information Management Series: Data Base Management* (Pennsauken, N.J.: Auerbach Publishers, Inc., 1977).

Jenkins, A. Milton, and Ron Weber. "Using DBMS Software as an Audit Tool: The Issue of Independence," *Journal of Accountancy* (April 1976), pp. 67–69.

Litecky, Charles R., and Ron Weber. "The Demise of Generalized Audit Software Packages?" *Journal of Accountancy* (November 1974), pp. 45–48.

Mair, William C. "Parallel Simulation—A Technique for Effective Verification of Computer Programs," *EDPACS* (April 1975), pp. 1–5.

Martin, James. *Computer Database Organization* (Englewood Cliffs, N.J.: Prentice-Hall, Inc., 1975).

Neumann, Albrecht J. *Features of Seven Audit Software Packages—Principles and Capabilities* (Washington, D.C.: U.S. Government Printing Office, 1977), S. D. Catalog No. C13.10:500-13.

Weber, Ron. "Audit Capabilities of Some Database Management Systems," Working Paper MISRC-WP-75-05, Management Information Systems Research Center, University of Minnesota, Minneapolis, Minn., 1975.

———. "Implications of Database Management Systems for Auditing Research," in Barry E. Cushing and Jack L. Krogstad, eds., *Studies in Accounting No. 7: Frontiers of Auditing Research* (Texas: Bureau of Business Research, The University of Texas at Austin, 1977).

Wilkinson, Bryan. "Selecting Audit Software," *EDP Auditing* (Pennsauken, N.J.: Auerbach Publishers, Inc., 1978), Portfolio 73-01-04, pp. 1–12.

Wooldridge, Susan. *Software Selection* (Philadelphia: Auerbach Publishers Inc., 1973).

CHAPTER 17

SYSTEM SOFTWARE AND SPECIALIZED AUDIT SOFTWARE

CHAPTER OUTLINE

SYSTEM SOFTWARE AS AN AUDIT TOOL
    Utility Software and Evidence Collection
    Reasons for Audit Use of Utility Software
    Audit Categorization of Utility Software
    Control of Utility Software
SPECIALIZED AUDIT SOFTWARE AS AN AUDIT TOOL
    Reasons for Developing Specialized Audit Software
    Development and Implementation of Specialized Audit Software
    Control of Specialized Audit Software
SUMMARY
REVIEW QUESTIONS
EXERCISES AND CASES
REFERENCES

Software constitutes a major means of evidence collection for the auditor. The previous chapter examined generalized audit software and its usefulness as an evidence collection tool. This chapter examines how the auditor can use system software and specialized audit software to collect evidence on an application system's ability to maintain data integrity and achieve its objectives efficiently.

SYSTEM SOFTWARE AS AN AUDIT TOOL

There are three reasons why the auditor is interested in system software. First, the extent to which an installation uses system software affects the auditor's assessment of the overall quality of systems within the installation. System software has been developed to facilitate the development and implementation of quality systems. Further, it usually is very reliable software, having been extensively tested by many users on a variety of applications. Second, as Chapter 12 pointed out, the auditor is concerned about the ways in which system software can be used to breach controls in computer systems. Some system software is designed to handle crises situations. It is designed to bypass normal controls (see, further, Perry [1975]). Thus, the auditor is concerned about what system software is used, by whom, when, for what purposes, and the controls that exist over its use. Third, the auditor can use system software to collect evidence about the quality of application systems. It is this last aspect of system software that is the focus of the remaining discussion.

Utility Software and Evidence Collection

Though all types of system software are useful to the auditor from time to time, a subset of system software is especially useful for evidence collection purposes. The programs in this subset often are called *utility* programs. It is difficult to define precisely what constitutes a utility program. However, in general, utility programs have two distinguishing characteristics. First, the functions they perform are less global than those performed by other system software. For example, a sort package usually is called a utility; a compiler usually is not considered to be a utility. Second, as a consequence of the first difference, utilities generally are smaller in size than other system software. However, it must be stressed that there are exceptions to these "rules" for categorization. Ultimately the term "utility software" is imprecise.

Reasons for Audit Use of Utility Software

For any given installation, the extent to which the auditor can use utility software to collect evidence depends in part on the types of utility software available. Most hardware vendors supply a wide range of utilities for use with their machines. However, some of this software is not free. The installation must decide whether or not to purchase it. Further, a large number of independent software vendors actively compete to supply supplementary or replacement software. The availability of system software also depends on other factors; for example, the size of the machine used by the installation. In general, there are fewer utility packages available for minicomputers and microcomputers than the larger machines.

The stimulus to use utility software as an audit tool comes from a number of sources. The following sections discuss some of the major reasons why the auditor may choose to use utility software as a means of collecting evidence.

Unavailability of Generalized Audit Software Most generalized audit software packages have been designed to run on IBM hardware/software configurations. This simply reflects IBM's dominant share of the market in commercial data processing and the difficulties involved in designing and maintaining audit software that will run on a variety of configurations.

However, inevitably auditors have to evaluate installations using hardware/software configurations on which specific audit software will not run. In some countries, for example, Australia, IBM does not dominate the market to the extent it does in the United States. With the rapid growth in the use of minicomputers and microcomputers, the unavailability of generalized audit software that runs on these machines may be a problem confronted increasingly by the auditor (see, also, McHugh [1978]). Further, at least in some cases, it is unlikely generalized audit software vendors will make major attempts to increase the availability of their packages on new hardware/software configurations. Increased availability means increased maintenance costs, decreased efficiency, and a greater risk of the integrity of the software being compromised (see, also, Canadian Institute of Chartered Accountants [1975]). Neither does it seem likely the major machine vendors will implement generalized audit software for their configurations. A task force group within the American Institute of Certified Public Accountants recently developed a set of common computer audit software specifications that they hoped the major machine vendors might implement. There has been little progress toward widespread implementation of these specifications. Thus, for those configurations on which generalized audit software will not run, the auditor either has to develop specialized software or use utility software for evidence collection purposes.

Functional Limitations of Generalized Audit Software With a few exceptions (generally in the statistical sampling and analytical review areas), the set of utility software packages available often provides a wider range of functional capabilities than generalized audit software. Chapter 16 discussed the various functional limitations of audit software: ex post auditing only, limited ability to verify processing logic, limited ability to determine the propensity for error (see, also, Will [1978] and Weber [1978]). With utility software, often these limitations are overcome. For example, utility software exists that permits the collection of audit evidence concurrently with application system running. Utility software includes a number of testing tools (for example, test data generators) that permit verification of processing logic and allow the auditor to determine the likelihood of errors occurring. Unlike generalized audit software, utility software sometimes runs in privileged mode to gather various evidence; for example, data relevant to assessing operational efficiency.

Efficiency Considerations Because audit software is generalized software, often it consumes more resources to perform a task than the utility software written for a particular hardware/software configuration. In some situations the costs of this inefficiency may be unacceptable. Large volumes of data may have to be processed so the increased costs become substantial. If the auditor uses software to perform a task repeatedly, again, over time the sum total of the costs caused by the inefficiency may be substantial. Though utility software may be somewhat more difficult to use than generalized audit software, the auditor may be unable to accept the increased costs caused by the processing inefficiency of generalized audit software.

Facilitates Use of Other Audit Tools Utility software includes programs that sort data, merge files, copy files, delete files, dump files, convert files produced by one machine into a form suitable for reading by another machine, restructure files, etc. These functions facilitate the use of other evidence collection tools. The following examples show how utility programs can be used to assist generalized audit software applications:

1 If generalized audit software is to compare data on two files, the files must be sorted in the same order.
2 Generalized audit software may be able to read only a small number of files simultaneously. Data on several files can be merged.
3 Generalized audit software may be unable to traverse a network data structure. A utility can be used to flatten the network into a sequential file.
4 If generalized audit software will not run on the hardware/software configuration of the installation being audited, a copy of the files to be examined can be made and these files then converted to a form suitable for processing on the hardware/software configuration on which the audit software will run.
5 Several records of a file can be dumped so the auditor can check the format of these records before the audit software application is run.
6 After an audit software run is complete, the work files created can be deleted.

Assists Development of New Audit Tools In some cases specialized audit software is needed for evidence collection purposes (discussed later in the chapter). When these tools must be developed and implemented, the process follows the steps described in Chapter 6. Further, the auditor can use the various software development aids described in Chapter 6 to assist in the production of high-quality software.

Audit Categorization of Utility Software

A major problem often confronting the auditor is identifying utility software that will fulfill an audit purpose. In any installation a large number of utility programs may exist. The documentation for these programs often is scattered and of varying quality. Usually it is written with the programmer rather than the auditor in mind. Thus, in some cases though the software may be well-documented, it may be difficult for the auditor to understand the purposes of the software and how to use the software. Effective and efficient use of utility software may require specialization within the EDP audit team.

To facilitate the EDP auditor's search for appropriate utility software, some machine vendors now have compiled listings of their utility software that are useful for audit purposes (see, for example, IBM [1977]). The software descriptions typically still are oriented toward the programming user and are couched in the jargon of the vendor; however, the listings are a convenient reference aid for the auditor. With the increased security consciousness of recent years, some software vendors also now highlight any audit and control features of their utility software in the documentation they produce for this software.

The following sections categorize and discuss utility software under five headings:

1 Programs that facilitate the auditor's understanding of application systems within an installation

2 Programs that facilitate gathering evidence on the quality of data within an installation

3 Programs that facilitate gathering evidence on the quality of other programs within an installation

4 Programs that facilitate development and implementation of specialized audit software

5 Programs that gather evidence on the efficiency (productivity) of an installation

The categorization scheme used here is not unique; other schemes have been used to classify utility software from an audit perspective (see, for example, Adams [1975]). The scheme below focuses on major functions the auditor will perform. As with most categorization schemes, there is some overlap of categories. Further, many of the programs listed have been discussed in previous chapters or will be discussed further in later chapters; they are listed here to illustrate the nature of the categories and for completeness. Whether or not some of the programs listed should be classified as "utilities" also might be debated. Again, both the terms "utility software" and "system software" are imprecise.

Software to Facilitate System Understanding A major problem confronting the auditor during the evidence gathering phase is the question of how to gain quickly an understanding of the programs and data within the installation being audited. Understanding program logic always has been a problem. However, with the increasing use of database management systems and the move away from sequential, index sequential, and random files to more complex data structures such as trees and networks, understanding data (especially the relationships between data items) is a growing problem.

The standards established by all professional auditing bodies stress the importance of the auditor understanding the system to be audited. The following utilities, designed primarily to assist the programmer maintain documentation on systems, also assist the auditor to understand programs and data within application systems. As a consequence, the use of other evidence collection techniques should be better directed.

Utility	Function
Flowcharter	Produces flowcharts from program source code.
HIPO Charter	Provides automated hierarchy plus input-process-output diagrams. Auditors can request a listing of HIPO charts for a program so they can better understand the functions performed by the program (see, also, Chapter 6).
Hierarchy Charter	Produces hierarchical function charts from structured code. A module and its associated lower level modules are diagrammed. The interfaces between modules (via PERFORMs, GO TOs, etc.) are indicated on the hierarchy chart.
Logic Path Mapper	Shows all the logic paths through a program by referencing paragraph names.
Cross-Reference Lister	Provides cross-reference listings for programs showing where a label (field) is referenced in a program.
Data Structure Charter	Produces charts from the database definition showing the structure of data within the database.
Transaction Profile Analyzer	Analyzes the characteristics of data updating the database; e.g., volume of a particular transaction type.
Data Dictionary	Describes the characteristics of all data items in the database. Facilities exist for selective retrieval of data from the data dictionary.
Text Manager	If system documentation is stored on magnetic media (word processing), text managers allow selective retrieval of text (based on key words) from the documentation.

Software to Facilitate Assessing Data Quality Utility programs that facilitate testing the quality of data within an installation assist the auditor in two ways. First, some utilities allow the auditor to test the quality of the data directly. For example, batch and online query facilities perform the same function as generalized audit software. Second, some utilities facilitate the use of other evidence collection tools. For example, a sort package can be used to order data for report purposes. The following utilities are widely available:

Utility	Function
Query Facility	Batch and online query facilities allow selected retrieval of data from a variety of data structure types.
Data Structure Conversion	Maps one data structure into another; e.g., a tree or network data structure into a flat (sequential) file.

Pointer Validation Utility	Searches storage structures that use pointers for invalid pointers; e.g., child nodes in a network that do not point back to their parent node (see, further, Thomas et al. [1977]).
Data Manipulation Utilities	Perform sundry functions; e.g., sort, merge, copy (selective copy), create, modify, delete, reorganize, format conversion, rename.
Dump/Lister	Printing (sometimes with partial editing) of file contents.
Data Comparison Utility	Compares two sets of data and lists the differences.

Software to Facilitate Assessing Program Quality These utilities allow the auditor to test a program's ability to maintain data integrity. The testing takes two forms. First, the validity of existing program logic is assessed. Second, the ability of the program to withstand abnormal conditions is assessed; for example, data input with severe outlier values can be submitted to the program. The following utilities developed primarily for programmers also assist the auditor to assess program quality:

Utility	Function
Test Data Generator	Automatic generation of test files with data having specified attributes. Various data and storage structures can be generated.
Trace	Batch or online monitoring of the status of programs as they step through various logic paths.
Online Debugging Facility	Permits online changes to object code and activitation of programs at selected start points.
Logic Path Monitor	Indicates whether test data has traversed all logic paths within a program.
Output Analyzer	Examines test output for various conditions; e.g., differences between output produced and a prior version of output.
Network Simulator	Allows batch or online simulation of a communications network without having to use the network hardware/software configuration.
Terminal Simulator	Allows batch simulation of online programs so testing can proceed without the online hardware/software configuration being available.
Test Manager/Driver	Manages the overall testing process for a program or set of programs.
Concurrent Monitor	Captures selected events as application systems are running.
Source/Object Code Comparison Utility	Compares two versions of the source/object code of a program and lists differences.
Change Tracker	Monitors changes to program source code libraries. May be a facility within a librarian package.

Software to Facilitate Program Development Sometimes neither generalized audit software nor utility software can be used for audit evidence collection purposes; generalized audit software may not run on the hardware/software configuration, utility software may not provide the required functions, etc. In these situations the auditor may be forced to develop specialized audit software to perform the evidence collection function. When developing this software the auditor has the same objectives as a programmer: fast, accurate development of a program that performs the required functions.

The utilities listed below have been developed to facilitate the program development process. One factor affecting the choice of a utility is the need for the specialized audit program to run efficiently. Many of the utilities described below facilitate fast, accurate development of code. Sometimes the code generated also may consume resources efficiently. However, in other cases the code produced executes inefficiently or consumes substantial core storage. If the auditor needs a one-off program, the program runs for only a short time, or it is run infrequently, efficiency considerations may be relatively unimportant. However, sometimes the motivation to develop specialized audit software is the need for processing efficiency. In these cases the auditor must be careful to use only those utilities that produce efficient code.

Utility	Function
Shorthand Preprocessor	Allows source code to be written in an abbreviated form.
Macro	Inserts standard code in a program.
Prompter	Supplies a "menu" for compiler option selection or parameter selection. Some prompters have been developed to facilitate structured programming (see, further, IBM [1977]).
Visual Display Utility	Permits abbreviated coding for visual display input and output. Manages a library of mock displays for training or experimental work to find the best formats/language for the displays.
Decision-Table Preprocessor	Converts decision tables into source code.
Library Copy	Copies source code from a library into a program.
Text Editor	Permits parameter-specified modification of source code.
Tidy	Formats source code so it is more readable.
Online Coding Facility	Permits programs to be coded and compiled in an interactive mode.
Report Generators	Simplifies coding of reports.
Language Subset Facility	Restricts source code used to an efficient subset.
Code Optimizer	Operates on the source or object code of a program to remove inefficient code.
Volume Test Facility	Shows the performance of a program under stress.

Software to Facilitate Assessing Operational Efficiency Like the auditor, EDP management is concerned with assessing the operating efficiency of an installation. Consequently, a large number of utilities have been developed to gather and report evidence on how efficiently the hardware and software resources in an installation are being used. Some of these utilities are designed primarily to be used by engineers and system programmers; thus, an auditor may have substantial difficulty understanding the output of these utilities without adequate training in performance monitoring methodologies. However, without the utilities it may be extremely difficult for the auditor to extract and report the data necessary for assessing operating efficiency.

Utilities that facilitate assessing operating efficiency perform three major functions. First, they gather the necessary source data on resource consumption. Second, they calculate statistics that reflect various aspects of operating efficiency on the basis of this source data. Third, they report these statistics in various forms: tables, bar charts, pie charts, histograms, frequency distributions, graphs, etc. Chapter 21 discusses these utilities further; however, some of the major types of performance data collected are:

1. CPU utilization
2. Core storage utilization
3. Secondary storage utilization
4. Channel utilization
5. Communication line utilization
6. Peripheral utilization
7. Task rates
8. Response times
9. Queue lengths
10. I/O buffer excesses and deficiencies
11. I/O concurrency
12. Direct access seek times
13. Paging rates/thrashing
14. Frequency of checkpoints/recovery
15. Storage media read/write errors
16. Effects of changes in memory allocations to tasks
17. Effects of changes in task priorities
18. Deviations from transaction profiles
19. Need for database restructuring/reorganization
20. Performance of hashing algorithms/indexes

Control of Utility Software

The use of utility software for evidence gathering purposes raises the same issues of audit independence discussed previously in Chapter 16 where database management systems were considered as an audit tool. Somehow the auditor must gain assurance the utility software has not been modified in an unauthorized way; for example, by the introduction of a Trojan horse.

If the auditor establishes and maintains an independently controlled library of utility software, there is less likelihood that unauthorized modifications will occur to the software. The library can be protected via access controls, or the auditor can hold the storage medium on which the library resides. For the external auditor the library provides an additional advantage: the audit is not constrained by the availability of utility software in the installation to be audited.

When establishing the library, if possible, the auditor should use software supplied by a third party; for example, the machine vendor. Utility software provided by a third party offers three advantages: (*a*) often it is better documented, (*b*) there is a higher level of assurance it functions correctly, and (*c*) unauthorized code is unlikely to be present in the software. However, utility software often is developed by an installation because of an unfulfilled need or because third-party software runs too inefficiently. Thus, the auditor may be forced to use some utility software developed in-house.

If it is possible for unauthorized modifications to occur to the utility software used by the auditor, several checks can be made to determine whether or not code changes have taken place. Chapter 16 discussed the blueprint approach, the hash total (checksum) approach, and the test data approach. If the installation uses a librarian facility, the audit trail of changes to source code can be examined. The operating system log also can be examined for unauthorized use of utility programs; for example, source code modifications and recompilation. As a further control, the source code can be protected by encrypting the code (see, also, Hoffman [1977]).

However, as Chapter 16 points out, these methods are not foolproof. Though the integrity of the utilities may have been preserved, other system components on which the utilities depend at run time may have been corrupted. For example, unauthorized modifications may have occurred to the operating system or machine microcode. These integrity violations may corrupt the processing integrity of the utility software.

SPECIALIZED AUDIT SOFTWARE AS AN AUDIT TOOL

Specialized audit software is software written in an assembler, procedure-oriented, or problem-oriented language to fulfill a specific set of audit tasks. The term "specialized" does not mean the software performs only a narrow range of functions. It may perform a wider range of functions than some utility programs. Rather, specialized means the auditor has developed and implemented software where the purposes and users of the software are well-defined before the software is written. Typically, when generalized audit software and utility software are developed and implemented, the purposes and users of the software are not as clearly defined.

Reasons for Developing Specialized Audit Software

When auditors require software for evidence collection purposes, they must choose either generalized audit software, utility software, or specialized audit software. The following sections discuss why the auditor may develop, implement, and use specialized audit software instead of using generalized audit software or utility software.

Unavailability of Alternate Software In some cases neither generalized audit software nor utility software is available to the auditor for evidence gathering purposes. Generalized audit software may not run on the hardware/software configuration of the installation being audited. The installation may not have purchased utility software that will fulfill the auditor's needs. A program must be written to perform the task.

Functional Limitations of Alternate Software Though generalized audit software and utility software may be available to the auditor, they may have functional limitations that prevent them fulfilling the auditor's needs. Suppose, for example, the auditor wants to undertake some form of statistical sampling or analytical review, and the necessary logic has not been incorporated in either generalized audit software or utility software. If the task is to be accomplished, specialized audit software must be developed.

Efficiency Considerations Since specialized audit software is written specifically to accomplish defined audit tasks, usually it will run more efficiently than generalized audit software or utility software. Over time the cost savings from this increased efficiency may outweigh expenditures on developing the software, especially if the software is run frequently or processes large volumes of data. For example, in a decentralized organization the software might be developed centrally and distributed to multiple sites for use by auditors at those sites. Alternatively, data may be dispatched to a centralized EDP audit facility—a competency center—where it is processed by a group of EDP auditors having high expertise. In both these cases, because of high run frequencies, small cost savings per run may accumulate to large amounts.

Increased Understanding of System If the functional limitations of generalized audit software or utility software prevent the auditor using this software to obtain evidence about an application system, often it means the application system is complex. One way for the auditor to gain an understanding of the system is to prepare detailed program specifications or write program source code for specialized audit software. Again, for one-off or infrequent audits, the costs may outweigh the benefits of undertaking these activities. However, if the application system is critical and the auditor must evaluate it on an ongoing basis, in-depth understanding of the system is essential to the performance of a high-quality audit.

Opportunity for Easy Implementation Often the development and implementation of specialized audit software will be costly. Further, if there is a high rate of change in either the installation's hardware/software configuration or application systems, specialized audit software may become obsolete quickly and high maintenance costs result. However, opportunities still exist for the easy development and implementation of specialized audit software. For example, some information useful to the auditor also may be useful to the users of the application system. Extracting this information may involve only a relatively simple modification to an existing application system program. Also, if the EDP audit staff has an expert programmer, opportunities for developing small specialized audit programs are more likely to be taken than if no programming expertise exists on the staff.

Increased Auditor Independence/Respect To some extent, if auditors can develop their own software for audit purposes, their independence increases. They have a better understanding of application systems, and they are not dependent on other people for the availability of software for evidence collection purposes. As a consequence, both management and the EDP staff may respect auditors more if they perceive auditors to have sufficient technical competence to write their own programs. Management's confidence in the audit staff performing high-quality work may increase. Improved relationships between the audit staff and data processing personnel also may result.

Development and Implementation of Specialized Audit Software

To ensure high-quality software is produced, the development and implementation of specialized audit software should follow the guidelines discussed in Chapter 6. Auditors at least must take responsibility for managing the programming process; they also may have responsibility for carrying out the various steps in the programming process.

Two types of specialized audit programs can be developed and implemented: (*a*) stand-alone programs, and (*b*) modified application system programs. Stand-alone specialized audit software is produced if the application system does not accomplish even partially the audit task to be performed, or it is cheaper to produce a stand-alone program. If the application system partially accomplishes the audit task, say, extracts the necessary data from a file, it may be cheaper to modify the application system program code to perform fully the audit task required.

Specialized audit software can be developed and implemented in three ways. First, the auditor can take total responsibility for developing and implementing the software. To do this the auditor must have the necessary programming skills; however, this approach provides the auditor with a high level of control over the programming process. Second, programmers in the installation to be audited may write the software. If specialized audit software also provides information useful to the application system users, they may be willing to bear some part of the development and implementation costs of the software. Third, an outside software vendor may prepare the software if the auditor is concerned about maintaining the integrity of the software. Though the costs may be higher, using the services of an independent third party provides extra assurance that integrity violations have not occurred.

Even though installation personnel or an outside programmer may code, test, debug, and document specialized audit software, the auditor still has responsibility for preparing program specifications, managing the programming process, performing acceptance testing, and preparing user documentation. Unless the auditor performs these tasks, reliance cannot be placed on the integrity of the program.

Control of Specialized Audit Software

Use of specialized audit software as an audit tool causes the same control problems as those involved with using utility software as an audit tool. Over a period of time, somehow the auditor must obtain assurance the integrity of the software is intact; that is, unauthorized modifications to the software have not occurred. The techniques previously described in the chapter—blueprints, checksums, etc.—still apply. However, again these techniques provide only limited assurance the processing integrity of the software has not been corrupted.

SUMMARY

Besides generalized audit software, the auditor can use two other software tools for collecting evidence on the quality of systems: (*a*) system software, and (*b*) specialized audit software. The auditor may use system software instead of generalized audit software for various reasons: generalized audit software may not run on the hardware/software configuration of the installation being audited, it may run too inefficiently, or it may be functionally limited. System software also may be used to facilitate the use of other audit tools such as generalized audit software or test data, or it may be used to facilitate the development of other audit tools such as specialized audit software.

The type of system software typically used by the auditor for evidence collection purposes is utility software. The auditor uses utility software in five ways: (*a*) to gain an understanding of the system to be audited, (*b*) to assess data quality, (*c*) to assess program quality, (*d*) to facilitate development of other evidence collection software, and (*e*) to assess operational efficiency.

For several reasons the auditor may develop, implement, and use specialized audit software rather than use generalized audit software or system software. Generalized audit software or system software that performs the audit task may be unavailable, if they are available they may be functionally limited, or they may be operationally inefficient. Use of specialized audit software also can improve the auditor's understanding of an application system, increase auditor independence, and enhance management and data processing personnel's respect for the auditor.

Specialized audit software may be either stand-alone software or modifications implemented in an existing application system program. The software can be developed and implemented by the auditor, installation personnel, or an independent third party. Whatever the approach adopted, the auditor must take steps to ensure unauthorized code does not exist in the software.

A problem confronted by the auditor when using utility software or specialized audit software is ensuring the software has not been subject to unauthorized modifications. Some level of assurance can be obtained by comparing the software with a blueprint, recalculating a hash total or checksum for the software, undertaking tests on critical modules, or examining an operating system or librarian log for unauthorized activities. However, these techniques still provide only limited assurance that unauthorized modifications have not occurred. The processing integrity of system software and specialized audit software is still dependent on the integrity of other system components such as the operating system used in the installation.

REVIEW QUESTIONS

17.1. Briefly explain the nature of utility software. Give three factors that affect the availability of utility software within an installation.

17.2. What problems does the use of minicomputers and microcomputers for accounting applications present for the auditor performing the evidence collection function?

17.3. Is it likely that generalized audit software will be available on a wider range of hardware/software configurations in the future? Explain.

17.4. The parts inventory master file for the manufacturing organization you are auditing is set up as a network data structure. The generalized audit software package available for you to use will not access network data structures; however, you consider it to be important that the quality of data in the file is evaluated. Outline how utility software might be used to overcome some of your problems.

17.5. Briefly explain the major ways in which utility software can be used by the auditor to facilitate evidence collection.

17.6. Give an example of an evidence gathering task where the external auditor might consider using utility software in preference to generalized audit software. Outline how the external auditor might go about finding out whether or not there is a utility program available in the installation that will perform the evidence gathering task.

17.7. What function might a transaction profile analyzer perform in the auditor's evidence collection process?

17.8. What function might a data structure charter perform in the auditor's evidence collection process?

17.9. Briefly explain why the auditor might be interested in using a pointer validation utility during the evidence collection phase of the audit. Give two implications of incorrect pointers existing in the database.

17.10. Compared to generalized audit software, give two disadvantages of using utility software for evidence collection purposes.

17.11. Briefly explain why the auditor is concerned with whether or not a Trojan horse has been inserted in utility software.

17.12. Give two advantages and two disadvantages of using utility software developed *within* the installation being audited.

17.13. Briefly explain why the various methods used for checking whether utility software has been modified do not guarantee the processing integrity of the software.

17.14. Briefly explain the nature of specialized audit software.

17.15. Outline a function that is unlikely to be performed by generalized audit software or utility software, thereby forcing the auditor to develop a specialized audit program.

17.16. Why is it likely that more specialized audit software will be developed if an organization develops a competency center; that is, a centralized EDP audit facility having highly skilled EDP audit staff?

17.17. Briefly explain how the development and implementation of specialized audit software can increase an auditor's understanding of a complex application system.

17.18. Briefly explain why the auditor might decide to develop and implement specialized audit software to age accounts receivable and analyze inventory turnover.

17.19. Compared to generalized audit software and utility software, give two disadvantages of developing and implementing specialized audit software.

17.20. How might the development and implementation of specialized audit software affect the auditor's relationships with management and data processing personnel?

17.21. What factors would affect the decision to modify application system program code versus write specialized stand-alone programs to perform audit evidence gathering tasks?

17.22. Outline the ways in which specialized audit software can be developed and implemented. List the relative advantages and disadvantages of each method.

17.23. Briefly describe three techniques the auditor can use to determine whether or not a specialized audit program written by a third party complies with its specifications.

17.24. If installation programmers or third parties code, test, and debug a specialized audit program, what are their responsibilities with respect to documenting the program? Explain.

17.25. Outline the advantages of both external and internal auditors building independently controlled libraries of system software and specialized software. How can auditors independently control these libraries?

17.26. Outline the major steps in a decision model the auditor can use when trying to choose between generalized audit software, system software, and specialized audit software for evidence collection purposes.

17.27. Are there any differences between the controls that should exist over system software and those that should exist over specialized audit software to prevent unauthorized modifications occurring?

EXERCISES AND CASES

17.1. As the manager of internal audit for a company, you are called one day to a meeting with the controller. The controller explains that a programmer has discovered accidentally some fraudulent code in an audit program written by a member of your staff. The audit program examined sales transactions as they were input to an online system and detected any unusual transactions that occurred so they could be examined by the audit staff. Unfortunately, the program also altered transactions for customers who seem to be relations of the auditor who wrote the program.

The controller asks you how this situation has arisen. You explain that your staff is small and overworked, and the auditor who wrote the program was the only member of your staff that could program.

Required: The controller asks you to prepare a brief report giving some recommendations to prevent a similar fraud occurring in the future.

17.2. You are the manager of internal audit for a company that uses a database management system for its applications systems. The database management system maintains a log, which includes all transactions that update the database.

One of your junior auditors asks you to approve a budget for $2000 so a program can be written to compare the log tape with the transaction files for the various application systems that use the database management system. You ask why the amount required is so high for a simple comparison program. He explains that the data is formatted and compressed in strange ways on the log tape and difficulties have been experienced on previous occasions when attempts have been made to read the tape.

Required: On the basis of the information given, what are your feelings on whether or not to have the program written? What errors or irregularities do you think the program might identify that other controls would not identify?

17.3. Consider an online realtime update system that has over 1000 terminals scattered in remote locations and connected to a central machine. One task of the EDP audit group is to ensure that all terminals connected to the central machine are authorized terminals and that the actual privileges allocated a terminal user correspond to the documented privileges.

Required: Where in the system would an auditor obtain the information needed to check that the terminals are authorized and the privileges assigned users are valid? Why would specialized or utility software probably be needed to obtain this information? What information would be needed?

17.4. Some external auditors claim they spend up to two-thirds of their time documenting controls in computer systems so they have a basis for evaluating these controls.

Required: Identify some utility software or specialized software that might be written to facilitate the documentation process carried out by the internal auditor. Should the external auditor be responsible for preparing the internal controls documentation for audit evaluation purposes?

REFERENCES

Adams, Donald L. "Alternatives to Computer Audit Software," *Journal of Accountancy* (November 1975), pp. 54–57.

Burch, John G., Jr., and Joseph L. Sardinas, Jr. *Computer Control and Audit: A Total Systems Approach* (New York: John Wiley & Sons, Inc., 1978).

Canadian Institute of Chartered Accountants. *Computer Audit Guidelines* (Toronto, Canada: The Canadian Institute of Chartered Accountants, 1975).

Cash, James I., Jr., Andrew D. Bailey, Jr., and Andrew B. Whinston. "A Survey of Techniques for Auditing EDP-Based Accounting Information Systems," *The Accounting Review* (October 1977), pp. 813-832.

Dorricott, Keith O. "Appraising Computer Assisted Audit Techniques," *CA Magazine* (August 1975), pp. 24-29.

Hoffman, Lance J. *Modern Methods for Computer Security and Privacy* (Englewood Cliffs, N.J.: Prentice-Hall, Inc., 1977).

IBM Corporation. *Auditability and Productivity Information Catalog* (New York: International Business Machines Corporation, 1977).

McHugh, Arthur J. "EDP and the Audit Function," *Accounting Education* (November 1978), pp. 34-54.

Perry, William E. "Audit Aspects of Utility Programs," *EDPACS* (October 1975), pp. 1-8.

Stanford Research Institute. *Systems Auditability and Control Study: Data Processing Audit Practices Report* (Altamonte Springs, Fla.: The Institute of Internal Auditors, Inc., 1977).

Thomas, D. A., B. Pagurek, and R. J. Buhr. "Validation Algorithms for Pointer Values in DBTG Databases," *ACM Transactions on Database Systems* (December 1977), pp. 352-369.

Weber, Ron. "On Some Aspects of Audit Software Attributes and User Needs," *Proceedings of the Eighth Australian Computer Conference* (Canberra: Australian Computer Society, Inc., 1978), pp. 1781-1794.

Will, Hart J. "Discernible Trends and Overlooked Opportunities in Audit Software," *The EDP Auditor* (Winter 1978), pp. 21-45.

Withington, Frederic G. *The Environment for Systems Programs* (Reading, Mass.: Addison-Wesley Publishing Company, Inc., 1979).

CHAPTER 18

CODE REVIEW, TEST DATA, AND CODE COMPARISON

CHAPTER OUTLINE

FACTORS THAT LOWER PROGRAM QUALITY: SOME EMPIRICAL EVIDENCE

PROGRAM SOURCE CODE REVIEW
    Objectives of Code Review
    Readability of Program Code
    Source Code Review Methodology
    Costs and Benefits of Code Review

TEST DATA
    Some Theoretical Considerations
    Designing Test Data
    Creating Test Data
    Automated Aids
    Costs and Benefits of Test Data

PROGRAM CODE COMPARISON
    Types of Code Comparison
    Use of the Technique
    Costs and Benefits of Code Comparison

SUMMARY

REVIEW QUESTIONS

EXERCISES AND CASES

REFERENCES

CHAPTER 18: CODE REVIEW, TEST DATA, AND CODE COMPARISON

This chapter discusses three evidence collection techniques used primarily to assess the quality of program logic. *Code review* involves the auditor reading program source code listings to determine whether unauthorized code exists and to generate hypotheses about potential errors in the logic. If the auditor is sufficiently skilled, code review also indicates potentially inefficient code and code that does not meet its objectives. *Test data* involves the auditor using a sample of data to assess whether logic errors exist in a program and whether the program meets its objectives. Again, the skilled auditor also can use test data to assess whether a program runs efficiently. *Code comparison* involves the auditor comparing two versions of the source or object code of a program; one version—the blueprint—has known attributes, and the auditor determines whether the other version has the same attributes. This technique has been discussed briefly in previous chapters. It is discussed more fully in this chapter.

Use of the three techniques sometimes follows a natural sequence (see Figure 18.1). First, the auditor reviews program code to generate hypotheses

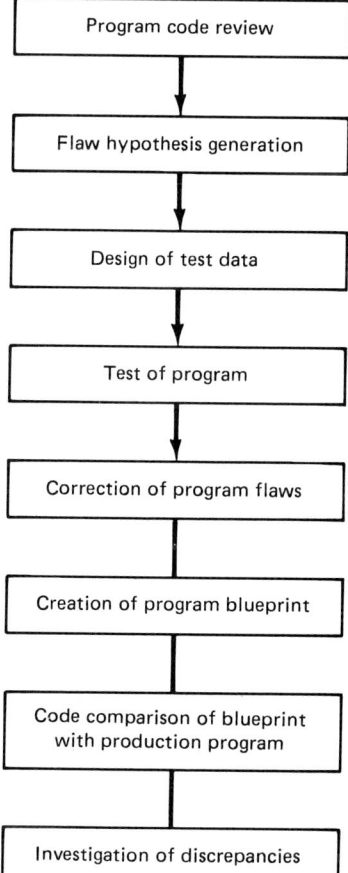

Figure 18.1
Integrated use of code review, test data, and code comparison for evidence collection purposes.

about erroneous code or code that is inefficient or does not meet its objectives. Second, the auditor uses test data to test these hypotheses. Any deficiencies found in the program logic then are corrected. Third, once the auditor is satisfied with the quality of the program code, this version of the program becomes a blueprint. At a later time, production versions of the program can be compared against this blueprint to determine whether any discrepancies exist.

FACTORS THAT LOWER PROGRAM QUALITY: SOME EMPIRICAL EVIDENCE

Code review and test data can be very time-consuming evidence collection techniques to use. They should be applied where they will have most effect; that is, where there is most likely to be erroneous code, unauthorized code, ineffective code, or inefficient code. Unfortunately, in spite of the enormity of the programming effort worldwide, relatively little is known about where the problem areas in programs lie. The studies described briefly below represent some of the few attempts to obtain empirical evidence on this issue.

Boehm et al. [1975] examined the errors discovered during the implementation of a large (100,000 lines of source code) software project. They classified the errors into two broad types: (a) design errors—those arising because the software did not comply with user requirements, and (b) coding errors— those arising because specifications were implemented incorrectly. Of the 224 errors found, 64% were design errors and 36% were coding errors. Further, of the 54% of errors found during or after acceptance testing, 45% were design errors and 9% were coding errors. On average the time taken to diagnose and correct design errors was twice the time required for coding errors.

Additional analysis undertaken on the errors indicated the nature of the design errors and the nature of the coding errors. The design errors arose primarily because of interface problems between the code and the database, input/output devices, and system users. The coding errors arose primarily because of incorrect computation, indexing, or control flow.

Endres [1975] studied the errors made in modifying IBM's DOS/VS operating system to produce Release 28; this release contained some of the most extensive changes ever made to the system. Of the 432 errors discovered when system modules were integrated and a system test (as opposed to a program test) was carried out, 46% were design errors and 38% were coding errors. The remaining 16% were a curious mixture; for example, they included spelling errors in system messages. Endres preferred not to classify them as design or coding errors.

Further analysis of the errors indicated the nature of the design and coding errors. The design errors arose primarily because the problems to be solved when implementing operating systems lack structure. The coding errors that arose were typical of assembly language programming: problems with initialization, addressability, name referencing, and counting and calculating. Interestingly, 85% of the errors that occurred could be corrected by changing only one module. Supposedly, major sources of errors in operating systems (and programs generally) are the interfaces between program modules. At least for this example the empirical evidence contradicts preconceived notions (see, also, Chapter 6).

Rubey et al. [1975] analyzed data from several studies that had collected program error statistics (see, also, Hartwick [1977]). Of 1202 errors discovered, they found 98% were identified by the programmer who coded the software; 2% were discovered during independent testing. Further analysis was undertaken on the errors discovered during independent testing. The errors were classified into 10 categories. The largest category, incomplete or erroneous program specifications, constituted 28% of the total errors discovered. Thus, design errors were again the major factor that lowered program quality. Major categories of coding errors were erroneous data accessing (10%), erroneous decision logic or sequencing (12%), and erroneous arithmetic computations (9%).

From an audit viewpoint, two tentative conclusions can be drawn from these studies about how evidence collection techniques such as code review and test data should be applied. First, if the techniques rely upon the integrity of program specifications, a large percentage (possibly 50%) of program errors will be missed (see, also, Mills [1976]). Coding errors may be identified; design errors will be missed. Second, when applying the evidence collection techniques the auditor should pay special attention to three areas of program code: data accessing, sequencing and control, and computation and indexing (see, also, Boehm [1973]). These areas seem especially prone to coding errors. However, since these conclusions are based on a limited number of studies, further empirical evidence is needed to assess their general validity.

Presumably, also, the more times a program is used for production running the more likely it is that design errors will be discovered and corrected. Thus, the auditor may have more confidence in the integrity of the specifications of older programs. However, it is also more likely that fewer coding (logic) errors exist in older programs.

PROGRAM SOURCE CODE REVIEW

Auditors use program source code review when they are unwilling to treat a computer program as a black box. Some evidence collection techniques permit only inferences to be made about the quality of code in a computer program. For example, generalized audit software can be used to examine the quality of data produced by a program. The quality of data reflects the quality of program code; however, little can be said about whether or not unauthorized code or inefficient code exists (see, further, Chapter 16).

Objectives of Code Review

Code review has five specific objectives: (a) to identify erroneous code, (b) to identify unauthorized code, (c) to identify ineffective code, (d) to identify inefficient code, and (e) to identify nonstandard code. The following sections discuss briefly each of these objectives.

Identify Erroneous Code The use of code review to identify erroneous code is well-established. Chapter 6 discussed this purpose under various headings: desk checking, structured walk-throughs, design and code inspections. The empirical evidence discussed earlier in the chapter suggests that coding errors are still a major cause of low-quality programs. The auditor can use code review to determine whether or not the code complies with the program specifications.

Identify Unauthorized Code Without directly examining a program's source code, it is unlikely that unauthorized program code will be identified. Unauthorized code normally is triggered by a specific data value or combination of data values; for example, an account number or an account number and date combination. A fraudulent programmer may modify a program so it does not print out an overdrawn account. Transactions having a certain account number and date value may be excluded from normal data validation processes. Unless the auditor submits test data having these specific values, the unauthorized code will not be identified. Code review also may deter a programmer from inserting unauthorized code in a program.

Identify Ineffective Code Ineffective code is code that does not achieve its objectives. The ineffectiveness of code can be gauged at two levels. First, the auditor can examine whether the code meets the documented program specifications. Second, the auditor can examine whether the code fulfills user requirements. The empirical evidence discussed earlier in the chapter suggests the documented program specifications and user requirements do not always correspond. Erroneous program specifications are a major cause of low-quality programs.

Identify Inefficient Code Code review may enable the auditor to identify inefficient segments of code. For example, in a sequence of tests of transaction types, the tests may not have been ordered according to their frequency of occurrence. Consequently, the program executes more of its code than it would have to if the tests were reordered. The auditor also might identify frequent use of instructions that execute inefficiently on the hardware/software configuration on which the program runs.

Identify Nonstandard Code Nonstandard code takes a variety of forms. It may be code that does not comply with installation standards covering data item names or internal documentation. It may be code that values an asset inconsistently with generally accepted accounting principles. It may be code that does not conform to legal or statutory requirements. In some areas, for example, the valuation of intangible assets or work-in-process inventory, the impossibility or difficulty of observing the entities that the data represents makes it even more important the code be correct (see, also, Burch and Sardinas [1978]).

Readability of Program Code

The use of program source code review as an audit tool assumes that the code reviewed is readable. The readability of the code under review affects how easily the technique can be applied and the likelihood of finding poor-quality code (aside from the lack of readability) using the technique.

In general, how readable is program code? Again, little empirical evidence has been obtained on this question. Elshoff [1976] studied the readability of 120 production PL/1 programs. He concluded that basically the programs in the study were unreadable. A nonprogrammer would be unable to understand any part of them; even an experienced programmer would have great difficulty understanding them.

Elshoff also found the complexity of the data flow and the control flow impaired the readability of the programs. On average, 384 identifiers appeared in a program; 107 were unreferenced, and the remainder were referenced 1195 times throughout the body of the program. One-third of the statements in an average program directed the flow of control; thus, for practical purposes the number of paths through the program was infinite.

As a further measure of complexity, Elshoff counted the number of statements spanned between two references to an identifier. Nearly 13% of the spans exceeded 100 statements. For the average-size program one span began every six statements. Thus, after 100 statements a programmer reading the program would have to remember as many as 16 separate data and control flows.

The extent to which Elshoff's findings are general within the computer industry is unknown. However, they highlight the difficulties an auditor may experience when trying to use program source code review as an evidence collection tool. In a computer installation, management must insist on the use of standard labeling conventions, code indentation to show the flow of control, internal documentation, etc. Top-down design, top-down coding, and structured coding clearly make program code more readable. These programming disciplines affect the ease with which programs can be maintained. From a control viewpoint they affect the auditability of programs (see, also, Chapter 6).

Source Code Review Methodology

There are seven steps involved in the review of program source code (see, also, Adams [1975]):

1 Select the program to be examined.
2 Review the installation's programming standards.
3 Obtain an understanding of the program specifications.
4 Obtain the source code listing.

5 Review the compiler language used for the program.
6 Review the source code.
7 Formulate flaw hypotheses.

The following sections discuss briefly each of these steps.

Program Selection Since program source code review can be a time-consuming evidence collection technique, the programs selected for review should be critical programs within the installation. Risk assessment techniques can be applied to determine the importance of a program for maintaining the overall integrity of an application system. However, not only must the program be critical, it also must be readable. Unless the program is readable, it may be extremely difficult for the auditor to evaluate whether it safeguards assets, maintains data integrity, achieves its objectives, and processes efficiently.

Review Programming Standards By reviewing the programming standards of the installation, the auditor develops a set of expectations about the code to be reviewed; for example, the way labels will be assigned and the way programs will be structured. The standards also may indicate likely deficiencies that will exist in the code—areas where the auditor has to be especially careful. Besides the installation programming standards, standards also may have been established for a particular application system. For example, programmers may be required to include certain documentation as notes in the program code.

Understand the Program Specifications By understanding the program specifications, the auditor is able to ask the question: Does the program do what it is supposed to do? Here the auditor must make a choice as to how an understanding of the program specifications is to be obtained. One alternative is to review the documented program specifications—those used by the programmer as the basis for constructing the code. By reviewing these specifications, the auditor will be able to check the correspondence of the code with the specifications. Further, deficiencies in the specifications may become apparent; for example, an important control may be missing in the specifications.

As a second alternative the auditor can attempt to understand the purposes of the program by consulting wider sources of information. The auditor can interview users of the program to check their understanding of what the program is supposed to do with the functions actually performed by the program. This alternative is more costly to undertake. However, the empirical evidence discussed earlier in the chapter shows erroneous specifications are a major cause of low-quality programs. The auditor must decide whether the likely additional benefits to be obtained from this alternative will exceed the extra costs involved.

Obtain Source Code The auditor must be careful to ensure the source code listing obtained for the program under review is the current version. The auditor has greater assurance the listing is current if the installation uses a librarian system to maintain program source code. If the auditor has doubts about the currency of the source code, it can be compiled and compared with the object code of the production version of the program. Any discrepancies identified alert the auditor to the fact that the source code is not current.

When obtaining the source code listing, the auditor can use various software tools to facilitate understanding the program; for example, cross-reference listers and flowcharters (see, further, Chapter 17). Use of these tools is especially important if the auditor does not intend to review the entire source code but only selected portions of the code; for example, the computations performed on a particular data item. A cross-reference lister would show where in the program the data item is used.

Review Compiler Language Used Many compiler languages contain nonstandard features incorporated in the compiler to facilitate implementation and testing of a program. For example, some COBOL compilers include verbs that are not ANS COBOL verbs to aid the programmer to debug a program.

Over time, internal auditors will build up experience with the features of the compiler used within their installation. Nonstandard verbs or clauses that pose threats to a program's processing effectiveness, efficiency, or integrity will become known. However, the external auditor confronts many different compilers for the one language. Before undertaking a review of program code, external auditors should examine carefully the documentation for the compiler. They should note any nonstandard features of the language that pose a threat to the quality of programs written in the language.

Review Source Code Currently, there is little theory or empirical evidence to indicate the "best" way of reviewing program code. Many questions remain unanswered. Do some ways of reviewing code identify more errors than others? Are some ways of reviewing code faster than others? Is the best way dependent on how the code is written (structured)? Should code be reviewed differently if efficiency is the main concern rather than data integrity? Is the effectiveness and efficiency of a code review technique dependent upon psychological and demographic characteristics of the person undertaking the review (see, further, Myers [1978]).

If only a selected portion of the code is to be reviewed, the auditor may simply focus on that section of the code and any interfaces it has with other sections of code. If the entire code is to be examined, one method of review is to focus first on input and output operations and then on processing.

In any programming language, certain verbs are more likely to be used to implement unauthorized code than others. Similarly, use of certain verbs is more error-prone than others. For example, when an auditor examines input/output in a COBOL program, special attention should be paid to the following verbs since they may be used in conjunction with unauthorized code:

COBOL verb	Audit concerns
SELECT	Relates a file to an input/output device. Can be checked to see the program processes only authorized files.
REDEFINES	Permits alternate record formats to be defined for the one file. Selection of a specific format generally is triggered by an "IF" clause. Can be checked to see the data items redefined are authorized data items.
OPEN/CLOSE	Makes a file available and unavailable for processing respectively. Multiple OPEN/CLOSE verbs in a program may mean a file is being made available for unauthorized processing.
COPY ... REPLACING	Used to change the definition of data items copied into a program from a source library. Can be checked to see the changes are authorized.

In general, during a complete code review of a program, the auditor should determine whether or not the data items and relationships processed by the program are the authorized set of data items and relationships. A cross-reference lister can be used to provide a listing of all data items and relationships (e.g., pointer fields will be listed). Those used within the FILE SECTION of a COBOL program can be checked against the file definitions in the program specifications; those used within the WORKING-STORAGE section must be evaluated independently. If the COBOL report writer facility is used, data items in the REPORT SECTION should be checked against program specifications. Literals and constants used in the PROCEDURE DIVISION must be verified independently.

With respect to processing, the following COBOL verbs (clauses) tend to be used in conjunction with unauthorized code:

COBOL verb	Audit concerns
IF	Typically the major conditional statement used in a program. Can be used to activate an unauthorized section of code when a certain condition is true or false.
GO TO ... DEPENDING	The GO TO without DEPENDING allows an unconditional branch in the logic flow; with the DEPENDING it provides a conditional branch. The branch may be to an unauthorized section of code.
ALTER	Changes the transfer point specified in a GO TO. The first transfer point may be authorized code; the second may be unauthorized code.
PERFORM ... UNTIL	The UNTIL statement permits a conditional branch to be carried out with the PERFORM. The branch may be to an unauthorized section of code.
CALL/ENTER	Used to call a subprogram (subroutine). The subprogram may contain unauthorized code. ENTER is used if the subroutine is written in a language other than COBOL.

DISPLAY	Can be used to breach the privacy of data by having the contents of a field displayed on a peripheral, e.g., the console.
ACCEPT	Program stops and awaits the input of data from a peripheral, e.g., the console. Can be used to input a code that will cause a conditional test to branch to unauthorized code.
EXAMINE	Used to replace certain occurrences of a given character in a field with another character. Might be inserted prior to and after a validation test so a specific transaction passes the test. The first instance changes the data item value so it passes the test; the second restores the data item to its original value.

Again, a cross-reference lister can be used to identify where in a program these verbs (clauses) are used. However, the auditor should be careful about examining any section of code in isolation. For example, a GO TO may branch to a section of authorized code. Further on in the program, however, the paragraph name referred to by the GO TO may be changed with an ALTER verb.

After examining the flow of logic and control in a program, the auditor may wish to examine any computations performed by the program. As discussed earlier in the chapter, empirical evidence shows computations often are a major source of error in programs. A cross-reference lister can be used to print out the COBOL verbs used for computations: ADD, SUBTRACT, MULTIPLY, DIVIDE, COMPUTE.

The auditor also should pay special attention to any nonstandard verbs used in the program. For example, some COBOL compilers provide various debugging verbs (TRACE, DEBUG) that are not part of ANS COBOL. These verbs could be used to breach the privacy of data.

Formulate Flaw Hypotheses Once a deficiency in the programming code has been identified, two further steps must be taken. First, the auditor must work out the implications of the deficiency for the effectiveness, efficiency, or integrity of processing. Second, the auditor must formulate a test to determine whether the postulated deficiency does, in fact, exist and the postulated results of the deficiency do, in fact, occur. These steps can be accomplished by careful desk checking of the code. Test data then might be used to verify the flaw hypotheses.

Costs and Benefits of Code Review

The primary advantage of reviewing program source code is that it provides a level of detailed knowledge about a program that is difficult to acquire using any other evidence collection technique. With other evidence collection techniques, inferences must be made about the quality of the code on the basis of some test result. With program source code review, the auditor examines the code directly.

The primary disadvantage of the technique is its cost. Earl [1977] concludes that, on average, an auditor can complete abut one code review per day, assuming the average program does not exceed 600 lines of source code. However, the speed with which a program can be read depends on the quality of the program code and the technical competence of the auditor performing the review.

TEST DATA

The use of a sample of data to assess the quality of a program is fundamental to many evidence collection techniques. It is based on the premise that it is possible to generalize about the overall reliability of a program if it is reliable for a set of specific tests.

The term "test data" usually is reserved for a technique where the set of tests is *designed* rather than based on a set of existing production data. In other words, the test data approach means data is created to test specific aspects of a program. The quality of the program is not inferred from the quality of application production data that has been processed already.

The test data technique goes under several names. It is sometimes called test decking. If a comprehensive set of test data is assembled for an application system, often the set is called a test bed. More recently the name "base case" has been used for a test bed and the testing technique called base case system evaluation (BCSE) (see Mullen [1978]). Some other variations of the basic test data technique also are described in the next chapter.

Some Theoretical Considerations

Like program source code review, test data can be used to evaluate the effectiveness and efficiency of a program and determine whether or not it safeguards assets and maintains data integrity. However, as an evidence collection technique it has been used primarily to assess whether or not a program maintains data integrity. Because the test data technique underlies many of the evidence collection techniques used, several researchers have investigated the theoretical underpinnings of using test data to assess whether programs contain errors. They have addressed two major issues. First, what are the attributes of a *reliable* set of test data for a program? Second, is it possible to generate automatically a reliable set of test data?

Reliable Test Data Suppose that P is a program for computing a function F whose domain is the set D. Let a finite subset $T \subset D$ be the set of test data used to determine whether P processes correctly; that is, that $P(d) = F(d)\ \forall d \in D$. Then T is defined to be a reliable set of test data for P if:

$$P(x) = F(x)\ \forall x \in T \Rightarrow P(x) = F(x)\ \forall x \in D$$

In other words, T is reliable if it reveals an error in P whenever P contains an error (see, further, Gerhart and Goodenough [1975] and Howden [1976]).

Clearly, the correctness of P can be determined by exhaustively testing P; that is, letting $T = D$. However, some programs have an infinite domain and testing would not terminate. The test data technique attempts to partition the input domain into a set of equivalence classes. By testing an element of each equivalence class, the correctness of the program for all elements of the equivalence class can be inferred. A reliable set of test data contains one element for every equivalence class of the input domain of the program to be tested.

Automatically Generating Reliable Test Data It would be a major breakthrough in proving the correctness of programs if there was some way of automatically generating a reliable set of test data. Unfortunately, Howden [1976] has proven that a computable procedure H does not exist which, given an *arbitrary* program P, a function F, and a domain D, generates a reliable set of test data T. Currently, the research is attempting to develop reliable test strategies for particular *classes* of programs (see, further, Howden [1976] and Geller [1978]).

Designing Test Data

Since the state of the art does not enable automatic generation of a reliable set of test data, test data still must be designed. The auditor should use a systematic approach to the design of test data. Unless a systematic approach is used, critical logic paths may be missed. There is also a tendency to believe that the greater the volume of test data, the more comprehensive is the testing carried out. Unfortunately, a large volume of test data neither ensures critical logic paths in a program will be tested nor does it result in the most economical test of a program. Given a cost constraint on the amount of testing that can be carried out, with a systematic approach to the design of test data, the auditor is better able to decide what program paths should be tested and what paths should be omitted from the test run.

Before commencing the test data design, the auditor first must decide on the objectives of the test, since this affects the source of the information on which the test data design is based. As discussed earlier in the chapter, design errors represent a major source of program errors. Simply basing the test data design on program documentation is likely to miss a large percentage of program errors. However, formulating user requirements as the basis for designing program test data usually is more costly than designing test data on the basis of the program documentation.

Once the auditor has made a decision as to the source of information on what the program is supposed to do, two approaches can be used to systematically design the test data: (*a*) the decision-table approach, and (*b*) the flowchart approach. The following two sections briefly discuss each of these approaches.

Decision-Table Approach Decision tables are useful for representing the logic of decisions (see, further, Montalbano [1974]). To create a decision table the auditor first must decide what program or section of a program is to be tested. If a top-down testing approach is to be used (see Chapter 6) and the program code has been written in a top-down manner, the auditor may attempt to test the mainline section of the code first and then proceed to lower level modules (see, further, Yourdon [1975]). Once the program or section of the program to be tested has been identified, the auditor can begin to formulate a description of the conditions (logic) relevant to the program's correct functioning.

To illustrate the decision-table approach to design of test data, assume the auditor interviews a payroll clerk about the payment of sales commissions. The auditor determines that most salepersons are paid a base salary plus 3% of sales if more than 100 units of the product are sold, and 4% of sales if more than 125 units of the product are sold. However, a salesperson can elect to sign a special contract, called a Type A contract, whereby no sales commission is paid until sales exceed 125 units. With a Type A contract, the sales commission then is paid at the rate of 6% of sales.

The auditor decides to test this processing aspect of the program. Table 18.1a shows the unreduced decision table constructed by the auditor, and Table 18.1b shows the reduced table. Montalbano [1974] provides a compre-

TABLE 18.1a
UNREDUCED DECISION TABLE

	Sales Commissions	Rules							
		1	2	3	4	5	6	7	8
Condition stub	Type A contract	Y	Y	Y	Y	N	N	N	N
	Sales > 125	Y	Y	N	N	Y	Y	N	N
	Sales > 100	Y	N	Y	N	Y	N	Y	N
Action stub	Salary = base			X	X				X
	Salary = base + 3% sales							X	
	Salary = base + 4% sales					X			
	Salary = base + 6% sales	X							
	Error		X				X		

TABLE 18.1b
REDUCED DECISION TABLE

	Sales commissions	Rules						
		1	2	3	4	5	6	7
Condition stub	Type A contract	Y	Y	Y	N	N	N	N
	Sales > 125	Y	Y	N	Y	Y	N	N
	Sales > 100	Y	N	—	Y	N	Y	N
Action stub	Salary = base			X				X
	Salary = base + 3% sales						X	
	Salary = base + 4% sales				X			
	Salary = base + 6% sales	X						
	Error		X			X		

TABLE 18.2
REDUCED DECISION TABLE WITH ASSOCIATED TEST DATA AND TEST RESULTS

	Sales commissions	\multicolumn{7}{c}{Rules}

	Sales commissions	1	2	3	4	5	6	7
Condition stub	Type A contract	Y	Y	Y	N	N	N	N
	Sales > 125	Y	Y	N	Y	Y	N	N
	Sales > 100	Y	N	–	Y	N	Y	N
Action stub	Salary = base				X			X
	Salary = base + 3% sales						X	
	Salary = base + 4% sales					X		
	Salary = base + 6% sales	X						
	Error			X			X	
Test data stub	Contract type	A	A	A	B	B	B	B
	Sales	130	–	120	130	–	120	130
Results stub	Expected result	17,800	–	10,000	15,200	–	13,600	10,000
	Confirmed	✔	–	✔	✔	–	X	✔

hensive description of the steps to be followed in constructing the table and checking it for completeness and consistency.

Note the unreduced decision table contains redundant rules 3 and 4 that can be combined. Further, there are some intrarule inconsistencies. For example, in rule 2 it is impossible for condition 2 (sales > 125) to be true and condition 3 (sales > 100) to be false. This condition could be satisfied only if some form of logic error exists.

To test the program logic the auditor simply constructs test data to satisfy each of the conditions in the reduced decision table. To document the test, two extra parts might be added to the decision table (see, also, Gerhart and Goodenough [1975]). The first part shows the test data for each rule in the decision table; the second part shows the expected result and whether or not the result was achieved when the program was tested. The two parts are the test data stub and the results stub respectively.

To illustrate the approach, assume the normal contract for a salesperson is a Type B contract. The base salary for both types of contracts is $10,000. The selling price per unit is $1000. Table 18.2 shows the test data constructed by the auditor and the results expected. Note, it is impossible to design test data for rules 2 and 5; that is, a data value cannot be constructed that is greater than 125 and less than 100. The "confirmed" row in the results stub of the table shows the result expected for rule 6 was not obtained. The auditor would have to investigate why this occurred. An "actual" results row also might be included in the results stub of the table.

Flowchart Approach In essence, the flowchart approach to the design of test data is the same as the decision-table approach. The major difference is the way in which the logic to be tested is documented. The auditor first must

462   PART 4: EVIDENCE COLLECTION

decide on the source of information for construction of the flowchart. Then the program or section of a program to be flowcharted must be chosen.

Figure 18.2 shows the flowchart for the salary example described in the previous section. Once the auditor has constructed the flowchart, test data

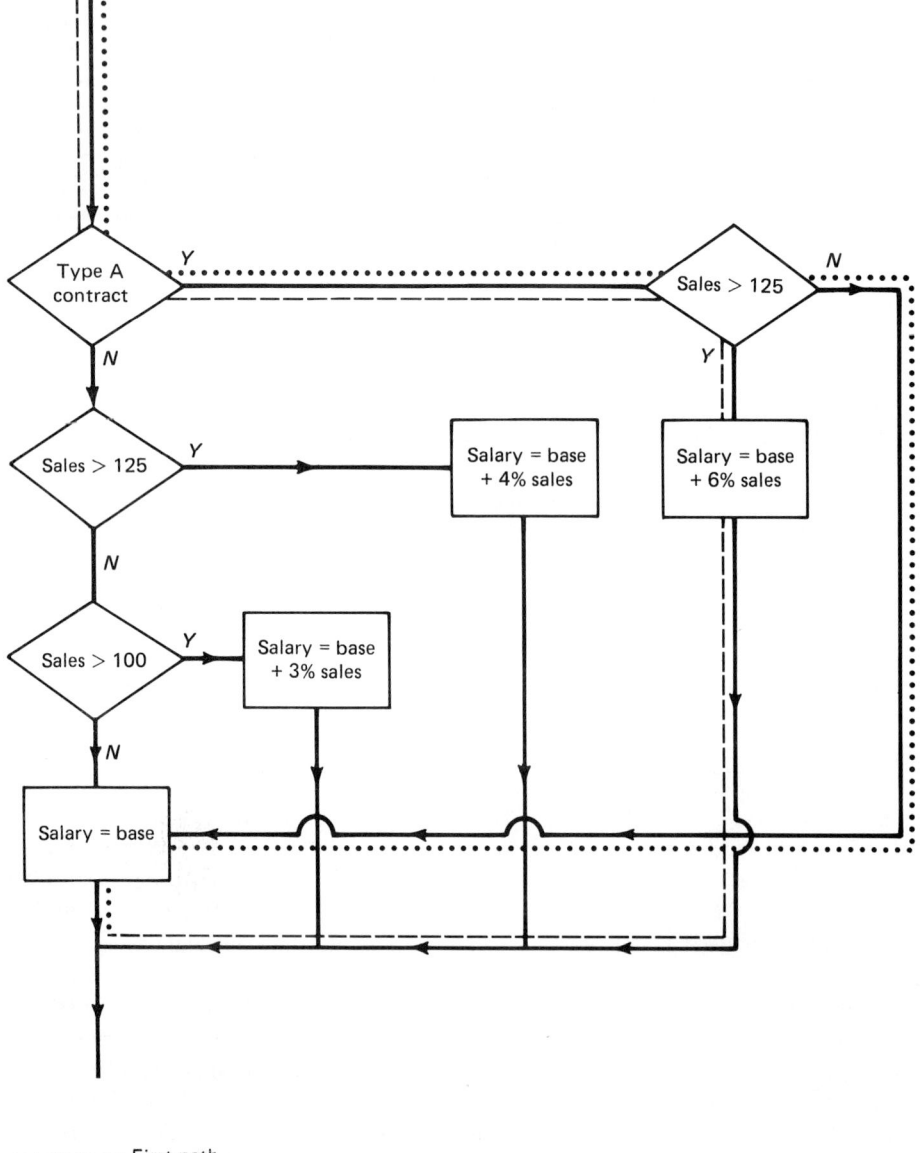

– – – – – First path
· · · · · · · · · Second path

Figure 18.2
Flowchart for test data design.

can be designed. The auditor must be careful to design test data for every path through the flowchart. A simple aid to identifying each path is to use different colored pencils to mark the different paths through the flowchart. As the auditor designs the test data for a path, the path should be marked off.

The auditor's choice of the decision-table or flowchart approach primarily depends on the auditor's facility with decision tables versus flowcharts. The decision-table approach has two major advantages. First, there is a set procedure for ensuring the completeness and consistency of the logic. Second, once the decision table has been constructed, it is easy to construct the test data; the auditor simply has to follow down a rule (column) in the decision table. However, for some types of situations it may be easier to construct a flowchart than a decision table. Whether or not decision tables lead to a more complete and faster test data design than flowcharts is a research issue.

Creating Test Data

Once the auditor has designed the test data needed for evidence collection purposes, the next step to be taken is to create test data that complies with the design. This can be a difficult and time-consuming step to complete. Master files may use complex data structures and storage structures that are difficult to create artificially. In some cases a large volume of test data may be required to carry out a comprehensive test. The following sections describe the approaches the auditor can use to create test data that complies with the test data design.

Use Production Data At least part of the test data required may be available in the form of production (live) data for the application system. Once the test data design has been formulated, the auditor can use generalized audit software or utility software to select off transaction files and master files data that complies with the design. For example, using the design in Table 18.2, the auditor could formulate a retrieval with generalized audit software to satisfy rule 1; that is, any live transaction for a Type A contract and sales in excess of 125 units would be selected. Similarly, master file records could be selected in the same way. A list of retrievals for which no production data exists must be kept, and test data created for the conditions expressed in the retrievals in some other way.

Use Installation Prepared Test Data Hopefully, the installation being audited attempts to carry out comprehensive testing of programs. The installation programming and systems staff should have prepared test data to assess the quality of the programs they have designed and implemented. If this test data exists on magnetic media, the auditor can use generalized audit software to select test data that complies with the design.

Develop New Test Data New test data must be created if it is unavailable from either production data or existing test data. One approach to creating new test data is to select data off production or existing test data files that partially fulfills a condition (rule) in the test design and modify those fields in the data that do not comply with the condition. These modifications can be carried out using generalized audit software or utility software. Alternatively, the auditor can code new test data, punch up the data, and use software to create the test records.

Automated Aids

Various automated aids that facilitate using test data to gather evidence on the quality of a program have been discussed previously in Chapters 6 and 17. Because of their importance, this section briefly reemphasizes the usefulness of some of these aids.

If new test data must be created, a test data generator reduces the time required to develop this data. Providing the auditor specifies correctly the parameter values for the generator, the test data generated will be accurate. This is important when the auditor has to create test data for complex data structures. Manual creation of test data for complex data structures is an error-prone process. Further, techniques for automatically generating test data are being refined continually (see, for example, Clarke [1976] and Ramamoorthy et al. [1976]).

A logic path monitor is an important aid for evaluating the completeness of a test data design. Since a logic path monitor indicates whether paths through a program have been traversed, the auditor is able to identify any unauthorized code or omissions made in the formulation of specifications for the test data design. However, before using the monitor, the auditor should check that the monitor is able to detect all paths through a program. For example, some monitors may be unable to detect conditional tests in a subroutine that is CALLed or ENTERed from the main COBOL program. The auditor also should check to see how the monitor handles such verbs as ALTER.

For some complex systems, simulators facilitate the testing process. For example, a network simulator allows testing of a data communications network without having to use the hardware/software configuration of the network. A terminal simulator permits simulation of multiple online terminals without having to use the hardware/software configuration of the online system. In both cases, without simulators the auditor may find it difficult to gather evidence on the quality of programs using test data.

Costs and Benefits of Test Data

The major benefit of using test data as an evidence collection technique is that it allows direct examination of the quality of program code. Well-designed test data tests specifically whether the program complies with specifications. The quality of the code need not be inferred from the quality of production data the program has processed.

Often it is claimed a major benefit of using test data is that auditors require little technical competence with computers to use the technique. For a very simple batch system or an undisciplined approach to the use of test data, this claim may be true. However, as the chapter illustrates, the effective and efficient design and creation of test data and the use of automated tools to support the test data approach requires the auditor to have substantial knowledge of computer technology.

The primary disadvantage of the test data approach is that it is often time-consuming and costly to use. As automated tools to support the approach are improved, this disadvantage may become less important.

The effectiveness and efficiency with which test data is employed also seems highly dependent on the capabilities of the individuals who use the technique. Myers [1978] had three groups of "above average" experienced programmers (average experience was 11 years) test a small program written in PL/1. Subjects in the first group were provided only with the program specifications. Subjects in the second group were provided with the specifications and a source listing. Subjects in the third group were organized into three-person teams and asked to test the program using the manual walk-through/inspection method (see Chapter 6). Each team was provided with the program specifications and a source listing. Myers found none of the groups different in their ability to detect errors; all performed poorly, detecting only about a third of the errors in the program. Further, there was significant variability in the individual results. The walk-through/inspection group took about 2½ times longer than the other groups to complete testing. Myers argues the most effective testing will occur if two programmers are used to test a program independently and their results combined. From his analysis of the types of errors detected and missed, he also concludes that programmers may pay too much attention to normal test conditions and insufficient attention to erroneous input and special conditions; the programmers focused on the program logic rather than input/output anomalies.

PROGRAM CODE COMPARISON

The auditor uses program code comparison for two reasons. First, it provides assurance the software being audited is the correct version of the software. For example, the auditor may wish to check correspondence between an audit version of an application program's code and the production version of an application program's code. Second, it provides assurance any software used as an audit tool is the correct version of the software. For example, the auditor may wish to compare an audit version of a specialized audit program with the installation version of a specialized audit program. If the auditor finds correspondence between the audit version and the installation version of the program, and the program has been tested comprehensively at a prior time, further testing should not be necessary. If the program has not been tested, the auditor obtains assurance the program to be tested is the production version of the program.

Types of Code Comparison

Software is available providing two types of program code comparison: (a) source code comparison, and (b) object code comparison. With source code comparison the software provides a meaningful listing of any discrepancies between the two versions of the program. Nevertheless, the auditor must obtain further assurance the source code version is the one used in production running.

With object code comparison it is difficult to identify the nature of any discrepancies found between the two versions of object code. Preferably, object code comparison is used to ask the simple question: Are there discrepancies? The major advantage of the technique is that it provides assurance the production version of a program is the authorized one. However, if discrepancies are identified, other techniques must be used to identify the cause of the discrepancies. Since compilers often are modified by their vendors and new releases provided, the auditor must be careful to ensure discrepancies do not arise because the same source code has been compiled with different versions of the compiler.

Use of the Technique

Source code and object code comparison are most effective as an audit technique when they are used in conjunction with each other. Figure 18.3 shows an overall approach to the use of program code comparison. The approach proceeds in the following way. First, the auditor compares the audit version of the program source code with that version the installation contends is the source code used to compile the production object code. Any discrepancies identified between the source code versions must be reconciled. Second, the auditor compiles either the audit or installation version of the source code with the compiler used to produce the production object code. Third, the auditor compares the object code produced with the production version of the object code. Any discrepancies identified mean either the wrong compiler has been used or the auditor has been supplied with the wrong version of the source code or object code.

Costs and Benefits of Code Comparison

The code comparison technique is an easy way of identifying changes made to programs. The software that performs code comparison usually is not costly to run. Further, the auditor requires little technical skill to be able to use the software. However, identifying the implications of any discrepancies found in the code requires some knowledge of programming.

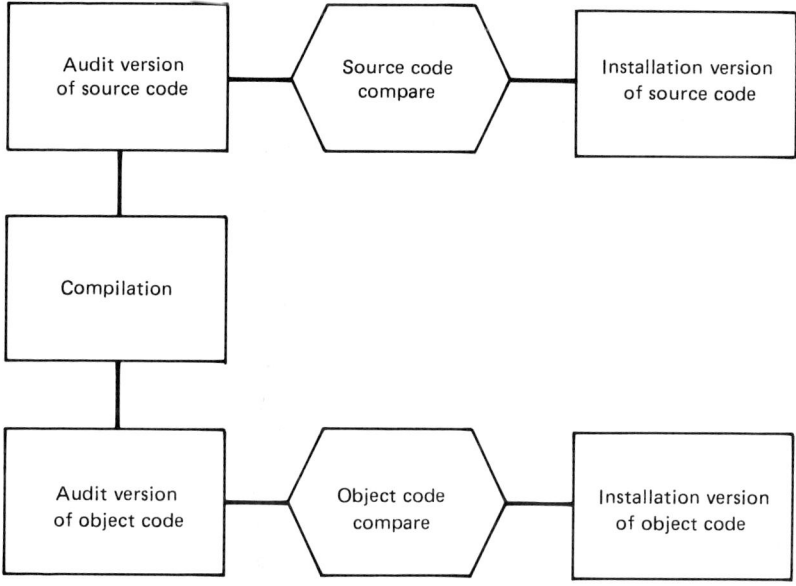

Figure 18.3
Use of code comparison for evidence gathering.

The technique is limited in that it does not provide any evidence on the quality of the code being compared unless one version of the code has been thoroughly tested by the auditor.

Code comparison programs also differ in the quality of their output. For example, if two files differ because a block of data (say, documentation text) has been shifted, some programs will show all data in the block as being changed rather than just the beginning and end (probably the more intuitive notion of the change). This may cause the auditor to overlook changes that may have been made within the block (see, further, Heckel [1978]).

SUMMARY

Three evidence collection techniques used primarily to evaluate the quality of program logic are code review, test data, and code comparison. The three techniques can be used together to perform an integrated test of the quality of program code. Code review provides a basis for generating flaw hypotheses about program logic. Test data enables these hypotheses to be tested. Code comparison allows the auditor to test whether the production version of a program used is the tested version.

A major decision that must be made when using code review or test data is how the specifications for the program to be examined will be formulated. Empirical evidence shows design errors are a major source of errors in programs. Thus, if the auditor relies on the documented program specifications as the basis for the code review or test data design, many errors may be missed.

The most effective and efficient ways of performing a code review or designing test data are still research issues. One recommended way of performing a code review is to examine input/output first and then examine processing. Two formal methods of designing test data are the decision-table approach and the flowchart approach.

Software is available to perform either source code or object code comparison. Source code comparison provides a meaningful description of discrepancies between two versions of a program; however, the auditor must obtain assurance the source code examined is the version used to compile the object code. It is difficult to determine the nature of any discrepancies when two object code versions of a program are compared. However, if one of the versions is the production object code, the auditor can test directly whether unauthorized modifications to the code have occurred.

REVIEW QUESTIONS

18.1. Briefly explain the nature of the code review, test data, and code comparison evidence collection techniques. Explain how they can be used as an interrelated set of techniques to examine the quality of a program.

18.2. Briefly outline the findings of the limited empirical research on where errors occur in programs. What implications do these findings have for the use of various audit evidence collection techniques?

18.3. As the auditor of a computer installation, list three factors that would affect your decision on whether or not to rely on the documented program specifications as the basis for code review or test data design for a program.

18.4. Briefly explain how code review can be used to identify ineffective code and nonstandard code in a program.

18.5. Construct a short section of COBOL code to show how you could use the ALTER verb to activate unauthorized code. Briefly explain how your program will work.

18.6. List the attributes of a COBOL program you would examine to see if the code is sufficiently readable for you to be able to carry out code review.

18.7. Briefly explain why it is important to review the documentation for the compiler used within an installation when carrying out program code review.

18.8. Briefly explain the procedures an auditor should follow upon encountering a CALL or ENTER statement during the code review of a program. Which statement usually presents more problems for the auditor in verifying the integrity of code? Explain.

18.9. Give three COBOL verbs that can be used to violate the *privacy* of data, and explain briefly how they can be used. How would the auditor go about detecting the use of these verbs?

18.10. Briefly explain the purpose of the auditor first reviewing input/output instructions when undertaking code review of a program.

18.11. In a COBOL program, what verbs would the auditor review to check any computations performed in the program? Which verbs do you think would be most error-prone?

18.12. Briefly explain what is meant by base case system evaluation. How does it differ from the "normal" test data approach?

18.13. What is meant by reliable test data? Is it possible to generate automatically reliable test data for any arbitrary program?

18.14. Why is it important to design test data before creating test data? What are the advantages and disadvantages of carrying out the design and creation activities concurrently?

18.15. Briefly explain how redundant rules are detected in a decision table and how they are removed. What is meant by interrule and intrarule inconsistency? How are these inconsistencies handled? How can the completeness of a decision table be checked? (*Hint:* See Montalbano [1974]).

18.16. Briefly explain how the auditor can use production data to create test data. Is production data sometimes still useful even though it does not meet exactly the test data design specifications?

18.17. Are there any hazards to using a logic path monitor to determine whether paths in a program have been traversed? Explain.

18.18. List the reasons why discrepancies may occur between two object code versions of a program.

18.19. Briefly compare the relative advantages and disadvantages of source code comparison versus object code comparison.

18.20. What steps can the auditor take to ensure the integrity of code comparison software has not been corrupted?

EXERCISES AND CASES

18.1 As the auditor responsible for examining the accounts receivable system within a computer installation, you decide to undertake code review of the program that prints out a list of customers who have exceeded their allowed credit limit. Since the source code is stored in a library and online facilities are available, you use an editor to retrieve all instances of various statements in the program. One of the "IF" statements you retrieve runs as follows:

```
IF ACBAL LE ALLOWBAL
OR ACNUM EQ C105-6A
    NEXT SENTENCE
ELSE PERFORM PRINT-ROUTINE
```

You are perplexed by this piece of code. None of the employees within the computer installation has an account with the company numbered C105-6A. Further, you cannot find any customer to whom this account number has been issued yet.

Required: Briefly explain why you are concerned with this piece of code and how you would proceed now.

18.2. You are the auditor in charge of the audit of the payroll system for an organization. One of your staff performs a code review of the input validation program for timecard data. She brings the following section of code to you as she is unable to understand the purpose of the code.

```
EXAMINE HRS-WORKED TALLYING UNTIL FIRST 9
    REPLACING BY 4.
IF HRS-WORKED LT ZERO OR HRS-WORKED GT 60
    PERFORM ERROR-ROUTINE
    GO TO NEW-CARD.
IF TALLY EQ 1
    EXAMINE HRS-WORKED UNTIL FIRST 4
    REPLACING BY 9.
GO TO SALARY-CALC.
```

Required: Briefly outline the advice you would give to her.

18.3. The input card for a payroll program contains the following fields:
Employee number
Regular hours
Overtime hours
Expenses
Commission
Vacation time
Sick time

Required: List five tests you might carry out to determine whether the input validation program processes the input data correctly.

18.4. You are the auditor responsible for evaluating an organization's invoicing program. You decide to use test data to test that section of the program relating to sales discounts. During an interview with the sales manager you make the following notes about how the program is supposed to operate:

Providing customers pay within 30 days, they are entitled to a sales discount. If the sales amount is over $5000, a 1% discount applies. If sales are over $10,000, a 1½% discount applies. However, for new customers a salesperson is allowed to override the standard discount. For sales less than or equal to $5000, the salesperson can give a 1% discount, over $5000 a 1½% discount, and over $10,000 a 2% discount. If the customer is the federal government, a 4% discount always applies providing payment is still received within 30 days.

Required: Using both the decision-table and flowchart approach, design test data to test this processing aspect of the program.

18.5. The specifications for a fixed assets program include the following paragraph.
Straight-line depreciation is to be charged on fixed assets at the following rates:

Code no.	Rate
100–199	10%
200–299	15
300–399	20

However, if the fixed asset is located in Alice Springs, a further 5% is to be added to the depreciation rate to allow for the higher deterioration that results from the more severe climate. Further, any asset in the 200–299 code category that produces over 10,000 units per year is to have an extra 2% added to the depreciation rate to allow for the higher deterioration that occurs when the asset produces at above normal output.

Required: Design test data using both the decision-table and flowchart approach to determine whether these specifications have been implemented correctly in the program.

REFERENCES

Adams, Donald L. "Audit Review of Program Code – I," *EDPACS* (August 1975), pp. 1–5.

Andres, Albert. "An Analysis of Errors and Their Causes in System Programs," *IEEE Transactions on Software Engineering* (June 1975), pp. 140–149.

Baker, F. Terry. "Structured Programming in a Production Programming Environment," *IEEE Transactions on Software Engineering* (June 1975), pp. 241–252.

Boehm, Barry W. "Software and Its Impact: A Quantitative Study," *Datamation* (May 1973), pp. 48–59.

⸺, Robert K. McClean, and D. B. Urfrig. "Some Experience with Automated Aids to the Design of Large-Scale Reliable Software," *IEEE Transactions on Software Engineering* (March 1975), pp. 125–133.

Burch, John G., Jr., and Joseph L. Sardinas, Jr. *Computer Control and Audit: A Total Systems Approach* (New York: John Wiley & Sons, Inc., 1978).

Canadian Institute of Chartered Accountants. *Computer Audit Guidelines* (Toronto, Canada: The Canadian Institute of Chartered Accountants, 1975).

Clarke, Lori A. "A System to Generate Test Data and Symbolically Execute Programs," *IEEE Transactions on Software Engineering* (September 1976), pp. 215–222.

Comptroller General of the United States. *Auditing Computers with a Test Deck* (Washington, D.C.: U.S. Government Printing Office, 1975).

De Millo, Richard A., Richard J. Lipton, and Alan J. Perlis. "Social Processes and Proofs of Theorems and Programs," *Communications of the ACM* (May 1979), pp. 271–280.

Earl, Michael J. "Program Auditing: A New Approach to Computer Audit," *EDPACS* (December 1977), pp. 5–14.

Elshoff, James L. "An Analysis of Some Commercial PL/1 Programs," *IEEE Transactions on Software Engineering* (June 1976), pp. 113–120.

Endres, A. "An Analysis of Errors and Their Causes in System Programs," *IEEE Transactions on Software Engineering* (June 1975), pp. 140–149.

Fitzsimmons, Ann, and Tom Love. "A Review and Evaluation of Software Science," *Computing Surveys* (March 1978), pp. 3–18.

Geller, Matthew. "Test Data as an Aid in Proving Program Correctness," *Communications of the ACM* (May 1978), pp. 368–375.

Gerhart, Susan L., and John B. Goodenough. "Toward a Theory of Test Data Selection," *IEEE Transactions on Software Engineering* (June 1975), pp. 156–173.

Hartwick, R. Dean. "Test Planning," *Proceedings of the 1977 National Computer Conference* (Montvale, N.J.: AFIPS Press, 1977), pp. 285–294.

Heckel, Paul. "A Technique for Isolating Differences between Files," *Communications of the ACM* (April 1978), pp. 264–268.

Hetzel, W. C., ed. *Program Test Methods* (Englewood Cliffs, N.J.: Prentice-Hall, Inc., 1973).

Howden, William E. "Reliability of the Path Analysis Testing Strategy," *IEEE Transactions on Software Engineering* (September 1976), pp. 208–215.

Huang, J. C. "An Approach to Program Testing," *Computing Surveys* (September 1975), pp. 113–128.

Lauesen, S. "Debugging Techniques," *Software-Practice and Experience* (January 1979), pp. 51–63.

Lemos, Ronald S. "An Implementation of Structured Walk-Throughs in Teaching COBOL Programming," *Communications of the ACM* (June 1979), pp. 335–340.

Mills, Harlan D. "Software Development," *IEEE Transactions on Software Engineering* (December 1976), pp. 265–273.

Montalbano, Michael. *Decision Tables* (Chicago: Science Research Associates, Inc., 1974).

Mullen, Jack B. "Defining a Base Case System Evaluation," *EDP Auditing* (Pennsauken, N.J.: Auerbach Publishers, Inc., 1978), Portfolio 73-01-03, pp. 1–8.

Myers, Glenford J. "A Controlled Experiment in Program Testing and Code Walkthroughs/Inspections," *Communications of the ACM* (September 1978), pp. 760–768.

Orr, Kenneth T. "Systems Design, Structured Programming and Data Security," *IBM Data Security Forum* (September 1974), paper 33 (pages unnumbered).

Ramamoorthy, C. V., S. F. Ho, and W. T. Chen. "On the Automated Generation of Program Test Data," *IEEE Transactions on Software Engineering* (December 1976), pp. 293–300.

Rubey, Raymond J., Joseph A. Dana, and Peter W. Biche. "Quantitative Aspects of Software Validation," *IEEE Transactions on Software Engineering* (June 1975), pp. 150–155.

Stanford Research Institute. *Systems Auditability and Control Study: Data Processing Audit Practices Report* (Altamonte Springs, Fla.: The Institute of Internal Auditors, Inc., 1977).

Weiss, Harold. "Audit Review of Program Code – II," *EDPACS* (August 1975), pp. 6–7.

Yourdon, Edward. *Techniques of Program Structure and Design* (Englewood Cliffs, N.J.: Prentice-Hall, Inc., 1975).

CHAPTER 19

CONCURRENT AUDITING TECHNIQUES

CHAPTER OUTLINE

BASIC NATURE OF CONCURRENT AUDITING TECHNIQUES

NEED FOR CONCURRENT AUDITING TECHNIQUES
    Advanced Systems Require Continuous Monitoring
    Increasing Difficulty of Performing Walk-Throughs
    Presence of Entropy in Systems
    Problems Posed by Service Bureaus and Distributed Systems

TYPES OF CONCURRENT AUDITING TECHNIQUES
    Integrated Test Facility
    Snapshot/Extended Record
    System Control Audit Review File

IMPLEMENTING CONCURRENT AUDITING TECHNIQUES
    Perform a Feasibility Study
    Interact with Groups Affected by Concurrent Auditing
    Ensure the Relevant Expertise Is Available
    Ensure the Commitment of Management and Data Processing Staff
    Make the Necessary Technical Decisions
    Plan the Design and Implementation
    Implement and Test
    Postaudit the Results

ADVANTAGES/DISADVANTAGES OF CONCURRENT AUDITING TECHNIQUES

SUMMARY
REVIEW QUESTIONS
EXERCISES AND CASES
REFERENCES

The previous chapters on evidence collection discussed techniques for gathering evidence *after* application system data has been processed. In some cases ex post evidence collection and evaluation is unsatisfactory. The auditor needs to identify problems in application systems on a more timely basis. For this reason techniques have been developed that collect evidence at the same time as application system processing occurs. These techniques are called "concurrent auditing techniques." This chapter discusses the basic nature of concurrent auditing techniques, the reasons why they were developed, the specific types of concurrent auditing techniques available and their relative advantages and disadvantages, and methods of implementing concurrent auditing techniques.

BASIC NATURE OF CONCURRENT AUDITING TECHNIQUES

Concurrent auditing techniques use two bases for collecting audit evidence. First, special audit modules are embedded in application systems to collect, process, and print audit evidence. Second, in some cases special audit records are used to store the audit evidence collected so the auditor can examine this evidence at a later stage. These records may be stored on application system files or on a separate audit file.

Though evidence collection is concurrent with application system processing, the timing of evidence reporting is a decision for the auditor. If a critical error is identified, the auditor may program the embedded audit routines to report the error immediately. The evidence may be dumped directly to a printer or terminal in the auditor's office. In other cases some time lag will exist between evidence collection and reporting. The auditor uses the special audit records to store the evidence collected during this interim period.

NEED FOR CONCURRENT AUDITING TECHNIQUES

The basic motivation for developing concurrent auditing techniques is the need for more timely evidence collection and evidence evaluation. However, the following sections discuss in more detail why concurrent auditing techniques are becoming more important.

Advanced Systems Require Continuous Monitoring

One characteristic of advanced systems is tight coupling between their subsystems. For example, Figure 19.1 shows a shared database situation where

CHAPTER 19: CONCURRENT AUDITING TECHNIQUES

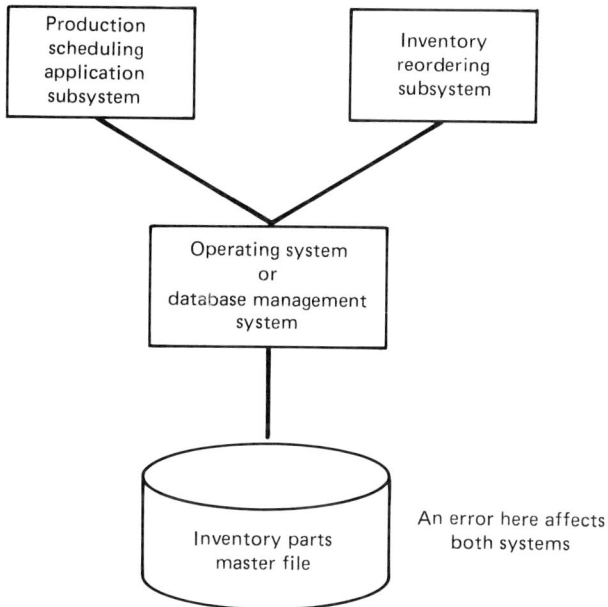

Figure 19.1
Tightly coupled subsystems accessing a shared database.

the production scheduling and inventory reordering subsystems concurrently access the inventory parts master file. Sharing the database causes these application subsystems to be tightly coupled; that is, each relies heavily on the correct functioning of the other.

Consider the implications of an erroneous update process in one subsystem. Incorrect processing in the production scheduling subsystem may result in the inventory reordering subsystem ordering insufficient inventory, thereby causing stockouts and lost sales; or too much inventory, thereby causing extra costs of obsolescence and storage. Concurrent auditing techniques enable faster identification of errors than ex post auditing techniques. Timely identification of errors is critical to the continuing operations of tightly coupled systems.

Increasing Difficulty of Performing Walk-Throughs

Auditors gain understanding of an application system by taking typical transactions of the system and tracing them through the various logic paths within the system. This also assists in identifying the system's strengths and weaknesses.

Advanced systems make the walk-through process more difficult because a large number of complex logic paths exist. Extensive coupling between different application systems also complicates matters. For example, understanding how a parts master file is updated may mean the auditor has to examine processes in the production scheduling system, inventory reordering system, purchasing system, receiving system, and warehouse system.

Concurrent auditing techniques facilitate the auditor's understanding of advanced systems by collecting all the information normally obtained from a walk-through in the one place. They capture images of a transaction as it traces its way through one particular logic path within a system and write this information to a file. When the auditor then attempts to understand a system and identify its strengths and weaknesses, all the information for different logic paths within the system exists in the one place.

Presence of Entropy in Systems

All systems have a characteristic called entropy (see Davis [1974]). Entropy is the tendency of a system toward disorder. There is never a question of whether entropy exists. The problem is to identify the *forms* of entropy that are present.

Some common forms of entropy exist in computer systems. One form arises because user information requirements change as the business expands and increased volumes of data have to be processed. These changes may place stress on the existing system design and the system's performance may start to degrade. The situation is further aggravated by hurried system and program maintenance to enable the system to cope with the changes. Errors creep into the system because of incomplete testing.

Because concurrent auditing techniques continuously monitor the system, increasing entropy can be identified at an early stage. They can be used to gather data on error frequencies and system exception frequencies and give advance warning of stresses being placed on the system. Thus, these techniques aid in understanding a system's evolution and assist in decreasing the future occurrence of errors.

Problems Posed by Service Bureaus and Distributed Systems

Sometimes it is difficult for the auditor to be physically present at a data processing installation to gather evidence. For example, a company's data processing may be performed by a service bureau, or data processing may be decentralized in the form of a distributed system. The auditor suffers two difficulties. First, valuable audit evidence cannot be collected because the auditor is unable to simply walk around the installation and gain impressions on the status of the installation's management, any changes occurring, the status of security, etc. Second, it is more difficult for the auditor to carry out data processing necessary for purposes of evidence collection. Even with data communications facilities the auditor may be forced to schedule any computer time required because files must be mounted at a remote installation, or the auditor's use of the system may unacceptably degrade response time.

A partial solution to these problems is to use concurrent auditing techniques. By embedding audit routines and records into application systems, evidence can be collected and the auditor can examine this evidence at a later stage when files are returned to the installation or time is available on the system for audit use.

TYPES OF CONCURRENT AUDITING TECHNIQUES

There are three major concurrent auditing techniques:

1 Integrated test facility (ITF)
2 Snapshot/extended record
3 System control audit review file (SCARF)

The above classification is generic in the sense that a number of specific techniques fall within each category. The specific techniques are simply variations on a basic idea. Furthermore, a technique or combination of techniques can be used to form a concurrent auditing system.

Integrated Test Facility

The integrated test facility (ITF) technique involves establishing a minicompany or dummy entity on an application system's files and processing audit test data against the entity as a means of verifying processing accuracy. For example, if the application is a ledgers system, the auditor sets up a dummy ledger account. If the application is a departmental costing system, the auditor sets up a dummy department.

The auditor submits test data to the application system as part of the normal system data for processing. In the case of a batch system, the auditor completes the system's source documents and submits them through the usual clerical channels. This allows the auditor to examine the quality of both the manual and machine processing within the system. In the case of an interactive system, the auditor keys in data while the system is online. Figure 19.2 shows the methods.

Using ITF involves two major design decisions:

1 What method will be used to enter test data?
2 What method will be used to remove the effects of ITF transactions?

Methods of Entering Test Data   Test data can be entered to an ITF application using two methods: (*a*) tagging live transactions, and (*b*) designing new test transactions. The first method involves using the normal transactions of the system and tagging them in some way so that the application system programs recognize them as ITF transactions. Thus, these transactions perform two updates instead of the normal one: one for the application system records and one for the dummy entity. The second method follows the normal procedures described in Chapter 18 for design of test data.

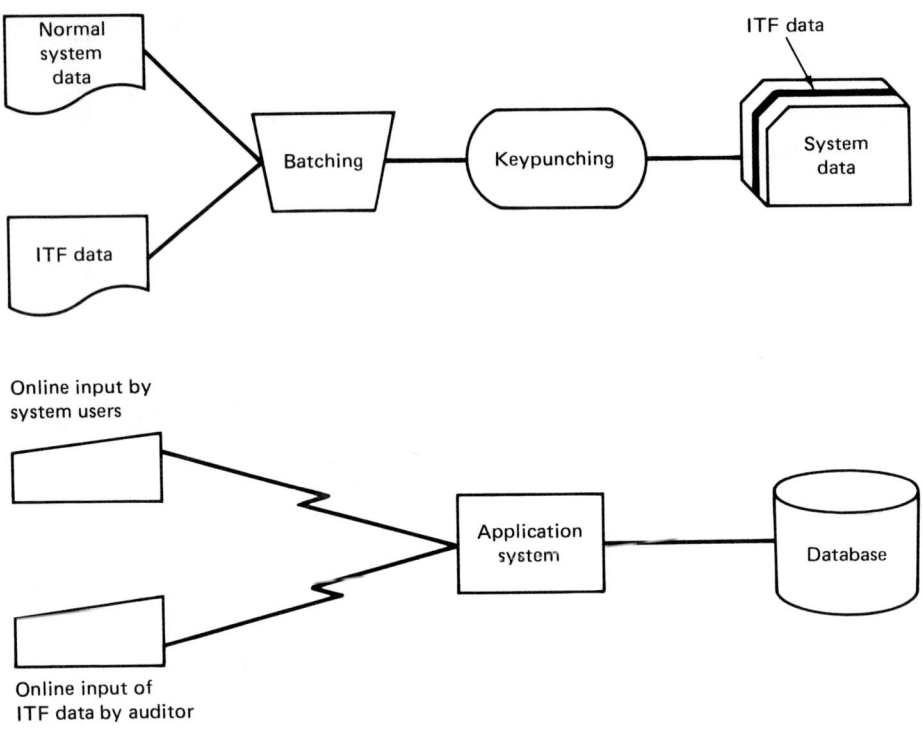

Figure 19.2
Submitting ITF data to an application system.

If the first method of entering test data is used, ITF transactions must be identified in some way. There are several alternatives. First, a special identifier field can be used to denote the transaction is also an ITF transaction. Space must be provided on the system's source documents for this field or the transaction tagged at the time of keypunching. Second, audit software modules can be embedded in the application system's programs to recognize transactions having certain characteristics of interest to the auditor. These modules then select and tag the transactions as ITF transactions. Third, sampling routines can be embedded in the application system programs that tag transactions as ITF transactions. This latter method attempts to select ITF transactions representative of the normal application system processing.

The first method of entering test data has two advantages: (*a*) ease of use, and (*b*) testing with transactions representative of normal system processing. It has two major disadvantages. First, using live data may mean the limiting conditions within the system are not tested. Second, because audit modules must be embedded in the application system, the presence of this extraneous code increases the risk of error occurring.

If the auditor uses the second method to enter test data and designs new test transactions, the auditor inserts the dummy entity's unique identifier in the key field of the transaction to denote the transaction as an ITF transaction. The transaction is processed as a normal transaction; no special routines need be embedded in the application system to tag the transaction. Though design of test data can be difficult, this method of entering ITF test data allows the auditor to test systematically all the controls within the application system.

Methods of Removing the Effects of ITF Transactions The presence of ITF transactions within an application system affects the output results obtained; for example, the control totals produced by the system. Unless the auditor discloses that ITF transactions have been used and manual adjustments are then made to output, the effects of ITF transactions must be removed. This can be accomplished in three ways: (*a*) application system program modification, (*b*) the auditor submitting reversal entries, and (*c*) the auditor submitting trivial or immaterial transactions so the effects on output are negligible.

Modifying the application system programs to recognize ITF transactions and not take them into account has two advantages. First, the method is simple to implement. Second, users are not affected by the auditor's activities. The auditor can covertly carry out testing of the application system. However, the method has two disadvantages. First, there is some cost in developing and maintaining the software to recognize the ITF transactions. If the system is stable or few modifications are made that affect ITF transactions, this cost may be relatively low. Second, the presence of extraneous code in the application system increases the risk of data integrity being violated through this code being in error.

If the auditor submits reversal entries to remove the effects of ITF transactions, this method has the advantage of simplicity since no programming costs are involved. It has several disadvantages. First, if the auditor wants to act covertly, the reversal entries must be submitted in the same run. Even then, control totals for the number of transactions processed are affected, and this may cause confusion for application system users. Second, the auditor must ensure the reversals are carried out correctly if data integrity is to be maintained. Third, the method causes problems in a shared database environment. Consider, for example, a company which borrows and lends daily on the short-term money market and which has a computer-based decision support system for its money market managers. This decision support system frequently may access the cash accounts master file during a day and use various fields. If the auditor affects these fields with ITF transactions and the reversal entries have not been processed (the lag may only be a matter of microseconds), this may cause the decision support system to provide wrong information to management, resulting in a costly investment error.

The third method of submitting trivial transactions to "remove" the effects (the effects are not really removed) of ITF test data has the advantages of simplicity and no costs and risks involved with program modification. However, unless users are informed that slight differences in control totals may be due to audit testing, time and effort may be wasted senselessly on trying to

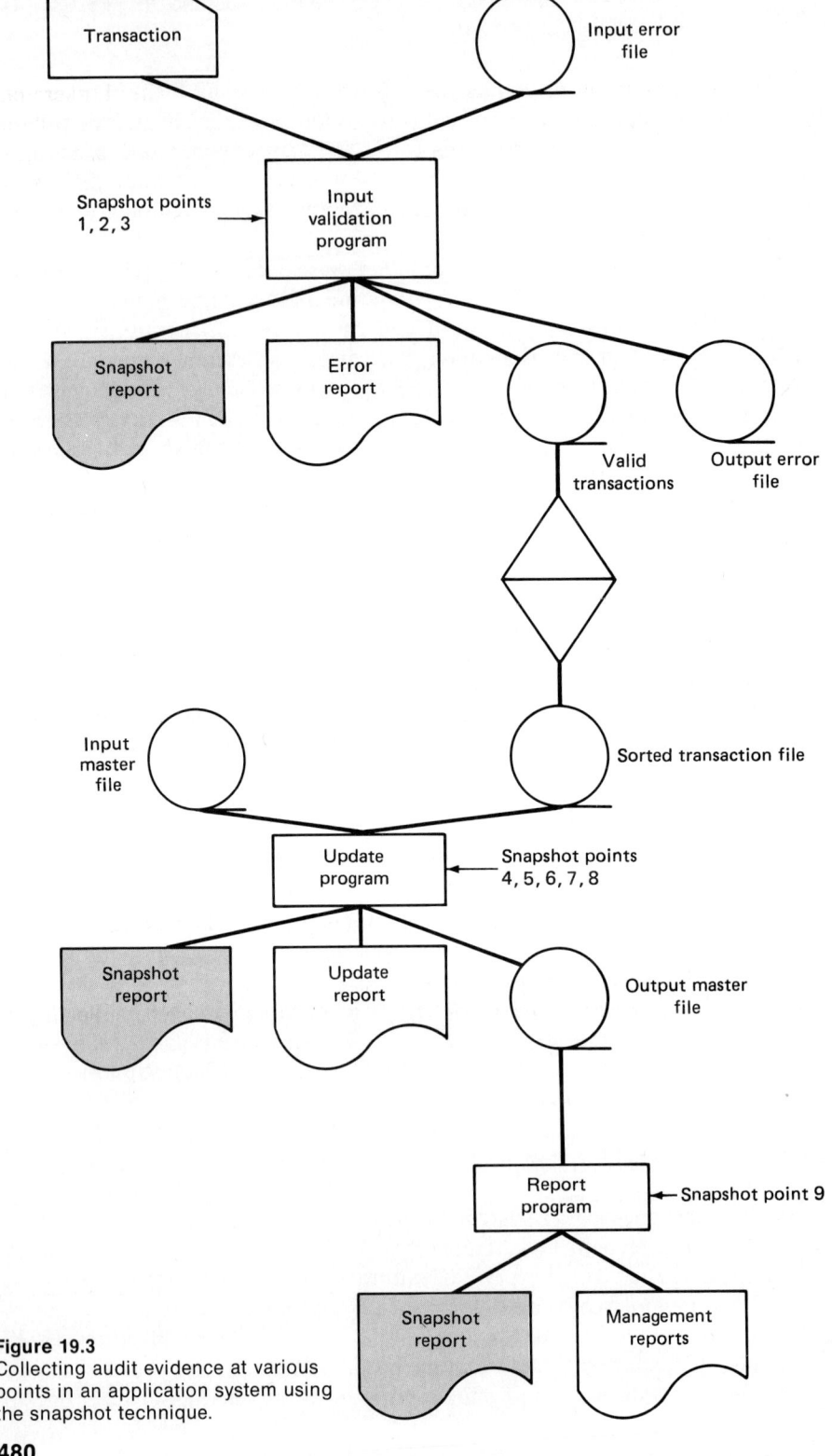

Figure 19.3
Collecting audit evidence at various points in an application system using the snapshot technique.

identify the source of the error. Even though the amount is trivial, users may be concerned that a logic error is present in the system. The auditor still may have to inform users of ITF testing and so lose covert testing capabilities. Another disadvantage is that it places limitations on the testing that can be carried out. Certain types of limit tests where large amounts are involved cannot be attempted.

Snapshot/Extended Record

For application systems that are large or complex, tracing the different logic paths through the system is difficult. The number of different possibilities can be enormous. The auditor who wants to perform a walk-through of a transaction faces a difficult task. A simple solution to the problem is to allow the computer to perform the walk-through.

The snapshot technique involves taking "pictures" of a transaction as it flows through the system. The auditor embeds software routines at different points within the application system to capture images of the transaction as it progresses through the various stages. To validate processing, the audit routines capture beforeimages and afterimages of the transaction. Figure 19.3 shows how the technique is used to obtain audit evidence at various points in a simple batch system.

A snapshot transaction first must be tagged by the auditor with a special indicator so that the audit software routines recognize it as a transaction for which an audit trail is to be printed. The different snapshot points must be numbered so that the auditor can identify which routine within the application system performed the processing. Audit trail reports must be printed for each snapshot point within the system. Alternatively, the snapshot can be written onto a file for later printing.

A modification of the snapshot technique is the extended record technique. Instead of writing one record for each snapshot point, a large record can be built up consisting of images from each snapshot point and carried through the system (Figure 19.4). This technique has the advantage of collecting all the snapshot data related to a transaction in one place. Again, the extended

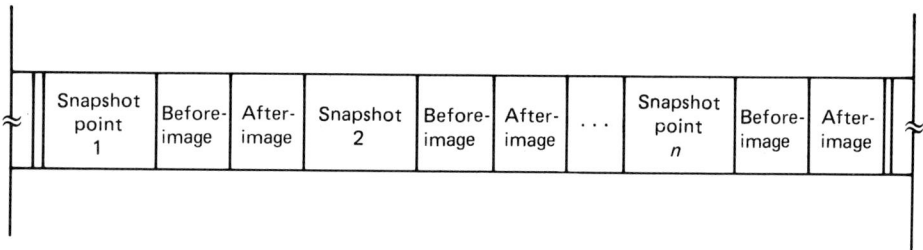

Figure 19.4
An extended record used with the snapshot technique.

record can be printed at the end of processing or written away to a file for later printing.

The snapshot and extended record techniques can be used in conjunction with the ITF technique to provide an extensive audit trail. ITF provides a master file record against which the auditor can test the processing of various transaction types. The snapshot and extended record techniques provide the audit trail as each transaction type progresses through the system.

System Control Audit Review File

The System Control Audit Review File (SCARF) technique is the most complex concurrent auditing technique. SCARF involves embedding audit software modules within a host application system to provide continuous monitoring of the system's transactions. These audit modules are placed at predetermined points to gather information about transactions that are of interest to the auditor. The information collected is then written onto a special audit file — the SCARF master file. Periodically the auditor examines the information contained on this file to see if some aspect of the system needs follow-up. Figure 19.5 illustrates the method for a master file update program.

Using SCARF involves two major design decisions:

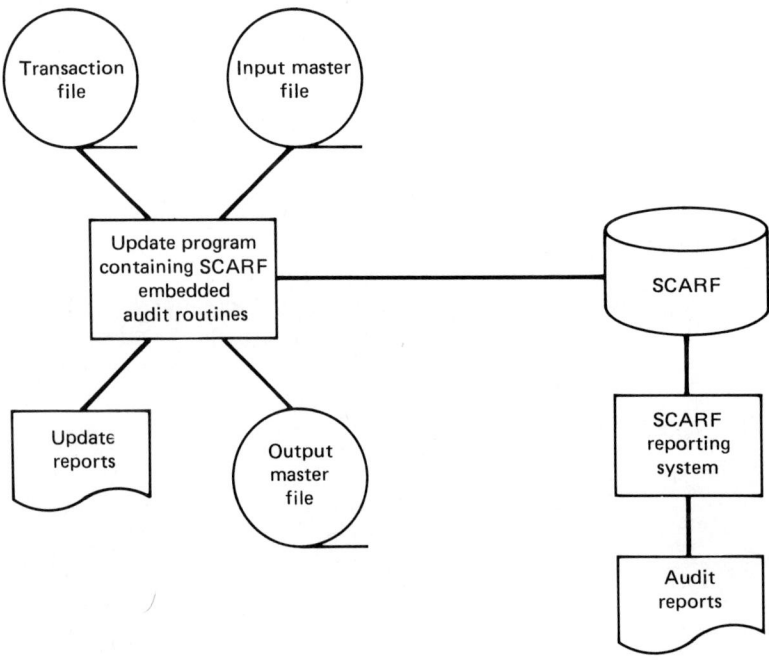

Figure 19.5
Use of SCARF with a master file update program.

1 Determining what information will be collected by SCARF embedded audit routines
2 Determining the reporting system to be used with SCARF

Information to Be Collected by SCARF The placement of embedded audit routines within the application system depends on the types of evidence the auditor wants to collect. Several types of information can be captured by the routines (see, also, Perry [1974a, 1974b]):

Information captured	Explanation
Application System Errors	Ideally an application system contains all the logic necessary to prevent and detect errors that occur. However, it is possible design and programming errors exist from the start, or errors may creep into the system as it is modified and maintained. SCARF audit routines provide an independent check on the quality of system processing.
Policy and Procedural Variances	Organizations have technical and administrative policies and standards to guide staff in their work. For example, a company may require one of its products to be sold in certain size lots. Industries often have accepted policies and standards to which members of the industry are expected to adhere. SCARF audit routines can be used to check variations from these policies and standards.
System Exceptions	SCARF can be used to monitor different types of application system exceptions. For example, certain errors may be allowed within the system provided they are within a specified tolerance. The auditor may wish to examine the frequency with which these errors occur. Salespersons may be given some leeway in the prices they charge customers. SCARF can be used to see how frequently salespersons override the standard price.
Statistical Samples	Some of the embedded audit routines may be statistical sampling routines. SCARF provides a convenient way of collecting all the sample information together on one file.
Snapshots and Extended Records	The printing of snapshots and extended records during normal application system processing may be inconvenient. The snapshots and extended records can be written onto the SCARF file and printed when required.
Performance Measurement Data	The auditor may use the embedded routines to collect various data useful for measuring or improving the performance of the system. For example, the frequency of certain kinds of transactions can be monitored and programs modified to test for the most frequent kinds of transaction first.

The auditor should give careful consideration to ways in which the integrity of the SCARF embedded audit routines can be maintained. Several measures can be undertaken. Application program listings should not contain the source code of the embedded audit routines. Call statements, only, should exist. The source code should be maintained on a special library file that is the responsibility of the audit staff. Alternatively, the source code can be maintained on the normal program library system and given special security locks to prevent it being read by unauthorized persons. Documentation for the routines should be kept by the auditor or require special authorization for withdrawal from the data processing library.

Structure of the SCARF Reporting System Determining the structure of the SCARF reporting system involves several design decisions: (*a*) how the SCARF file will be updated, (*b*) sort codes and report formats to be used, and (*c*) the timing of report preparation. If SCARF is to be used in conjunction with ITF and the snapshot/extended record techniques, care must be taken to ensure decisions made on the SCARF reporting system satisfy the requirements of the other techniques.

With respect to the method of updating the SCARF file, one alternative is to have each application system create a temporary SCARF work file that in due course is copied onto the master SCARF file using utility software. This method has the advantage of simplicity and the disadvantages of possible loss of the work file and delay until it has been written to the master file. A second alternative is to allow the SCARF master file to be updated concurrently by several application systems. Since the SCARF file is used primarily for reporting, many of the problems with concurrent update processes, discussed in Chapter 12, do not arise.

Careful thought must be given to the report formats and SORT codes used with SCARF. The quality of reporting in part determines the effectiveness with which the evidence collected is communicated to the auditor. The report design should follow the guidelines described in Chapter 13.

The report formats affect the sort codes assigned the SCARF records. Two kinds of sort codes are needed. First, a unique identifier must be assigned the record that identifies it as being needed for the preparation of a specific report. This code enables the records to be selected from the unordered SCARF file. Second, sort codes are needed that are application-specific so data can be presented on the report in some logical order. For example, for a parts inventory audit report, records for subcomponents may have to be sorted by major components, or critical variances detected by the audit modules may be assigned a high priority so they sort to the front of the audit report.

The decision on the length of the reporting period primarily depends on the importance of the audit evidence collected and the costs of generating the SCARF reports. Until report formats and reporting periods stabilize, generalized audit software can be used to prepare reports. Once stability has been attained, report generation can be made automatic. Part of the SCARF reporting system can be a timing facility whereby a file or program table is examined to determine when a SCARF report should be produced.

IMPLEMENTING CONCURRENT AUDITING TECHNIQUES

When implementing concurrent auditing techniques, the auditor should follow the same steps necessary to achieve any well-implemented system. Since these steps have been described extensively in Chapter 5, the following sections provide only a brief overview and highlight those aspects having special relevance for concurrent auditing.

Perform a Feasibility Study

Concurrent auditing techniques result in overheads for application systems because of the presence of special audit records and embedded audit routines. Sometimes these overheads may be unacceptable; for example, in an online system where response times are critical. The auditor must consider carefully the costs and benefits of using concurrent auditing techniques.

Interact with Groups Affected by Concurrent Auditing

Because of the ongoing support needed for concurrent auditing techniques, they are typically the responsibility of the internal audit staff. However, external auditors should be contacted as they may have requirements that can be met by a concurrent auditing system. In any case they should be informed of progress with concurrent auditing since it will affect their assessment of the reliability of internal control.

Data processing staff may be both developers and users of concurrent auditing techniques. If the audit staff does not have sufficient expertise to be able to program the audit modules required, data processing staff may be made responsible for this task. Concurrent auditing techniques also constitute a useful system testing vehicle for data processing staff.

It is also critical that a viable communications system exists between data processing staff and the audit staff. In the past, one of the major reasons why concurrent auditing techniques have failed is neglect in communicating to the audit staff changes in the application system that affect the concurrent auditing system.

Application system users also must be informed if concurrent auditing affects their normal tasks; for example, the possibility of minor discrepancies existing in control totals because of ITF transactions. Users also may be interested in concurrent auditing techniques as a means of training new staff. This matter is discussed further later in the chapter.

Ensure the Relevant Expertise Is Available

For two reasons, concurrent auditing techniques should be used only after the audit staff has gained some expertise with EDP auditing. First, even if the audit staff has insufficient expertise to perform the programming of the embedded audit modules, at least they still must be able to evaluate the work of data processing staff or consultants who perform the programming. Otherwise, the usual questions of audit independence arise. Second, without EDP audit expertise, it is doubtful whether the auditor will be able to choose those points in a system where audit modules can be placed most profitably. Even with EDP audit experience, auditors first should implement concurrent auditing techniques on simple systems so they gain experience with the techniques.

Ensure the Commitment of Management and Data Processing Staff

If management is not committed to concurrent auditing, they may be unwilling to allocate future resources for its maintenance. If data processing staff are not committed, they may directly sabotage the techniques or contribute to their downfall through neglecting to communicate application system changes to the audit staff.

Make the Necessary Technical Decisions

When implementing concurrent auditing techniques, several key technical design decisions have to made. For ITF the test data method to be used and the method of removing the effects of the ITF transactions must be chosen. For snapshot/extended records and SCARF, the auditor must decide on those points in the system where data will be captured and the type of data that will be captured. The structure of the SCARF reporting system also must be determined.

Plan the Design and Implementation

Once the necessary technical decisions have been made, the specific design for the concurrent auditing system can proceed and the implementation can be planned. Especially important is the design of the audit support system. This support system includes procedures for follow-up of detected variances, procedures for maintenance of the concurrent auditing system, and standards for documentation of the system, its associated support procedures, and the results produced.

Implement and Test

The normal procedures for orderly and controlled implementation of a system should be used when implementing concurrent auditing techniques. Great care must be taken in testing the techniques. Since an error in a concurrent auditing technique may cause an error in an application system, the continuing support of management, data processing staff, and application system users depends on the techniques being error-free.

Postaudit the Results

After concurrent auditing techniques have been running for some time, the auditor should evaluate the costs and benefits of the techniques. This postaudit identifies weaknesses that possibly can be corrected. It also may lead to the conclusion that concurrent auditing techniques should be scrapped. In addition, the postaudit formalizes the experience gained and establishes guidelines for the design and implementation of concurrent auditing techniques in other application systems.

ADVANTAGES/DISADVANTAGES OF CONCURRENT AUDITING TECHNIQUES

Concurrent auditing techniques provide the following major advantages for the auditor, data processing staff, and application system users:

Advantage	Explanation
Viable Alternative to Ex Post Auditing and Auditing Around the Computer	Though the use of concurrent auditing techniques is not widespread (Perry [1977a]), some organizations have successfully implemented the techniques. By using the techniques the auditor need not infer the quality of application system processing through examining only the input and output of the application system. The evidence obtained is more timely and more comprehensive.
Surprise Test Capability	Using concurrent auditing techniques, the auditor can unobtrusively gather evidence. Because data processing staff and application system users normally are not aware that evidence is being collected, the techniques provide the auditor with a surprise test capability.
Test Vehicle for Data Processing	With respect to the quality of application system processing, data processing staff have the same concerns as the auditors. Those organizations that use concurrent auditing techniques report strong support for the techniques by data processing staff. The auditor must consider trading off some independence for the improved testing capabilities provided to data processing staff by concurrent auditing techniques.
Training Vehicle for Users	Some organizations use ITF as a training vehicle for new staff. Training need not proceed by simulating the preparation of input data and its submission to the application system. Instead, new staff can prepare data on the system's source documents, submit the data to the application system, and obtain feedback on any mistakes made via the system's error reports.

In spite of these advantages a study by Stanford Research Institute [1977] found few organizations use concurrent auditing techniques, and furthermore the researchers believe the techniques have questionable or minimal future potential. The conclusions of the study are debatable; however, they illustrate concurrent auditing techniques also have their disadvantages.

A primary disadvantage of concurrent auditing techniques is the need for auditors to have extensive EDP expertise before they are capable of successfully designing and implementing the techniques. Whether this is a failing of the techniques or the auditors who use the techniques is questionable. As Perry [1978] points out, a key feature of concurrent auditing techniques is that they provide detailed evidence on the quality of individual programs in the application system rather than general evidence about the application system. However, the Stanford researchers seem to believe investigating individual programs will not be a primary activity of auditors in the future. Rather, they argue auditors will play a more active role in the system development process. Some experienced EDP auditors would debate this issue. It is an interesting question for further research.

The costs of implementing concurrent auditing techniques can be substantial. The Stanford researchers found the following costs to be typical:

1 ITF – 3-10% of system development cost
2 Snapshot – 2 weeks planning plus 2½ days programming per audit module
3 Extended records – may be as high as 5% of system development effort
4 SCARF – 3-month development effort

The costs of implementing concurrent auditing techniques will be less if they are designed and implemented when the application system is initially developed.

Finally, concurrent auditing techniques require an ongoing commitment. Modifications and maintenance to the application system may necessitate changes to the concurrent auditing techniques. Otherwise, the techniques may start to collect useless data or cause errors in application system processing.

SUMMARY

Concurrent auditing techniques collect audit evidence at the same time as application system processing occurs. This evidence is written to a file and periodically printed for the auditor to analyze and evaluate. The auditor has control over the time lag between evidence collection and reporting.

Three major concurrent auditing techniques exist. The integrated test facility technique (ITF) involves establishing a dummy entity on the application system's files and processing audit test transactions against the entity. The snapshot/extended record technique involves embedding audit modules in the application system and capturing images of a transaction as it passes through the system. The system control audit review file technique (SCARF) also involves embedding audit modules within the application system and capturing variances and exceptions of interest to the auditor.

The implementation of concurrent auditing techniques should follow the project management procedures established to achieve effective and efficient systems. These procedures include the auditor interacting with groups affected by the techniques, a feasibility study, planned implementation and testing, and postaudit. Several key design decisions must be made including the method of entering test data and removing its effects, the types of variances and exception data to be collected, the points where audit modules will be embedded in the application system, and the structure of the reporting system to be used.

REVIEW QUESTIONS

19.1. Explain the nature of concurrent auditing.
19.2. Why might a cash receipts and payments system be coupled tightly with an investments decision support system? What could be the implications of an error made in either system? How might concurrent auditing techniques assist in preventing errors?
19.3. What is entropy? Data processing installations are often characterized by a high staff turnover. Is this a form of entropy? If so, how can concurrent auditing techniques help arrest entropy?
19.4. What might prevent snapshot and SCARF being used if a service bureau performs routine data processing (e.g., payroll, accounts receivable) for a company? Would there be any restrictions on the form ITF can take if the auditor decides to implement it in the application systems processed at the service bureau?
19.5. Using ITF, what form will the dummy entity take if there are multiple record types on an application system's files? What form will the dummy entity take if there is a single record type of variable length?
19.6. Suppose a file is set up hierarchically; for example, projects within departments within subdivisions within divisions within the company. There may be up to 10 levels within the hierarchy, and because of the nature and size of some of the operations carried out within the company, various levels in the hierarchy can be present or missing. Thus, a large number of possible forms of the hierarchy exists. How would you set up an ITF dummy entity for such a file?
19.7. Discuss some methods of setting up a dummy entity on a file. Outline the advantages and disadvantages of each method depending on whether the file is hierarchical or flat and has fixed length or variable length records.
19.8. Describe the two methods of entering test data for an ITF application and discuss the relative advantages and disadvantages of each method.
19.9. After some time, clerical personnel may start to recognize the code used for ITF transactions and so treat them in a special way; for example, take special care on coding associated source documents such as the batch cover sheet. How can the auditor prevent this occurring?
19.10. Describe the methods of removing the effects of ITF transactions and the relative advantages and disadvantages of each method.
19.11. Outline the difference between the snapshot and extended record techniques.

19.12. In a large system an extended record may grow to a size that is unacceptable because of the size of the input/output buffer required in a program, an installation standard, or system software limitations. What must the auditor do in this situation?

19.13. Describe the SCARF concurrent auditing technique. Discuss how snapshot and SCARF can be integrated.

19.14. A properly written input program should contain the necessary subroutines to validate input data. Why might the auditor also be interested in using SCARF embedded audit modules to check input data is valid?

19.15. Why might the auditor use a concurrent auditing technique to collect periodically the volumes of different transaction types? When the auditor wishes to "turn off" the collection of this data for a time, how can this be accomplished?

19.16. Who are the groups affected by concurrent auditing techniques and how are they affected?

19.17. Why is it unlikely external auditors will be responsible for implementing and maintaining concurrent auditing techniques in an organization?

19.18. Describe the various design and implementation steps to be undertaken with a SCARF reporting system.

19.19. When report records are selected from the SCARF file and printed, should they then be deleted from the SCARF file? If so, why? If not, what should be the basis for deletion?

19.20. What should be the components of the manual audit system supporting a concurrent auditing system? Why is it important to carefully design the audit support system?

19.21. What methods can be used to test a concurrent auditing system? Can the test data used to test the application system be used to test the concurrent auditing system without any alterations being made?

19.22. "If you can't formally document in audit working papers the results of concurrent auditing and the audit analyses undertaken, you shouldn't use concurrent auditing." Agree or disagree?

19.23. What are some of the major factors affecting the cost of concurrent auditing? Which concurrent auditing technique do you think would most likely be more costly? What are the incremental benefits for the added costs of this technique?

EXERCISES AND CASES

19.1. A large diversified company has divisions scattered around the country. These divisions do not necessarily carry out the same kinds of activities. The company has a distributed data processing system to support its operations. Each division has its own costing system but aggregate cost information is transmitted to head office for centralized planning and control purposes. The costing system is relatively new and the internal audit staff has not examined thoroughly its operations. Because of budget constraints for the current financial year, the audit staff is unable to fly to different divisional locations.

Required: How might the audit staff use concurrent auditing techniques to assist them in a preliminary evaluation of the system before they undertake a detailed investigation for the coming year? Note, this preliminary evaluation may form the basis for deciding which divisions they will then visit.

19.2. The internal audit manager is involved in a debate with management over the implementation of concurrent auditing techniques in a payroll system. She argues the system is a critical system and, as such, there is no need to undertake a feasibility study with respect to implementing the techniques. Further, she points out there are several recurring errors in the system and the source of these errors, as yet, cannot be identified. Management is not so sure of the benefits to be derived from implementing concurrent auditing techniques and they want a detailed feasibility study. Is a detailed feasibility study necessary? Why or why not?

19.3. The internal audit manager has just returned from a course on concurrent auditing techniques and he decides there are many systems where implementing the techniques would be beneficial. He decides to start out with the most critical application system, an online inventory system that supplies information to divisions scattered around the country. How would you advise the internal audit manager to proceed?

19.4. Because of his concern with audit independence, the internal audit manager decides to implement concurrent auditing techniques within an application system and tell as few people as possible. He argues he has an expert programmer on his staff and so he does not need data processing to perform the work. What problems might arise from this strategy?

19.5. With the active support of all groups affected, the audit staff implements its first concurrent auditing system, a SCARF system, in a large ledgers application system. However, on the second day of live operations for the SCARF system, the data processing manager calls the audit manager to complain. She is furious because the SCARF file has already grown to consume an entire disk pack and processing time for the ledgers system has degraded by 15%. She accuses the audit manager of failing to test the embedded audit routines. He argues all the logic was thoroughly tested, and what's more, data processing programmers wrote the routines. What might have happened?

19.6. You are the internal auditor for a company that is implementing a new online realtime update order entry system. Salespersons enter transactions at intelligent terminals, which validate the input data, and a centralized orders master file is updated. The system also is to be integrated with other application systems: inventory, purchasing, billing, accounts payable, cash receipts and disbursements, general ledger.

Required: Identify three economic events that you might monitor using concurrent auditing techniques. Explain what control objectives you hope to achieve by monitoring the events and why you have chosen these events for monitoring purposes.

19.7. As the manager of internal audit for a company, one day you receive a telephone call from the data processing manager. She is upset because a major inventory update run has had to be aborted. The reason why is that some audit modules implemented in the inventory system had commenced to process data erroneously. She points out that this is the fifth time in the last few months that this action has had to be undertaken because of problems with the audit modules.

When you question the junior auditor responsible for the audit modules, he complains that the reason why failures are occurring is because the data processing department has been making changes to the inventory system but failing to notify him of changes that affect the audit modules. He has tried on several occasions to get data processing personnel to send him notification of changes to the inventory system but he has been unsuccessful.

Required: Outline the steps you would follow in an attempt to remedy the problems that have occurred.

REFERENCES

Davis, Gordon B. *Management Information Systems: Conceptual Foundations, Structure, and Development* (New York: McGraw-Hill Book Company, 1974).

Mair, William C., Donald R. Wood, and Keagle W. Davis. *Computer Control and Audit*, 2d ed. (Altamonte Springs, Fla.: The Institute of Internal Auditors, Inc., 1976).

Munson, James E. "We Tried ITF—We Like ITF," *EDPACS* (August 1977), pp. 1-3.

Perry, William E. "Try ITF, You'll Like ITF," *EDPACS* (December 1973), pp. 1-6.

_____. "Concurrent EDP Auditing: An Early Warning Scheme," *EDPACS* (January 1974a), pp. 1-7.

_____. "Concurrent EDP Auditing: An Implementation Approach," *EDPACS* (February 1974b), pp. 1-6.

_____. "Snapshot—A Technique for Tagging and Tracing Transactions," *EDPACS* (March 1974c), pp. 1-7.

_____. "Computer Audit Practices," *EDPACS* (July 1977a), pp. 1-9.

_____. "Skills Needed to Utilize EDP Audit Practices," *EDPACS* (November 1977b), pp. 1-13.

_____. "Selecting Computer Audit Practices," *EDPACS* (March 1978), pp. 1-11.

Porter, W. Thomas, and William E. Perry. *EDP Controls and Auditing* 2d ed. (Belmont, Calif.: Wadsworth Publishing Company, Inc., 1977).

Stanford Research Institute. *Systems Auditability and Control Study: Data Processing Audit Practices Report* (Altamonte Springs, Fla.: The Institute of Internal Auditors, Inc., 1977).

Weber, Ron. "Auditing Computer Systems Using Integrated Test Facility," *The Australian Accountant* (May 1975), pp. 232-235.

CHAPTER 20

INTERVIEWS, QUESTIONNAIRES, AND CONTROL FLOWCHARTS

CHAPTER OUTLINE

INTERVIEWS
    Some Conceptual Issues
    Preparing for the Interview
    Conducting the Interview
    Analyzing the Interview
QUESTIONNAIRES
    Design of Questionnaires
    Reliability and Validity Issues
    Effective Use of Questionnaires
CONTROL FLOWCHARTS
    Constructing a Control Flowchart
    Advantages and Limitations of Control Flowcharting
SUMMARY
REVIEW QUESTIONS
EXERCISES AND CASES
REFERENCES

This chapter examines three manual techniques used to collect evidence on the quality of computer systems: interviews, questionnaires, and control flowcharts. Interviews and questionnaires have been widely used evidence collection techniques in manual systems. Their importance has not diminished in computer systems. Particularly during the evaluation of the management control framework, interviews and questionnaires constitute a primary means of testing compliance (see Chapter 2 and, for example, Chapters 4 and 5). Control flowcharting also has been used with manual systems; however, its use is now more widespread because of the general popularity of flowcharting techniques as an analysis and documentation aid in computer systems.

INTERVIEWS

When assessing the quality of a computer system, the auditor may use interviewing for a variety of reasons; for example:

1 Systems analysts and programmers who designed and implemented the system may be interviewed so the auditor can obtain a better understanding of functions and controls within the system.

2 Clerical staff may be interviewed to determine whether or not there are problems in submitting data to the system.

3 Users of the system may be interviewed to determine the impact of the system on their quality of working life.

4 If a fraud is discovered, personnel may be interviewed to try and track down who perpetrated the fraud.

5 Operators may be interviewed to identify systems that seem to consume abnormal amounts of resources at run time.

6 The controller may be interviewed to identify the critical systems within an organization.

Interviews can be used to obtain both qualitative and quantitative information. Ultimately the objective is to elicit frank, complete, and honest answers from a respondent who has more information about a particular topic than the auditor.

A distinction should be made between interviewing and interrogation. The motivation for an interrogation is some type of wrongdoing—a fraud. The respondent often may be antagonistic and uncooperative; possibly the suspected culprit. In an interview, hopefully respondents bear no antagonism toward the interviewer, although this may be the case if respondents believe the auditor will bring about a change that has an unfavorable impact on their work life. Most auditors will perform an interview task. However, effective interrogation requires special skills; it should be left to experts (see, further, Krauss and MacGahan [1979]).

Some Conceptual Issues

Effective interviewing requires the auditor to have a basic understanding of what motivates a person to respond to a question. This knowledge allows the auditor to design better interviews and to identify why problems sometimes arise (see, further, Kahn and Cannell [1966] and Bouchard [1976]).

A respondent's motivation to reply to questions asked in an interview is a function of the extent to which they perceive the interview to be a means of obtaining their own goals. If respondents see the interview as helping them attain their goals, they will respond favorably. If they see the interview as hindering their goal attainment, they may be antagonistic toward the interviewer.

Different interviews require different levels of respondent motivation if the interview is to be successful. Questions vary in the stress they place on the respondent—the amount of time required to answer, the recall effort required, the threats and fears generated, etc. More stressful interviews require higher levels of respondent motivation. The auditor can control the level of stress caused by an interview by limiting the number of difficult questions asked in any one interview, making more stressful interviews shorter, and alleviating any fears that may arise as a result of the interview before the interview is commenced.

In any interview there are two forces that sometimes conflict: the desire of the interviewer to obtain answers to questions on a problem and the desire of the respondent to pursue topics that are of interest to the respondent with a responsible person (the interviewer). Unfortunately the interviewer's task is to try and foster the respondent's interest in the topic of the interview. The interviewer must communicate clearly the purpose of the interview to the respondent, show empathy toward the respondent, and promote a spirit of mutual trust and respect.

Preparing for the Interview

Conducting a successful interview requires careful preparation. The following sections discuss some of the major steps to be taken by the auditor during the preparation phase.

Perform Background Research Before undertaking an interview, the auditor must ensure the information required is not readily available elsewhere; otherwise, respondents may become upset if they consider the interview to be a waste of their time. The auditor should be convinced an interview is the best evidence collection technique to use for the problem at hand.

Background research allows the auditor to become familiar with the organization's policy and terminology relating to the interview topic. Further issues that might be pursued during the interview sometimes are identified. Alternate sources of information also may be found.

Identify the Respondents It is important to identify those personnel within the organization who can provide most information on the interview topic. Interviews can be costly and time-consuming; wasted effort should be minimized.

Organization charts often are a first source of information on the appropriate respondents. The auditor also might seek the help of senior management when identifying the respondents. It is useful to enlist the help of senior management since they should be aware of any interviews carried out within their area. Further, senior management can introduce the auditor to the respondents (perhaps at a group meeting) prior to the conduct of the interviews so the respondents have advance notice of the reasons for the interview.

Prepare the Interview Content During the preparation phase the auditor should identify clearly the objectives of the interview and make a list of the information to be sought during the interview. If other auditors are conducting interviews, the interview process must be coordinated so a respondent is not asked the same question by different auditors.

After the information sought has been identified, it can be structured in a time sequence for the interview. General information should be requested at the beginning and end of an interview; specific information should be requested toward the middle of an interview. Information requested at the beginning of the interview should not be controversial or sensitive; this allows the respondent time to relax. Information requested at the end of the interview should give the respondent an opportunity to express opinions on central issues. There is a tendency for respondents to leave significant points they wish to make to the end of the interview (see, also, Hartman et al. [1968]).

After the information sought has been structured, the questions to be asked during the interview can be prepared. Formally preparing questions does not mean the interview has to be inflexible. If necessary the auditor must be willing to adapt and diverge from the formal structure.

Either closed or open questions can be used. A closed question requires a "yes" or "no" response; thus, closed questions should be used infrequently and only toward the middle of the interview when specific information is requested. In general, open questions should be asked, especially at the beginning and end of the interview. Open questions may lead to closed questions. For example, the open question, "What types of controls do you exercise over the preparation of batches?" may lead to the closed question, "Do you prepare hash totals on document numbers?"

The types of questions formulated for the interview depend on the tasks performed by the respondent and the respondent's seniority within the organization. The tasks performed determine the nature of the information requested. The level of seniority determines whether the questions focus on operational issues or policy issues.

After the interview has been structured and the questions prepared, the auditor should review its content to determine whether it is satisfactory. It may be too long, ask too many difficult questions, require too much respondent recall, ask too many sensitive questions, omit questions that need to be asked, etc. The opinions of other auditors also might be solicited. This review may lead the auditor to restructure or modify questions, or break the interview into two or more interviews.

Schedule Time and Place of Interview When the auditor has finished preparing the interview content, a respondent can be contacted and the time and place of the interview scheduled. By scheduling the interview in advance, the respondent has time to think about the interview and, if necessary, collect material relevant to the interview.

Lunchtime and late afternoon interviews should be avoided; the respondent is hungry, tired, or concerned with terminating the interview. Midmorning interviews often work well; the respondent is fresh and has had time to clear any urgent business.

If possible, the interview should be conducted at the respondent's work place. The respondent is familiar with the surroundings and has access to any materials needed during the interview. However, a different venue should be chosen if there is a high risk of distractions occurring (e.g., frequent telephone calls) or there is insufficient privacy.

Check the Background of the Respondent Before conducting the interview the auditor should check the background of the respondent. This check may cause the auditor to avoid certain topics in the interview as they may evoke antagonistic responses. Further, if the auditor knows the respondent's biases before the interview, the interview may be directed better to obtain objective responses. The auditor also may be able to couch the interview in terms of the respondent's interests so the respondent is more motivated to answer questions.

Conducting the Interview

At the start of the interview the auditor should reiterate the purpose of the interview so the respondent can confirm the interview to occur corresponds with the arranged interview. The respondent also may have some questions about the objectives of the interview. At this time it is especially important for the auditor to establish rapport with the respondent.

The interview should follow basically the structure established during the preparation phase. During the interview the auditor should apply certain rules of protocol:

1 Minimize digressions from the main thrust of the interview.
2 For the most part be a listener.
3 Allow the respondent some thinking time.
4 Avoid condescension and criticism; be polite.
5 Avoid sarcasm and be careful of humor.
6 Avoid jargon and buzzwords; state clearly the questions.
7 Be attentive and interested.
8 Avoid disagreements and confrontations.
9 Answer courteously the respondent's questions.
10 Maintain a relaxed formality; avoid familiarity.

To facilitate recall of the content of the interview, the auditor may have to maintain a record. Either notes can be taken or a tape recorder used. Tape recorders often make respondents nervous; however, they relieve the auditor of notetaking so the auditor can focus better on the interview. Notetaking keeps the auditor's mind on the interview, especially items to be recorded. However, the time spent on notetaking should be minimized; it may distract the respondent and interrupt the flow of the interview. Whatever recording method is used, the auditor first should ensure its acceptability to the respondent at the start of the interview. The respondent also should have the right to review the transcript of the interview or notes taken during the interview to assess their accuracy.

In some cases the interview might be conducted by two auditors—a tandem interview. Tandem interviews have several advantages (see, further, Bouchard [1976]). First, they allow more efficient use of time; one interviewer can ask questions while the other makes notes. Second, since a respondent has one interviewer's complete attention, increased rapport results. Third, the questioning, recording, and analysis of the interview are more in depth, complete, and accurate. However, since a tandem interview places greater stress on the respondent, they are best used with people whose time is at a premium.

At the end of the interview the auditor should review the material covered with the respondent. Both the auditor and the respondent may wish to clear up ambiguities or omissions. The interview should be concluded promptly but not abruptly.

Analyzing the Interview

As soon as possible after the termination of the interview, the auditor should prepare a report on the interview. Recall of events usually deteriorates rapidly within a few hours of the interview. During the preparation of the report the auditor has two major objectives. First, the auditor attempts to separate fact from opinion. If there is some doubt about the factual content of the information provided, independent verification may be necessary. Where opinion is involved, for verification purposes the auditor may need to show the interviewer a copy of the interview write-up. Second, the auditor attempts to assimilate the information obtained during the interview and determine what it means for the overall objectives of the interview. Is the process well-controlled? Has the system decreased the respondent's quality of working life?

Some follow-up may be required after the interview. The auditor may need to contact the respondent to obtain further information or clarify some issues. The respondent may have comments on the auditor's report of the interview. Information obtained during the interview may cause the auditor to investigate aspects of the system that previously were to be left untouched.

QUESTIONNAIRES

Questionnaires have been used traditionally to evaluate controls within systems. Responses to questions indicate the presence or absence of a control or the nonapplicability of a control. However, questionnaires have other purposes as an evidence collection tool. They can be used to evaluate system effectiveness. For example, Maish [1979] used questionnaires to assess users' overall feelings about an information system. Users were asked about the quality of the information system staff, the quality of data input to the system, the quality of batch output obtained from the system, and the quality of the online part of the system. Lucas [1978] used questionnaires to assess whether users thought a file was up-to-date, contained relevant information, and was complete. Bostrom and Heinen [1977] used questionnaires to assess a system's impact on the quality of working life of its users.

Questionnaires also may be used to identify areas within an information system where potential inefficiencies exist. For example, operators may be surveyed to determine whether or not they think a system consumes resources inefficiently at run time. Clerical staff who supply input to a system may be surveyed to determine whether or not they think procedures for submission of data can be streamlined.

Design of Questionnaires

Extensive research has been carried out on questionnaire design (see, further, Moser and Kalton [1971]); however, for the most part successful questionnaire design is still an art. The following three sections focus on some major aspects of questionnaire design: (a) design of the questions, (b) design of the response scale, and (c) design of the layout and structure of the questionnaire.

Question Design Three major factors affect the design of questions for a questionnaire: (a) the respondent group, (b) the nature of the information sought, and (c) how the questionnaire will be administered.

The respondent group for an audit questionnaire may be either the auditors themselves or the users of a system. For example, the well-known internal control questionnaire is completed by the auditor as the evidence gathering task proceeds. However, if the auditor is attempting to elicit attitudes on various attributes of system quality, the respondent group will be the users of the system. For example, customer satisfaction may be surveyed as a measure of system effectiveness; analysts and programmers may be asked their opinions on how easy the system is to maintain and modify. If auditors are the respondent group, questions can be specific, terms can be left undefined, instructions for completing the questionnaire can be minimized, etc.; the auditors should have been trained to use the questionnaire. If the respondent group is the users of the system, these liberties usually cannot be taken.

Questionnaires can be used to obtain either factual information or opinions. A factual question would be: Is there a fire extinguisher in the computer room? An opinion question would be: Do you feel the members of the information system staff are competent? The primary problem in designing factual questions is to ensure the respondent group understands precisely the facts required. Thus, the questionnaire designer may provide different kinds of information (some redundant) on the questionnaire in an attempt to ensure the respondent understands what facts are required. The primary problem in designing opinion questions is to ensure the wording of the question does not bias the response either by leading the respondent or being argumentative. Consider the question: Shouldn't the response time of the system be faster? User responses to this question could be biased positively.

The way in which the questionnaire is administered affects the extent to which questions have to be self-explanatory. If auditors are completing internal control questionnaires themselves, the questionnaire designer can presume the respondent group has substantial prior knowledge of the questionnaire. If auditors administer questionnaires to users, the questionnaire designer may assume the auditor can answer any questions or clarify any ambiguities which arise. However, if the questionnaire is self-administered by the user group, the questionnaire designer must word the questions carefully; the respondent may not be able to ask the auditor for assistance. For example, the auditor may be measuring the effect of an online data communications system on job satisfaction. Users may be dispersed physically over wide areas. The auditor may have to use a mail questionnaire to assess users' opinions on how the system has impacted their job satisfaction.

Though the design of questions depends on the factors described above, some general design guidelines can be given (see, further, Moser and Kalton [1971], Kerlinger [1973], and Bouchard [1976]):

1 *Ensure Questions Are Specific* The question, "Are controls over input adequate?" is too general to be of much use. The question, "Are hash control totals for batches calculated?" is much more specific. It provides the respondent with a frame of reference to answer the question.

2 *Use Simple Language and Avoid Jargon* In some cases technical terms have a very precise meaning; for example, the auditor should know what the term "encryption" means. However, if the respondent group is the user of an interactive language, the question, "Are the semantics of the language sufficient for you to be able to perform your job?" may cause confusion. The users may or may not know what the term "semantics" means.

3 *Avoid Ambiguous Questions* The question, "Does the system allow you to perform your job faster and improve your job satisfaction?" is ambiguous. What does a "no" answer mean? There are several possibilities: the job may be performed faster but job satisfaction remains unchanged, the job may be performed faster but job satisfaction decreases, both the speed with which the task is performed and job satisfaction remain unchanged, job satisfaction may increase but the speed with which the job is performed is unchanged, etc. Questions should focus on a single item; they should be clear and unambiguous.

4 *Avoid Leading Questions* Leading questions suggest the answers a respondent should give. For example, suppose a manager is asked about use of an interactive system. The question, "Does your secretary use the system to obtain the information for you?" is unlikely to be answered truthfully. The question may be taken to imply something bad about managers not directly using the system themselves.

5 *Avoid Presumptuous Questions* Questions should not presume anything about the respondent. The question, "How often do you use the system?" presumes the respondent uses the system. The respondent may or may not use the system.

6 *Avoid Hypothetical Questions* The question, "Would you like the system to provide a faster response time?" is likely to evoke a positive response. Most users would not object to having a faster response time in an interactive system; however, whether they would be willing to pay for a faster response time is another issue.

7 *Avoid Embarrassing Questions* At times the auditor may use a questionnaire to obtain information that is personal, delicate, or controversial. Care must be taken to formulate the question in such a way that it does not embarrass the respondent. For example, suppose the auditor is exploring the quality of the system design process within an installation. If the auditor asks system designers, "Do you consider the impact of the systems you design on the user's quality of working life?" a positive response is likely to be obtained. To answer otherwise implies socially unacceptable behavior.

8 *Avoid Questions Involving Extensive Recall* Factual questions involve the respondent recalling information. The accuracy of the response depends upon the extent of recall needed. The question "How many times in January did you use the system?" is unlikely to produce an accurate response if it is asked in the following December, unless the respondent maintains a diary of uses.

9 *Avoid Questions About Which the Respondent Has Little or No Knowledge* Respondents tend to answer questions on a questionnaire, even when they have little or no knowledge about the subject matter covered by the question. If responses to factual questions are being elicited, respondent ignorance with respect to the question asked may be detected by the auditor. Where opinion is being elicited, however, respondent ignorance may go undetected.

Choosing a Response Scale The type of response scale chosen for a questionnaire depends upon the nature of the question asked. If the question asked requires a factual response, the choice of response scale usually is straightforward. Figure 20.1 shows three examples of response scales that might be used. Typically the scales involve checking a "yes" or "no" response or inserting some piece of information; for example, a make of machine.

When opinions or attitudes are solicited, the choice of a response scale is a more complex decision (see, further, Nunnally [1967], Kerlinger [1973], and Brown [1976]). Figure 20.2 shows three types of scales that might be used for

Disposal of Output:

	Yes	No	N/A
1 Are sensitive reports shredded?			
2 Is disposal of carbon paper secure?			
3 Is disposal of waste paper from computer room secure?			

Figure 20.1a
Excerpt from internal control questionnaire.

Fire Protection:
_____ 1 Fire exits marked clearly
_____ 2 Portable fire extinguishers placed at strategic points
_____ 3 Fire drills conducted regularly

Figure 20.1b
Excerpt from fire protection checklist.

Hardware Configuration:
Vendor:
_____ Burroughs   _____ IBM
_____ Control Data   _____ ICL
_____ Digital   _____ Univac
_____ Facom
_____ Honeywell   Other _____
Model: _____
Number of disk drives: _____   Number of tape drives: _____

Figure 20.1c
Excerpt from hardware configuration questionnaire.

questions on various aspects of system effectiveness (see, further, Chapter 23). Figure 20.2a shows a common seven-point scale. Figure 20.2b shows a Likert scale. Responses to individual items on a Likert scale are summed and the average calculated. Figure 20.2c shows a semantic differential scale used to assess users' attitudes toward an information system. Other types of scales can be used; for example, Thurstone scales and Guttman scales (see, further, Moser and Kalton [1971] and Nunnally [1967]). The choice of an appropriate response scale to measure attitudes or opinions requires substantial expertise. Unless the auditor is well-trained in psychometrics, consulting advice should be employed whenever a new questionnaire is to be designed.

Choice of Layout and Structure The layout and structure of a questionnaire impact how accurately the questionnaire will be completed. If the questionnaire is used in a mail survey, layout and structure also affect the response rate (see, further, Bouchard [1976]).

The Job I Perform Offers:

```
                           Low                              High
Variety                    1 __|__|__|__|__|__|__ 7
Opportunities for learning 1 __|__|__|__|__|__|__ 7
Challenge                  1 __|__|__|__|__|__|__ 7
```

Figure 20.2a
Seven-point scale used to assess users' attitudes about the jobs they perform.

Feelings about the Information System Staff:

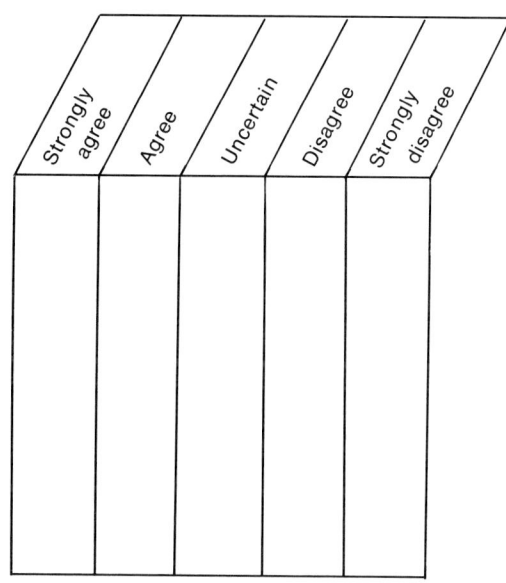

Are technically competent
Design systems with the user in mind
Deal well with people

Figure 20.2b
Likert scale used to assess users' feelings about the information system staff.

```
                 The System
1. Pleasant  :__:__:__:__:__:__:__:__:__:  Unpleasant
2. Ugly      :__:__:__:__:__:__:__:__:__:  Beautiful
3. Heavy     :__:__:__:__:__:__:__:__:__:  Light
```

Figure 20.2c
Semantic differential scale used to assess users' attitudes about the system.

The length of a questionnaire affects the morale of the respondent. If a questionnaire is too long, respondents become fatigued. They either refuse to answer the questionnaire or answers given toward the end of the questionnaire become more unreliable.

If the respondent has not been trained to complete the questionnaire, care must be taken to show clearly the flow of questions through the questionnaire, especially if the responses to some questions cause branches to other questions. The questionnaire should appear uncluttered; questions and sections of the questionnaire should be spaced adequately.

Questions placed at the beginning of the questionnaire should be general in nature and place little stress on the respondent. More difficult questions — those that require high recall, are controversial, etc. — should be placed toward the middle and end of the questionnaire.

Reliability and Validity Issues

If a questionnaire is designed to elicit factual information, providing the questions are expressed unambiguously, the responses obtained should be unequivocal. When opinions and attitudes are elicited, however, the auditor faces the problem of designing a questionnaire that is reliable and valid (see, further, Kerlinger [1973]).

A *reliable* questionnaire is one that gives the same measurements over repeated administrations. In other words, assuming all factors are held constant, if a respondent completed the questionnaire twice, the scores obtained on the second administration of the questionnaire would be the same as those obtained on the first administration.

Test-retest reliability is difficult to establish by having respondents complete the questionnaire twice. At the second administration, respondents may remember the ratings they gave at the first administration; thus, the administrations are not independent. It is also difficult to assess whether all other factors remain constant. Nevertheless, the theory of reliability has been researched extensively and techniques for assessing the reliability of questionnaires are well-developed (see Nunnally [1967]).

A *valid* questionnaire measures what it sets out to measure. A questionnaire may be reliable but it may not be valid; it may measure something other than the attitude or opinion it is supposed to measure.

There are three major types of validity:

Type of validity	Explanation
Predictive Validity	Scores (ratings) on the questionnaire are used to predict some criterion. Predictive accuracy is a measure of validity.
Content Validity	How representative are the sample items on the questionnaire of the universe of content? The items on the questionnaire should cover the full range of the attitude or opinion being measured.
Construct Validity	What trait does the questionnaire measure? On the basis of theory, associations between scores on the questionnaire and other variables are postulated and these hypotheses are tested empirically.

Again, the theory underlying validity has been researched extensively and techniques for assessing validity are well-developed (see, further, Brown [1976]). The American Psychological Association [1966] has issued standards that define reliability and validity criteria that a test (questionnaire) should meet.

Clearly, then, the auditor must be careful when designing questionnaires to elicit attitudes or opinion. Design is not simply a matter of listing questions that the auditor believes to be important. The resulting questionnaire may be neither reliable nor valid, and actions may be taken on the basis of flawed measurements; for example, a system may be redesigned on the basis of an inaccurate measure of the quality of working life of users.

When attitudes must be measured, if possible, the auditor should use a standard instrument. A large number of questionnaires (tests, instruments) have been developed to measure a wide range of attitudes and opinions. For example, if the auditor wishes to measure job satisfaction as part of the evaluation of system effectivenesss, Robinson et al. [1969] contains 13 instruments that measure general job satisfaction, five instruments that measure job satisfaction for particular occupations, and eight instruments that measure satisfaction with specific job features. Other collections of instruments are available (see, for example, Chun et al. [1975] and Robinson and Shaver [1969]). These collections also provide discussions of the instrument's validity and reliability, references to its use, the name and address of the publisher of the instrument, and instructions for administering the instrument.

If the auditor must have a new questionnaire developed, the services of a psychometrician should be employed. Until the reliability and validity of the questionnaire have been established, the measures of attitudes or opinions obtained should be interpreted cautiously.

Effective Use of Questionnaires

Even though a questionnaire may be well-designed, it may not be used effectively. The auditor must know when to use the questionnaire, how to use it, and what the responses mean.

Mailed questionnaires are useful when the auditor must obtain information from physically dispersed locations. They are a cheap means of collecting data. However, the auditor must be able to ensure a high response rate is obtained. The auditor also must ensure the questionnaire is well-designed so response errors are minimal.

Auditors may complete questionnaires themselves during the course of an interview or observation of a system. Questionnaires structure the interview or review process and provide a convenient recording schedule. However, the auditor must be trained to use the questionnaire. Further, if a questionnaire is used on a regular basis, there is a risk the auditor will complete the questionnaire mechanically or copy answers from previous questionnaires.

There is sometimes a problem in choosing the right questionnaire to use.

For example, if the auditor wishes to assess a system's impact on job satisfaction, several questionnaires are available. The auditor must evaluate carefully the purposes for which the instrument was designed, how its reliability and validity were assessed, and how well the purposes of the questionnaire correspond with audit purposes.

Care must be taken when questionnaires are administered. A hurriedly completed questionnaire increases the likelihood of response errors occurring. Standardized questionnaires have instructions on how they should be administered. The reliability of the questionnaire depends on these instructions being followed.

The auditor also must know what the responses obtained on a questionnaire mean. For example, what score indicates a high level of job satisfaction exists? When is an internal control system weak? The instructions for standardized questionnaires discuss how scores should be interpreted. If auditors have designed their own questionnaires, they must derive a rule for assigning a global evaluation to the individual or aggregate ratings obtained.

CONTROL FLOWCHARTS

A control flowchart shows *what* controls exist and *where* these controls exist in the flow of data through a system. Control flowcharting can be used during the system development process as a design aid; the analyst can construct a control flowchart as a focal point for the design of controls. The auditor can use a control flowchart as an evaluation aid; controls existing in the system can be noted on the flowchart and the flowchart examined for control deficiencies.

Constructing a Control Flowchart

Constructing a control flowchart involves two major steps. First, a system flowchart must be constructed. Second, controls then must be narrated on the flowchart. The control flowchart should show only the control flow; the data flow should be shown on a separate flowchart (see, also, Benjamin [1971]).

Jenkins and Carlis [1975] suggest using Chapin's sandwich rule when constructing a system flowchart as the basis for a control flowchart (see Chapin [1970]). The sandwich rule simply says a flowchart must begin and end with a data symbol — the bread layers of the sandwich — and the data symbols should be separated by a process symbol — the filling in the sandwich (Figure 20.3). Providing standard flowcharting symbols are used with the sandwich rule, a system flowchart with high communicative power can be achieved (see, also, Skinner and Anderson [1966]).

Once the unnarrated system flowchart has been constructed, the designer or auditor can commence to insert controls on the flowchart. Jenkins and Carlis [1975] identify three points on the flowchart where controls may be located. First, controls may be needed where processing symbols exist. For example, if a processing symbol represents an input validation program, the various checks that should be performed by the program can be documented.

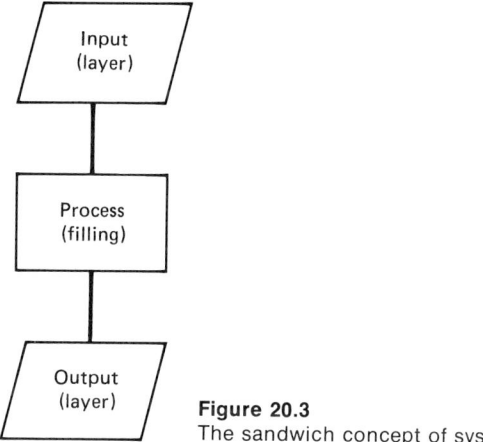

Figure 20.3
The sandwich concept of system flowcharting.

Second, controls may be needed where data symbols exist. For example, if the data symbol represents a disk master file, the control flowchart may show the data on the file is encrypted. Third, controls may be specified for the flowlines on the flowchart. For example, if a flowline shows the transit of data from a user department to the computer installation, the control flowchart may show a batch log as the control used to ensure all data is received after transit.

Figure 20.4 shows a section of a completed system flowchart. Note the conventional top to bottom, left to right flow. Figure 20.5 shows the corresponding control flowchart. On the system flowchart the narrative focuses on data; on the control flowchart it focuses on controls.

Advantages and Limitations of Control Flowcharting

Stanford Research Institute [1977] investigated an organization that developed control flowcharts at a detailed level. The organization found control flowcharts useful in designing better controls and communicating the controls existing in a system to personnel who had to become familiar with the system. The technique was simple to use and required little training time.

However, control flowcharts have several limitations. They are subject to the problems of all flowcharting techniques: time-consuming to develop, difficult to modify and maintain, etc. Effective use of the technique requires the auditor to have a good understanding of controls within systems; otherwise, control strengths and deficiencies cannot be identified on the flowchart. Jenkins and Carlis [1975] also point out the difficulty of applying the sandwich rule to event-driven systems (compared to data-driven systems). Control flowcharting may be more difficult to use as an evidence gathering and evaluation technique in advanced systems.

Research carried out by Shneiderman et al. [1977] also calls into question the usefulness of flowcharts. Experiments were run to test whether flowcharts aided program composition, comprehension, debugging, and modification. No

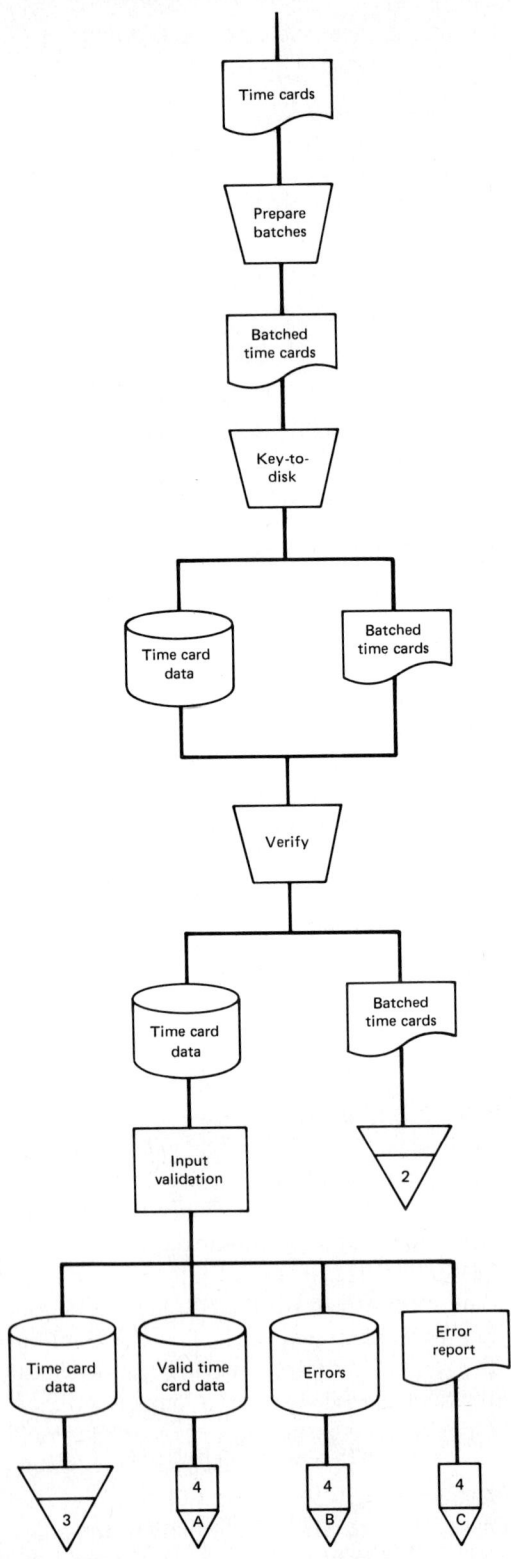

Figure 20.4
Section of a system flowchart for a payroll application.

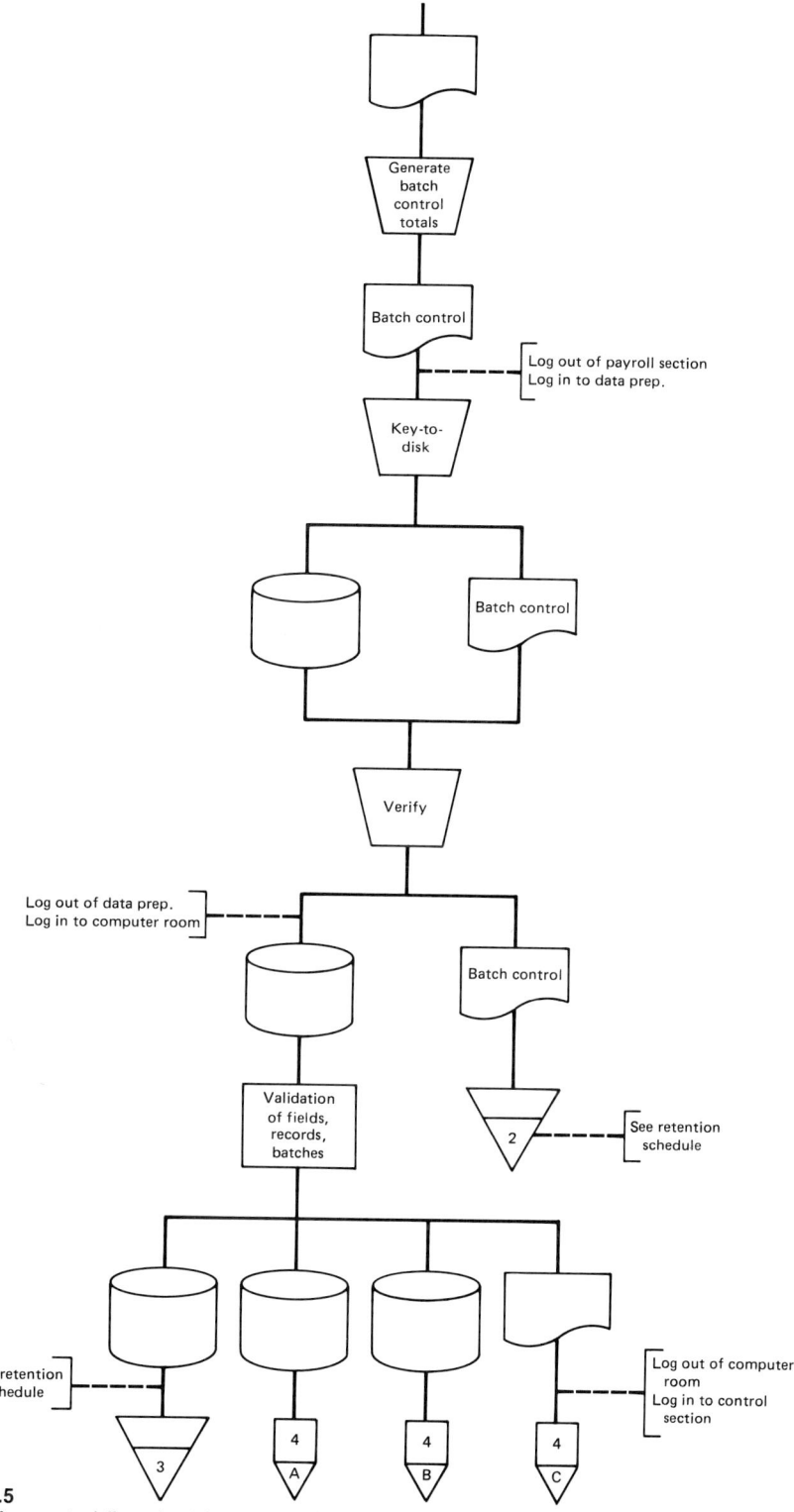

Figure 20.5
Section of a control flowchart for a payroll application.

statistically significant differences were obtained between groups using flowcharts and groups who did not use flowcharts. In some cases flowcharts seemed to hinder rather than help task performance.

Several human factors research studies support the usefulness of flowcharts (see, for example, Kammann [1975]). However, in general, the studies have examined whether prose or a flowchart is understood more easily and they have been carried out using noncomputer tasks. Thus, the usefulness of control flowcharts is still a research issue.

SUMMARY

Three manual techniques that the auditor can use to collect evidence on the quality of computer systems are interviews, questionnaires, and control flowcharts. These techniques were used before the advent of computers. Their importance has not diminished in computer systems.

Interviews consist of three major phases: preparing for the interview, conducting the interview, and analyzing the interview. Interviews reduce the time required to find out information if someone is willing to provide the answers. However, effective interviewing requires that various rules of protocol be followed carefully.

Questionnaires can be used to elicit factual information or opinion. The most difficult design problems arise when opinion must be obtained. The auditor must be careful to use a questionnaire that is valid and reliable.

Control flowcharts show what controls exist where in a system. The auditor can use a control flowchart to identify control deficiencies in a system. However, the overall usefulness of control flowcharts is still a research issue. There is some evidence to suggest flowcharts generally may not be as useful as they were initially thought to be.

REVIEW QUESTIONS

20.1. Other than those given in the chapter, give an example of how an interview might be used to gather evidence on some aspect of:
  a. system effectiveness
  b. system efficiency
  c. data integrity
20.2. Briefly explain the difference between interviewing and interrogation. Why should the auditor be careful about becoming involved in an interrogation?
20.3. Why do people respond to questions in an interview? Why is it important the auditor has an understanding of what motivates a person to respond?
20.4. Why do different types of interviews require varying levels of respondent motivation? Give two examples of interviews the auditor might conduct, one that requires a high level of respondent motivation and one that requires a low level of respondent motivation.
20.5. In the structure of an interview, where should general questions be placed? Where should specific questions be placed? Why is placement of questions important?

20.6. Briefly explain the difference between a closed and an open question. What factors affect whether the auditor uses a closed or an open question during an interview?

20.7. Briefly outline the factors that the auditor should consider when choosing a time and place for the interview.

20.8. What is meant by the auditor establishing rapport with the interviewee? Why is rapport important in an interview? Give three ways in which the auditor can set about establishing rapport.

20.9. What can the auditor do if a confrontation situation arises during an interview?

20.10. Briefly explain what is meant by a tandem interview. What are the advantages and disadvantages of a tandem interview? Give an example of where the auditor might use a tandem interview.

20.11. What tasks does the auditor perform during the analysis of an interview? When should the analysis be carried out?

20.12. Why must the auditor consider who will be the respondent group in the design of a questionnaire? What impact does the type of respondent group have on the design?

20.13. How will the characteristics of a self-administered questionnaire differ from the characteristics of a questionnaire administered by the auditor? When should a self-administered questionnaire be used and when should a questionnaire administered by the auditor be used?

20.14. How do response scales differ for questions asked to obtain factual information versus questions asked to obtain attitudes or opinions?

20.15. What is meant by the reliability and validity of a questionnaire? Why must the auditor be concerned with reliability and validity issues?

20.16. What advantages do standardized questionnaires offer the auditor? Does their use have any disadvantages?

20.17. One problem with using the same questionnaire on a routine basis is the problem of "cheating." Explain.

20.18. Give three problems of mail questionnaires. Outline some techniques the auditor can use to overcome these problems.

20.19. What is a control flowchart? How does it differ from a system flowchart? How does it differ from a program flowchart?

20.20. What is the importance of the sandwich concept for constructing a control flowchart? Why do event-driven systems sometimes present problems for applying the sandwich principle?

20.21. At what points on a control flowchart are controls narrated? Give an example of a control that might exist at each of these points for an online retrieval system.

20.22. Briefly explain why the usefulness of control flowcharts might be debated. To what extent would use of an automatic flowcharter overcome any of the objections raised to control flowcharting?

EXERCISES AND CASES

20.1. What problems, if any, exist with the following questions on a self-administered questionnaire given to users to assess their feelings about a system:
   a. Do you ever have trouble using the system?
   b. Does your terminal have a fast enough baud rate?
   c. Would you like graphical reports to be prepared?
   d. Do you make better decisions using the output of the new system?

e. Has the system made many of the tasks you perform trivial?
f. On average, how many times per week during the last year has the system been unavailable when you needed it?
g. Does your secretary use the system more than you do?
h. Has the system caused you to think about changing your job?
i. Do you make more errors when preparing input for the new system than you did with the old system?
j. How does your husband/wife feel about you using a system that has put some of your work colleagues out of a job?

20.2. The chapter identifies various deficiencies in the following questions:
a. Are the semantics of the language sufficient for you to be able to perform your job?
b. Does the system allow you to perform your job faster and improve your job satisfaction?
c. Does your secretary use the system to obtain the information for you?
d. How often do you use the system?
e. Would you like the system to provide a faster response?
f. Do you consider the impact of the systems you design on the user's quality of working life?
g. How many times in January did you use the system?

Required: Propose alternatives to the above questions that remedy their deficiencies.

20.3. You are a senior on the external audit team for a bank that has an online realtime update system for its customer accounts file. The customer accounts file uses a network data structure that is maintained by a database management system.

Required: As part of the evaluation of application controls, your manager decides that you should interview the project manager for the online realtime update system to assess the adequacy of backup and recovery for the system. She asks you to outline the subject matter that you intend to cover in the interview and the chronological order in which you intend to cover the subject matter.

20.4. Design an internal control questionnaire that could be used to evaluate the database administration function.

20.5. Construct a control flowchart for the following system flowchart that shows an online update system used by bank tellers. You should show the controls that you think should be used in the system.

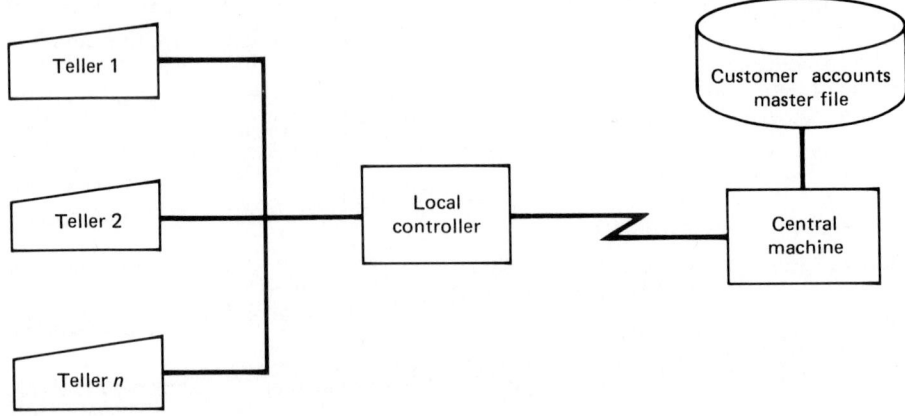

REFERENCES

American Psychological Assocciation. *Standards for Educational and Psychological Tests and Manuals* (Washington, D.C.: American Psychological Association, 1966).

Benjamin, Robert I. *Control of the Information System Development Cycle* (New York: John Wiley & Sons, Inc., 1971).

Bostrom, Robert P., and J. Stephen Heinen. "MIS Problems and Failures: Socio-Technical Perspective – Part II: The Application of Socio-Technical Theory," *Management Information Systems Quarterly* (December 1977), pp. 11–28.

Bouchard, Thomas J., Jr. "Field Research Methods: Interviewing, Questionnaires, Participant Observation, Systematic Observation, Unobtrusive Measures," in Marvin D. Dunnette, ed., *Handbook of Industrial and Organizational Psychology* (Chicago: Rand McNally College Publishing Company, 1976), pp. 363–413.

Brown, Frederick G. *Principles of Educational and Psychological Testing*, 2d ed. (New York: Holt, Rinehart and Winston, 1976).

Burch, John G., Jr., and Joseph L. Sardinas, Jr. *Computer Control and Audit: A Total Systems Approach* (New York: John Wiley & Sons, Inc., 1978).

Chapin, Ned. "Flowcharting with ANSI Standard: A Tutorial," *Computing Surveys* (June 1970), pp. 119–146.

Chun, Ki-Taek, Sidney Cobb, and John R. P. French, Jr. *Measures for Psychological Assessment* (Ann Arbor, Mich.: Institute for Social Research, The University of Michigan, 1975).

Clifton, H. D. *Business Data Systems: A Practical Guide to Systems Analysis and Data Processing* (London: Prentice-Hall International, Inc., 1978).

Hartman, W., H. Matthes, and A. Proeme. *Management Information Systems Handbook: Analysis, Requirements Determination, Design and Development, Implementation and Evaluation* (New York: McGraw-Hill Book Company, 1968).

Jenkins, A. Milton, and John V. Carlis. "Control Flowcharting for Data Driven Systems," Working Paper MISRC-WP-76-02, Management Information Systems Research Center, University of Minnesota, Minneapolis, Minn., 1975.

Kahn, R. L., and C. F. Cannell. *The Dynamics of Interviewing: Theory, Techniques and Cases* (New York: John Wiley & Sons, Inc., 1966).

Kammann, R. "The Comprehensibility of Printed Instructions and the Flowchart Alternative," *Human Factors* (April 1975), pp. 183–191.

Kerlinger, Fred N. *Foundations of Behavioral Research*, 2d ed. (New York: Holt, Rinehart and Winston, 1973).

Krauss, Leonard I., and Aileen MacGahan. *Computer Fraud and Countermeasures* (Englewood Cliffs, N.J.: Prentice-Hall, Inc., 1979).

Lucas, Henry C. "The Use of an Interactive Information Storage and Retrieval System in Medical Research," *Communications of the ACM* (March 1978), pp. 197–205.

Mair, William C., Donald R. Wood, and Keagle W. Davis. *Computer Control and Audit*, 2d ed. (Altamonte Springs, Fla.: The Institute of Internal Auditors, Inc., 1976).

Maish, Alexander M. "A User's Behavior toward His MIS," *Management Information Systems Quarterly* (March 1979), pp. 39–52.

Moser, C. A., and G. Kalton. *Survey Methods in Social Investigation*, 2d ed. (London: Heinemann Educational Books, 1971).

Nadler, David A., Philip H. Mirvis, and Cortlandt Cammann. "The Ongoing Feedback

System: Experimenting with a New Managerial Tool," *Organizational Dynamics* (Spring 1976), pp. 63–80.

Nunnally, Jum C. *Psychometric Theory* (New York: McGraw-Hill Book Company, 1967).

Robinson, John P., and Phillip R. Shaver. *Measures of Social Psychological Attitudes* (Ann Arbor, Mich.: Institute for Social Research, The University of Michigan, 1969).

———, Robert Athanasiou, and Kendra B. Head. *Measures of Occupational Attitudes and Occupational Characteristics* (Ann Arbor, Mich.: Institute for Social Research, The University of Michigan, 1969).

Sharratt, J. R. *Data Control Guidelines* (Manchester, England: NCC Publications, 1974).

Shneiderman, Ben, Richard Mayer, Don McKay, and Peter Heller. "Experimental Investigations of the Utility of Detailed Flowcharts in Programming," *Communications of the ACM* (June 1977), pp. 373–381.

Skinner, R. M., and R. J. Anderson. *Analytical Auditing* (Toronto: Sir Isaac Pitman, 1966).

Stanford Research Institute. *Systems Auditability and Control Study: Data Processing Audit Practices Report* (Altamonte Springs, Fla.: The Institute of Internal Auditors, Inc., 1977).

CHAPTER **21**

PERFORMANCE MONITORING TOOLS

CHAPTER OUTLINE

THE OBJECTS OF MEASUREMENT
GENERAL CHARACTERISTICS OF PERFORMANCE MONITORS
TYPES OF PERFORMANCE MONITORS
    Hardware Monitors
    Software Monitors
    Firmware Monitors
    Hybrid Monitors
PERFORMANCE MONITORING AND DATA INTEGRITY
    Ensuring Correct System Instrumentation
    Ensuring Maintenance of Data Privacy
SUMMARY
REVIEW QUESTIONS
EXERCISES AND CASES
REFERENCES

Performance monitoring tools enable the auditor to obtain evidence on factors relating to system efficiency. The measurements taken are used in two ways. First, for systems that already are operational, they provide the basic data for diagnosis of problems and construction of tuning therapies. For example, data on the frequency of page faults may be used to select a paging algorithm in a virtual storage system. Second, the measurements may be used to estimate the values of parameters in analytic and simulation performance evaluation models of computer systems. For example, to evaluate the effects of a changed hardware configuration on throughput, a simulation model may be constructed. Performance monitoring tools can be used to estimate the characteristics of existing workloads (e.g., service demands) for input to the simulation model. Chapter 24 discusses these matters further.

This chapter provides an overview of performance monitoring tools. The whole subject area of performance monitoring and evaluation has been extensively researched in recent years (see, for example, Kobayashi [1978] and Ferrari [1978]). To be capable of using the various performance monitoring tools to carry out performance evaluation requires substantial expertise. For those EDP audit groups that have responsibility for evaluating system efficiency, either a member of the group must specialize in the area or the services of a consultant must be employed because of the complexity of performance monitoring tools and the consequences of their improper use.

The chapter proceeds as follows. The first section briefly discusses some of the objects of measurement; that is, those factors that affect overall system efficiency. The second section examines the general characteristics of performance monitoring tools. The third section surveys specific types of monitors. Finally, the chapter discusses some implications of performance monitoring for maintenance of data integrity.

THE OBJECTS OF MEASUREMENT

It is not especially meaningful to give a general listing of what objects in a computer system might be measured to evaluate performance. *All* resources in a computer system can be the objects of measurement. For any particular evaluation some subset of the total resources of a system will be measured. The particular subset selected will depend on what aspect of system performance is to be evaluated and whether or not the auditor (analyst) performing the evaluation believes the resources are impacting system performance.

To illustrate these notions, assume the auditor is concerned about the slow response time in an online system. The auditor believes two factors may be causing the slow response time: channel bottlenecks and inefficient algorithms in the online program. To determine whether these factors are a problem, the auditor decides to measure CPU and channel utilization. Two further decisions now must be made. First, the auditor must determine where information on CPU and channel utilization can be found in the system. Various system state memories may be accessible to provide this information; for example, the CPU wait/busy bit, the CPU supervisor/problem state bit, and the channel interrupt bit. Second, the auditor must determine how the information is to be extracted, recorded, and presented. In this case, the auditor may choose a hardware monitor to extract and record the information. A software package then may be used to summarize and present the information, perhaps in graphical form.

GENERAL CHARACTERISTICS OF PERFORMANCE MONITORS

Performance monitors have five basic structural elements (Figure 21.1). The *sensor* detects the occurrence or nonoccurrence of an activity and the magnitude of the activity. The *selector* designates the subset of activities to be measured from the set of all activities that the monitor can measure. The *processor* transforms the data collected into a form suitable for storage and output; for example, it may count the instances of an activity that have oc-

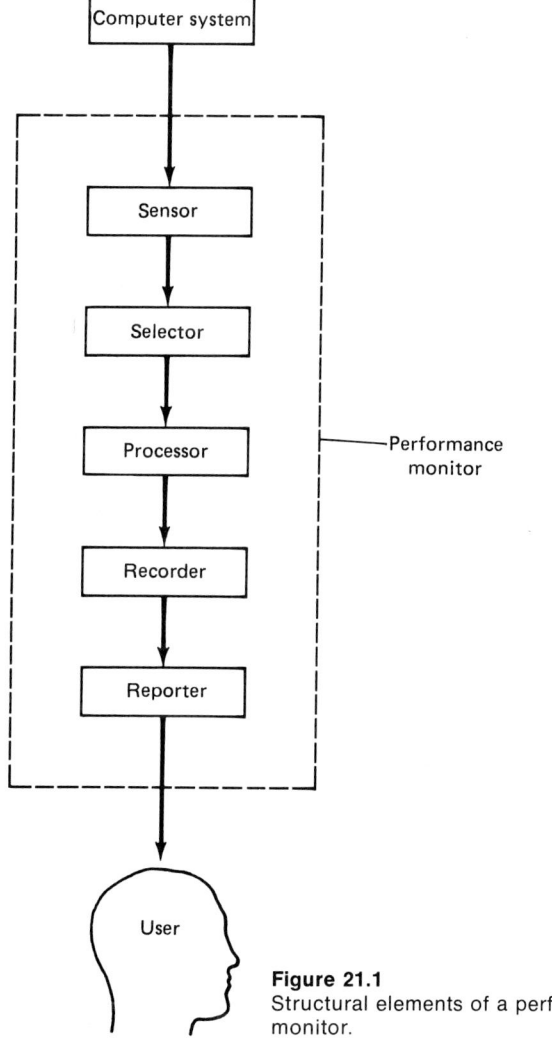

Figure 21.1
Structural elements of a performance monitor.

curred over a time period. The *recorder* writes the processed data to the storage medium used by the monitor. The *reporter* summarizes the information stored and presents it to the user of the monitor.

Performance monitors take five types of measurements of resource consumption activities (see, also, Svobodova [1976]):

Measurement	Explanation
Trace	Recorded sequence of occurrence of activities
Activity Duration	Realtime consumed by activity
Relative Activity	Ratio of total realtime for the activity to total elapsed time
Activity Frequency	Number of times the activity occurs over a given time period
Distribution of Activity	Distribution of activity times over some elapsed time period

Not all monitors are capable of making these measurements equally well. Some are designed primarily to measure certain kinds of resource consumption activities. The more expensive monitors usually have greater measurement capabilities. The overall capabilities of a monitor are a function of seven attributes of the monitor (see, for example, Ferrari [1978] and Svobodova [1976]):

Attribute	Explanation
Monitor Artifact	Extent to which presence of the monitor interferes with the normal operations of the system
Monitor Domain (Scope)	Set of resource consumption activities that the monitor can detect
Resolution (Input Rate)	Maximum frequency at which events can be detected and recorded correctly
Input Width	Number of bits of input data a monitor can extract and process when an event occurs
Data Reduction Capabilities	Extent to which data can be summarized before it is stored
Data Storage Capabilities	Amount of memory available for storage of data
Precision	Number of digits available to represent data

Other factors affect the usefulness of a monitor. For example, the external auditor involved with performance monitoring would be concerned with the number of makes and models of machines on which the monitor will run. Monitors also vary with respect to how easy they are to install and use.

TYPES OF PERFORMANCE MONITORS

There are four types of performance monitors available to measure resource consumption activities: hardware monitors, software monitors, firmware monitors, and hybrid monitors. The following sections discuss the nature of each type of monitor and their relative strengths and limitations.

Hardware Monitors

A hardware monitor is a device connected to a host computer (the computer to be measured) that detects pulses in the host computer's electronic circuitry. Assume, for example, that the auditor is interested in the extent of overlap between the operations of the CPU and two channels (see, also, Stimler [1974]). Further, the auditor wishes to distinguish between problem state and supervisor state operations in the CPU. Thus, the auditor must monitor four flip-flops in the host computer: the CPU busy/idle flip-flop, the busy/idle flip-flop for channel 1, the busy/idle flip-flop for channel 2, and the problem/supervisor flip-flop for the CPU. Using logical AND combinations of the states of the flip-flops, 12 measurements can be obtained:

1. CPU busy in problem state only
2. CPU busy in supervisor state only
3. Channel 1 busy only
4. Channel 2 busy only
5. CPU in problem state and channel 1 busy
6. CPU in problem state and channel 2 busy
7. CPU in problem state and both channels busy
8. CPU in supervisor state and channel 1 busy
9. CPU in supervisor state and channel 2 busy
10. CPU in supervisor state and both channels busy
11. Both channels busy only
12. CPU busy only

Note that measurement 12 is simply the addition of measurements 1 and 2. The measurements can be printed out as counts or perhaps graphically to better illustrate the overlap that occurs.

Figure 21.2 shows the basic structure of a hardware monitor. Probes are connected to the host system. A concentrator reduces the number of cables from the host system to the monitor. A comparator performs a test on two or more registers and outputs a pulse depending on the result of the test. The processor has three major components. A patchboard allows the logic for different kinds of tests to be specified. Counters are available to count either event occurrences or the time interval between events. A clock generates timing pulses. The final component of the monitor is a magnetic tape unit used to store the measurement data (see, also, Arndt and Oliver [1972]).

Types of Hardware Monitor Ferrari [1978] identifies three types of hardware monitors that exist: (*a*) fixed hardware monitors, (*b*) wired-program monitors, and (*c*) stored-program monitors.

Fixed hardware monitors are incorporated in the host system at design time. For example, the system clock and various register displays are fixed

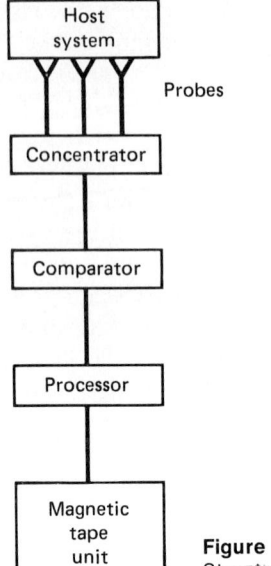

Figure 21.2
Structure of a simple hardware monitor.

hardware monitors. The contents of these monitors can be displayed at a console or accessed by programs. The monitors are useful both for measurement and program debugging purposes. For example, the system clock can be accessed to determine the start and stop time for a job so system throughput can be calculated. However, fixed hardware monitors have only limited usefulness for measurement purposes. Neither the events they monitor nor the actions they take upon measurement can be controlled by a user.

Wired-program hardware monitors provide the user with some control over the events to be monitored and the actions to be taken on the occurrence of an event. The monitor is connected to the host system via probes onto the circuitry pins of the host computer. Different events can be monitored by changing the placement of the probes on the circuitry pins. The monitor has some type of plugboard or patch panel that allows the user to specify various Boolean functions to be performed on the events monitored; for example, an AND function on a CPU busy event and channel busy event.

The storage capabilities of wired-program hardware monitors vary. Some simply have counters; the contents of these counters are dumped periodically on magnetic tape. Others have random access memory in addition to secondary storage capabilities. The random access memory can be used, for example, to store bit patterns that enter the monitor in parallel or to maintain a histogram of event types as they occur.

Stored-program hardware monitors are driven by sets of microprograms or user-coded programs. An integral part of a stored-program hardware monitor is a minicomputer that controls the operations of the monitor. Thus, the stored-program hardware monitor is the most flexible type of hardware monitor. It allows the user to modify the measurement process during the measurement period depending upon the set of conditions that occur. For example, assume a database management system is partitioned; one part resides in core and the other part on a drum. The auditor wants to evaluate whether the present partitioning could be improved. Other system software also resides on the drum. The map of the drum showing the address ranges for the various system software can be stored in the monitor. When the monitor detects a reference to the drum, it can check the memory reference that is stored in fixed core resident operating system tables and compare the address with the drum memory map. If the address falls within the range for the database management system, it increments a counter by one (see, also, Ferrari [1978]).

Capabilities of Hardware Monitors Because hardware monitors measure electronically the state of a system, they are able to detect very short duration events in a computer system; for example, a change of the CPU from a busy to an idle state. Thus, they are high-resolution tools. They also are able to monitor several events simultaneously, even events occurring on independent hardware units.

Hardware monitors usually have a broad domain; many types of resource consumption activities can be monitored by attaching probes or some type of interface to the circuitry of the system. However, the size of the monitor domain is affected by the architectural design of the system being measured. If the system does not provide access to important measurement points, then the domain of the hardware monitor is restricted. Architectural design to facilitate measurement becomes more important with the more widespread use of large-scale integrated circuits.

Hardware monitors cause no artifact and they are portable. The monitor functions independently of the host system. Further, it simply recognizes pulses; thus, it can be used on any system.

The input width, data reduction capabilities, data storage capabilities, and precision of hardware monitors vary. The input width depends on the number of available probes. The data reduction capabilities and data storage capabilities depend on what logical operations the monitor can perform, the types of secondary storage devices attached to the monitor, and whether or not the monitor has random access memory. Precision is a function of the word length of the counters and storage used by the monitor.

Limitations of Hardware Monitors Effective use of hardware monitors requires substantial expertise. Probes can be connected to incorrect points. Care must be taken so stress is not placed on the probes and hardware is damaged.

Perhaps the major limitation of hardware monitors is their inability to trace software-related events. For example, a hardware monitor cannot detect a program's access to a data structure; it is unable to monitor directly the contents of random access memory. Similarly, it is unable to determine whether a program variable has been modified. When evaluating the performance of individual programs, often it is important to be able to trace the sequence of state changes that occurs within the program.

Software Monitors

A software monitor is a program (subroutine, instruction) inserted into the code of a system to collect performance measurement data. The monitor may be incorporated into the operating system to examine the performance of systemwide functions, or it may be incorporated into an application program to gather specific data on that program.

Software monitors detect the execution of an instruction in a program. Thus, if the instruction results in the modification of a variable, the time series of modifications can be monitored. Similarly, if the instruction results in access to a data structure, the time series of accesses can be monitored. Any event that can be detected by the execution of a program instruction can be monitored.

In effect there is no difference between a concurrent auditing technique such as Snapshot and a software monitor. Both evidence collection techniques are invoked when a particular instruction in a program is executed. In fact, software such as IBM's SMF can be used to collect both performance measurement data and evidence on how well data integrity is maintained.

Types of Software Monitors There are two types of software monitors: (*a*) event-driven monitors, and (*b*) sampling monitors. The distinction rests on the manner in which the monitors are activated.

Event-driven software monitors undertake a measurement when some type of event occurs internally to the system or program; for example, a CPU interrupt is generated or a program checkpoint is reached. Assume, for example, the auditor wants to assess the efficiency with which an interactive program executes different decision models that users call selectively to aid their decision-making process. The auditor wants to focus first on those models that are used most frequently and consume most time.

The code below is an excerpt from the interactive program (written in COBOL) and the software monitoring instructions inserted in the program.

```
WHAT-DEC-MØD.

      IF DECNØ IS EQUAL TØ 6
      CALL CLØCKTIME USING STARTTM
      PERFØRM DEC-MØD6
      CALL CLØCKTIME USING ENDTM
      PERFØRM STATS.
```

The instructions execute in the following way. First, when the interactive program identifies that decision model 6 is required (DECNØ = 6), it calls a subroutine that accesses the system clock to obtain the start time of the execution of the subroutine that performs the processing related to decision model 6. Second, the program performs the subroutine that executes the decision model. Third, when the subroutine returns control, the program again accesses the system clock to determine the finish time of the event. Finally, the program performs a subroutine that writes away to some storage device the decision model number, the start time, and the finish time. At the end of the measurement period the auditor can access this data, determine the number of times a particular decision model was used, plot the distribution of execution times, and calculate relevant statistics such as the mean and variance of execution times for each decision model.

The major device used to collect data in an event-driven software monitor is a checkpoint instruction. These checkpoints may be either permanent or temporary. Permanent checkpoints are always resident in the host system, though they may be deactivated at times. For example, many permanent checkpoints exist in operating systems; the job accounting checkpoints and instructions identify the start and finish of a routine, the resources used, etc. Temporary checkpoints are inserted in a program only for the measurement period and removed when the measurement period is over.

Sampling software monitors collect performance data when a signal is received from some timing device. The timing device may generate signals randomly or after constant intervals. When a signal occurs, the software monitor accesses system tables to obtain resource consumption data.

Sampling software monitors cause less system interference than event-driven software monitors because they are invoked less often; they sample the population of events rather than measure each event in the population. However, only estimates of the true characteristics of the population of events can be calculated.

The major decision to be made when using a sampling software monitor is how often events will be sampled. The auditor must trade off the benefits of increasing the accuracy of the estimates of resource consumption by more frequent sampling with the increased costs caused by more system interference. Decisions on the sampling rate should be based on (*a*) the frequency with which the event to be measured occurs, (*b*) the required accuracy of the estimates, and (*c*) the costs of measurement, which include both the cost of execution and the cost of system interference (see, also, Kobayashi [1978]).

Capabilities of Software Monitors The primary advantage of using a software monitor rather than a hardware monitor is the greater flexibility the software monitor usually provides to measure system events. The domain of a software monitor sometimes contains more elements; however, the elements in its domain are more macroscopic events than those in the domain of a hardware monitor, though there is some overlap of domains. With a software monitor, events are detected at the instruction level, whereas events in a hardware monitor are detected at the level of a pulse in the circuitry.

Theoretically, the input width of a software monitor is unlimited. As many checkpoints as the auditor needs to monitor events can be inserted in a program. In comparison, the input width of hardware monitors is limited by the number of probes available. Practically, the input width of a software monitor is limited by the extent of system interference (artifact) that can be tolerated.

In general, software monitors are easier to install than hardware monitors. They are also less susceptible to external interference (for example, accidental removal of probes) than hardware monitors.

Limitations of Software Monitors Probably the major limitation of software monitors is the artifact they introduce in the system they measure. This artifact takes two forms: time and space. Time artifact occurs because the checkpoint instructions must be executed. Space artifact occurs because the checkpoint instructions must be stored in the machine. In some cases it is possible to correct for this artifact. For example, the time taken to execute a checkpoint instruction may be known and this time can be subtracted from the length of the interval affected by the instruction.

Software monitors also are not as portable as hardware monitors. Whereas in general a hardware monitor can be attached to any CPU, for efficiency reasons a software monitor often must be written in the assembly language of a specific machine; thus, it can run only on that machine. Implementing a software monitor also requires detailed knowledge of the host system or program so the checkpoints can be inserted at the correct place in the code.

Firmware Monitors

Some instructions used to collect performance measurement data can be implemented as microcode. Firmware monitors operate in a similar way to software monitors. However, they have three major advantages over software monitors. First, the execution time for a microinstruction is shorter; thus, less interference is produced. Second, microinstructions allow access to some hardware indicators that cannot be accessed with a programming language; consequently, the domain of a firmware monitor overlaps both hardware and software monitors (Figure 21.3). Third, firmware monitors have higher resolution.

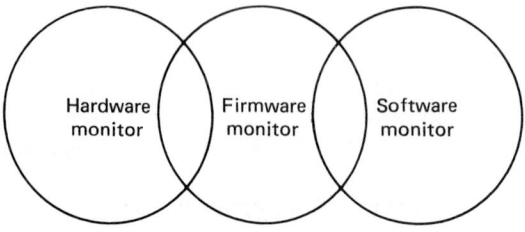

Figure 21.3
Relationship between domains (scope) of hardware monitors, firmware monitors, and software monitors.

Relative to software monitors, firmware monitors have several disadvantages. Unlike ordinary program instructions, microinstructions usually have a very constrained space that they are permitted to occupy in the machine; thus, fewer probes can be inserted for monitoring purposes. Since firmware monitors have a high resolution, they can degrade considerably the execution speed of the host system, thereby producing a large monitor artifact. To reduce this artifact, firmware monitors often have low data reduction capabilities. Measurement data collected simply is stored as a trace, and the data then must be summarized at a later time.

Hybrid Monitors

A hybrid monitor has hardware, software, and perhaps firmware elements. The monitor consists of an external hardware device to receive, process, store, and present data collected by an internal software or firmware component (see Rose [1978]). For example, a microinstruction in a hybrid monitor may be used to output certain bit patterns that can be accessed by a hardware device having probes connected to the appropriate pins in the circuitry.

Svobodova [1976] describes various methods of implementing a hybrid monitor. Special monitor registers can be kept in main memory; software writes the events to be monitored to these registers and the hardware component of the hybrid monitor detects changes to these registers. The monitor also can be installed in a memory bus; again, software detects signals passing along the bus and writes them to registers that are read by the hardware component of the monitor. Whatever the technique used, the basic design principle is the same. An interface exists between the software (firmware) component of a hybrid monitor and the hardware component. The software component writes events monitored as signals to the interface, and the hardware component reads and processes these signals (Figure 21.4). The software component also may control the external hardware component.

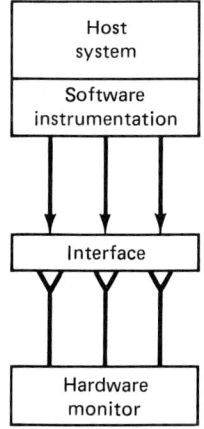

Figure 21.4
Basic structural components of a hybrid monitor.

Hybrid monitors have two major advantages. First, they reduce the artifact caused by the monitoring process. The domain of hybrid monitors includes the domain of hardware monitors plus some subset of the domain of firmware and software monitors. However, they do not cause as much interference as software and firmware monitors. Second, in general, it is easier to instrument a system with a hybrid monitor than a software monitor. Placement of software probes in the host system can be a complex task. The placement of probes with a hybrid monitor is more well-defined.

The major limitation of hybrid monitors is that they are not able to monitor all the types of events that can be monitored by a software or firmware monitor.

PERFORMANCE MONITORING AND DATA INTEGRITY

Auditors should have two concerns about data integrity whenever a performance monitor is used. First, they must determine whether the monitor has been installed correctly in the host system. Here the concern is with the integrity of the measurements made by the monitor and the integrity of the host system processes after instrumentation. If the host system is not instrumented correctly, the measurements taken will be erroneous and wrong decisions may be made that have serious consequences; for example, an unnecessary change may be made to a hardware/software configuration. Further, the integrity of processes in the host system may be corrupted; again, this could have serious consequences if the host system is the operating system, a compiler, a database management system, or a teleprocessing monitor. Second, auditors must try to determine whether a monitor has been used to violate data integrity. Here the concern is with unauthorized use of the monitor to breach data privacy. The following two sections briefly discuss each of these concerns.

Ensuring Correct System Instrumentation

The proper placement of the probes of a hardware monitor and the checkpoints of a software monitor is a difficult task. Stimler [1974] recommends using test programs to check proper placement of probes with a hardware monitor. If test programs are not available from the monitor vendor, he argues special assembly level programs should be prepared that execute loops of known instructions a predetermined number of times. Resource utilization by these programs should be calculated and compared with measured resource utilization to validate the placement of probes.

Proper placement of checkpoints is facilitated if the auditor uses a software monitor that automatically inserts checkpoints at user-specified locations in the host system. Ferrari and Liu [1975] describe a software monitor that can be used interactively to instrument a program. The monitor automatically inserts the checkpoints that issue calls either to standard predefined measurement routines already included in the monitor or user-coded measurement routines. Further, the monitor checks that checkpoints are not inserted at locations in the host system where they might cause errors; for example, at locations referenced in the program as data and not instructions.

Some software monitors also validate any user-supplied measurement routines. These monitors impose various restrictions on the code supplied by the user; for example, it must not contain illegal or privileged instructions, it cannot modify itself or other measurement routines, it must not store data or branch into the host system, and it must not contain backward branches (see, further, Ferrari [1978]). Still other types of checks can be applied. For example, the monitor may check whether a checkpoint would cause intolerable interference, thereby destroying the integrity of a time-critical host system process.

Ensuring Maintenance of Data Privacy

Use of a performance monitor within an installation must be controlled carefully. Since monitors have access to lower-level elements within the system hierarchy of resources (for example, memory ports and input/output channels), they can be used to breach the privacy of data. For each user the permitted domain of the monitor must be defined and enforced via access controls (see, also, Chapter 10). Application users should be restricted to monitoring resource consumption of their own processes only. The database administrator may be granted more global privileges to optimize overall resource consumption.

The usual types of access controls should be applied to a monitor. In the case of hardware monitors, physical access to the monitor must be restricted. Even if the hardware monitor is installed permanently in the machine, physical access to its controls should be prevented. Saltzer [1974] expresses his concerns about how the lights and switches on an operator console can be used for unauthorized purposes. In the case of software monitors, access to the monitor should be controlled by the operating system. A log of users of the monitor also can be kept.

The performance monitor itself also must be protected. As a piece of software that may be used widely within an installation, a software monitor is a suitable target for a Trojan horse (see, further, Chapter 12).

SUMMARY

Performance monitoring tools enable the auditor to obtain evidence on hardware and software resource consumption within an installation. This evidence is used as a basis for making decisions on how resource utilization can be improved.

Four types of performance monitoring tools are available: (*a*) hardware monitors, (*b*) software monitors, (*c*) firmware monitors, and (*d*) hybrid monitors. Hardware monitors take measurements through probes attached to the circuitry of the system hardware. Software monitors take measurements through checkpoints inserted into the software that runs on the system. Firmware monitors take measurements through the microcode inserted in the system. Hybrid monitors use an external hardware device to process data collected by an internal software/firmware component. The different types of monitors have varying capabilities with respect to their scope, resolution, input width, data reduction and storage capabilities, precision, portability, and the artifact they produce.

When using a performance monitor, the auditor must ensure that the monitor is installed correctly; otherwise, the measurements taken may be invalid, or the integrity of the host system may be corrupted. When a hardware monitor is used, test programs should be run to determine whether or not the probes have been placed correctly. If possible, a software monitor should be used that automatically inserts user-specified checkpoints into the host program.

Use of a performance monitor also must be controlled. Monitors can be used to breach data privacy. The normal access controls should be applied to monitors. The monitor itself also must be protected against unauthorized modifications.

REVIEW QUESTIONS

21.1. What is a performance monitor? Why does use of a performance monitor require special expertise?

21.2. Give three examples of objects in a computer system that might be measured by a performance monitor. Briefly explain why each of these objects may be measured.

21.3. What constitutes the sensor in (a) a hardware monitor, and (b) a software monitor?

21.4. Briefly explain why it may be necessary to carry out some form of reduction on data collected by a monitor before it is stored. Give two examples of reductions that may be applied to trace measurements.

21.5. Briefly explain why the auditor may be interested in obtaining the distribution of disk seek times for an online realtime program when attempting to improve the efficiency of the program.

21.6. What is meant by monitor artifact? Why is it important for the auditor to know the extent of artifact that a monitor may produce? Is it possible to control for artifact? Explain.

21.7. If an auditor wants to measure the extent of CPU and channel overlap, how can he or she set up the Boolean AND operator required in a hardware monitor?

21.8. Briefly explain the difference between a wired-program hardware monitor and a stored-program hardware monitor. Which type of hardware monitor provides the user with more flexibility? Why?

21.9. Give an example of a fixed hardware monitor and an example of how the monitor might be used during an evaluation of system efficiency.

21.10. Why does a hardware monitor have greater resolution than a software monitor?

21.11. Give two factors that limit the domain of a hardware monitor, and briefly explain how they limit the domain.

21.12. Briefly explain the relative capabilities of hardware monitors and software monitors with respect to input width.

21.13. Briefly explain the difference between an event-driven software monitor and a sampling software monitor. What are the relative advantages and disadvantages of each type of monitor?

21.14. How does a checkpoint instruction in a software monitor work? What is the difference between a permanent checkpoint and a temporary checkpoint? Give an example of each.

21.15. Give two examples of standard (vendor-written) measurement routines you would expect to see in software monitors. Give an example of a measurement routine the user may have to write.

21.16. Briefly explain how a software monitor may be used to measure disk seek time. What type of output might be generated for the user to examine?

21.17. Theoretically, the input width of a software monitor is unlimited; however, practically it is limited by the extent of interference it produces. Explain.

21.18. How do the domains of hardware and software monitors differ? Give an example of an event that would be only in the domain of a hardware monitor, one that would be only in the domain of a software monitor, and one that would be in both domains.

21.19. Briefly explain what is meant by time and space artifact.

21.20. Give two advantages that firmware monitors have over software monitors. What problems may arise because of the high resolution capabilities of firmware monitors?

21.21. Briefly explain the purpose of the interface in a hybrid monitor.

21.22. Why do hybrid monitors produce a lower artifact than software monitors but a higher artifact than hardware monitors?

21.23. What is meant by instrumenting a system for performance monitoring? Why is it desirable for vendors to consider instrumentation during the design stages of a computer system?

21.24. What problems arise during performance monitoring if a system is incorrectly instrumented? How can incorrect instrumentation be detected in a hardware monitor and a software monitor?

21.25. Give two advantages of using a software monitor that instruments a system automatically.

21.26. Why is it important to control who gains access to a performance monitor? Why is a performance monitor a likely target for someone wishing to carry out unauthorized activities in a computer installation?

21.27. Why must the domain of a performance monitor be controlled? Briefly explain how it is possible to limit the domain for different types of users of a monitor.

21.28. In general, why should the operator console not be used for display purposes by a hardware monitor?

EXERCISES AND CASES

21.1. As the manager of internal audit for an organization, you are called one day to a meeting with the controller and the data processing manager. The controller informs you that a limited amount of funds has been made available to hire a consultant to carry out some performance evaluation within the data processing department. Since the funds are limited, however, the controller wants the consultant to focus on those application systems where there is most likely to be a payoff. She asks you and the data processing manager to provide her with a list of recommendations on the systems that should be evaluated.

Required: Outline how you would go about determining which systems you would recommend be subject to performance evaluation. Be sure to indicate the variables/attributes of the systems on which you would base your decision.

21.2. As more users are added to an interactive system, response times get longer. The project manager responsible for the system is perplexed because he believes the system should be able to cope with many more users without any noticeable increase in response times. He cannot determine whether the response time problem is hardware or software based.

Required: Identify five system activities that might be measured to determine whether the response time problems are hardware or software based. Explain the type of measurement you would undertake — trace, activity, duration, etc. — and why you would measure the activities you list in the manner that you specify. For your information, terminals in the system are located in clusters in remote locations. These clusters are connected to a local controller that in turn is connected to a front-end communications controller for the central machine. The software that handles the interactive system consists of a master program that calls subroutines from a library to handle the various functions to be performed in an interactive request.

21.3. Refer to Exercise and Case 21.2. For *each* activity you intend to measure, indicate whether you would use a hardware or software monitor for measurement purposes, and explain the reasons for your choice.

21.4. You are the manager of internal audit for a large company that uses advanced computer systems: distributed, online realtime update, database management, etc. Management of your company has decided that computer operations are sufficiently large that it is worthwhile to employ a full-time person with expertise in computer performance evaluation. This person will be responsible for setting up and carrying out a program of performance review of all computer operations.

Management recognizes that the person responsible for performance evaluations at times will be in a position to breach the integrity of systems. They are concerned that the powers vested in the person not be abused.

Required: Management asks you to write a brief report recommending some controls that might be implemented and exercised over the person to ensure proper performance of duties.

REFERENCES

Arndt, Fred R., and G. M. Oliver. "Hardware Monitoring of Real-Time Computer System Performance," *Computer* (July–August 1972), pp. 25–29.

Ferrari, Domenico. "Architecture and Instrumentation in a Modular Interactive System," *Computer* (November 1973), pp. 25–29.

———. *Computer Systems Performance Evaluation* (Englewood Cliffs, N.J.: Prentice-Hall, Inc., 1978).

———, and Mark Liu. "A General-Purpose Software Measurement Tool," *Software-Practice and Experience* (April–June 1975), pp. 181–192.

Kobayashi, Hisashi. *Modeling and Analysis: An Introduction to System Performance Evaluation Methodology* (Reading, Mass.: Addison-Wesley Publishing Company, 1978).

Lucas, Henry C. "Performance Evaluation and Monitoring," *Computing Surveys* (September 1971), pp. 79-91.

Miller, Edward F., Jr. "Bibliography on Techniques of Computer Performance Analysis," *Computer* (September-October 1972), pp. 39-47.

Ramamoorthy, C. F., K. H. Kim, and W. T. Chen. "Optimal Placement of Software Monitors Aiding Systematic Testing," *IEEE Transactions on Software Engineering* (December 1975), pp. 403-411.

Rose, Clifford A. "A Measurement Procedure for Queueing Network Models of Computer Systems," *Computing Surveys* (September 1978), pp. 263-280.

Saltzer, Jerome H. "Protection and the Control of Information Sharing in Multics," *Communications of the ACM* (July 1974), pp. 388-402.

Shermer, Jack E., and John B. Robertson. "Instrumentation of Time-Shared Systems," *Computer* (July-August 1972), pp. 39-48.

Stimler, Saul. *Data Processing Systems: Their Performance, Evaluation, Measurement, and Improvement* (Trenton, N.J.: Motivational Learning Programs, Inc., 1974).

Svobodova, Liba. *Computer Performance Measurement and Evaluation Methods: Analysis and Applications* (New York: American Elsevier Publishing Company, Inc., 1976).

PART

EVIDENCE EVALUATION

Once the evidence on a system has been collected it must be evaluated. The evaluation process involves the auditor weighting and combining piecemeal evidence to make a global decision on whether a system safeguards assets, maintains data integrity, achieves organizational goals effectively, and consumes resources efficiently.

It is the evidence evaluation process that requires auditors to make the most use of their judgment capabilities. Little is known about how various evidence should be weighted and combined to make a global evaluation. To a large extent, auditors must rely on their intuition and experience when assessing the impact of a system strength or weakness on the overall quality of the system.

The next three chapters examine the evidence evaluation process for the four major decisions the auditor must make: whether the system safeguards

Chapter	Overview of contents
22 Evaluating Asset Safeguarding and Data Integrity	Measures of asset safeguarding and data integrity; formal evaluation techniques; cost-effectiveness guidelines
23 Evaluating System Effectiveness	Task accomplishment goals; quality of working life goals; operational effectiveness; technical effectiveness; economic effectiveness
24 Evaluating System Efficiency	Performance indexes; workload models; system models

533

assets, whether it maintains data integrity, whether it is effective, and whether it is efficient. Until more is known about the evaluation process, the chapters can provide only some guidelines to assist making high-quality evaluation decisions. Currently, it is this area that requires the most intensive research effort.

CHAPTER 22

EVALUATING ASSET SAFEGUARDING AND DATA INTEGRITY

CHAPTER OUTLINE

MEASURES OF ASSET SAFEGUARDING AND DATA INTEGRITY
EVALUATING ASSET SAFEGUARDING AND DATA INTEGRITY: FORMAL TECHNIQUES
   Analytical Techniques
   Simulation Techniques
COST-EFFECTIVENESS CONSIDERATIONS
   Costs and Benefits of Controls
   Calculating the Ongoing Costs of Control Systems
   Controls as an Investment Decision
SOME INFORMAL GUIDELINES FOR EVALUATION
   Ensure Identification of Relevant Cues
   Ensure Proper Weighting of Cues
   Carefully Organize and Present the Evidence
SUMMARY
REVIEW QUESTIONS
EXERCISES AND CASES
REFERENCES

When auditors evaluate how well assets are safeguarded, they attempt to determine whether or not the asset could be destroyed, stolen, or used for unauthorized purposes. When auditors evaluate how well data integrity is maintained, they attempt to determine the completeness, soundness, purity, and veracity of the data. In both cases the auditor is concerned with expected losses given the controls in place.

This chapter examines both the decision on how well assets are safeguarded and the decision on how well data integrity is maintained. It considers these decisions jointly because there is a large overlap in the evaluation methodologies that can be used for each decision.

The chapter first discusses measures of asset safeguarding and data integrity and then various formal models for determining values for these measures. Since asset safeguarding and maintenance of data integrity are not costless processes, the evaluation decision is considered next within a cost-effectiveness framework. Finally, the chapter discusses some informal guidelines for performing the evaluation process and examines some problems and pitfalls encountered.

MEASURES OF ASSET SAFEGUARDING AND DATA INTEGRITY

To evaluate how well assets are safeguarded and data integrity is maintained, the auditor needs some kind of measurement scale. Asset safeguarding and maintenance of data integrity are not all or nothing affairs; assets are safeguarded and systems maintain data integrity to varying degrees.

The measure of *asset safeguarding* that the auditor uses is the expected loss that occurs if the asset is destroyed, stolen, or used for unauthorized purposes. The auditor may assign different probabilities to the different losses that could occur; that is, if there is uncertainty surrounding the size of the dollar losses that result if assets are not safeguarded, the losses can be described via a probability distribution.

The measure of *data integrity* used by the auditor depends on the nature of the data item on which the auditor focuses. In general, the auditor is interested in the extent to which a system of internal control can produce errors. If the auditor is concerned with a monetary data item, data integrity will be evaluated in terms of the *dollar error* that could have been produced. If the auditor is concerned with a quantity figure, say, the amount of an inventory item, data integrity will be evaluated in terms of the *quantity error* that could have been produced. If the auditor simply is concerned with whether or not a data item is in error, say, a name and address record, data integrity will be evaluated in terms of the *number* of data items that might be in error. For these last two cases, however, ultimately the auditor still must translate a quantity error and a number error into a dollar consequence so the cost-effectiveness of controls can be evaluated.

Since most computer systems contain stochastic elements, data integrity must be assessed in terms of a *probability distribution* of possible error. If all errors in computer systems were deterministic, a single point estimate of error would suffice. For example, assume the only error that occurs in a computer system is a program error relating to transaction type Z where a quantity amount is multiplied by $5 instead of $4. Estimating the error produced is simple: the total quantity amount for transaction type Z can be determined and multiplied by the $1 error to obtain the total error.

However, some controls in computer systems fail probabilistically. For example, a clerk randomly may transcribe a wrong amount onto a source document, which the input validation program may be unable to detect. Data communications controls may not detect all errors resulting from noise on a communications line. Thus, the *actual* error produced depends on the nature and seriousness of the errors that occur, the timing of the errors, the ways in which they compound and compensate, the extent to which errors are deterministic or probabilistic, etc. These factors affect the mean, variance, skewness, and kurtosis of the probability distribution of error that could occur.

To illustrate these concepts, Figures 22.1*a*, 22.1*b*, and 22.1*c* show examples of probability distributions of errors that a system might produce. Figure

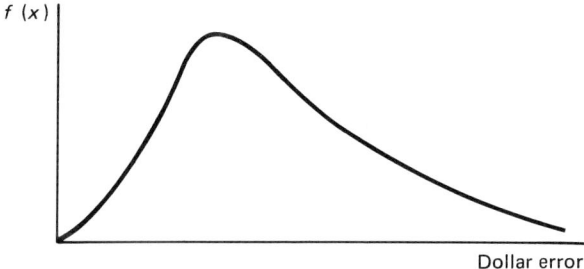

Figure 22.1a
Right-skewed probability distribution of dollar error a system could produce.

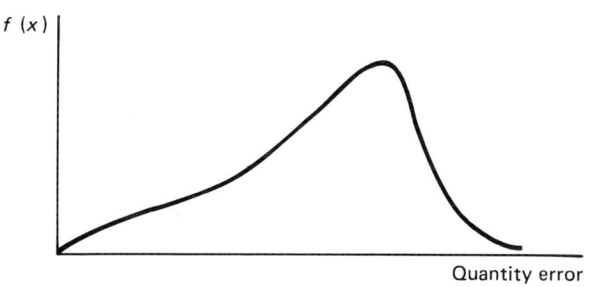

Figure 22.1b
Left-skewed probability distribution of quantity error a system could produce.

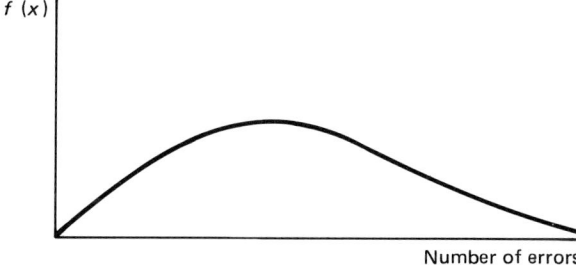

Figure 22.1c
Probability distribution with kurtosis of number of errors a system could produce.

22.1a shows a probability distribution of error for a dollar data item; note how the distribution is skewed to the right. Figure 22.1b shows a probability distribution of error for a quantity data item; note how the distribution is skewed to the left. Figure 22.1c shows a probability distribution of error for the number of data items that could be in error; note the flatness (kurtosis) of the distribution. Thus, the shapes of the probability distributions of error are important indicators of the risk an auditor faces when making a decision about the materiality of the error that a system could produce. For example, Figure 22.1c shows it is most likely that the error produced will be "small"; however, there is a possibility that a large error could be produced.

EVALUATING ASSET SAFEGUARDING AND DATA INTEGRITY: FORMAL TECHNIQUES

There has been little research undertaken on decision models that auditors could use as an aid when evaluating how well assets are safeguarded and systems maintain data integrity. For the most part auditors must apply their best judgments. Clearly, the judgments to be made are complex. Somehow the auditor must weight and combine piecemeal evidence on the probability of an error or irregularity, control strengths and weaknesses, the ways in which controls compensate, compound, and interact, the characteristics of data passing through systems, etc., to come up with a global evaluation. Little research has been undertaken on how well auditors make these global evaluation judgments.

The few studies that have been carried out on the quality of the global evaluation judgment produce some conflicting evidence. For example, Ashton [1974] found a high level of consensus among auditors in their judgments on the reliability of an internal control system for payroll. He asked the auditors to rate the overall strength of the internal control system on a 6-point scale ranging from extremely weak to adequate to strong. Weber [1978] found auditors were moderately accurate when estimating the *mean* of the probability distribution of dollar error that an inventory system could produce. The auditors gave inaccurate estimates, however, of the *range* of the dollar error that could occur. This inaccuracy could have grave implications for materiality decisions when the mean of the error distribution is not considered to be a material amount but the extremes of the distribution are considered to be material errors. Both studies were carried out using manual systems. The results could be different for judgments made on computer systems since a larger number of *deterministic* errors usually occurs in a computer system (because of program error), and the ratio of stochastic to deterministic errors may affect the quality of the decision made.

The following sections examine some of the research undertaken to develop models that would assist the auditor to evaluate how well assets are safeguarded and data integrity is maintained. Two types of models have been developed: (a) analytical models, and (b) simulation models. None of the models have been implemented on a widespread basis. Nevertheless, examining the models provides important insights into the problems of evaluating asset safeguarding and data integrity.

Analytical Techniques

An analytical approach to solving a model requires the derivation of mathematical equations to express the relationships between the dependent variables of interest and the independent variables that affect the values of the dependent variables. In other words, to use an analytical technique the auditor must be able to formulate equations showing the relationship between a measure of asset safeguarding or data integrity and the variables that affect asset safeguarding or data integrity. If the parameters of the equations require single point values, the set of equations is a deterministic model of the system; if the parameters are stochastic, the model is probabilistic.

Deterministic Models Deterministic models may be useful when evaluating part of a system of internal control or obtaining a first approximation of how well a computer system safeguards assets and maintains data integrity.

Consider, for example, the access control mechanism in an operating system. Assume the auditor discovers an integrity flaw in the system that allows, under certain conditions, the privacy of a data file to be violated; that is, the flaw can be exploited so the data file (asset) is no longer safeguarded against unauthorized use. To determine the consequences of the flaw, the auditor might access the system log to determine how many times the flaw has been exploited; assuming, of course, that the integrity of the log has been preserved. Calculating the loss that has resulted because of the flaw involves estimating the loss on each occasion that the flaw was exploited and summing the losses. Thus, the model used in this example is deterministic, providing there is no uncertainty about the losses involved.

Consider, also, a batch computer system. Any errors that the auditor identifies in the programs within the system are deterministic; if a program processes a data item incorrectly, it will always process the data item incorrectly. The auditor simply has to determine the frequency with which the data item occurs and the magnitude of the error that occurs. Audit software can be used to retrieve all instances of the data item from the audit trail so the total error for the data item can be determined. The ways in which different errors compound and compensate, however, still must be considered.

Even if the system to be evaluated contains stochastic elements, a deterministic model still might be used. A *mean value* deterministic model simply replaces each probabilistic element with its mean value. To obtain some idea of the probability distribution of errors that may result, *extreme value* deterministic models can be used; that is, the probabilistic elements can be replaced by their lowest and highest values.

Deterministic models are relatively simple models to construct. The auditor might use them to perform a pencil and paper analysis of how well a system safeguards assets and maintains data integrity. The models provide only limited information, however, about the forms of the probability distribution of error that can be produced when a system contains stochastic elements.

Probabilistic Models Probabilistic models have more potential than deterministic models for representing the sometimes complex, variable phenomena in systems relating to asset safeguarding and maintenance of data integrity. Though the research is still meager, some progress has been made on the formulation of probabilistic models of internal control systems that would aid the auditor during the evaluation process.

The probabilistic models proposed tend to be based either on Markov theory or engineering reliability theory. For example, Yu and Neter [1973] modeled a payroll system as a Markov process. Cushing [1974] and Bodnar [1975] used reliability theory to analyze the overall reliability of an internal control system (see, also, Ishikawa [1975]). There also have been some aggregate probabilistic models constructed. For example, Schick [1974] proposes introducing induced errors into a system and having another person attempt to rediscover them. During this process the second person discovers both induced and indigenous errors. Statistical theory then can be used to predict the remaining number of indigenous errors (see, also, Schick and Wolverton [1978]). However, since the reliability approach perhaps is the most straightforward and easily understood, the model described below is a modified version of a model proposed by Cushing [1974].

Figure 22.2a shows a simple system where there is one process, a single control, and a single error correction process. Assume, also, only one type of error or irregularity occurs within the system. The reliability of the system, that is, the probability the system will not have an error or an irregularity, is computed as follows:

$$R = p + (1 - p) P(e) P(c)$$

where R = system reliability
p = probability the process executes correctly
$P(e)$ = probability the control detects an error or irregularity when one exists
$P(c)$ = probability an error or irregularity is corrected when the control detects an error or irregularity and one exists

In other words, the reliability of the system equals the probability the process executes correctly plus the probability it executes incorrectly but the control identifies the error or irregularity and the error or irregularity is corrected.

Consider, first, how the model can be used to assess how well an asset is safeguarded. Assume, for example, the system to be assessed is a fire detection and extinguisher system. Assume the probability $(1-p)$ of a fire to be .005. In other words, the probability of the "process" executing correctly—there is no fire—is .995. The probability $P(e)$ of the detector system signaling a fire when one occurs is .95. The probability of the system correctly activating the extinguisher and putting out the fire when a fire is signaled and one exists $P(c)$ is .90. Thus, the reliability of the detection and extinguisher system is:

$$R = .995 + (.005)(.95)(.90)$$
$$= .999275$$
$$(1 - R) = .000725$$
$$(R - p) = .004275$$

Note, the probability of a fire occurring even with the detection and extinguisher system $(1 - R)$ is .000725. The detection system may fail to signal a fire, the extinguisher may fail to put the fire out, etc. However, the probability of a fire causing destruction is reduced by .004275; that is, $R - p$.

Consider, also, how the model can be used to assess how well a system maintains data integrity. Assume, for example, the "system" to be evaluated is the keypunching operation in an application system. The control process is verification of the data that has been keypunched. The probability of data being keypunched correctly is .9; thus, the probability of incorrect keypunching $(1 - p)$ is .1. $P(e)$ is the probability .9 that the verifier operator detects a key-

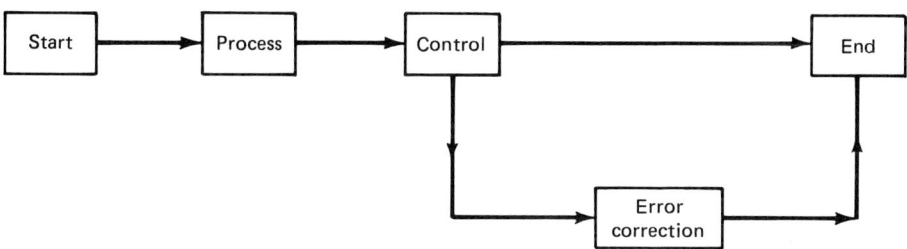

Figure 22.2a
System with one process and one control.

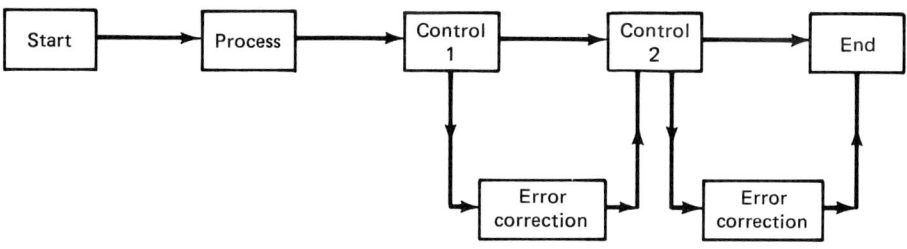

Figure 22.2b
System with one process and two controls.

punch error when one exists. $P(c)$ is the probability .95 that the verifier operator corrects a detected error. The reliability of the process R is:

$$R = .9 + (.1)(.9)(.95)$$
$$= .9855$$
$$(1 - R) = .0145$$
$$(R - p) = .0855$$

Note, the probability of an error occurring even with verification is .0145; the verifier operator may omit verifying some incorrectly keypunched data, the verifier operator may make the same mistake as the keypunch operator, the wrong character may be punched during the correction process, etc. However, the verification control improves the overall reliability of the process by $R - p$, that is, .0855.

The above example assumes only one type of error or irregularity occurs within the system. For more than one error or irregularity type, the parameters in the formula can be suitably subscripted. Thus, R_i the reliability of the system for the ith error or irregularity type can be computed as follows:

$$R_i = p_i + (1 - p_i) P(e_i) P(c_i)$$

The overall reliability of the system for all error or irregularity types is $R = \prod_{i=1}^{n} R_i$. For example, if $R_1 = .9$ and $R_2 = .8$, then $R = (.9)(.8)$, that is, .72.

Figure 22.2b shows the case of a simple system where only one error or irregularity type occurs, a single process exists, and two controls operate. Extending the previous keypunch system example, assume the keypunch machine also automatically checks batch totals. However, verification as a second control still would identify compensating errors that were not detected by the batch total check. After the second control point the reliability of the system is:

$$R^2 = R^1 + (1 - R^1) P(e_2) P(c_2)$$

Thus, the reliability of the system after the second control point R^2 is dependent upon the reliability of the system after the first control point R^1. Note in this case only, $P(e_2)$ and $P(c_2)$ are probabilities for the second control point and not the second error type.

More generally, in a single system where $i = 1, n$ error or irregularity types can occur and $j = 1, r$ controls exist, the reliability of the system after the jth control for the ith error or irregularity type is:

$$R_i^j = R_i^{j-1} + (1 - R_i^{j-1}) P(e_{ij}) P(c_{ij})$$

To illustrate the application of this formula, Table 22.1 shows the reliability calculations for a single process system where there are two controls and two error or irregularity types. Note that the second control is unable to identify any of the first error or irregularity type; thus, $R_1^2 = R_1^1$.

By itself a reliability (probability) figure is not especially meaningful. The auditor needs to know what dollar or quantity error a system can produce or how many data items are likely to be in error. For example, if auditors are assessing data integrity and they are dealing with monetary or quantity error types, the effect of error type i on a data item can be calculated by:

$$A_i = Ne_{ir} \times Ve_i \times T_r$$

where A_i = dollar or quantity error produced
Ne_{ir} = average number of errors of type i which remain undetected after r control processes
Ve_i = estimated average dollar or quantity effect of an undetected type i error
T_r = frequency with which the set of r controls is performed

The expected total dollar or quantity error is simply the sum of the individual error effects; that is, $A = \sum_{i=1}^{n} A_i$

TABLE 22.1
RELIABILITY CALCULATIONS FOR SYSTEM WITH SINGLE PROCESS, TWO CONTROLS, AND TWO ERROR TYPES

$p_1 = .8$ $\quad\quad\quad\quad$ $p_2 = .85$
$P(e_{11}) = .85$ $\quad\quad\quad\quad$ $P(e_{21}) = .85$
$P(c_{11}) = .95$ $\quad\quad\quad\quad$ $P(c_{21}) = .90$
$P(e_{12}) = 0$ $\quad\quad\quad\quad$ $P(e_{22}) = .80$
$\quad\quad\quad\quad\quad\quad\quad\quad$ $P(c_{22}) = .95$

$R_1^1 = p_1 + (1 - p_1)P(e_{11})P(c_{11})$
$\quad\,\, = .8 + (.2)(.85)(.95)$
$\quad\,\, = .9615$
$R_2^1 = p_2 + (1 - p_2)P(e_{21})P(c_{21})$
$\quad\,\, = .85 + (.15)(.85)(.90)$
$\quad\,\, = .96475$
$R_1^2 = R_1^1 + (1 - R_1^1)P(e_{12})P(c_{12})$
$\quad\,\, = .9615 + (.0385)(0)$
$\quad\,\, = .9615$
$R_2^2 = R_2^1 + (1 - R_2^1)P(e_{22})P(c_{22})$
$\quad\,\, = .96475 + (.03525)(.8)(.95)$
$\quad\,\, = .99154$
$R = (R_1^2)(R_2^2) = (.9615)(.99154) = .953366$
$p = (p_1)(p_2) = (.8)(.85) \quad\quad = .68$
$R - p = .953366 - .68 = .273366$

If the auditor is attempting to estimate the *number* of data items that are likely to be in error, the formula is:

$$H = \sum_{i=1}^{n} H_i$$

where $H_i = Ne_{ir} \times T_r$.

Note that A and H are expected (mean) values. Thus, the auditor still must estimate the probability distributions of these variables. The distributions of A and H are a function of the distributions of Ne_{ir}, Ve_i, and perhaps T_r if T_r is stochastic.

The model described so far also needs further refinement if it is to be used in practice to evaluate how well a system safeguards assets and maintains data integrity. It must be extended to handle the multiple-process case. It also must be extended to handle redundant processes and redundant controls.

Cushing [1974] and Bodnar [1975] both argue the reliability approach currently is feasible to use to evaluate controls in a system. Since there are only a few reported applications of the model, however, it is not known generally how difficult it is to formulate the model for any specific system.

Probably the major problem encountered in using the model is estimating the values of the model parameters. In the examples given previously, each error or irregularity type was assumed to be statistically independent of the occurrence of any other error or irregularity type. This assumption may not always hold in practice; thus, at times the auditor may have to determine how error types interact.

As with the output of all analytic models, the accuracy of a probabilistic model's output is a function of how accurately it has been formulated, whether or not there are solution inaccuracies caused by the use of approximation methods, and how accurately the parameter values of the model have been estimated. As always, the problem is to achieve a computationally tractable model that provides sufficiently accurate output.

Simulation Techniques

Analytic models should be used whenever possible since the values of the dependent variables can be evaluated usually at low cost over a wide range of values of the independent variables and variations in the structure of the model. However, sometimes analytic models are not mathematically tractable; the equations of the system are not obvious or they may be insolvable. In these cases, simulation often can be used to evaluate the values of the dependent variables. Simulation allows the behavior of the system to be studied over time.

Simulation might be used to evaluate how well assets are safeguarded if the system to be evaluated is complex and there are several levels of controls that can fail stochastically. For example, there may be some probability that a guard will fail to detect an intruder, some probability that a surveillance system also may fail to detect the intruder, some probability that the intruder can crack a safe lock combination, etc., and eventually the intruder gains access to and steals sensitive data files. Often an analytical model can be used to determine the probability of all controls failing. Nevertheless, if controls compound and compensate in different ways, a simulation model may be necessary for gaining insight into the reliability of the system of controls.

The use of simulation to evaluate how well a system maintains data integrity has been suggested by Burns and Loebbecke [1975]. Methodologies for constructing simulation models have been described extensively elsewhere (see, for example, Emshoff and Sisson [1970]); however, the following simplified example illustrates the use of the approach to help solve an auditing problem.

Assume a clerk uses a terminal connected to a minicomputer to perform complex pricing calculations for a product. A counter maintained by the minicomputer shows that in the past year 8000 calculations were performed. During the evidence collection phase the auditor finds that the size of transactions follows a normal distribution with a mean of 100 units and a standard deviation of 30 units.

The auditor also discovers two errors have occurred during the pricing process. First, an estimated 5% of the time the clerk types the wrong transaction amount as input to the program. The clerk sometimes overstates the amount and sometimes understates the amount. The best description the auditor can give of the error is that it appears to be distributed normally with a mean of 3 units and a standard deviation of 7 units (overstatements occur more often than understatements). Second, the program contains an error; it prices wrongly if the transaction amount is between 120 and 125 units.

Figure 22.3 shows the flowchart for a simulation program written to estimate the dollar error that could have occurred. Note the program simulates the year's transactions a thousand times. At the end of the simulation the program prints out the probability distribution of total error that might have resulted because of the stochastic error (the clerk typing in the wrong amount) and the deterministic error (the incorrect pricing calculation). Of course, in practice the simulation program needed to evaluate how well a system maintains data integrity usually would be much more complex.

As with analytical models, the accuracy of simulation output is a function of model formulation inaccuracies, solution inaccuracies, and parameter inaccuracies. Techniques for calibrating and validating simulation models are well-developed (see Emshoff and Sisson [1970]). The auditor should be careful not to rely on simulation output until these activities have been performed.

COST-EFFECTIVENESS CONSIDERATIONS

So far the discussion has proceeded without considering the costs of safeguarding assets or maintaining data integrity. However, how well a system of

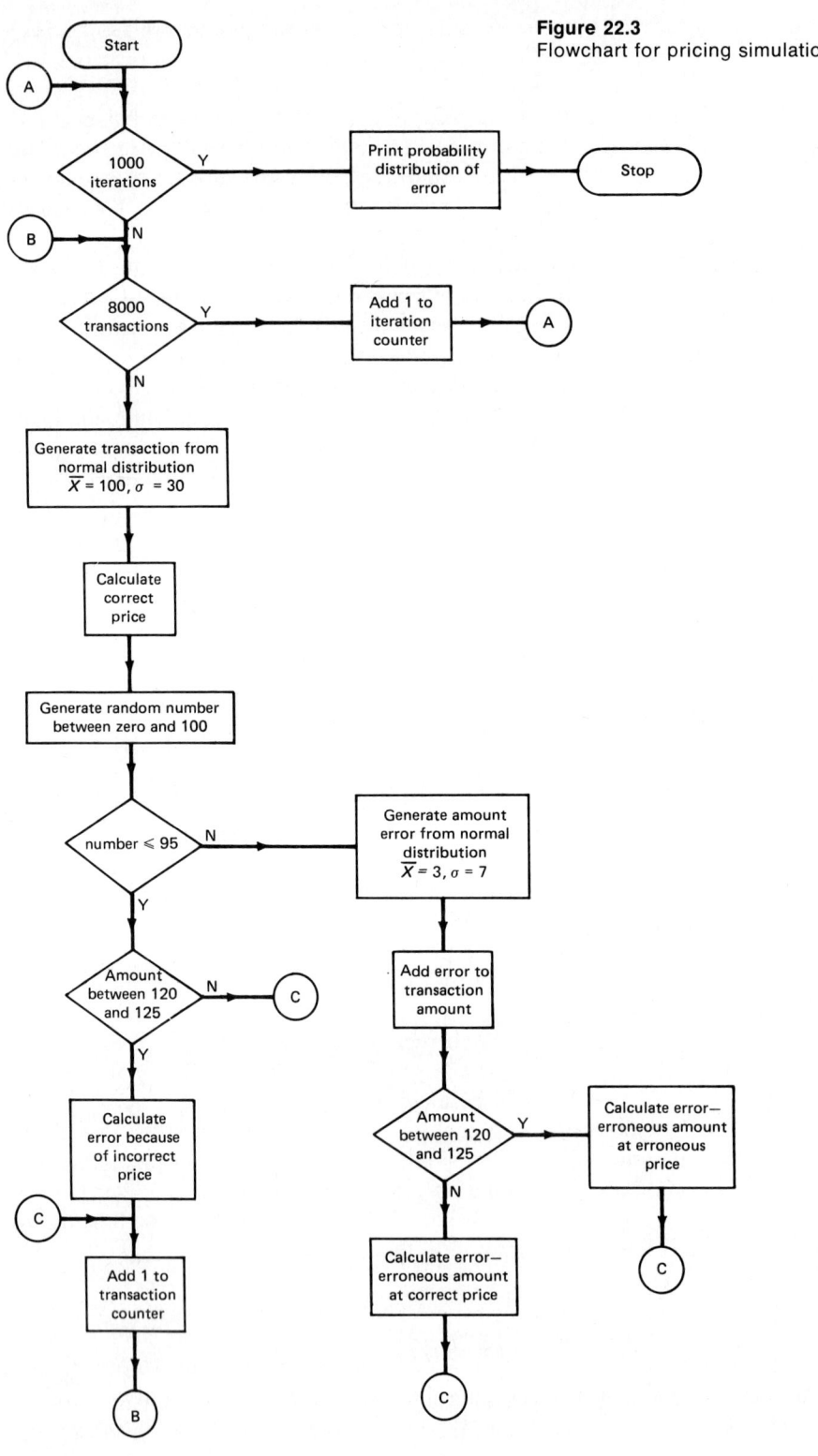

Figure 22.3
Flowchart for pricing simulation.

controls safeguards assets or maintains data integrity must be considered within a cost-effectiveness framework. A system might prevent all types of errors or irregularities occurring but at a prohibitive cost. Always the question must be asked: Do the benefits obtained from having a control exceed the costs of that control?

The following sections outline the elements of a decision model that the auditor can use to evaluate whether a system is cost-effective in its asset safeguarding or maintenance of data integrity. Again, the model provides important insights into this evaluation problem; however, its use is not widespread so little is known about the problems of implementing the model.

Costs and Benefits of Controls

Implementing and operating controls in a system involves four costs. First, initial setup costs must be incurred to design and implement controls; for example, magnetic card door locks must be installed or validation routines must be written into programs. These are one-off costs. Second, execution costs are incurred; for example, the wages of a security officer must be paid or CPU charges arise from executing validation routines. Third, there are costs involved in searching for an error or irregularity, determining whether one exists, and then correcting any error or irregularities that are found. Fourth, costs arise because the controls do not detect some errors or irregularities and these errors or irregularities cause losses; for example, an uncorrected error or irregularity may allow a defalcation to occur. The first cost is the outlay for a system of controls. The last three costs are the ongoing operational costs of a control system.

The benefits derived from having a control system relate to the decreased occurrence of errors or irregularities that results. In some cases errors or irregularities would occur routinely without the control; for example, transposition errors regularly will be made and perhaps remain undetected unless a check digit is used. In other cases the control acts as a deterrent; for example, a burglar alarm may deter unauthorized intruders. The benefits of a control system are calculated when the losses that would result from errors or irregularities that the control system does not detect are compared with the losses that would result from errors or irregularities that an alternate control system does not detect.

Calculating the Ongoing Costs of Control Systems

Perhaps the most difficult part of the evaluation of cost-effectiveness of control systems is assessing the ongoing costs of a system. The reliability approach discussed earlier in the chapter can be extended to provide a basis for calculating these costs. Let C_t be the ongoing costs of a control system in period t. Then:

$$C_t = \sum_{j=1}^{r} Cc_j + \sum_{i=1}^{n} (1 - R_i^r)Ce_i$$
$$+ \sum_{i=1}^{n} \sum_{j=1}^{r} \{R_i^{j-1}[1 - P(s_{ij})][1 - P(d_{ij})] + (1 - R_i^{j-1})P(e_{ij})\}Cs_{ij}$$

where $P(s_{ij})$ = probability the jth control will not signal the ith error or irregularity when an error or irregularity does not exist

$P(d_{ij})$ = probability a failure in the jth control is detected and no action taken when the control signals an error or irregularity type i and no error or irregularity exists

Cc_j = cost of executing control j

Cs_{ij} = cost of searching for error or irregularity type i, detecting whether it exists, and correcting the error or irregularity

Ce_i = average cost of an uncorrected error or irregularity type i

R_i^j, $P(e_{ij})$ have the usual meaning

In other words, the total ongoing costs of a control system in any period equal the costs of executing the control plus the losses resulting from uncorrected errors or irregularities plus the costs of identifying whether errors or irregularities exist when they are signaled and correcting them if they do exist.

If no controls are implemented, the formula simply reduces to:

$$C_t = \sum_{i=1}^{n} (1 - p_i)Ce_i$$

To illustrate the approach, first, with respect to asset safeguarding, consider again a fire detection and extinguisher system (see, also, State of Illinois [1974]). Assume the probability $(1 - p)$ of a fire in any year to be .005 and the loss Ce that would occur because of the fire to be $3,000,000. Thus, the expected loss in any one year is $15,000. The maintenance cost of the system Cc is $500 per year. The probability $[1 - P(s)]$ of the detector system falsely signaling a fire and activating the extinguishers is .001. If this occurs, the probability $P(d)$ of detecting the false signal in time before the extinguishers are activated is .5. The probability of the system correctly signaling a fire and activating the extinguishers $P(e)$ is .995. The cost of a cleanup operation after the extinguishers have been activated is $4000.

With the fire detection and extinguisher system, the probability $(1 - R)$ of a fire causing damage is $(1 - p)[1 - P(e)]$; that is, the probability of a fire occurring multiplied by the probability of the detection and extinguisher system not detecting the fire. Thus:

$$(1 - R) = (.005)(.005)$$
$$= .000025$$

The yearly cost of the fire detection and extinguisher system is calculated as follows:

$$C_t = Cc + (1 - R)\,Ce + \{p[1 - P(s)][1 - P(d)] + (1 - p)P(e)\}Cs$$
$$= 500 + (.000025)\,(3{,}000{,}000) + [(.995)\,(.001)\,(.5) + (.005)\,(.995)]\,4000$$
$$= 500 + 75 + [.000498 + .004975]\,4000$$
$$= 596.892$$

In other words, the ongoing costs of the fire detection and extinguisher system equals the cost of maintaining the system plus the expected loss which would result from an undetected fire plus the costs of a cleanup operation which results either from incorrect activation or correct activation of the extinguisher system.

Consider, now, use of the model for evaluating how well data integrity is maintained. Assume a simple system where there is one transaction type, one process, two controls, and two possible error types. For example, assume the process is an online update program. The user submits data at a terminal and periodically, with some probability, the user makes two types of error: (*a*) a wrong account number is submitted, and (*b*) a wrong dollar amount is submitted.

The program performs two types of validation checks. First, the account is checked against the master file to determine whether or not it is a valid account number. Second, a reasonableness check is performed. Account numbers are coded to indicate the expenditure limits imposed on an account; thus, the program checks the amount is reasonable given the account number.

Even with the program validation checks, errors still may get through and affect the master file. The wrong account number may be submitted but it still may be a valid number on the master file. The account number check will not identify this error. However, possibly the reasonableness check will identify the error; the dollar amount (submitted correctly) will be unreasonable for the invalid account number.

The reasonableness check also will identify dollar errors that fall outside the allowed range for an account number. However, some amount errors made will fall within the allowed range and remain undetected by the control.

Table 22.2 shows the reliability calculations for the system using the formula discussed earlier in the chapter. Table 22.3 shows example ongoing cost calculations for three alternate control systems: (*a*) no controls, (*b*) the account check only, and (*c*) the account check then the amount check. Note the assumption that the program performs the validation checks correctly; thus, $P(s_{ij})$ the probability of an error signal arising when there is no error is zero. Note, also, the user may not correct an error correctly. Data identified in error and resubmitted in error still may pass the validation checks.

Even with only two controls, two other control systems can be considered. First, a control system using only the *amount* check might be evaluated. Second, a control system using the amount check then the account check might

TABLE 22.2
RELIABILITY CALCULATIONS FOR ONLINE UPDATE PROGRAM

p_1(correct account) = .85 p_2(correct amount) = .9
$P(e_{11})$ = .97 $P(e_{21})$ = .0
$P(c_{11})$ = .95 $P(e_{22})$ = .9
$P(e_{12})$ = .25 $P(c_{22})$ = .8
$P(c_{12})$ = .95

$$R_1^1 = p_1 + (1 - p_1)P(e_{11})P(c_{11})$$
$$= .85 + (.15)(.97)(.95)$$
$$= .988225$$

$$R_2^1 = p_2 + (1 - p_2)P(e_{21})P(c_{21})$$
$$= .9 + (.1)(0)$$
$$= .9$$

$$R_1^2 = R_1^1 + (1 - R_1^1)P(e_{12})P(c_{12})$$
$$= .988225 + (.011775)(.25)(.95)$$
$$= .991022$$

$$R_2^2 = R_2^1 + (1 - R_2^1)P(e_{22})\,P(c_{22})$$
$$= .9 + (.1)(.9)(.8)$$
$$= .972$$

$$R = (R_1^2)(R_2^2) = (.991022)(.972) = .963273$$
$$p = (p_1)(p_2) = (.85)(.9) \qquad = .765$$
$$R - p = .963273 - .765 = .198273$$

be evaluated. The order of controls could be important when the cost-effectiveness of alternate control systems is considered.

The above procedure provides only the expected (mean) ongoing costs of a control system. Consider, for example, the alternative of no controls shown in Table 22.3. The value 35, the ongoing costs *per transaction*, is an expected value. To illustrate, if A is the event "account error" and B is the event "amount error," then the expected value is calculated as follows:

$$p(A \cap \sim B) = p(A)p(\sim B) = (.15)(.9) \quad = .135$$
$$p(A \cap B) = p(A)p(B) = (.15)(.1) \quad = .015$$
$$p(\sim A \cap B) = p(\sim A)p(B) = (.85)(.1) \quad = .085$$
$$p(\sim A \cap \sim B) = p(\sim A)p(\sim B) = (.85)(.9) = \underline{.765}$$
$$\underline{\Sigma p(E) = 1.000}$$

Event	p(E)	Cost	Expected cost
$A \cap \sim B$	.135	100	13.5
$A \cap B$	.015	300	4.5
$\sim A \cap B$	.085	200	17.0
$\sim A \cap \sim B$	.765	0	0
			$\Sigma(EC) = \underline{35.0}$

The variance of the probability distribution is an important indicator of the riskiness of the cash flows in any period.

Perhaps the most difficult part of using the above model is estimating the probabilities of the various events that can occur. Again, methods of risk analysis can be applied to obtain these probabilities and the associated losses that result (see, for example, Gerberick [1979]).

Controls as an Investment Decision

So far, only the ongoing operational costs of a control system to safeguard assets or maintain data integrity have been considered. When evaluating cost-

TABLE 22.3
ONGOING COSTS FOR ALTERNATE CONTROL SYSTEMS IN ONLINE UPDATE PROGRAM

$Cc_1 = .01$ $Cc_2 = .02$
$Cs_{11} = 1.00$ $Cs_{21} = -$
$Cs_{12} = 1.25$ $Cs_{22} = 1.10$
$Ce_1 = 100.00$ $Ce_2 = 200.00$
$P(s_{11}) = 1$ $P(s_{22}) = 1$
$P(d_{11}) = 1$ $P(d_{22}) = 1$
$P(s_{12}) = 1$
$P(d_{12}) = 1$

1. No controls
$C_t = (1 - p_1)Ce_1 + (1 - p_2)Ce_2$
$= (.15)(100) + (.1)(200)$
$= 15 + 20$
$= 35$

2. Account check only
$C_t = Cc_1 + (1 - R_1^1)Ce_1 + (1 - R_2^1)Ce_2$
$\quad + \{p_1[1 - P(s_{11})][1 - P(d_{11})] + (1 - p_1)P(e_{11})\}Cs_{11}$
$\quad + \{p_2[1 - P(s_{21})][1 - P(d_{21})] + (1 - p_2)P(e_{21})\}Cs_{21}$
$= .01 + (.011775)(100) + (.1)(200)$
$\quad + [(.85)(0)(0) + (.15)(.97)]1$
$\quad + [(.9)(0)(0) + (.1)(0)]0$
$= .01 + 1.1775 + 20 + .1455$
$= 21.333$

3. Account check then amount check
$C_t = Cc_1 + Cc_2 + (1 - R_1^2)Ce_1 + (1 - R_2^2)Ce_2$
$\quad + \{p_1[1 - P(s_{11})][1 - P(d_{11})] + (1 - p_1)P(e_{11})\}Cs_{11}$
$\quad + \{R_1^1[1 - P(s_{12})][1 - P(d_{12})] + (1 - R_1^1)P(e_{12})\}Cs_{12}$
$\quad + \{p_2[1 - P(s_{21})][1 - P(d_{21})] + (1 - p_2)P(e_{21})\}Cs_{21}$
$\quad + \{R_2^1[1 - P(s_{22})][1 - P(d_{22})] + (1 - R_2^1)P(e_{22})\}Cs_{22}$
$= .01 + .02 + (.008978)(100) + (.028)(200)$
$\quad + [(.85)(0)(0) + (.15)(.97)]1 + [(.988225)(0)(0) + (.011775)(.25)]1.25$
$\quad + [(.9)(0)(0) + (.1)(0)]0 + [(.9)(0)(0) + (.1)(.9)]1.10$
$= .01 + .02 + .8978 + 5.6 + .1455 + .00368 + 0 + .099$
$= 6.77598$

effectiveness, however, the outlay cost for the control system also must be taken into account.

Whether or not to implement a control system can be evaluated just like any other asset investment decision using the decision models that are well-developed within the finance literature (see, for example, Bierman and Smidt [1975] and Sharpe [1978]). Since control systems so far have been considered only in terms of costs (not benefits), the simple decision rule is to implement that system which has the lowest net present value of costs.

Consider, again, the online update program example discussed in the previous section. Three control systems were considered: (a) no controls, (b) an account check only, and (c) an account check and then amount check. If I_j is the implementation cost of the jth control and k is the required rate of return on an investment for an organization, then TC_m the net present value of the mth control system can be computed as follows:

$$TC_m = \sum_{j=1}^{r} I_j + \sum_{t=1}^{T} \frac{C_t}{(1+k)^t}$$

The control system having the minimum TC_m should be chosen.

Table 22.4 shows the calculations for the online update program example. Assume the cost of implementing the account check control is $1000 and the cost of implementing the amount check control is $2500. Assume, further the life of the system is three years, the required rate of return is 10%, and 500

TABLE 22.4
NET PRESENT VALUE CALCULATIONS FOR CONTROL SYSTEM ALTERNATIVES

$I_1 = 1000$
$I_2 = 2500$
$k = 10\%$
$T = 3$ years
Number of transactions per year = 500

1 No controls

$$TC_1 = \frac{35 \times 500}{(1.1)^1} + \frac{35 \times 500}{(1.1)^2} + \frac{35 \times 500}{(1.1)^3}$$
$$= 43{,}520$$

2 Account check only

$$TC_2 = 1000 + \frac{21.33 \times 500}{(1.1)^1} + \frac{21.33 \times 500}{(1.1)^2} + \frac{21.33 \times 500}{(1.1)^3}$$
$$= 1000 + 26{,}522$$
$$= 27{,}522$$

3 Account check then amount check

$$TC_3 = (1000 + 2500) + \frac{6.78 \times 500}{(1.1)^1} + \frac{6.78 \times 500}{(1.1)^2} + \frac{6.78 \times 500}{(1.1)^3}$$
$$= 3500 + 8430$$
$$= 11{,}930$$

transactions occur per year. Thus, the control system having both the account check and the amount check should be chosen since it has the lowest net present value of total costs.

Obtaining the required rate of return k to carry out the discounting process is a difficult problem. Current finance theory defines k as:

$$k = k_f + \beta(\bar{k}_m - k_f)$$

where k_f = risk-free rate of return
$\bar{k}_m$ = expected rate of return on the market portfolio
β = beta coefficient of a security

The β coefficient of a security indicates the riskiness of returns on the security relative to returns on the market portfolio. The value of β can be obtained by regressing returns on the security against returns on the market portfolio (see Van Horne [1977]).

However, what is β for an investment in a control system? There is no easy answer to this question. One approach to calculating β would be to regress the returns on a security for an organization involved in designing and implementing control systems with the returns on the market portfolio. But there are still further theoretical and practical problems involved in calculating β for multiperiod investments under uncertainty (see Fama [1977]). These matters are left for further study.

As a final point, note also the net present value of cost calculated using the above formula is an expected (mean) value. Recall, there is a probability distribution over the ongoing costs of a control system; thus, there is a probability distribution over the net present value of costs for a control system. The variance of the probability distribution of net present values can be calculated using the following formula (see, further, Van Horne [1977]):

$$\sigma = \sqrt{\sum_{t=1}^{T} \frac{\sigma_t^2}{(1+k)^{2t}}}$$

where σ_t^2 is the variance of the probability distribution of costs (cash outflows) in period t. The variance of the net present value of costs reflects the risk of the investment in a control system.

SOME INFORMAL GUIDELINES FOR EVALUATION

Ideally, the quality of auditor decision making on how well a system safeguards assets and maintains data integrity could be assessed by determining the accuracy of auditors' judgments. Unfortunately, assessing the accuracy of judgments in this area is a difficult if not impossible task. Inaccurate judgments only become obvious some time after the judgment has been made. Further, the judgment must be blatantly wrong for its poor quality to be apparent; for example, a system on which the auditor gives an unqualified judgment fails. For a vast range of intermediate cases, a system that does not safeguard assets or maintain data integrity causes an organization losses, but these losses do not cripple the organization.

In the absence of an accuracy measure, two other measures used to assess the quality of auditor judgment are consensus and consistency. Consensus means different auditors would make the same judgment on how well a system safeguards assets or maintains data integrity. Consistency means a single auditor would make the same evaluation judgment on a system if the same system was to be evaluated again at a later time.

The following sections briefly present some guidelines to assist obtaining consensus and consistency in auditor evaluation judgments. Unlike the previous sections in the chapter, the guidelines presented involve mainly informal techniques. Until formal techniques of evaluation have been better developed and implemented on a more widespread basis, informal techniques are an important means of obtaining higher-quality judgments. The guidelines discussed below have three objectives: (*a*) to ensure the auditor identifies all cues (factors) relevant to the evaluation decision; (*b*) to ensure each cue is weighted properly in the evaluation decision; and (*c*) to ensure the evidence is organized and presented in a way that facilitates the global evaluation decision.

Ensure Identification of Relevant Cues

As a first step in evaluating how well a system safeguards assets or maintains data integrity, the auditor should ensure all cues relevant to the evaluation process have been identified. The cues are simply the system characteristics that impact asset safeguarding or data integrity; for example, controls and data volumes for different transaction types. The evaluation process can be flawed badly if important cues are omitted.

A traditional technique used to ensure all relevant cues are considered is a checklist. Use of a checklist simply recognizes the auditor may forget to gather evidence on particular aspects of asset safeguarding or data integrity. FitzGerald [1978] extends the traditional checklist to form a control matrix (see, also, Chapter 2). The rows of the matrix constitute various resources or assets to be protected; for example, people, records, output devices. The columns constitute various concerns and exposures; for example, errors and omissions, message loss, privacy breaches. At the intersection of a row and column, controls are listed that protect the asset (row) from the exposure (column).

Like a checklist, the control matrix focuses the auditor's attention on the controls that should be present; however, it has the additional advantage of showing how the controls assist in safeguarding assets and maintaining data integrity. Different control matrices can be constructed and used for the major components of a data processing system.

Ensure Proper Weighting of Cues

One of the more difficult tasks to perform when evaluating how well a system safeguards assets or maintains data integrity is determining the relative weighting that should be given to different internal control cues. For example, what overall impact does the absence of a control have on data privacy? How sensitive is the overall dollar error produced to varying error rates in a system component? The ways in which factors (cues) interact and compound to affect asset safeguarding or data integrity sometimes are complex. Psychological evidence suggests decision makers who must make judgments on these types of complex processes often tend to have poor insight into the importance that they attach to various cues (see Slovic and Lichenstein [1971]). They overestimate the importance of minor cues and underestimate the importance of a few major cues.

How can auditor decision making on the importance of cues be improved? The formal decision models described earlier in the chapter provide one means. An important advantage of formal decision models is that they allow sensitivity analyses to be undertaken. For example, changes in system reliability can be assessed as the error rates in controls are varied. In this way those attributes of a system that are critical to safeguarding assets or maintaining data integrity can be assessed. Auditors then can focus their attention on these attributes.

Another technique for improving decision making is to provide feedback to auditors on the weights they attach to various cues when they make a judgment on asset safeguarding or data integrity. These weights can be determined by regressing the auditor's overall judgment with the values of the attributes that affect asset safeguarding or data integrity. For example, the auditor might make a judgment on overall system reliability on a scale ranging from zero (totally unreliable) to one hundred (perfect). This rating constitutes the dependent variable in the regression model. For each decision the values of the factors that affect the decision must be determined; these factors are the independent variables in the regression model. For example, the presence or absence of a control can be coded as a binary variable, or an error rate can be coded as a continuous variable.

The beta values for the independent variables provide "objective" measures of the weighting that an auditor attaches to these factors. It is useful to compare the weightings auditors think they give to factors (subjective weightings) with the objective weightings calculated by the regression model (see, further, Ashton [1974]). The divergence of the subjective and objective weights is a measure of auditors' insight into their decision processes. By knowing the extent of this divergence, auditors can evaluate better the weights they attach to various cues.

Carefully Organize and Present the Evidence

If many pieces of evidence have been collected on a system, the auditor often has difficulty assimilating this evidence to perform a global evaluation. To aid the judgment process, a data reduction technique can be applied to the evidence. Hopefully, in this way the auditor is better able to grasp the overall significance of the evidence collected.

Perhaps the most basic data reduction technique that can be used is some form of tabular presentation of the evidence. Mair, Wood, and Davis [1976] recommend using the control evaluation table discussed in Chapter 2. Other types of data reduction methods might be used; for example, filtering out unimportant evidence or some type of aggregation method. More research is needed on data reduction techniques that can be used and the effectiveness of the techniques.

SUMMARY

When evaluating asset safeguarding and data integrity, the auditor attempts to determine whether assets could be destroyed, damaged, or used for unauthorized purposes, and how the completeness, soundness, purity, and veracity of data is maintained. The evaluation process involves the auditor making a complex global judgment using piecemeal evidence collected on the strengths and weaknesses of an internal control system.

To evaluate how well an internal control system safeguards assets and maintains data integrity, measures of asset safeguarding and data integrity are needed. Common measures are the dollar loss for asset safeguarding and the dollar error, quantity error, and number of errors a system can produce for data integrity. Since a system of internal control usually contains stochastic elements, these measures should be expressed probabilistically.

To aid the evaluation process, formal models for assessing internal control system reliability have been developed. Both analytical and simulation models exist. Some of the models incorporate cost-effectiveness considerations when evaluating asset safeguarding and data integrity.

Because formal models for evaluating asset safeguarding and data integrity are still in the developmental stages, several informal methods for improving the judgment process have been advocated. These methods aim to ensure all relevant cues are considered, the cues are properly weighted, and the evidence is presented for the global evaluation process in an organized manner.

REVIEW QUESTIONS

22.1. List three measures of data integrity and give an example of where each measure would be used. Briefly explain why measures of data integrity usually need to be expressed probabilistically.

22.2. Why is it important the auditor considers the variance of the probability distribution of error a system could produce?

22.3. Briefly explain the difference between analytical techniques and simulation techniques for evaluating asset safeguarding and data integrity. What are the relative advantages and disadvantages of the techniques?

22.4. During the test of a program the auditor discovers the program incorrectly calculates the discount given for certain types of customers. Outline how the total amount of dollar error that results because of the incorrect calculation could be determined.

22.5. Briefly explain what is meant by a mean value and an extreme value deterministic model for evaluating data integrity. Why might the auditor use these types of models?

22.6. Briefly explain *in words* what is meant by the overall reliability of a system of internal control.

22.7. Briefly discuss three problems encountered if probabilistic models are used to evaluate how well a system safeguards assets and maintains data integrity.

22.8. Briefly describe how an auditor could use a simulation model to determine the extent of errors that exist in data received over a communications line even after error detection and correction controls have been exercised.

22.9. The flowchart shown in Figure 22.3 shows the simulation program iterating 1000 times. Why is it necessary to iterate 1000 times through the year's transactions? Outline one method the auditor might use to determine whether 1000 iterations is enough.

22.10. Why must asset safeguarding and maintenance of data integrity be considered within a cost-effectiveness framework?

22.11. Briefly explain the major types of costs involved in implementing and operating a control system. How are the benefits of a control system assessed?

22.12. What costs are represented by the following formula:

$$\sum_{i=1}^{n} \sum_{j=1}^{r} \{R_i^{j-1}[1-P(s_{ij})][1-P(d_{ij})]\} \, Cs_{ij}$$

22.13. Why is the net present value of costs for a control system typically an *expected* value? Why must the auditor be careful in dealing with expected net present values only?

22.14. Briefly explain why it is difficult to assess whether auditors make *accurate* decisions when they evaluate how well an internal control system safeguards assets and maintains data integrity.

22.15. What are the overall purposes of the various informal guidelines proposed in the chapter for evaluating asset safeguarding and data integrity?

22.16. Why may it be useful to provide feedback to auditors on how they weight the various cues they consider during the evaluation of asset safeguarding and data integrity? Briefly outline a method that can be used to provide the feedback.

22.17. What is the purpose of applying a data reduction technique to the evidence collected on the reliability of system components?

EXERCISES AND CASES

22.1. An auditor wishes to calculate the reliability of a validation program with respect to a particular error type. The probability of a clerk submitting the data item in error is .2. The program can identify the error 80% of the time, and 95% of the time it will be corrected properly by the clerk. What is the reliability of the program with respect to the error?

22.2. Given the following values, calculate the overall reliability of a system having a single process, two error types, and two controls:

$$p_1 = .7 \qquad p_2 = .85$$
$$P(e_{11}) = .8 \qquad P(e_{21}) = .9$$
$$P(c_{11}) = .9 \qquad P(c_{21}) = .95$$
$$P(e_{12}) = .75 \qquad P(e_{22}) = .8$$
$$P(c_{12}) = .6 \qquad P(c_{22}) = .75$$

22.3 Calculate the reliability of the online update program evaluated in Table 22.2 if the amount check is performed before the account check.

22.4. Calculate the value of A_i the total dollar error produced in a year by a validation program run monthly if on average the program fails to detect 10 errors and the estimated average effect of each error is $2.

22.5. Calculate the ongoing costs of operating the amount check only and the amount check then the account check for the system evaluated in Table 22.3. Using the data given in Table 22.4, which of the five possible control systems for the on-line update program would you choose?

22.6. Determine whether or not to invest in the fire detection and extinguisher system described in the chapter if the installation cost of the system is $80,000, the life of the system is 10 years, and the required rate of return is 10%.

22.7. If the fire detection and extinguisher system described in the chapter is installed, show the probability distribution of costs that may occur in any one year.

22.8. Maintaining the privacy of data is a form of asset safeguarding. For an online realtime update system with remote entry terminals and a centralized shared database, list the various controls to preserve privacy that you would examine to assess reliability. Describe the evidence collection technique you would use for each of these controls to assess their reliability. Describe, also, a *formal* model that you could use to assess the *overall* reliability of the internal control system.

REFERENCES

Ashton, Robert. "An Experimental Study of Internal Control Judgments," *Journal of Accounting Research* (Spring 1974), pp. 143–157.

Bierman, Harold, and Seymour Smidt. *The Capital Budgeting Decision*, 4th ed. (New York: Macmillan Publishing Co., Inc., 1975).

Bodnar, George. "Reliability Modeling of Internal Control Systems," *The Accounting Review* (October 1975), pp. 747–757.

Burch, John G., Jr., and Joseph L. Sardinas, Jr. *Computer Control and Audit: A Total Systems Approach* (New York: John Wiley & Sons, Inc., 1978).

Burns, David C., and James K. Loebbecke. "Internal Control Evaluation: How the Computer Can Help," *Journal of Accountancy* (August 1975), pp. 60–70.

Cushing, Barry E. "A Mathematical Approach to the Analysis and Design of Internal Control Systems," *The Accounting Review* (January 1974), pp. 24–41.

———. "A Further Note on the Mathematical Approach to Internal Control," *The Accounting Review* (January 1975), pp. 151–154.

Emshoff, James R., and Roger L. Sisson. *Design and Use of Computer Simulation Models* (New York: The Macmillan Company, 1970).

Fama, Eugene F. "Risk-Adjusted Discount Rates and Capital Budgeting Under Uncertainty," *Journal of Financial Economics* (August 1977), pp. 3-24.

FitzGerald, Jerry. *Internal Controls for Computerized Systems* (San Leandro, Calif.: E. M. Underwood, 1978).

Gerberick, Dahl A. "Security Risk Analysis," *EDPACS* (April 1979), pp. 1-11.

Hoffman, Lance J. *Modern Methods for Computer Security and Privacy* (Englewood Cliffs, N.J.: Prentice-Hall, Inc., 1977).

Ishikawa, Akira. "A Mathematical Approach to the Analysis and Design of Internal Control Systems: A Brief Comment," *The Accounting Review* (January 1975), pp. 148-150.

_____, and Charles H. Smith. "A Feedforward Control System for Organizational Planning and Control," *Abacus* (December 1972), pp. 163-180.

Mair, William C., Donald R. Wood, and Keagle W. Davis. *Computer Control and Audit*, 2d ed. (Altamonte Springs, Fla.: The Institute of Internal Auditors, Inc., 1976).

Ramamoorthy, C. V., and Siu-Bun F. Ho. "Testing Large Software with Automated Software Evaluation Aids," *IEEE Transactions on Software Engineering* (March 1975), pp. 46-58.

Schick, George J. "Modeling the Reliability of Computer Software," *Decision Sciences* (October 1974), pp. 529-544.

_____, and Ray W. Wolverton. "An Analysis of Competing Software Reliability Models," *IEEE Transactions on Software Engineering* (March 1978), pp. 104-120.

Sharpe, William F. *Investments* (Englewood Cliffs, N.J.: Prentice-Hall, Inc., 1978).

Slovic, Paul, and Sarah Lichtenstein. "Comparison of Bayesian and Regression Approaches to the Study of Information Processing in Judgment," *Organizational Behavior and Human Performance* (June 1971), pp. 649-744.

State of Illinois. "Elements and Economics of Information Privacy and Security," *Data Security and Data Processing Volume 3 Part 2 Study Results: State of Illinois* (New York: IBM Corporation, 1974), pp. 23-244.

Van Horne, James C. *Financial Management and Policy*, 4th ed. (Englewood Cliffs, N.J.: Prentice-Hall, Inc., 1977).

Weber, Ron. "Auditor Decision Making on Overall System Reliability: Accuracy, Consensus, and the Usefulness of a Simulation Decision Aid," *Journal of Accounting Research* (Autumn 1978), pp. 368-388.

Yu, Seongjae, and John Neter. "A Stochastic Model of the Internal Control System," *Journal of Accounting Research* (Autumn 1973), pp. 273-295.

CHAPTER **23**

EVALUATING SYSTEM EFFECTIVENESS

CHAPTER OUTLINE

GOALS OF AN INFORMATION SYSTEM
THE EVALUATION PROCESS
    Task Accomplishment Objectives
    Quality of Working Life Objectives
    Operational Effectiveness Objectives
    Technical Effectiveness Objectives
    Economic Effectiveness Objectives
THE GLOBAL EVALUATION JUDGMENT
SUMMARY
REVIEW QUESTIONS
EXERCISES AND CASES
REFERENCES

An effective system achieves its goals. When evaluating the effectiveness of a system the auditor often confronts two major problems. First, the goals of the system may have been left vague and ill-defined. Second, as a consequence of the first problem, if system effectiveness is to be evaluated, the auditor may face the difficult tasks of trying to elicit system goals and construct measures that allow goal accomplishment to be assessed.

This chapter identifies the major sets of goals that high-quality information systems seek to achieve. It discusses how the auditor can evaluate a system in terms of these goals. Finally, the chapter focuses on the problem of how a global judgment on system effectiveness can be made.

GOALS OF AN INFORMATION SYSTEM

What are (should be) the goals of a high-quality information system? This is a frustrating and difficult question to attempt to answer. One answer might be that the overall objective of an information system is to increase the effectiveness of the organization it services. But this response simply shifts the problem; for the next question must be: What are the goals of an effective organization? The goals of an information system and the goals of the organization it serves are inextricably intertwined. Information systems are developed to help an organization meet its goals; thus, whether or not a system is effective must be assessed in terms of organization goals.

Unfortunately there is little consensus on what constitute the goals of an organization. Steers [1977] in his review of the literature on organizational effectiveness shows the diversity of indicators used to measure goal accomplishment. They include profitability, growth, turnover, absenteeism, job satisfaction, stability, flexibility, morale, and readiness. Whether some of these indicators measure goal accomplishment or the state of factors that affect goal accomplishment might be debated. For example, an economist might argue that ultimately the effectiveness of an organization is solely a function of its profitability. Turnover, stability, readiness, absenteeism, etc., all affect profitability. However, an organizational theorist might argue that profitability is too gross a measure of effectiveness. It might be possible, for example, to increase the quality of working life of employees without affecting profitability.

Given the problems, then, of defining organization goals, it is unlikely any uncontroversial statement can be made on what should be the goals of an information system. This chapter discusses the evaluation of effectiveness in terms of five major goals (Figure 23.1):

Information system goal	Explanation
Improved Task Accomplishment	Users of the system should be more productive and produce higher-quality output.
Improved Quality of Working Life	The system should contribute positively to a user's overall quality of life.
Operational Effectiveness	The system should be easy to use; it should be used frequently.
Technical Effectiveness	The system should be supported by the appropriate hardware and software technology.
Economic Effectiveness	The benefits of the system should exceed the costs.

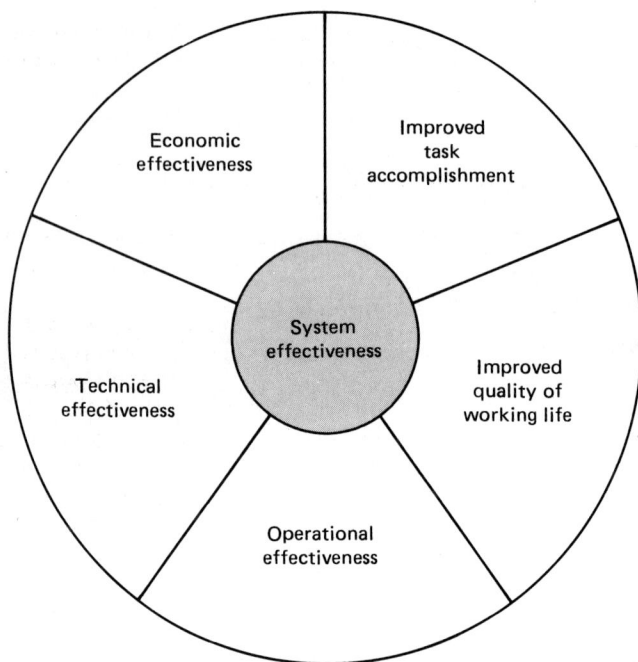

Figure 23.1
Major goals of an effective information system.

The choice of these goals for evaluating effectiveness simply reflects the biases, experience, and training of the author. The utility of the choices made is an empirical question. Further, the five goals must be considered in conjunction with three other major goals discussed in the previous chapter and the next chapter: (*a*) asset safeguarding, (*b*) maintenance of data integrity, and (*c*) operational efficiency. The following section examines the evaluation process in terms of each of these five goals.

THE EVALUATION PROCESS

When assessing system effectiveness the auditor carries out two kinds of evaluations: (*a*) a relative evaluation, and (*b*) an absolute evaluation. In a relative evaluation the auditor compares the state of goal accomplishment after the system has been implemented with the state of goal accomplishment before the system is implemented. In an absolute evaluation the auditor assesses the size of the goal accomplishment after the system has been implemented.

Relative evaluations can be applied to two goals: (*a*) improved task accomplishment, and (*b*) improved quality of working life. With these two goals the auditor attempts to assess what changes have occurred with the implementation of the system. Has task performance improved or deteriorated? Has the quality of working life gone up or down?

Relative evaluations involve six steps:

1 *Identify the Attributes of the Goal to Be Measured*   There may be some debate over what attributes of a goal should be measured. In part, the choice may be affected by the cost of measuring various attributes and the perceived importance of these attributes.

2 *Select the Measures to Be Used*   Tools for measuring the attributes next must be chosen. Chapter 20 described how questionnaires and interviews might be used. Data on some attributes may be collected routinely by the organization.

3 *Identify the User Group to Be Measured*   It is important to identify both the primary and secondary users of a system. Improved task accomplishment and increased quality of working life for the primary user group may be attained at a cost of decreased task accomplishment and lowered quality of working life for the secondary user group.

4 *Obtain Ex Ante Measures*   Before the system is implemented, the state of goal accomplishment must be measured.

5 *Obtain Ex Post Measures*   After the system is implemented the state of goal accomplishment must be measured. The difficulty here is determining what time period should elapse before the measures should be taken.

6 *Assess the Change in Goal Accomplishment*   The ex ante and ex post measures are compared to assess the changes in goal accomplishment. If ex post measures are taken periodically, the time series of changes in goal accomplishment can be plotted.

Absolute evaluations can be applied to three goals: (*a*) operational effectiveness, (*b*) technical effectiveness, and (*c*) economic effectiveness. With these three objectives an ex ante measure of goal accomplishment cannot be taken; for example, system use cannot be measured before the system is operational. Thus, the auditor must consider an absolute measure of goal accomplishment after the system has been implemented and judge whether the level of accomplishment is satisfactory.

Absolute evaluations follow the same steps to be taken for relative evaluations except that an ex ante measure of goal accomplishment is not taken (step 4) and the process of assessing goal accomplishment (step 6) is different. Initially a judgment must be made on whether the absolute level of goal accomplishment is satisfactory; however, changes in this level over time also may be traced as part of the evaluation process.

Task Accomplishment Objectives

An effective information system improves the task accomplishment of its users. Unfortunately, providing specific measures of task accomplishment that the auditor can use to evaluate an information system is difficult. Performance measures for task accomplishment differ considerably across applications (and sometimes across organizations).

Consider, for example, the ways in which task accomplishment might be assessed for a manufacturing control system, a sales system, and a welfare system that supports counselors in their work. Some of the measures of task accomplishment used for the manufacturing control system might be:

1 Number of units output
2 Number of defective units reworked
3 Number of units scrapped
4 Amount of waste produced
5 Amount of downtime
6 Amount of idle time

For the sales system, some of the measures of task accomplishment might be:

1 Dollar value of sales made
2 Changes in customer satisfaction ratings
3 Amount of doubtful/bad debts that arise
4 Average time for delivery of goods to customer
5 Number of new customers acquired
6 Number of sales made to old customers

For the welfare system, some of the measures of task accomplishment might be (see, also, Kling [1977]):

1 Number of clients successfully counseled
2 Average cost per client
3 Number of clients returning for counseling
4 Client satisfaction ratings of counseling service provided

One of the major problems encountered when evaluating task accomplishment is choosing a measure that is neither too global nor too detailed. In many cases a measure such as profitability probably is too global. It is important to know the factors that affect profitability so they can be manipulated favorably. On the other hand, continuously monitoring, say, 100 measures of task accomplishment would be too detailed a measurement process. The data collection process would be costly. Further, it is doubtful whether the data could be assimilated to assess the impact of changes in the variables monitored on overall effectiveness. The auditor must attempt to identify a small set of indicators that provide most information about goal accomplishment.

It is also important to trace task accomplishment over time. If the system designers have not carried out the process of refreezing (see Chapter 5), users of the system may revert to their old behavior patterns. The level of task accomplishment may fall back to the level existing before the implementation of the system; it may be even lower if the system interferes with these old behavior patterns.

Quality of Working Life Objectives

The Report of a Special Task Force to the U.S. Secretary of Health, Education, and Welfare [1973] claimed fundamental relationships exist between the quality of working life of individuals and their physical and mental health. The report examined, among other things, relationships between work and longevity, work and heart disease, work and peptic ulcers, work and arthritis, work and psychosomatic illness, work and alienation, and work and suicide. The message in the report is clear: the overall welfare of a nation is vitally dependent on the quality of working life of its people.

There is now general acceptance that achieving a high quality of working life for users of a system is a major objective in the design process. There is less agreement on the definition and measurement of the quality of working life. Lawler [1975] argues disputes exist because different groups in an organization have vested interests in how the quality of working life is defined; for example, some consider the quality of working life from a productivity perspective, some from a physical conditions and wages perspective, and some from an alienation perspective.

Even if agreement existed on the attributes of a high quality of working life, some difficult measurement problems remain (see, also, Lawler [1975] and Seashore [1975]). It is not easy to construct a measure that has face validity; that is, one that interested parties perceive to be a legitimate measure. Measurement instruments that have high test-retest reliability are not common. Further, the measure must be objective and verifiable and not subject to manipulation; otherwise, responses may be biased intentionally by a particular interest group. Somehow the measure must take into account that individuals in the same work environment may respond differently; for example, a person who has had several jobs is likely to have a higher level of job satisfaction than a person who is employed for the first time. The time span for measurement also must be chosen; employees subject to poor working conditions may report a high quality of working life if they have high expectations of better things to come.

Surrogate Measures One way of assessing the quality of working life is to use surrogate measures; that is, measures that act as indicators of the level of the quality of work life existing instead of directly measuring attributes of the quality of working life. Some of the surrogate measures that have been used are (see, further, Macy and Mirvis [1976]):

Measure	Possible definitions
Absenteeism rate	$= \dfrac{\text{total absent days}}{\text{total working days}}$
Tardiness rate	$= \dfrac{\text{total incidents of tardiness}}{\text{total working days}}$
Strike rate	$= \dfrac{\text{total strike days}}{\text{total working days}}$
Work ban rate	$= \dfrac{\text{total work bans}}{\text{total working days}}$
Stoppage rate	$= \dfrac{\text{total stoppages}}{\text{total working days}}$
Grievance rate	$= \dfrac{\text{total grievances}}{\text{average work force size}}$
Turnover rate	$= \dfrac{\text{total turnover incidents}}{\text{average work force size}}$
Accident rate	$= \dfrac{\text{total accidents}}{\text{total working days}}$
Sick rate	$= \dfrac{\text{total sick days}}{\text{total working days}}$
Theft/sabotage rate	$= \dfrac{\text{total theft/sabotage incidents}}{\text{average work force size}}$

Changes in these measures are the outcome of changes in the quality of working life. For example, a lowered quality of working life may cause increased turnover of employees or a greater number of strikes. Thus, to assess the effectiveness of a system, the focus is on how these measures change after the system has been implemented.

There are three advantages of using surrogate measures to assess the quality of working life. First, the measures are objective, verifiable, and difficult to manipulate. Second, the data required for the measures is relatively easy to obtain. Most of the data should be maintained routinely by an organization. For example, the personnel department of the organization should keep records on sickness, absenteeism, strikes, etc. Third, the cost of changes in the measures can be assessed. For example, the cost of absenteeism can be measured by calculating the cost of wages and fringe benefits of replacement workers, the opportunity cost of profit lost during the replacement process, the cost of the personnel department's time in dealing with the absenteeism, etc. (see, further, Macy and Mirvis [1976]).

The major disadvantage of using surrogate measures is that management (or a union) does not always know why the quality of working life has been lowered or raised. What attributes of the quality of working life have been affected by the implementation of a system still must be determined; otherwise, if the quality of working life has been lowered, there is little basis for corrective action. Use of surrogate measures does not alleviate the need to investigate cause-effect relationships.

Direct Measures Direct measures attempt to gauge the levels of the attributes of the quality of working life; thus, a decision must be made on what is meant by a high quality of working life.

Various researchers have proposed different lists of attributes of a high quality of working life (see, for example, Davis and Cherns [1975]). The following list provided by Walton [1975] includes some of the major attributes commonly proposed:

Quality of work life attribute	Explanation
Adequate and Fair Compensation	The income received from work should meet social standards of sufficiency and bear an appropriate relationship to the income received from other work.
Safe and Healthy Working Conditions	The physical work conditions should minimize the risk of illness and injury. There should be limitations on hours worked.
Opportunity to Use and Develop Human Capacities	Jobs should provide autonomy, involve both planning and implementation activities, allow use of multiple skills, and be meaningful. Employees should obtain feedback on their actions.
Opportunity for Continued Growth and Security	There must be ongoing opportunities to develop and use new skills. Employment and income security should exist.
Social Integration in the Work Organization	The work place should be free of prejudice, allow interpersonal openness, and encourage a sense of community.
Constitution in the Work Organization	The work place should preserve personal privacy, allow free speech, provide equitable treatment, and allow due process when disputes arise.
Balanced Work Role and Total Life Space	Work should be integrated with the total life space; e.g., it should not place unreasonable demands on leisure and family time.
Social Relevance of Work Life	The worker should perceive the work place to be socially responsible.

Measurement of these attributes is a difficult task. In some cases instruments have been developed and their validity and reliability tested. For example, Hackman et al. [1975] have developed an instrument to measure how well a job matches a worker's needs in terms of variety, challenge, decision making autonomy, opportunities for learning, perceived relevance and contribution, and future prospects. Instruments to measure job satisfaction (as an attribute of the quality of working life) are well-developed. Nadler et al. [1976] describe an instrument developed to assess ongoing attitudes in an organization related to job satisfaction, the quality of supervision, and the availability of regular feedback on job performance. However, in general, directly measuring the quality of working life still constitutes a major problem.

Operational Effectiveness Objectives

When assessing operational effectiveness the auditor examines how frequently a system is used, the way in which it is used, and how easily it can be used. The following three sections discuss how each of these attributes of operational effectiveness can be evaluated.

Frequency of Use Frequency of use has been employed widely by researchers as a measure of the implementation success of computer systems (see, for example, Schultz and Slevin [1975] and Lucas [1978b]). Intuitively, this relationship is appealing; however, Danziger [1977] obtained empirical evidence showing a relationship existed between information system use and the extent to which managers believed computer systems achieved operational and information efficiencies (see, also, Guthrie [1974]).

When measuring information system use a distinction must be made between voluntary use and involuntary use (Figure 23.2). In an online inquiry system a decision maker may be able to choose whether or not to use the system to aid performance of the task; other sources of information may be available. Where use is voluntary, a monitor can be built into the system to collect data on system use (see Lucas [1978a]).

However, some systems do not allow the user to choose whether or not output will be provided. Many systems generate routine reports for their users. Where use is not discretionary, the auditor must be careful to determine whether use is "real" or "apparent." Reports provided may play no part in decision-making activities; individual items or reports may not be used.

To determine the extent of "real" use of system output, questionnaires that obtain satisfaction measures can be employed. Maish [1979] describes a ques-

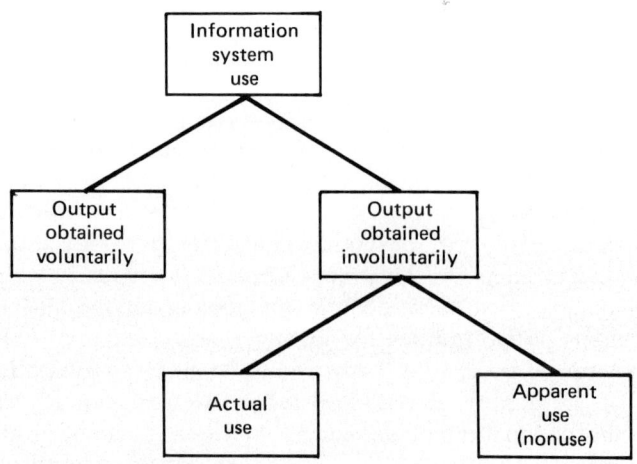

Figure 23.2
Types of information system usage.

tionnaire he used to determine whether routine reports provided by an information system contained the data decision makers required and whether the reports provided too much or too little information. King and Rodriguez [1978] employed a questionnaire to measure decision makers' perceptions of the *urgency* of the information provided by a system; that is, their need to have the results in spite of the costs that may be involved.

Nature of Use The overall success of a system also seems to depend on the way it is used. Ginzberg [1978] investigated the relationship between users' ratings of system success and the level of individual change that occurred when the systems were implemented. He identified four levels of individual change that a system may evoke:

Level of change	Explanation
Management Action	The user simply treats the system as a black box and uses the information or solution to the problem provided by the system.
Management Change	The user must have an elementary understanding of the system. The user treats the system as a tool that can be applied to find answers to specific problems.
Recurring Use of the Management Science Approach	The user develops a fundamental appreciation of the analytic approach used by the system to solve problems. The user attempts to apply this analytic approach to other problems.
Task Redefinition	The system causes users to rethink their view of the job, the way in which they perform the job, etc. The user employs the system to help redefine tasks.

Ginzberg hypothesized that different types of systems required different types of change (levels of adoption) if they were to be successful. For example, at one extreme a clerical replacement system such as a payroll system requires only a "management action" level of change. At the other extreme a decision support system for portfolio managers requires a "task redefinition" level of change. Further, he argued that attempting to adopt a level of change other than the one appropriate to the type of system was a waste of effort. In essence, Ginzberg's hypothesis is based on a contingency theory of implementation; successful systems require different levels of adoption depending upon the nature of the system (see, also, Alter [1978] and Moore [1979]).

Ginzberg found empirical evidence to support his hypothesis. He investigated 29 systems and employed a questionnaire administered to users of the system to identify the characteristics of the system, the level of change that it had evoked, and the perceived degree of success the system had achieved. Successful systems had evoked the appropriate level of change that his theory predicted; unsuccessful systems had not achieved the required level of change.

The auditor should be careful not to imply high operational effectiveness if a system is used frequently. Ginzberg's research suggests the level of change brought about by the system also must be examined. A user may have no choice but to use the output of a system. However, this does not mean that the users consider the system to be successful (see, also, Dutton and Kraemer [1978]).

Ease of Use Maish [1979] found positive associations between a user's feelings about systems and the extent to which the systems were easy to use. Sterling [1974] presents a number of design guidelines to facilitate use of a system; for example, the language of the system should be easy to understand, the system should recognize that it deals with different types of individuals, the system should allow an individual a choice on how to deal with the system, the system should relieve the user of unnecessary chores.

When evaluating ease of use, the auditor again must be careful to identify both the primary and secondary users of a system. A system may have been designed to facilitate use by one class of users with little thought being given to other classes of users. For example, middle managers of an exception reporting system may find the system easy to use; the clerical staff who collect the input data may have great difficulty in meeting the data submission deadlines imposed by the system (see, also, Chapter 5).

Questionnaires can be used to evaluate user's perceptions of how easy a system is to use. Maish [1979] describes a questionnaire he employed to evaluate various attributes of ease of use: terminal location convenience, availability of user instructions, flexibility of reporting formats, ease of error correction, etc. Individual items on a questionnaire will depend on the characteristics of the system used. For example, evaluation of an online system would include questions relating to the interactive language; a questionnaire for a batch system would not include these questions.

Technical Effectiveness Objectives

The evaluation of technical effectiveness involves deciding whether or not the appropriate hardware and software technology has been used to support a system. In essence the question asked is: Would a change in the support hardware/software technology enable a system to meet its goals better? The following three sections briefly examine some major aspects of this evaluation process.

Hardware Effectiveness Chapters 21 and 24 provide detailed discussions of how hardware performance can be evaluated. This evaluation may enable the throughput of the existing configuration to be improved. However, it also may indicate a new hardware configuration is needed; in other words, the benefits of a new configuration would exceed the costs of the change. Since in-depth evaluation of hardware often is a costly and time-consuming process (see, also, Chapter 4), the regular effectiveness evaluation simply may examine gross measures of hardware performance; for example, system response time, downtime, idle time.

Software Effectiveness The software technology supporting an application system can be evaluated by examining three attributes of application programs: (*a*) the history of program repair maintenance, (*b*) the history of program modifications, and (*c*) run-time resource consumption.

The history of program repair maintenance indicates the quality of logic existing in a program. Repair maintenance is carried out to correct program logic errors. Extensive repair maintenance means inappropriate design, coding, or testing technologies have been used to implement the program — inexperienced programmers have not been supervised adequately, system testing has not been carried out, a top-down design approach has not been used, etc.

There are two reasons why modifications to program specifications occur. First, the designer may formulate incorrect specifications; consequently, the specifications have to be changed and the program logic altered. Second, user requirements may change; the program has to be altered to meet these new user requirements. Incorrect program specifications mean the technology used to develop the specifications should be examined. Frequent modifications to meet changes in user needs may mean the system is inflexible; it has not been designed to accommodate change.

If at run time an application program consumes resources inefficiently, it may mean the logic is structured poorly or the programming language or compiler used is inappropriate for the task to be performed. Again, the auditor should examine the technology supporting these aspects of software implementation; there may be inadequate code review, the installation may be using a poor quality compiler, testing may be inadequate, etc. (see Chapter 6).

The designers and programmers responsible for carrying out program modification and repair maintenance and the operators responsible for running programs are important sources of information on the appropriateness of the software technology used for an application system. Designers and programmers can make judgments on the overall quality of programs; they know whether a program is easy to modify or repair. Operators often can make judgments on whether a program consumes abnormal amounts of resources at run time. These judgments can be elicited using questionnaires or interviews (see Chapter 20).

Independence Goals A major objective in choosing the technology to support an information system is to attain independence within and among the major resources that support the system: hardware, software, and data. Independence is a desired goal for three reasons (see, also, Gilb [1977]). First, it allows a system to be adapted more readily to a future environment. Second, it allows a system to be adapted more readily to multiple existing environments. Third, it allows a system to be adapted more readily to a backup environment.

Halloran et al. [1978] identify six resource relationships where the extent of independence should be assessed:

Resource relationship	Independence criteria
Data–Data	The system should minimize data redundancy, "fixed" data, and the number of interrelationships existing between data items.
Software–Software	Programs should maximize module strength and minimize module coupling.
Hardware–Hardware	Generalized hardware components should be used to reduce interface problems.
Data–Software	The definition of data should be maintained independently of the programs that operate on it.
Data–Hardware	The definition of data should be separated into a logical definition and a physical definition. The logical definition should remain intact when the hardware on which the data is stored changes.
Software–Hardware	To the extent possible, the logical structure and source code of a program should be independent of the hardware on which the program operates.

The development of measures of independence is still a research area. Halloran et al. [1978] provide some guidelines as to the measures that can be used. However, judgment still must be exercised. Designers, programmers, and operators again are important sources of information on the extent of independence existing within and among the resources supporting an application system.

Economic Effectiveness Objectives

When evaluating the economic effectiveness of an information system, the auditor attempts to determine whether the net present value of the investment in the information system is greater than or equal to zero; in other words, the return on the investment in the information system is greater than or equal to the required rate of return. The evaluation involves carrying out three tasks: (*a*) identifying the costs and benefits of the information system, (*b*) valuing these costs and benefits, and (*c*) determining the net present value of these costs and benefits. The following sections provide a brief overview of each of these tasks (see, further, Kleijnen [1980]).

Identifying Costs and Benefits Identifying the costs and benefits of an information system is a difficult task. To some extent, specific costs and benefits depend on the nature of the information system. For example, at least some of the benefits derived from an information system to support welfare counselors would be different from those derived from a manufacturing process control system.

There is also the problem of identifying *all* benefits and costs. The omission of a cost or benefit from a cost-effectiveness analysis may render the analysis invalid. Two types of costs and benefits present particular problems. First, the intangible benefits and costs of an information system often are difficult to identify as well as value. Does a system "enhance morale"? If so, what is the value of the enhanced morale? Second, externalities or spillover effects often are difficult to identify. For example, if an organization implements an advanced computer system, to what extent is the data processing department now able to hire better computer personnel because of the greater job challenge that exists?

Table 23.1 shows some relatively global classifications of the more tangible benefits and costs of an information system. King and Schrems [1978] present a more detailed listing. Ultimately the benefits of an information system translate into cost savings or revenue increases. Cost savings arise because fewer resources are needed to complete a task or existing resources become more productive. For example, a computerized payroll system eliminates many clerical positions needed with a manual system; a process control system may improve the productivity of machines in the job shop. Revenue increases arise because the demand for existing products increases or the organization is able to expand its markets. For example, a sales system may allow salespersons to improve their service to customers, thereby increasing demand for the organization's products; a strategic planning system may identify opportunities for expanding markets.

TABLE 23.1
BENEFITS AND COSTS OF AN INFORMATION SYSTEM

Benefits	Costs
Cost savings	Implementation costs
Labor	Hardware/software purchases
Fewer needed	System development costs
More productive	Labor: System analysis and
Machines	programming
Fewer needed	Hardware usage and supplies
More productive	Documentation
Overhead	Overhead
Revenue increases	Ongoing operational costs
More sales of existing products	Hardware usage and supplies
Expanded markets	Labor
	Program maintenance
	Operations personnel
	Clerical support
	Overhead

Two major types of costs arise with information systems: implementation costs and ongoing operational costs. Implementation costs include the cost of any new hardware and software that must be purchased to support the system, labor costs associated with system analysis and programming work for the system, hardware usage and supply costs associated with program compilations and tests, documentation costs associated with the preparation of user manuals, etc., and various overhead costs, for example, administrative costs. The ongoing operational costs include charges for computer time and supplies, system maintenance costs, clerical support costs associated with data capture and preparation and running the system, and overhead costs.

Valuing Costs and Benefits Once the individual costs and benefits have been identified, they must be valued. The auditor may be involved in several ways in valuing the costs and benefits of an information system. Before the system is implemented the auditor may be asked to assist in estimating the costs and benefits of an information system or act as an objective judge of the quality of these estimates. After the system has been operational the auditor may be involved in the ex post assessment of whether or not the required rate of return was achieved with the investment in the information system.

Ex ante valuation of costs and benefits is the more difficult task; usually there is high uncertainty about the cash inflows and outflows that will arise. Even relatively straightforward costs and benefits sometimes may be difficult to estimate. For example, estimating the clerical support costs may not be simply a matter of calculating wages and salaries for the clerical personnel involved. The auditor may feel the system will have an unfavorable effect on the quality of working life of the clerical staff. Thus, the auditor may want to include an estimate of the extra costs that will arise because of increased staff turnover, higher training costs, strikes, increased absenteeism, etc.

Uncertainty can be incorporated into the cost-effectiveness analysis by expressing the anticipated costs and benefits in the form of a probability distribution. Chapter 22 showed how the probability distribution can be constructed. Assume there are only three operational costs for an information system: labor, machine, and overhead. The auditor estimates that each of these costs will take on one of two possible values with some probability, namely:

Labor		Machine		Overhead	
Cost	Probability	Cost	Probability	Cost	Probability
100,000	.6	7,000	.7	20,000	.8
120,000	.4	8,000	.3	25,000	.2

The resulting joint probability distribution consists of eight mutually exclusive events:

Amount	Probability
100,000 + 7,000 + 20,000 = 127,000	(.6)(.7)(.8) = .336
100,000 + 7,000 + 25,000 = 132,000	(.6)(.7)(.2) = .084
100,000 + 8,000 + 20,000 = 128,000	(.6)(.3)(.8) = .144
100,000 + 8,000 + 25,000 = 133,000	(.6)(.3)(.2) = .036
120,000 + 7,000 + 20,000 = 147,000	(.4)(.7)(.8) = .224
120,000 + 7,000 + 25,000 = 152,000	(.4)(.7)(.2) = .056
120,000 + 8,000 + 20,000 = 148,000	(.4)(.3)(.8) = .096
120,000 + 8,000 + 25,000 = 153,000	(.4)(.3)(.2) = .024
	$\Sigma(p) =$ 1.000

Ex post estimation of costs and benefits usually is less difficult since some costs and benefits are known with certainty; for example, the costs of running a system at a service bureau. In some cases, however, valuation still may be difficult. For example, it may be hard to identify what cost savings or resource increases the system has produced; other factors in the organization that affect costs and revenues may have changed and it may be difficult to disaggregate the effects.

If benefits cannot be estimated directly, a surrogate estimate can be made. Managers who use the information system can be asked to value the information it produces. Davis [1974] identifies two approaches to obtaining this estimate: the direct estimation approach and the less than/greater than approach. Using the first approach, managers are asked to indicate how much they would be willing to pay for the different reports produced by the system. Using the second approach, a series of questions are asked of the type: Is the value of the report greater than $100 per month? Is it less than $500 a month? Thus, a range estimate of value is obtained. Some convention then must be adopted to incorporate the estimate into the analysis; for example, the midpoint of the range might be taken as the estimate or a uniform or normal probability distribution over the range might be assumed.

Determining the Net Present Value Once the benefits and costs of an information system have been estimated, the net present value of the system can be determined using the formula (see, also, Chapter 22):

$$\text{NPV} = \sum_{t=0}^{n} \frac{B_t - C_t}{(1+k)^t}$$

where $B_t =$ benefits of information system in period t
$C_t =$ costs of information system in period t
$n =$ life of project in periods
$k =$ required rate of return

As discussed in Chapter 22, k is determined using the formula:

$$k = k_f + \beta(\bar{k}_m - k_f)$$

where k_f = risk-free rate of return
$\bar{k}_m$ = expected rate of return on the market portfolio
β = beta coefficient of a security

Estimating β is still a problem. In this case, conceptually, it is estimated by regressing the returns on a security of an organization involved in designing, implementing, and marketing information systems of the type being considered with the returns on the market portfolio.

Again, as pointed out in Chapter 22, the net present value estimated is an *expected* value. Since there is uncertainty surrounding the benefits and costs of the information system, there is uncertainty surrounding the net present value that will occur. The variance of the probability distribution over the net present values is an important indicator of the risk involved in investing in the information system.

THE GLOBAL EVALUATION JUDGMENT

So far the discussion has focused on evaluating how well the system achieves five major goals: improved task accomplishment, improved quality of working life, operational effectiveness, technical effectiveness, and economic effectiveness. Ultimately, however, an overall judgment must be made — a global judgment on whether or not the system is effective.

Chapter 22 also discussed the problem of making a global judgment in terms of how well a system maintains data integrity. The problems of making the judgment on system effectiveness are the same; similarly, the recommendations made for improving the quality of the judgment process apply to the evaluation of system effectiveness.

As with the evaluation of data integrity it is difficult, if not impossible, to determine the *accuracy* of auditor decision making on whether or not a system is effective. Thus, primarily the quality of auditor judgment must be assessed in terms of whether or not there is consensus among different auditors and consistency in the judgments made by the same auditor over time.

Judgment consensus and consistency can be improved in three ways: (*a*) ensuring the auditor identifies all the relevant cues, (*b*) ensuring the auditor understands what weighting he or she gives to the cues, and (*c*) ensuring the evidence is carefully organized and presented. The techniques recommended in Chapter 22 for accomplishing these objectives apply equally well here.

SUMMARY

The evaluation of system effectiveness involves assessing how well a system meets its goals. Perhaps the major problem in making this evaluation is knowing what the goals of an information system should be. Often these goals are left vague and ill-defined.

In general, a high-quality information system achieves five major goals. First, it improves the task accomplishment of its users by allowing them to be more productive or to produce higher quality output. Second, it improves the overall quality of users' working lives. Third, the system should be operationally effective in the sense that users find the system easy to use and they use it frequently. Fourth, the system should be supported by the appropriate hardware and software technology. Fifth, the benefits derived from the system should exceed the costs of implementing and operating the system.

How well the system meets each of these major goals first must be assessed; then, a global evaluation must be made. Little is known about how a quality global judgment can be obtained. Only a few guidelines exist: ensuring all the evidence is considered, the evidence is weighted properly, and the evidence is presented in an organized manner.

REVIEW QUESTIONS

23.1. Briefly explain what is meant by a relative evaluation and an absolute evaluation. What goals of an information system are subject to a relative evaluation?

23.2. Why is it difficult to give any general listing of task accomplishment objectives for an information system? For each of the following systems give five task accomplishment objectives:
  a. personnel system
  b. online insurance system
  c. energy information system

23.3. Briefly explain the problem of choosing too global versus too detailed a measure of task accomplishment.

23.4. Give two reasons why the auditor may wish to trace a measure of task accomplishment over time.

23.5. "Auditors are concerned with controls, not the quality of working life! That should be left to the personnel people in an organization." Discuss.

23.6. Briefly explain why different groups might define a high quality of working life differently. If there is dispute in the organization over what constitutes a high quality of working life, whose viewpoint should the auditor use as the basis for assessing the effectiveness of an information system?

23.7. Briefly explain why current measurement instruments for assessing the quality of working life still have validity and reliability problems.

23.8. Briefly explain the difference between surrogate measures and direct measures of the quality of working life. List the relative advantages and disadvantages of using each kind of measure.

23.9. Why is frequency of use an indicator of the operational effectiveness of an information system? Briefly explain how an auditor might measure the frequency of use of:
  a. an online inquiry system
  b. a batch reporting system

23.10. Why is it important to distinguish between voluntary and involuntary use of an information system? How might the auditor identify involuntary use of an information system?

23.11. Why is it important to identify the *nature* of use of an information system?

What type of change (level of adoption) should the following systems evoke if they are to be operationally effective:
   a. inventory reordering system
   b. accounts receivable system
   c. system designed to assist short-term money market operators with their investment decisions
23.12. List three attributes of an online inquiry system that would make it easy to use. Similary, list three attributes of a batch system that would make it easy to use for *secondary* users.
23.13. Briefly describe three ways in which the auditor can assess the technical effectiveness of the software supporting a system. Give two major reasons for software sometimes being technically ineffective.
23.14. How does resource independence affect the technical effectiveness of a system? How can the auditor assess the extent of independence between the software of a system and the hardware on which it operates?
23.15. There are two types of data independence:
   a. logical data independence (data-software)
   b. physical data independence (data-hardware)

   How does data independence make a system more technically effective? How can the auditor assess the extent of data independence in a system?
23.16. Briefly explain what is meant by an externality or spillover effect of an information system. What problems do externalities cause for evaluating the economic effectiveness of an information system? Give an example of an externality that might be caused by an information system that improved utilization of beds in a hospital.
23.17. For each of the following cost categories give three examples of costs that would be included in the category:
   a. ongoing operational costs – overhead
   b. system development costs – documentation
   c. ongoing operational costs – hardware usage
   d. implementation costs – overhead
23.18. Briefly explain the difference between an ex ante valuation of the costs and benefits of a system and an ex post valuation. Which valuation usually is more difficult to perform? Why?
23.19. One of the parameters in the net present value formula is the life t of the investment. What are the major factors that affect the life of an information system? Give an example of a system that probably would have a short life and one that probably would have a long life.
23.20. In the global evaluation judgment, is it likely that technical effectiveness might be weighted as being more important for some systems than others? If so, give an example and explain why.

EXERCISES AND CASES

23.1. During the evaluation of the economic effectiveness of an information system you interview the manager of the user department for which the system was developed. You ask her about the benefits obtained from having the system. She responds that all the benefits obtained are intangible; however, she has no doubts that the benefits obtained via the improved decision making of her staff exceed the costs of the system.

Required: Discuss briefly how you would now proceed in the evaluation study.

23.2. You are trying to estimate the likely increases in revenue that will result from a new sales system. Your best estimate of the increased revenue that will result for the two products the system supports is as follows:

Product A		Product B	
Revenue increase	Probability	Revenue increase	Probability
90,000	.7	60,000	.15
115,000	.2	65,000	.3
120,000	.1	70,000	.25
		78,000	.25
		80,000	.05

Required: Construct the joint probability distribution of revenue increase you expect to be produced by the system.

23.3. Over one year ago your organization—a travel company—installed a new online realtime update system that allows travel agents to inquire about the available space in hotels, airlines, etc. As the manager of internal audit for the company, management asks you to undertake a postimplementation review of the system to assess whether or not the system has met its objectives. There is some uncertainty in several areas about whether the system has been successful.

You assign two of your staff to undertake a review of the system. After two months you receive a brief memorandum from them informing you that they have completed their review. In the memo they also rate the system on how well it has achieved each of five major sets of objectives. Their ratings are as follows:

Set of objectives	Rating
Task accomplishment objectives	9
Quality of working life objectives	6
Operational effectiveness objectives	8
Technical effectiveness objectives	5
Economic effectiveness objectives	8

Note: The rating is on a 10-point scale; 10 is the highest and 1 is the lowest.

Required: Given only this small amount of information, what is your global assessment of whether or not the system has been successful? Briefly explain your reasons. How would you now proceed to prepare a final report for top management?

23.4. One of the systems in your organization is an old online system that supports advance planning in the marketing department. A variety of data is collected for the system: sales data, general economic indicators, data on competitors, etc. The system produces over 50 reports: some are online and some are batch.

Because the existing hardware/software configuration is becoming saturated with respect to use, management questions whether or not the system can be streamlined. As the manager of internal audit, they ask you to undertake an evaluation of whether or not all the data currently collected to support the system needs to be collected, whether or not all the reports prepared need to be prepared, and whether or not the existing batch and online reports should be changed.

Required: Outline how you will carry out your evaluation task. You should be specific, however, when you describe how you will collect the data needed to answer management's questions.

23.5. Your organization has decided to purchase a database management system and begin to modify existing systems so there is greater sharing of data; for example, the payroll and personnel files will be combined.

Currently there exists an extensive set of standards for carrying out an evaluation of whether systems meet their objectives. However, the standards have been prepared assuming there is no sharing of data among multiple users.

As the manager of internal audit in the organization, management asks you determine what changes, if any, will be needed to the effectiveness evaluation standards now that a policy of sharing data, wherever it is cost-effective, should be followed.

Required: Prepare a brief report outlining any changes to the standards that you think will be necessary.

23.6. Assume that a postimplementation review (postaudit) of systems in an organization is optional; that is, not all systems necessarily have to be evaluated after they have been implemented. The factor that affects whether or not a postaudit will be undertaken is the level of uncertainty surrounding the effectiveness attributes of a system. This uncertainty may exist in (*a*) the mind of the person responsible for the postaudit decision, or (*b*) the minds of other members of the organization (e.g., top management).

Required: Identify those characteristics of a system that would tend to affect the level of uncertainty surrounding the effectiveness of a system. In other words, why is the person responsible for the postaudit decision or top management more uncertain about the effectiveness of some systems than others?

REFERENCES

Alter, Steven. "Development Patterns for Decision Support Systems," *Management Information Systems Quarterly* (September 1978), pp. 33–42.

Biggs, Stanley F. "Group Participation in MIS Project Teams? Let's Look at the Contingencies First!" *Management Information Systems Quarterly* (March 1978), pp. 19–26.

Bostrom, Robert P., and J. Stephen Heinen. "MIS Problems and Failures: A Socio-Technical Perspective—Part I: The Causes," *Management Information Systems Quarterly* (September 1977*a*), pp. 17–32.

_____, and _____. "MIS Problems and Failures: A Socio-Technical Perspective—Part II: The Application of Socio-Technical Theory," *Management Information Systems Quarterly* (December 1977*b*), pp. 11–28.

Cherns, Albert. "The Principles of Socio-Technical Design," *Human Relations*, vol. 29, no. 8, pp. 783–792.

Danziger, James N. "Computers and the Frustrated Chief Executive," *Management Information Systems Quarterly* (June 1977), pp. 43-53.

———, and William H. Dutton. "Computers as an Innovation in American Local Governments," *Communications of the ACM* (December 1977), pp. 945-956.

Davis, Gordon B. *Management Information Systems: Conceptual Foundations, Structure, and Development* (New York: McGraw-Hill Book Company, 1974).

Davis, Louis E., and Albert B. Cherns, eds. *The Quality of Working Life: Volume 1 – Problems, Prospects, and the State of the Art* (New York: The Free Press, 1975).

Dutton, William H., and Kenneth L. Kraemer. "Management Utilization of Computers in American Local Governments," *Communications of the ACM* (March 1978), pp. 206-218.

Gilb, Tom. *Software Metrics* (Cambridge, Mass.: Winthrop Publishers, Inc., 1977).

Ginzberg, Michael J. "Redesign of Managerial Tasks: A Requisite for Successful Decision Support Systems," *Management Information Systems Quarterly* (March 1978), pp. 39-52.

Guest, Robert H. "Quality of Work Life – Learning from Tarrytown," *Harvard Business Review* (July-August 1979), pp. 76-87.

Guthrie, A. "Attitudes of the User-Managers Towards Management Information Systems," *Management Informatics* (October 1974), pp. 221-232.

Hackman, J. R., G. R. Oldham, R. Janson, and K. Purdy. "A New Strategy for Job Enrichment," *California Management Review* (Summer 1975), pp. 57-71.

Halloran, Dennis, Susan Manchester, John Moriarty, Robert Riley, James Rohrman, and Thomas Skramstad. "Systems Development Quality Control," *Management Information Systems Quarterly* (December 1978), pp. 1-13.

King, John Leslie, and Edward L. Schrems. "Cost-Benefit Analysis in Information Systems Development and Operation," *Computing Surveys* (March 1978), pp. 19-34.

King, William R., and Jaime I. Rodriquez. "Evaluating Management Information Systems," *Management Information Systems Quarterly* (September 1978), pp. 43-51.

Kleijnen, Jack P. C. *Computers and Profit* (Reading, Mass.: Addison-Wesley Publishing Company, 1980).

Kling, Rob. "The Organizational Context of User-Centered Software Designs," *Management Information Systems Quarterly* (December 1977), pp. 41-52.

Lawler, Edward E. "Measuring the Psychological Quality of Working Life: The Why and How of It," in Louis E. Davis and Albert B. Cherns, eds., *The Quality of Working Life: Volume 1 – Problems, Prospects, and the State of the Art* (New York: The Free Press, 1975), pp. 123-133.

Lucas, Henry C. "Behavioral Factors in System Implementation," in Randall L. Schultz and Dennis P. Slevin, eds., *Implementing Operations Research/Management Science* (New York: American Elsevier Publishing Company, Inc., 1975a), pp. 203-215.

———. *Towards Creative System Design* (New York: Columbia University Press, 1975b).

———. *Why Information Systems Fail* (New York: Columbia University Press, 1975c).

———. *The Implementation of Computer-Based Models* (New York: National Association of Accountants, 1976).

———. "The Use of an Interactive Information Storage and Retrieval System in Medical Research," *Communications of the ACM* (March 1978a), pp. 197-205.

_____. "Empirical Evidence for a Descriptive Model of Implementation," *Management Information Systems Quarterly* (June 1978*b*), pp. 27–42.

Macy, Barry A., and Philip H. Mirvis. "A Methodology for Assessment of Quality of Work Life and Organizational Effectiveness in Behavioral-Economic Terms," *Administrative Science Quarterly* (June 1976), pp. 212–226.

Maish, Alexander M. "A User's Behavior Toward His MIS," *Management Information Systems Quarterly* (March 1979), pp. 39–52.

Manley, John H. "Implementation Attitudes: A Model and a Measurement Methodology," in Randall L. Schultz and Dennis P. Slevin, eds., *Implementing Operations Research/Management Science* (New York: American Elsevier Publishing Company, Inc., 1975), pp. 183–202.

Matlin, Gerald L. "How to Survive a Management Assessment," *Management Information Systems Quarterly* (March 1977), pp. 11–17.

Moore, Jeffrey H. "A Framework for MIS Software Development Projects," *Management Information Systems Quarterly* (March 1979), pp. 29–38.

Mumford, Enid, and Harold Sackman, eds. *Human Choice and Computers* (Amsterdam: North-Holland Publishing Company, 1975).

Nadler, David A., Philip H. Mirvis, and Cortlandt Cammann. "The Ongoing Feedback System: Experimenting with a New Managerial Tool," *Organizational Dynamics* (Spring 1976), pp. 63–80.

Report of a Special Task Force to the Secretary of Health, Education, and Welfare. *Work in America* (Cambridge, Mass.: The MIT Press, 1973).

Schultz, Randall L., and Dennis P. Slevin. "Implementation and Organizational Validity," in Randall L. Schultz and Dennis P. Slevin, eds., *Implementing Operations Research/Management Science* (New York: American Elsevier Publishing Company, Inc., 1975), pp. 153–182.

_____, and _____, *Implementing Operations Research/Management Science* (New York: American Elsevier Publishing Company, Inc., 1975).

Seashore, Stanley E. "Defining and Measuring the Quality of Working Life," in Louis E. Davis and Albert B. Cherns, eds., *The Quality of Working Life: Volume 1 — Problems, Prospects, and the State of the Art* (New York: The Free Press, 1975), pp. 105–118.

Senn, James A. "A Management View of Systems Analysts: Failures and Shortcomings," *Management Information Systems Quarterly* (September 1978), pp. 25–32.

Steers, Richard M. *Organizational Effectiveness: A Behavioral View* (Santa Monica, Calif.: Goodyear Publishing Company, Inc., 1977).

Sterling, T. D. "Guidelines for Humanizing Computerized Information Systems: A Report from Stanley House," *Communications of the ACM* (November 1974), pp. 609–613.

_____. "Consumer Difficulties with Computerized Transactions: An Empirical Investigation," *Communications of the ACM* (May 1979), pp. 283–289.

Walton, Richard E. "Criteria for Quality of Working Life," in Louis E. Davis and Albert B. Cherns, eds., *The Quality of Working Life: Volume 1 — Problems, Prospects, and the State of the Art* (New York: The Free Press, 1975), pp. 91–104.

Wetherbe, James C., and V. Thomas Dock. "A Strategic Planning Methodology for the Computing Effort in Higher Education: An Empirical Evaluation," *Communications of the ACM* (December 1978), pp. 1008–1015.

CHAPTER **24**

EVALUATING SYSTEM EFFICIENCY

CHAPTER OUTLINE

THE EVALUATION PROCESS
PERFORMANCE INDICES
    Timeliness Indices
    Throughput Indices
    Utilization Indices
WORKLOAD MODELS
    Natural Workload Models
    Artificial Workload Models
SYSTEM MODELS
    Analytical Models
    Simulation Models
    Empirical Models
SUMMARY
REVIEW QUESTIONS
EXERCISES AND CASES
REFERENCES

There are two reasons why auditors may become involved in evaluating system efficiency. First, they may be asked to evaluate an existing operational system to determine whether its performance can be improved. For example, it may be possible to decrease the response time of an interactive system by increasing the memory partition size allocated to each user of the system. Second, they may be asked to evaluate alternate systems that the installation is considering purchasing, leasing, etc. For example, management may be considering two systems having different storage hierarchies. The auditor may provide advice on which of the two storage hierarchies is likely to allow faster throughput of the installation's workload.

This chapter discusses methodologies the auditor can use to determine whether a system is efficient; that is, whether it achieves its objectives in a least-cost manner. Most of these methodologies have been developed within the area that has been generally called "computer performance evaluation." However, as Ferrari [1978] points out, the focus of research in the performance evaluation area is somewhat narrow; it is concerned primarily with system efficiency and not broader performance issues such as ease of use, reliability, user's productivity, etc.

The chapter proceeds as follows. The first section provides an overview of the evaluation process relating to system efficiency. The second section defines several major performance indices used to assess system efficiency. The third section discusses various ways of modeling system workloads. Finally, the chapter discusses various ways of modeling the computer system to be evaluated so experiments can be run to assess the efficiency of the system.

THE EVALUATION PROCESS

Figure 24.1 shows eight major steps to be taken during an evaluation of system efficiency. Note that at each step one outcome may be the revision of work done at prior steps. For example, the formulation of a suitable workload model may be more costly than anticipated at the outset of the evaluation process; thus, the estimate of the costs and benefits of the evaluation may have to be revised. One possible consequence of this revision may be that the evaluation is terminated because the expected benefits of the evaluation do not exceed the costs.

The paragraphs below provide an overview of the work to be performed at each step in the evaluation process:

1 *Formulate the Objectives of the Study* As with all evaluation studies it is important to define the objectives of the study at the start. The objectives determine the boundaries of the system to be evaluated, and they suggest the nature of the performance indices that will be required to assess the efficiency of the defined system. The objectives may be global; for example, improve the performance of the online registration system. They may be specific; for example, improve the CPU utilization. The objectives also should specify the constraints that apply; for example, improve the response time of the interactive system without purchasing any more hardware resources.

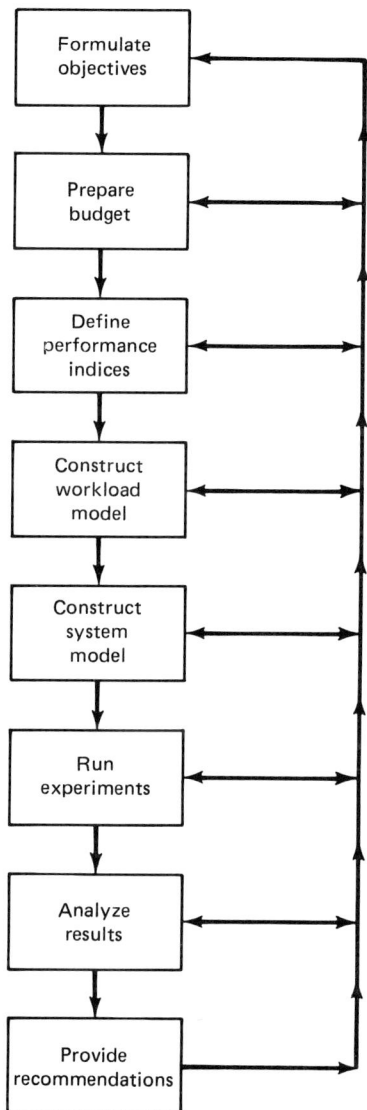

Figure 24.1
Major steps in the evaluation of system efficiency.

2 Prepare the Budget for the Evaluation Efficiency evaluations can be costly to carry out. The benefits obtained from the evaluation should exceed the costs of the evaluation and the costs of any changes necessary to achieve the benefits. Estimating the costs of the evaluation usually is reasonably straightforward. Unfortunately, estimating the benefits of the evaluation and the costs of changes to achieve these benefits often is difficult. Only after the evaluation is complete will the auditor know whether or not efficiency can be improved, what benefits can be expected from the improved efficiency, and the cost of the changes necessary to achieve the improved efficiency. Ultimately, experience in carrying out efficiency evaluations is a major determinant of quality decisions when the budget for the evaluation is prepared.

3 *Define Performance Indices* The performance indices provide the standard against which the efficiency of the system is assessed. What performance indices are chosen for an evaluation study depends on the objectives of the study. For example, if the objective of the study is to improve the timeliness of the output of an interactive system, clearly an index of performance is response time. Response time now must be defined, however; there may be some debate as to whether response time ends upon receipt of the first character of output or the last character of output. If the system is overloaded it may take some time for the output to print so the latter definition may be used.

4 *Construct a Workload Model* Figure 24.2 shows a structural model of a computer system. The performance of a system is some function of the workload the system must process. When evaluating system efficiency the auditor must construct a workload model that is representative of the real system workload. If the system to be evaluated is operational, the workload model may be based on the real workload. If the system to be evaluated is in the design stages, an artificial workload model must be constructed; that is, one based on the expected characteristics of the workload to be processed.

5 *Construct a System (Configuration) Model* The performance of the system to be evaluated is studied using a model of the system. Again, if the system is operational, the workload can be processed and the values of various performance indices calculated. However, if the effects of a changed hardware/software configuration are to be determined or the purchase of a new system is considered, some type of artificial model of the changed or new system must be constructed. In essence, the system model maps the attributes of the workload into values of the performance indices chosen.

6 *Run Experiments* Once the workload and system models have been constructed, experiments can be run to determine the values of the performance indices. Sensitivity analyses may be carried out by varying both the characteristics of the workload and the system.

7 *Analyze Results* When evaluating efficiency the auditor hypothesizes certain relationships between the values of the performance indices and the characteristics of the workload and system models. For example, the auditor may hypothesize that varying the time quantum allocated each job in an interactive system will have a major impact on response times, or that changing the device to channel assignment of a system's disk drives will cause a marked change in throughput. Once experiments have been run with these changed parameters and the values of the performance indices determined, the data can be analyzed to determine whether the relationships hypothesized do, in fact, exist.

8 *Provide Recommendations* After the data from the experiments is analyzed, the auditor can make recommendations on how system efficiency can be improved. The recommendations will depend on whether or not the data supported the hypotheses that the auditor postulated about relationships

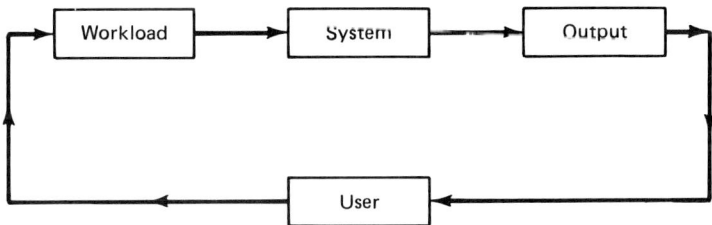

Figure 24.2
Structural model of a computer system.

between performance indices and system and workload characteristics, and the relative benefits and costs of changes to improve system efficiency.

PERFORMANCE INDICES

A performance index is a measure of system efficiency; it expresses quantitatively how well the system achieves an efficiency criterion. Performance indices have several functions: they allow users to decide whether a system will meet their needs, they permit comparison of alternate systems, and they show whether changes to the hardware/software configuration of a system have produced the desired effect.

Performance indices must be expressed as a probability distribution. For example, the response time in an online system may have considerable variation—perhaps from one second to one minute or more. If a performance index is expressed only as a mean value, it may hide important information from the user. In the example given, a user may be unaware that at certain times of the day effective problem solving using an online decision model may be inhibited by the slow response time of the system. The mean, variance, and shape of the distribution alert the user to the possibility of these types of problems occurring.

Performance indices also must be expressed in terms of a workload. The response time of an interactive system will vary depending on the number and the nature of the jobs in the system.

Stimler [1974] and Svobodova [1976] provide extensive lists of various performance indices that have been used to assess system efficiency. The following sections discuss briefly only some of the more important and widely used indices.

Timeliness Indices

Timeliness indices reflect how quickly a system is able to provide users with the output they require. The measure of timeliness for a batch system typically is turnaround time. *Turnaround time* is the length of time that elapses between submission of a job and receipt of the complete output. For interactive systems the measure of timeliness is the response time. Typically the *response time* is defined to be the length of time that elapses between submission of an input transaction to the system and receipt of the first character of output.

Timeliness indices must be defined in terms of a unit of work and the priority categorization given to the unit of work. In a batch system the unit of work usually is a job. In an interactive system it may be a job (multiple transactions) or a single transaction. Higher priority units of work are given access first to available computing resources; thus, these units of work should have faster turnaround and response times.

Timeliness indices also are user-oriented performance indices; they reflect the primary concerns of the system user. Other indices discussed below are system-oriented indices; they are the concern of the data processing managers who seek to obtain maximum returns on their investment in hardware and software.

Throughput Indices

Throughput indices are measures of the productivity of a system; that is, they indicate how much work is done by the system over a period of time. The *throughput rate* of a system is the amount of work done per unit time period. The *capability* of a system is the maximum achievable throughput rate. Again, throughput indices must be defined in terms of some unit of work: a job, a task, an instruction, etc. Relative throughput indices can be used to compare the throughput of one system with the throughput of another system (see, further, Stimler [1974]). Note, also, the interdependencies between timeliness indices and throughput indices; in general, the more responsive a system the greater its throughput.

Utilization Indices

Utilization indices measure the proportion of time a system resource is busy. For example, the *CPU utilization* index is calculated by dividing the amount of time the CPU is busy by the total amount of time the system is running. Similarly, *channel utilization* is defined to be the amount of time the channel is busy divided by the amount of time the system is running. Utilization indices may be defined for any hardware, software, or data resource within the system.

WORKLOAD MODELS

A system workload is the set of resource demands imposed upon the system by the set of jobs that occur during a given time period. Conceptually, the workload can be characterized as a matrix. The rows in the matrix are the set of jobs that occur for the time period under consideration. The columns in the matrix are the hardware, software, and data resources of the system. The elements of the matrix are the amounts of each resource demanded by each job. System performance (efficiency) must be defined in terms of a given workload.

When evaluating system efficiency there are several purposes for formulating a workload model. First, using the real workload of the system for evaluation purposes may be too costly. To measure efficiency for a representative workload, the time period for evaluation may be long. Second, the real workload cannot be used if the system to be evaluated is not operational. If the auditor is evaluating competing systems (say, proposed hardware/software configurations for a system yet to be implemented), an artificial workload must be created for purposes of the evaluation. Third, the auditor may want to carry out sensitivity analyses when evaluating system efficiency. If the behavior of the system is to be examined under varying workloads, it may be easier to change the characteristics of a workload model than the real workload to carry out these sensitivity analyses.

The objective of workload model design is to obtain a drive workload (the workload to be used during the evaluation) that is *representative* of the real workload. Unfortunately, what is meant by a representative workload model is still unclear. Ferrari [1972] defines representativeness in terms of the set of performance indices used for the evaluation. A representative workload model is one that produces the same values of the performance indices as the real workload. For example, if a single performance index, throughput rate, is used for the evaluation, the throughput rate values for the workload model and the real workload should be equal. Recall, performance indices often are stochastic variables, so the mean, variance, and higher moments of the distributions of the performance indices for the workload model and the real workload should be compared.

This notion of representativeness may be conceptually useful but it is not always practically useful. For a system that is not operational, the real workload is not yet known; thus, determining the representativeness of the workload model is difficult if not impossible. Even if the values of performance indices for the real workload and the workload model are known, there is the problem of determining whether the workload model will remain representative when the system structure is changed. A workload model is devised to provide a cheaper means of undertaking sensitivity analysis than the real workload; however, the costs of inaccurate performance measurements must not exceed the costs savings obtained by using a model. Ideally, the model's representativeness will be invariant across system structures.

Besides representativeness there are other desirable attributes of a workload model. It should not be costly to construct and use. It should facilitate change to workload parameters. It should be portable across different system structures.

How these attributes of a workload model are obtained is still an extensive research issue. Currently there are few design guidelines. The following sections present an overview of some of the major workload models that have been devised. Following Ferrari [1972], the models are classified either as natural workload models or artificial workload models. The sections also examine briefly how well the models achieve the desired characteristics of workload models discussed earlier.

Natural Workload Models

Natural workload models are constructed by taking some subset of the real workload. There are two methods of obtaining the subset required. First, time subsets can be chosen; the content of the workload model is the same as the real workload but the time interval over which performance indices are calculated is less than the interval for the real workload. Second, content subsets can be chosen; sample jobs from the real workload are selected in some way. Natural workload models sometimes are called *benchmarks*.

If the auditor constructs a natural workload model on the basis of a time subset, the only decision to be made is when the evaluation period should start and end. The start time and duration of measurement should be chosen so as to maximize representativeness and minimize evaluation costs; unfortunately, these objectives conflict.

If the auditor constructs a natural workload model on the basis of a content subset, a decision must be made on how the subset will be selected from all jobs executed within the interval for the real workload. One method is to choose a random sample of jobs from the real workload. Another method is to partition jobs into defined classes and choose at random a job from each class for inclusion in the workload model (see, further, Ferrari [1972]). The size of the sample chosen depends on the tradeoff made between representativeness and workload model construction and use costs; smaller samples are less representative but enable cheaper workload models to be constructed and used.

Natural workload models have two major strengths. First, since they are constructed from jobs in the real workload, their representativeness can be high. Second, the cost to construct a natural workload model usually is low; however, this cost increases as the representativeness of the model increases.

A natural workload model has several limitations. Modifications to the workload model are not always easy to make; thus, sensitivity analyses using the model may be difficult to carry out. The operational costs of using the model may be high since they are often less compact than an artificial workload model. Also, natural workload models can be used only if a real workload exists already; the system to be evaluated must be operational.

Artificial Workload Models

If a workload model is not constructed from jobs in the real workload, it is an artificial workload model. The auditor may construct an artificial workload model for several reasons. Some types of system models chosen for evaluation studies are unable to process natural workload models. For example, queuing models can process only an artificial workload model. As discussed previously, if the system to be evaluated is not operational the real workload is unknown and an artificial workload must be constructed. In general, artificial workload models are more flexible and compact than natural workload models. They facilitate sensitivity analyses and are less costly to use. However, these advantages are attained only at a cost. Artificial workload models usually are more costly to construct, less representative, and less portable than natural workload models.

A large number of different types of artificial workload models have been constructed. They vary widely in their capabilities with respect to representativeness, cost, compactness, etc. To illustrate the diversity that exists, the following sections survey some of the major types of artificial workload models that have been used (see, also, Lucas [1971], Svobodova [1976], and Kobayashi [1978]).

Instruction Mixes An instruction mix specifies the frequency with which different instructions occur or are expected to occur within an application. The mean execution time for a system can be computed using the following formula:

$$\bar{t} = \sum_i p_i t_i$$

where $\bar{t}$ = mean execution time
p_i = probability of the ith instruction being executed
t_i = execution time of the ith instruction

The relative frequencies of the different types of instructions in the mix can be determined in three ways. First, if the system is operational, a trace of instructions in the real workload can be taken and the incidence of the different types of instructions counted. Second, standard instruction mixes such as the Gibson mix can be used (see Svobodova [1976]). Third, the frequencies of the different types of instructions can be estimated on the basis of the expected workload.

An instruction mix is a very limited workload model. It provides a basis for quickly comparing the speeds of different CPU architectures. Also, it is a cheap workload model to use. However, obtaining a representative instruction mix may be difficult. A set of representative programs must be chosen and the frequencies of instructions used estimated or counted. Instruction mixes usually do not take into account instruction overlap nor do they include I/O instructions. Thus, instruction mixes permit only a partial evaluation to be carried out.

Kernel Programs A kernel program is a program or subroutine that has been coded as a representative job within the system to be evaluated. For example, in a scientific installation the kernel may be a matrix inversion routine; in a commercial installation it may be a file updating routine. From the list of instructions in the kernel and the execution times of the instructions in the system being evaluated, the total execution time of the kernel can be calculated; thus, the execution times of two competing systems can be compared.

Instruction mixes and kernel programs have similar strengths and limitations. Kernel programs usually contain more representative instructions; for example, they may include I/O instructions. Like instruction mixes, however, they provide only a first approximation of system efficiency and they are a very limited form of workload model.

Synthetic Jobs A synthetic job is a representative job (or set of jobs) that is coded and executed on the systems being evaluated. Synthetic jobs are similar to benchmarks; however, whereas benchmarks are based on some subset of the real workload, a synthetic job is an artificial workload model. Synthetic jobs usually are prepared because the systems being evaluated are not yet operational so a real workload does not exist.

Providing the synthetic job used is representative of the real workload, it allows more accurate estimates to be made of system efficiency than instruction mixes or kernel programs. However, synthetic jobs are less compact so they are more costly to develop and use. Synthetic jobs also can be constructed so they are flexible to use. The resources consumed by a synthetic job can be changed by altering its parameters; for example, the number of CPU processing demands and the frequency of disk accesses.

Care must be taken if a synthetic job is used to evaluate alternate hardware/software configurations. Erroneous decisions may be made if synthetic jobs are not written so they execute efficiently on the hardware/software configuration they use. Program structures are not always independent of hardware/software structures.

Probabilistic Workload Models In a probabilistic workload model, resource demands are described by a probability distribution. Various types of distributions may be used; for example, the Poisson distribution, the exponential distribution, and the normal distribution. A time series of resource demands is generated by sampling from the probability distribution.

Probabilistic workload models are used extensively in analytic and simulation studies of computer system performance. The system model used may impose constraints on how the workload model is formulated. For example, if the auditor uses a queuing model to evaluate system efficiency, it is difficult, if not impossible, to obtain a tractable model if the workload model takes into account correlations between service times.

Probabilistic workload models differ in their representativeness of the real workload. To the extent that the workload model is not constrained by tractability requirements imposed by the system model, the workload model has high potential for representativeness. Probabilistic workload models are compact and flexible. Resource demands are described by a probability distribution; changing the workload simply involves changing the parameters of the distribution. Development costs usually are low. However, usage costs depend on how many samples are taken from the distribution when system efficiency is evaluated.

SYSTEM MODELS

To determine whether or not a system can be changed to improve efficiency, the system must be modeled. The modeling process involves specifying the system components, the interfaces between the components, how the system operates, and the functional relationships between outputs and inputs.

Once the system has been modeled, various control parameters in the model can be changed to determine their impact on system efficiency. For example, the auditor may investigate the impact of changes in the priority assigned different jobs, the size of the time slice allocated a job, the amount of memory allocated a job, the device to channel assignment, the paging algorithm used, the number of users allowed to access the system simultaneously, and the maximum allowed paging rate. Using the performance indices discussed earlier in the chapter, the auditor can run experiments to determine the effects of changes in a particular workload or system control parameter when the other parameters are held constant.

One of the more difficult problems in constructing a system model is knowing how to decompose the system into subsystems so the evaluation problem can be conceptualized. In general, the methodologies discussed by Simon [1969] are applicable; the boundaries to subsystems are defined so the relationships between elements of the subsystem are strong and the interfaces between the subsystem to be evaluated and other subsystems are weak. Kobayashi [1978] points out that very often when modeling computer systems to evaluate efficiency, the subsystem boundaries can be identified by major differences in the time interval between events in the subsystems. For example, to evaluate cache memory algorithms, the auditor must work with a subsystem having time intervals of nanoseconds or microseconds. In contrast, if the auditor evaluates I/O scheduling by the operating system, the time interval usually can be expressed in milliseconds. Note that a single event in the latter subsystem may be represented by multiple events in the former subsystem. To evaluate performance of the I/O subsystem, the model should not be defined at the level of the cache memory subsystem; otherwise, it is unlikely that a tractable model will result.

The following three sections provide an overview of the three major types of system models used to evaluate efficiency: (*a*) analytical models, (*b*) simulation models, and (*c*) empirical models. An extensive literature exists relating to each of these models (see, for example, Miller [1972]); thus, the auditor who specializes in this area must undertake substantial further study.

Analytical Models

A variety of analytical models have been developed to evaluate system efficiency; however, queuing models have received the most widespread use (see, for example, Ferrari [1978]). Perhaps the major reasons for this development are the availability of substantial theoretical support for queuing models and the ability of queuing models to represent complex probabilistic phenomena in computer systems.

It is easy to conceive a computer system within a queuing framework. Jobs (customers) make demands on various computer resources (servers). For example, a job submitted by a user at an online terminal will request CPU time, memory, I/O devices, etc. As resource contention among jobs arises, queues result. There will be a queue of jobs waiting for CPU service, an I/O queue, a system software queue, etc.

The output of queuing models includes the timeliness, throughput, and utilization indices discussed earlier in the chapter, as well as such measures as the mean waiting time in a queue, the mean waiting time in the system, the mean number of jobs waiting for service, and the mean number of jobs in the system. Thus, queuing models enable system efficiency to be evaluated and strategies for improving system efficiency to be devised. Often, queuing models are used to focus on a specific resource management problem; for example, hierarchical memory management, channel scheduling, and buffer allocation.

The following sections discuss briefly the major steps to be undertaken when constructing a queuing model to evaluate system efficiency. The sections assume basic familiarity with queuing theory (see, for example, Allen [1975]). Nevertheless, the discussion is somewhat superficial so the interested reader should consult, for example, Kobayashi [1978] and Ferrari [1978] for an in-depth treatment of the topic.

Model Formulation The first step to be taken when using a queuing model to evaluate system efficiency is to formulate the model. This step involves choosing the type of queuing model to be used to represent the system.

The earliest queuing models constructed to evaluate computer systems were simple single-server models (see Graham [1978]). The model consists of a single process (server) and a single queue of jobs (Figure 24.3). Jobs are described by a distribution of arrival times and requested service times. The underlying assumptions of the model are restrictive; for example, the inter-

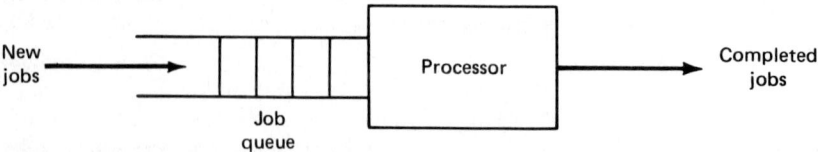

Figure 24.3
Single process single queue model of a computer system.

arrival times and service times are statistically independent, all interarrival times are distributed identically, and all service times are distributed identically. Since there is only one resource queue, the model user has to consider the entire system as a black box. In computer systems where one resource dominates (for example, the CPU), the model may be appropriate. In multiple resource systems, however, its usefulness is limited.

Currently, computer systems are modeled as a network of single resource models (Figure 24.4). Substantial advances have been made in the theory sup-

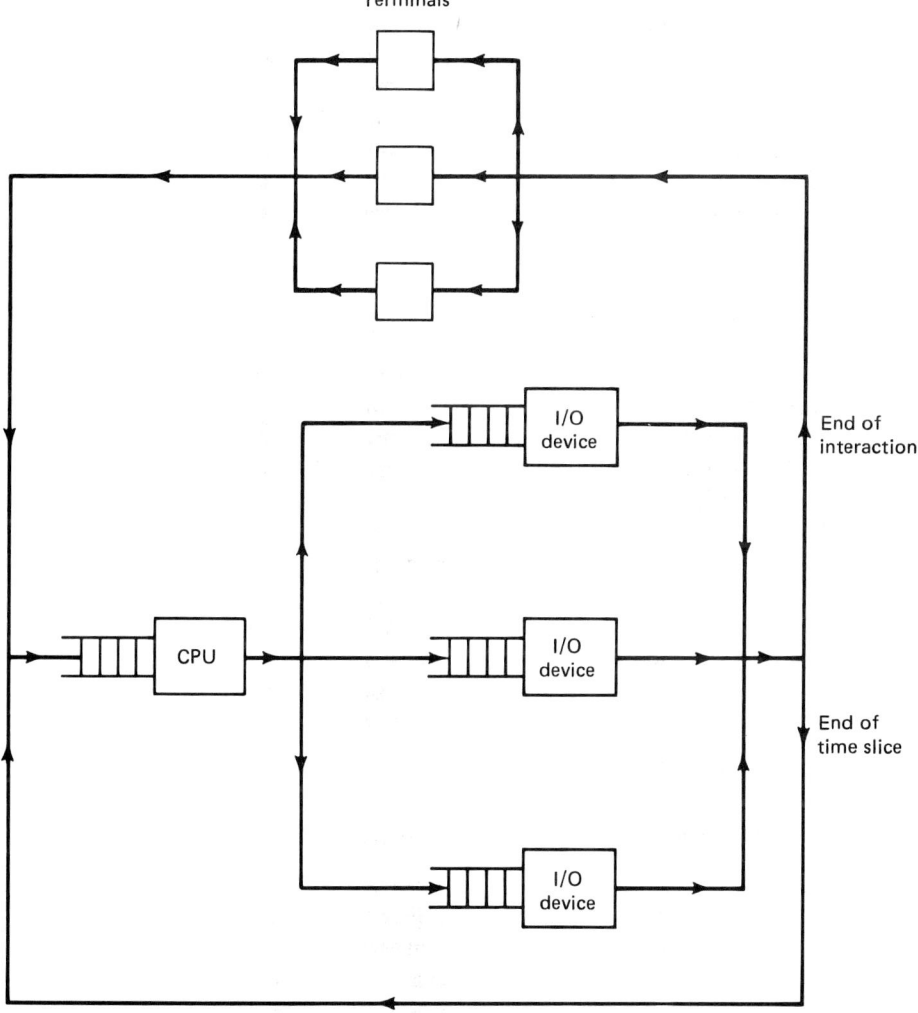

Figure 24.4
Queuing network model of a computer system.

porting these models (see Denning and Buzen [1978]). Buzen [1978], Bard [1978], and Wong [1978] describe applications of these queuing network models.

The queuing model used may be a closed model, an open model, or a mixed model (see, further, Kobayashi [1978]). In a closed model, for all classes of jobs, the number of jobs in that class is fixed and constant. New jobs are generated internally to the model. In an open model, for all classes of jobs, there exists an external source of jobs. Mixed models have some job classes that are closed and some that are open.

Open models usually are easier to solve mathematically than closed models. Closed models, however, are sometimes more representative of real systems. For example, assuming an infinite population source (open model) is unrealistic for an interactive system where there is a finite number of terminals (see, further, Kobayashi [1978]).

Estimating Model Parameter Values Once the queuing model has been formulated, the values of the parameters in the model must be estimated. If the system to be modeled is operational, the parameter values may be estimated from data obtained using a performance monitoring tool; otherwise, the expected parameter values must be used.

The major input parameters to be obtained for a queuing network model are (see Rose [1978]):

Parameter	Explanation
Number of Job Classes	The jobs in the system must be categorized; for example, as either batch or time-sharing or into different priority classes.
Arrival Pattern	The interarrival time distribution for each job class must be specified; for example, a Poisson process may be used.
CPU Queuing Discipline	How jobs are scheduled and served by the CPU must be specified; for example, a first-come-first-served basis may be used or a processor sharing (round robin) basis may be used.
Degree of Multiprogramming	The number of jobs that can be in the system simultaneously must be specified; this depends on whether a finite or infinite population source has been assumed or a closed or open model has been used.
I/O Device Routing Frequencies	Jobs are processed alternately by either the CPU or an I/O device. The routing frequency for an I/O device is the proportion of total I/O operations executed that apply to that device.
Service Time Distribution	The service time distributions must be specified for the CPU and I/O devices; for example, exponential distributions might be used.

Solving the Model Denning and Buzen [1978] survey the formulas used to solve queuing network problems. These solutions can be obtained using exact analysis or approximate analysis (see Muntz [1978]). Exact analysis is used when the assumptions underlying the model are satisfied. Since some queuing model assumptions are restrictive and often may be violated, approximate analysis may be used to solve the model. Approximate analysis also can be used if exact analysis will be too expensive to undertake or alternate more credible models such as simulation will be too expensive to use.

Model Validation and Calibration Once a queuing model has been constructed, it should be validated to determine how accurately it predicts the values of the various performance indices. If the system to be evaluated is operational, the auditor can compare the results of the queuing model with those obtained using performance monitoring tools. The robustness of the model over changing workloads and changing system parameters also can be examined. If the system to be evaluated is not operational, the auditor must examine the model and its output for face validity.

Validation allows the size of the error in the output of the queuing model to be determined. In light of whether or not the size of the error is acceptable, calibration then might be undertaken. Calibration reduces the size of the output error by reducing or eliminating model formulation inaccuracies, inaccuracies caused by the use of approximate solution methods, and inaccuracies caused by incorrect estimates of parameter values (see, also, Chapter 22).

Simulation Models

The auditor may decide to use simulation to evaluate system efficiency for several reasons. First, an analytical solution may not be available; the model may not be tractable. Second, the system to be evaluated may not be operational; thus, empirical performance measurement cannot be carried out. Third, the simulation model may be used to validate the analytical model. Fourth, simulation may be cheaper to use than empirical performance measurement.

The following sections provide an overview of the steps to be taken when constructing a simulation model to evaluate system efficiency. Stimler [1974], Ferrari [1978], and Kobayashi [1978] provide examples of the use of simulation to evaluate efficiency. They also discuss the theoretical bases underlying the use of simulation methodologies in a performance monitoring context.

Model Formulation It is essential at the start of the design of a simulation model to know how the model will be used for performance evaluation purposes. These objectives impact the design of a simulation model in several ways. They determine the input (workload) parameters, internal (system) parameters, and output variables needed in the model. The output variables to be measured are the performance indices of interest in the evaluation. The input and internal parameters included in the model reflect the auditor's decisions on what variables will be manipulated to determine their impact on the performance indices.

The objectives also determine the level of system detail to be included in the model. Simulations can be expensive to implement and run; therefore, the model should focus only on those variables of interest, and the level of detail in the model should be sufficient simply to produce results that contain an acceptable level of error. If the system to be modeled is the CPU, the simulator must be sufficiently detailed to study instruction execution. However, if the system to be modeled is an application system, the simulator must be formulated at a more macroscopic level.

Simulators differ in their structure depending on whether the auditor focuses on processes or events. If the auditor focuses on processes, time is incremented by constant intervals. If the auditor focuses on events, time is incremented when the simulator changes its state (see, further, Ferrari [1978]).

Model Implementation When implementing a simulator a choice must be made on how the workload model will be implemented and how the system model will be implemented.

The workload model can be implemented using a probabilistic workload model or a trace. If the auditor chooses a probabilistic workload model, resource requests are generated as random samples from specified distributions. If the auditor chooses a trace, the time series of resource requests for an artificial or operational system must be kept. Trace-driven simulators usually produce more accurate results. The correlations between resource requests by jobs can be preserved, and a more detailed description of the workload is possible. However, traces often are more costly to construct and run than probabilistic models. Further, the simulation results tend to be less accurate when sensitivity analyses involving major modifications to the workload or system structure are carried out.

The major decision to be made when implementing the system model is what simulation language will be used. This choice can have a significant impact on the overall cost of using simulation methodology to evaluate efficiency. Some simulation languages facilitate implementation of event-structured models; others facilitate implementation of process-structured models. Several special simulation languages have been written specifically to facilitate efficiency evaluations of computer systems; for example, CSS, CASE, and SCERT (see, further, Kobayashi [1978] and Ferrari [1978]). These languages contain libraries of performance specifications for the hardware and software configurations of various vendors.

Model Validation and Calibration As with queuing models, validation of simulation models is not always an easy task. If the system being modeled is operational, the values of the performance indices produced by the model can be compared with the values of performance indices for the real system obtained using performance monitoring tools. If the system being modeled is not operational, the auditor must carefully examine the model for face validity. On the basis of the validation results the simulator then can be calibrated.

The auditor also must attempt to determine how robust the model is over changes in the input parameters and system parameters. The simulator must produce accurate results for the range of parameter changes to be made during experiments with the model.

Conduct Experiments Once the auditor is satisfied that the simulator has been adequately validated and calibrated, experiments can be conducted. The values of input and system parameters can be changed to determine their impact on the output performance indices. For example, the auditor can increase the rate at which jobs are submitted to the system to see the effect on throughput. Procedures for analyzing the results produced are discussed further in the next section.

Empirical Models

If the computer system to be evaluated is operational and the auditor can obtain values for the performance indices of interest and the various workload and system parameters of interest, an empirical model can be used to estimate the relationships between the performance indices and workload and system parameters. An empirical model also may be used to estimate relationships between the output of a simulator and changes in its parameters.

The major empirical model used in performance evaluation is the general linear model. The model is a statistical model; both the underlying theory and the practical application of the model are well-developed (see, for example, Neter and Wasserman [1974]). In essence, the model considers the system to be a black box. The model estimates the extent to which variations in the independent variables (workload and system parameters) explain variations in the dependent variables (performance indices).

The following sections provide an overview of three forms of the general linear model used to evaluate system efficiency: (*a*) the analysis of variance, (*b*) multiple regression, and (*c*) the analysis of covariance. The sections assume basic familiarity with these forms of the model; thus, the focus of the sections is the application of the model to performance evaluation questions. Huck et al. [1974] provide an introduction to the various forms of the general linear model.

Analysis of Variance The analysis of variance model is used when the workload and system parameters to be changed are measured at a nominal or ordinal level. Assume, for example, the auditor is interested in the effects of changes in the memory size allocation and the page replacement algorithm on

TABLE 24.1
TREATMENT MEANS FOR TWO FACTOR ANALYSIS OF VARIANCE

		Memory size allocation		
		10 frames	20 frames	Row mean
	LIFO	5.622	2.306	3.964
Paging algorithm	LRU	5.546	2.364	3.955
	Column mean	5.584	2.335	3.9595

the response time in an interactive system. The auditor tries two different memory allocations — 10 page frames and 20 page frames — and two different page replacement algorithms — last-in-first-out (LIFO) and least-recently-used (LRU). For a given workload the auditor obtains the response time for 100 jobs using each of the four combinations of memory allocation and paging algorithm; thus, 400 measurements of response time are taken.

Table 24.1 shows the mean response time for each combination (treatment) of the memory allocation and paging algorithm (factors). Analysis of variance allows the auditor to answer three important questions. First, does the memory size allocation and the paging algorithm used interact in a statistically significant way to impact response time? Second, if no statistically significant interaction exists, does the memory size allocation or the paging algorithm used independently impact the response time in a statistically significant way? Third, if the memory size allocation or the paging algorithm does affect the response time, what is the size of the effect?

Table 24.2 shows a hypothetical analysis of variance table for the above example. The table shows that only the memory size allocation has a statistically significant effect on the response time. The size of the effect then can be estimated. From Table 24.1 the point estimate of the difference is 5.584 − 2.335 = 3.249 seconds. However, statistical estimation must be undertaken to determine a confidence interval for the difference between the means (see, further, Neter and Wasserman [1974]).

TABLE 24.2
ANALYSIS OF VARIANCE TABLE FOR TWO FACTOR EXPERIMENT

Source of variation	Sums of squares	Degrees of freedom	Mean square	F
Memory allocation (A)	215.927	1	215.927	20.541*
Paging algorithm (P)	12.047	1	12.047	1.146
A × P	.999	1	.999	.095
Error	4162.752	396	10.512	
Total	4391.725	399		

*$p < .05$

Regression A regression model is used when the workload and system parameters to be changed are measured at an interval or ratio level. For example, the auditor may be interested in the impact of the number of simultaneous jobs allowed in the system and the number of logons per hour that occur on the response time of an interactive system. To examine the effects, the following regression model might be used:

$$Y = \beta_0 + \beta_1 X_1 + \beta_2 X_2 + \epsilon$$

where Y = system response time
X_1 = number of simultaneous jobs allowed in the system
X_2 = number of logons per hour that occur
β_j = regression coefficients
ϵ = error term, normally distributed with constant variance

Using the regression approach, the auditor can test whether the overall model is statistically significant and the individual terms in the model are statistically significant. The variation in response times explained by the independent variables also can be determined, and confidence intervals for the beta coefficients can be estimated.

Assume, using the ordinary least-squares method, the following model is obtained:

$$Y = .342 + .051 X_1 + .011 X_2 \quad (R^2 = .24)$$

Assume, also, the overall model is statistically significant and the individual terms are statistically significant. The number of jobs simultaneously in the system (X_1) and the number of logons per hour (X_2) account for 24% of the variation in response times. Further, each extra job in the system adds .051 second to the response time and each extra logon per hour adds .011 second to the response time. The values .051 and .011 are point estimates of the beta coefficients; thus, the auditor may wish to determine a confidence interval for each beta coefficient, say, at the 95% level.

Analysis of Covariance If the auditor investigates the effects of changes to both workload and system parameters, some of which are measured at the nominal or ordinal level and some of which are measured at the interval or ratio level, an analysis of covariance model can be used (see, for example, Friedman and Waldbaum [1975]). The analysis of covariance model can be formulated as a regression model where the variables measured at a nominal or ordinal level can be included as dummy variables (see, further Neter and Wasserman [1974]). Kobayashi [1978] discusses the use of analysis of covariance for efficiency evaluation purposes.

SUMMARY

The auditor evaluates system efficiency either to determine whether the performance of an existing system can be improved or to assess the relative capabilities of proposed hardware/software configurations to process an installation's workload. The evaluation process consists of eight steps: (a) formulate study objectives, (b) prepare a budget, (c) define performance indices, (d) construct a workload model, (e) construct a system model, (f) run experiments, (g) analyze results, and (h) provide recommendations.

There are three types of performance indices used to evaluate system efficiency. Timeliness indices measure how quickly a system can process user jobs. Throughput indices measure the productivity of the system. Utilization indices measure how often a system resource is busy.

The major objective in the design of a workload model is representativeness with respect to the real workload. Either natural or artificial workload models can be constructed. Natural workload models are constructed by taking some subset of the real workload; any other type of workload model is artificial.

To assess the impact of workload and system variables on performance indices, a system model must be constructed. The auditor can choose from three types of system models: (a) analytical models, (b) simulation models, and (c) empirical models.

REVIEW QUESTIONS

24.1. Give two purposes of defining clearly the objectives of an efficiency evaluation study.

24.2. Why is it usually difficult to estimate the benefits of an efficiency evaluation study?

24.3. Briefly explain the difference between a workload model and a system model. To what extent can the workload model be formulated independently of the system model?

24.4. Briefly explain the nature of the three major types of performance indices. For each type, give an example of a specific performance index that might be used in an efficiency evaluation study.

24.5. Why must a performance index usually be described by a probability distribution rather than a single point estimate?

24.6. Even if the system to be evaluated is operational, why might the auditor decide to use a workload model to evaluate system efficiency rather than the real workload?

24.7. What is meant by the representativeness of a workload model? How can the representativeness of a workload model be measured? Why is it sometimes difficult to evaluate the representativeness of a workload in practice?

24.8. Briefly explain the difference between a natural workload model and an artificial workload model. What are the relative advantages and disadvantages of each type of model?

24.9. Briefly explain the difference between constructing a natural workload model on the basis of a content subset and a time subset. Which model is likely to be more representative of the real workload?

24.10. What is the nature of the *system* model used with an instruction mix workload model? Give three limitations of the output of the system model.

24.11. What is the difference between a synthetic job and a kernel program? How will the system models for these two types of artificial workload models differ?

24.12. Why is it important to focus on the interevent times when decomposing a system so it can be modeled for efficiency evaluation purposes? When a decision is made on the level of the system to be modeled, how must events in a lower level system be described in the model?

24.13. What is the attribute of a computer system which allows it to be modeled as a queuing system? Are there any types of computer systems where queuing theory would not provide a useful basis for modeling the system?

24.14. Briefly explain the difference between an open queuing model and a closed queuing model. What factor might cause the auditor to model a system as an open model even though a closed model is more realistic?

24.15. Even though the system to be modeled is operational, why might the auditor use a queuing model of the system instead of a simulation or empirical model for efficiency evaluation purposes?

24.16. What is meant by the CPU queuing discipline? How does the queuing discipline affect the nature of jobs awaiting service at the CPU?

24.17. Why have queuing theorists been concerned with developing approximate methods for solving queuing models?

24.18. How can the auditor determine which parameters in a queuing model are more important to calibrate?

24.19. Briefly explain the nature of a trace-driven simulation model of a computer system. What are the strengths and limitations of a trace-driven simulation? How can a trace be constructed for a system that is not operational?

24.20. What advantage does a simulation package such as SCERT offer over a simulation language such as GPSS?

24.21. Give two attributes of a simulator that the auditor might examine when assessing the face validity of the simulator as a vehicle for efficiency evaluation.

24.22. Using a simulator, the auditor changes the device to channel assignment to assess the impact on system throughput. How can the auditor determine *formally* whether the change is significant?

24.23. What factor determines whether the auditor uses an analysis of variance, regression, or analysis of covariance model when constructing an empirical model to assess the impact of changes to the system on efficiency?

EXERCISES AND CASES

24.1. Briefly explain how resource demands are generated in a probabilistic workload model. If the demand for processor time by jobs is distributed normally with a mean of 5 microseconds and a variance of 2.5 microseconds, and the random number generator you use for your workload model is functioning correctly, what percentage of the jobs generated should request more than 7 microseconds of processor time? How could you check that, in fact, this is the case with your workload model?

24.2. The auditor obtains the following results for a regression model used to assess the impact of the number of jobs per hour that request over 5 microseconds of CPU time (X_1) and the number of jobs per hour that require more than one work space in main memory (X_2) on the response time of a system (measured in seconds):

$$Y = .106 + .371X_1 + .402X_2 \quad (R^2 = .16)$$

Required:
a. What is the expected impact on response time of introducing two more jobs into the system that request more than 5 microseconds of processor time?
b. What is the impact on response time of introducing one more job that requests more than 5 microseconds of processor time and four jobs that require more than one work space?
c. What is the expected response time if there are no jobs in the system requiring more than 5 microseconds of processor time or more than one work space.

24.3. Your organization uses an online realtime update system for several of its application systems. Recently, there has been concern over increasing response times with the system. The workload has been increasing; nevertheless, since two of the online realtime update systems are used by clerical staff who deal directly with customers, customer goodwill depends upon fast response times being maintained. One suggestion made by the data processing manager to decrease response times is to see whether the introduction of job priority classes and an increase in the time slice allocated jobs would improve system throughput.

As the internal auditor in your organization having expertise in performance evaluation, management asks you to evaluate the changes proposed by the data processing manager. You decide to evaluate the changes using an experiment.

Required: Outline how you would set up the experiment. Describe how you would determine whether the changes proposed are worthwhile.

24.4. Spreaditround Ltd., is a large fertilizer company with offices scattered throughout the United States. A communications network links the various offices to the head office in Detroit. The offices have online realtime update capabilities to several centralized databases.

Response times in the network have been deteriorating. After an investigation into the possible reasons why response times are increasing, the system programming group suggests two alterations to the network that they feel may remedy the situation. The first option is to purchase a new model of network controller; however, they are uncertain as to which of two models of controller to purchase. The second option is to change the method of polling terminals in the system from roll-call to hub polling.

The system programming group constructs a simulation model of the network and runs the model for 2000 iterations. The first 1000 iterations allow the simulation to stabilize. During the second 1000 iterations, response times for a particular controller-method of polling configuration are measured. The experiment is run four times, one for each controller-method of polling combination.

As the manager of internal audit for Spreaditround, you receive a report from the system programming group on their simulation runs that contains the following table:

TABLE 1
MEAN RESPONSE TIMES IN SECONDS FOR 1000 ITERATIONS OF EACH CONTROLLER-METHOD OF POLLING COMBINATION

	Type of controller		
Method of polling	Type 1	Type 2	Row mean
Roll-call	5.002	4.157	4.5794
Hub	5.001	3.062	4.0315
Column mean	5.0015	3.6095	4.3055

Required: On the basis of the simulation results, what do you conclude about the proposed changes? If a statistical analysis (ANOVA) of the results was undertaken, what variables do you think would be statistically significant?

24.5. During the design of a new motor vehicle registration system for a state highway department, the systems analysts must decide on the number of terminals that are needed for the clerks who serve customers at the front desk. Customers can come to the counter, pay their registration renewals, and receive their stickers for the coming year. The system also provides answers to queries about registration rates for the different types of motor vehicles, the status of registration on a particular vehicle, etc.

The systems analysts believe that one terminal will serve two clerical staff adequately but they are not sure whether it will serve three without a queue developing, especially during peak periods; for example, around lunchtime.

Required: Outline how you would construct a queuing model to help the analysts with their problem. Note, assume there is excess capacity with the central processor, disks, etc.

REFERENCES

Allen, A. O. "Elements of Queuing Theory for System Design," *IBM Systems Journal* vol. 14, no. 2, 1975, pp. 161–187.

Anderson, H. A., Jr., M. Reiser, and G. L. Galati. "Tuning a Virtual Storage System," *IBM Systems Journal,* vol. 14, no. 3, 1975, pp. 246–263.

Arndt, Fred R., and G. M. Oliver. "Hardware Monitoring of Real-Time Computer System Performance," *Computer* (July–August 1972), pp. 25–29.

Bard, Y. "The VM/370 Performance Predictor," *Computing Surveys* (September 1978), pp. 333–342.

Boyse, John W., and David R. Warn. "A Straightforward Model for Computer Performance Prediction," *Computing Surveys* (June 1975), pp. 73–93.

Buzen, Jeffrey P. "A Queueing Network Model of MVS," *Computing Surveys* (September 1978), pp. 319–331.

Callaway, P. H. "Performance Measurement Tools for VM/370," *IBM Systems Journal,* vol. 14, no. 2, 1975, pp. 134–160.

Chandy, K. Mani, and Charles H. Sauer. "Approximate Methods for Analyzing Queueing Network Models of Computing Systems," *Computing Surveys* (September 1978), pp. 281–317.

Denning, Peter J., and Jeffrey P. Buzen. "The Operational Analysis of Queueing Network Models," *Computer Surveys* (September 1978), pp. 225–261.

Ferrari, Domenico. "Workload Characterization and Selection in Computer Performance Measurement," *Computer* (July–August 1972), pp. 18–24.

———. "Architecture and Instrumentation in a Modular Interactive System," *Computer* (November 1973), pp. 25–29.

———. *Computer Systems Performance Evaluation* (Englewood Cliffs, N.J.: Prentice-Hall, Inc., 1978).

———, and Mark Lin. "A General-Purpose Software Measurement Tool," *Software-Practice and Experience* (April–June 1975), pp. 181–192.

Friedman, H. P., and G. Waldbaum. "Evaluating System Changes under Uncontrolled Workloads: A Case Study," *IBM Systems Journal*, vol. 14, no. 4, 1975, pp. 340–352.

Graham, G. Scott. "Queueing Network Models of Computer System Performance," *Computing Surveys* (September 1978), pp. 219–224.

Grochow, Jerrold M. "Utility Functions for Time-Sharing System Performance Evaluation," *Computer* (September–October 1972), pp. 16–19.

Huck, Schuyler W., William H. Cormier, and William G. Bounds, Jr. *Reading Statistics and Research* (New York: Harper & Row Publishers, 1974).

Kobayashi, Hisashi. *Modeling and Analysis: An Introduction to System Performance Evaluation Methodology* (Reading, Mass.: Addison-Wesley Publishing Company, 1978).

Lipsky, Lester, and J. D. Church. "Applications of a Queueing Network Model for a Computer System," *Computing Surveys* (September 1977), pp. 205–221.

Lucas, Henry C. "Performance Evaluation and Monitoring," *Computing Surveys* (September 1971), pp. 79–91.

Miller, Edward F., Jr. "Bibliography on Techniques of Computer Performance Analysis," *Computer* (September–October 1972), pp. 39–47.

Muntz, Richard R. "Queueing Networks: A Critique of the State of the Art and Directions for the Future," *Computing Surveys* (September 1978), pp. 354–359.

Neter, John, and William Wasserman. *Applied Linear Statistical Models* (Homewood, Ill.: Richard D. Irwin, Inc., 1974).

Ramamoorthy, C. V., K. H. Kim, and W. T. Chen. "Optimal Placement of Software Monitors Aiding Systematic Testing," *IEEE Transactions on Software Engineering* (December 1975), pp. 403–411.

Rose, Clifford A. "A Measurement Procedure for Queueing Network Models of Computer Systems," *Computing Surveys* (September 1978), pp. 263–280.

Saltzer, Jerome H. "Protection and the Control of Information Sharing in Multics," *Communications of the ACM* (July 1974), pp. 388–402.

Shermer, Jack E., and John B. Robertson. "Instrumentation of Time-Shared Systems," *Computer* (July–August 1972), pp. 39–48.

Simon, Herbert A. *The Sciences of the Artificial* (Cambridge, Mass.: The M.I.T. Press, 1969).

Stimler, Saul. *Data Processing Systems: Their Performance, Evaluation, Measurement, and Improvement* (Trenton, N.J.: Motivational Learning Programs, Inc., 1974).

Svobodova, Liba. *Computer Performance Measurement and Evaluation Methods: Analysis and Applications* (New York: American Elsevier Publishing Company, Inc., 1976).

Wong, J. W. "Queueing Network Modeling of Computer Communication Networks," *Computing Surveys* (September 1978), pp. 343–351.

PART

FUTURES

In the previous twenty-four chapters of this book we have ranged widely over the subject matter of EDP auditing. Clearly the EDP auditor's task is complex. There is a large set of controls from which the auditor can choose to design a system so it safeguards assets, maintains data integrity, achieves its goals effectively, and consumes resources efficiently. There is a large number of techniques from which the auditor can choose to gather evidence. The global evaluation process is complex and not well understood. Even so, we have examined primarily the status quo. Perhaps unfortunately, it is apparent the EDP audit function is in a state of flux.

The final section of this book consists of a single chapter on the changing EDP audit function. The chapter discusses some of the possible futures of EDP auditing.

Use of the plural form "futures" rather than the singular form "future" is intentional. It is impossible to predict with too much confidence a single future for EDP auditing; instead, a number of future scenarios can be described, all of which are possible. The plural form "futures" emphasizes the uncertainty surrounding the prediction process.

Chapter	Overview of contents
25 Futures	Toward professionalism; legal and social influences; impact of the changing technology; research and pedagogy

607

Since the final chapter of the book often is speculative, it represents the opinion of the author. The reader may have alternate viewpoints. Hopefully, however, there is at least some agreement on the sources and areas of impact of the changes examined.

CHAPTER 25

THE CHANGING EDP AUDIT FUNCTION

CHAPTER OUTLINE

TOWARD PROFESSIONALISM
    Motivations toward Professionalism
    EDP Audit Professionalism
LEGAL INFLUENCES
    Privacy Legislation
    Foreign Corrupt Practices Act
SOCIAL INFLUENCES
    Computers and the Worker
    Computers and the Consumer
IMPACT OF THE CHANGING TECHNOLOGY
    Impact at a General Level
    Impact at a Detailed Level
RESEARCH AND PEDAGOGY
SUMMARY
REVIEW QUESTIONS
EXERCISES AND CASES
REFERENCES

This final chapter of the book reviews a number of forces acting on the EDP audit function that may cause it to change in some way. These forces have a variety of origins. Some arise because the society has been focusing critically on the professions and there have been major pressures for change and improvement. Others arise because there has been widespread concern about how computer technology should be used; consequently, there has been more questioning about the global benefits and costs of using computers. Still others arise because technological advancements have not stood still; if anything, at least in some areas of computer technology, the rate of change has increased.

The chapter proceeds as follows. The first section examines moves made by EDP auditors toward increased professionalism. The motivation for and likely outcome of these moves are discussed. The second and third sections review possible changes that may arise because of the enactment of laws and the increased focus of a more informed public on computer use. The fourth section examines some of the major implications of advanced systems for the EDP audit function. Finally, the chapter discusses some changes that may arise as research and pedagogy within the EDP audit area improves.

TOWARD PROFESSIONALISM

In 1969 the EDP Auditors Association was formed in Los Angeles. The Association started out with approximately 100 members. By the end of 1979 it had over 3500 members and over 35 chapters scattered throughout the United States, Canada, Mexico, Costa Rica, and Australia. The Association was the first organization formed to cater solely for individuals in the EDP audit area. Its explosive growth, however, was paralleled by the rapid formation of other EDP audit interest groups within the various professional societies of external auditors and internal auditors.

Implicitly the EDP Auditors Association always has considered itself to be a professional organization. Indeed, those EDP auditors who were certified external or internal auditors regarded themselves as having professional status. Nevertheless, in the late 1970s there were formal moves to have EDP auditors recognized as professionals.

Motivations toward Professionalism

During the 1970s the various professions—medicine, law, accounting, etc.— were subjected to intense scrutiny. There was general dissatisfaction with the professions. Both governments and the public questioned whether professionals were overpaid, whether they were performing their duties with sufficient care, whether their ethical and performance standards might not be improved, whether professional organizations had acted in restraint of trade, etc. In essence the professions were asked to be more accountable. Were the benefits of their outputs exceeding their costs? Could these benefits be attained in a cheaper way?

In December 1976 the U.S. Senate Subcommittee on Reports, Accounting and Management issued a report titled: "The Accounting Establishment: A Staff Study." The report was highly critical of the accounting profession. It recommended, inter alia, direct involvement by the federal government in establishing financial accounting standards and auditing standards, promulgating standards of conduct for auditors, and reviewing periodically the work performed by auditors. In other countries the accounting profession was experiencing similar criticisms. For example, in Australia the New South Wales Attorney General announced his support for an Accounting Practitioner's Act to regulate and discipline the accounting profession, and an Accounting Standards Board that would endorse or reject accounting standards proposed by the accounting profession, company directors, stockbrokers, bankers, and other interested groups.

In November 1977 the U.S. Senate Subcommittee on Reports, Accounting and Management issued a second report titled: "Improving the Accountability of Publicly Owned Corporations and Their Auditors." In this report the Sub-Committee tempered the recommendations made in its initial report. It encouraged private reform of the profession rather than mandatory reform as the preferred mode of action. However, the Subcommittee issued a warning that mandatory reform would be forthcoming if private reform was not timely.

Since many auditors were members of the various EDP audit groups that had been formed, they recognized that the criticisms levied at the accounting profession in general soon might focus on EDP auditors (see, for example, Barnes and Bariff [1978]). Thus, there were substantial motivations to seek formal recognition of professional status for EDP auditors.

EDP Audit Professionalism

The U.S. Taft-Hartley Act identifies five conditions for defining a profession: (*a*) a common body of knowledge, (*b*) standards of competency, (*c*) examination of competency, (*d*) a code of ethics, and (*e*) a disciplinary mechanism (see, further, Canning [1976]). In an attempt to comply with these requirements, the EDP Auditors Association has been defining a common body of knowledge for EDP auditors; it also has set up a certification program (see, further, Barnes and Bariff [1978]).

From July 1, 1979 individuals wanting to obtain a Certified Data Processing Auditor (CDPA) certificate must pass a written examination, provide evidence of two years satisfactory EDP audit experience, and adopt the CDPA Code of Professional Conduct. The common body of knowledge developed by the Association provides the basis of the written examination. The examination is modified as the common body of knowledge is updated. Holders of the CDPA also must fulfill continuing education requirements.

Hopefully, certification will provide a number of benefits. First, the formalization of EDP audit knowledge should lead to higher-quality EDP audits being performed. Second, the certification program reduces the information search costs incurred by an employer when seeking out a suitably qualified and competent EDP auditor. The CDPA certificate defines the minimum skills the employer should be able to expect. If the certificate skill level is too high for the employer's needs, a noncertified EDP auditor can be hired, presumably at a lower price. Third, if the disciplinary mechanism of the Association is effective, certification provides a means of penalizing those EDP auditors who violate ethics or perform substandard work.

Nonetheless, these benefits are attained at a cost. Professional organizations must be supported by membership fees. Further, members normally incur substantial personal costs both in terms of time and money to be certified. Thus, the employer must expect to pay for the benefits obtained by the existence of a certification program.

If a certification program also is supported by government licensing of the professional, the society tends to bear other costs. Licensing enables the profession to restrict entry. It is difficult, if not impossible, for other competing professional organizations to be set up or for the noncertified individual to practice. Thus, consumer choice is restricted. The profession has all the powers of a cartel. It can extract monopoly profits and the level of output of the services provided is less than the level that would be attained in a freely operating market (see, further, Friedman [1962]).

LEGAL INFLUENCES

Throughout the 1970s several laws were enacted that have had or may have a substantial impact on the EDP audit function. These laws have extended the scope of the EDP audit function and the responsibilities of the EDP auditor. Since some of the laws are still evolving, their final impact is unclear.

The following sections examine two major sets of laws that affect the EDP audit function: (*a*) those relating to privacy, and (*b*) those relating to foreign corrupt practices. There has been widespread activity internationally relating to privacy laws; thus, EDP auditors in many countries have been or potentially will be affected. Legal activity with respect to foreign corrupt practices has been confined primarily to the United States. However, the effects of this activity are examined here because the United States EDP audit function is so large; also, there are many U.S.-based multinational companies affected by the law relating to foreign corrupt practices.

Privacy Legislation

Data privacy refers to the right to have data protected from inadvertent or unauthorized disclosure. Inadvertent disclosure occurs, for example, when a system crash results and the contents of a user's files are displayed publically at a terminal. Unauthorized disclosure occurs when a person having access rights uses the data for an unintended purpose. Thus, authorization has two dimensions: (*a*) the authority to access data, and (*b*) the authority to use data only for specified purposes (see, also, Hsiao et al. [1979]).

Scope of Privacy Legislation Many countries already have enacted privacy laws; for example, Sweden, the United States, West Germany, Denmark, Norway, Canada, France, and Austria. Various states have enacted their own privacy laws; for example, Minnesota in the United States and the West German Land of Hesse. There have been a number of specific laws to protect certain kinds of data; for example, New Zealand's Wanganui Computer Centre Act that regulates how police may process and use personal data. Still other countries have given power to various organizations to mediate on privacy issues. For example, in Australia the New South Wales Privacy Committee with limited powers has been successful in resolving a wide range of privacy disputes (see, further, Kirby [1979]). At the international level, the Council of Europe and the Organization for Economic Cooperation and Development have been active in the privacy area.

The forms of legislation passed vary considerably. Some Acts apply only to the public sector, some apply only to the private sector, and some cover both sectors. There are differences relating to whether the laws cover only personal data or both personal and organizational data. The means of enforcing the laws are different. Some countries have established powerful supervisory agencies, some rely on the courts, and some have created an ombudsman position. There are still other differences; for example, whether the laws apply to both manual and computer systems, whether they cover transborder data flows, and whether they cover third-party use of data.

However, there are some emerging principles that are common, at least to some extent, in the laws. Stadlen [1979] identifies seven such principles:

1 Individuals should be able to discover the existence and ownership of automated personal data systems. Usually, organizations that establish such systems must register them publically.

2 Individuals should be able to discover whether information about them exists in a personal data system. Usually, the owner of the system must respond to a request by an individual about whether data on them exists in the system.

3 Individuals should be able to examine data held about them.

4 Individuals should be able to correct or delete data held about them that is inaccurate, outdated, or irrelevant.

5 Data should be collected lawfully and fairly.

6 Data collection on some individual attributes should be prohibited; for example, racial origin, political philosophy, religious views, and sex life details.

7 Special measures over and above the normal computer security measures should be taken to preserve the privacy of personal data.

The extent to which these principles become pervasive or further principles emerge is yet unknown. However, the trends in privacy legislation are relatively clear and with increasing international flows of data there are pressures toward standardization.

Implications for the EDP Auditor The scope and extent of the impact of privacy legislation on the EDP auditor depends on the particular form of the legislation existing in the country in which the EDP auditor resides or the form of the legislation applying to the organization audited. However, there are four broad ways in which privacy legislation may impact the auditor:

1 *Need to Be Familiar with Statutes* Auditing standards generally require auditors to be familiar with statutes affecting the organizations they audit. In the case of privacy statutes, the laws applicable may have both domestic and foreign origins. For example, under the Swedish Data Act the Data Inspection Board must give approval for the release of data about Swedish citizens to foreign countries. The Board occasionally has refused to release permission because it considers the foreign organization to have inadequate security to protect data privacy.

2 *Need to Audit for Legislative Compliance* Because of the risk of penalties arising under a privacy act, EDP auditors may be responsible for ensuring the organization complies with the statutes. Internal auditors also may be responsible for preparing a privacy impact statement and constructing a comprehensive privacy plan (see, further, Goldstein and Nolan [1975]). In some cases external auditors may have to determine whether there is a possibility of contingent liabilities arising because of noncompliance with an act.

3 *Auditor as a User of Personal Data* How privacy legislation will eventually affect the auditor as a user of data is still unclear. In some ways it appears that, because of the statutes, an organization may have to identify its auditor and the ways in which the auditor will use personal data in advance. Approval for any deviation from these stated purposes may have to be sought. The timing of audits may be affected if substantial lead time is required for notification and approval of deviations from stated purposes. Audit reports also may be delayed if some dispute arises over how the data will be used. If organizations must keep a log of uses made of personal data and individuals have access to data about them on this log, the auditor's ability to carry out confidential investigations is impaired. Further, audit techniques may become widely known and ways of circumventing these techniques devised more readily.

4 *Auditor as a Maintainer of Personal Data* In the course of an audit the EDP auditor may extract personal data from files for inclusion in working papers. Thus, auditors must ensure that adequate security exists over their own files, just as this security must exist over the files of the organizations they audit. In fact, the organization audited may be unable to transfer personal data to the auditor unless the auditor's files are secure.

Foreign Corrupt Practices Act

In December 1977 the Foreign Corrupt Practices Act became law in the United States. The Act was the outcome of post-Watergate investigations that revealed corporations making illegal domestic and foreign contributions to governments, politicians, and civil servants for purposes of obtaining business.

The Act has international importance in that it applies to multinational U.S. firms; thus, EDP auditors involved with these firms in foreign countries are affected. For example, the firm's primary external auditor in the United States has responsibility for ensuring that audits carried out by foreign external auditors comply with the Act. Similarly, the firm's management will require foreign internal auditors to ensure the firm complies with the Act.

Scope of the Act The Act has two major sections: the Antibribery Provisions and the Accounting Standards Provisions (see, further, McKee [1979]). The Antibribery Provisions make it a criminal offence for a firm under the Act to pay a bribe to obtain business. Penalties are prescribed; companies may be fined up to $1,000,000 and individuals fined up to $10,000 and imprisoned up to five years. The Accounting Standards Provisions, in general, require a firm under the Act to devise and maintain a sound system of internal control. In a prior study of firms who had made bribes, the SEC found in each case a weak internal control system facilitated the illegal payments.

Implications for the EDP Auditor In essence, the Act does not change the existing responsibilities of both internal and external auditors. Ensuring the firm has a sound internal control system always has been a concern of the auditor. What does change, however, is the risk auditors confront when performing their duties. The penalties for nonperformance of duties are now even higher.

Roberts [1978] argues that in the event of a firm failing to comply with the Act, EDP auditors may find themselves subject to a private suit brought by the firm's management. Ultimately, management is responsible for the firm's internal control system. Management might argue, however, that it was technically unable to perform an evaluation of a computer-based internal control system. Thus, it discharged its responsibility by hiring individuals competent to perform such an evaluation; namely, EDP auditors. Though the collection of significant damages from EDP auditors is unlikely, the penalties levied on management for violating the Act may be lessened.

As a consequence, greater resources may be devoted to establishing a viable internal EDP audit function. McKee [1978] argues the Act will accelerate the trend toward professionalism and certification and strengthen the position of EDP auditors within organizations.

From the auditor's viewpoint, it now becomes more important for a firm under the Act to have a sound corporate code of conduct and a sound internal control system. EDP audit resources may have to be shifted away from other areas (e.g., operational audits) to ensure compliance with the Act. More extensive auditing also may have to be carried out. Under the Act the level of materiality of an error changes. The Act prohibits paying "anything of value" as a bribe. What was considered previously as immaterial from an audit viewpoint may now constitute something of value in terms of the Act.

SOCIAL INFLUENCES

The ability of organizations to survive depends in part on how well they monitor changing values within the society. Failure to monitor these changing values results in one of two outcomes. First, individuals in the society signal to the legislature via their votes that laws should be enacted to force the organization to comply with their wishes. Second, the organization produces goods or services that the society does not want — at least at the selling price offered. Organizations better attuned to the market's wishes can increase their profitability, usually at the expense of less responsive organizations.

Today the society is forming stronger values about how computers should be used. The ACM Committee on Computers and Public Policy [1974] identified 16 major problem areas that arise because of the interaction between computers and people. All of these issues are important to an organization wanting to survive in the marketplace. Ultimately, they infringe upon the characteristics of the products and the prices of these products that the organization offers to consumers.

To identify potential areas of impact of the society's changing values with respect to computers, management of an organization must make some group within the organization responsible for monitoring these changes. As individuals primarily concerned with control of computer implementation and use, more and more the EDP auditor may perform this function. Thus, increasing their awareness of the social influences affecting how computers are used may be an increasingly important part of the EDP auditor's changing job function.

The following two sections examine two major forces within the society that currently appear to have the potential to impact significantly the way organizations will use computers. The first force arises because of a growing concern about the effects of computers on unemployment. The second force arises because of a growing concern about the quality of the computer systems that are designed and implemented.

Computers and the Worker

In 1979 the Australian Government made available $.75 million to carry out research on the impact of technological change. The nation had experienced a series of crippling strikes, primarily in the telecommunications industry, over disputes about how new technology (primarily computer technology) should be introduced into organizations. On the one hand unions claimed the technology was resulting in widespread displacement of workers and substantial unemployment. On the other hand employers argued that to remain competitive internationally it was necessary for the technology to be introduced as quickly as possible. In terms of lost output the strikes cost millions of dollars. The strikes also were very controversial and bitter ones. Friendships were lost, work relationships were strained, and some employees at all levels within the organizations involved have continued to be ostracized. The social patterns within the organizations have been changed irrevocably.

In the aftermath of the strikes, one of the major questions asked was whether or not the strikes could have been avoided by introducing the technology differently within the organization. The problems caused by technological change are not new. They were experienced by organizations in the nineteenth century when the technological innovations of the Industrial Revolution were introduced. What is clear is that economic survival in the long run depends upon technological innovation being accommodated in some way; otherwise, an organization not introducing the technology is driven from the marketplace by an unfavorable cost structure relative to organizations that have introduced the technology. In the Australian situation, however, there was little evidence to show that organizations attempting to introduce the technology also had planned carefully the implementation of change from a social viewpoint using, for example, some of the strategies discussed in Chapter 5. Further, there was little evidence to show the unions involved had attempted over the long run to prepare their members for those technological changes that were inevitable.

The problems caused by the effects of technological innovation on the workplace are not peculiar to Australia; they are common to most countries where the use of computers has reached an advanced stage. What the resulting problems emphasize is the need for organizations to plan technological changes and to monitor carefully the changes; otherwise, the social problems arising from the changes may be costly. It is unlikely that changes will be successful unless they are the joint product of management and the worker.

As part of a changing job function, the EDP auditor may be made responsible, at least to some extent, for planning and monitoring technological change involving computers within organizations. Whereas in the past EDP auditors have developed skills primarily to handle the technology supporting maintenance of data integrity, a new range of skills now may need to be developed in the industrial relations area.

Computers and the Consumer

EDP auditors always have been concerned with users' perceptions of the quality of a computer system. Users often provide important insights into the strengths and weaknesses of a system. To date, however, who EDP auditors have considered to be the users of a computer system has been a narrow group.

Chapter 5 pointed out the tendency among many system designers (and EDP auditors) to focus on the primary users of a system and not the secondary users who often have the most direct contact with the system. The conception of who constitutes the user group is narrow in still another way. It tends to include only users who are internal to the firm. The external users, the consumers of the organization's product, often are forgotten or ignored. Evidence collection on the quality of a computer system remains internal to the organization. Rarely are the external users consulted. If the internal users are happy with the system and the auditor's tests suggest there are few problems with the system, it is assumed the external users are receiving high-quality output.

There is now some research that shows external users of a computer system are an important source of evidence on the quality of the system. For example, Sterling [1979] surveyed a random sample of members of the Consumer's Association of British Columbia to determine the extent to which they experienced errors in their dealings with computer systems. Of the individuals responding to the survey questionnaire, 40.5% reported they had encountered one or more errors within the preceding 12 months. Eighty-one percent of the errors reported were billing errors involving charges that were not justified, overcharges, etc. Further, 7.2% of the consumers reporting errors gave up trying to correct the errors after initial unsuccessful attempts. Similar results have been obtained in other studies of consumer experiences with computer systems (see, further, Sterling [1979]).

Sterling's study provides some initial evidence of a potential consumer backlash against further moves toward a cashless and checkless society (see, also, Kling [1978]). Respondents in the study reported they often experienced considerable difficulties trying to correct the errors they encountered. The average time spent by a consumer dealing with the organization involved was 2.6 hours, and the average length of time between discovery of the error and its correction was 8 weeks. Further, the consumers reported their experiences trying to correct the error often were unpleasant; some were coerced to pay a disputed amount and some were treated as troublemakers.

One consequence of these experiences was a move by the consumers back to using cash rather than credit to transact business. Such a move is in direct conflict with business organizations that want to move even more to electronic transfer of funds.

It is difficult to understand why such a large percentage of consumers encounter difficulties with well-established systems like billing systems. The design principles for these types of systems are known widely and many standard packages are available. Consumer difficulties also provide direct feedback on errors in the system. Nevertheless, long-run problems still seem to persist. Either organizations are inflexible and not responsive to these problems, the systems are badly designed or badly managed, consumers are at least partially responsible for some of the errors themselves, or the error rate for the systems must be considered normal. Whatever the reasons, it appears there is still considerable scope for improvement of basic computer systems. Further, organizations wishing to introduce new technology that increases the consumer's dependence on correct processing by computer systems may experience problems unless they are able to demonstrate convincingly to the consumer that the benefits of the technology exceed the costs.

The problems described above highlight the need for EDP auditors to ensure they include consumers within the user group they consult on matters affecting data integrity and system effectiveness. Sterling's study shows consumers can provide important information on errors existing within a system, or failure by the system to meet its objectives, at least from a consumer viewpoint. This information might be solicited not only after systems have been implemented and made operational but also during the design phase.

IMPACT OF THE CHANGING TECHNOLOGY

The previous section examined the indirect effects produced on the EDP auditor as a consequence of the impact of the changing technology on the worker and the consumer. This section briefly examines some of the possible *direct* effects of the changing technology. What will be the impact on the EDP auditor of more widespread use of database management systems, data communications, minicomputers and microcomputers, electronic funds transfer systems, online realtime systems, word processing systems, distributed systems, etc.? Clearly, there is a need for futures research in EDP auditing. The development of EDP audit tools and methodologies (e.g., audit software and its use) often has been a slow and painful process. A greater understanding of the implications of future technology for EDP auditing would result in better-directed EDP audit developmental work.

The following sections examine the impact of the changing technology on EDP auditing at a general level and a detailed level. The effects on the basic nature of EDP auditing are discussed; then the effects on controls and audit procedures are examined.

Impact at a General Level

At a basic level it is difficult to see how the changing technology can have any major impact on the role of EDP auditors or fundamental EDP audit methodologies. The auditor still will need to perform the attest function. Further, the auditor still will need to evaluate management controls, application system controls, and the quality of data in an organization's database. These aspects of auditing are invariant across technologies.

Where the impact of the changing technology will be felt is at the margin. At least five possible areas of impact can be identified. First, clearly the auditor will need to understand the new technology. Without this understanding the auditor is unable to make an informed judgment nor adequately perform evidence collection tasks. Second, there may be a greater number of more well-defined levels of EDP audit work. At one extreme an organization may use a complex system implemented in assembly level programming. For this system the auditor will require detailed technical knowledge to audit the system. At the other extreme an organization may use a package where most of the logic has been implemented as read-only microcode. Further, the system may be certified as to the adequacy of its controls and it may contain inbuilt routines for collecting audit evidence. Thus, the auditor may work at a higher level of system detail than current audits. Third, more systems should contain features that facilitate audit work. There is now a heightened awareness of the importance of data integrity. Many vendors emphasize the auditability of their systems during marketing efforts. Fourth, in the short run, system design audits may become increasingly important. Because of the difficulty of changing complex systems, the auditor will need to ensure controls are incorporated during the design phase. However, in the long run systems may have greater evolvability; thus, it may be relatively easy to modify systems to incorporate better controls in light of experience with the system. Fifth, in some areas there will be a scarcity of audit tools. Currently, few generalized audit software packages run on minicomputers. As the makes and models of minicomputers and microcomputers proliferate, the problems caused by the lack of availability of audit tools may become more acute.

Impact at a Detailed Level

Though the changing technology may have little impact on EDP auditing at a general level, at a detailed level the EDP auditor must make and evaluate decisions on the controls and audit procedures that need to be changed when the new technology is introduced into an organization. How can the auditor determine what changes need to be made to controls and audit procedures when an organization changes from using its existing technology to using new technology for its data processing?

Davis and Weber [1981] propose a conceptual model that the auditor can use to think about the consequences of a change to new technology for controls and audit procedures. They argue that a change to new technology occurs because an organization is responding to some stress; for example, a stress to be more responsive to customer demands or a stress to operate more efficiently. The use of new technology helps the organization accommodate this stress and survive. Understanding the impact of a stress on controls and audit procedures involves understanding the nature of the stress itself and the nature of the adjustment processes that are (should be) undertaken by the organization.

Figure 25.1 shows an organization as consisting of various suprasystems, systems, and subsystems. For example, if the organization is considered to be the system, its suprasystem is its environment and its subsystems consist of various functional units, one of which is the computer installation. A stress imposed by one level of system eventually permeates all the lower levels of systems. For example, if the task environment faced by the organization be-

CHAPTER 25: THE CHANGING EDP AUDIT FUNCTION   621

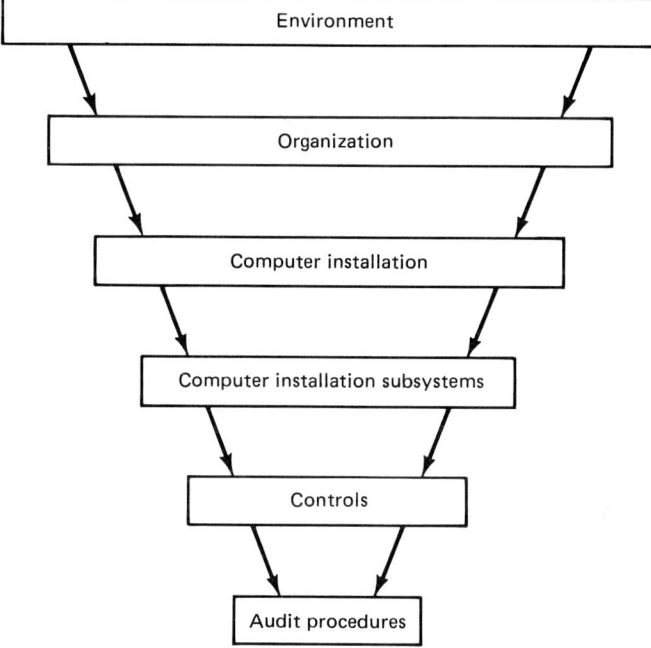

Figure 25.1
Stress imposed by higher-level systems on lower-level systems.
By permission, The Limperg Institute, The Netherlands.

comes more uncertain (see Chapter 5), the organization may respond by altering its organization structure. Eventually, pressures may be imposed on the computer installation to change so management information can be provided on a more timely basis for the new organization structure.

Within this framework, then, of levels of systems, consider the system of audit procedures within an organization. What forces drive a change to audit procedures? Davis and Weber [1981] argue that the suprasystem for the system of audit procedures is the controls system; thus, changes to controls (in response to stress) drive changes to audit procedures.

This relationship can be demonstrated by example. Assume an organization changes from using a batch system to using an online realtime update system for its data processing. Many of the controls exercised over the batch processes disappear; for example, verification of keypunched data and batch control registers. Audit procedures used to examine the reliability of these controls are no longer required.

At the next level of systems within an organization, what forces drive changes to controls? Davis and Weber [1981] argue that the suprasystem for the system of controls is the set of computer installation subsystems that exist. Changes to a computer installation subsystem drive a change to controls.

Table 25.1 shows a conceptualization of the various computer installation

TABLE 25.1
COMPUTER INSTALLATION SUBSYSTEMS

Application systems
- data capture/transaction origination
- access (e.g., to programs and data)
- input (terminal transaction entry or offline data preparation and input)
- data transmission
- transaction processing (computation, classification, and summarization)
- update of data for addition, modification, and deletion purposes
- use of system resources (e.g., core memory, system software)
- retrieval of data
- output/report preparation and distribution
- output/report use by decision makers

Systems management
Application system design and implementation
Modification and maintenance of application systems
File/database design
Modification and maintenance on file/database designs
Computer operations
Backup and recovery operations

subsystems within an organization. Consider how a change to the form of the structure or processes within these subsystems drives a change to controls. Again, assume an organization changes from using batch processing to using an online realtime update system for its data processing. The form of the structure and processes in the input subsystem changes from using source document preparation and offline keypunching to online data entry. Consider how controls change as a consequence. Controls such as keypunch verification and dual signature authorization disappear. New controls are needed; for example, checking the validity of the terminal identification number for the terminal used to enter the data.

Given, then, that changes to computer installation subsystems drive changes to controls and changes to controls drive changes to audit procedures, the auditor's problem is to determine what computer installation subsystems, if any, are affected in terms of the form of their structure and processes when an organization implements new technology. By identifying what subsystems change, the auditor can determine *where* changes to controls and audit procedures are most likely to occur.

Obviously the specific adjustments made to computer installation subsystems depend on the form of the stress. At a conceptual level, however, Davis and Weber [1981] propose two "principles" for identifying what subsystems will be adjusted to accommodate a stress. The first principle states that those subsystems "closest to the stress" will be the subsystems that adjust primarily to accommodate the stress. "Closeness" is measured in terms of *functional* closeness; that is, the extent to which a subsystem performs the *function* that must be adjusted to accommodate the stress. The rationale for this principle is that the system consumes less resources to accommodate the stress by adjusting those subsystems closest to the stress. Note, *all* subsystems may be affected in some way by the stress; the principle simply states there is a rank order of effects.

The second principle states that systems will attempt to *localize* the impact of a stress to a subset of subsystems. In other words, when a system undergoes stress and it adjusts to accommodate the stress, it attempts to confine the adjustments to only some of its subsystems. Again, the rationale behind this principle of stress localization is that the system consumes less of its resources by accommodating the stress in this way. Recall, also, from Chapter 6 that complex systems survive by maximizing the cohesiveness of their subsystems and minimizing coupling between their subsystems. In this way changes to one subsystem have minimal impact on other subsystems.

To illustrate how these two principles can be applied, assume once again that the organization changes from using batch processing to using an online realtime update system so the data in the database is more current. What computer installation subsystems will have to adjust to accommodate this timeliness stress? According to the "closeness to stress" principle, all subsystems that inhibit the timely update of the database must be adjusted. According to the principle of stress localization, only a few subsystems will undergo major change. In terms of the example, the input subsystem must be adjusted to allow faster input of data—offline keypunch preparation no longer satisfies timeliness requirements. The access subsystem can be streamlined. Dual signature authorizations constrain the speed of the input process; program access controls can be exercised instead. Similarly, the data capture subsystem can be streamlined. Rather than having clerks perform detailed manual validation of data before data entry, programmed validation checks can be used with immediate feedback on errors. The backup and recovery subsystem also must be adjusted to recover the system more quickly if the timeliness stress is to be accommodated. Other computer installation subsystems primarily remain unchanged.

Nevertheless, even after having identified where control and audit procedure adjustments must be made, two issues still remain. First, the auditor still must determine the *specific* control and audit procedure adjustments to be made. Unfortunately, at a conceptual level, all that can be said is that this issue is a cost-benefit question. The specific values of the costs and benefits must be determined empirically. Second, even if the auditor makes a "correct" decision on how controls and audit procedures should be adjusted, an incorrect decision on adjustments to be made at high levels of systems can nullify the auditor's decision. For example, an incorrect decision on how a system should be distributed may cause so many behavioral problems that the system fails even with sound controls. Thus, the relationship between stresses and the adjustment processes needed to accommodate these stresses is still a major research area.

RESEARCH AND PEDAGOGY

Two hallmarks of a strong profession are a sound theoretical and empirical knowledge base and well-developed pedagogical support for passing on this knowledge base. Unfortunately, in both areas the record of the EDP auditing profession is dismal.

To date there has been little research carried out in the EDP audit area. Boutell [1975] surveyed the literature appearing in *The Accounting Review* and *Journal of Accountancy* between 1969 and 1975. He found only 12 articles dealing with EDP audit; further, only three of these articles involved any type of empirical work. The picture has not changed much.

Fundamentally, the dearth of research reflects lack of interest in the area by academics. Primarily the literature consists of practitioner writings; thus, the experiences of EDP auditors are reasonably well-documented but basic research is lacking. Ultimately, the speed with which the profession advances depends on the availability of basic research.

There also has been within the profession a lack of awareness of relevant research undertaken in other fields. For example, many computer scientists are carrying out research in the area of operating system integrity; but there is little reference to their research in the EDP audit area. Again, this reflects the lack of interest by accounting academics in the EDP audit area. Since it is the academic side of a profession that usually is most aware via journals and their interactions with colleagues of relevant developments in other fields, it is unlikely that a cross-fertilization of ideas in the EDP audit area will be forthcoming without more academic participation.

EDP audit pedagogy is in a similar state. Regarding the U.S. experience, Schneidman [1979] comments that "eleven years after the publication of the common body of knowledge for certified public accountants 'Horizons for a Profession' we find that the bulk of the accounting profession is still protesting that it does not need knowledge of computers." Thus, the market has imposed few pressures on academics to offer EDP auditing courses. To date, EDP audit education has come primarily from on-the-job training and short courses.

Fortunately there are changes occurring in the areas of research and pedagogy. In recent years more funds have been made available by business and the accounting profession to encourage EDP audit research and support development of teaching materials. The trend toward professionalism and certification provides an added incentive for tertiary institutions to develop and offer courses in EDP auditing. Hopefully the outcome will be higher-quality decision making among EDP auditors and more effective and efficient dissemination of EDP audit knowledge.

SUMMARY

Currently there are several forces at work that may change the EDP audit function. As a result of pressures applied by governments and the public, professions have attempted to improve their standards of conduct and performance and be more accountable. EDP auditors have responded by trying to increase their professionalism by developing a common body of knowledge, a code of ethics, and a certification program.

The legislative process also has impacted the EDP audit function, especially with the enactment of data privacy laws in various countries and the Foreign Corrupt Practices Act in the United States. In some cases privacy laws have extended the EDP auditor's responsibilities to ensure compliance of an organization with the laws. EDP auditors also may be subject to the laws as maintainers and users of data. The Foreign Corrupt Practices Act has increased the possible penalties faced by an EDP auditor who makes a wrong judgment about the quality of an internal control system.

New computer technology has impacted the EDP audit function both indirectly and directly. Indirectly, the effects have occurred because of problems experienced by workers and consumers with changing technology. Organizations need to be increasingly aware of the society's attitudes toward computer use. EDP auditors may perform some part of this monitoring function required. Directly, the effects have occurred because the EDP auditor must evaluate systems based on the new technology. The role of the EDP auditor and the basic audit methodologies remain unchanged; however, the EDP auditor must understand the new technologies, be capable of determining their impact on controls and audit procedures, and ensure that evidence collection tools and techniques have been developed.

Finally, the EDP audit function is changing because research and pedagogy in the area is improving. More research will provide a better-developed theoretical and empirical knowledge base for the function. Improved pedagogy will allow more effective and efficient dissemination of this knowledge base.

REVIEW QUESTIONS

25.1. What impact did moves by various governments to regulate the accounting profession have on the development of the EDP audit profession?
25.2. List five identifying characteristics of a profession. What actions have EDP auditors taken to ensure compliance with these characteristics?
25.3. Give two benefits and two costs of professional certification. What problems can arise when professional certification is supported by government licensing?
25.4. List three ways in which international privacy laws differ. What implications do these differences have for EDP auditing in a multinational corporation?
25.5. List four privacy "principles" that are common, at least to some extent, in international privacy laws. Choose one principle and outline how it might affect the EDP audit function.
25.6. What implications do privacy laws have for EDP auditors as maintainers of personal data?
25.7. How may a contingent liability arise because of privacy laws? Why might the EDP auditor be concerned with contingent liabilities when auditing an organization for compliance with privacy laws?

25.8. What implications do privacy laws have for EDP auditors as users of personal data?
25.9. The Foreign Corrupt Practices Act does not change the responsibilities of EDP auditors; however, it changes the risks they face. Explain.
25.10. Why does the concept of materiality change under the Foreign Corrupt Practices Act? How might the evidence collection phase of an EDP audit change as a consequence?
25.11. Even though the Foreign Corrupt Practices Act is a United States act, why may it affect foreign EDP auditors?
25.12. Why may the EDP auditor become increasingly involved in monitoring social attitudes toward computer technology?
25.13. Briefly discuss the dilemma facing management and workers over the introduction of new computer technology within organization. What part might the EDP auditor have to play in resolving some of the problems caused by the dilemma?
25.14. What evidence exists to show EDP auditors may have a narrow conception of who constitutes the user group of a computer system? Give two potential consequences if this focus continues to be narrow.
25.15. How might consumer experiences with batch billing systems affect moves toward further implementation and use of electronic funds transfer systems?
25.16. Briefly describe two ways in which an EDP auditor might better monitor the attitudes of consumers toward an organization's computer systems.
25.17. Why is it unlikely that the changing technology will affect the basic role of the EDP auditor and fundamental EDP audit methodologies?
25.18. Why might the changing computer technology allow the EDP auditor to work at a higher level of detail? Give two implications of the EDP auditor being able to work at this higher level of detail.
25.19. Briefly explain the relationship between the form of the computer installation subsystem and the form of controls, and between the form of controls and the form of audit procedures.
25.20. How is the principle of stress localization useful when considering the impact of new technology on controls and audit procedures?
25.21. What is meant by futures research? How would futures research aid the development of the EDP audit function?
25.22. Give two reasons why EDP audit research and pedagogy have been slow to develop. Why is it likely the pace will quicken in the future?
25.23. Briefly discuss why it is necessary for the survival of a profession to have a sound theoretical and empirical knowledge base and an effective and efficient means of disseminating this knowledge base.

EXERCISES AND CASES

25.1. In terms of the general principles of privacy legislation, identify those aspects likely to impact only the external auditor, those aspects likely to impact only the internal auditor, and those aspects that impact both external and internal auditors. Be sure to explain the nature of the impact in each case.
25.2. As auditors we tend to think of the impact of computers on jobs other than our own. Over the next 10 years, to what extent will the computer cause job displace-

ment within the auditing profession? If you believe displacement will not occur, explain why we will be "saved."

25.3. How much do we know about where computers will have an impact over the next 10 years? To what extent is there agreement among the experts? As someone having some knowledge of computers and their capabilities, rate the extent to which computers will cause work displacement in the following jobs over the next 10 years. A score of 10 means high job displacement will occur; a score of one means there will be little or no impact.

 Real estate salesperson
 Medical practitioner (doctor)
 Assembly line worker
 University academic
 Farmer
 Auto mechanic
 Accounts clerk
 Biochemist
 Homemaker
 Surveyor
 Civil engineer

Compare your ratings with other members of your class to determine consensus.

25.4. Using the conceptual framework proposed by Davis and Weber [1981] for considering the impact of new technology on controls and audit procedures, what computer installation subsystems would be affected (see Table 25.1) when an organization implements a database management system to promote sharing of data? For each subsystem that you list as being affected, explain why you think it will be affected. Furthermore, list some control changes and audit procedure changes that you expect to occur as a consequence of the subsystem changes.

25.5. What computer installation subsystems will be affected by a stress imposed on the computer installation cannot be determined unless the stress is understood. Explain this statement in terms of a move by a computer installation from centralized to distributed data processing. *Hint:* You should consider what is meant by distributed data processing.

REFERENCES

ACM Committee on Computers and Public Policy. "A Problem-List of Issues Concerning Computers and Public Policy," *Communications of the ACM* (September 1974), pp. 495-503.

Barnes, Stanley H., and Martin L. Bariff. "Professionalism and the EDP Auditor," *The EDP Auditor* (Winter 1978), pp. 4-11.

Becker, Lawrence C. *Property Rights: Philosophic Foundations* (London: Routledge & Kegan Paul, 1977).

Boutell, Wayne S. "Auditing and Research," in Gary J. Previts, ed., *Accounting Research Convocation* (Alabama: University of Alabama, 1975), pp. 87-102.

Canning, Richard G. "Professionalism: Coming or Not," *EDP Analyzer* (March 1976), pp. 1-12.

Davis, Gordon B., and Ron Weber. *Auditing Advanced EDP Systems* (Altamonte Springs, Fla.: The Institute of Internal Auditors, Inc., 1981).

Friedman, Milton. *Capitalism and Freedom* (Chicago: The University of Chicago Press, 1962).
Goldstein, Robert C., and Richard L. Nolan. "Personal Privacy Versus the Corporate Computer," *Harvard Business Review* (March–April 1975), pp. 62–70.
Hsiao, David K., Douglas S. Kerr, and Stuart E. Madnick. *Computer Security* (New York: Academic Press, Inc., 1979).
Kirby, M. D. "Data Protection and Law Reform," *Computer Networks* (June 1979), pp. 149–163.
Kling, Rob. "Value Conflicts and Social Choice in Electronic Funds Transfer System Developments," *Communications of the ACM* (August 1978), pp. 642–657.
McKee, Thomas E. "Auditing Under the Foreign Corrupt Practices Act," *The CPA Journal* (August 1979), pp. 31–35.
Mason, John O., Jr., and Jonathan J. Davies. "Legal Implications of EDP Deficiencies," *The CPA Journal* (May 1977), pp. 21–24.
Novotny, Eric J. "Restrictions on the Transnational Flow of Corporate Information: New Challenges for the Auditing Profession," *The EDP Auditor* (Summer 1979), pp. 13–33.
Report of the Secretary's Advisory Committee on Automated Personal Data Systems, U.S. Department of Health, Education and Welfare. *Records, Computers, and the Rights of Citizens* (Boston, Mass.: The Massachusetts Institute of Technology, 1973).
Roberts, Ray. "Impact on the Auditor of Recent Developments Relating to Internal Control," *The EDP Auditor* (Winter 1978), pp. 12–20.
Ross, Steven L. "The Legal Review of Data Processing Systems," *The EDP Auditor* (Summer 1979), pp. 1–11.
Ruder, Brian. "Privacy and Data Base Administration," *EDP Auditing* (Pennsauken, N. J.: Auerbach Publishers, Inc., 1978*a*), Portfolio 73-02-04, pp. 1–12.
———. "Privacy and the Data Center," *EDP Auditing* (Pennsauken, N. J.: Auerbach Publishers, Inc., 1978*b*), Portfolio 72-03-05, pp. 1–12.
Schneidman, Arnold. "Need for Auditors' Computer Education," *The CPA Journal* (June 1979), pp. 29–35.
Shattuck, John H. F. *Rights of Privacy* (Skokie, Ill.: National Textbook Company, 1977).
Stadlen, Godfrey. "Survey of National Data Protection Legislation," *Computing Networks* (June 1979), pp. 174–186.
Sterling, T. D. "Consumer Difficulties with Computerized Transactions: An Empirical Investigation," *Communications of the ACM* (May 1979), pp. 283–289.
Westin, Alan F., and Michael G. Baker. *Databanks in a Free Society: Computers, Record-keeping and Privacy* (New York: Quadrangle/The New York Times Book Company, 1972).

NAME INDEX

Abbott, R. P., 317, 319
Abdel-Khalik, A. Rashad, 91
Accounting Review, The, 624
ACM Committee on Computers and Public Policy, 616
Adams, Carl R., 344
Adams, Donald L., 78, 153–154, 157, 160, 173, 192, 254, 370–371, 423, 435, 453
Alexander, Christopher, 130
Allen, A. O., 594
Allen, Brandt, 210, 331
Alter, Steven, 569
Altshuler, Gene P., 172
American Federation of Information Processing Societies (AFIPS), 76, 196
American Institute of Certified Public Accountants, 10, 28, 42, 47, 250
American Psychological Association, 505
Anderson, Lane K., 235
Anderson, R. J., 506
Antonelli, D. C., 223
Arens, Alvin A., 46
Arndt, Fred R., 519
Arthur Andersen & Co., 42
Ashton, Robert, 538, 555
Automation Training Center, Inc., 55, 56
Awad, Elias M., 260
Axelrod, C. Warren, 346–347

Baker, F. T., 144
Bard, Y., 596
Bariff, Martin L., 611
Barnes, Stanley H., 611
Bates, John E., 91
Belady, L. A., 143
Benbasat, Izak, 345
Benjamin, Robert I., 506
Bierman, Harold, 73, 552
Biggs, Charles L., 101
Bjork, L. A., Jr., 360, 365
Bodnar, George, 540, 544
Boehm, Barry W., 129, 154, 450–451
Bohl, Marilyn, 260–261

Böhm, C., 137, 141
Boritz, J. Effrim, 11
Bostrom, Robert P., 101, 111, 122, 499
Bouchard, Thomas J., Jr. 494, 498, 500, 502
Boutell, Wayne S., 624
Brandon, Dick H., 84, 90
Bright, Herbert S., 280
Brooks, Frederick P., Jr., 153
Brown, D., 262
Brown, Frederick G., 501, 505
Burch, John G., Jr., 453
Burns, David C., 545
Buzen, Jeffrey P., 596–597

Canadian Institute of Chartered Accountants, 34, 42, 47, 91, 433
Cannell, C. F., 494
Canning, Richard G., 129, 131, 134, 136, 140–141, 144, 150, 152, 611
Cardenas, Alfonso F., 189
Carlis, John V., 117, 506–507
Chapdelaine, P. A., 232
Chapin, Ned, 506
Cherns, Albert B., 567
Chun, Ki-Taek, 505
Clarke, Lorie A., 464
Cleland, David I., 76
Clifton, H. D., 216
Combelic, Donn, 136
Conrad, R., 232
Conway, R. W., 257–259
Courtney, Robert H., Jr., 195
Crook, B. H., 324
Cushing, Barry E., 540, 544
Cypser, R. J., 260

Daniels, Alan, 236
Danziger, James N., 568
Davis, Gordon B., 32, 35, 74, 81, 117, 140, 344, 351, 476, 575, 620–622, 627
Davis, Keagle W., 556
Davis, Louis E., 567
Davis, William P., 77
Denning, Dorothy E., 14
Denning, Peter J., 14, 596–597

NAME INDEX

Dickson, Gary W., 90
Dijkstra, Edsger W., 137
Ditri, Arnold E., 72
Dolan, William J., 250
Doll, Dixon R., 260
Drury, Donald H., 91
Duhne, Ricardo, 117
Dunnette, Marvin D., 87
Dutton, William H., 570

Earl, Michael J., 457
EDP Auditors Foundation for Education and Research, 35
Ehrsam, W. F., 272–275
Elshoff, James L., 129, 453
Emshoff, James R., 545
Endres, A., 450
Enison, R. L., 272
Equity Funding Corporation, 16–17
Everest, Gordon C., 4, 165, 167, 170, 172, 251, 253–254, 314–315, 364, 384–385, 389, 391, 417

Fagan, M. E., 142–143
Fama, Eugene F., 553
Fayen, E. G., 340, 345–346
Feltham, Gerald A., 344
Ferranti, Barry Z. de, 51
Ferrari, Domenico, 516, 518–519, 521, 526–527, 584, 589–590, 594, 597–598
FitzGerald, Jerry, 76, 195–196, 555
Fossum, Barbara M., 315
Friedman, H. P., 601
Friedman, Milton, 612

Galbraith, Jay R., 80, 93, 115
Geller, Matthew, 459
Gerberick, Dahl A., 76, 551
Gerhart, Susan L., 458, 461
Gerrity, T. P., 345
Gilb, Tom, 571
Ginzberg, Michael J., 569
Gladney, H. M., 258
Goldstein, Robert C., 614
Goodenough, John B., 458, 461
Gore, Marvin, 233, 245
Gould, John D., 342
Graham, G. Scott, 594
Greenwald, Bruce M., 358
Gustafson, L. M., 57
Guthrie, A., 568

Hackman, J. Richard, 113, 567

Haga, Clifford I., 243
Halloran, Dennis, 572
Hansen, Morris H., 257
Hartman, W., 100, 496
Hartwick, R. Dean, 451
Heckel, Paul, 467
Hedberg, Bo, 114
Heinen, J. Stephen, 101, 111, 122, 499
Henshall, Don, 106, 111
Hippert, R. O., 224
Hoffman, Lance J., 14, 440
Howden, William E., 458–459
Hsiao, David K., 613
Huck, Schuyler W., 599

Institute of Internal Auditors, 55, 56, 59, 61
International Business Machines (IBM), 78, 134, 144, 146, 262, 435, 450
International Data Corporation, 4
International Telegraph and Telephone Consultative Committee (CCITT), 262
Ishikawa, Akira, 540

Jacopini, G., 137
Jancura, Elise G., 47
Jenkins, A. Milton, 419, 506–507
Journal of Accountancy, 51, 624

Kahn, David, 270–271
Kahn, R. L., 494
Kammann, R., 510
Katton, G., 499–500, 502
Keen, Peter G. W., 117
Kelly, John R., 129, 147
Kerlinger, Fred N., 500–501, 504
Kimbleton, Stephen R., 260, 266
King, John Leslie, 573
King, William R., 76, 569
Kirby, Michael D., 613
Kirschner, Leslie S., 373
Kleijnen, Jack P. C., 572
Kline, Charles S., 274
Kling, Rob, 564, 618
Knuth, Donald E., 258
Kobayashi, Hisashi, 516, 523, 591, 593, 596–598, 601
Koontz, Harold, 70, 86, 87
Kraemer, Kenneth L., 570
Krauss, Leonard I., 494
Krenz, G., 316

Lancaster, F. W., 340, 345–346
Lawler, Edward E., 565

Lawrence, Paul R., 58, 79
Lehman, M. M., 143
Lempel, Abraham, 274
Lennon, R. E., 272
Lichenstein, Sarah, 555
Lientz, B. P., 129
Linde, Richard R., 321
Litecky, Charles R., 414
Liu, Mark, 526
Loebbecke, James K., 23, 46, 545
Lohman, Guy M., 383, 392
London, Keith R., 90
Lorsch, Jay W., 58, 79
Lucas, Henry C., Jr., 14, 90, 499, 568, 591
Lusk, Edward J., 91
Lyon, John K., 167

MacGahan, Aileen, 494
McGee, W. C., 315
McGowan, Clement L., 129, 147
McHugh, Arthur J., 357, 433
McKee, Thomas E., 615
McKinsey and Company, 90
McNurlin, Barbara C., 194
Macy, Barry A., 565–566
Mair, William C., 22, 99, 407, 556
Maish, Alexander M., 499, 568, 570
Marschak, Jacob, 8
Martin, James, 196, 199, 228–230, 260–262, 414
Matyas, S. M., 273–274
Merkle, Ralph C., 274
Merten, A. G., 117
Meyer, C. H., 273–274
Miles, Raymond E., 109, 112
Miller, Edward F., Jr., 593
Miller, George A., 232
Miller, J. O., 51
Miller, James Grier, 60, 82
Miller, Lance A., 345
Miller, Robert B., 229, 345
Mills, Harlan D., 129, 451
Mirvis, Philip H., 565–566
Mock, Theodore Jaye, 344
Montalbano, Michael, 459–460, 469
Moore, Jeffrey H., 569
Moser, C. A., 499–500, 502
Mullarkey, John F., 423
Mullen, Jack B., 458
Mumford, Enid, 106, 111, 114
Muntz, Richard R., 597
Munz, R., 316
Myers, Glenford J., 131, 133–134, 139, 455, 465

Nadler, David A., 567
Naftaly, Stanley M., 150–151, 154
National Bureau of Standards, 272, 317
National Computing Center, 77, 236
Naumann, J. David, 103–104
Neter, John, 540, 599–601
Neumann, Albrecht J., 425
New York Times, The, 144–145
Nolan, Richard L., 60, 88–90, 92, 614
Nunnally, Jum C., 501–502, 504

Oberlander, Gary, 358
O'Donnell, Cyril, 70, 86, 87
Oliver, G. M., 519
Owsowitz, S., 232

Parker, Donn B., 6, 318, 331
Perry, William E., 39, 54–57, 60, 64, 153, 156, 160, 368, 371, 432, 483, 487–488
Peterson, W., 262
Pinchuk, P. L., 188
Plagman, Bernard K., 172
Popek, Gerald J., 274
Powers, Richard F., 90
Price Waterhouse & Company, 10

Radner, Roy, 8
Raiffa, Howard, 77
Ramamoorthy, C. V., 464
Rittenberg, Larry E., 36, 47, 57
Roberts, Ray, 615
Robinson, John P., 505
Rodriguez, Jaime I., 569
Rose, Clifford A., 525, 596
Roussey, Robert S., 250
Rubey, Raymond A., 451

Sackman, Harold, 148
Saltzer, Jerome H., 253, 255, 259, 527
Sardinas, Joseph L., Jr., 453
Sawyer, Lawrence B., 46, 57
Schaller, Carol A., 250, 367–368
Schick, George J., 540
Schneider, G. Michael, 260, 266
Schneider, Jerry, 17–18, 331
Schneiderman, Ben, 341, 507
Schneidman, Arnold, 624
Schrems, Edward L., 573
Schroeder, M. D., 253, 255, 259
Schroeder, Roger G., 345
Schultz, Randall L., 568
Scott Morton, Michael S., 117, 345
Seashore, Stanley E., 565

Senko, Michael E., 116
Severance, Dennis G., 117, 383, 392
Shannon, Claude E., 272
Sharpe, William F., 552
Shaver, Phillip R., 505
Short, G. E., 193, 199, 319
Shultis, Robert L., 241, 243
Simmons, Gustavus J., 274
Simon, Herbert A., 130, 593
Sinkov, A., 270
Sisson, Roger L., 545
Skinner, R. M., 506
Sleeper, Richard C., 77
Slevin, Dennis P., 568
Slovic, Paul, 555
Smidt, Seymour, 73, 552
Smith, Barry W., 51
Stadlen, Godfrey, 613
Stanford Research Institute, 51, 54, 63, 227, 488
Stay, J. F., 134
Steers, Richard M., 561
Stepczyk, F. M., 319–320
Sterling, T. D., 618
Stimler, Saul, 519, 587–588, 597
Stubbe, John, 233
Sutton, Jimmy A., 90
Svobodova, Liba, 518, 525, 587, 591
Swanson, E. B., 129
Sweetland, A., 232

Thomas, D. A., 437
Thomas, John C., Jr., 342, 345

Union Dime Savings Bank, 18–19
U.S. Department of Commerce, 91
U.S. Secretary of Health, Education, and Welfare, 565

Van Horne, James C., 553
Van Leer, P., 139
Van Tassel, Dennis, 271

Waldbaum, G., 601
Walton, Richard E., 567
Wasserman, William, 599–601
Watson, Richard W., 260
Weber, Ron, 167, 321, 341, 414, 417–419, 433, 538, 620–622, 627
Weinberg, Gerald M., 148
Weir, Mary, 111, 114
Weiss, Harold, 51
Wilkinson, Bryan, 422
Will, Hart J., 433
Withington, Frederick G., 250
Wolverton, Ray W., 540
Wong, J. W., 596
Wong, K. K., 76
Wood, Donald R., 556
Woodward, Joan, 114
Wooldridge, Susan, 216, 224–225, 294, 337, 346, 424
Wu, Margaret, 221

Yasaki, Edward K., 51
Yeates, Donald, 236
Yourdon, Edward, 130, 137, 142, 148, 156, 378, 460
Yu, Seongjae, 540

Zuber, George R., 23

SUBJECT INDEX

Access control mechanism:
   functions of, 251–257
   implementation of, 257–260
Access monitor security kernel, 320
Accounting audit trail:
   creation of, 358–359
   deletion of, 362
   design of, 364–366
   modification of, 359–362
   nature of, 356
   operational requirements for, 358–363
   problems of change to, 363–364
   purposes of, 356–358
   retrievals from, 362–363
   and statutory requirements, 357–358
ACK-NAK logic, 263
Action privileges, 256–259
   conditional, 257, 259
   unconditional, 257, 259
Action research, 110–111
Adaptive team, 148
Afterimage, 362, 365, 388–390, 481
Alarms, 196, 199
Amplitude modulation, 263–265
Analysis of covariance, 601
Analysis of variance, 599–601
Analytical models:
   of asset safeguarding, 539–544
   of data integrity, 539–544
   of system efficiency, 594–597
Analytical review, 409
Archival system, 297–298
Artifact, monitor, 518
Artificial workload models, 590–593
Asset safeguarding:
   analytical models of, 539–544
   cost-effectiveness of, 545–553
   measures of, 536
   objectives of, 7
   simulation models of, 544–545
Association codes, 233–234
Attenuation distortion, 264
Audit approach, 36–40, 99, 409–410
   around the computer, 36–38
   selecting application systems to audit, 38–40

Audit approach (*Cont.*):
   through the computer, 38
Audit modules, 111, 358–359
   (*See also* Concurrent auditing techniques)
Audit opinion (*see* Evaluation judgment)
Audit procedures, timing of, 35–36
Audit software (*see* Generalized audit software; Specialized audit software)
Audit trail:
   accounting (*see* Accounting audit trail)
   defined, 355
   disappearance of, 11, 357
   with ITF and snapshot, 482
   minicomputer, effects on, 11
   operations (*see* Operations audit trail)
   types of, 355–356
Auditor independence:
   effects of design phase participation on, 35–36
   methods of strengthening, 36, 47–48
   use of database management systems and, 416–419
   use of specialized audit software and, 442
Authentication, 251–256
Authorization, approaches to, 257–259
Authorization dynamics, problems of, 259–260
Authorization matrix, 258
Availability, objective of, 166, 169

Backup:
   of data (*see* Backup and recovery)
   of data preparation resources, 189–190
   of documentation, 78, 194–195
   of hardware, 78
   of input data, 294
   of software, 78
Backup and recovery:
   nature of, 376–377
   need for, 377–378
   strategies for, 378–392
   testing of, 393–394
Backup programmer, 146–147
Base case system evaluation (*see* Test data)
Batch controls, 237–239
Batch cover sheet, 238

SUBJECT INDEX

Batch register, 239–240, 294
Batches:
  design of, 239
  logical, 237
  physical, 237
Beforeimage, 365, 385–387, 390, 392, 481
Behavioral problems, causes of, 101–102
Benchmarks, 590
Benefits:
  of controls, 547–551
  of information systems, 572–574
  valuation of, 574–575
Binding, 364
Blackouts, 197
Block sequence codes, 232–233
Blueprint, 419, 440, 443, 449–450
Bounded context, 132
Brownouts, 197
Browsing, 318
Bugs, electronic, 199
Bursting controls, 338–339
By-product data capture, 219

Capability, system, 588
Cards, punch, 216–217
Career advancement:
  for computer installation personnel, 85
  for EDP auditors, 59–60
Cassettes, 219
Centralization:
  of computer facilities, 81–82
  of the EDP audit function, 50–51
Certification, software, 620
Certified Data Processing Auditor (CDPA) certificate, 611–612
Change process, management of, 105–106
Changeover plan, 73–74
Chargeout, 91–92, 191
Check digits, 234–237
  calculation of, 234–235
  efficiency of, 235–236
  use of, 237
Checkpoint, 323–324, 388, 391
Chief programmer team, 146–148
Cipher system:
  cryptographic key in, 272
  encipherment algorithm in, 271–272
Ciphers, types, of, 270–271
Ciphertext, 270, 272
Cleaning:
  of computer room, 198
  of magnetic media, 193
Clippings, magnetic tape, 193
Closed routine, 289, 311

Code comparison (*see* Program code comparison)
Code optimizer, 158
Code review (*see* Program code review)
Codes (*see* Communications codes; Data codes; Error codes)
Coding errors, 450–451
Communications:
  electronic: controls over, 199
    traffic, growth in, 250
  human, and management controls, 88
Communications codes, 261–263
Communications line:
  analog, 266
  conditioning of, 264, 266
  digital, 266
  errors in, treatment of, 261–263
  optical fiber, 266
  private, 265–266
  public, 266
Communications network:
  completely connected, 267, 269
  failure in, 260–261
  reliability of, improvement of, 263–270
  ring, 267, 269
  star, 269–270
  topology of, 266–270
Competency center, 51
Completely connected network, 267, 269
Complexity, theory of, 130
Compliance testing phase, 31
Composite design, 130
Computation and indexing errors, 450–451
Computer abuse:
  cases of, 16–19
  defined, 6
  losses from, 6
Computer audit specialists:
  need for, 46–48
  placement of, 48–50
  training of, 46–47, 53–56
Computer operations, 185–189
Computers:
  need for control and audit of, 4–7
  use of, 4, 7
Concentration, 260–261
Concurrency, 170, 311–313, 388, 390, 392, 474–475
Concurrent auditing techniques, 482
  advantages of, 487
  disadvantages of, 488
  implementation of, 485–487
  nature of, 474
  need for, 474–477

Consumers, computers and, 617–619
Contingency theory, 79–81
　and job design, 112–113
　and levels of adoption, 569–570
　and normative models of system
　　development, 103–104
　and organization structures, 79–81,
　　113–114
Control flowchart:
　advantages of, 507
　construction of, 506–507
　limitations of, 507, 510
　nature of, 506
Control section, functions of, 190–191,
　　294, 337–338
Control totals, 288, 306, 310–311
　(*See also* Batch controls)
Controlling, management function of,
　　88–92
Controls:
　application, 26–27
　batch, 237–239
　bursting, 338–339
　communications (*see* Communications
　　network)
　compensating, 30, 32
　corrective, 28
　costs and benefits of, 547–551
　decollation, 338–339
　detective, 28, 214
　horizontal, 27
　internal (*see* Internal control)
　investment in, 551–553
　management, 24–26
　nature of, 24–28
　preventive, 27–28, 214
　procedures, 239–240
　stationery, 334–337
　user, 38–39, 339
　vertical, 27
Conversion, 120–121
Coordinating mechanisms, 107–112
Copy facility, 151
Costs:
　of controls, 547–551
　of information systems, 572–574
　valuation of, 574–575
Coupling, 474–475
Covariance, analysis of, 601
Cross-reference lister, 154, 436
Cryptanalysis, 270
Cryptographic key, 273–275
　distribution of, 274
　generation of, 273–274

Cryptographic key (*Cont.*):
　installation of, 274–275
Cryptography, 270–275
　for databases, 275
　(*See also* Encryption)
Cryptology, 270
Cryptosystem, 270
Cyclic codes, 262

Data:
　creation of, 168–169
　defined, 168–169
　　(*See also* Data dictionary)
　integrity of (*see* Data integrity)
　loss of, 4–5
　retirement of, 168–169
Data accessing errors, 450–451
Data capture:
　controls over, 214
　methods of, 211–215
　overview of, 210–212
Data codes, 231–234
　design of, 231
　errors in, 231–232
　types of, 232–234
Data dictionary, 172–175, 436
　audit aspects of, 173–175
　elements of, 172–173
Data encryption standard (DES), 272
Data entry:
　cost-effectiveness of, 545–553, 563
　methods of, 211, 216–224
　overview of, 210–212
Data integrity:
　analytical models of, 539–544
　defined, 8, 166
　formal evaluation techniques, 538–545
　maintenance of, 170–171
　measures of, 536–538
　objectives of, 8
　simulation models of, 544–546
Data preparation:
　controls over, 214
　functions of, 189–190
　methods of, 211, 216–224
　overview of, 210–212
Data privacy, 7, 612–614
　EDP auditor and, 614
　legislation for, scope of, 613–614
　principles of, 613
Data set (*see* Modem)
Database:
　cryptography for, 275
　definition of, 165

Database administrator:
  audit considerations, 166–167
  control over, 175–178
  functions of, 167–171, 388, 393
Database management, objectives of,
    165–166
Database management system, 165–166,
    414–419, 435
  host language features of, 416–417
  self-contained features of, 417–418
Database tools, control problems of,
    176–177
Deadlock, 313–316
  conditions for, 314
  prevention of, 315–316
  solutions to, 314–315
Decentralization:
  of computer facilities, 81–82
  of the EDP audit function, 50–51
Decision support system, 117
Decision table, 151–152, 438, 459–461
Decollation controls, 338–339
Decomposition, 131–134
Degaussing, 193
Delay distortion, 264
Design and code inspections, 142–143
Design of systems (see System design)
Design errors, program, 450–451
Design phase, audit participation in,
    35–36, 99
  effects on independence, 36
Detailed review phase, 30–31
Deterministic models:
  extreme value, 539
  mean value, 539
  (See also Analytical models)
Diagnosis phase in system development,
    107–110
Dialog, authentication using, 254
Dialog generators, 230
Direct entry data capture, 215
Directing, management function of, 86–88
Disaster, 76–78, 196–198
  categories of, 77
Disaster recovery plan, 76–78
Diskettes, 219
Distortion, 264
Distributed system, 476–477
Document-based data capture, 213–215
Documentation:
  backup of, 78, 194–195
  control over use of, 194–195
  in a database environment, 169
  maintenance of, 194–195
Documentation library, 194–195

Documentation standards, 90–91
Domain, monitor, 518
Dual recording, 380–381
Dumping, 381–383, 389–392
  logical, 382–383
  physical, 381–383
  residual, 389–392

Eavesdropping, 198–200
Economic effectiveness, 572–576
Edits (see Input validation checks)
EDP audit, steps in, 28–32
EDP auditing:
  defined, 7
  foundations of, 12–14
    behavioral science, 14
    computer science, 14
    information systems management, 13
    traditional auditing, 13
  as a separate function, 46–50
  as a staff function, 48, 57–59
Effectiveness of systems (see System
    effectiveness)
Efficiency:
  of audit software, 433–434, 441
  of systems (see System efficiency)
Electronic funds transfer systems (EFTS),
    250, 618
Embezzlement (see Computer abuse)
Empirical models of system efficiency,
    599–601
Encryption, 270
  and control of utility software, 440
  and masquerading, 255–256
Encryption standard, data (DES), 272
End-of-file protocols, 307
Energy variations, 197
Engineering tools, control problems of,
    188–189
Engineers, control of, 188–189
Entropy, 476
Entry phase in system development,
    106–107
Equity Funding Corporation, 16–17
Error codes, 293–294
Error correcting codes, 262–263
Error detecting codes, 261–262
Error file, 289–291, 296–297
Error handling, 289–291
Error reporting, 291–294, 297
Error statistics, 294
Evaluation judgment, 33–35
  accuracy of, 553–554, 576
  consensus in, 554–556, 576
  studies of, 538

Evaluation judgment (*Cont.*):
  consistency in, 554–556, 576
  identification of factors affecting,
    554–555, 576
  informal guidelines for, 553–556, 576
  matrix conceptualization of, 33–35,
    554–555
    columnar evaluation, 34
    global evaluation, 34
    row evaluation, 34
  presentation of evidence affecting, 556,
    576
  weighting of factors affecting, 555, 576
Evolvability, objective of, 166
Ex post audit, 99, 409–410
Expected loss, 22
  (*See also* Loss)
Extended record, 481–482

Feasibility study, 71–73, 106–107
  feasibility study proper, 72–73
  preliminary survey, 72–73
Files, magnetic, 191–194
  controls over, 287–288, 343
  maintenance of, 193–194
  use of, 191–193
Fire damage, 196
Firmware monitor, 524–525
Fishbowl effect, 340
Fixes, direct, 185–186, 335, 387
Flaw hypothesis generation, 449–450, 457
Flowchart (*see* Control flowchart)
Flowcharters, 155–156, 436
Foreign Corrupt Practices Act, 615
Forms, design of, 118–119
Fraud (*see* Computer abuse)
Frequency modulation, 263–265

Generalized audit software:
  accessing complex data structures using,
    414–419
  audit tasks and, 406–409
  differences among, 422–423
  functional capabilities of, 403–406
  functional limitations of, 409–410,
    433–434, 441
  impact of life cycle, 410–411
  managing an application of, 412–414
  and minicomputers, 620
  need for, 402–403
  purchase of, 419–426
  semantics of, 422–423
  syntax of, 423–424
  and test data creation, 463–464
  unavailability of, 433, 441

Generalized audit software (*Cont.*):
  uses of, 357, 371
  vendors of, 420–421
Generalized audit trail system, 364
Generalized input validation module, 296
Gibson mix, 591
Goals of information systems, 561–562
Grandfather, father, son strategy, 379–380

Hardware effectiveness, 570–571
Hardware errors, 321–323
Hardware monitor, 519–522
  capabilities of, 521
  fixed, 519–520
  limitations of, 521–522
  stored-program, 520–521
  wired-program, 520
Hierarchical codes, 233
HIPO (hierarchical plus
    input-process-output) chart,
    134–136, 436
Host language extensions, 416–417
Human information processing, limitations
  of, 131, 232, 344–346, 555
Human motivation, 87
Hybrid methods of data capture, 215
Hybrid monitor, 525–526

Identification, 251–256
Independence:
  of auditor (*see* Auditor independence)
  resource, 571–572
Information analysis phase, 107–110
Information quality, 344
  (*See also* Data integrity)
Input/output pool, 296, 335–336
Input validation checks, 285–288
  batch checks, 287
  field checks, 286
  file checks, 287–288
  record checks, 286–287
Input validation program, 288–294
Instruction mixes, 591–592
Insurance, 77–78
Integrated test facility (ITF), 477–481
Integrity of data (*see* Data integrity)
Interactive languages:
  design of, 227–230
  semantics of, 342–343
  syntax of, 341–342
Internal control:
  and the audit approach, 22
  effects of EDP on, 10–12
    access to assets, 10–11
    audit/management trails, 11

Internal control, effects of EDP on (*Cont.*):
  comparing recorded accountability with
    assets, 11
  consequences of error, 11–12
  separation of duties, 10
  types of, 11
Interviews:
  analysis of, 498
  conceptual issues, 494–495
  conduct of, 497–498
  content of, 496
  preparation for, 495–497
  purposes of, 494
Intrusion, unauthorized, 198–200
Investment:
  in computing facilities, 73
  in controls, 551–553
  in information systems, 575–576
Isolation, principle of, 320
ITF (integrated test facility), 477–481

Job satisfaction (*see* Quality of working life)

Kernel programs, 591–592
Key-to-disk devices, 218–219
Key-to-tape devices, 217–218
Keypunch methods of data capture,
    216–219
  design of keying tasks and keying
    environment, 241
Kiting, 422

Language subset, 158
Leadership styles, 87–88
Least privilege, principle of, 320
Levels of abstraction approach, 130
Levels of adoption, 569–570
Librarian:
  of chief programmer team, 146–147
  functions of, 191–195
Librarian package, 192, 440
Library:
  documentation, 194–195
  file, 191–194
  program production, 147
Life cycle:
  of the computer installation, 70–71,
    88–90, 410–411
  of the EDP audit group, 60–61, 411
  of programs, 118, 129
  of the system development process,
    100–101, 104
Line (*see* Communications line)
List-oriented authorization, 257–259

Log(s):
  of changes to source code, 440
  database administrator,
    control of, 177
  files: maintenance of, 193
    use of, 191–192
  operators, control of, 186
  report software for, 370–371
  user subroutines and, 371
  (*See also* Operations audit trail)
Logging, 383–389
  of afterimages, 388–389
  of beforeimages, 385–388
  of change parameters, 389
  of input transactions, 384–385
Logic path monitor, 157, 437
Loop check, 261
Loss:
  causes of, 22–24
  effects of controls on, 22

M-out-of-N codes, 262
Machine use, authorization of, 186–187
Macro or subroutine facility, 151
Magnetic ink character recognition
    (MICR), 220–221
Maintenance:
  of data preparation equipment, 189
  of files, 193
  of hardware, 187–189
  of programs, 129, 143–144
  of systems, 121
Maintenance engineers, control of,
    188–189
Management trail (*see* Audit trail)
Manual(s):
  operator run, 185, 194
  of specifications, 73, 82–83
  user, 194
Masquerading, 254–256, 318
Master plan, 74–75
Memoranda, 169, 194
Metacode, 139–140
Methods standards, 83–84
Microcomputers (*see* Minicomputers)
Microfilm, 195
Minicomputers:
  and audit/management trails, 11
  and generalized audit software, 620
  and separation of duties, 10
  use of, 4
Modem, 260–261, 263–265
  equalization of, 264
Modulation, 263–265

SUBJECT INDEX

Module:
  audit, 111, 358–359
  coupling, 133–134
  strength of, 133–134
Monitor (see Hardware monitor;
    Performance monitor)
Multilist, 386–387, 414, 417

Natural workload models, 590
Network (see Communications network)
New York Times project, 144–145
Noise, studies of, 261–262
Nondisclosure agreements, 189
Normative models of the system
    development process, 99–103

Online coding facility, 151–153
Online debugging facility, 155–157
Operating system:
  and audit trail, 367
  evolutionary dynamics of, 143–144
  integrity of, 317–320
    flaws in, 319
    threats to, 318
Operation of systems, 121
Operational effectiveness, 568–570
Operations audit trail:
  control of, 371
  nature of, 366–367
  purposes of, 367–369
  retrieval from, 369–371
  [See also Log(s)]
Operations management, functions of,
    184–185
Operator intervention, minimization of, 311
Operators, 185–186
  controls over, 185–186, 335–337
  duties of, 185
Optical character recognition (OCR), 221
Optical fiber transmission, 266
Optical mark sensing, 222
Organizational relationships between
    management and other groups,
    57–59
  EDP auditing as a staff function, 48,
    57–59
    methods of improving, 48, 58–59
    problems experienced, 57–58
Organizing:
  of computer installation, 78–84
    functional structure, 78–79
    project structure, 78–79
  of database administrator, 171–172
  of operations management function, 184

Organizing (Cont.):
  of programmers, 144–148
    adaptive team, 148
    chief programmer team, 146–148
    functional structure, 145–146
    project structure, 145–146
Output analyzer, 155
Overflow, 226–227, 305

Paper tape, 217
Parallel simulation, 407–408
Parity check, 261–262, 322
Passwords, 251–253
Pattern recognition data capture, 220–222
Pedagogy, 624
Peephole effect, 345
Performance indices, 587–588
Performance measurement:
  objects of, 516–517
  types of, 518
  (See also Performance monitor)
Performance monitor:
  characteristics of, 517–518
  instrumentation of, 526–527
  and privacy breaches, 527
  types of, 518–526
Performance standards, 90
Person–machine dialogs, 229
Personal characteristics, authentication
    using, 254
Personnel (see Staffing)
Phase modulation, 263–265
Piggybacking, 318
Plaintext, 270
Planning, 70–78
  changeover, 73–74
  disaster recovery, 76–78
  feasibility study, 71–73
  master, 74–75
  project, 76
  steering committee and, 71–72
Point-of-sale terminals, 223–224
Pollution, 198
Polynomial codes, 262
Possessed objects, authentication using,
    253–254
Postaudits, 91, 121
Preventive maintenance, 187–188
Printer file controls, 335–336
Printer ribbons, 337
Printing controls, 336–337
Privacy of data (see Data privacy)
Probabilistic models:
  of asset safeguarding, 540–544

Probabilistic models (*Cont.*):
  of data integrity, 540–544
  of system efficiency, 594–597
  of workloads, 592–593
Problem recognition in system development, 104–105
Procedural review, 190–191, 241
Procedures, design of, 118–119
Procedures controls, 239–240
Processing validation checks, 305–306
Product cipher, 271
Professionalism:
  conditions for, 611
  EDP auditing, 611–612
  motivations toward, 610–611
Program:
  analysis and design of, 130–136
    aids for, 134–136
  coding of, 136–140
  errors in, 450–451
  operation and maintenance of, 129, 143–144
  testing of, 140–143
  (*See also* Test data)
Program code comparison:
  costs and benefits of, 466–467
  methodology of, 466–467
  objectives of, 465–466
  types of, 466
Program code review:
  of COBOL verbs, 455–457
  costs and benefits of, 457–458
  methodology of, 453–457
  nature of, 449, 451
  objectives of, 451–453
Program production library, 147
Program quality:
  characteristics of, 130
  factors lowering, 450–451
Program specifications, 117–118
Programmer:
  backup, 146–147
  chief, 146–147
  support, 146–147
  system, 148–150
Project plan, 76
Proofs of program correctness, 140–141
Protocols:
  end-of-file, 307
  of operators, 185–186
Pseudocode, 139–140

Quality of working life, 101–102, 107–108, 114, 121, 565–567

Quality of working life (*Cont.*):
  measures of, 565–567
  questionnaires on, 499, 505, 567
Questionnaires:
  design of, 499–504
  effective use of, 505–506
  layout and structure of, 502–504
  and operational effectiveness, 568–570
  purposes of, 498–499
  and quality of working life, 499, 505, 567
  reliability of, 504
  response scales for, 501–502
  validity of, 504–505
Queuing models, 594–597

Recertification, magnetic media, 193
Reentrant program, 324
Refreezing of organizations, 105–106
Regression, 601
Reliability theory, 540–544
Remedial maintenance, 187–188
Report collection controls, 337
Report distribution controls, 339
Report program controls, 335
Reports:
  controls over: batch, 331–339
    online, 331, 340
  effectiveness of, 344–346
  efficient production of, 346–349
  presentation method of, 344–345
  use of, 568–569
Representativeness, workload, 589
Research, 624
Response time, 228–229, 345–346, 586–588, 599–601
Restart, 323–324
Retention controls:
  file, 288, 343
  input data, 189
  reports, 339
Ring network, 267, 269
Risk:
  pure, 76
  residual, 77
  speculative, 76
Risk management, 76–78
  risk control, 77–78
  risk identification, 76–77
  risk measurement, 77
Rollback, 377, 385–390, 392
Rollforward, 377, 386, 388, 390–392
Rounding, 307–309
Run-to-run control totals, 306, 310

S-shape curve, 60, 88–90
Sandwich rule, 506–507
Sanitization, 193
SCARF (System Control Audit Review File), 482–485
Schneider, Jerry, 17–18, 331
Security, physical, 195–200
Security administrator, functions of, 195
Separation of duties:
  database administrator, problem of, 175–176
  effects of EDP on, 10
  minicomputers, problem of, 10
Sequence check, 287
  of master and transaction files, 306–307
Sequencing and control errors, 450–451
Serial codes, 232
Service bureaus, 250, 476–477
Sharability:
  objective of, 165–167
  problems arising from, 166–167
Shorthand preprocessors, 150–151
Shredding, 189, 339
Simulation languages, 598
Simulation models:
  of asset safeguarding, 544–545
  of data integrity, 544–546
  of system efficiency, 587–599
Simulators, testing, 437, 464
Snapshot techniques, 481–482
Social influences, 616–619
Sociotechnical design, 101–103, 110–112
  major phases of, 102–103
Software:
  demand for, 129
  supply of, 129
  system (*see* System software)
  utility (*see* Utility software)
  (*See also* Generalized audit software; Program; Specialized audit software)
Software development aids, 150–158
  coding, 150–153
  debugging/testing, 153–157
  execution, 157–158
Software effectiveness, 571
Software monitor, 522–524
  capabilities of, 523–524
  event-driven, 522–523
  limitations of, 524
  sampling, 523
Source code, readability of, 453
Source documents, design of, 224–227
Specialized audit software:
  control of, 443

Specialized audit software (*Cont.*):
  development and implementation of, 442–443
  nature of, 440
  need for, 440–442
  types of, 442–443
Spikes, 197
Spoofing, 318
Spooling, controls over, 335–336
Staffing:
  of computer installation, 84–86
  of EDP audit function, 50–53
Stage growth hypothesis, 88–90
Standards:
  documentation, 90–91
  methods, 83–84
  performance, 90
Standing data, 310–311
Star network, 269–270
Stationery controls, 334–337
Statistical databases, 257
Statistical sampling, 405, 408–409, 483
Steering committee, 71–72
Stepwise refinement, 130
Strategic design, 109–110
Structural damage, 197–198
Structured design, 130
Structured programming, 137–140
  and code readability, 453
Structured walk-throughs, 142–143
Substantive testing phase, 32
Substitution cipher, 271
Support programmer, 146–147
Suspense account, 310
Synchronization point, 391
  (*See also* Checkpoint)
System control audit review file, 482–485
System design, 110–118
  database, 116–117
  decision support system, 117
  information flow, 115–116
  information processing system, 114–118
  job design, 112–113
  organization structure, 113–114
  procedures and forms, 118–119
System designers, limited perceptions of, 101–102
System development life cycle, 100–101
  major phases of, 100, 104
System effectiveness:
  defined, 9
  objectives of, 9
  steps in evaluation of, 563

System efficiency:
    analytical models of, 594–597
    defined, 9
    empirical models of, 599–601
    objectives of, 9
    simulation models of, 597–599
    steps in evaluation of, 584–587
System programmers, 148–150
    control measures, 150
    control problems, 149
System software:
    audit of, 320–321
    audit use of, 432–440
    integrity of, 316–320, 432

Tables, internal, 310–311
Tandem interview, 498
Task accomplishment, 561–565
    measures of, 563–565
Task closure, 229, 345–346
Task uncertainty, 79–81, 103, 114–115, 145–148
    strategies for reducing, 80
Technical effectiveness, 570–572
Technology, changes in:
    audit procedures impact, 620–623
    and consumer backlash, 618–619
    controls impact, 620–623
    EDP audit impact, 619–620
    and strikes, 617
Terminals, 222–224
    point-of-sale, 223–224
Test bed (see Test data)
Test data:
    costs and benefits of, 464–465
    creation of, 463–464
    design of, 459–463
        decision-table approach, 459–461
        flowchart approach, 461–463
    with ITF, 477–481
    nature of, 449, 458
    reliability of, 458–459
Test data generator, 154–155, 437, 459, 464
Test manager, 157, 437
Testing:
    acceptance, 119–120
    program, 119, 140–143
        (See also Test data)
    system, 119
    user, 119
Text editors, 153

Throughput indices, 588
Ticket-oriented authorization, 258–259
Tidy facility, 153
Timeliness indices, 587–588
Top-down approach:
    coding of programs, 136–137
    design of programs, 130
    and readability of source code, 453
    testing of programs, 141–142, 453
Trace facility, 154
Training:
    of computer installation personnel, 85
    of data preparation personnel, 241–242
    of EDP auditors, 53–56
        amount needed, 53–54
        types needed, 54–56
Transaction simulator, 230
Transfer price, 91–92, 191
Transposition cipher, 270–271
Trojan horse, 318, 439, 527
Turnaround documents, 219–220, 292–293
Turnaround time, 586–588

Unfreezing of organizations, 105–106
Union Dime Savings Bank, 18–19
Universal product code (UPC), 223
User controls, 38–39, 339
Utility software:
    audit categorization of, 434–439
    audit use of, 432–434
Utilization indices, 588

Variance, analysis of, 599–601
Verification, 216–218, 241
Visual display units (VDU), 222–223
Virtual machine, 250

Walk-throughs, 475–476, 481
    structured, 142–143
Water damage, 196–197
Wire transfer (see Electronic funds transfer systems)
Wiretapping, 199, 254, 266, 340
Word processing, controls over, 194–195
Work factor, 270
Workers, computers and, 616–617
Working life (see Quality of working life)
Workload models, 586, 588–593
    artificial, 590–593
    natural, 590